KU-556-867

H46 551 142 6

THE OFFICIAL HISTORY OF BRITAIN AND THE CHANNEL TUNNEL

This authoritative volume presents the first official history of the British Government's evolving relationship with the Channel Tunnel project from the early nineteenth century to 2005.

The building of the Channel Tunnel has been one of Europe's major projects and a testimony to British-French and public-private sector collaboration. However, Eurotunnel's current financial crisis provides a sobering backcloth for an examination of the British Government's long-term flirtation with the project, and in particular, the earlier Tunnel project in the 1960s and early 1970s, which was abandoned in 1975. Commissioned by the Cabinet Office and using hitherto untapped British Government records, this book presents an in-depth analysis of the successful project of 1986–94. It provides a vivid portrayal of the complexities of quadripartite decision-making (in two countries, with both public and private sectors), revealing new insights into the role of the British and French Governments in the process.

Written by **Terry Gourvish**, Britain's leading transport historian, this book will be essential reading for general readers and specialists with an interest in business history, international relations, public policy and project management.

WHITEHALL HISTORIES: GOVERNMENT OFFICIAL HISTORY SERIES

ISSN: 1474–8398

The Government Official History series began in 1919 with wartime histories, and the peacetime series was inaugurated in 1966 by Harold Wilson. The aim of the series is to produce major histories in their own right, compiled by historians eminent in the field, who are afforded free access to all relevant material in the official archives. The Histories also provide a trusted secondary source for other historians and researchers while the official records are not in the public domain. The main criteria for selection of topics are that the Histories should record important episodes or themes of British history while the official records can still be supplemented by the recollections of key players; and that they should be of general interest, and, preferably, involve the records of more than one government department.

THE UNITED KINGDOM AND
THE EUROPEAN COMMUNITY
Vol. I: The Rise and Fall of a National Strategy, 1945–1963
Alan S. Milward

SECRET FLOTILLAS
Vol. I: Clandestine Sea Operations to Brittany, 1940–1944
Vol. II: Clandestine Sea Operations in the Mediterranean, North Africa and the Adriatic, 1940–1944
Brooks Richards

SOE IN FRANCE
M.R.D. Foot

THE OFFICIAL HISTORY OF THE FALKLANDS CAMPAIGN
Vol. I: The Origins of the Falklands War
Vol. II: War and Diplomacy
Lawrence Freedman

THE OFFICIAL HISTORY OF BRITAIN AND
THE CHANNEL TUNNEL
Terry Gourvish

THE OFFICIAL HISTORY OF BRITAIN AND THE CHANNEL TUNNEL

Terry Gourvish

Research: Mike Anson

LONDON AND NEW YORK

First published 2006
by Routledge
2 Park Square, Milton Park, Abington, Oxon OX14 4RN

Simultaneously published in the USA and Canada
by Routledge
270 Madison Ave, New York, NY 10016

Routledge is an imprint of the Taylor & Francis Group, an informa business

Typeset in Times New Roman by
Newgen Imaging Systems (P) Ltd, Chennai, India
Printed and bound in Great Britain by
Biddles Digital, King's Lynn

British Library Cataloguing in Publication Data
A catalogue record for this book is available
from the British Library

Library of Congress Cataloging in Publication Data
A catalog record for this book has been requested

ISBN10: 0–415–39183–0 (hbk) ISBN13: 978–0–415–39183–2 (hbk)
ISBN10: 0–203–96949–9 (ebk) ISBN13: 978–0–203–96949–6 (ebk)

The author has been given full access to official documents. The data and factual information in the report is based on these documents. The interpretation of the documents and the views expressed are those of the author.

There was a young lady of Rye
Who said, with a smile in her eye
'If a tunnel they bore
From France to our Shore
Goodbye, little basin goodbye'*

*Quoted in Claude Boillot–TSI, 23 December 1959, TSI Archive, Vol. 60, HBS.

CONTENTS

List of figures ix
List of cartoons x
List of tables xi
Preface xiii
Acknowledgements xvi
Abbreviations and acronyms xvii

1 Beginnings, 1802–1945 1

2 New aspirations: the Channel Tunnel project, 1945–64 16

3 Another false start: the Wilson Governments and the Tunnel, 1964–70 46

4 The Heath Government and the Tunnel: reaching agreement, 1970–2 79

5 The Heath Government and the Tunnel: taking the project forward, 1972–4 107

6 Abandonment, 1974–5 134

7 Keeping hopes alive, 1975–81 171

8 The Thatcher Governments and the Tunnel: from hope to eternity, 1981–4 207

9 The Thatcher Governments and the Tunnel: choosing a promoter, 1984–6 247

10 Eurotunnel: finance and construction, 1986–90 285

11 From Tunnel to transport facility, 1988–94 322

12 The Channel Tunnel: postscript, 1994–2005 364

Notes 386
Index 511

FIGURES

1.1	Sartiaux-Fox Channel Tunnel scheme with strategic viaduct, 1906	8
1.2	Channel Tunnel Co. scheme, 1929–30	12
2.1	CTSG scheme, 1960: proposed alignment	27
3.1	Options for Channel Tunnel terminals, 1968	75
5.1	The 1970s Tunnel	110
6.1	Route of proposed Channel Tunnel Rail Link, 1973	150
7.1	The Channel Tunnel circle	205
9.1	Thatcher and Mitterand's signed announcement to proceed with a Channel Tunnel, 20 January 1986	278
10.1	Channel Tunnel organisational chart	288
11.1a	Channel Tunnel Rail Link: British Rail's four route options, 1988	332
11.1b	British Rail's four route options, 1988: London termini	333
11.2	Channel Tunnel Rail Link: options, 1989–94	338
12.1	The 'Eurotunnel System', 1994	367

CARTOONS

1	Channel Tunnel phobia, 1907	9
2	Anglo-French differences, 1963	39
3	Cynicial about project management, 1966	61
4	Abandonment, 1975	166
5	The illusive Tunnel dream, 1981	208
6	Thatcher and Ridley encounter opposition, 1985	259
7	Alastair Morton accuses TML, 1989	320
8	Escalating costs and financial crisis, 1991	353
9	The Tunnel opens, 1994	365
10	The banks' continuing anxieties, 1996	374
11	Eurotunnel wins a Concession extension, 1997	375
12	The Channel Tunnel Rail Link's financing problems, 1998	379

TABLES

1.1	Select list of early proposals for a fixed channel link, 1803–89	2
2.1	Channel Tunnel Study Group Report, March 1960: estimated construction costs, and prospects for a rail-only tunnel	28
2.2	Channel Tunnel Study Group, estimate of the Channel Tunnel's 'economic benefits', July 1960	32
2.3	Tunnel v. Bridge: Joint working party's 1963 traffic forecasts for 1980	36
2.4	Tunnel v. Bridge: Joint working party's 1963 assessment of economic and financial returns	37
3.1	The 1963 and 1966 estimates of economic and financial returns	55
3.2	Traffic forecasts: revisions of April and August 1966, compared with Anglo-French report, 1963	57
3.3	Shortlisted consortia for Channel Tunnel, May 1967	65
3.4	Channel Tunnel terminal facilities: options, 1959–69	76
4.1	The Channel Tunnel consortium, July 1970	82
4.2	'Interim' study results, 1972, compared with 1963, 1966 and 1969	96
4.3	Participation in the private consortium, October 1972	105
5.1	The 1973 studies: estimated financial return	113
5.2	Channel Tunnel, 1973: cost-benefit analysis for the United Kingdom	113
5.3	Traffic forecasts, 1973, compared with those in 1963 and 1966	114
5.4	Suggested remuneration proposals (based on lower growth estimate), July 1973	120
5.5	Agreed remuneration package, September 1973	126
6.1	Channel Tunnel Rail Link: analysis of increases in cost between June 1973 and August 1974	159
7.1	Cross-channel passenger and freight traffic: actual, 1962–73, and Cairncross Report forecast, 1980–90	180

7.2	Cairncross Report estimate of Tunnel costs and benefits (UK share), 1975–2030	182
7.3	Cairncross Report estimate of rail investment costs and benefits (UK share), 1975–2030	183
7.4	BRB and SNCF single-track rail tunnel: estimate of capital investment, 1978	191
8.1	Channel Fixed Link options, December 1981	215
8.2	Cross-channel traffic forecasts, 1980–2000	229
8.3	Channel Fixed Link: estimated rates of return and resource costs, April 1982	230
9.1	Evaluation of Channel Link options by Banking Report, 1984	248
9.2	Competing bids for the Channel Fixed Link concession, October 1985	262
9.3	Comparison of promoters' capital cost and revenue estimates, December 1985	269
10.1	Toll payments agreed under the Railway Usage Contract, July 1987	304
10.2	Progress with tunnelling, 1987–91	311
10.3	Increases in Channel Tunnel construction and project costs, 1985–90	320
11.1	British Rail's four options for new route capacity, July 1988	331
11.2	Eurotunnel's estimate of cost consequences of IGC and Governments' interventions, November 1993	361
12.1	Channel Tunnel outturn, 6 May 1994, compared with November 1987 forecast	368
12.2	Channel Tunnel traffic, 1994–2004	370
12.3	Eurotunnel operating results and profit and loss, 1994–2004	372

PREFACE

In 2001 I was appointed by Prime Minister Tony Blair to write a history of the Channel Tunnel as part of the programme of official histories run by the Cabinet Office. My broad remit was to analyse in some depth the involvement of the British Government, its ministers, civil servants and advisers, in the project management of this, one of the largest, if not the largest, infrastructure mega-projects in Europe. It is important at the outset to explain what this book deals with and what it does not. While I was asked to cover events from the beginning, that is, from the early nineteenth century, the initial efforts to build a Channel crossing have naturally attracted the attention of generations of historians. Furthermore, when the Tunnel became a reality in the late 1980s, it stimulated a mini-boom in publications. Some of the books were written by those who, like Michael Bonavia, Donald Hunt and Colin Kirkland, had been actively involved in its history; others dealt at length with the construction phase, again from the perspective of the expert. With no previously unexploited archives to trawl, there was little point in going over much of the same ground in detail. I therefore decided to concentrate upon the periods which had not been covered in depth before, that is, the full story of the 1970s Tunnel and its abandonment in 1975, and of course, the successful promotion of the mid-1980s. The book does not attempt to provide a rounded Anglo-French analysis of this great joint venture, nor does it attempt to write from the perspective of the numerous private sector corporations which were engaged in lobbying, promoting, constructing and operating the Tunnel. This is not to say that the role of French ministers, officials and companies is neglected, nor indeed that of bodies such as Eurotunnel, TML (Transmanche-Link), and the numerous financial institutions involved in the capital investment in the Tunnel. Rather it is concerned with the complexity of project management, where more than one country is involved, and a multiplicity of actors is involved. The security aspects relating to defence, terrorism and immigration were not examined in depth in the contemporary period.

The book therefore reflects the privileges I enjoyed in being permitted to consult the archives of the British Government, before the complexities introduced by the Freedom of Information Act (my contract with the Cabinet Office terminated in January 2005). Although there were some exceptions, in general this privileged access was not extended elsewhere. However, I must express my thanks to the following, who allowed me to consult material dealing with the Tunnel: the Bank of England Archive (Chief Cashier's papers, 1959–63); Centre des Archives du Monde du Travail, Roubaix (Rothschild, Chemin de fer du Nord papers); Churchill Archives Centre, Cambridge (Channel Tunnel Co., Bonavia and Churchill papers); Glasgow University Archive Services (Cairncross papers); Harvard Business School's Baker Library, Boston (Technical Studies Inc. papers); HSBC Archive, London (Midland Bank's Channel Tunnel papers, mid-1980s); ING Bank, London (Baring Partners papers, 1957–76); London Business School Library; Modern Records Centre, University of Warwick (TUC and TGWU papers); Lady Parker (Sir Peter Parker's papers); Rio Tinto plc (RTZ, RTZ-DE papers); Rothschild Archive, London (N.M. Rothschild & Sons papers, 19th century); Royal Archives, Windsor (Queen Victoria's papers); Strategic Rail Authority (British Railways Board's Channel Tunnel papers, 1970s–94).

I benefited greatly from the assistance offered by those who agreed to be interviewed, or shared their experience of the Tunnel with me. Of the British politicians the following were particularly helpful: Sir Edward Heath, Prime Minister when the 1970s Tunnel was promoted, and Lord Peyton, his Transport Minister; Sir David Mitchell, junior minister to Nicholas Ridley in the critical period in the mid-1980s; and Lord Heseltine, Environment Secretary. Among the civil servants, I owe a particular debt to John Noulton, who was actively involved in the project first at the DTp, then at TML and finally at Eurotunnel as Director of Public Affairs. John not only agreed to be interviewed on a number of occasions, but also hosted a visit to Eurotunnel's control centre and the service tunnel, allowing me to view the crossing point with Sir Edward Watkin's tunnel of the 1880s, and the 'public sector' section bored in 1975. Also extremely helpful were Lord Armstrong, Guy Braibant, Brig. John Constant, Lady Harrop (Margaret Elliott-Binns), Sir Peter Kemp, Andrew Lyall, Sir David Serpell and Sir Edward Tomkins. I enjoyed the help of Alan Bennett, Andy Heslop and David Williams, from British Rail and its successors; Graham Corbett, Jean-Loup Dherse, Patrick Ponsolle and Peter Ratzer from Eurotunnel; Pen Kent, from the Bank of England; Lady Jill Parker, who helped me to unearth some of Sir Peter Parker's missing papers; and Frank P. Davidson, former President of Technical Studies Inc. and tunnel promoter extraordinaire. I was also able to draw on interview material collected for my earlier book on British Rail with Sir Peter Baldwin, David Blake, Richard Edgley, Sir Norman Fowler, Gil Howarth, Lord Howell, Lord Kelvedon, David Kirby, Lord MacGregor, John Palmer, Sir Peter Parker, Lord Parkinson, John Prideaux, Sir Robert Reid (Bob Reid I), Sir Robert Reid (Bob Reid II), Malcolm Southgate, Sir Alan Walters, and John Welsby. I also received invaluable help from Professors Stefan Szymanski and Roger Vickerman, who very generously shared their Tunnel archives with me. Preliminary thoughts were presented to conferences in Athens, Canterbury and Gothenberg, where valuable comments were received. I should also like to thank Melanie Aspey, Laurent Bonnaud, Camilla Brautaset, Frances Cairncross, Sonia Copeland, Gerald Crompton, Stephen Freeth, Patrick Fridenson,

Henry Gillett, Edwin Green, John Jenkins, John Kelsey, Alex Kemp, James King, Pierre Longuemar, Fiona Maccoll, Alan Milward, Mary Morgan, John Orbell, Leslie and Sheila Pressnell, Lesley Richmond and Peter Trewin.

I was assisted in my work by the support offered by a Project Board chaired by Tessa Stirling, Head of the Histories, Openness and Records Unit at the Cabinet Office. Most of its members had had direct experience of the Tunnel in their professional lives. I was therefore extremely grateful for the wisdom of Peter Thomas, John Henes and Deborah Phelan (DTp), Irene Ripley (Treasury), Richard Edgley (ex-BRB, EPS), Rosemary Jeffreys (Treasury Solicitor), and Heather Yasamee (FCO). I should also like to thank the staff at the Cabinet Office, and in particular, Tessa, for her unfailing support, Richard Ponman, whose birthday proved to be a critical element in the project's administration, and Sally Falk. Valuable assistance was provided at the Cabinet Office by Deb Neal, Joan Davies, Norman Rainnie, Chris Grindall, Naomi Tobi, at the DTp by John Sheard, and at the DTI by David Tookey. The figures were drawn most professionally by Mark Lacey of *Picture This*. The search for cartoons was once again aided by Jane Newton and the Centre for the Study of Cartoons and Caricature at the University of Kent, and the British Library at Colindale.

In preparing the book my greatest debt was to my researcher on the project, Mike Anson. Mike not only showed an unflagging and seemingly limitless appetite for processing the voluminous and often challenging files of government, but exhibited a strong sense of the contemporary period and its political economy, and was able to steer me away from some (but not all) of my well-known idiosyncrasies. Our working relationship was also influenced by the fact that the fortunes of his football teams – Exeter City and Stafford Rangers – invited comparisons with Eurotunnel's at several points. Mike's wife Jo, crossword puzzler par excellence, was, as ever, a wonderful proof-reader. Last, and certainly not least, my family were supportive whenever I retreated into the world of tunnels and tunnelling. Sue made valuable comments on the last chapter and was sufficiently inspired to travel on Eurostar for the first time, thereby taking actual numbers a little bit closer to the optimistic forecasts. Like the Tunnel itself, this book has been a collaborative effort and I thank all who helped me to produce it. Responsibility for the text is of course, mine alone.

TRG
London, June 2005

ACKNOWLEDGEMENTS

The author and the publishers wish to thank the following for kind permission to reproduce material.

Cartoons

Jane Newton and the Centre for the Study of Cartoons and Caricature, University of Kent for locating and providing prints for Cartoons 1–3 and 6; Derek Alder and News International for Cartoon 4; Steve Bell and the *Guardian* for Cartoon 12; Peter Brookes and News International for Cartoon 8; *Daily Mirror* for Cartoon 1; *Evening Standard* for Cartoon 2; Nicholas Garland and the *Daily Telegraph* for Cartoon 6; News International for Cartoon 3; Plantu and *Le Monde* for Cartoon 10; *Private Eye* Magazine for its cover, reproduced as Cartoon 9;. Varney and *Building* for Cartoon 5; Kipper Williams and the *Guardian* for Cartoon 11; and Richard Wilson and News International for Cartoon 7.

Figures

Cabinet Office for Figure 9.1. Figures 1.1 and 1.2 were drawn from original material in the Cabinet Office, Figures 2.1, 3.1, 5.1, 6.1 and 11.2 from material provided by the Department for Transport and its predecessors, Figure 11.1 from a British Railways Board Report, and Figure 12.1 from a Eurotunnel original.

ABBREVIATIONS AND ACRONYMS

ACTG	Anglo Channel Tunnel Group
AF63	MT, *Proposals for a Fixed Channel Link*, September 1963, Cmnd.2137
AF66	MT, Joint Report by British and French officials on the construction and operation of the Channel Tunnel, August 1966
AF82	DTp, Report of Anglo/French Study Group, April 1982 (published version: DTp, *Fixed Channel Link. Report of UK/French Study Group*, June 1982, Cmnd.8561)
AMD	Aviation and Maritime Department (FCO)
APS	Assistant Private Secretary
APT	Advanced Passenger Train
ASLEF	Associated Society of Locomotive Engineers and Firemen
Asst	Assistant
BAA	British Airports Authority
BBC	British Broadcasting Corporation
BC	Borough Council
BCTC	British Channel Tunnel Company
BICC	British Insulated Callenders Cables
BOAC	British Overseas Airways Corporation
BOE	Bank of England
BoT	Board of Trade
BP	British Petroleum
BR	British Rail
BRB	British Railways Board
BSC	British Steel Corporation
BTC	British Transport Commission
BTR	British Tyre and Rubber
CAB	Cabinet Office
CBI	Confederation of British Industry
CE	Channel Expressway
CEO	Chief Executive Officer
CFL	Channel Fixed Link (Divn, DTp)

CGE	Compagnie Générale d'Electricité
CGE-DE	CGE-Développement
CID	Committee of Imperial Defence
Co. Co.	County Council
CPRS	Central Policy Review Staff
CT	Channel Tunnel
CTA	Channel Tunnel Administration (MT)
CTAG	Channel Tunnel Advisory Group (Cairncross)
CTAWP	Channel Tunnel Agreement No. 2 Working Party (DOE)
CTD	Channel Tunnel Developments (1981) Ltd
CTE	Channel Tunnel Engineering (MT)
CTG	Channel Tunnel Group (MT)
CTG	Channel Tunnel Group (company)
CTG-FM	Channel Tunnel Group/France-Manche
CTIC	Interdepartmental Committee on the Channel Tunnel (DOE)
CTPC	Channel Tunnel Parliamentary Committee
CTRL	Channel Tunnel Rail Link
CTSG	Channel Tunnel Study Group
CTSU	Channel Tunnel Studies Unit (DOE)
CTU	Channel Tunnel Unit (DTp)
DCF	Discounted Cash Flow
DEA	Department of Economic Affairs
Dep	Deputy
Dept	Department
DETR	Department of Environment, Transport and the Regions
DG	Director General
DHB	Dover Harbour Board
Divn	Division
DOE	Department of the Environment
DoT	Department of Trade
DSIR	Department of Scientific and Industrial Research
DTI	Department of Trade and Industry
DTp	Department of Transport
E	Cabinet Ministerial Committee on Economic Strategy
E(A)	Cabinet Sub-Committee on Economic Affairs
EC	European Community
ECD	European Community Department (FCO)
ECTG	European Channel Tunnel Group
ECU	European Currency Unit
ED(O)	Cabinet Economic Development (Official) Committee
EDC	Cabinet Ministerial Committee on Economic Development
EEC	European Economic Community
EFL	External Financing Limit
EFTA	European Free Trade Association

EIA	Environmental Impact Analysis
EIB	European Investment Bank
EP	European Parliament
EPC	Cabinet Ministerial Committee on Economic Policy
EPS	European Passenger Services
EWS	English Welsh and Scottish Railway
FCO	Foreign and Commonwealth Office
FM	France-Manche
FO	Foreign Office
FTI	Finance Transport Industries (Divn, DTp)
GDP	Gross Domestic Product
GEC	General Electric Company
GLC	Greater London Council
GM	General Manager
GNP	Gross National Product
GoCo	Government-owned Company
H&LG	Housing and Local Government
HBS	Harvard Business School
HC	House of Commons
HGV	Heavy Goods Vehicle
HL	House of Lords
HO	Home Office
HSBC	Hongkong and Shanghai Banking Corporation
ICI	Imperial Chemical Industries
IFR	Investment and Financing Review
IGC	Channel Tunnel Intergovernmental Commission
IND	Immigration and Nationality Department (Home Office)
IRA	Irish Republican Army
IT	International Transport (Divn, DTp)
ITN	Independent Television News
JEXIM	Export-Import Bank of Japan
Jnc.	Junction
L&H	Livesey and Henderson
LCR	London and Continental Railways
LP of C	Lord President of the Council
LSE	London School of Economics
LUL	London Underground Ltd
MAED	Maritime, Aviation and Environment Department (FCO)
MD	Managing Director
MdO	Maître d'Oeuvre
MEP	Member of the European Parliament
MHLG	Ministry of Health and Local Government
MIT	Massachusetts Institute of Technology
MMC	Monopolies and Mergers Commission

MoD	Ministry of Defence
MP	Member of Parliament
MPA	Major Projects Association
MT	Ministry of Transport
MTCA	Ministry of Transport and Civil Aviation
MUC	Minimum Usage Charge
MVA	Martin Vorhees Associates
NATO	North Atlantic Treaty Organisation
NatWest	National Westminster (Bank)
NEDC	National Economic Development Council
NEDO	National Economic Development Office
NPV	Net Present Value
NUR	National Union of Railwaymen
OECD	Organisation for Economic Co-operation and Development
OFT	Office of Fair Trading
OPEC	Organisation of Petroleum Exporting Countries
PAC	Public Accounts Committee (HC)
P&O	Peninsular and Oriental Steam Navigation Company
Parl.	Parliamentary
Parl.Deb.	Parliamentary Debates (Hansard)
PBKA	Paris-Brussels-Köln-Amsterdam (rail network)
PCA	Parliamentary Commissioner for Administration
PE	Public Enterprises (Group, Treasury)
PESC	Public Expenditure Survey Committee
PFI	Private Finance Initiative
PID	Project Implementation Division (Eurotunnel)
PM	Prime Minister
PP	Parliamentary Papers
PPP	Public–Private Partnership
PPS	Principal Private Secretary
PQ	Parliamentary Question
PREM	Prime Minister's Office
PRO	Public Record Office (now The National Archive)
PS	Private Secretary
PTR	Public Transport and Research (DTp)
PUSS	Parliamentary Under-Secretary of State
RACHEL	Rainham to Channel Tunnel
RE	Railway Executive (BRB)
REC	Railway Executive Committee (BRB)
RfD	Railfreight Distribution
RIBA	Royal Institute of British Architects
Rlys	Railways
RT	Rio Tinto
RTZ	Rio Tinto-Zinc

RTZDE	RTZ Development Enterprises
S&O	Systems and Operations
SC	Select Committee
SCREG	Société Chimique Routière et d'Entreprise Générale
Sec	Secretary
SEPM	Société d'Etude du Pont sur la Manche
SETCM	Société d'Etude du Tunnel Complet routier et ferroviaire sous la Manche
SETEC	Société d'Etudes Techniques et Economiques
SFTM	Société Française du Tunnel sous la Manche
SHAPE	Supreme Headquarters, Allied Powers Europe
SNCB	Société Nationale des Chemins de Fer Belges
SNCF	Société Nationale des Chemins de Fer Français
SOGEI	Société Générale d'Exploitation Industrielle
SOLAS	International Convention for the Safety of Life at Sea
SoS	Secretary of State
TALIS	Thames Alternative Link International System
TBM	Tunnel Boring Machine
TGV	Train à Grande Vitesse
TGWU	Transport and General Workers' Union
TML	Transmanche-Link
TPRU	Transport Policy Research Unit (DTp)
TRRL	Transport and Road Research Laboratory
TSG	Tunnel Signalling Group
TSI	Technical Studies Inc
TUC	Trades Union Congress
UAC	Unit of Account
UBS	Union Bank of Switzerland
UIC	Union International des Chemins de Fer
UMIST	University of Manchester Institute of Science and Technology
UNESCO	United Nations Educational, Scientific and Cultural Organisation
U-Sec	Under-Secretary
UWIST	University of Wales Institute of Science and Technology
VP	Vice President
WED	Western European Dept (FCO)

1

BEGINNINGS, 1802–1945

1. The early possibilities

Interest in the idea of linking Britain to the continent of Europe and specifically to France is usually identified as beginning in the early nineteenth century. In the middle of the French Wars, a French mining engineer, Jacques-Joseph Mathieu-Favier, apparently made the somewhat implausible suggestion that the time was ripe to link countries who were then enemies. His proposal envisaged a two-gallery tunnel from Cap Gris Nez to Folkestone, to be constructed from each side to an artificial island on Varne bank in mid-channel. Services were to be provided by horse-drawn coaches. It seems that during the brief peace of Amiens in 1802–3 Napoleon expressed an interest in the proposal, and in informal discussions with Charles James Fox, a former foreign secretary, it was suggested that the scheme was ambitious enough to require the two countries to undertake it jointly. However, the resumption of war for a further decade and a half put paid to such exploratory discussions.[1]

In the first half of the century the initiatives for a fixed link crossing came mainly from the French. Bridges, bored tunnels, and immersed tubes were all suggested. In the 1830s the mining engineer Thomé de Gamond began four decades of investigation of the Channel strata, making a significant contribution by asserting that the chalk strata were continuous.[2] Another leading figure was Hector Horeau, who advanced the idea of a submerged tube in 1851. However, the British were never far behind, as the work of James Wylson, William Low and John Hawkshaw demonstrates (Table 1.1). In 1855 Wylson proposed an ingenious if somewhat implausible *floating* tunnel, anchored by ties and buoys, costed at £15 million. More importantly, it was the work of the British engineers Low and Hawkshaw in the 1860s that had the most influence in engineering terms. Low teamed up with de Gamond and another British engineer, John Brunlees, to produce the first serious plan for a tunnel, between Dover's South Foreland and Sangatte, near Calais.[3] Hawkshaw's privately funded trial borings in 1865–7 convinced de Gamond to abandon the idea of using Varne bank for a more direct route through the chalk between St. Margaret's Bay, east of Dover, and Sangatte. De Gamond was also encouraged to join an Anglo-French consortium led by

Table 1.1 Select list of early proposals for a fixed channel link, 1803–89

Date	*Proposer*	*Country of origin*	*Mode*
1803	Jacques–Joseph Mathieu–Favier	France	tunnel
1833–67	Louis Joseph Aimé Thomé de Gamond	France	tube, bridge, tunnel
1843	Cyprien Tessié du Mottay and Charles Franchot	France	immersed tube
1851	Hector Horeau	France	immersed tube
1855	James Wylson	Britain	immersed tube
1855	Léopold Favre	France	tunnel
1856	William Austin	Britain	tunnel
1865	John Hawkshaw and Hartsinck Day	Britain	trial borings
1867	William Low *et al.*	Britain	tunnel
1869, 1875	A. Mottier	France	bridge
1872	Channel Tunnel Co.	Britain	tunnel: borings
1875	Chemin de Fer Sous-Marin	France	tunnel: borings
1881–2	South Eastern Railway/ Submarine Continental Co.	Britain	tunnel: borings
1889	Hildevert Hersent *et al.*/ Schneider et Cie	France/ Britain	bridge

Source: Alphonse de Longuemar, 'Tunnel sous-marin anglo-français', *Journal de la Vienne*, 29 December 1857; Peter A. Keen, 'The Channel Tunnel Project', *Journal of Transport History*, III (1957–8); Humphrey Slater and Correlli Barnett, *The Channel Tunnel* (1958); Thomas Whiteside, *The Tunnel under the Channel* (1962); Mick Hamer, 'La [sic] rêve de Napoleon ... *et al*!', in Bronwen Jones (ed.), *The Tunnel: The Channel and Beyond* (Chichester, 1987); Donald Hunt, *The Tunnel: The Story of the Channel Tunnel 1802–1994* (Upton-upon-Severn, 1994); Keith Wilson, *Channel Tunnel Visions, 1850–1945: Dreams and Nightmares* (1994); Bertrand Lemoine, *Le Tunnel sous la Manche* (Paris, 1994); Richard Rogers, 'England & the Channel Tunnel', University of Amsterdam PhD thesis, 1998.

Lord Richard Grosvenor, MP for Flintshire, and Michel Chevalier, the Inspector-General of Mines in France, to take the project forward in a more commercial sense.[4]

While the technical feasibility of such a tunnel may have seemed somewhat remote at first, it is clear that by the early nineteenth century enthusiasts could point to the success of a number of striking engineering feats, particularly in British canal-building. Some of the tunnelling extended for over a mile, notably James Brindley's Harecastle Tunnel on the Trent & Mersey Canal in 1777, $1\frac{2}{3}$miles long, and the two-mile Sapperton Tunnel on the Thames & Severn of 1789. The biggest of all was the Standedge Tunnel traversing the Pennines on the Huddersfield Canal, completed in 1811 and over three miles long.[5] These were all land-based projects, of course. The first under-river tunnel for public use was Marc Isambard Brunel's crossing of the Thames in London. His Thames Tunnel, from Wapping to Rotherhithe, took 18 years to complete (1825–43) and encountered serious problems of safety and financing as construction costs rose (the final cost was £468,250). However, this was a major achievement in the science of tunnelling, in demonstrating the feasibility of under-water tunnelling, and the successful use of Brunel's invention, the tunnelling shield.[6]

The introduction of railways provided further impetus to the art of the possible. This revolutionary technology, the most important of the century, embraced significant advances in civil engineering, and in difficult terrain bridges and tunnels were critical elements of the new infrastructure. Thus, as early as 1832 officials of the newly opened Leicester & Swannington Railway invited disconcerted passengers to enter Robert Stephenson's impressive, even frightening Glenfield Tunnel near Leicester, then Britain's longest at just over a mile. Six years later, the London & Greenwich Railway – London's first – was operating trains over nearly four miles of continuous viaduct.[7] The Sheffield, Ashton-under-Lyne & Manchester Railway's Woodhead Tunnel was one of the wonders of the world on its opening in 1845, though at 3 miles 22 yards its length was merely a tenth of what was required for the crossing of the channel. The major railway tunnel of the late nineteenth century in Britain, Sir John Hawkshaw's Severn Tunnel of 1886, was over a mile longer at 4 miles 628 yards, and on the continent of Europe the Mont Cenis (1871) and St. Gotthard (1882) tunnels were respectively, 8 miles 868 yards and 9 miles 562 yards long. These larger works were also significant in engineering terms. They offered more instructive precedents for a channel tunnel since they could not be constructed by traditional methods, that is by connecting a series of ventilation shafts sunk from the surface, a method adopted by most of the canal and railway tunnels. Instead they made use of compressed air boring machines, a new technology.[8] However, it was not until the building of London's underground railways that something approaching the length of tunnel was actually attempted. In 1884 the Inner Circle line extended to 13 miles, though it was barely below ground, having been constructed on the 'cut and cover' principle.[9] The small-bore, 'tube' lines built in the early twentieth century offered a closer approximation to the engineering challenge of a channel crossing. When the Piccadilly line was opened in 1906 its tunnel length was $7\frac{3}{4}$ miles; by 1926, however, the City & South London/Hampstead (Northern) line's extensions had produced an unbroken tunnel from Morden to Highgate (Archway) of over 16 miles in length.[10] Building to the appropriate length was not enough, of course. Cost and safety considerations were also critical, and here difficulties were experienced in all developed countries. Sceptics were able to point to several examples of faulty forecasting, major cost over-runs, and, on some occasions, to failures and disasters. The loss of life in constructing the Great Western Railway's Box Hill Tunnel between Chippenham and Bath in the late 1830s was particularly distressing. Half a century later the Severn Tunnel project encountered numerous engineering problems and cost £1.8 million to build, about £150 million in 2005 prices. The most spectacular disaster was, of course, the collapse during a gale of the Tay Bridge in December 1879.[11]

2. The commercial possibilities: Lord Richard Grosvenor, Sir Edward Watkin and the 'Manchester to Paris Railroad'

Early engineering effort and speculation gave way to more substantial proposals in the 1870s. By this time free trade was gaining ground, the benefits of linking Britain and France had been fully demonstrated by the submarine telegraph cable constructed in 1851, while the domestic railway network in both countries provided good communications with Folkestone, Dover, Boulogne and Calais.[12] A fixed link was clearly consonant with the Liberal vision of free trade and international co-operation espoused by Richard Cobden and John Bright.[13] The Anglo-French consortium met Napoleon III in 1868, and were given considerable encouragement. The group included, on the British side, Grosvenor, and prominent engineers such as Low, Hawkshaw, Brunlees and Thomas Brassey, and on the French side, Chevalier, Paulin Talabot, the Chief Engineer of Roads and Bridges, and de Gamond. While numerous schemes had surfaced for improving transport links in the early 1870s, it was this consortium which first turned ideas into tangible venture capitalist activity. By 1872 it had obtained declarations from both the British and French Governments that they had no objection in principle to the construction of a tunnel. The British were more cautious than the French, however. There were fears of sanctioning a perpetual private monopoly, and the personal objections of Queen Victoria.[14] Nevertheless, these difficulties were surmounted, and Benjamin Disraeli's Government, having inherited the issue from William Gladstone's previous administration, joined with France in 1875 in appointing a joint commission to examine the basis for a treaty. The commission's protocol of May 1876 provided the ground rules for a formal treaty by determining important points of principle, for example the boundary between the two countries, each country's rights to purchase the tunnel, suspend services, or destroy it for security reasons, and the extent of the concessions to be granted. It also recommended that a permanent international commission be set up to regulate construction, operation and maintenance.[15] At the same time steps were being taken by commercial interests in the two countries to turn promotional intention into corporate activity. In France a tunnel company, the Société du Chemin de Fer Sous-Marin Entre la France et l'Angleterre, was formed in 1875, with Chevalier as chairman. Enjoying the financial support of the Chemin de Fer du Nord and the French house of Rothschilds, the company was granted a concession for construction and went on to undertake preparatory geological investigations.[16] After the renewal of its concession for a further three years in 1880, it continued with the boring of a pilot tunnel, which extended to about 1,840 metres (*c.*$1\frac{1}{4}$ miles) by March 1883. Further progress depended on the company reaching agreement with a British counterpart, and it was here that difficulties arose.

In Britain two rival groups emerged. The interests headed by Grosvenor lost no time in forming a company, the Channel Tunnel Co. Ltd, in 1872, with an initial capital of £30,000.[17] Like its counterpart in France it obtained legislation in 1875, though in the British case the Act enabled it merely to purchase land at St. Margaret's Bay, in order to conduct experimental boring operations. However, despite enjoying the blessing of the joint commission, the company was prevented from proceeding by a lack of resources. An attempt to raise £80,000 with the help of its bankers, the English house of Rothschilds,[18] failed. No financial support was provided by the two principal railway companies, the London Chatham & Dover, led by James Staats Forbes, and the South Eastern, led by Sir Edward Watkin. Their companies were not only short of cash but also locked in bitter rivalry. The French promoters had hoped that their English counterparts would match their investment of £80,000, and the Nord Railway hoped that the two British railway companies would match its investment of £40,000. The South Eastern had agreed to put up £20,000 if the London Chatham & Dover did the same, but there was little prospect of the two companies agreeing, and the South Eastern refused to co-operate while the Channel Tunnel Co. insisted on St. Margaret's Bay as its preferred site on the English side. A prospectus issued by the Channel Tunnel Co. in 1876 stated that the London Chatham & Dover and N.M. Rothschild had each agreed to put up £20,000, but the remaining £40,000 did not come from the market. Progress was thus limited, and no Anglo-French treaty emerged.[19]

Watkin, a buccaneering entrepreneur, was determined to pursue his own ambitions, a Manchester to Paris railroad created from the railway companies he controlled, viz. the Manchester Sheffield & Lincolnshire (from 1897 the Great Central), the Metropolitan in London, and the South Eastern.[20] In 1874 he was elected Liberal MP for Hythe in Kent and encouraged the South Eastern to include in its Act for that year powers to undertake experimental works.[21] First he sounded out the leading members of the French company, Chevalier, his successor, Léon Say, the President of the French Senate, the engineer Alexandre Lavalley, and Fernand Raoul-Duval. Then, by 1880 he was ready to press for a tunnel route more favourable to his own railway, that is starting from Abbot's Cliff and Shakespeare Cliff, between Dover and Folkestone. Under the direction of the South Eastern's engineer, Francis Brady, the South Eastern engaged Col. Frederick Beaumont and others to employ the newly-patented Beaumont-English compressed-air boring machine to drive pilot tunnels in the area. Work began in 1881, thanks to further powers obtained in that year. After discussions with the French company, the Submarine Continental Railway Co. was formed in December 1881 with a capital of £250,000 to take over the South Eastern's works. Initial shareholders included the South Eastern Railway, and William Low, who had left Grosvenor's group after bitter arguments with Hawkshaw.[22] By July 1883 the company had spent £56,000 in driving three tunnels through the lower chalk stratum, including 2,026 yards of tunnel (diameter: 7ft.) out to sea from Shakespeare Cliff.[23]

There were limits to Watkin's promotional zeal, however. It is clear that while he accepted that the railway companies would build the connecting lines, neither the South Eastern nor the London Chatham & Dover had the resources to finance half a tunnel. In the 1870s he argued that given the project's long gestation period the private sector would be unwilling to take on the risk, and the two governments should therefore provide a financial guarantee. When tunnelling began in the 1880s he tried to persuade Joseph Chamberlain, then President of the Board of Trade, that the tunnel itself should be undertaken as a public investment. Neither proposal was palatable.[24] There were other difficulties, too. In 1882 the Board of Trade asserted that the South Eastern had acted *ultra vires* in tunnelling beyond the low-water mark without its permission and further work was halted after a reference to the High Court.[25] Watkin's abrasive style hindered agreement between the main parties, as is evident from his correspondence with Grosvenor and Say. Furthermore, Sir Nathaniel and Alfred de Rothschild were upset by the failure of Watkin and Forbes to reach an understanding, and finding Watkin's methods of doing business particularly unappealing, they quickly lost interest in the project.[26] Efforts by the two competing tunnel companies to obtain further powers in 1882–3, the Channel Tunnel Co. in association with the London Chatham & Dover, and the Submarine Continental with the South Eastern, were then frustrated by a groundswell of opposition which emerged within Britain's ruling circles. Work on both sides of the channel then ceased. The French were particularly resentful, having invested £80,000 in their tunnelling (1,825 yards).[27]

If in the 1870s the rivalry of the competing railway companies had proved a barrier to progress, in the following decade military objections were paramount. The Government's action in halting the works was clearly driven by military advice which emphasised the threat to Britain from an invasion. This became clear during Gladstone's next administration. In response to Watkin's announcements of success with the tunnel boring machine, the Board of Trade, War Office and Admiralty established a departmental committee to examine the issue in 1881–2. The committee, consisting of Thomas Farrer, Vice-Admiral Phillimore and Col. J.H. Smith, was immediately presented with entirely opposite views. On the one hand, Lt.-General Sir John Adye, Surveyor-General of the Ordnance, referred to the commercial advantages of a tunnel and expressed little fear of any danger to the integrity of Britain. On the other hand, Lt.-General Sir Garnet Wolseley, the Adjutant-General, carried most support with a highly emotive memorandum. He argued passionately that a tunnel would destroy all the strategic advantages of the channel for a major naval power. It would be difficult, he contended, to prevent the tunnel being used as a springboard for invasion, in which case Britain's comparatively small standing army would be at a distinct disadvantage. Invoking both Wellington and Napoleon, he claimed that the tunnel would be 'a constant inducement to the unscrupulous foreigner to make war upon us … Surely, John Bull will not endanger his birth-right, his liberty, his property … simply in order that men and women may cross to and fro between Britain and France without running the risk of sea-sickness.'[28] Wolseley's view received sympathetic support from the Admiralty, and from Foreign Office officials. Lord Tenterden and Sir Charles Dilke, permanent under-secretaries in the Foreign Office, also raised the spectre of French or German soldiers disguised as civilians seizing the tunnel in peacetime, and emphasised the commercial waste involved in destroying the tunnel in the event of either a war with France or another Franco-German conflict to follow the Franco-Prussian War of 1870–1.[29] With the committee unable to reach a firm decision, the issue of military safeguards passed to a special 'scientific' committee appointed by the War Office to advise it on ways of making the tunnel useless to an enemy.[30] The process helped to produce more staunch opponents, notably Hugh Childers, Secretary of State for War until December 1882 and then Chancellor of the Exchequer, the Duke of Cambridge, Commander-in-Chief of the British Army, and outside government, petitioners such as Cardinal Manning, Lord Tennyson, Herbert Spencer and the Governor of the Bank of England, Henry Grenfell. A much smaller group of enthusiasts included John Bright, MP, Colonel Sir Andrew Clarke, the Inspector-General of Fortifications, and representatives of the working class, notably the London Trades Council.[31] The debate culminated in the appointment in 1883 of a joint parliamentary select committee chaired by Lord Lansdowne, a future foreign secretary. While Lord Lansdowne himself was enthusiastic about the commercial prospects of a tunnel and felt the military apprehensions to be exaggerated, his colleagues were bitterly divided. Only three of his nine colleagues were prepared to sign his report, and in the end the committee was only able to express the opinion, by a majority of six to four, that parliamentary sanction should not be given.[32] The Foreign Office was also hostile. Its anxiety about a long-term commitment to France, given numerous disagreements (e.g., over Egypt and the Sudan, culminating in the Fashoda Crisis of 1898) and the abundant evidence of its political instability, proved to be another enduring element.[33] As time went on, Anglo-German rivalry intensified, providing further ammunition for the tunnel sceptics.[34]

There the matter rested. Subsequent co-operation among the competing commercial interests provided some hope for supporters of a tunnel, who included (in later life) William Gladstone. The Submarine Continental purchased the Channel Tunnel Co. in 1886 following an increase of capital to £275,000 and adopted the latter's name in 1887. All this made little difference in practice, however. While several bills and motions were introduced in parliament, in fact on eleven further occasions to 1895,[35] all foundered on the rock of military objection, fed from time to time by reports raising the spectre of invasion and by efforts to ward off cuts in defence spending.[36] More determined efforts were made to revive the scheme in the Edwardian period, when the Liberals were returned to power. Inter-railway rivalry had been dissipated with the merger of the South Eastern and London Chatham & Dover companies in 1899. Electric traction now offered a more practical solution to the problems of steep gradients and ventilation in a long tunnel. There was also enthusiastic support in France, notably from Albert Sartiaux, General Manager of the Nord railway, who with Sir Francis Fox (of Sir Douglas Fox & Partners) prepared a tunnel scheme in 1904–6 costed at £16 million. An attempt was made to allay military fears by proposing that a viaduct be built over the sea close to the tunnel's mouth to make it easier to disable if circumstances demanded it (Figure 1.1).[37] Serious consideration was given to the issue within government in 1906–7 and again in 1913–14. On both occasions the recently-formed Committee of Imperial Defence provided the principal forum for

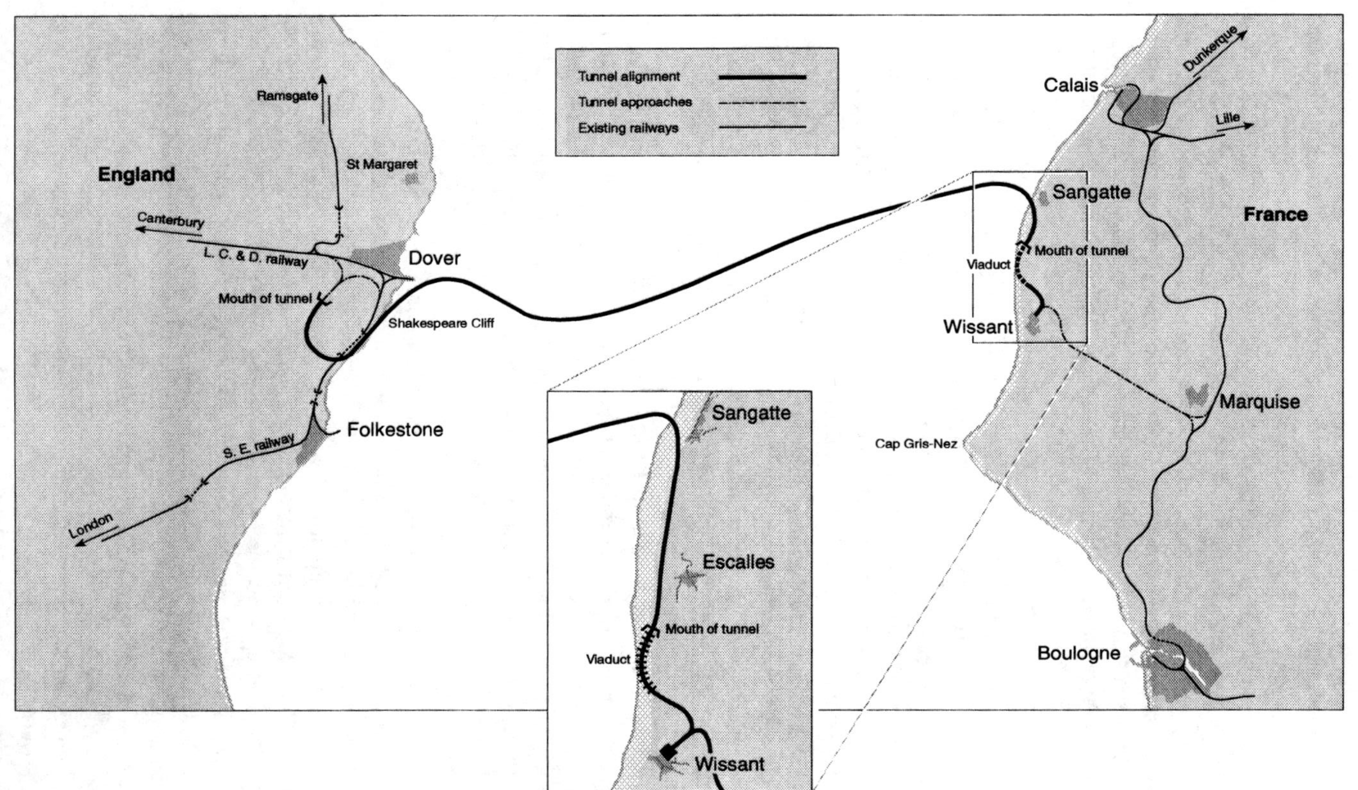

Figure 1.1 Sartiaux-Fox Channel Tunnel scheme with strategic viaduct, 1906.

debate within government circles. In 1906–7, Sir George Clarke (subsequently Lord Sydenham), the Secretary to the Committee, argued strongly for the tunnel, in the wake of the Anglo-French Entente Cordiale of 1904. He asserted his long-held view that the military arguments about Britain's vulnerability to attack were largely specious.[38] Opinion within the Board of Trade, on the other hand, was rather lukewarm. The commercial impact was uncertain, it was argued, but the likelihood was that imports from France and neighbouring countries would rise. Sir Herbert Llewellyn Smith's revealing view was that whatever the reality of the military risks, the danger of popular panic, and the encouragement this would give to an increase in military spending, provided the biggest single argument against the tunnel. The Prime Minister, Sir Henry Campbell-Bannerman,

Cartoon 1 Channel Tunnel phobia: military fears about the Tunnel, W.K. Haselden, *Daily Mirror*, 18 February 1907 [Centre for the Study of Cartoons and Caricature].

confined the debate to the narrow military aspects, helping to ensure that, given the opposition of the Admiralty and General Staff, the proposal was rejected.[39]

In 1913–14 pressure exerted by Arthur Fell, Conservative MP for Great Yarmouth and Chairman of the newly-formed House of Commons Channel Tunnel Committee, led to a re-examination of the issue. Fell's committee, which had the backing of a large number of MPs, formed a deputation which met the Prime Minister, Herbert Asquith, in August 1913, and extracted a promise that the Committee of Imperial Defence would conduct another review. Here the military interest was seriously split for the first time. Within the army Sir John French, the Chief of the Imperial General Staff, and General Sir Henry Wilson, Director of Military Operations, were now stressing the value of a tunnel to assist Britain in operations on the continent in alliance with France, though critics pointed to the associated and self-serving emphasis on the need for a larger standing army. French went so far as to argue that submarines and aircraft had subverted the defence offered by the sea, and that a tunnel would be militarily advantageous in the event of a war with Germany. The First Lord of the Admiralty, Winston Churchill, was also in favour of a tunnel. However, views like these were resisted, with the help of Maurice Hankey, now secretary of the Committee of Imperial Defence, who exploited the various differences of opinion, notably the inconsistent stance of the Admiralty, and the position of Asquith, who was characteristically equivocal.[40] Thus, in 1914, as in 1907, military and naval objections, fed by a sentimental appeal to insularity pervasive among opinion formers, proved dominant.[41]

3. The inter-war years

After the First World War the mood changed again and the Government exhibited less hostility to the idea of a link. Wartime experience, and shipping losses in particular, had led to popular belief, set out at length in several newspapers, that the tunnel would have been beneficial to the war effort. Pressure to build it was exerted by Fell, Sir Francis Dent and Sir Percy Tempest of the South Eastern & Chatham Railway, and Baron Emile d'Erlanger, now Chairman of the Channel Tunnel Co.[42] The climate was encouraging enough for the Channel Tunnel Co. to try out a new tunnelling machine designed by Douglas Whitaker of Leicester.[43] Military opposition had eased a little too, with Marshal Foch, the Commander-in-Chief of the French armies, going so far as to assert that a tunnel would have helped Britain to defeat Germany and shortened the war by two years.[44] Moreover, during the Paris Peace Conference of 1919 the Prime Minister, Lloyd George, revealed that he regarded the construction of a Channel Tunnel as an important element in any Anglo-American guarantee of support for France against Germany.[45] In France lobbying increased after 1921, when the Comité Français du Tunnel sous la Manche was created by Paul Cambon.[46] In Britain Parliament returned to the subject in 1919–20 and in 1924. Once again the public records indicate the continuing strength of scepticism within Whitehall, typified by Sir Maurice Hankey, and the armed services, which won the day once the post-war diplomatic euphoria had evaporated.[47] On the latter occasion a deputation led by Sir William Bull, Fell's successor as Chairman of the Channel Tunnel Committee, met the Prime Minister, Ramsay MacDonald, who again referred the proposal, a twin-bore tunnel costed at £29 million, to the Committee of Imperial Defence.[48] On this occasion, thanks to Hankey, the committee's membership was strengthened by the presence of four former Prime Ministers (Balfour, Asquith, Lloyd George and Baldwin). Its advice, apparently arrived at after only forty minutes of deliberation, was accepted by the Government. It was argued that the commercial advantages of a tunnel were outweighed by the disadvantages in terms of security. Although some of the more extreme fears of invasion had eased somewhat, the majority opinion was that a tunnel would lead to significant demands for additional defence spending to protect it.[49] There was dismay among supporters. In a trenchant article for the *Weekly Dispatch* Winston Churchill asked: 'Should Strategists Veto the Tunnel?' He went on: 'In forty minutes five ex- or future-ex Prime Ministers dismissed with an imperial gesture the important and complicated scheme for a Channel Tunnel ... One spasm of mental concentration enables these five super-men, who have spent their lives in proving each other incapable and misguided on every other object, to arrive at a unanimous conclusion'.[50]

Further lobbying by enthusiasts, including Gordon Selfridge, the department store magnate,[51] accompanied by supportive noises from the French,[52] built up to such an extent that Stanley Baldwin's Conservative Government was moved in April 1929 to appoint a Channel Tunnel Committee to examine the 'economic aspects of proposals for the construction of a Channel Tunnel or other new form of cross-Channel communication'. The Committee, chaired by Edward Peacock, a Director of the Bank of England, concluded, in its report in March 1930, that notwithstanding the need to verify the feasibility of construction through the lower chalk, a tunnel, which should be built by the private sector without subsidy, would be economically beneficial. Two serious proposals had been examined: the first presented by the d'Erlangers' Channel Tunnel Co.; the second advanced by another erstwhile campaigner, William Collard, of the woollen merchants Collard Parsons & Co. Collard, Chairman of London and Paris Railway Promoters Ltd, dusted off an ambitious and expensive scheme first conceived in 1895. He proposed to build the tunnel together with a new, broad-gauge (7ft) railway from London to Paris, and sought legitimacy by engaging the services of the noted railway manager Philip Burtt, former Deputy General Manager of the North Eastern Railway and lecturer in railway economics at the London School of Economics. Construction costs were estimated at £189 million.[53] The Channel Tunnel Co. developed a more realistic and much cheaper scheme in association with the Southern Railway (a company created in 1923 with the merger of the South Eastern & Chatham, London & South Western and London Brighton & South Coast railways). Its 36 miles of twin tunnel (diameter: 18.5 ft) would take eight years to build and cost about £30.45 million. Additional infrastructure would be required at each end of the tunnel, but there would be no new, high-speed railway (Figure 1.2).[54] The Committee favoured the latter scheme but was not unanimous

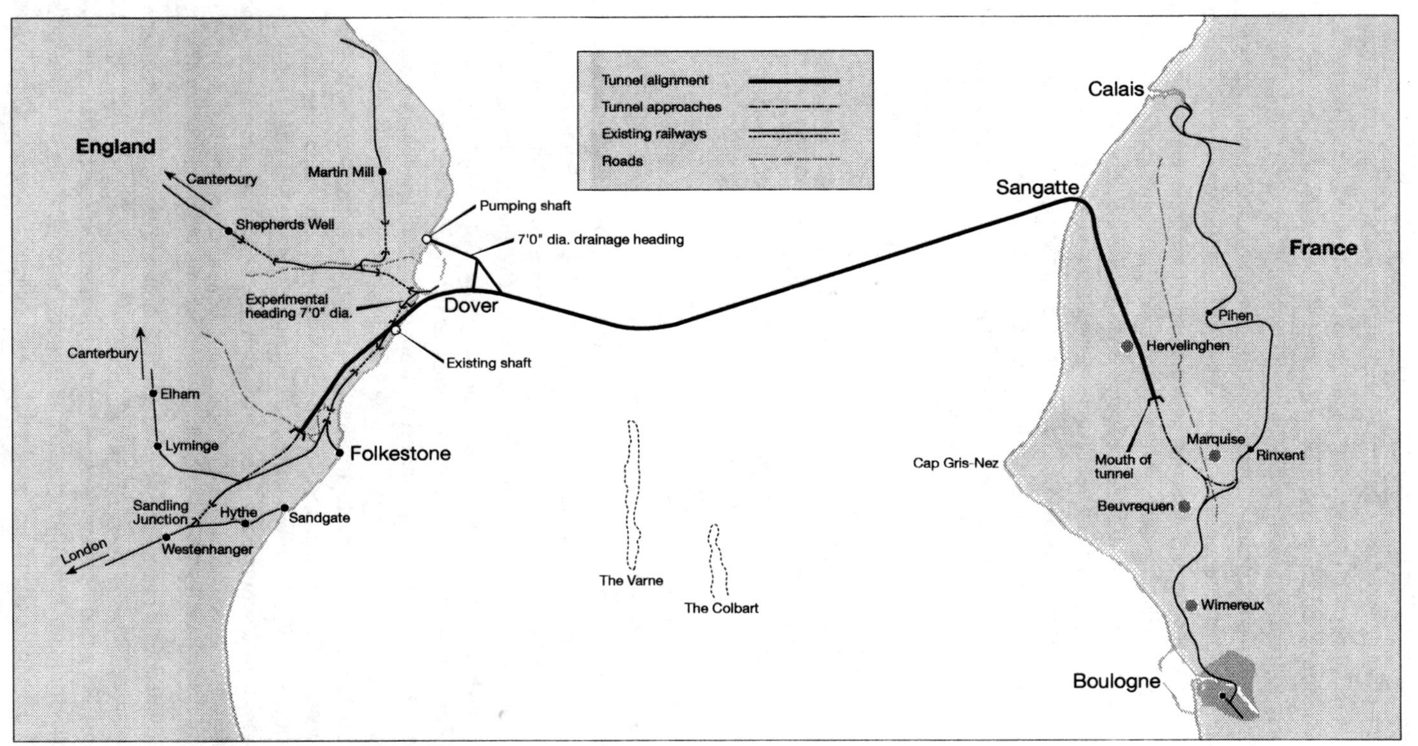

Figure 1.2 Channel Tunnel Co. scheme, 1929–30.

in its enthusiasm for the project. A minute of dissent recorded by Lord Ebbisham, a recently-appointed director of the Southern Railway and former Conservative MP for Epsom, opposed the tunnel on economic grounds. Ebbisham considered the traffic projections to be inflated, and argued that the most predictable effects were likely to be an adverse impact on British shipping and agriculture.[55]

It was evident that opposition within Whitehall was still entrenched. A statement by the Government, now a Labour administration led by Ramsay MacDonald, in June 1930, poured cold water on the Committee's Report. MacDonald's stance was assisted on the one hand by Hankey's continuing machinations and on the other by the scepticism of Philip Snowden, the Chancellor, and the Treasury.[56] The latter's views were given additional force by the recommendations of a special policy committee which included Sir Andrew Duncan (chairman), John Maynard Keynes and Ernest Bevin among its members.[57] This committee was briefed by a single Treasury paper heavily critical of the presented case for a tunnel. Unsurprisingly, then, its principal recommendation was that should the private sector fail to produce the required financial support, the advantages of a tunnel as presented appeared insufficient to justify either construction by the public sector or financial assistance from the Government. The committee also cocked a snook at the Channel Tunnel Committee for failing to bring forth the necessary information on expected revenue and traffic generation. However, in a parting shot the committee gave some comfort to tunnel supporters. Should the tunnel be shown to be in the national interest, it argued, there was a 'strong case' for government participation, either in whole or in part.[58] The Government's statement saw no promise of gains in the national interest, however. It emphasised the engineering and economic risks, encouraged by equivocal reactions from the Board of Trade, which challenged the freight traffic benefits, noted the 'lukewarm' response from British industry and agriculture, and contended that defence costs would rise substantially, a view which continued to be expressed by the Committee of Imperial Defence.[59] Some Foreign Office officials were more enthusiastic, but their views were not shared by either their Minister, Austen Chamberlain, or their Permanent Under-Secretary, Sir Ronald Lindsay.[60] There was no consensus in railway circles either. The cause was scarcely helped by the somewhat detached evidence presented to the Committee of Sir Herbert Walker, General Manager of the Southern Railway (see below). And the railway press included expressions of scepticism about the traffic forecasts supplied by the promoters, notably a paper given by E. Godfrey, to the Great Western Railway (London) Lecture and Debating Society in January 1930.[61] Supporters were therefore unable to reverse a half-century of opposition to the tunnel. A Commons motion in support was presented by Ernest Thurtle as a private member on 30 June 1930. In the event the free vote was very close, the motion being defeated by just seven votes (179–172).[62]

Three times a Channel Tunnel project had emerged – in 1883, 1913 and 1930, and three times it failed to obtain the support of government. Throughout the period from 1880 to 1945 military objections of various kinds remained a sticking point, reinforced by the opinions of those who preferred the status quo to radical change. The tunnel was thought unlikely to offer an expeditionary force an advantage over sea transport, while the commercial tunnel operations would have an adverse effect on channel steamer services at ports such as Folkestone and Newhaven, which the military might wish to use in the event of war.[63] Furthermore, the railway companies had invested in alternatives, operating a large fleet of steamships and developing the train-ferry. The ferry concept was first employed by the London & North Eastern Railway's freight-only Harwich-Zeebrugge service in 1924. In 1936 the Southern Railway introduced a train-ferry service from Dover to Dunkerque for both freight and passengers, the latter travelling by the much-vaunted 'Night Ferry'.[64]

In fact, the attitude of the Southern was not entirely helpful in the inter-war years. Committed to an ambitious electrification programme, but strapped for cash, as all the 'Big Four' companies were, it could only emphasise the financial burden it would face in providing railway works should the tunnel be built. When representatives of the Channel Tunnel Co. met with those of the Southern in April 1929, it was agreed that a large station would have to be built near the tunnel entrance at Sandling Jnc., and that the continental or 'Berne' loading gauge should be adopted for the line to London. The total cost was put at a challenging £10–12 million, and on top of this, the Southern wanted compensation for the loss of shipping revenue (about £0.5 million a year) and for liabilities relating to capital expenditure at the channel ports.[65] It is true that the costs were scaled down when the General Manager, Walker, first appeared before the Committee in July. In the intervening three months he had been informed by the Nord Railway Co. that the continental railways would be prepared to receive (and even build) rolling stock to the smaller, English loading gauge. This concession would reduce the capital burden facing the Southern to something nearer £3 million.[66] Nevertheless, Walker's overall lack of enthusiasm did not go unnoticed. He maintained that the Southern would incur a net loss of £450,000 in the first year of the tunnel's operation, and there was a lively debate with one of the Committee members, the banker Sir Henry Strakosch, about the traffic forecasts which the railway manager favoured. Strakosch observed rather pointedly that while a survey of trends since 1850 suggested that cross-channel traffic had been growing by over 4 per cent, Walker's more limited projections suggested a growth of under 2 per cent.[67] The promoters' cause was scarcely helped by such joustings. Not for the first (nor the last) time, the railways' attitude to the tunnel scheme played a part in its rejection.[68]

However, it is clear that the appeal to military risks dominated the arguments against a tunnel. And the backcloth to the debate was a widely-held view that Britain derived advantages, social and otherwise, from its physical separation from the rest of Europe. Ebbisham hinted at this in his dissenting minute, referring to the advisability, 'in the case of an island people such as ourselves', of keeping 'open all possible channels of communication'. Hostility to the idea was often cloaked in emotional reactions to perceived social dangers. Many within

Britain's ruling elite exhibited a profound insularity, nursing varying degrees of xenophobia about the likely effect of a physical connection with continental Europe upon the 'British way of life'. Rarely articulated publicly, such views came to the surface, for example in the evidence given by the Earl of Crawford to the Channel Tunnel Committee in 1929. Educated at Eton and Magdalen College Oxford, Lord Crawford (1871–1940) had been Conservative MP for Chorley, 1895–1913, was a former chief whip and wartime minister and had served as Chancellor of Manchester University since 1923. He explained that a tunnel would expose Britain to a torrent of criminality, homosexuality, pornography and drug trafficking – elements which, he claimed, were the particular preserve of foreigners. Such views, which as many scholars have shown, have a long provenance, were not to be underestimated when MPs came to vote.[69] Campbell-Bannerman's personal opinion of the tunnel was characteristic of so many Prime Ministers when in power over the 70 years to 1945: 'I have never thought much of the so-called military objections or seen actual danger in the proposed tunnel; but undoubtedly it would cause great uneasiness and might lead to panic… Besides, I doubt its commercial advantages to this country.' Unwilling to take on the military, sceptical about the commercial prospects and wider economic benefits of a tunnel, successive governments were, above all, determined to avoid making a substantial financial commitment to the project. For justification they fell back on the more emotional appeal to 'Britishness' and the protection offered by the 'silver streak' or the 'moat defensive' in keeping Britain '*virgo intacta*'.[70]

The onset of the Second World War did not prevent discussion on the tunnel. In the months before hostilities began, the French were actively promoting a new scheme. André Basdevant's ambitious single-bore tunnel, which incorporated a four-lane motorway and, above it, a double-track railway, had been presented at the International Exhibition of 1937. It was then sponsored in the French Chamber of Deputies by Marcel Boucher.[71] On the British side parliamentary lobbyists pressed Prime Minister Neville Chamberlain for his support, but without success. When the War began, the French Minister of Public Works, Anatole de Monzie, made a statement advocating the construction of a tunnel after the War, but this too fell on Chamberlain's deaf ears.[72] After the Dunkirk evacuation in 1940 the Cabinet's Scientific Advisory Committee was drawn into the investigation of rumours that the Germans were secretly constructing a tunnel as the precursor to an invasion; once again Hankey attempted to exploit the occasion to maintain an anti-tunnel stance.[73] However, in one thing the War provided a positive stimulus to this much-debated project. The transformation of military technology which it produced – aircraft, rockets, and finally the atomic bomb – made the idea of barriers redundant, producing a major chink in the military objections to a tunnel in the post-war period. From this point the barriers to progress were other than military.

2

NEW ASPIRATIONS

The Channel Tunnel project, 1945–64

1. The Military threat recedes, but economic scepticism resurfaces

After the Second World War the military objections to the tunnel became progressively weaker.[1] Initially, however, opposition in Whitehall was still entrenched. Thus, when in May 1949 the Cabinet agreed to define its present attitude 'in case the matter should be raised by European Governments, either in the Council of Europe or otherwise', the Prime Minister, Clement Attlee, asked the interested departments to submit their views in writing. The exercise, reviewed by the Chancellor of the Duchy of Lancaster, Hugh Dalton, revealed not only that ministers were unanimous in opposing the early construction of a tunnel, but also that many of them opposed it in the longer-term. Sir Stafford Cripps, the Chancellor, was particularly hostile: 'This seems a vast waste of time', he noted.[2] The Chiefs of Staff noted that developments in military technology, for example the atomic bomb, more effective bombing by aircraft and rockets, advances in mining and submarine warfare, the use of aircraft for moving troops, and the increased weight of military equipment, strengthened the case for a tunnel, though they continued to argue that the military advantages were outweighed by the military disadvantages.[3] And inside the Foreign Office, the archives revealed that 'opinion... both official and ministerial, has always been heavily against the tunnel'. There were dangers: 'It is quite on the cards that France may fail to recover spiritually, economically, politically and militarily; and that she will succumb to Communism'. Lord Balfour's observation was repeated – 'As long as the ocean remains our friend, do not let us deliberately destroy its power to help us'. Finally, those familiar 'psychological' objections resurfaced. 'There is still an obvious significance, for the British people, in inhabiting an island having no land communication with its neighbours', the memorandum to Cabinet observed. 'An important element in the character of our national life would be altered by the creation of a land connection... one effect might for example be the weakening of that unquestioning sense of superiority over the peoples of the continent which forms an essential element in British self-confidence.'[4]

On the other hand, it was clear that by 1949 the Chiefs of Staff were ready to concede that 'the military considerations are of minor importance relative to any strong political and economic arguments for or against the project, always provided adequate means of putting the tunnel out of action are incorporated in its construction'. There were glimmers of opposition. In July 1954 Lance Mallalieu, joint chairman of the Channel Tunnel Parliamentary Committee, pressed Alan Lennox-Boyd, the Minister of Transport and Civil Aviation, about the long-standing objections. The Minister replied: 'I could not say that the old objections have been all removed'. At the same time wartime sceptics, such as Lord Montgomery, continued to echo Wolseley with their references to the benefits of 'our island home'. However, such arguments enjoyed less support in the late 1940s and 1950s than they had in the 1880s and 1920s.[5] In the post-NATO world, the western military establishment seemed to be more positive than negative. For example, in 1952 Supreme Headquarters Allied Powers Europe [SHAPE] had spent some time evaluating the advantages of André Basdevant's scheme for a large road-rail tunnel.[6] In the following year a report by the Ministry of Defence's Joint Administrative Planning Staff concluded that a tunnel might offer 'logistic advantages' in maintaining the line of command from Britain to the continent, though it would be vulnerable to attack in wartime, and its cost, together with the length of time it would take to build, scarcely made it an attractive proposition.[7] In the more public arena, most commentators agree that 16 February 1955 was a defining moment. In the Commons Mallalieu asked the Minister of Defence, Harold Macmillan, 'to what extent strategical objections still prevent the construction of a road-rail tunnel under the Channel from England to France'. Macmillan's pithy response was: 'Scarcely at all'.[8] By 1959 the British Chief of the Defence Staff was able to brief his Minister that 'the military advantages of a Channel tunnel now slightly outweigh the disadvantages… Subject to the incorporation of means of putting the tunnel out of action in an emergency, there are no valid military objections to the project'.[9]

The major stumbling blocks now were political and economic. The major change in post-war Britain was the Labour Government's nationalisation of the basic industrial infrastructure. Britain's private sector railway companies now joined their French counterparts (nationalised in 1937) in the public sector, with the establishment of the British Transport Commission in 1947. This meant that from the standpoint of central government the consideration of the project moved from that of sanctioning and regulating a private sector venture to that of having to fund it within what later became known as the 'public sector borrowing requirement'. With Britain's railways nationalised, Whitehall assumed initially that the tunnel would have to be undertaken by the British Transport Commission, in partnership with the Société Nationale des Chemins de Fer Français [SNCF]. As the MP Christopher Shawcross, founder of the revived Channel Tunnel Parliamentary Committee (see below), put it in a note to Churchill in 1949: 'It is agreed by all parties that the ownership and maintenance of the Tunnel could not now be, as originally proposed, in the hands of private enterprise'.[10] And in the climate of post-war austerity this was a remote prospect in 1945, or even in the early 1950s. The departmental memoranda circulated inside the Cabinet in 1949 make this clear. Both the Treasury and Board of Trade felt that such a large public investment – put at £90–100 million – would have a 'crowding-out' effect at a time when the post-war economic crisis was producing severe constraints upon capital investment in transport.[11] The latter found the economic case fragile. The tunnel was unlikely to either produce a significant reduction in transport costs – 'There is no sense in spending a fortune to save a bagatelle' – or, given the development of air transport, attract large amounts of additional traffic. The Ministry of Transport's view was that there were many transport schemes 'which would make a far higher economic return… The maintenance of the present shipping routes and particularly the improvement and development of the train ferry services (at an infinitely less cost than a tunnel) are probably the right policy for us to pursue'.[12] In this way, economic considerations replaced military objections as the principal obstacle.

Negative views persisted within the Ministry of Transport into the 1950s. After lobbying from the French at a conference of European ministers of transport in October 1954, the department re-examined the idea, but saw no reason to change its mind as a letter to the Foreign Office in February 1955 made clear. Its conclusion was that: 'having regard to the present facilities already provided by rail-ferries, ships and air services across the Channel and to the future development of air transport, there is no place for the Channel Tunnel in our transport system. Moreover, whatever economic grounds may at one time have been advanced, these are progressively disappearing. The project could only be undertaken at great capital expense and would be unremunerative'.[13] Eighteen months later, support for closer co-operation with the French inside the Foreign Office produced a memorandum in September 1956 suggesting that the tunnel be revived as part of the possibilities. However, there was no enthusiasm for this at Cabinet level and therefore no minuted discussion.[14]

2. Enthusiasm reasserted: the Channel Tunnel Company and the Channel Tunnel Study Group

As military and civil service objections became less effective, the lobbyists took up the challenge with renewed vigour after the War. The long-established Channel Tunnel Company awoke after several decades in the doldrums. Essentially a speculative fiefdom of the d'Erlanger banking family, it had reduced its capital to £91,351 in 1897; paid-up capital in 1900 amounted to just under £80,000; the remainder was called up in 1907. Annual general meetings were sparsely attended; capital expenditure crept up slowly, reaching £73,000 in 1918, and £89,000 in 1938.[15] In 1931 William Collard of London and Paris Railway Promoters Ltd had suggested to the d'Erlangers that the two companies should merge and proposed an alliance of the d'Erlangers, the Rothschilds and an American house. However, given the depressed circumstances of the time the proposal was clearly a kite-flyer and was not taken seriously.[16] The future of the company was put in doubt following the death of the Chairman, Emile d'Erlanger, in 1939, and the loss of the shareholders' registers, along with other key documentation, in the blitz in 1941. However, rescue came from within the controlling interest, the d'Erlangers, with about 24 per cent of the capital, and the Southern Railway, with 26 per cent. In 1940 Leo d'Erlanger and Sir Herbert Walker, now a Southern director, were co-opted onto the Board, and Walker took the chair in 1941. On his death in 1949 he was succeeded by Leo d'Erlanger. The latter's enthusiasm for the tunnel, notwithstanding his interest in airlines, and Walker's change of heart were critical to the survival of the company. Walker's conversion at the age of 72, prompted in part by a seat on the board of United Steel, echoed that of Prime Minister Gladstone in the nineteenth century – and others who opposed in youth, but supported in old age. Under this new leadership the Channel Tunnel Co. took a decisive step in encouraging the revival of the Channel Tunnel Parliamentary Committee and the creation of a Channel Tunnel Study Group.[17]

In January 1947, at a dinner attended by members of both houses of parliament, Sir Herbert Walker, Gerard d'Erlanger, Harold Carvalho (Manager of the Channel Tunnel Co. since 1929) and others, Christopher Shawcross, the Labour MP for Widnes, revived the Channel Tunnel Parliamentary Committee. Shawcross made the suggestion that it should take the form of a small study group which would draw up a considered case for the tunnel. A group of 34 MPs was then established, with Shawcross as chairman, Capt. Malcolm Bullock and George Hicks as joint vice-chairmen, the inter-war campaigner Ernest Thurtle as treasurer, and other notables as members, among them Ernest Davies, Arthur Lewis and Francis Noel-Baker.[18] Its initial report, produced in July 1947, repeated the case for a twin-bore rail tunnel and put the cost at £45–65 million, depending on the choice of lining material.[19] Advice was then taken from consulting engineers, and liaison was made with a similar group established in France. Walker provided revised estimates of revenues, costs and returns in 1948, and the Basdevant road-rail alternative was dismissed, with the help of George Ellson, who had succeeded Sir Percy Tempest as engineer to the Channel Tunnel Co. in 1927.[20]

Revival in Britain was matched in France, where a parliamentary group was also set up and, notwithstanding the disappointments of the previous 70 years, a fresh wave of enthusiasm emerged. However, it was to be almost a decade after the initial expression of support in the two countries in 1947–8 before anything very tangible emerged. By this time there were a number of supportive and dynamic individuals in prominent positions in France. They included Réné Mayer, President of the Council and a former Vice-President of the Nord Railway, Louis Armand, Director-General of the SNCF, Jacques Chaban-Delmas, Minister of Transport, Paul Leroy-Beaulieu, economic adviser at the French embassy in London, and Joseph Laniel, related to the Fougerolles, developers in the 1920s of an innovative, slurrying method of waste extraction. In England, too, there was a change of personnel. Shawcross left the Commons in 1950 and the chairmanship of the Parliamentary Committee passed to William (later Sir William) Teeling,

Conservative MP for Brighton (Pavilion). The two sides then came together. In 1955–6 Leroy-Beaulieu, a director of the Chemin de Fer Sous-marin and grandson of its first chairman, Michel Chevalier, met Leo d'Erlanger, grandson of Frederick d'Erlanger, a chairman of the British company. They agreed that a more concerted effort should be made to progress the project by enlisting the support of the Suez Canal Company (Compagnie Universelle du Canal Maritime de Suez), whose concession was due to run out in 1968.[21] In fact, Colonel Nasser's seizure of the Canal in July 1956 encouraged the Suez Co., then led by Jacques Georges-Picot as Director-General, to contemplate new opportunities more rapidly than had been expected, though direct participation was hindered initially by the existence of a disputed claim for compensation from the Egyptian Government.[22]

At the same time, there was a promise of support from the United States, the result of an apparent case of contingency theory. A New York lawyer, Frank P. Davidson, and his French wife, Izaline, made a trip to Europe in 1956 and encountered bad weather on the channel crossing. They then got together with a number of influential members of their family and friends to 'do something' about a tunnel. The most important were Mrs Davidson's brother-in-law, Comte Arnaud de Vitry d'Avaucourt, a senior executive with Socony Mobil Oil; Professor Cyril J. Means, Jr., former arbitration director of the New York Stock Exchange; William Buchan, a well-connected British public relations consultant; Claude Arnal, an engineer; and Davidson's brothers, Alfred and John.[23] In December 1956 Davidson wrote to the British and French tunnel companies to offer them the prospect of 'dollar funds'.[24] Then in February Means was sent to Europe to make contact with the tunnel and Suez companies and offer American backing. This was the first of a number of visits. Later on, accompanied by Buchan, he spoke to officials in the Foreign Office, the British Embassy in Paris, and the French Ministry of Public Works. Additional lobbying was conducted in Britain by the consulting engineer, Brian Colquhoun.[25] The outcome was that Davidson and de Vitry established Technical Studies Inc., with backing from Dillon Read, J.P. Morgan and Morgan Stanley, to provide American finance for a full technical investigation.[26] The move was followed, in July, by the creation of a more substantial Channel Tunnel Study Group (CTSG). The new Group was operated as a financial syndicate, putting up an initial sum of £100,000, later raised to £255,000. Stakes were held by the old British and French tunnel companies (30 per cent each), the Suez Co. (30 per cent), and Technical Studies (10 per cent). The Group was administered by a supervisory board led by René Massigli, former French Ambassador in London, as chairman, and subsequently by Sir Ivone Kirkpatrick, former Permanent Under-Secretary at the Foreign Office, as co-chairman.[27] This was able to draw upon the services of some particularly influential managers, including: Louis Armand of the SNCF, which was a major shareholder in the French Channel Tunnel Co.; Baron Charles de Wouters d'Oplinter, President of the International Road Federation (Paris), a minority shareholder in the French group; and Alec Valentine, representing the British Transport Commission, which had acquired the Southern Railway's stake in the

British Co. in 1947.[28] The new Group was no less assertive than Watkin and his colleagues had been three-quarters of a century before; and, like its predecessors, it was to experience a long and frustrating period of 'stop-go' in its relations with government – in this instance for some 18 years.[29]

Blissfully unaware of the way history was about to repeat itself, the Channel Tunnel Study Group lost no time in undertaking work of its own. A preliminary report from Brian Colquhoun & Partners, commissioned by Technical Studies Inc. and the Channel Tunnel Parliamentary Committee, was produced in April 1957. It provided an historical resumé and made numerous recommendations as to how the promoters might pursue the necessary investigations. Although Colquhoun noted that existing knowledge of the strata between the coasts was 'almost entirely conjectural', he reaffirmed the opinion of the Victorian engineers that the lower chalk offered the best prospects for tunnelling, and followed the position adopted by William Low, and later by Sir Francis Fox, that the Folkestone-Sangatte route was to be preferred.[30] The Colquhoun report acted as the basis for further research, presided over by the engineering consultants René Malcor, Ingénieur en Chef des Ponts et Chaussées, and Harold Harding, Vice-president of the Institution of Civil Engineers. Work was commissioned on five fronts: traffic forecasting; geological; civil engineering; finance; and legal. It gave every impression of being a most thorough exercise. Preliminary technical advice was provided by a small committee led by Léon Migaux, President of the Compagnie Générale de Geophysique in Paris. Evaluations of the economic prospects were made using the firms Société d'Etudes Techniques et Economiques [SETEC], the Economist Intelligence Unit and de Leuw, Cather & Co. of Chicago. Geological work was progressed by two advisers, Professor J.M. Bruckshaw of Imperial College, London, and Professor Jean Goguel, Ingénieur Général des Mines, together with Dr William Smith, seconded to CTSG from the United States Geological Survey,[31] and a number of specialist firms, including Richard Costain and George Wimpey.[32] Civil engineering was commissioned from four consulting firms: Société Générale d'Exploitations Industrielles [SOGEI]; Sir William Halcrow & Partners; Livesey & Henderson; and Rendel Palmer & Tritton.[33] Financial advice was provided by an impressive array of banking associates, including de Rothschild Frères, Banque de l'Union Parisienne, Erlangers, and Morgan Grenfell.[34] In all, the Group and its constituent companies spent over £500,000 in preparing what was in effect a preliminary prospectus.[35] The culmination of its efforts was the publication on 28 March 1960 of a 30-page report, which was presented to both the British and French Governments. It was followed on 25 July by a more considered statement of the economic benefits. The Group's work was the most comprehensive evaluation of the prospects for a tunnel yet produced.[36]

3. The Government's response, 1957–60

While the Study Group went about its work the British Government necessarily retained an interest in its activities. First of all, the Government was in essence one of the promoters. Its public corporation for transport, the British Transport Commission, held a 26 per cent stake in the British Channel Tunnel Co., and it retained a substantial (44 per cent) shareholding in the Suez Co. (though without commensurate control).[37] Second, its attitude to the tunnel was shaped by the changing political and economic environment that emerged with the post-war recovery of France and West Germany, and the establishment of a 'Common Market' bloc following the Treaty of Rome. Thus, while the promoters' heightened activity in 1956–7 obviously attracted the attention of Whitehall, it was Britain's decision to participate in a European free trade area, and support for closer economic ties with France, which encouraged the Cabinet to re-examine the issue in May 1957. By this time the Foreign Office had become more bullish, in marked contrast with its stance over the previous 70 years. In January the British Minister in Paris, Sir George Young, had suggested that a positive announcement about the Tunnel might be made at the time of the Queen's visit to Paris in April. Once again, a rough sea crossing served to concentrate the mind: 'In the course of a recent hellish crossing on the Night Ferry', he remarked, 'my thoughts inevitably turned, as so often before, to the Channel Tunnel'.[38] Inside the Foreign Office, civil servants did not regard the Ministry of Transport's sceptical position as unassailable. The participation of American financial interests from 1956 raised the possibility that private sector financing might be feasible. As a percipient minute by C.M. Anderson, Assistant to the Head of the Western Department, noted: 'The project would clearly be very costly, but there is no evidence that full consideration has ever been given to (a) raising the capital privately and/or recovering the cost by means of tolls; (b) distributing the cost in such a way that the British share of it was small…; (c) relating the cost of the project itself to the likely increase in revenue to the economy as a whole from an increased tourist trade and other possible benefits'.[39] Furthermore, the potential participation of the Americans was an attraction to some inside the Treasury. Lord Harcourt of Morgan Grenfell, who was in Washington as head of the Treasury delegation, had formed the opinion that about two-thirds of the $300 million required might be raised in the United States and Canada. Such an investment would be a welcome relief to dollar-starved Britain and France, and the episode was reported by Sir Herbert Brittain, Second Secretary to the Treasury, in a letter canvassing departmental opinion in April 1957.[40]

On the other hand, for others the prospect of American participation was problematic. There was a case for excluding American finance in order to retain the 'essentially European' character of the project. Concern about the bona fides of some of the promoters was also evident.[41] More importantly, there was a fair amount of scepticism inside Whitehall about the economic case for a tunnel, and the voices of the doubters became louder the closer one got to the departments with a more direct interest in it, viz. the Ministry of Transport and the Board of Trade. The Minister of Transport and Civil Aviation, Harold Watkinson, raised the matter both in the Cabinet's Economic Policy Committee and in the full Cabinet, but his initial proposals, to highlight the issue by announcing a re-evaluation in parliament, and to contact the French Government about a possible joint approach to preliminary surveys, fell on deaf ears.[42] Discussion at the Cabinet meeting on 2 May carried the message that Britain should avoid being rushed into any commitment and should make no public announcement. 'The Cabinet were reluctant to conclude, without further enquiry, that the balance of considerations would favour the construction of a Channel Tunnel. Our economic interests might be better served by devoting our share of a possible expenditure of £200 millions to the improvement of our roads and ports. Germany would probably become our most important market in the proposed free trade area and the development of an adequate ferry service to the Rhine might prove a more valuable investment. The construction of a Channel Tunnel would make it easier for European manufacturers to compete effectively in our home market'. Instead it was agreed that the Minister of Transport, in consultation with the Chancellor, should make a study of the best way to handle continental European *freight* traffic (passenger traffic was not to be examined), taking into account revived interest in the Channel Tunnel.[43] Young, the British Minister in Paris, was disappointed with the response. Encouraged by some of his Foreign Office colleagues to expect an expression of benevolent support, he noted that the tone of the Cabinet minute suggested that the Government was 'veering towards malevolent neutrality'.[44]

The inter-departmental study was neither a deep nor rigorous affair. Undertaken in a few weeks, it drew on a conventional, and rather gloomy, memorandum prepared by the British Transport Commission. The origins of this document lay in a report by Leslie Harrington to the Commission's shipping and international services' sub-commission in March 1957, which was as cautious as the Southern Railway responses had been in the 1920s and 1930s. The capital required for the tunnel was estimated to be £180 million, before any provision for compensation or write-offs in connexion with shipping and harbours. Gross revenue was put at £12.5 million; after deducting operating costs, maintenance, interest (at 5 per cent) and amortisation charges, there was a small surplus of £489,000. Harrington thus concluded, with characteristic understatement, that 'this might not seem an attractive investment'.[45] The report passed on to government departments on 10 May 1957 was essentially the same calculation. The capital cost was raised to £235 million by including the cost of servicing capital during construction and the losses on port and shipping assets; gross revenue was increased by 12 per cent to £14 million (46 per cent of which was to come from freight). The estimated net revenue of £11.5 million promised a return of about 5 per cent, reckoned to be 'well below a reasonable commercial return for the risks involved…the tunnel would appear to be a viable though not a very profitable undertaking'.[46] There was some dissatisfaction with the Commission's rather unadventurous approach. A.T.K. Grant of the Treasury felt that the Commission's calculations were 'highly conventional'. Existing traffic levels and rates had been taken as the basis for the estimated return and no attempt had been made to model price elasticities at lower rates.[47] On the other hand, as Matthew Stevenson, an Under-Secretary, pointed out, manufacturing industry was accustomed to gross returns of 20 per cent, and if the calculation of 5 per cent were correct 'this project would probably never start on a private basis'.[48] And the Ministry of Transport, preoccupied with road transport at home,[49] was not persuaded to depart from its rather jaundiced view of prospects. Passenger traffic benefits were accepted, but largely discounted on the basis that the outward flow of tourists would greatly exceed the inward flow. As for freight, a tunnel would obviously limit traffic to a fixed route. A road tunnel would be preferable to a rail one, but would be prohibitively expensive to construct. As an alternative, the prospect of roll-on roll-off ferry services attracted the department's support. These would provide more route flexibility and lower transport costs. The reassessment thus produced the conclusion, conveyed to the Cabinet on 25 July by Watkinson, that there was 'no pressing need for the construction of a Channel Tunnel'. There was 'no clear *prima facie* case for building a tunnel in order to help our trade with the Continent… goods might be moved almost as quickly, and with greater flexibility as to route at much less cost, by other methods such as ferry ships.'[50] One should have some sympathy for this caution given the economic environment of the mid-late 1950s. Fuel rationing during the Suez crisis had disrupted road transport, and railway deficits were building up within the British Transport Commission. The railways' net operating account revealed a deficit – of £16.5 million – for the first time in 1956, and the overall deficit, after deducting a contribution to 'central charges', was £57.5 million.[51] Later on, in January 1958, a Chancellor of the Exchequer, Peter Thorneycroft, and his team resigned after failing to convince the Cabinet about the need for deflationary measures, including public expenditure cuts.[52] The Government's attitude to the newly-created Study Group, if cool, was not entirely hostile. While it felt that the Suez Co. should refrain from investing in speculative ventures such as the tunnel, it made no objection to the company taking a stake in the Study Group. The Government felt it 'unwise' to allow one of the British Government directors to serve on the syndicate since this 'might appear to commit the Government to support the project'. Instead, a watching brief on the syndicate's activities was established through the appointment of Valentine, a member of the British Transport Commission and a director of the British Channel Tunnel Co., as an informal Government representative.[53]

Thereafter the trail went a bit cold. However, in June 1958, six months before his election as President of France, General de Gaulle had spoken enthusiastically about the channel tunnel at a meeting with the British Prime Minister, Harold Macmillan, and a year later Leo D'Erlanger, Chairman of the British Channel Tunnel Co., had made a bullish and much-publicised address to the company's AGM. Consequently, when in June 1959 Macmillan told the Chancellor, Derick Heathcoat Amory, that he was 'a little worried' about the tunnel the Whitehall machine swung into action again. Because Macmillan was anxious though by no means enthusiastic – 'there seems to be a lot going on, and some people may be getting committed', he noted – there was a need for the Government to clarify its position once more, and the Minister of Transport was asked to bring his 1957 paper up to date.[54] By this time the Channel Tunnel Study Group had made considerable progress with its numerous surveys and reports, and the several departments endeavoured to monitor the process with their intelligence gathering. Expectations were that the Group would be ready to publish a report by the end of the year, and that the several consultants favoured a rail-only tunnel. The private sector was expected to provide most of the finance. Civil servants noted that the cost of construction was likely to be nearer to £100 million than to £200 million. The latter figure, put forward by the British Transport Commission, was now reckoned to have been 'in the nature of a wild guess', before the type of fixed link had been identified.[55] At the Cabinet meeting on 23 July, Watkinson was able to state that the tunnel 'seems feasible from the geophysical and engineering point of view, and shows a reasonable prospect of paying its way'. Officials from five departments were then asked to examine some of the problems raised by the tunnel project without waiting for publication of the Study Group's Report.[56] They also assessed the prospects for funding, in particular from the Suez Co. and the French Government.[57] Their tentative conclusions represented a considerable softening in attitudes. The tunnel was expected to bring trading advantages by offering new services at lower rates, and there would be no objection to it if it remained a privately-funded venture. There would be little impact on the 'tourist balance of trade' and distinct political advantages in improving relations with the rest of Europe, particularly with the six common market countries, who were concerned about Britain's refusal to join and its plans for a free trade alternative.[58] The latter point was pressed by representatives of the Foreign Office, where both Sir Gladwyn Jebb [later Lord Gladwyn], the British Ambassador in Paris, and Sir Anthony Rumbold, an Under-Secretary, were self-professed 'keen tunnellers'.[59]

Not all Cabinet members were warming to the tunnel. A notable sceptic was Lord Hailsham, Lord President of the Council, who in a terse note to Watkinson had remarked: 'I certainly hope that we shall not go in for a Channel Tunnel. The economic case is at best 'not proven'. I regard de Gaulle's enthusiasm as anything but a commendation. And, despite everything the experts say, I am quite unconvinced that there is not a defence risk. There is always a risk in defence when you create a new postern'.[60] And there were anxieties elsewhere, not least about the funding of the project. Here the British Government appeared to want it both ways. On the one hand officials wished to avoid a financial commitment and to keep any contribution small. The Bank of England's view was that Britain's participation 'should be nothing more than a token and a small one at that'.[61] There was also some amusement at the flurry of correspondence from one of the British Government directors of Suez Financière, Sir Francis Wylie, who not only sought to stir up some anti-tunnel sentiment aimed at Georges-Picot but made it clear that the company's financial contribution was unlikely to be larger than £2 million.[62] On the other hand, alarm was expressed when Alfred Davidson of Technical Studies Inc. reported that about half of the capital might come from the Americans, a concern compounded by initial reports that the French Government were reluctant to participate financially.[63] The uncertainty of the funding situation remained perplexing for the Government, and on the other side the promoters were naturally worried by the silence from Whitehall. Delay in providing a response to Sir Ivone Kirkpatrick, Co-chairman of the Study Group, who had asked the Government for an indication of its views, was only to be expected given a general election in October and a change of minister at Transport.[64] However, when at last the Cabinet considered the state of play, in February 1960, the general attitude was supportive. The Minister of Transport, now Ernest Marples, in presenting the officials' report, noted that the Tunnel was technically, economically and legally feasible, and its military advantages outweighed the disadvantages. He suggested that he should inform Kirkpatrick in fairly warm terms that the Government was prepared to look sympathetically at a commercially viable scheme. The Foreign Secretary, Selwyn Lloyd, while nursing 'a slight prejudice for emotional reasons against the project', argued that given the enthusiasm of the French Government there was much to be said for supporting it. The Tunnel 'could be made a symbol of Her Majesty's Government's desire to draw closer to Europe and of our realisation that the days of "splendid isolation" are no more'.[65] The Cabinet, at its meeting on 18 February duly concluded that 'on grounds of international policy' an indication of the Government's attitude be given to the promoters along the lines suggested by Marples.[66]

4. The Channel Tunnel Study Group's 1960 Reports

The Study Group's initial report of March 1960 was a rather slim document, though the authors made it clear that it was derived from numerous reports and $2\frac{1}{2}$ years of detailed study.[67] Not only did it refer to investigations of all the possibilities for a continental connexion, including a bored tunnel, immersed tube, bridge, and a bridge-tunnel combination, but it also provided engineering and financial support for its preferred option – a twin-bore, rail-only tunnel or single-bore immersed tube, with road vehicles to be conveyed on flat trucks. The former was given greater prominence in the text, and was thus in many ways a reworking of that advocated by William Low in the 1870s (see Figure 2.1 and above, pp. 1–6), the only substantial change being the addition of a service tunnel. It also provided the basis for both the scheme of 1966–75 and its successor in 1985. The geological surveys, incorporating new 'sonar' techniques, confirmed the opinion of the French engineers in 1875–6 that the lower chalk stratum was continuous. A rail tunnel, 32 miles long (23 miles under the sea) would take five years to construct and would cost £109.8 million, including £80 million for the engineering work, £9.8 million for railway installations, and £20 million for terminal stations and rolling stock. French road improvements would add £2.2 million to the cost, while the cost of financing the construction was put at a further £20 million, making £129–32 million in all. The consultants' traffic survey produced forecasts of 3.2 million passengers, 676,000 cars and 1.2 million tons of freight on opening in 1965, with increases of 52, 67 and 29 per cent respectively after 15 years (see Table 2.1). A return on capital was not given in the

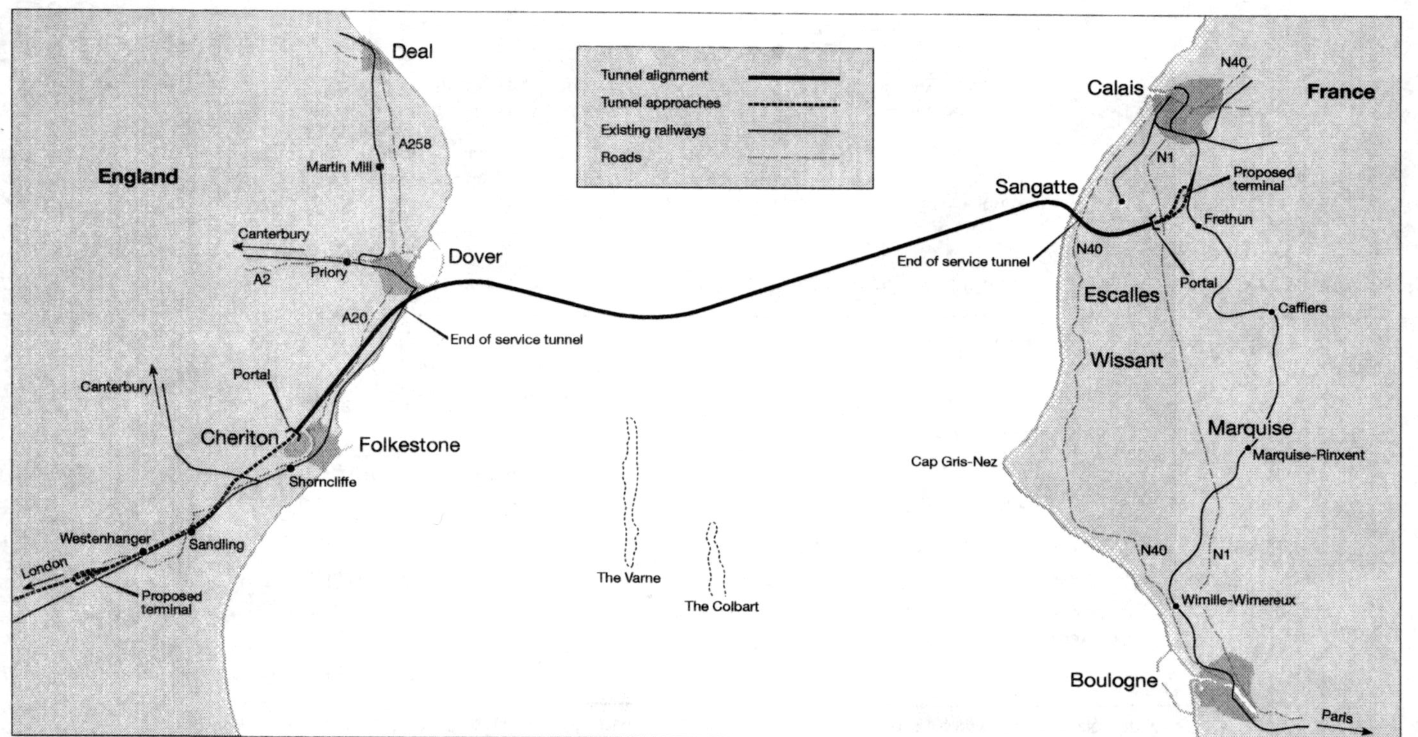

Figure 2.1 CTSG scheme, 1960: proposed alignment.

Table 2.1 Channel Tunnel Study Group Report, March 1960: estimated construction costs, and prospects for a rail-only tunnel

(i) Estimated construction costs (£m.)

Rail-only tunnel	Road-only tunnel	Rail-only tube	Road-only tube	Road-rail tube	Road-rail bridge
109.8–112.0[a]	129.0–152.0[b]	112.9	104.2–114.9[c]	201.1	181.0

(ii) Rail-only tunnel

	Traffic: Passengers (no.)	mkt-share (%)	Cars (no.)	mkt-share (%)	Freight (tons)	mkt-share (%)	Capital Cost (£m.)	Revenue Gross (£m.)	Net, pre-tax (£m.)	Implied Return (Gross) (%)	(Net) (%)
1957	2,241,000	(39)	285,900	(90)	1,168,000	(34)	130.0[d]	—	—		
1965	3,180,000		676,000		1,230,000			13.5[e]	10.4	10.4	8.0
1980	4,831,000		1,127,000		1,587,000			19.9[e]	16.2	15.3	12.5

Source: CTSG, *Report 28th March 1960*, pp. 11, 20, 22–5, enclosed in Kirkpatrick-Macmillan, 29 March 1960, PREM11/3576, PRO; CTSG, 'Economic Benefits of a Channel Tunnel: July 25, 1960', p. 19 (MT124/1090, PRO).

Notes

a £112.0 m. includes £2.2 m. for French road improvements. A further £3.0 m. would be required for terminal stations by 1980.
b £129.0 m. with one island , £152.0 m. with two islands.
c £104.2 m. with one island, £114.9 m. with two islands.
d £110 m. + £20 m. for terminals and rolling stock.
e The published report gave 'net' receipts as £13.0 m. in 1965 and £21 m. in 1980. However, the 'Economic benefits' document of July 1960 gave *gross* revenue as £13.5 m. in 1966 and £19.9 m. in 1980. Net revenue here excludes 'indirect revenue' estimated in the July report.

published Report, but if the promoters were correct in assuming that an investment of about £130 million would be required, then their estimated revenue figures suggested a net return of 8.0 and 12.5 per cent respectively (Table 2.1).

The promoters did not spell out the operating economics on which their optimism was founded, however, and their financial survey provided some surprises for those who had been encouraged to believe, during the three years of preparatory evaluation, that the private sector would bear all of the risk. Indeed, the promoters' failure to convince either the Government or the media of the scheme's financial viability was a major weakness and played into the hands of the (still considerable number of) opponents. 'In view of the magnitude of the project', the Report stated, 'the conclusion has been reached that if it is desired that the undertaking be financed exclusively by private capital, then various assurances would have to be forthcoming without which private capital could not be expected to run the risks involved.' The preferred course of action was to create an international company to finance, construct and own the tunnel. The company would be highly geared, with 80 per cent of the capital in the form of fixed-interest bonds (6 per cent, with a convertibility option, was suggested), and it would require numerous 'exemptions, guarantees and assurances' from the two governments. These embraced: an exclusive 99-year concession for construction and operation with power to assign; specified conditions for government purchase at an agreed price; exemption from company taxation; and protection against construction cost 'over-runs'. Then, because it was envisaged that British Railways and the SNCF would jointly operate services under a long-term leasing arrangement, the promoters required the governments to either enter into the lease themselves or provide a guarantee of the obligations undertaken by the railway enterprises as lessees. These included a guaranteed minimum annual payment, protection of toll levels in real terms, and responsibility for the construction and maintenance of the railway infrastructure and rolling stock. On top of all this, it was expected that the Channel Tunnel bonds themselves would carry a direct guarantee from either the two governments or the railways. The promoters demanded that investors be protected from the risks of abandoned construction, a delay in completion, or the tunnel 'becoming unusable through operation of *force majeure*.' They also required a commitment to make available the necessary foreign exchange to enable the company to pay dividends, interest on securities issued in other currencies (presumably dollars).[68]

While from a contemporary standpoint some of these demands were scarcely surprising and even prescient, in 1960 the list seemed so extensive as to turn the project into a public venture. David Serpell, newly-appointed Deputy Secretary at the Ministry of Transport, noted on 5 April 1960 that 'the financial proposals, which involve a great deal of Government support, were not expected nor very welcome.' His former Treasury colleague, Stevenson, went further: 'I doubt whether H.F. (Home Finance Division) need read more than Chapter V ('Financial Study'). This proposition has turned out a good deal less private and a good deal more governmental than was at one time expected and even those who were sympathetic to the Tunnel at an earlier stage are going to have second thoughts'.[69] Marples, in briefing Macmillan, felt that the demand for government financial backing precluded his speaking to Kirkpatrick in 'sympathetic' terms. The Chancellor, Heathcoat Amory, wrote on his copy of the letter: 'This information is useful. It rules out the possibility of our 'blessing the scheme'.[70] Fed by the criticisms of vested interests, the private enterprise ferry companies such as Townsend, those developing the hovercraft, and Eoin Mekie, Chairman of the vehicle air ferry operator Silver City Airways, the reaction of the media was also cool. The *Times*, for example, referring to the Report on the same day that the proposal to build a London motorway ring [M25] was announced, made much of the guarantees expected from government. In a leader entitled 'Taxpayers' Tunnel?', it found that the suggested financial arrangements 'do not make sense. British and French tax-payers would be asked to underwrite, directly or indirectly through their railways, £110 m. out of a total £130 m. investment. At that rate they might as well have the equity and any residual profits as well... there is no justification whatever for committing taxpayers to big risks against the expectation only of profits accruing to others'. The *Economist*, in an article headed 'Pie Under the Sea', took the same view, and went on to assert that nobody believed the tunnel 'would pay as a private commercial enterprise'. The reception was clearly not what the promoters either expected or wanted.[71]

While a Whitehall working party led by David Serpell presided over a further round of departmental soundings,[72] the promoters lobbied energetically in an attempt to rescue the situation. The attention of ministers and civil servants naturally focussed on the extent of the required guarantees,[73] though doubts were also expressed about the robustness of the tunnel traffic estimates, and the strength of support from the French Government, which also found 'le plan financier' unacceptable and did not apparently want to do anything to appear to integrate the UK into Europe.[74] One of the most worrying aspects for the two governments was the request for a guarantee on cost over-runs. Here, previous British experience, with the Clyde tunnels (a 200 per cent over-run), the M1 and the Runcorn-Widnes bridge (about 100 per cent), was far from reassuring. As one Treasury official correctly observed, 'there have been tremendous differences between early estimates and final costs when they have been separated by a number of years... Even if the Channel Tunnellers did much better and suffered an error of only 50% this would mean H.M.G. footing the bill for £40 m., apart from any allowance for possible increases in the cost of materials and wages.'[75] A further complication was the investment required from the British Transport Commission, which had welcomed the Study Group's Report.[76] Not only had its handling of the railways' major investment programme of 1955 – the 'Modernisation Plan' – inspired sharp criticism by 1960, but its finances had also deteriorated sharply since 1956. The railways' operating loss amounted to £84 million in 1959 and was set to exceed £100 million. Indeed, in March 1960 the Commission's affairs were made the subject of a secret inquiry conducted by major industrialists led by Sir Ivan Stedeford of Tube Investments, together with civil servants Matthew Stevenson and David Serpell. Since the Ministry of Transport had placed an embargo on all major new projects by the Commission, the proposal that it should invest in tunnel infrastructure and make financial guarantees of tunnel revenue was naturally disturbing.[77] However, before the Ministry of Transport could produce a considered evaluation of the March 1960 Report,[78] the promoters came up with a revised set of proposals. On 15 July 1960 Leo d'Erlanger sent Macmillan a memorandum containing modified proposals; ten days later a supplementary report on 'economic benefits' was produced. The promoters then met senior officials from the Treasury (Sir Frank Lee, Sir Thomas Padmore) and Ministry of Transport (Sir James Dunnett and David Serpell) to explain their proposals.[79]

More reassuring noises were now made about the proposed financial arrangements. The Study Group accepted that the British Government were reluctant to see substantial investment by the British Transport Commission, and therefore offered to raise the capital for the British railway terminal and associated infrastructure (but not the rolling stock), adding £29 million to the private sector's share of the investment.[80] It was also made clear that the Tunnel Co. shareholders would bear the risk of their investment (20 per cent of total) in the event of delay, over-run or abandonment. Finally, the Group offered to dispense with some of the guarantees and assurances required from the two governments. It argued that the bonds might be marketed *without* direct government guarantees provided that a head lease of the Tunnel were entered into directly by the governments in return for an amount sufficient to cover interest on and amortisation of the Bonds. The governments would then sublet to their railways. A supplementary document on economic benefits spelt out the results of the consultants' cost-benefit analysis. It was pointed out that the Tunnel would have four times the capacity of an expanded ferry fleet necessary to carry the estimated traffic in 1966. It would also provide 'substantial economic benefits to passengers, motorists, shippers and other users, to the Railways...and to the British and French nations'. User benefits were computed at £469 million over the period 1966–2015. The gross economic value of the tunnel, discounted at 5 per cent, amounted to £419 million over the same period, exceeding that of a ferry operation by £342 million. The 'net return', that is, the gross economic value minus net ferry revenue summed to an impressive £1,149 million (Table 2.2), implying a 'time adjusted rate of return' of 14.2 per cent.[81]

While the Study Group made this message of substantial economic benefits the subject of a public relations campaign, orchestrated by E.D. O'Brien, the former publicity director for the Conservative party,[82] the two governments embarked on a further examination of the proposal. On the British side, a final report by Whitehall officials was completed in October 1960 and, as in 1957, was considered by both the Economic Policy Committee and the full Cabinet. There was little new in the process. The revised financial package made the tunnel intrinsically more attractive, but the Government continued to nurse reservations. It was considered extremely risky to assess the tunnel's prospects in a period of rapid technological change in transport, and there was now the additional complication of introducing a mix of public and private investment in Britain's railways. As Stevenson put it, 'I cannot

Table 2.2 Channel Tunnel Study Group, estimate of the Channel Tunnel's 'economic benefits', July 1960

Period	*User benefits (£m.)*	*Gross economic value (£m.)*	*Gross economic value discounted at 5% (£m.)*	*Benefits over ferry services*		
				Gross (£m.)	*Gross discounted at 5% (£m.)*	*Net return (£m.)*
1966	4.8	15.2	14.4	12.1	11.6	13.6
1980	9.0	25.2	12.1	20.6	9.9	22.8
1985	10.6	27.7	10.5	22.9	8.6	25.2
1966–75	60.4	183.6	139.6	148.1	101.5	165.0
1976–85	91.4	252.3	118.5	206.3	96.8	228.2
1986–2015	317.2	832.3	160.7	685.8	143.5	755.6
1966–2015	469.0	1268.2	418.8	1040.1	341.8	1148.8

Source: CTSG, 'Economic benefits' (July 1960).

Notes

Definitions: 'user benefits' = passengers: 2s. fare saving + 1 hr 35 mins time saving, motorists £3 3s. fare saving + 2 hr 30 mins time saving; freight 75% cost saving; 'gross economic value' = gross direct revenue + user benefits minus operating costs; 'gross benefits over ferry services' = gross economic value of tunnel minus gross economic value of ferries; 'net return' = gross economic value of tunnel minus net ferry revenue (after financial charges).

Assumptions: nil inflation, 1966–2015; constant tunnel costs; ferry charges increase by 2% p.a., 1966–85.

help thinking that this project comes up a generation too late in terms of economics and finance'.[83] When Marples reported to the Economic Policy Committee in November, he noted that there was some uncertainty about the estimates of capital costs and revenue. However, the main stumbling block was financial. The promoters were still asking for tax exemption and a government lease operating from a fixed date which would in effect guarantee their obligations to bondholders.[84] These proposals were 'quite inappropriate to a private venture' and therefore 'unacceptable as they stand'. Notwithstanding d'Erlanger's assurances that three-quarters of the capital might come from outside the UK, the investment would crowd out other worthy transport schemes. This view was accepted by the Committee and endorsed by the Cabinet on 25 November. However, there was some nervousness about informing the Study Group since the Government did not wish to be placed in a position where the French were able to blame Britain for having rejected the project. Consequently, its decision to reject the revised financial proposals remained confidential.[85]

5. Bridge v. Tunnel 1960–3

By this time, there was a further complication. Before the Study Group could make its main report public in April 1960, a consortium of three construction firms, the Compagnie Française d'Entreprises, Dorman Long in Britain, and Merritt-Chapman and Scott of the United States, had approached it with a new proposal for a bridge. This was the first serious scheme of its kind since the Hersent-Schneider bridge of 1889 and that put before the Channel Tunnel Committee by Sir Murdoch MacDonald & Partners and A. Huguenin in 1929.[86] When the Study Group maintained its preference for a tunnel, the French promoters went on in December 1960 to form their own organisation, the Société d'Etude Du Pont sur la Manche (Channel Bridge Study Group), in order to lobby for the alternative. Their £211–15 million bridge was to extend for 20.3 miles from Dover to Calais and provide two railway tracks, five lanes of motorway and two cycle tracks, resting on 164 reinforced concrete piers. This new entrant in the field enjoyed substantial support in France. Led by Jules Moch, a former Minister, it had the backing of road interests such as the Union Routière de France, trade associations for iron & steel and petroleum, major firms (Creusot, St. Nazaire-Penhoët) and leading banks such as Crédit Lyonnais and the Banque Nationale pour le Commerce et l'Industrie.[87] In Britain, the steel industry was anxious to back such an output-consuming venture, and the promoters were also able to secure the lobbying assistance of the former British Ambassador in Paris, Lord Gladwyn. Moreover, with a Minister of Transport in Marples, who was a firm supporter of road transport (and indeed had a background in the industry via his road construction company Marples Ridgeway), and civil servants in Dunnett (Permanent Secretary from April 1959) and Serpell, who favoured a smaller, more cost-effective railway industry, it was only to be expected that this new development should throw the whole matter into the melting pot again.[88]

The Channel Tunnel Study Group continued to lobby hard for the tunnel in 1961,[89] but there was something of a stalemate in government circles since no fresh financial proposals were being put forward, and this impasse was reflected in bouts of fencing at parliamentary question time.[90] Indeed, there were other distractions too, although some of these had a bearing on the tunnel debate. First, it was announced in a White Paper in December 1960 that the financially ailing British Transport Commission would be dismantled and divided into bodies responsible for each of the separate modes of transport, and notably, for railways, the British Railways Board. The change was anticipated by the appointment in June 1961 of Dr Richard Beeching, a member of the Stedeford Advisory Group, as chairman of the Commission (and chairman-elect of the British Railways Board) in place of General Sir Brian Robertson. This fundamental shake-up of nationalised transport, which was accompanied by further restraints on spending and the publication in April 1961 of a key Treasury White Paper requiring public sector corporations, *inter alia*, to achieve defined rates of return on investment, did not suggest that there would be room for investment in the luxury of a channel tunnel.[91] Nor, indeed, did the emergence of a competing Anglo-French venture, the supersonic plane Concorde, whose origins lay in design work in 1959–60 and which by 1961 had seen British Government opinion favour collaboration with the French rather than with the Americans.[92] On the other hand, the United Kingdom had applied to join the European Economic Community in July 1961, and Foreign Office officials regarded the Tunnel as a minor but not insignificant element in the negotiations between the parties.[93] Thus, by the time the bridge promoters had revealed their scheme in September 1961, it was clear that something more had to be done at governmental level. Indeed, in August the French Government had finally decided to initiate discussions with the British about the 'ouvrage fixe' [fixed link], whether tunnel or bridge.[94]

In November Marples and Robert Buron, the transport ministers of the two governments, met in Paris and agreed with Marples's suggestion that a joint working group of civil servants be established to evaluate the two proposals on the table.[95] Marples was characteristically cagey. When pressed on the bridge v. tunnel issue on his return from Paris, he replied, 'I never back the horse until I see the form'.[96] But he was also representing the views of his officials, who were thought in more enthusiastic Foreign Office circles to be using the issue as an excuse to shelve the project. Roderick Sarell, for example, 'was distressed by the atmosphere of sceptical destructiveness'.[97] The outcome was yet another long period of exhaustive investigation, and it was not until September 1963 that the findings of the working group were published simultaneously in Britain and France (in Britain via a White Paper from the Ministry of Transport).[98] The new inquiry was led by a steering group chaired by David Serpell and Robert Vergnaud (the latter was replaced by Jean Ravanel, Commissaire du Tourism, in June 1962). There were four sub-groups, finance (Evan Maude, P. Dargenton), technical (Peter Scott-Malden, J. Mathieu), economic (Gordon Bowen, Philippe Lacarrière), and diplomatic (Roderick Sarell, A. Jordan).[99] The civil servants conducted a full evaluation of the fixed link and the two competing proposals, and, as with earlier work, covered technical, legal, economic and financial aspects.[100] In the course of the inquiry there were some complications. First, the bridge promoters submitted an outline proposal for a composite structure (bridge-tunnel-bridge), then in March 1963 a body calling itself SETCM advanced the idea of an immersed tube for joint road-rail use. Both schemes came too late to be given a full examination.[101]

The final report was presented to the respective transport ministries in July 1963 and published in the following September. Unsurprisingly, given its civil service origins, it was a cautious document. Nevertheless, the working group did record its preference for the rail-only tunnel scheme developed by the Channel Tunnel Study Group, which was also in line with railway opinion, and, indeed, with earlier thinking in Whitehall.[102] Reduced to bare essentials, while both projects would take six years to construct and reduce London-Paris journey times from 7 to 4½ hours, the tunnel would cost £143 million in 1962 prices, while the bridge would cost more than double this at a rather exact £298.5 million.[103] The economic and financial assessments did little to disturb this hierarchy of preference. Of course, much hinged on the traffic estimates accepted by the civil servants. Here they faced a considerable variation. In addition to the figures offered by the Tunnel promoters in 1960, the bridge promoters offered two sets of calculations, the second of which was based on the optimistic belief that the bridge would confer all the advantages of a land frontier. In addition, the joint working group came up with four estimates of its own, ranging from 'very low' to 'very high', though for purposes of assessment it elected to steer a fairly conservative course through the minefield by selecting its middle-range estimates of 'lower' and 'upper'.[104] Nevertheless, the five published estimates exhibited a fairly wide range, with coefficients of variation for the year 1980 ranging from 54 per cent for freight to 126 per cent for accompanied vehicles (Table 2.3). The Report's own data suggested that passenger and freight traffic flows would be similar whether undertaken by bridge or tunnel; only vehicle traffic would be higher with a bridge. These estimates were higher than those of the Channel Tunnel Study Group for freight, but lower than those offered by the promoters for passenger traffic. They were used to support the contention that there was no justification whatever for spending twice as much on a bridge (Table 2.3). The bridge was also found to require technical modifications as a protection against damage from ships, and in any case, there were serious safety and regulatory issues involved in, as the *Economist* had put it in 1961, 'straddling one of the most crowded, and at times foggiest and windiest, shipping lanes in the world'.[105] Both the Admiralty and the Ministry of Defence felt that in an emergency a bridge would restrict shipping to an unacceptable degree.[106] Calculations of economic benefits (based on a 7 per cent discount rate) and financial returns underlined this support for the Tunnel (Table 2.4). The Tunnel would produce an overall net benefit of either £74 million or £153 million in 1969 prices, and an economic return of either 10.4 or 13.3 per cent, results which were superior to those for the bridge (where the net

Table 2.3 Tunnel v. Bridge: Joint working party's 1963 traffic forecasts for 1980

Traffic in 1980	*CTSG tunnel*	*SEPM bridge*		*Working party tunnel*		*Bridge*		*Coefficient of variation (%)*
		First estimate	*Revised estimate*	*Lower bound*	*Upper bound*	*Lower bound*	*Upper bound*	
Cars and Accompanied Passengers ('000s)	1,127[a]	1,674	8,917	880	1,260	950	1,390	126
Unaccompanied Passengers ('000s)	4,831[a]	5,300	21,437	3,000	3,700	3,000	3,700	104
Freight ('000 tons)	1,587[a]	1,905	7,350	3,000	4,000	3,000	4,000	54

Source: MT, *Proposals for a Fixed Channel Link*, September 1963, P.P. 1962–3, ix, Cmnd.2137, pp. 6, 53–5.

Note

a As in CTSG, Reports, 1960; the MT document presented rounded figures of 1,130 [cars] and 4,850 [unacc. pass.] and a revised figure of 2,609 for freight.

Table 2.4 Tunnel v. Bridge: Joint working party's 1963 assessment of economic and financial returns (£m., in 1969 prices)

	Tunnel upper traffic estimate		*Tunnel lower traffic estimate*		*Bridge upper traffic estimate*		*Bridge lower traffic estimate*	
Estimated economic return, 1969–2018, discounted at 7%								
Capital + operating costs of existing transport	308		247		308		247	
Capital + operating costs of fixed crossing: initial[2]	141		141		351		352	
Post-1969	67		58		72		65	
Total	208		199		423		417	
Overall net benefit of fixed crossing over existing transport	153		74		−46		−135	
Economic return[1]	13.3%		10.4%		6.2%		4.2%	
Prospective financial return, 1969–2005								
Capital required	160		160		329		329	
	[a]	[b]	[a]	[b]	[c]	[d]	[c]	[d]
Return: years 1–7	8.35%	8.0%	5.7%	6.1%	3.3%	3.7%	2.0%	2.6%
Years 31–37	14.25%	17.45%	8.6%	10.65%	5.65%	4.0%	2.4%	1.55%

Source: MT, *Proposals for a Fixed Channel Link*, September 1963, pp. 7–10, 30.

Notes

1 Discount rate at which additional return from fixed link cancels out the additional investment.

2 These figures include a credit representing the estimated initial costs of the assets less straight-line depreciation.

[a] 20% equity, rising to 33.3% after exercise of warrants.

[b] 25% equity.

[c] 74% equity.

[d] 100% equity.

benefit was shown to be negative). Furthermore, the expected financial returns on the tunnel were substantially higher than those for its competitor (cf. Table 2.4).

When Marples raised the matter of the joint report in Cabinet in July 1963, he was authorized to secure the agreement of the French to its early publication.[107] This was effected two months later, on 19 September, but by then it was clear that this was not a propitious time for a confident steer from the British Government. Battered by allegations of scandal and sleaze, and at the end laid low by an enlarged prostate, Macmillan resigned as Prime Minister on 18 October and was succeeded by the Earl of Home, subsequently Sir Alec Douglas-Home. But whatever the political climate, the impact of the joint report was weakened by the fact that Anglo-French relations had already begun to cool. They were exacerbated by de Gaulle's action in vetoing Britain's application to join the Common Market in January 1963. Thus, although the French were reportedly more anxious to proceed with the rail tunnel, with de Gaulle apparently stating that the British decision on the issue would be taken as a further test of their attitude towards European co-operation, the British were happier to draw breath. As the Cabinet noted on 8 October, 'very large issues of economic policy were at stake; and it would be premature to seek to reach a decision on the project until they had been examined'. These included the economic return relative to other investments, the benefit to British trade, the effect on railways, roads and the airlines, and the impact on the Government's regional development policies.[108] Furthermore, the joint inquiry had done nothing to resolve the difficulties posed by the request for government guarantee of bonds and tax exemption, and there was the additional problem of inserting such a large project into national investment programmes, where civil engineering and public works resources would be undoubtedly stretched. On all these matters, the tone of the report, derived from Treasury thinking, was negative. Tax relief was 'difficult to contemplate', and to guarantee the loan capital of a profit-seeking private company, while considered preferable to either leasing or tax concessions, would represent 'an entirely new departure in at least one of the countries' [UK]. In these circumstances the working party raised another possibility, the alternative of a public or public-private company which, given the special nature of the project – high capital cost, long gestation period, the demand for fiscal/financing concessions – might be preferable. The position of the Treasury had been decisive here. An early paper on financing from the British side had concluded that the tunnel was not viable as a private enterprise 'in the normal sense of that phrase'.[109] There were other complicating factors, too. The conclusion of the joint working party was that the tunnel, while clearly an economic asset, would be difficult to finance given the size of the capital required and the uncertainties of the financial outcomes. On top of this, some doubt was placed on the geological basis for proceeding, and the tunnel promoters were asked to spend another £1 million on 'supplementary soundings and seismic studies'.[110] As an insider put it, 'the 1963 report was clearly not the end of the story'.[111] The pioneering promoters in the Channel Tunnel Study Group may have had some cause for optimism, but their prevailing reaction was

Cartoon 2 Anglo-French differences on the Channel Fixed Link, as seen by Vicky, *Evening Standard*, 19 September 1963 [Centre for the Study of Cartoons and Caricature].

one of frustration with the processes of joint governmental evaluation. Speculation in the shares of the Channel Tunnel Co. was evident, for the share price rose and fell with every new piece of information. During one of the periods of optimism, the *Times* was moved to record: 'the company retains an unbroken record of having never paid a dividend in its 80 years' existence without the marketability of its shares being in any way affected'.[112] There were also indications that the Group's public relations were not all they might have been. For example, Means was critical of d'Erlanger for his lack of diplomacy – apparently, 'his sense of public relations went out with the Assyrians' – and when Marples met American interests informally in January 1960 he was quick to criticise Kirkpatrick and others for buttonholing politicians without having the necessary mastery of technical and financial details. If governments were frustrating, the promoters could be equally exasperating.[113]

6. The Governments make a commitment to the Tunnel 'in principle', 1964

In September 1963 a special sub-committee of the Cabinet's Economic Steering (General) Committee was established to produce a speedy report on the Report. Chaired by Scott-Malden of the Ministry of Transport, it comprised representatives at under-secretary level from the Treasury, Foreign Office, Board of Trade, Ministry of Housing and Local Government, Department of Scientific and Industrial Research, and the Office of the First Secretary of State, Rab Butler. Its remit was to evaluate the 'balance of advantage' for the UK and give an opinion on the best form of organisation for construction and operation. The Scott-Malden committee considered media reactions to the report, the views of interested parties, and various planning implications, including the effects on road infrastructure, and was expected to assess the broader interest, and not merely narrow investment criteria.[114] Reporting at the end of October 1963, during Douglas-Home's brief residency at Number Ten (until the general election in the following October), the committee provided the most positive expression of support for the Tunnel yet produced by British civil servants. First, it concluded that 'an early decision of principle should be taken in favour of a fixed Channel link in the form of a rail tunnel', which was to be preferred to continuing with existing transport alternatives. The scheme was consonant with British foreign policy, which was 'to maintain and foster the European-mindedness of the United Kingdom'. The Tunnel would be 'a striking and dramatic gesture in pursuance of these policies'. Second, it argued that the project should be carried out with *public* finance as a joint Anglo-French project. The committee calculated that the internal rate of return was likely to fall within the range 9–11 per cent, which it regarded as acceptable. It was also more sanguine than its predecessors about the impact on UK investment as a whole – at the peak it would consume no more than 1 per cent of public investment expenditure and 4–5 per cent of civil engineering capacity. On the critical issue of organisation, the Scott-Malden committee concluded that the two governments would need to retain prime responsibility for safety, defence, regulation of tolls and freedom of access. The two railway institutions, the British Railways Board and SNCF, would have to provide the day-to-day running of services. For construction and tunnel management it was essential that responsibility be clear and unequivocal – a percipient observation. The two latter functions might be combined, but the key issue concerned the prospects for a private venture. The Channel Tunnel Study Group offered some further concessions in its financing proposals while the Scott-Malden committee was sitting. It was willing, apparently, to give up its demand for favourable tax treatment and to divide the risk capital between equity and low-interest, convertible debentures. However, the committee stuck to its guns. It took the view that there was little prospect of a tunnel being built by private enterprise with no government assistance of any kind. And whatever the adjustments offered by the Study Group the scheme involved a government guarantee and as such provided government subsidy. Since a subsidy would have to be counterbalanced by some form of government participation in the project, it was appropriate to consider a public-private partnership. However this 'hybrid' option would present problems of complexity, and therefore it was reasonable to conclude that the balance of argument lay with an entirely public enterprise.[115]

The optimism of the Scott-Malden report was not shared by the more senior civil servants of the Treasury-led Economic Steering (General) Committee, chaired by Sir William Armstrong, a Joint Permanent Secretary. These officials had significant reservations about the tunnel. The economic case was not felt to be conclusive, and the Tunnel's advantage over existing means was questioned. The financial rate of return of 9–11 per cent was felt to be lower than that which would be expected of new projects from bodies such as British Railways (a rather disconcerting position given the recommended use of a benchmark 8 per cent return from 1961[116]). The calculation of the broader, economic returns rested on the novelty of cost-benefit analysis, which made it difficult to interpret; at least one voice regarded the railway as an 'old-fashioned' form of transport. More importantly, the impact on Britain's resources and therefore the health of the economy was also raised, and in consequence the option emerged of postponing construction, say for five years, or longer. The Treasury challenged the Scott-Malden committee's view that a 1 per cent addition to the public investment programme (in the peak year of construction) was insignificant.[117] On the contrary, the department contended that the Tunnel, which would require about £75 million, £55 million of this in 1968–70, would add substantially to the strain on the economy represented by public sector investment, which was already expected (via the Public Expenditure Survey Committee mechanism) to outpace GNP growth in rising by about 23 per cent, over the period 1963/4–1967/8. Competing demands on limited resources included major house-building and roads programmes, provision for a 'bulge' generation of schoolchildren, and investment in electricity, with an increasing nuclear element. Investment in the tunnel was equivalent to a year's school-building; four new universities; a new town of 50,000; 2,500 megawatts of electricity; London Underground's Victoria Line; or 20 VC10 s for BOAC. The Treasury may have stated that the case for the tunnel was 'very evenly balanced', but it was clear that the doubters outnumbered the enthusiasts. Thus, the Ministers in the Cabinet's Economic Policy Committee were given a less prescriptive assessment of the pros and cons of proceeding with a tunnel, shorn of the sub-committee's recommendations and conclusions.[118] Further discussions took place at three meetings of the Economic Policy Committee held on 22 November and 10 December 1963, and 16 January 1964. By the time of the third meeting the argument had become polarized. The Treasury's concern with priorities and economic impact was strengthened by references to alternative projects such as decimalisation, raising the school leaving age, nuclear research and Concorde, and warnings about increased taxation. The Ministry of Transport, on the other hand, were demanding a quick decision, preferably in favour.[119] Marples, having met his French counterpart, Marc Jacquet on 6 December 1963, had become intensely frustrated with what he saw as the Treasury's stalling tactics. Memoranda presented by the Chancellor of the Exchequer, Reginald Maudling, for the committee meeting on 16 January 1964 did nothing to dispel this notion. An investigation of ways of fitting the tunnel into forward planning 'without excessive strain' contained some gloomy prognostications, and invited a decision to postpone the project for three years. Moreover, a further look at the key issue of organisation and finance, and in particular the

French interest in public-private funding – a Société d'Economie Mixte – produced the conclusion that 'no decision in principle . . . should be announced publicly before decisions in principle can also be announced on organisation and financing.'[120] Marples, encouraged by his officials, who were intensely critical of the Treasury's somewhat dubious tactics,[121] responded by producing a 'last-minute' paper of his own. This expressed his personal belief in the tunnel. He pointed out that the economic case was favourable and based on conservative estimates, 'incidentally prepared with Treasury help'. Above all, he urged that a decision be taken quickly to avoid embarrassment with the French.[122]

The matter went to Cabinet in this unresolved state. Maudling set out the arguments of civil servants 'for and against a decision in principle in favour of British participation in a Channel Tunnel', and their review of the prospects of obtaining external private finance. His memorandum, considered at the Cabinet meeting on 23 January, injected a more cautious tone. Thus, while the arguments for the tunnel – clear long-term savings over established transport modes, 'realistic' economic benefits, 'acceptable' financial returns and compatibility with Britain's European policy – were repeated, they were counterbalanced by 'arguments against'. The Tunnel would have to compete with other public investment projects, and was regarded as being more 'optional' than other items: 'the harsh fact remains that the accommodation of the tunnel within the investment resources available gives rise to great difficulty'. Much of the economic benefit would pass to users rather than the operator, and the expected financial returns were not large in private sector terms. Since the British and French railway systems were nationalized the two governments would be 'morally committed' to see the project through to completion and were therefore bound to take a close interest in its construction, financing and operation, including safeguards against monopoly profits. For this reason the success of a sizeable equity issue was doubtful. But in any case, the project as advanced by the Channel Tunnel Study Group was essentially a public venture, since a guarantee of bonds would involve the two governments in sharing risks with the ordinary shareholders. There were complications. It was the British practice to make Exchequer issues rather than make bond guarantees, the French were understood to be interested in taking up what private capital was available, and the prospects of raising money in foreign markets was not to be ruled out. These elements clearly required further consultations with the French. Sir Burke Trend, the Cabinet Secretary, interpreted the position as follows, in a brief for Douglas-Home: 'The Cabinet may feel that . . . the case for committing ourselves now to the Channel tunnel is, at best, not proven . . . The only counter-argument in favour of immediate commitment is the political contention that, if we endorse the project, we should be seen to be good Europeans whereas, if we reject it, General de Gaulle will notch up another black mark against us. But is this a respectable reason for overloading the British economy and provoking a new round of inflationary pressure? . . . Might the right course be to state publicly that we are well-disposed to the project in principle but that it does not offer us so clear a prospect of economic advantage during the next ten years as to be able to claim priority over other more urgent demands on our resources . . . and that we must therefore defer a decision until we are ready to take it?[123] The discussion in Cabinet largely followed this line. Some ministers pressed for an early decision to demonstrate Britain's 'truly European' stance; others agonized about the private v. public possibilities and the dangers of 'crowding-out'. Although not minuted explicitly, the Cabinet appeared to give a favourable if lukewarm blessing to the Channel Tunnel. Maudling and Marples were then invited to give further consideration to the terms in which the British Government's response might most appropriately be announced.[124]

Further memoranda in the following week indicated a difference of opinion between the two Ministers. Both were worried about the possibility of stimulating an undesirable speculation in the shares of companies concerned with the tunnel. But while Marples argued that it would be 'intolerably discourteous and a clear breach of faith' were the British Government to issue a unilateral statement without consulting with the French, Maudling thought it essential to issue an announcement before there were any damaging leaks. This would convey the Government's tentative decision to proceed, noting that there was likely to be little scope for private equity capital.[125] Both views were taken on board. On 30 January 1964 the Cabinet formally agreed in principle to proceed with the construction of the Channel Tunnel, subject to concluding satisfactory agreements with the French on technical and financial arrangements and the timing of construction. The Lord Chancellor, Lord Dilhorne, was invited to prepare a statement in consultation with Maudling and Marples, and Rab Butler, the Foreign Secretary, was asked to instruct the British Ambassador in Paris to seek the agreement of the French to a simultaneous announcement by the two governments.[126] This decision was passed to the French Government, and a week later, on 6 February, the two ministers of transport, Marples and Jacquet, announced that their Governments considered that a rail tunnel was 'technically possible' and 'in economic terms' a 'sound investment'. They had therefore 'decided to go ahead with this project'. However, much remained to be done in technical, legal and financial terms, and caution remained the watchword. In the Commons Marples noted: 'Bearing in mind the very heavy burden of the two countries' existing commitments and the many other competing claims on their national resources, it remains to be decided when and how best the expense involved can be sustained'. He went on to point out that the two governments had 'not yet decided whether there is a rôle – and, if so, in what form – for the participation of private equity capital in the enterprise.' Furthermore, in response to questioning, much of it displaying impatience, he revealed that the choice of bored tunnel or immersed tube had still to be resolved, and would follow the results of 'further geological surveys and tests'.[127]

A deputation from the Channel Tunnel Parliamentary Group met Douglas-Home and Marples on 9 April, and expressed dismay at the apparent abandonment of a role for private capital. Sir William Teeling felt that with a publicly financed scheme the Tunnel might go to the bottom of the Government's list of priorities.[128] This was but one of a number of issues to be resolved between the two governments. At this time, the pursuance of a further geological survey was the most pressing item. In March, at a meeting of British and French officials with the promoters, the Channel Tunnel Study Group, outline agreement was reached on the terms for undertaking a survey. In June the two governments signed a joint protocol (formal exchange of notes) setting up a joint commission (the Commission of Surveillance) to supervise the progress of the geological studies,[129] and a contract with the CTSG was signed in July.[130] However, it is clear that the project was still very much in the developmental stage. We were now seven years from the foundation of the CTSG.

A mixture of political and economic factors served to extend the period of 'evaluation'. With the benefit of hindsight, we can see that the economic circumstances were much more favourable to such an investment in the 1960s than they were to become after the 'oil shock' of 1973.[131] However, politicians and their advisers were more preoccupied with short-run problems, and concerns associated with the 'stop-go' policies of Selwyn Lloyd and Reginald Maudling as chancellors tended to overshadow contemporary admiration for French planning and the search for strategies of economic modernisation. On top of this, the Conservative administrations of Macmillan and Douglas-Home were battered by allegations of 'sleaze' associated with the Profumo affair, which proved a considerable distraction and enabled their Labour opponents to condemn 'thirteen years of Tory misrule' during the election campaign in 1964. Thus, while the tunnel had been endorsed by both the British and French Governments in 1964, progress was slow. A constant theme in the post-war story, however, was the nervousness of Whitehall, coupled with the fact that the sponsoring department, Transport, a Cinderella founded in 1919, was scarcely the strongest in the Cabinet. It tended to attract ministers who were either inexperienced or second-rate, both groups viewing the job as something to be done for a short time before moving on to something better. Transport ministers were unlikely to succeed in challenging the prevailing view within the Treasury, where the customary policy of caution and restraint was strengthened by its view that public sector management of the railways, as seen in the parlous state of the balance sheet and the mistakes of the Modernisation Plan, had largely failed. A weak ministry and a trenchant Treasury would be evident again.[132] But the fact was that in the early years of the 1960s there was a fair amount of diffidence in both Britain and France. Plans for undertaking higher levels of public expenditure were taking shape, but this was scarcely an adventurous time in terms of public investment. Macmillan's famous 'wind of change' may have been blowing elsewhere in politics but not in the corridors of the Treasury and Ministry of Transport. Much had been accomplished by private enterprise to establish the feasibility of the tunnel project, and to assess costs and benefits. From the late 1950s it was accepted that in terms of Britain's relations with Europe there were advantages. But in the commercial sense, the uncertainties and long gestation period were too much for the private sector and the Treasury maintained its customary stance of parsimony and risk-aversion. By deciding that the tunnel would have to become a public sector project, its organisation and financing required a substantial re-evaluation. There was clearly a great deal for the incoming Labour administration of October 1964 to determine.

Another caveat may be appropriate at this stage. It should not be assumed that all the opposition to a fixed link came from the British. The French are often credited with making supportive gestures about a link, but the fact was that at several stages they, like the British, were not prepared to underwrite a project which had been presented to them as a paying, private-sector operation. The enthusiastic noises of the French, and those of de Gaulle in particular, for a rail tunnel, should not be taken to prove that they could have or were willing to translate this into firm capital investment in 1960–4. There was a certain amount of 'blowing hot and cold' on both sides. If de Gaulle had been enthusiastic about the tunnel in 1958, he did not show it when he met Macmillan at Rambouillet in March 1960, where the conversation on the subject had been apparently 'desultory'. Indeed, the French Ambassador had let it be known that the French 'were not prepared to put any money into the project'.[133] The diplomatic relations leading to a further meeting in January 1961 were equally frustrating. It was difficult to discover which country was anxious to discuss the Tunnel, and which one wished to avoid discussing it.[134] However, over the course of 1961 the policy 'drift' which so exasperated John Hay, a Parliamentary Secretary in the Ministry of Transport, and Bill Harpham, a British Embassy official in Paris, appeared to have been the result of French, rather than British, procrastination.[135] Discussions in June 1962 between Macmillan, de Gaulle and Georges Pompidou (who as a director of Rothschild Frères had been interested in the tunnel project in the 1950s) were more enthusiastic, but the record of the meeting reveals little more than informal pleasantries.[136] In the course of the joint working party's work both sides accused the other of dragging its feet, and nervousness about publication of the joint report in 1963 was as much a French as a British phenomenon. As in Britain, the French were somewhat nervous about the prospect of government financing, and the Minister of Finance was said to be inclined to the view that the money might be better spent on purely French projects.[137] By February 1964 it was evident that the British had done much more work than the French in developing their ideas after the publication of the joint report.[138] Finally, the French caused some consternation when shortly after agreeing in principle to proceed with the geological survey, they announced that as a result of a budgetary crisis they were unable to raise the money for their share of the estimated £1.2 million cost. The Ministry of Transport and Foreign Office both pressed for the British to find the whole of the amount, but the Prime Minister and Chancellor refused to countenance this. In the event, the French portion was put up by the SNCF.[139] This was a rather inauspicious start to Anglo-French co-operation, and proof that whatever the rhetorical enthusiasm of de Gaulle and some of his colleagues a practical caution was evident in Paris as well as in London. Clearly, a simple 'French enthusiasm, British caution' hypothesis is rather misleading.

3

ANOTHER FALSE START

The Wilson Governments and the Tunnel, 1964–70

1. The Labour Government and the Tunnel

When the Labour Party was returned to power in October 1964 it inherited the work on the Tunnel begun under the Conservatives. Eight months earlier the joint announcement by the British and the French Governments had stimulated a more committed administrative response. In Britain a special department called the Channel Tunnel Group was constituted within the Ministry of Transport in February 1964. Led by an Under-Secretary, O.F. (Overy) Gingell, a committed tunneller, its function was to co-ordinate further inter-departmental studies on the Tunnel. A similar group was put in place in France, led by Philippe Lacarrière.[1] At the same time, the British and French railway institutions continued their close co-operation on more detailed technical and operating issues, a process begun as early as 1958, in response to the work of the CTSG.[2] In September 1964, following pressure exerted by André Segelat, President of the SNCF, the British Railways Board (BRB) agreed to create its own Channel Tunnel committee, which was to form the British half of a joint working party or steering group.[3] The co-chairmen were Philip Shirley, Vice Chairman of BRB and its representative on the CTSG, and Roger Guibert, Deputy Director-General of SNCF. Together they presided over a comprehensive if rather cumbersome set of eight committees and working parties convened to examine technical, commercial, financial, and legal implications.[4]

However, in the upper echelons of government the Tunnel was scarcely one of Labour's top priorities. Indeed, the project was not considered officially at any Cabinet meeting during Harold Wilson's first term as Prime Minister (1964–6).[5] It is true that within a fortnight of taking office a statement was made by Tom Fraser, the incoming Minister of Transport, to the effect that the current work would continue. However, it is also clear that the statement was reactive rather than proactive. It was prompted by a meeting between Roy Jenkins, Labour's Minister of Aviation, and Marc Jacquet in Paris on 28 October to discuss the more pressing issue of the future of Concorde, and was designed to reassure the French about the Tunnel and avoid unnecessary speculation about the project.[6] Furthermore, in the winter of 1964–5, there was a real danger that the existing activity would be halted. The new Chancellor, James Callaghan, having issued a statement on the worsening economic situation on 26 October, ordered a strict review of government expenditure, and the Treasury task group asked to undertake it nominated the Tunnel for inclusion.[7] At the Ministry of Transport, Fraser and Sir Thomas Padmore, his Permanent Secretary, fought successfully to avert this. They argued that a unilateral review could damage relations with France, a view shared by Patrick Gordon-Walker, the Foreign Secretary. But their main objection was that the Tunnel was not a committed item in the investment programme of either country.[8] The Ministry's view prevailed, but it appears to have been a close call. Otto Clarke, leading the review, was not inclined to exempt it from scrutiny. Treasury officials only gave ground when Padmore assured them that 'there were in fact so many matters to be discussed on the financial, technical and juridical problems which arose, that there was almost infinite scope for the United Kingdom to drag its feet if it wished to do so.' Nevertheless, impressed by new developments in cross-channel transport (new car ferries, and the promise of hovercraft), the task group would not budge from its view that the project should be reviewed again at a later stage.[9]

In this rather unpromising environment the project continued to progress via the groups led by Gingell and Lacarrière. The pace was somewhat leisurely, and a Treasury official was able to refer in August 1965 to 'this sleepy subject'.[10] In the same month the Channel Tunnel Parliamentary Group, frustrated with the lack of progress, sent yet another deputation to meet with the Prime Minister. Lance Mallalieu, Sir William Teeling and their colleagues pressed once again for an early decision, and although Wilson said that he saw no reason for delay, there was clearly little sense of urgency elsewhere.[11] In theory at least, the project was certainly consonant with the reformist, modernising stance that Labour's first administration since 1951 brought with it. Wilson had already referred to his party's enthusiasm for economic planning and modernisation through scientific and technological development – the 'white heat of the technological revolution'. New departments were created to give expression to these aspirations. The Department of Economic Affairs (DEA) was set up under George Brown to orchestrate economic growth through the mechanisms of industrial rationalisation and a National Plan. It also shared responsibility with the Treasury for projects such as the Tunnel, though very much in a subordinate position.[12] At the same time, a Ministry of Technology was created under Frank Cousins (and subsequently, Tony Benn) to harness science and technology and give impetus to civil, rather than military, applications.[13] However, it is clear from accounts of the period that the Tunnel did not occupy a prominent place in the new, technological agenda. And, in any case, projects both old and new (and especially Concorde, Polaris and the TSR2 aeroplane) were affected by the economic crises which preceded devaluation in 1967.[14] Thus, while the Ministry of Transport pressed for the inclusion of the Tunnel in Labour's National Plan of September 1965, largely because the French had decided to include it in their Plan, the agreed reference was distinctly *sotto voce*. A short paragraph emphasised its 'long-term significance' and made the point that since the engineering work 'would take at least five years to complete' the project would not be operational during the planning period.[15]

2. Preparing the ground: the geological survey, 1964–6

The immediate task of the more focused Channel Tunnel teams established after the joint announcement of February 1964 was to progress the geological survey inherited from the Conservative administration. While both the joint report of 1963 and the February 1964 announcement accepted the need for further geological work, it is evident that within Whitehall there were some anxieties about how this should be pursued. The CTSG, who were reported to have expressed 'modified rapture' with the February 1964 announcement,[16] pointed out that it was necessary to determine the precise alignment of the Tunnel and in particular to confirm the integrity of the chalk stratum close to the coasts. They offered to pay for the work in return for being granted the Tunnel concession, or on a reimbursement basis, the money to be charged to equity once they obtained the concession.[17] Inside the Ministry of Transport it was conceded that the civil servants, in recommending that a survey be undertaken, had merely accepted the advice of the CTSG's consultants without developing a case of the kind needed to convince the Treasury that the expenditure was justified. However, given the earlier relationship with the CTSG, and their undoubted expertise, the Ministry felt it was entirely reasonable to act in co-operation with them.[18] The Treasury's initial response had been to question whether the CTSG should be involved in the survey. There was some nervousness about whether they would seek to use their first-mover advantage to lock out rivals in tendering for the Tunnel proper, and consequently the Treasury favoured employing the Group on a reimbursement basis rather than as co-partners.[19] Agreement in principle was reached at meetings held in London on 25 March. The only pressing difficulty was on the French side, where there was a preference for delaying the start of the work due to budgetary constraints in 1964.[20] Eventually, as we have seen, the SNCF agreed to put up the French share of the costs. Under the eventual contracts signed in July 1964 the Group undertook to invite tenders for work to verify the continuity and thickness of the lower chalk and to determine the best alignment for a bored tunnel or immersed tube. The two governments agreed to reimburse the Group for the cost of the survey work, marine borings, geophysical and land investigations, and an initial schedule of estimated maximum cost ran to a total of £1.1 million. The intention was to charge the cost to whatever organisation was set up for the Tunnel. Meanwhile, the results were to remain the property of the two governments, and, as we have already noted, the work was to be supervised by an Anglo-French Commission of Surveillance.[21]

In May 1964 the tendering procedure for the survey work began under the direction of the CTSG, subject to endorsement by the Commission of Surveillance and the Ministry of Transport. No fewer than 31 contractors from five countries were invited to tender for the various works. Twenty-two firms were asked to tender for the marine boring contracts, but only eight did so, and only two bids were deemed compliant: an Anglo-French tender of £770,000 for 70 boreholes by George Wimpey and Forasol of Paris; and an Anglo-American tender of £900,000 (also for 70 boreholes) from Richard Costain and Raymond International. The cheaper tender was accepted.[22] Before the geophysical survey was awarded, three firms participated in trials of the available techniques ('Hydrosonde', 'Sparker' and 'Boomer'), and following this assessment, the contract was awarded to an American firm, Edgerton, Germeshausen & Grier of Boston, who undertook to use the 'Sparker' equipment. A British and a French firm competed for the contract to supply and operate the position-fixing equipment, and the British firm, Decca Navigator, which offered rates less than half of its rival, SERCEL, was consequently successful.[23] Preparatory work began in August 1964, and the project was officially marked in the last month of the Conservative administration, when on 14 September Marples and Jacquet visited the site of boring operations near Dover and held a press conference. The mood was optimistic. According to the *Times*, 'after a blustery day in the Channel' the two Ministers 'agreed that the Channel tunnel was now a certainty'.[24]

However, when the Labour Government took office a great deal remained to be done. The geophysical survey proved to be a straightforward exercise. In October, Edgerton completed its work within the estimated cost of £17,000, producing results of 'unexpectedly' high quality. Unfortunately, the marine boring was to prove a much more challenging affair. Operations began in September but quickly ran into difficulties. Wimpey-Forasol had tendered to use five drilling ships, but eventually four were employed. Delays were caused by competition for ships from North Sea oil explorers, and, once the vessels had been acquired, by the need to refit two of them. Thus, while the contractors had been given authority to proceed in July, only two ships were ready by the end of September, and a third, the *Sauvetur*, was wrecked on 2 November, two days after putting out to sea.[25] Indeed, exceptionally bad weather was responsible for curtailing activities to a significant extent. As concern mounted in Whitehall about the financial implications of the various problems, it also emerged that relations between the CTSG and Wimpey-Forasol had deteriorated to the extent that the latter were threatening to withdraw from some of their obligations.[26] The project was re-evaluated by the Commission of Surveillance in January 1965. Its recommendations represented a radical revision of the marine boring work. The French came to the rescue by supplying two oil-drilling platforms; Wimpey-Forasol settled their differences with the CTSG and agreed to scale down their programme; and a revised estimate of cost of £2.1 million, 90 per cent higher than the £1.1 million estimated in July, was accepted by the two governments in April. At this stage only eight boreholes had been completed, the same number as had been sunk under the direction of the CTSG in 1959–60.[27] The reconstitution of the project, together with better weather, led to an immediate improvement. Marine boring was completed in October 1965, and in all 88 marine and land borings were sunk. Preliminary results were encouraging, although the main reports did not emerge until 1966, and the final report was not submitted until June 1969.[28] The geological survey highlighted all the difficulties of project management where responsibility is divided, a feature which was to re-emerge several times in the Tunnel's history. Subsequent inquests accepted that the CTSG had failed conspicuously to manage the project and that the administrative arrangements had been unduly complex. It was also recognised that some geological loose ends remained.[29] However, at this stage, the delays and cost escalation produced by the survey, while irksome, were overshadowed by more serious obstacles to progress, namely the requirement to resolve complex questions of organisation and financing. It is to these issues that we now turn.

3. Preparing the ground: questions of organisation, finance and economic viability

Work on the more fundamental issues surrounding the project began in 1964, but progress was decidedly slow. The first Anglo-French meeting of any substance was not held until the end of the year, and a second, with wider departmental involvement, did not take place until May 1965, 15 months after the teams had been established.[30] There was more than a hint that the French were reacting to a cooling of British enthusiasm for Concorde.[31] Meanwhile British officials toiled away with the details of a complex subject and produced a substantial documentation on organisation and finance, some of it, in the view of one civil servant, 'almost of Royal Commission length'.[32] In November 1965, seven months after the basic British position had been put to the French, Fraser wrote to senior Ministers (Callaghan, Brown, Michael Stewart, the Foreign Secretary, and Douglas Jay, President of the Board of Trade) in some frustration. His progress report revealed that the French had deliberately avoided discussion on the key issue of public v. private funding (see below) and thus the initiative had remained with the British.[33] It was not unknown in Anglo-French relations for the French to put up a wall of silence only to surprise the British with a substantial contribution. And so it proved. At the time of Fraser's report the French side had promised to produce a comprehensive memorandum outlining their views and when this document, which ran to 172 pages and 80,000 words, was received, a few weeks later, officials from the two governments embarked once again on a period of 'intense technical, organisational and economic studies'.[34]

It was not difficult to reach unanimity on the scope of the government controls required, irrespective of the type of organisation and financing plan. These embraced the basic physical characteristics of the Tunnel and its terminals, safety, provision for repairs, commercial policy (tariffs) and so on. However, there was less agreement about organisation and finance, and since it was accepted by both sides that they should work towards a common and practicable solution, the discussions were necessarily protracted. The basic criteria were not in doubt. An agreed scheme had to: ensure that the public interest of Britain and France was paramount; establish a capital structure that squared with the organisation's 'commercial needs in a competitive situation'; establish a compatibility with legal frameworks; and safeguard 'technical and managerial continuity'. But the methods of achieving these aims were 'fundamentally divergent', and the battle lines were essentially those drawn up in 1960 and 1963. French officials proposed that the Tunnel should be constructed by private enterprise, or failing that by a 'société d'économie mixte', that is a private-public partnership, but one in which private capital predominated. Since the company would be internationally financed, it should itself be established as an international institution. The British, on the other hand, felt that a private sector solution was precluded by the project's special circumstances, a position they had taken earlier (see Chapter 2). They therefore argued that the Tunnel should be constructed and operated by a public corporation.[35]

The method of financing was a long-standing question which, in the words of one Treasury official, had been 'discussed ad nauseam'.[36] Since 1960, as we have seen, most of those involved on the British side, including sceptics, had accepted that the necessity for government guarantees would turn the project in effect into a public one. A considerable effort was made to ascertain precisely what the French meant by 'private' financing, and the Bank of England was asked for its assistance. There was much reference to the French enthusiasm for sociétés d'économie mixte, organisations in which a substantial degree of control was retained by the State through direct participation. Indeed, the SNCF itself was one such institution, the French Government holding 50.7 per cent of the capital; the Mont Blanc Tunnel Co. was another, with a 52.5 per cent state holding. In Britain, there was little direct experience of this model, which differed substantially from the Morrisonian public corporation.[37] But in any case the French were by no means certain about their intentions. The British had picked up indications that there were departmental disagreements about the issue, and officials in the Ministry of Finance had expressed the private opinion that there was little scope for raising private capital. Indeed, when Chancellor Maudling had met his French counterpart, Valéry Giscard d'Estaing, in May 1964 the latter had said that the Tunnel 'should be done as a public enterprise, though some room might be found for private participation (he did not make it very clear what he had in mind)'.[38]

The British position was scarcely helped by the CTSG, which continued to lobby hard for the private financing of the Tunnel under its auspices. The arguments were set out in a widely circulated booklet entitled *The Channel Tunnel: the Facts*, produced in April 1964. While it was clear that the document, which claimed that a privately-financed tunnel would be in the national interest, was a piece of self-promotion, the Treasury expressed concern that Britain might be backed into a corner on the finance issue. Consequently, aided by the Bank of England, it took the trouble to address the document in some depth.[39] It was not difficult to criticise the booklet, but the CTSG could not be dismissed so easily. Through the committee led by Louis Armand the Group had developed a special relationship with French officials which bordered on 'capture'; and it was able to make its presence felt with British politicians and civil servants.[40] There were fears in some quarters that the Group's special position would make it difficult to resist awarding it the concession to build and operate the Tunnel. But whatever the motivations, both British and French officials felt it necessary to obtain its co-operation during this critical period of policy formation. In July 1965 the Group was sent a jointly-prepared questionnaire that sought to ascertain the scope for private financing given the likely extent of government controls. Three alternatives were put forward: private financing alone; mixed private-public financing, with either a single or twin company structure; and public financing alone.[41] The CTSG responded by reiterating its preference for private financing, but emphasised that in order to attract investors the level of government control would have to be much lower than that envisaged. For example, it required the removal or dilution of controls on tariffs, new investment, the disposal of earnings, and the transferability of shares. In British eyes this confirmed the belief that a large measure of private financing was unrealistic, something they wished to get out into the open in the presence of French officials.[42]

A meeting of British and French officials with the CTSG was duly held in Paris on 5 August 1965, but although the fragility of the CTSG's position was exposed, the French being unwilling to concede anything on controls, it was apparent that the two countries were some distance from resolving both the method of financing and the type of organisation required.[43] At this stage the attitude of the French was clearly causing disillusionment within the Ministry of Transport. There was little sign of any serious input from them, either in producing their own proposals or in studying those prepared on the British side.[44] In addition, there was a broader measure of exasperation over the unwillingness of the French civil servants to discuss the question of finance, on the grounds that this was a matter entirely for ministers to determine. In London, the French fixation with private capital was difficult to understand, but at the same time, the French found the British insistence on a public authority to be academic, even doctrinaire. One thing was clear: the CTSG had stated that the maximum they would be able to raise as equity would be £30–35 million. As a Treasury official observed, 'for the sake of a mere £18 m. or so on each side it did not seem right to concede managerial control and the greater part of the profits to private enterprise'.[45]

The much anticipated and weighty French memorandum, known after its academic architect as the Rigaud report, reached Whitehall on 22 November 1965. Dated 'August' it came down firmly in support of a single international company.[46] However, it was accompanied by a more conciliatory paper from French officials which offered three possible solutions: (1) a single international tunnel company, privately financed; (2) an international tunnel company in which half the capital was subscribed by a British public authority and half by a société d'économie mixte; and (3) the British suggestion of two public bodies, one constituted under British law, the other under French law. Nevertheless, since the French repeated their strong reservations about options two and three, the British felt that, after all the waiting, the Rigaud report took things no further in terms of serious and detailed debate.[47] Indeed, the document was quickly sidelined as steps were taken to break the impasse in December. A compromise solution then emerged. Since a satisfactory single institution could not be devised, an alternative, suggested by Lacarrière on 15 December, envisaged *two* distinct organisations: a privately-funded international construction company, which would build the Tunnel; and a public authority (or possibly two authorities), which would operate it under a leasing arrangement. This inevitably introduced more complexity into the arrangements, but the French were adamant that construction should be undertaken by private enterprise, though they were willing to move towards the British position by accepting that operation could be managed by a public concern.[48] The compromise solution received a mixed reception in Whitehall. It was not clear whether it was a stalling tactic; certainly, it was held to be vague, and the way in which private capital would be stitched into such a dual structure did not appear to have been thought out fully.[49] Nevertheless, the compromise had political as well as economic attractions, and it certainly helped to resolve the policy gridlock. In a private meeting in London at the end of January 1966, Gingell and Lacarrière agreed that the compromise solution 'was the only one on which they saw any real hope of finding the basis for agreement'. They agreed to sound out their newly-appointed Ministers of Transport: Barbara Castle, who had succeeded Fraser in December 1965; and Edgard Pisani, who had replaced Jacquet in the following month as Minister of Equipment (including Transport). If accepted, the proposal would be incorporated into a further joint report. At last there appeared to be something resembling real progress.[50] The Gingell-Lacarrière meeting was considered to have been 'more useful than the whole series of mass gatherings so far'.[51] Unfortunately, the announcement of a British general election interrupted plans for the Ministers of Transport to meet.[52]

While the compromise solution to organisation and finance surfaced, the British Treasury intervened to press for an immediate economic and financial assessment of the project, the fourth to date. This, they suggested, should be a unilateral exercise, kept from the French. As we have seen, it had been accepted that a reappraisal would be necessary before a final decision was taken. The Ministry of Transport had envisaged that this would be tackled jointly in co-operation with French officials. But Callaghan insisted that the review should be started immediately, completed speedily (by the end of January 1966, i.e. within two months) and, notwithstanding earlier qualms, undertaken from the British perspective alone.[53] An inter-departmental steering group, led by Gingell, was formed to conduct the review. The exercise may have been devised as another wrecking manoeuvre by sceptics such as Otto Clarke.[54] Certainly, some of the arguments put up by the Treasury prior to the review pointed in this direction; others were rather specious. One of the more bizarre suggestions was to make the Tunnel too small for large lorries to be carried on flat wagons, in order to give British Rail the bulkier traffic. Sceptics also drew comfort from a re-examination of the exact wording of the February 1964 announcement. The British version – 'The two Governments have...decided to go ahead with this project' – appeared less committed in the French translation – 'Les deux Gouvernements se déclarent, en conséquence, favorables à ce projet'.[55] However, taken at face value, a reassessment was justified on the following grounds: the market for cross-channel transport had changed since

1963, with Townsend's investments in drive-through car ferries, the introduction of Scandinavian ferries (e.g. Thoresen's Southampton-Cherbourg service in 1964), and greater hopes for the hovercraft technology; new traffic statistics had become available; the problem of financing had received more attention; and the geological studies made it possible to estimate construction costs with more precision.[56] The work was proceeding to a conclusion when Wilson, whose government's position in the Commons was fragile, called a general election in March 1966.

After the election Labour was returned to power with a healthy majority, and although once again the subject had not been raised in the manifesto, the Prime Minister soon called for some action on the Tunnel.[57] On 10 May his Private Secretary, Michael Halls, sent a note to the Ministry of Transport asking for information on the state of play. Other documentation indicates that Wilson wanted the subject handled with 'all reasonable speed'.[58] The Department responded with a position paper on 23 May, from which it was clear that officials had reached a substantial measure of agreement on the outstanding issues: geological feasibility, organisational structure, financing methods, and economic and financial viability.[59] Indeed, Barbara Castle, continuing as Minister of Transport, had already informed Callaghan, on 20 April, that the economic reappraisal had produced a positive outcome (see below). Then, on 25 May, she told Brown that events had moved so quickly that it was not necessary to wait for the civil servants to produce their final report.[60] The consensus view on the Tunnel was then taken through the Cabinet committee structure. First, on 7 June the Economic Development (Official) Committee found 'a clear, indeed a strong case for a decision in principle in favour of going ahead with the Channel Tunnel without delay'.[61] Its reception was more mixed at the next stages, the Ministerial Committee on Economic Development, on 13 June – and the full Cabinet on 21 June. However, a process which had consumed four months in 1963–4 took a mere two weeks in 1966. After proceeding at a rather leisurely pace during its first 18 months in office, the re-elected Labour government moved relatively quickly to a new position on the Tunnel.

Castle, who enjoyed the support of Brown and Stewart, argued, first of all, that the geological survey had demonstrated the technical feasibility of a bored tunnel. There was insufficient evidence to permit a considered judgement on the alternative, immersed tube technology, but prevailing opinion was sceptical. 'In the light of the marine risks this method would be open to', the Ministry noted, 'it cannot be viewed with confidence'. For a tunnel, on the other hand, it was safe to conclude that 'no technical obstacle stands in the path of the project'.[62] On organisation and finance her department accepted the compromise solution drawn up by British and French officials. The Tunnel should be built by private enterprise, then handed over to a public operating authority. The construction company would receive pre-determined rental payments to cover interest and redemption of its bonded debt and a variable toll to remunerate its equity holders. Finally, Britain's confidential and unilateral reappraisal of the Tunnel had only strengthened the arguments in its favour. The project was declared to be a sound investment of UK resources and an attractive financial proposition.[63] As Table 3.1

Table 3.1 The 1963 and 1966 estimates of economic and financial returns (£m.)

	Lower estimate			*Upper estimate*		
				'Upper'	*'Probable'*	*'Most favourable'*
	Joint 1963	*British April 1966*	*Joint August 1966*	*Joint 1963*	*British April 1966*	*Joint August 1966*
Capital + operating costs of existing transport	247	410	416	308	499	524
Capital + operating costs of tunnel						
Initial	141	135	182	141	135	161
Post-1969/1974	58	71	71	67	82	86
Total	199	206	253	208	217	247
Cost difference:	48	204	163	100	282	177
Overall net benefit of fixed crossing over existing transport	74	249	217	153	343	356
Prospective financial return	9%[a]	17%	14%	11%[a]	21%	20%

Source: MT, *Proposals for a Fixed Channel Link*, September 1963 (AF63) and see Table 2.4; CT Economic Steering Group, Channel Tunnel Economic Reappraisal, 12 April 1966, MT144/89; MT, Joint Report, August 1966, PREM13/1244, PRO.

Notes

Economic return: 1963: 1969–2018, discounted at 7%, 1969 prices
1966: 1974–2023, discounted at 8%, 1974 prices.

Two calculations were offered for the 'probable' estimate, one assuming traffic growth to 1990 only, the other assuming growth to 2005. The latter has been used here. Calculations with a 7% discount rate were also shown.

a Not shown in AF63.

shows, the 1966 exercise produced higher financial returns and higher economic benefits than those shown in the White Paper of 1963. Taking the capital cost to be £134 million, £9 million lower than the figure used in 1963, and using a discount rate of 8 per cent (instead of 7 per cent), the net economic benefit over ships and aircraft (the hovercraft option was dismissed) was found to be £249–343 million, substantially higher than the £74–153 million shown in 1963. The financial return, calculated on a discounted cash flow basis, was given as 17–21 per cent, again much higher than the 9–11 per cent calculated in 1963. Higher estimates of traffic lay at the root of this 'improvement'. From 1962 to 1965 cross-channel traffic had grown by twice the expected rate, and consequently the 1963 report was based on a significant underestimation of the prospects. For example, the actual number of accompanied vehicles in 1965 – 860,000 – was 34 per cent higher than the 1963 report's upper-bound estimate for that year of 640,000, and was equivalent to the 1963 upper-bound prediction for *1981*. Consequently, higher traffic data were fed into the new calculation. For 1980–2005 the increase amounted to 81–122 per cent. Estimates of freight traffic were also increased, by 50–236 per cent (see Table 3.2, April 1966 cols).[64] The additional burden on the UK construction industry and manpower resources was not regarded as serious, and the point was also made that the railways, which badly needed a boost, would benefit from the opportunities for developing through traffic. The exercise was a substantial encouragement to a 'yes' vote. As Castle and Brown noted, even if the Tunnel were to cost £200 million and was not used at all after 30 years, it would still produce a net economic benefit of £164-252 million.[65]

There was more than a hint of *déjà vu* about the ministerial debates, and, of course, there was much similarity with previous evaluations of the Tunnel's prospects, in 1960, 1963 and 1964. Thus, issues raised in committee and at Cabinet included: on the plus side, the Tunnel's political value in Britain's tortuous European policy, and the absence of defence objections; and on the minus side, the opportunity cost of construction, and arguments for postponing a decision, including concerns over the challenge to regional policy and (surprisingly) the absence of sufficient information on traffic and costs. The Secretaries of State for Scotland and Wales, respectively Willie Ross and Cledwyn Hughes, were understandably worried about the implications of giving a further boost to the South-east. Some views were new. The new car ferries and the promise of hovercraft technology were helping to widen the potential market for the Tunnel, but some experts were arguing that these modes would continue to prosper after it was opened, and their opinions were taken seriously by Ministers such as Brown and Callaghan.[66] In a discussion described by one Minister as 'desultory', the most serious criticism came from Frank Cousins, the Minister of Technology, who argued that the Tunnel should be both operated and constructed by the public sector. This belief, presented as an 'overriding' objection was countered by Chancellor Callaghan's view that there were advantages in letting the private sector find the money for construction.[67] With additional support from Roy Jenkins, the Home Secretary, Richard Crossman, Minister of Housing, and Anthony Crosland, Secretary of State for

Table 3.2 Traffic forecasts: revisions of April and August 1966, compared with Anglo-French report, 1963

Traffic	*1963 Report*			*Modification (%) April 1966 Reappraisal*			*August 1966 Joint report*		
	1980	*1985*	*2005*	*1980*	*1985*	*2005*	*1980*	*1985*	*2005*
1 Lower estimate									
Accompanied vehicles ('000s)	880	980	980	+122	+122	+122	+116	+117	+137
Unaccompanied passengers ('000s)	3,000	3,040	3,040	0	+3	+18	+8	+11	+24
Freight ('000 tons)	3,000	3,400	3,400	+74	+89	+203	as reappraisal		
2 Upper estimate									
Accompanied vehicles ('000s)	1,260	1,400	1,400	+81	+81	+100	+102	+104	+161
Unaccompanied passengers ('000s)	3,700	3,800	3,800	−4	−3	+10	+3	+6	+22
Freight ('000 tons)	4,000	4,500	4,500	+50	+72	+236	as reappraisal		

Sources: MT, *Proposals for a Fixed Channel Link*, September 1963 (AF63), p. 6 and see Table 2.3; CT Economic Steering Group, Channel Tunnel Economic Reappraisal, April 1966, cit.; MT, Joint Report, August 1966, PREM13/1244, PRO.

Education and Science, the balance of opinion was in favour of going ahead with the Tunnel.[68] After the Cabinet meeting a form of words was agreed for use at Wilson's meeting with Georges Pompidou, the French Prime Minister, and Maurice Couve de Murville, the French Foreign Minister, on 6–8 July.[69]

There was a hiccup before the politicians met. The consultants produced a revision of their earlier estimate of the construction costs, largely as a result of enhanced engineering requirements. The new estimate, £156–71 million in 1966 prices, represented an increase of 16–28 per cent. Although this clearly unsettled those who, with George Brown, feared that the Tunnel would prove to be another escalating project like Concorde, it appeared that even at the higher costs the economic benefit would fall by only 10 per cent, and the financial return would be closer to 15–19 per cent instead of 17–21 per cent.[70] After this panic was over, the Prime Minister discussed the Tunnel with Pompidou on 8 July, with Castle present. The geological report 'was extremely encouraging', Wilson pointed out, and the British 'wished to make all possible progress' on the basis of construction with private capital and operation using public funds. Pompidou welcomed an important project, but felt that 'several points still needed to be clarified', not least the construction costs and the financing issue. Both sides accepted that they should agree on the kind of arrangements that could be made with private capitalists before discussions were started with the interests concerned. Other matters took centre stage, of course. The joint communiqué referred to the leaders' talks on Britain's entry into the EEC, in which the two sides adopted rather entrenched positions, and to the decision to proceed with Concorde, in spite of spiralling costs. But in relation to the Tunnel, Pompidou accepted Wilson's view that the statement should be more encouraging following the geological survey, giving a 'green light' to the Tunnel.[71] The outcome remained cautious, however. Shorter than originally drafted, after intervention from a sceptical Couve de Murville, and more 'yellow' than 'green', the communiqué stated that the Tunnel should be built, but subject to the important proviso that questions of finance and construction had still to be agreed.[72]

Why did the British Government display such a sense of urgency in the summer of 1966? Castle's appointment as Minister of Transport had been followed by a shake-up of the department, which appeared to have taken its foot off the pedal under Fraser and Padmore, the latter being dismissed by Castle for having become 'lackadaisical' and 'utterly bored with Transport'.[73] Planning was given greater emphasis with the appointment of Christopher Foster as Director-General of Economic Planning in January 1966. Castle was also determined to inject some co-ordination into this 'sprawling jungle' of 7,000 civil servants, 12 Under-Secretaries and somewhat autonomous departments (the main sections were highways, railways and nationalised transport, and planning), an intention which culminated in the Transport Act of 1968.[74] However, important as Castle's revolution was, the origins of the decision to accelerate consideration of the Tunnel lay elsewhere. Major issues at the centre of Anglo-French relations encouraged the British Government to resolve the matter quickly. First, there was de Gaulle's personal statements in favour – notably, 'Le tunnel se fera [the tunnel will be built]', backed by an equally enthusiastic Minister of Transport in Pisani.[75] Second, there was some real anxiety that the 'compromise solution' had already leaked out, and more specifically that the CTSG had already learned about it through their close contacts with French officials.[76] Third, it is clear that after the 1966 election Wilson had put European matters and improved relations with France higher up the political agenda. He had appointed George Thomson as Chancellor of the Duchy of Lancaster with the specific brief of reconsidering Britain's entry into the EEC. In this context, de Gaulle's announced withdrawal from NATO in March 1966 was a potentially explosive area of disagreement with the French. So too were the arguments over the rising cost of two joint European ventures, Concorde and the European rocket launcher, ELDO, where the British were keen to extricate themselves or else reduce their financial commitments.[77] With Pompidou set to visit London in early July, there was every reason to prevent the Tunnel from becoming a negative pawn in a wider and more complex diplomatic game.

Nevertheless, one could easily exaggerate the extent of the progress made in July 1966. The joint statement of the two governments was another expression of agreement 'in principle' which did not commit anybody to going ahead, leaving more to be agreed at a later stage. As Castle so aptly put it during the EDC discussions, 'If it was now decided to go ahead with further study of the project, the Government would not be finally committed'. She was equally candid during the Wilson-Pompidou talks, noting that 'The problem... was the desirability of conveying the impression that we had moved further than the statement of February 1964 without, at the same time, giving a false impression that all the problems had been settled'.[78] Indeed, the 'slow, slow, quick quick' waltz was intensely frustrating for those outside government who did not appreciate the intricacies of inter-departmental and inter-country negotiation. Tunnel promoters could only speculate why, in the six years between the publication of the CTSG Report in March 1960 and the second major joint statement in principle in July 1966, there was so much still to be decided. Outstanding issues included: the details of the rental agreement; the terms and timing of the governments' option to acquire the Tunnel at the end of the concessionary period (also not determined), the distribution of equity and the participation of overseas capital; the British Government's insistence that it be allowed to participate in the equity; the appropriate remuneration to shareholders given their reduced risk; the need to secure unrestricted access to the Tunnel for traffic from continental countries other than France; and a further examination of the regional planning implications. In British eyes, the French were mainly responsible for the feet-dragging, as they had been in 1961–3, and there was press speculation that some of the delays were caused by French exasperation with the British over Concorde.[79] But the difficulties were also caused by genuine disagreements within the two governments. In France, as we have seen, the Finance Ministry saw some merit in the public capital argument, while the Transport Ministry did not. The degree of enthusiasm for the Tunnel was also much stronger in the latter department than in the former. Furthermore, economists in the Foreign Ministry were known to be hostile to the project.[80] British civil servants and Bank of England officials accepted that there were genuine difficulties in the French position *vis-à-vis* government expenditure. The Finance Ministry had placed a balanced budget at the top of its priorities, and having succeeded in achieving this goal in 1965 – 'the first time for decades' – was not keen to find any capital for the Tunnel from the public purse. In addition, there was a constitutional obstacle. Unless a large proportion of private capital were raised for a single tunnel company, it would be deemed in French law to be a public sector venture, and would thus be included in the national accounts, where budgetary difficulties would rule it out.[81] Political instability in both countries also presented numerous opportunities for delaying tactics. In Britain, the small majority of Wilson's first administration pushed new and expensive projects to the bottom of the list of priorities. And in France, instability was also evident. Voters were called to the polls no fewer than 15 times during de Gaulle's presidency (1958–69); his narrow re-election win at the end of 1965 heralded 15 months of almost continuous electioneering.[82] The departure of enthusiasts did not help the tunnellers' cause. Overy Gingell was given broader responsibilities in March 1966 on becoming a Deputy-Secretary, but then died unexpectedly in the following month.[83] Pisani, an enthusiast who was prepared to take matters into his own hands if civil servants failed to share his sense of urgency, gave up his responsibility for transport in April 1967.[84] But these were exceptions. Given the numerous complications surrounding the Tunnel there was just not enough unequivocal support either in Whitehall, l'hôtel Matignon (Prime Minister's office) or the Quai d'Orsay (Foreign Ministry) to really push the project home.

4. The search for private sector partners, 1966–70

In spite of the apparent progress in the first half of 1966, there was little chance of taking matters further until the completion of the second joint report of British and French officials. This document, dubbed 'AF66' to distinguish it from the earlier study in 1963 ('AF63'), appeared in August. It contained no surprises. The only substantive change over the advance summary text considered by the Cabinet in June was the incorporation of the revised estimate of construction cost (see above). Traffic estimates were also revised, most being raised by between 5 and 30 per cent (cf. Table 3.2, cols 4–6 and 7–9). However, these modifications had only a marginal impact on the calculations of net economic benefit and financial return, which remained healthy (see Table 3.1), and AF66 gave the seal of Anglo-French approval to the work which the British had done earlier. The summary results of the geological survey, endorsed by the joint Commission of Surveillance, were that there was sufficient information to enable the tunnel line to be plotted with precision. The lower chalk offered an uninterrupted medium and the engineering risks were regarded as slight. Consequently, there was confidence in the revised estimate of costs, which provided for a portal-portal service tunnel and more generous contingencies. The figure was £120.5 million, plus

"All dates are tentative at the moment, but we expect the financial backing in 1968, planning and execution of approaches in 1969, work on the tunnel started in 1970 and the whole project abandoned in 1971 due to escalating costs."

Cartoon 3 Cynical but prophetic observation about the project management of the Channel Tunnel after the Anglo-French report of 1966, Kenneth Mahood, *Times*, 4 November 1966 [Centre for the Study of Cartoons and Caricature].

£51 million for the associated rail and road infrastructure. The Commission felt that given the provision for contingencies the total cost would lie in the range £157–71 million. The immersed tube alternative was not ruled out entirely, but given the enthusiasm for a tunnel it had not been subjected to the same degree of rigorous study.[85] Of course, further work was required. A detailed design of the Tunnel was needed, together with agreement on construction techniques, ventilation methods, and operational criteria. More legal work was needed to draw up a Franco-British Treaty, together with the necessary domestic legislative instruments, and concession agreements. The two governments also had to agree a joint negotiating position, with suitable prospectus documentation, so that serious negotiation with interested private interests could begin. This in itself meant that a detailed specification and corporate profile of the construction and operating companies had to be determined, resolving all the outstanding issues identified in July (rental, equity participation, profit distributions, etc. see p. 59), and establishing the relationship of these new bodies with British Rail and SNCF.[86]

The joint report pointed the way to formal acceptance of the plan by the two governments. It had been known for some months that Pisani was coming to Britain in September and was keen to meet Castle to discuss the Tunnel. Castle obtained the support of her senior Cabinet colleagues for the policy, and officials, anticipating an extensive discussion, worked on a lengthy communiqué.[87] However, there was insufficient time for the French Government to endorse AF66 officially, and the status of the meeting had to be reduced hastily to that of an informal talk.[88] Held on 9 September, it was the first time that the two Ministers had met face to face to discuss the project. The mood was upbeat. Castle confirmed British acceptance of the private construction/public operation compromise, and declared 'that she was convinced that the time was now right for decisions on the Tunnel, a project on which she personally was very keen'. Pisani was characteristically bullish. He 'also wanted decisions as quickly as possible' and regarded the joint report as an 'excellent' basis for proceeding. 'He agreed that it was "now or never" so far as the project was concerned.' However, if the British were to introduce legislation in the 1967/8 session there was very little time to determine the outstanding issues identified in the joint report. The preliminary discussions on these issues and, in particular, on government participation in the equity, were frank but, as in July, a short communiqué had to serve. It referred very briefly to receipt of AF66 and announced that the Ministers were to meet again in Paris on 28 October. By this time it was anticipated that the Pompidou Government would have given AF66 its formal blessing.[89]

The British were disconcerted by French reticence to reach a decision, and contingency plans were made to withdraw from the meeting if a formal endorsement did not materialise. On the other hand, there was more than a hint that the French were perplexed by British coolness towards the CTSG and its insistence first on a public solution, then on a government stake in the equity, both of which were regarded in some circles as stonewalling tactics. As Castle noted in her diary, 'The French obviously came along thinking *we* were dragging our feet'.[90] After more Franco-British fencing the two Ministers met again on 28 October. Castle and Pisani established a rapport and a more substantial joint communiqué was quickly agreed and launched at a press conference. With the support of an optimistic outline timetable drawn up in the Ministry of Transport, Castle announced that the Tunnel should be open by 1975. The meeting was followed by visits to the car-ferry rail terminal at Fontainebleau and, on the following day, to the Mont Blanc road tunnel.[91] The new statement took the project further forward in a public sense by revealing the terms of the compromise. The Tunnel would be built by private capital 'drawn to the greatest possible extent from the international capital market'; however, it would be operated by an Anglo-French public authority. Government participation in the risk capital 'would not be excluded'. It was also announced that British and French railways would be 'closely associated' with the operation of tunnel services, and that 'unrestricted access . . . would be guaranteed, without discrimination, to all users'. Nevertheless, sceptics could be forgiven for their belief that the extent of this 'progress' was limited. The communiqué conceded that the financing 'would have to be secured on terms acceptable to the two Governments'. And yet more 'study' was promised, the work to be undertaken by permanent working groups in each country.[92] Furthermore, a minor embarrassment in the aftermath of the statement revealed in microcosm the difficulties in managing the project as a joint Anglo-French government venture. *Le Monde*, using an information circular from the Ministry of Equipment issued two days before the meeting, had asserted that the immersed tube alternative had been abandoned. Castle was then moved to write to Pisani to point out that 'no irrevocable choice has been made at this stage'. Although a tunnel was the most likely choice, the intention was to wait until negotiations with private interests were nearing completion before making a final decision. The episode did not augur well for the resolution of other, more pressing, problems.[93]

The October 1966 announcement marked the beginning of a two-year period of protracted negotiations which ultimately produced little advancement of the project. To undertake the programme of work identified in the communiqué, the British and French Governments appointed John Barber and Roger Macé to head teams with special responsibility for the Tunnel. Barber, an Assistant Secretary reporting directly to Scott-Malden, led the Channel Tunnel Project Team and chaired an inter-departmental committee with representatives from the Treasury, DEA, Board of Trade, Foreign Office, Inland Revenue and the Bank of England. The first task was to produce a prospectus to issue to private interests.[94] In spite of the new spirit of optimism engendered by the Castle-Pisani talks, and the new players, the somewhat pedestrian nature of Anglo-French negotiations scarcely altered. Macé proved extremely elusive in his early months in office, and given the pressing timetable, this produced renewed frustration on the British side. Once again, there were complaints that, 'as has happened throughout the history of this project, the British side is making all the running'. By the end of January 1967 the British team had met 18 times and produced 14 working papers; the French, in contrast, had done little; Macé had not moved into his offices in the Ministry of Equipment and his inter-departmental team was not complete. An impending general election, to be held in March, was an obvious distraction.[95] Nevertheless, the two sides were able to agree on the wording of an information memorandum in the following month. This was also something of a compromise. Inviting expressions of interest by 15 April, it contained the minimum necessary in British eyes to avoid serious delay and the maximum that could be revealed in French eyes to avoid perceived difficulties before their election.[96] On 22 February Castle was thus able to announce, as an aside during the Commons debate on the Transport Policy White Paper, that the two governments were seeking expressions of interest from private groups wishing to finance or construct the Tunnel.[97] The procedure may have appeared a rebuff to the CTSG, which had invested about £1 million in advancing the project since 1957. However, British officials fully expected the Group to be the front runner, since no major competitors appeared to be in the wings.[98] In fact, interest was expressed from a wider base. In all there were 41 requests for information, most of them from potential bidders, and five serious applications were submitted by the April deadline. After the study teams had examined the replies, the Ministers, Castle, and Jean Chamant, head of a reconstituted Ministry of Transport, announced on 22 May that three financial consortia had been invited to submit more detailed bids by 15 July and enter into further discussions with the two governments. The groups were the CTSG; an Anglo-French-American group headed by the British merchant bankers, S.G. Warburg, and the Banque de Paris et des Pays-Bas; and an Anglo-French-American-Italian group, also led by a British merchant bank, Hill Samuel, in association with the French bank Louis-Dreyfus (Table 3.3).[99]

Once again, British and French officials took a very different view of the way in which talks with these private parties would be conducted. Barber's team had been busy working on a detailed statement of the British negotiating position, with the help of Hambros Bank as consultants. The documentation was intended to be used in discussions with the French Government and subsequently with the private consortia. The French, on the other hand, made it known that they preferred to wait until the consortia had submitted detailed proposals before committing themselves.[100] Notwithstanding this difference of approach, British officials went on to secure ministerial approval for the position they wished to adopt. In April Castle consulted with Callaghan, Stewart (now First Secretary) and Brown (now Foreign Secretary), and took additional advice from Thomas Balogh, Reader in Economics at Oxford University and Economic Adviser to Wilson's Cabinet, and Lord Campbell of Eskan, a businessman sympathetic to Labour and a friend of Castle.[101] Balogh had already made some characteristically trenchant comments on the prospects for private financing of the Tunnel.[102] In May, Castle identified five basic negotiating issues. Should there be any equity? If so, how much? Were the suggested periods for amortisation and the length of the concession right? What was the appropriate return on equity? And, finally, should the Government participate in the equity? In discussions with her advisers Castle agreed that the cheapest way to raise capital would be via government-guaranteed, fixed-interest bonds. However, the compelling argument for including a portion of risk capital was the fact that without it, the French might refuse to go ahead with the project. It therefore followed that the British strategy should be to maximise the extent of fixed-interest bonds and minimise the equity element (to say 10 per cent) consistent with satisfying the French. If any concessions were made in the direction of rewarding risk capital, it was suggested that they be limited to the 'extra costs involved in a share capital of the order of £10 million'. Given the expectation of a highly geared capital structure, the Minister suggested that officials should not exclude the possibility that the period of debt amortisation might have to be longer than the 20–25 years originally envisaged.[103] The negotiating position was then put to Castle's colleagues. Offering broad support, their criticisms were limited. Stewart and Brown made a plea for flexibility in handling the equity issue, while Callaghan expressed his department's preference for a shorter period of amortisation.[104]

Table 3.3 Shortlisted consortia for Channel Tunnel, May 1967

Consortium 1		*Consortium 2*	
Channel Tunnel Study Group		S.G. Warburg	UK
Channel Tunnel Co.	UK	Banque de Paris et des Pays-Bas	Fra
Société du Chemin de Fer Sous Marin	Fra	White, Weld	USA
Compagnie Financière de Suez	Fra	*Consortium 3*	
Technical Studies Inc.	USA	Hill Samuel	UK
Associated parties		Banque Louis-Dreyfus	Fra
Baring Brothers	UK	Freeman Fox & Partners	UK
Lazard Brothers	UK	Kleinwort Benson	UK
Robert Fleming	UK	Midland Bank	UK
Morgan Grenfell	UK	Banque Nationale de Paris	Fra
N.M. Rothschild	UK	Crédit Commercial de France	Fra
J. Henry Schroder Wagg	UK	Société Générale	Fra
MM. de Rothschild Frères	Fra	Union Européenne Industrielle et Financière	Fra
Banque de Suez et de l'Union de Mines	Fra	Banca Nazionale del Lavoro	Ita
Banque de l'Union Parisienne	Fra	First Boston Corporation	USA
Crédit Lyonnais	Fra		
Morgan Stanley	USA		
Dillon, Read	USA		

Source: MT Press Release, 22 May 1967, MT144/68, and supplementary material, MT144/69, PRO.

Discussions with the three consortia began in the summer of 1967 and went on into 1968. The financing and organisational proposals of each group were first elaborated through the submission of detailed documents in July 1967, then clarified in answers to separate questionnaires, and at face-to-face meetings with British and French officials in November and December 1967.[105] The two governments responded by issuing a further set of guidelines inviting the consortia to confirm any modifications and indicate the parameters within which their proposals might be varied.[106] These 'rounded-off' submissions were received by the beginning of February 1968. However, it immediately became clear that the prospects of resolving the bidding process were slim. The sheer complexity of the proposals was one element, but the more fundamental problem was that of selecting one of the groups. In March Barber warned Scott-Malden that the choice would be difficult because 'no one group stands head and shoulders above the others and…no one group is quite clearly out of the running'. At the same time, none of the three submissions looked like being acceptable 'without negotiated modifications'. In fact, a combination of groups might be required because 'the group whose proposals most readily fit in with the French point of view may not be the same as that whose proposals suit the British side best'. Barber's initial analysis of the situation was to prove perspicacious as the deliberations continued.[107]

British and French officials scrutinised the proposals and prepared reports with the aim of producing a set of joint recommendations for their respective ministers. By early April the British position was clear. Hill Samuel's bid was the most attractive because it proposed a small equity component which would earn moderate returns for a lower acceptance of risk. The group also found favour in London because it was British-led and its initial proposals had been presented first, and 'in the clearest, least evasive format'. On the other hand, the bid of the CTSG did not command support. The Group had shaped a proposal much closer to French requirements. It offered to put up the highest amount of equity itself – £5 million – and was prepared to take on higher risks in return for higher returns. It also had the advantage, from a French point of view, of a larger input from French financial interests. Some elements of 'lock-in' were also recognised. The CTSG would seek compensation for past work if not selected, and the SNCF, which had put up the French money for the geological survey, might also seek repayment. However, British officials felt that the CTSG had shown 'too little evidence of being able to act as a coherent team' and required 'an injection of new blood – particularly on the British side'. Nor could the third bid, that of Warburg's, be accepted as a compromise. It possessed 'considerable quality and attractiveness', but was less developed than the other two, and was criticised for being 'individualistic' and 'somewhat idiosyncratic'. Barber's team therefore agreed to state an initial preference for Hill Samuel and, failing French support, to suggest a compromise involving this group and the CTSG.[108]

A frank exchange between the British and French teams took place in Paris on 8 and 9 April. Barber declared his preference for Hill Samuel, Macé for the CTSG. The latter then made it clear that he would not be averse to a merger of two groups if satisfactory terms could be agreed.[109] But in spite of this willingness to compromise, the problem of finding a way through the labyrinth persisted. There was more than a hint of impatience with the failure to complete the negotiations, and there were some ministerial exchanges in May, since by this time a further reshuffle had occurred. Michael Stewart, who had been reinstalled as Foreign Secretary on 16 March, offered the new Minister of Transport, Richard Marsh (he had succeeded Castle on 6 April), the help of Foreign Office staff in breaking the log-jam. He also pressed for a speedy resolution of the matter, so that 'the economic advantages of getting on quickly with the project will not be diminished by over-elaboration on methods of financing, and on administration in the preliminary stages'. Marsh, stung by this observation, defended his Department's performance. The problem was not over-elaboration so much as the failure of the financing groups to come up with an acceptable proposal. As proof of the Ministry's concern for the legislative timetable, he referred to the insertion of clauses into the Transport Bill (Transport Act 1968). These provided powers to purchase land for the Tunnel, and, as a matter of urgency, to establish a Channel Tunnel Planning Council as the forerunner of an operating company on the British side.[110] Another factor in the delay, not referred to by either Stewart or Marsh, was the outbreak of serious political disturbances in the French capital in the same month. The strikes and direct action of students and workers, soon to pass into history as 'mai 68' or the 'Paris Spring', certainly gave the French a legitimate reason for distraction.[111]

The British team completed its report in June and agreed joint recommendations with its French counterpart in early July. It was readily accepted that none of the financing proposals was acceptable as it stood, and that the way forward was to invite the three consortia (Warburg was not ruled out) to respond to a second round, with more specific guidelines. The impasse over the amount and phasing of the successful group's contribution to risk capital was more difficult to resolve, however. Appeals to complex mathematical models indicating risk and returns during both the initial 'study' period (yet more study!) and the construction period, and arguments over the operation of 'perverse incentives' were eventually abandoned in favour of 'horse-trading', and a compromise deal was reached. It was agreed that the proportion of equity would lie within the parameters 5 and 15 per cent of total capital, and would be fixed after the study period had revealed the Tunnel's financial prospects with more accuracy. The winning consortium would be required to put up at least 20 per cent of the risk capital subscribed by the early years of construction. It would have to find £2 million in this form for the study period (the remaining study costs, expected to be another £2 million, would be financed by short-term bank loans, convertible into fixed-interest debt). The precise returns to equity were to emerge after a further round of negotiation with the consortium.[112] Shortly afterwards, these recommendations were submitted formally in the two countries. Marsh, in briefing his colleagues, expressed regret about the failure to select a winner, but felt the revised guidelines would reduce the time spent in negotiating once the selection was made. He therefore expected the successful group (or groups) to be identified by the end of October and a preliminary agreement reached by the end of the year. He intended to make the timetable public during parliamentary question time on 24 July.[113]

The worsening political and economic crisis in France put paid to this timetable. The new government elected in June, in the wake of 'mai 68', provided no comfort for 'tunnelistes' since Couve de Murville, a known sceptic, became Prime Minister. The French also had a genuine difficulty in matching the British initiative in providing for the establishment of an embryonic operating body.[114] The lack of progress was disturbing to British officials and an embarrassment for Marsh. His intended announcement was abandoned and he was forced to stall.[115] It was not until 18 October, over three months after the letter had been drafted, that Marsh was able to write to Chamant to seek formal endorsement of the compromise.[116] Five days later the British Minister was able to inform the Commons that the two sides had agreed to embark on a second round of negotiation with the private groups. The Governments remained 'confident that this final stage of talks will reach a successful conclusion leading rapidly to the choice of a private group'.[117] On the same day the three consortia received letters inviting them either to submit supplementary proposals or to combine in presenting joint proposals. The suggested deadline for the process was 1 January 1969. A response from the CTSG was made contingent upon agreement of its claim for compensation (see below).[118]

Once again, only limited 'progress' had been made in the tortuous process of constructing a Channel Tunnel. As a British official conceded, the statement did not even commit governments to the choice of a group, 'let alone to the reaching of any particular agreement with that group, or to the building of the tunnel itself'.[119] Furthermore, entrepreneurs could be forgiven for some astonishment at the slow pace of project management. In spite of all the work accomplished over the period 1957–68, the new guidelines required both the successful consortium and the two governments to go over much of the ground again in a 'study period'. This was to include another estimate of cost, another appraisal of viability (traffic, tolls, receipts, etc.), and more geological work, in addition to the preparation of detailed engineering designs, and tender documents. And, of course, the two governments reserved the right to abandon the project 'for any reason'.[120] Unsurprisingly, press reaction was muted. The *Financial Times*, in a leader entitled 'Slow progress on the tunnel', suggested that the request for resubmitted proposals was 'a roundabout way of saying that both Governments are less enthusiastic about the project than they were two years ago'.[121] The *Times* included a short paragraph headed 'Channel Tunnel decision delayed', and went on to add to its earlier bouts of Cassandra-like forecasting by including scare stories about escalating costs, one in November planted by anti-tunnel lobbyist, William Deedes, the Conservative MP for Ashford.[122] With the three groups invited to return to the drawing board, the CTSG had the additional problem of formulating its demand for compensation. In the circumstances, there could be no instant response to the Governments' compromise on financing and risk capital. The risks that continuing delay might scupper the project emerged in a Commons debate in July 1969, which revealed the strength of opposition in Kent.[123] It was not until November, by which time the compensation issue had been resolved (see below), that the CTSG and Hill Samuel began a series of informal talks with British and French officials to explore the possibility of producing a set of financial proposals from the consortia acting on a joint basis. Unsurprisingly, the private parties were sceptical about the complexity involved in the stipulation that two companies, a 'study company', followed by a 'construction company', be set up. Instead, they favoured a single company, with a single system of finance.[124] By this time Marsh had moved on, as had Chamant,[125] and detailed negotiations were proceeding when the Conservatives were returned to office in June 1970 (see Chapter 4).

An important consequence of the October 1968 decision was to effectively end the aspirations of the CTSG to independently finance, build and operate the Tunnel. The Group's immediate challenge was therefore to pursue the thorny matter of compensation. As we have seen, when the contract for the geological survey was signed in 1964, provision was made for reimbursement, and the two governments had always conceded that the CTSG had a moral, if not necessarily a legal, claim for work undertaken and for rights and property acquired.[126] When the Group submitted its detailed proposals in July 1967 it emphasised that no provision had been made for remunerating it 'for the considerable time, study and expense... devoted to the Channel Tunnel since the Study Group was formed in 1957, or for remunerating certain of its constituent parties for their work since the latter part of the last century'. It was accepted that an agreed sum should be added to the liabilities of the successful construction company. But how much was justified? When pressed for a detailed statement, the Group responded in October 1967 by placing a value on its work and activities, 'including fair recognition of its initiative', of £4 million.[127] No progress was made until after the October 1968 decision. On 4 November the CTSG submitted an itemised claim for £3.3 million in 1971 values, excluding profit, or £3.96 million with a profit element of 20 per cent. Explanatory accounts of Group expenses followed, including bills of £173,000 and £100,000 from SNCF and British Rail respectively.[128] The initial reaction of officials on the British side was that a more reasonable figure was £2–3 million and bargaining with the Group began at £1.5 million.[129] But with Technical Studies Inc. adopting a hard line, and with elements of the claim originating in the nineteenth century, the legal and financial niceties were challenging, to say the least. A *modus vivendi* between the CTSG and the two Governments was not reached until September 1969, when a payment of £3 million was provisionally agreed.[130]

The haggling over compensation added a somewhat bitter taste to the CTSG's important involvement in the Tunnel project. What had the Group achieved? First and foremost, it had pressed for the Tunnel in a thoroughly entrepreneurial spirit and had provided enthusiasm and determination whenever civil service caution and the nervousness of Ministers threatened to bring proceedings to a halt. The abiding memory among tunnel watchers was of Leo d'Erlanger presiding over annual meetings of the Channel Tunnel Company in London, or of Lord Harcourt, with his impeccable governmental and banking pedigree, pursuing the cause in numerous meetings behind the scenes. Most characteristic of all was Alfred Davidson, striding the boards in London and Paris and exasperating the British and French in equal measure, but, above all, promising American entrepreneurship of a kind which had financed the London Underground at the turn of the century, and, more recently, the 23-mile Chesapeake Bay bridge-tunnel complex in Virginia, completed in 1964.[131] Second, there is no doubt that this was a truly international consortium, with significant French support, from Suez, de Rothschild and the SNCF, although the American component appears to have grated on the French, at a time when Jean-Jacques Servan-Schreiber was warning Europe about the dangers of the American challenge.[132] Finally, it was self-evident that the pioneering work begun by the Group in 1957 and continued after the submission of its initial plans in 1960, provided the template from which all else since has followed. As British officials readily conceded, although the two Governments had carried out their own studies since 1960, the project was 'still, in essence, that of the CTSG; the Government studies having served to confirm and develop the original proposal, rather than produce a new one ab initio'.[133] On the other hand, the Group failed to sustain its clear lead in the field. Because it was so firmly identified with French prescriptions for the project, it helped to muddy the waters of Anglo-French relations while giving the French Government a rather optimistic picture of the prospects for private investment. The shortcomings of a somewhat ill-fitting amalgamation of speculators, financiers, and mixed economy companies were revealed during the consortia competition of 1967–8 and by 1969 there was evidence that some of its players were ready to step down.[134] Even so, the legacy of the CTSG persisted in that it played a full part in the inter-consortium negotiations of 1969–70, and transformed itself, without the American involvement of Technical Studies, Inc., into the new grouping (see Chapter 4).

5. The railway dimension, 1966–9

Although dominated by financial questions, the project also demanded parallel work on the operating element, which in turn required the two Governments to clarify the role of, and their relationship with, the two railway systems. The joint report of 1966 had set out the basic structure. An Anglo-French public authority would assume a planning function during the study and construction periods before taking executive responsibility for the running of the Tunnel, including maintenance and future enhancements, the setting of commercial policy and the remuneration of the construction company. But once again, the devil was in the detail, and potentially complex issues surfaced in the period 1968–9 in relation to functional responsibilities, the precise division of assets, and relationships with other parties. As one working paper observed, there was a 'triple duality' in the role of the operating body. First, it had to perform a planning function followed by a managerial one; second, it had to pursue a single-minded commercial strategy while balancing the needs of multiple interests; third, it had to reconcile differences in the approaches of the two countries. Initial thinking envisaged a small executive body of four–six members reporting to the governments through a joint commission of officials, with an advisory council representing the interests of users and consumers.[135] Limited steps were also taken to establish the Channel Tunnel Planning Council. Expecting that the new organisation would be required imminently, officials worked on the details of its budget, structure and staffing over the course of 1969. In December Sir Eugene Melville, an experienced diplomat and UK representative to the United Nations in Geneva, indicated that he was prepared to accept an offer of appointment as chairman of the new body.[136] However, the continued drift of the project meant that the powers obtained in the 1968 Transport Act remained unused at the end of the second Wilson Government.[137] Of course, a key issue in terms of operating was the public authority's future interaction with the two national railway systems. The British Railways Board (BRB) had already expressed the view that it should operate the Tunnel in conjunction with SNCF, but the 1966 Report had dismissed this suggestion for practical and competitive reasons. There was also a potential conflict of interest in that the two railways were, through their shareholdings, members of the CTSG.[138] Nevertheless, the railway corporations were critical to the operating equation. First, they had a pivotal role to play in determining technical aspects, such as the Tunnel's internal diameter, ventilation, fire-fighting, the impact of train speeds and the choice of loading gauge. Second, they had a dual role as customer and contractor. As a customer, British Railways and SNCF would pay tolls for running through trains between their respective networks. As a contractor, the railways were expected to enter into agreements with the operating authority for the haulage of car-carrying shuttle trains, and possibly to undertake signalling and track maintenance work. Third, there was the railway investment associated with the Tunnel, most notably in terminal facilities (see below).[139]

As we have seen, the railways had established mechanisms for planning connected with the Tunnel (p. 46), although there was little urgency given the uncertainty surrounding the project. However, with the more optimistic climate in 1966 the Ministry of Transport felt that BRB should be the subject of some 'vigorous prodding'.[140] In September, Castle informed Stanley Raymond, Beeching's successor as Chairman, that, since the Government had decided that the Tunnel should be built, her department would be looking 'more and more' to the Board for advice, particularly in relation to technical and planning aspects. She also pressed him to ensure that the maximum commercial benefit was extracted. Raymond's reply was scarcely enthusiastic. Although 'pleased' to learn that a final decision was expected, much of his response was taken up with rather negative observations on the commercial implications. The Tunnel would have an adverse impact on the railways' shipping services, raising the possibility of financial compensation. Commercial benefits would also be affected if BRB were excluded from all direct operating. He was therefore disinclined to commit scarce management resources to the project while BRB's precise role had still to be clarified.[141] The subject was raised again when Castle met Raymond during the Labour Party conference at

Brighton in October. The meeting had been convened to tackle a number of pressing issues affecting the railway industry, but there was time for Scott-Malden to make it clear that BRB was expected to make a full-time Tunnel appointment, and the pressure was kept up in subsequent weeks.[142] The Board eventually conceded by appointing Michael Bonavia, Director of Training and Education, as Director, Channel Tunnel Studies in December.[143] In the following year the rather cumbersome Anglo-French committee structure was streamlined. A Railways (Channel Tunnel) Joint Committee was established to improve the railways' responsiveness at a senior level. Its initial composition was three officials on each side: from BRB, two board members, John Ratter (Co-chairman), Philip James, and a general manager, David McKenna; from SNCF, the Deputy Director-General, Roger Hutter (Co-chairman), M. Legrand and R. Parès. The railways regarded the change as a means to provide a single railway voice in negotiations with the operating authority. However, the move did not square with Ministry of Transport thinking, which much preferred mechanisms to produce a united *British* voice, rather than having to cope with the complexities of two rival Anglo-French camps, one for officials, the other for railways.[144]

In fact, the evidence indicates that far from providing a unified voice, the two railway administrations differed markedly in their approach to the Tunnel project. In contrast to the stance taken by French ministry officials, it was the SNCF that took the lead and devoted more resources to the Tunnel than their British counterparts. The difference was exemplified by the stance taken by successive BTC/BRB chairmen. While Robertson had been in favour, his successors, Beeching, Raymond and (from 1968) Henry Johnson, were patently less enthusiastic, a position which contrasted with that of French railway leaders.[145] Lower down there was no consensus. David McKenna, a Board Member from 1968, was a strong advocate of the Tunnel. While General Manager of the Southern Region he had expressed alarm at the 'extraordinary slowness' with which this important subject was proceeding.[146] However, the attitude of his more junior colleagues was very different. They felt that the resources required to run the existing railway should not be diverted into planning a project that would probably not come to fruition. Dubiety about the Tunnel was also reflected in the appointment and standing of Bonavia. Ratter had been adamant that the project did not justify the appointment of a top ranking manager.[147] Bonavia, who experienced several changes of title – 'Director of Planning', 'Chief Officer (Special Duties)' – as the project was moved from one department to another, clearly lacked the authority and command of resources enjoyed by his opposite number in SNCF, Hutter. Unsurprisingly, SNCF was found to have been more active than BRB in research and development work.[148] One British civil servant felt in 1966 that it was difficult to get the Board to 'spark', while another complained in 1969 that the railways, having been 'pushing very hard' for the Tunnel 'a few years ago', were now displaying a 'lukewarm attitude'.[149]

There were also doubters within BRB's Shipping Division, where the Tunnel clearly represented a competitive threat. We have already noted the attention given by Whitehall to the prospects of hovercraft and car ferries. These were modes of transport in which British Railways made significant investments in the late 1960s and early 1970s.[150] The initial effect of the Tunnel on cross-channel shipping was expected to be 'fairly abrupt'.[151] Consequently, Raymond made the point that the Board might receive some compensation for displaced profitable services, or else a share in the Tunnel's operating profits. These suggestions were not well received at the Ministry, which expected a more entrepreneurial approach.[152] Furthermore, the procrastination over the Tunnel project did little to assist the Division's investment planning. There was the challenge of deciding whether to expand port facilities, for example, and a more pressing matter, what to do about the train ferries, which were life-expired and unlikely to be serviceable to 1974.[153] The late 1960s also saw the beginnings of the deep-sea container revolution. The growth of this sector, while benefiting Freightliners, BRB's own fledgling container business,[154] raised doubts in some managers' minds about the existing projections for freight traffic through the Tunnel. While it was only to be expected that such thinking would emanate from planning departments in Whitehall, it was more disconcerting to find railway staff quoted in newspaper articles questioning the value of the Tunnel. For example, the statement of a senior shipping manager in 1966 that BRB's new container ship operations would produce speedier transit and major cost reductions encouraged the *Times* to take this to be a distinct threat to Tunnel economics. Once again, British Railways had divided loyalties, since it was making a large investment in the container concept at Harwich.[155]

Expectations of the Tunnel were also affected by more fundamental debates within BRB about the wider strategy for freight, and by differences in the character of international freight operations by rail. The break up of the BTC in 1963 had produced only short-term relief from the railways' financial problems, and Beeching's major rationalisation plan of 1963 acquired more authority as deficits increased (BRB made losses of £150 million per annum, 1967–8). For freight the strategy was to concentrate on block train-load traffic and container flows, while eliminating the unprofitable wagon-load traffic.[156] However, in continental Europe wagon-load operations remained the critical component of the railways' international freight traffic, and containerisation had scarcely developed. Furthermore, Britain's more restricted loading gauge was clearly a barrier to the movement of continental-gauge wagons. These differences made it very difficult to forecast the railways' share of tunnel freight traffic, which at this stage rested on the assumption that a high proportion of rail freight, initially at least half, would be in containers. The possibility that BRB might abandon wagon-load traffic altogether raised the prospect that a much higher percentage of tunnel freight would reach its destination by road rather than rail, with consequent implications for the provision of terminals.[157] However, these issues, which have had a continuing resonance, did not prevent senior railway managers from sharing the views of British civil servants that the prospects for tunnel freight were good. The 1966 Report had predicted that freight would contribute about a third of the Tunnel's gross revenue in 1980, rising to just under a half by 2005, and that much of this would be rail-borne. Even Raymond agreed that the opportunities here were greater than on the passenger side. Great play was made of the beneficial effects of pushing back customs frontiers to inland depots and of reducing transit and handling times. Ratter was particularly bullish in predicting that the Tunnel would integrate Britain closely with Europe's railway network through long-distance Freightliner services.[158]

6. Infrastructure issues, 1966–70

Three main infrastructure requirements for tunnel traffic were identified: (1) a ferry terminal for the shuttle trains; (2) a passenger station; and (3) a railway freight terminal. Although new rail connections would have to be made to link to the British Railway network, at this stage line capacity was thought sufficient to meet traffic forecasts. The London-Folkestone line had recently been modernised, and thus no provision for a dedicated rail link was made. However, some expenditure in London was envisaged, including enhancements at Victoria station and an option to develop a car terminal at Kensington (Olympia).[159] The location of these facilities demonstrated differences between the British and the French approach to infrastructure planning and development. In France, a site at Coquelles, between Sangatte and Calais, had already been chosen. However, Kent, in contrast to the Pas-de-Calais, had a strong lobby of wealthy commuters with a 'nimbyist' attitude to economic development, and there was much more hostility to possible sites. Initial proposals, formulated during the CTSG's studies in 1959–60, were for a terminal at Sellindge, near Ashford, on the line to Folkestone (see Figure 3.1), and alongside the A20 road. However, in June 1966, BRB indicated informally to the Ministry of Transport that another location, Cheriton, closer to Folkestone, had been identified as superior on grounds of cost and operational convenience, and this alternative was promoted in subsequent meetings.[160] Shortly after his appointment, Bonavia had made it clear to Barber that the location of terminals was a fundamental factor in the planning process and should be dealt with as a matter of urgency.[161] However, Ministry officials were far from convinced about the advantages of switching from Sellindge to Cheriton, where there were environmental objections, and it was a further year before a British Terminals Working Party was established by the Ministry, in December 1967.[162] Made up of representatives from the interested departments (Transport, Housing and Local Government), BRB and Kent County Council, it was chaired by Brigadier John Constant, a newly-appointed full-time engineer in the Ministry's Channel Tunnel Division. Constant's appointment, which was followed by the creation of separate divisions for Channel Tunnel Administration and Engineering, reflected the increasing importance of physical planning in the project's development.[163]

The Terminals Working Party produced an interim report in April 1968. It quickly found that basic considerations heavily circumscribed the choice of

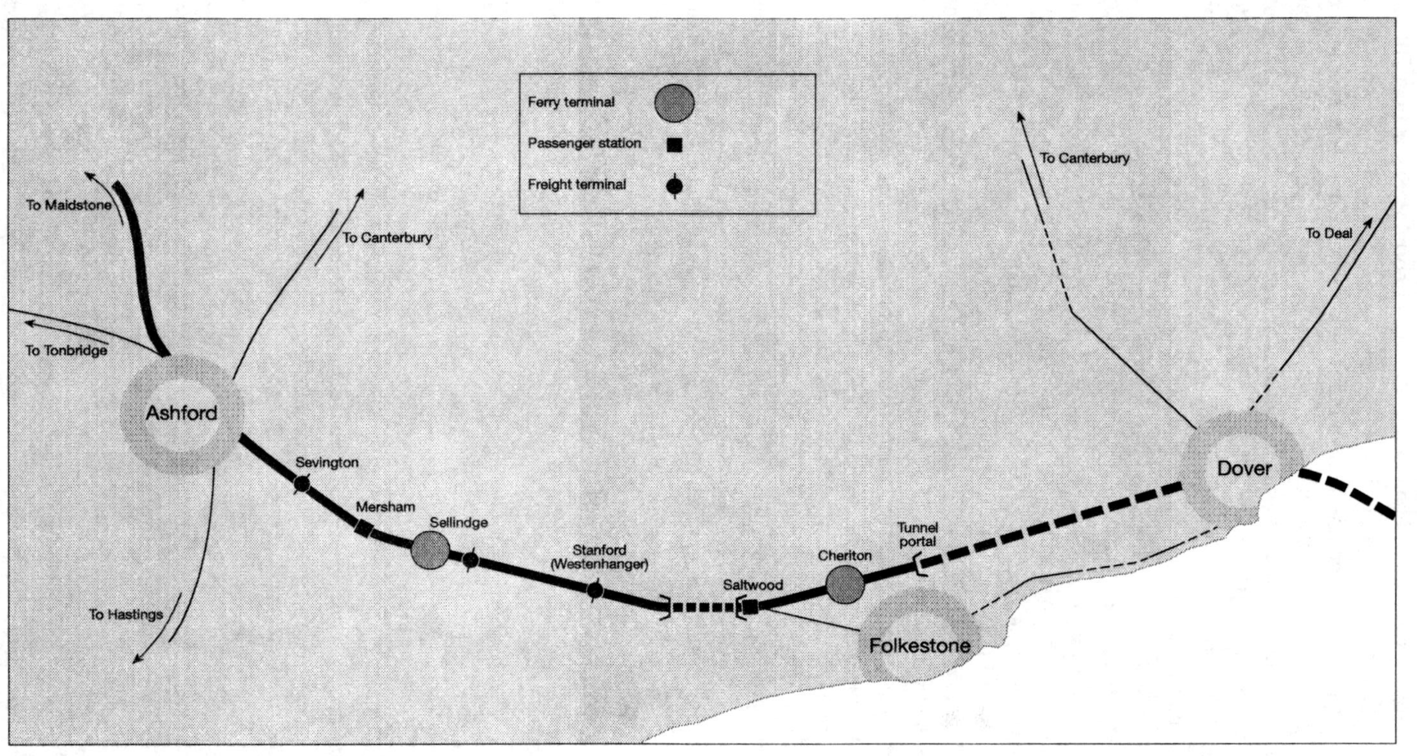

Figure 3.1 Options for Channel Tunnel terminals, 1968.

location. The terminal had to be close to the tunnel portal at Sugar Loaf Hill and the Folkestone-Ashford railway line, and the parameters were narrowed further by the topography and amenity value of the available land, and more particularly by the need to provide for future expansion. These requirements challenged the assumption that the terminal facilities could be located on a single site. The Working Party therefore concluded that the three elements of tunnel operations should be located separately: the ferry terminal at Cheriton; the passenger station at Saltwood; and the freight facilities at Sellindge (Figure 3.1).[164] Officials were aware that both the substance and the timing of any public announcement would be sensitive issues. A particular concern was to avoid the kind of controversy that had occurred in 1967 with the proposal to build the third London airport at Stansted, where the Government, in rejecting the recommendations following a public inquiry, had given the impression that it had already made up its mind before consultation.[165] On the other hand, there was an anxiety to avoid a lengthy public inquiry of the Stansted type. After an exchange between Scott-Malden and Idwal Pugh, Deputy Secretary at the Ministry of Housing and Local Government, it was agreed that the matter was sufficiently important to merit a submission to ministers.[166] In September 1968 Marsh obtained the approval of his colleagues on the Ministerial Committee on Environmental Planning to the publication of a short discussion document setting out tentative proposals and inviting public comment.[167] Three months later a discussion paper produced by the Ministry of Transport was published as a consultative booklet by Kent County Council. It presented the public with two broad ‘packages’, based on Cheriton and Sellindge respectively (Table 3.4).[168] The consultation exercise generated some 200 replies from local authorities, other statutory bodies and individuals. Many displayed outright opposition to the Tunnel *per se*, but of those that expressed an opinion on terminal sites, the balance was overwhelmingly for Cheriton, and this package, with the freight terminal at Stanford (Westenhanger), was adopted at a meeting of Kent County Council in February 1969.[169] Armed with

Table 3.4 Channel Tunnel terminal facilities: options, 1959–69

Date	*Source*	*Ferry terminal*	*Passenger station*	*Freight terminal etc.*
1959/60	CTSG/BTC	Sellindge	Sellindge	Sellindge
1966	BRB	Cheriton	Cheriton	Cheriton
April 1968	Joint Terminals Working Party	Cheriton	Saltwood	Sellindge
Dec. 1968	KCC/MT Discussion Doc.	i Cheriton	Saltwood	Stanford (Westenhanger) or Sellindge or Sevington
		ii Sellindge	Mersham	Sevington
July 1969	MT announcement	Cheriton	Saltwood	Stanford or Sevington

this 'Kent view', the arguments were rehearsed again in Whitehall, with more discussions about the presentational challenge and the adequacy of the consultation process. The Ministry, in a decision circulated to Ministers in July, endorsed the Cheriton package, but exploiting British Railways' uncertainty about its freight requirements, hedged its bets on the freight terminal, where two of the potential sites were retained. The details were then made public. The roll-on roll-off ferry terminal would be located at Cheriton, the passenger station and sidings at Saltwood, and the freight yard at either Stanford or Sevington.[170]

The challenge of selecting the terminal sites, the need for associated road and rail improvements and the continuing uncertainty over the future of the Tunnel project drew attention to the potential impact of the facility on South-east England in general and on Kent in particular. The concept of environmental planning had by this time assumed a growing significance within government. Under the previous Conservative administration Keith Joseph, when Minister for Housing and Local Government, had taken a leading role and in March 1964 he published a White Paper assessing future developments in the South-east. The document, produced in conjunction with the Board of Trade, made it clear that the Tunnel would have no detrimental impact on the region, since its beneficial effects would be 'spread... far beyond the South East'.[171] A further report, produced in response to a Labour Cabinet resolution in July 1966 (see above, p. 58 and n.71), was undertaken by a working group led by the DEA, discussed at the Official Committee on Environmental Planning in July 1967, and endorsed by Ministers in November. This reaffirmed the findings of the 1964 White Paper. There would be no serious or controversial implications for regional planning. The Tunnel would not challenge the Government's regional policies and, indeed, would have a positive impact on regions outside the South-east. In addition, the report was sanguine about the impact of terminal requirements, pointing out that road improvements, particularly for the A20, were already envisaged.[172] The decision not to designate Ashford as a new town, announced in March 1968, provided further relief from planning complexities in the area.[173] However, such reassurances had a hollow ring for many in Kent, and debates in the Commons in 1968–9 provided evidence of the considerable anxiety and discontent over the impact of the Tunnel on the local infrastructure. A short debate on the terminal issue in May 1968 produced a miscellany of local planning concerns affecting Folkestone, Ashford and Canterbury.[174] Concern about planning 'blight', a depreciation in the value of property caused by the knowledge that it was required for future development, surfaced in a more general and sharper debate in July 1969. The Tunnel, declared Deedes, was 'already casting a long shadow'. Albert Costain's straw poll of his Folkestone constituency had produced 88 per cent against the Tunnel and only 12 per cent in favour.[175] Opposition was scarcely assuaged by the decision to place planning protection on a 14-mile strip of land for the terminals and their approaches, or by continuing uncertainty about the freight terminal (as late as 1973 the choice of site had still to be made).[176] The strength of opposition expressed through local MPs in the late 1960s, articulated before the idea of a dedicated high-speed rail link had been mooted (see Chapter 4), was merely a precursor to the more intense environmental battles which were to follow.

7. Conclusion: another phoney war

What, then, was achieved during Labour's Governments of 1964–70? A major geological survey, though not without its difficulties, had found that there were no technical obstacles to construction. The British and French Governments had reached an accord on going ahead 'in principle'. And planning had been undertaken in some depth on the financial formulae for the preferred opinion – private sector construction and public sector operation – and on the railway infrastructure required to support it. However, as in earlier periods, genuine political optimism, on this occasion represented by the Castle-Pisani talks in 1966, was quickly eroded by the realities of detailed decision-making. This meant that with each government statement, the project seemed little further forward. Some writers, notably Bonavia and Donald Hunt, have suggested that the problem in the 1960s was caused by the chasing of an elusive hare, the compromise private-public solution. The concept was complex, demanded a government guarantee, satisfied neither country and was doomed to fail. Hunt was particularly hard on the two governments: 'Five years had been wasted in a tedious repetitive spectacle – the consequence of indecision, indifference, and procrastination – coupled with a total lack of imagination'.[177] This view may be overdrawn. However, it is interesting to find contemporary and private support for it from Transport's Permanent Secretary, Padmore, who wrote: 'I cannot pretend that to my way of thinking the prospect of raising capital on this basis, for a project of this nature, makes any real sense'.[178] On the other hand, each negotiation, and each new study produced a learning curve in the management of large, international projects, and it has to be said that the difficulties were by no means all a government responsibility. The complexities of the bids presented by the private sector consortia with their numerous financial and mathematical calculations proved a nightmare for civil servants to evaluate. And as the project limped on, a new dimension surfaced: local opposition for environmental reasons. Debate and delay merely played into the hands of opponents and nimbyists. Indeed, there were as many opponents as supporters in parliament, Whitehall and private industry. As Wilson's second term in office came to a close, critics could be forgiven for complaining that the reality of a tunnel seemed as far away in 1970 as in 1960. One of the players, Bonavia, encapsulated the situation perfectly. The 1966 statement, he wrote, was merely the prelude to a 'stately minuet that was to last some half-dozen years, and seemed to involve orders of "take your partners and advance; retreat and change partners; advance again; pause and retreat; finally advance and honour your partners".'[179]

4

THE HEATH GOVERNMENT AND THE TUNNEL

Reaching agreement, 1970–2

1. A new government

With the initiative having passed to the private sector consortia in October 1968, the period of Labour administration came to an end some twenty months later, while the parties were still considering their response to the Government's invitation to come up with a new scheme. The election date – 18 June 1970 – had been chosen for a number of reasons, not least the good local election results in May. There was even a suggestion that Labour expected to derive some advantage from a successful performance by England in the football World Cup. In the event, England fell at the quarter-final stage on 14 June, and Labour's overall majority of 96 in 1966 was turned into an unexpected Conservative majority of 30.[1] Of course, football was not an election issue – the main concerns in a rather pallid campaign were the state of the economy and industrial relations. But neither was the Channel Tunnel, which was not mentioned in any of the manifestos and does not appear to have attracted debate at the hustings.[2] Edward Heath, like Harold Wilson before him, was no *a priori* enthusiast for a Tunnel.[3] Indeed, his belief in the need to reform Whitehall and move ministers towards strategic planning rather than day-to-day matters may lead us to assume that he would have eschewed direct involvement in a specific project such as this. In the autumn of 1970 he announced the establishment of two new super ministries, the Department of the Environment [DOE], a merger of Housing & Local Government, Public Building & Works and Transport, and the Department of Trade and Industry [DTI], together with a 'think-tank', the Central Policy Review Staff [CPRS]. These important innovations suggested that the detailed consideration of a tunnel would have to pass through several layers in the new structure before reaching the top.[4] Furthermore, the establishment of the unwieldy DOE, a reform anticipated by steps taken by the previous administration, did nothing to elevate the concerns of transport and the Tunnel within the Whitehall hierarchy. The new department may have functioned satisfactorily under Peter Walker, Secretary of State until November 1972. However, it was less effective thereafter, and there seems little doubt that as a result the old Ministry of Transport functions ran less smoothly until they achieved their 'independence' again in 1976.[5] The responsible minister also experienced a downgrading. When the new Government took office in 1970 John Peyton was appointed Minister of Transport (but without Cabinet status, like his predecessor, Fred Mulley). Four months later he became Minister for Transport Industries, a junior post within the DOE, 'that great spongy heap', as he described it.[6] On the other hand, Heath's stance on Europe may have predisposed the Government to arguments linking the project to improved Anglo-French relations. There was no doubt that the Prime Minister was enthusiastic about joining the EEC, his manifesto pledging that Britain would enter into negotiations. He had also doubted Wilson's conviction about membership, notwithstanding the latter's application to join, which had produced a second veto from de Gaulle, in November 1967. President Pompidou had apparently let it be known that the Tunnel would be seen as a test of 'British conversion to the European ideal', and Heath may have been susceptible to this argument, even if there is no direct evidence to substantiate it.[7]

2. Negotiations with the new consortium, 1970–1

As we have seen in the previous chapter, attempts to find a suitable consortium to finance and construct the Tunnel were left hanging by Marsh's October 1968 statement and the need to resolve the CTSG compensation issue. With tentative agreement on the latter reached in September 1969 the way was cleared for informal discussions to recommence and in November representatives of the Study Group and Hill Samuel met British and French officials. The parties were prepared to follow the governments' guidelines of October 1968, but put forward some important modifications. First, they argued that there should be one company, instead of two, to handle the study and construction periods, and one system of finance, applying the same proportions of private equity and publicly guaranteed fixed-interest debt throughout. Second, they were not prepared to accept such a high level of risk in the study period. As Dallas Bernard of Morgan Grenfell noted, 'Governments do not appear to understand the absurdity of requiring that the more risky the project appears to be the more equity capital should be raised'.[8] The capital structure should therefore be amended, enabling the consortium to put up only £1 million (instead of £2 million) of the initial £4 million expenditure in the form of equity. Third, the financing group asked for a management fee in recognition of their 'role as bankers rather than entrepreneurs'. The £5 million in equity promised initially by the CTSG had not materialised. Thus, British officials felt that their 'bluff', which had so impressed the French, had been called.[9]

British and French officials quickly rejected the idea of a management fee. They also insisted that the group should put up an equity stake of at least £2 million in the initial 'study' period, though they were willing to provide safeguards in the case of abandonment. If the two governments unilaterally scrapped the scheme, the companies would be entitled to compensation in full; if the project were abandoned for any other reason, the governments would underwrite the non-equity element. This represented a substantial concession on the part of the French.[10]

British officials then sought the approval of the Minister of Transport, Fred Mulley, to indicate to the CTSG and Hill Samuel that a formal submission along these lines would be given serious consideration by the two governments. Ministerial agreement was obtained in March 1970 and British civil servants anticipated that the group would submit its proposals in the following month.[11]

Such optimism proved unjustified. Negotiations with the group continued to address the fine details of the financing package. In particular, there was a fair amount of haggling over the remuneration the consortium should receive as founding shareholders for the special risks they were prepared to bear, and in particular, for the non-transferability of, and nil return on, their equity until construction was completed.[12] In Paris Roger Macé was unhappy with the suggestion that the two governments should intervene to fix in advance the precise extent of the risk-reward for the founders. He was happier for the consortium to set itself a ceiling on the reward, though he quickly came round to the British viewpoint.[13] The CTSG/Hill Samuel group, on the other hand, wished to see the rate fixed in advance, and towards the top end. It was also irritated by the protracted negotiations. At times, the discussions were clearly somewhat acrimonious.[14] Delay in arriving at an agreed text for draft heads of agreement was also occasioned by the appearance of new players, with S.G. Warburg and White Weld joining the group in April.[15] The position of the banks in the emerging French consortium was another restraining factor. There were a number of ‘sticking points’, not least about the remuneration formula. It was clear that while the British preferred to specify ‘objectives’ rather than ‘mechanics’ in the heads of agreement, in France the reverse was true. There were also anxieties about the production of suitable clauses covering possible abandonment.[16] Consequently, the discussions were protracted, prompting numerous questions in the House of Commons.[17] Officials had not managed to resolve all the outstanding issues when Wilson announced the dissolution of Parliament on 18 May, and discussions went on into June.[18]

By July 1970 a position had been reached where formal proposals could be put.[19] Lord Harcourt (Chairman of Morgan Grenfell) and Jock Colville (Executive Director, Hill Samuel) saw Peyton on 9 July and told the Minister that the new combined group was ‘virtually agreed’ on new proposals for the financing and conduct of the period of final study and construction.[20] Six days later the proposals were sent to the British and French Ministers of Transport.[21] A number of coincidental events – the tabling of parliamentary questions, an annual general meeting of the Channel Tunnel Company, a visit by the British Foreign Secretary, Alec Douglas–Home, to Paris, and a meeting of French channel tunnel officials – led to an announcement on 15 July.[22] Thus, only a month after the election, Peyton was able to tell the House of Commons that a new consortium had been formed.[23] Referred to initially as the ‘Group’, it was an amalgam of the core elements of the previous three bidders. The notable exception was Technical Studies Inc., which dropped out. The suggestion was that the Davidson Brothers and their bankers were unhappy with the lack of progress. However, the Davidsons regarded themselves more as industrial entrepreneurs than as financiers. In any case, the presence of Technical Studies was felt to inhibit the choice of consultants and contractors and as an American institution it was a rather expensive partner.[24] This left a 'British Sub-Group', consisting of the Channel Tunnel Company, together with seven supporting banks from Britain and the United States; and a 'French Sub-Group', consisting of the Compagnie Financière de Suez, SNCF and eight French financial institutions (see Table 4.1). The consortium asked the Ministers to approve 'heads of terms' covering the three phases of the project: the study period; construction period; and remuneration period. The first phase was to be governed by a definitive and legally binding 'Preliminary Agreement' between the Anglo-French Group and the two governments, which the former expected to be signed within nine months. Prior to its signature the consortium members undertook to: (1) submit management proposals for government approval; (2) reach a legally binding agreement with the CTSG for the transfer of assets and rights; and (3) form two companies, one British and one French, to finance and carry out the remaining studies, and, if the results proved positive, undertake the construction (under a 'Main Agreement'). The share capital of each company was to be £1 million or its equivalent in francs, with the Group undertaking to subscribe a minimum of 75 per cent, and no single member subscribing more than 25 per cent. The major provisions for the study and construction periods were, with the exception of the corporate structure, in accordance with the October 1968 guidelines. The private sector agreed to find up to £4 million to finance the first stage (studies and preliminary works), £2 million in shares, and £2 million in loan capital, the latter to be indemnified by the two governments should the project be abandoned.[25] It accepted the idea that 5 to 15 per cent of the total cost should be met from equity, with the governments asked to guarantee bond issues for the remaining 85 per cent.[26] On the other hand, the Group, in

Table 4.1 The Channel Tunnel consortium, July 1970

British Sub-Group	*French Sub-Group*
The Channel Tunnel Company	Compagnie Financière de Suez et de l'Union Parisienne
Morgan Grenfell & Co. Ltd	Compagnie du Nord
Robert Fleming & Co.Ltd	Banque Louis-Dreyfus et Cie
Hill, Samuel & Co. Ltd	Banque de Paris et des Pays-Bas
Kleinwort, Benson Ltd	Société Nationale des Chemins de fer Français
S.G. Warburg & Co. Ltd	Banque Nationale de Paris
White, Weld & Co. (USA)	Crédit Commercial de France
The First Boston Corporation (USA)	Crédit Lyonnais
	Société Générale
	Banque de l'Union Européenne Industrielle et Financière

Source: Lord Harcourt-J. Barber (MT), 15 July 1970, enclosing letter to Minister of Transport, n.d., and subsequent documentation, MT144/159, PRO.

committing itself to underwrite the lower-bound 5 per cent in equity, went beyond the commitment originally asked for. It promised to find 33⅓–100 per cent of the equity – instead of 20 per cent, though, as we have seen, it also expected a reward, of up to 2.8 times its founding stake of £2 million. Finally, the remuneration period was specified. It was to last for 50 years, with the debt amortised within the first 25 years. A reward formula for the companies' shareholders was referred to, though not finalised. It was based on a suggested benchmark return of 12 per cent net of corporation tax in the first year of operation.[27] There was to be a two-stage mechanism involving a fixed percentage of gross revenue plus a clawback of any excess net revenue on a tapering scale.[28] Of course, in spite of nine months of informal but detailed discussion in the two countries, the proposals, as before, merely represented a starting point for further negotiations with the two governments.

The new consortium's submission made it necessary for the British and French governments to determine their positions once again. At the end of July 1970, the two countries consulted at a senior level. Delegations headed by Lacarrière and Scott-Malden met in Paris with the specific intention of reaching common ground. The parties recognised that the 'heads of terms' contained a number of points to be resolved, but agreed that once this had been done, each side would submit separate papers to their respective ministers, Peyton and Raymond Mondon. Although no specific timetable was fixed, the evidence suggests that on this occasion it was the French who were anxious to press ahead. The British, frequent critics of French 'feet-dragging' in the past, wished to avoid the same smear. However, progress in Whitehall was hindered by the fact that a Conservative government had not considered the Channel Tunnel since 1964 and it was therefore necessary to take the project once again through the machinery of Cabinet.[29] Lobbying of ministers was a natural accompaniment. Colville of Hill Samuel pressed Douglas-Home to help put an end to this 'wearisome exercise'; the consortium were 'at last about to hoist the mainsail, or at any rate pull up the anchor.' Colville and Harcourt also met Geoffrey Rippon, Chancellor of the Duchy of Lancaster, with responsibility for Europe, seeking an assurance that 'there would be full government support'. No doubt General Philippe Maurin, former chief of the French Air Staff, leading the French Sub-Group, was engaged in similar activities in France.[30]

Peyton may have been equivocal about the Tunnel at the outset,[31] but it seems he readily accepted the advice of his civil servants that the project, which in its present form had been started by a Conservative administration in 1964, appeared to be economically sound. He also noted that it was backed by a 'very powerful and respectable group of private interests'. Peyton was told that 'the project was a rail tunnel or nothing', since other suggestions, for example, a bridge and/or road tunnel 'could be considered out of court from a practical point of view'. The current proposal, 'for private construction and public operation stemmed from compromise', but it was unlikely that the French would wish to put up any public money for construction. Finally, 'the latest economic and financial forecasts, which derived from a report commissioned by the French government, were impressive'.[32] In October he embarked on the customary procedure of consultation, as Watkinson, Marples (twice) and Castle had done before him, in 1957, 1960, 1963 and 1966. First of all, he sent a draft paper intended for the Cabinet Economic Policy Committee [EPC] to the key ministers concerned: Anthony Barber, the Chancellor of the Exchequer; Foreign Secretary Douglas-Home; and the Lord President, William Whitelaw. Peyton's position was clearly stated. He recommended acceptance of the Group's proposals, subject to a similar acceptance by the French and some reservations.[33] Agreement to embarking on a final study period did not, of course, bind the Government to actually build the Tunnel. The Conservatives, committed to a policy of reducing the size of the public sector, had no intrinsic enthusiasm for a scheme which rested on public control of tunnel operating. However, Peyton accepted that a substantial measure of government control was essential to ensure safety, equality of treatment for users and to prevent abuse of a quasi-monopolistic position. He wrote: 'If we were starting from scratch, we would possibly devise a different pattern but I am sure, in the circumstances, that it is best to get the final studies under way on the general basis of the present proposals, which the French Government seem likely to agree, rather than run the risk of extensive delays on the French side by asking them to consider any "root and branch" change.... The saying "the best is enemy of the good" is, I think, particularly true of Anglo-French projects, where the search for a solution perfectly acceptable to both sides can effectively put a stop to all progress. The present proposals are the result of long and arduous negotiations. They offer a means to Anglo-French agreement on a way of putting in hand the studies which precede the final decision on the future of the project.'[34]

While ministerial consultations were proceeding, there were developments affecting the membership of the consortium. The possibility of other institutions being added to the Group had not been excluded, and in the course of 1970 the Ministry of Transport learned that the mining conglomerate, Rio Tinto-Zinc (RTZ) was interested in acting both as project manager and investor. In fact, its involvement began in August 1969 when Lord Gladwyn asked Sir Val Duncan, Chairman and Chief Executive, if the company were interested in his alternative scheme for a bridge-tunnel-bridge, based on the Chesapeake Bay facility. This led RTZ to examine the possibilities under the codename 'Rollercoaster'.[35] In October Alistair Frame, its chief engineer, threw his weight behind the rail tunnel and contacts were made with the consortium led by Harcourt.[36] Links already existed, since Sir Mark Turner, the Deputy Chairman of consortium member Kleinwort Benson, also sat on the board of RTZ. Duncan and Turner had not only rescued Rio Tinto in the 1950s; they proved to be dynamic players in the diversification–fuelled acquisitions of the 1960s and early 1970s, which had seen the creation of RTZ (in 1962) and its expansion into large-scale, capital-intensive natural resource projects.[37] Turner was well aware that the banks could not build a tunnel without professional assistance, and that effective management of the engineering side was critical. Duncan had told Harcourt at an early stage: 'we are naturally interested if the set-up is right'.[38] There were of course a number of possible candidates, including Freeman Fox, the Bechtel Corporation, and Brown & Root. However, RTZ claimed to possess extensive experience and was in many ways hand-picked by the Government. Heath apparently knew Duncan. The company was regarded in Whitehall as the only British concern with the necessary capability. It soon gained the approval of permanent secretaries such as Sir David Serpell (DOE) and Sir Frank Figgures (Treasury).[39] Finally, it had recently impressed civil servants with a presentation to a project management seminar at Peterhouse Cambridge on the part it had played in the ambitious hydro-electric scheme at Churchill Falls in Canada (opened in 1971).[40]

In August 1970 Duncan met Harcourt to discuss the potential for RTZ's involvement in the Tunnel as project managers on the British side. It was to prove an episode with wider ramifications.[41] Shortly after the meeting RTZ set up a subsidiary company, RTZ Development Enterprises (RTZDE), to provide 'large-scale project management capability'. Led by heavyweights such as Duncan Dewdney as Chairman (an executive director of RTZ, 1968–72) and Lord Shackleton, Labour's leader in the Lords (1968–74), the subsidiary was to handle the management and supervision of building and construction for RTZ activities where expertise was lacking. The Tunnel, retaining the codename 'Rollercoaster', was one of its first concerns.[42] By September, talks between the British Sub-Group and RTZ had reached the stage where it was thought appropriate to involve the Minister,[43] and after a series of exploratory discussions between the parties, including the French, Peyton met Harcourt and Duncan on 16 October.[44]

The problem was that Rio Tinto executives were far from enamoured with what they termed a typical bankers' deal. They disliked the fact that the proposed 'equity' was essentially equivalent to preference shares with limited participation, while the two-stage remuneration formula was criticised for giving too much to the public operating authority. The banks had accepted this arrangement, thought RTZ, because they favoured a risk-averse, low-return strategy and expected to derive the main benefits from financing and debt management activities. RTZ much preferred to take a large equity stake in partnership with the governments.[45] By this time, of course, the 'heads of terms' had been submitted, and Harcourt was at pains to point out that the document, unsatisfactory as it might appear to a private sector outsider, was the product of months, if not years, of protracted negotiations with the two governments and their officials.[46] Consequently, RTZ, like its predecessors, was forced to compromise. At the meeting with Peyton, the company argued that it believed a greater expenditure would be required both in the pre-study and study periods; the cost of the former should be raised from £100,000 to £600,000; the cost of the latter would be at least £9 million, rather than the £4 million envisaged. It also reaffirmed its desire to participate in the equity, and here a stake of £5–10 million was mentioned. Finally, it argued that a unitary management structure was required for the several stages of the project. The possibility that the French were envisaging construction by two separate and autonomous national teams was regarded with some dismay. This approach would hamper technical and cost control, and encourage significant cost overruns. Duncan went further than this. He argued that it would be preferable if a single organisation (50 per cent public, 50 per cent private) handled both construction and *operation*. However, Ministry officials pointed out that given the tortuous negotiations required to get this far, 'it would not be timely' to raise such a major modification at this stage. RTZ was therefore encouraged to consider its fall-back position, a willingness to work within the existing framework for an adequate return on an equity stake.[47] Even so, these negotiations, conducted on the British side only, required a fair amount of diplomacy with French officials, who were kept informed of progress. While not opposed to the involvement of Rio Tinto, the French were clearly wary about any new ideas being presented outside the current framework. They had approached project management in a quite different way, arranging for an engineering consortium – SOGEI and SETEC, acting together as 'Sofremanche', and subsequently SITUMER – to work on a strictly fee-only basis. The possibility that RTZ's requirements might upset the delicate balance of British and French participation – the 'moitié-moitié' principle[48] – was an obvious concern. The negotiations with RTZ were thus still in an unresolved state when Peyton sent his draft paper on the Channel Tunnel to his colleagues.[49]

The reactions of Ministers who saw Peyton's draft were mixed. In November 1970 Douglas-Home conceded that the Tunnel would be politically popular in France and was prepared to support it on those grounds. His 'only question' was a pertinent one: 'how far this will call on resources which could be devoted to other purposes'.[50] At the Treasury, officials recommended acceptance of the paper. The Chief Secretary, Maurice Macmillan, had initially opposed the project and continued to harbour reservations about the small equity element in the investment. However, he agreed to support the proposals at the EPC.[51] It was the Lord President, William Whitelaw, who expressed unequivocal opposition, in spite of his pro-European stance. When learning of the revival of interest in July he had minuted: 'I hope it is not too late to stop this. We must save money here'. His reaction to Peyton's draft paper in October was equally hostile: 'I am against the whole project and would like to cut our losses now'.[52] Peyton, stung by this 'somewhat sharp' comment, wrote to Whitelaw, pointing out that until the final study period was complete there were 'very few losses to cut'. Like Whitelaw, he had been sceptical at first, but after a closer look had changed his mind. Referring to the Government's moral commitments to both the French Government and the private sector, he appealed to his colleague's better judgement with the observation that 'Rejection now would probably kill the project for all time'. Unfortunately, his plea fell on stony ground, and Whitelaw remained 'pretty unrepentant'.[53] However, it was the intervention of Peyton's Secretary of State, Peter Walker, which threatened to give the project the *coup de grâce*. Shortly after the Peyton-Whitelaw exchanges, the Ministry of Transport became operationally part of the conglomerate DOE. In late November, with Peyton's paper ready for formal consideration at EPC, Walker was briefed in detail on the Tunnel for the first time. His reaction, expressed at a meeting on 2 December, was surprisingly acerbic in view of his earlier equanimity. He found the existing proposals 'an unhappy mixture of "public" and "private" interests for which it would be almost certainly impossible to obtain the support of Government backbenchers', and suggested that the EPC should be asked to provide only an outline approval of the project. He then asked for the accompanying paper to be rewritten to encompass broader aspects, including alternative ways of dealing with the rapid increase in cross-channel traffic. The intervention was thought likely to delay a submission to the EPC until the New Year.[54]

Walker's actions were made all the more exasperating by the fact that on 9 December the French Council of Ministers had taken an 'unreservedly positive attitude' towards the existing proposals. In a tedious repetition of many of the negotiations that had gone on before, British officials sought to forestall French accusations of 'bad faith' for a project which had already been subject, in the words of one civil servant, to 'endless quibbling and delay'.[55] Peyton was due to visit Paris in the following week for a meeting of European transport ministers, where the Tunnel was likely to be raised. Officials feared that a year would be lost if the traffic studies were not put in place. These concerns were intensified by anxiety about how a negative decision on the Tunnel might affect Anglo-French relations in general and Britain's application to join the EEC in particular.[56] Peyton wished to inform the French that a decision would be delayed and deliver a hint that the British Government did not favour the present proposals. But this suggestion caused some alarm in Downing Street and drew Heath into the debate. The Prime Minister, briefed by his Principal Private Secretary, Robert Armstrong, agreed that alternatives to the Tunnel should be reviewed, but warned Peyton against saying too much to the French. He then injected some urgency into the debate by asking that the project be discussed at Cabinet before his visit to the Commonwealth Conference in Singapore in early January. Among the arguments made was the point that 'there is every reason to believe that Monsieur Pompidou regards the Channel Tunnel as one of the principal indices of British conversion to the European ideal'. Walker was therefore required to take his revised paper to the EPC meeting just before Christmas. Policy was thus conducted at a somewhat frenetic pace.[57]

The Secretary of State's hastily rewritten memorandum of 16 December was considered by the EPC on the 21st. Walker accepted the economic case for a rail tunnel, based on the results of the further appraisal commissioned from SETEC-Economie by the French and completed in 1969.[58] The Tunnel, now expected to cost £280 million to build in 1970 prices, was forecast to produce an internal rate of return of over 14 per cent compared with existing means of transport. However, the memorandum also reiterated his concerns that the existing proposals, with their complex structure of risks and rewards, represented an unattractive and awkward division between private construction and public operation. Nevertheless, the political concerns about the state of play with the French were taken on board. Walker argued that it was important not to delay matters while the financial arrangements were being challenged. He therefore proposed that the Government should put up a sum of up to £500,000 for the first stage (ten months) of the final study period. Of course, as in the past, this was not to be taken as a commitment to actually build the Tunnel.[59] The Committee, like its predecessor in 1966, accepted the proposal for a rail tunnel 'in principle', and endorsed government funding of stage 1. Private funding of the rest of the study exercise was to be contingent upon resolving the Government's qualms about the extent of public sector involvement in the Tunnel.[60]

The Cabinet discussed the project on 5 January 1971. Burke Trend, the Cabinet Secretary, briefed Heath on the subject. Comparisons could be drawn with the long-serving Maurice Hankey in the inter-war years (see Chapter 1, pp. 10–15), since Heath was the fourth Prime Minister to be advised on the subject by Trend. And like Hankey, his personal position was scarcely enthusiastic, though his advice to Heath was carefully measured.[61] The Cabinet conclusions were equally measured, and scarcely a ringing endorsement of the scheme. Walker's recommendations were supported by Barber and Heath. It was agreed that the possibilities for reducing public sector support should be explored as a matter of urgency. Meanwhile, the main pre-occupations were: first, how best to handle the French; and second, how to ensure that the funding of stage 1 involved no commitment to construct the Tunnel, whether implicit or implied – there was an anxiety to 'avoid another Concorde agreement with no let-out'.[62] The French were informed of the British Government's revised position shortly afterwards. The news was conveyed via the British Ambassador in Paris, Christopher Soames, because the Transport Minister, Mondon, who had been ill for some time, had died on New Year's Eve. Mondon's successor, announced on 7 January, was Jean Chamant. His return to the post he had occupied in 1967–9 was viewed with some mixed feelings inside Whitehall, given his role in approving the 1968 guidelines (Chapter 3, pp. 64–6).[63] In fact, the French lost no momentum with the change of ministers, and with Peyton expressing his willingness to see Chamant, the two met in Paris on 22 January. It was clear that while both sides wished to see a greater degree of private sector financing (perhaps up to 30 per cent), the French were insistent that the talks should proceed on the basis of the existing proposals. However, they had no objection to the British suggestion that stage 1 – the *economic* studies – could start before the financing details were finalised, and the Ministers undertook to brief members of the Anglo-French Group. The EPC, and then the Commons, were given a short report on the position reached.[64]

Despite the apparent progress, some officials considered that this meeting had merely papered over the cracks, and so events proved.[65] Within the British and French groups there was both frustration and divergence, and the January meeting did nothing to resolve the situation. Nor did the French press release about the meeting, which put a much more optimistic gloss on the situation than Peyton did in his Commons statement, enabling the French press to refer to British 'shilly-shallying' and 'hesitation'.[66] Harcourt noted that the French banks were still wedded to the heads of agreement drawn up in July 1970, whereas the British side, prodded by RTZ, considered these now 'out of date and inapplicable'. He also claimed that the French banks were 'getting bored' with the project, their leading protagonists, Georges-Picot and Guy de Rothschild, having apparently 'lost interest'. Peyton was pressed to name the Anglo-French Group as the Governments' 'chosen instrument', but the Minister replied that this would result in 'great difficulties' since other ministers were 'not uniformly in favour of the project' and he therefore lacked a mandate to do so.[67] A note on the 'state of play' prepared by John Barber of the DOE's Channel Tunnel Division in early February 1971 was far from optimistic. The French Government were 'not really being so helpful as they wish to seem', since they were insisting that the Group had to be designated as 'chosen instrument' before they were prepared to underwrite stage 1 of the study period. For their part the French banks were being 'more royalist than the King' in interpreting their Government's position as hawkish in relation to the existing proposals. 'The present situation could easily develop into a sort of continuous loose maul. Someone has got to blow the whistle and start play again.' It was difficult for Peyton to do this. He had been given the impossible negotiating brief of 'go thou and do better!' without either enjoying the unequivocal support of his colleagues for 'a precise and attainable objective' or having a firm steer on the concessions he might make in the name of Anglo-French relations.[68] Peyton repeated the gloom in a note to Walker on 15 February, pointing out that Britain's desire to review the financing structure was seen in France as an 'unwillingness to enter into firm long-term commitments'. Behind the scenes RTZ's interventions, which had revived hopes of more private equity, were regarded in Paris as an irritating 'nuisance'. British 'temporising' appeared to have replaced French 'feet-dragging'.[69]

Although there was some amelioration when Chamant sent a conciliatory letter to Peyton suggesting further talks and a ministerial meeting in mid-March,[70] the climate remained unpromising. There were strong indications that the French banks would withdraw if agreement were not reached by the end of March. Peyton proposed a move in the French direction, by accepting the 1970 proposals as a starting point and giving the existing Group 'first refusal' of any revised financing scheme, but seeking to limit the governments' capital guarantee to about 70 per cent of total investment.[71] The strategy was endorsed by the Treasury.[72] But as the date for the ministerial meeting (22 March) drew closer, Peyton wrote to the Chancellor, Tony Barber, warning that he saw 'a real prospect of the project floundering altogether unless I can convince the French that we genuinely intend to make progress'. He enclosed a draft letter to Chamant designed to break the log-jam.[73] Unfortunately, its contents, which had been cleared with the British Sub-Group, ruffled feathers at the highest level. Peyton wanted to suggest that the two governments accept the rail tunnel in principle, and accept the Group as the chosen instrument for constructing and financing it. Heath asked that the passage about acceptance in principle be removed, since it went beyond what had been authorised in Cabinet, but Peyton replied that he regarded the terms set out in the letter as 'the minimum required to keep the project alive'.[74] The Transport Minister received some support, notably from Lord Jellicoe, the Lord Privy Seal, and Geoffrey Rippon, who referred the Chancellor to the 'very serious consequences which a breakdown would mean for our relations with the French and therefore indirectly for our negotiations for entry into the EEC.'[75]

At this point an important corner was turned. An accepted text, incorporating what Peyton wanted but at the same time strengthening the reference to the right to withdraw from the project if necessary, was sent to Chamant on 15 March.[76] The French Minister then came to London a week later. The meetings of ministers, held at Lancaster House, were full-blown affairs, attended by officials and the financing groups. Afterwards the two governments agreed to give their approval in principle to the Anglo-French Group's proposals and to the commencement of the preliminary (stage 1) studies (the Group agreed to make an immediate start on these at its own expense). The range of private risk capital was to be doubled from 5–15 per cent to 10–30 per cent, with a corresponding increase in the share of profits for the private sector. The French also agreed to consider Britain's preference for a single private company to both construct and operate the Tunnel if the level of private sector finance could be further increased. A press notice was released on the following day. The final approval to construct was expected in 1973, with the opening in 1978.[77] Shortly afterwards Sir Eugene Melville, who had been expecting to serve as chairman of the now redundant Channel Tunnel Planning Council (Chapter 3, p. 67) was appointed Special Adviser on Channel Tunnel Studies, and head of the Channel Tunnel Studies Unit [CTSU] within the DOE.[78] His brief was to advance the study programme, and later to assist in the negotiation of the financial agreement and Anglo-French Treaty. No doubt his experience as Ambassador to the United Nations in Geneva was held to be invaluable in dealing with the French. However, his direct knowledge of the Tunnel was limited, and the early loss of John Barber, who moved to Housing and Construction within the DOE, provided him with a rather steep learning curve.[79]

There was a distinct air of optimism after the March meetings.[80] It was also encouraged by the news that the British Sub-Group had been strengthened with the addition of RTZ, the British Railways Board, and the American Bank, Morgan Stanley. RTZ had agreed to join in return for an option to take 20 per cent of the British founders' capital of £1 million. British Rail and Morgan Stanley had agreed to join the consortium too, but with much lower stakes.[81] Nevertheless, as with so much in channel tunnel history, the path was not straightforward. It took another six months of frustrating negotiations before the signature, on 22 September 1971, of the 'Heads of Terms for the Preliminary Agreement', and a formal exchange of notes between the two governments. No fewer than ten weighty DOE (transport industries) files bear testimony to the complications, which involved haggling over the technical, legal and financial niceties.[82] The issues included: governmental acceptance of budgets for the studies (and, in particular, costs incurred by the Group before 1 April 1971); clarification of the respective governments' responsibility for costs in the event of abandonment; private sector concerns about the remuneration formula for holders of equity and its role in determining tunnel operations and tariffs (all still to be settled); and the need to ensure comparability of intentions in the two languages.[83] The anxiety of RTZ to increase the 'private sector' element of the project was a further irritant. It was also insisting on adequate rewards, including 'substantial management fees', and requested an additional payment to finance the 'supplementary' work for the British Government on a new, 'British only' cost-benefit study.[84]

However, by the autumn it could be said that progress had been made. The September 1971 agreement, broadly similar to the Heads of Terms of July 1970, contained the following changes. The British and French construction companies, now constituted as the British Channel Tunnel Co. and the Société Française du Tunnel sous la Manche (SFTM), undertook to increase their capital to £1 million each when the Preliminary Agreement was signed (no later than 1 May 1972). In the construction period the Group undertook to raise a minimum of 10 per cent, and up to 30 per cent, as risk capital. Government requirements and responsibilities were redefined as *Ministerial* requirements and responsibilities. A clause giving the ministers power to require the raising of loan capital from outside the UK and France was added. As to remuneration, an undertaking was made to increase the return to share capital over that specified in 1970 in response to the increase in risk capital, though nothing was spelled out. The technical studies, and responsibility for study costs, were specified more tightly. There was also an annexe providing for the transfer of rights and assets owned by the CTSG for a sum of £3 million in 30 June 1971 values.[85] At the DOE Scott-Malden, stepping down in January 1972 after a decade of involvement in the project, appeared to have something to show for his endeavours at last.[86]

What did this tentative start in 1970–1 reveal about Conservative intentions? Did the Heath Government really want to proceed with the Tunnel? There was certainly no genuine champion of the project. Peyton has recorded that none of his colleagues had shown any trace of enthusiasm for it; indeed, at the January 1971 Cabinet, no fewer than four ministers, including Margaret Thatcher, the Minister of Education, had voiced their opposition to it.[87] Peyton himself had originally been sceptical, but his conversion was not enough by itself since he clearly lacked the political muscle to push things forward. When his department was subsumed within Walker's empire, he found a Secretary of State who had considerable doubts about the Tunnel and remained unsure about it even when it was under construction.[88] It is also apparent that as the project gained momentum, greater attention was focussed on how the Government might invoke an escape clause and thereby avoid the risk of a Concorde-style entanglement. But while nobody was very keen, neither did anyone, Whitelaw excepted, wish to pull the plug on it. There was certainly unanimity about one hardy perennial. No firm commitment was to be given, no start was to be made on the project, until all the facts were available. This obsession with reappraisal and re-evaluation every time the government changed irritated the private sector, but it was clearly a fact of political life. But so too was the looming importance of Britain's efforts to join the EEC, which made it more and more difficult to continue the perpetual cycle of further studies and delay.[89] The Tunnel was merely one of the smaller leaves in the artichoke of negotiation,[90] but there was a growing recognition that in the eyes of some key players support for the project might be taken as an affirmation of British faith in Europe. Foreign Office officials had certainly noticed that whenever the subject of British entry was raised, President Pompidou 'nearly always referred in that connexion to the Channel Tunnel', though his motives in so doing were harder to read.[91] It is not too fanciful to suggest that with the negotiations for entry at a delicate stage in 1970–1, leading politicians were more disposed to give their blessing to the final study period. Rippon was particularly trenchant here. 'To attempt to withdraw from the Channel Tunnel project at this stage', he minuted in November 1970, 'after having promoted it when we were in Government in 1962–64, would have a deplorable effect on our international relations. Quite apart from the immediate effects on our current negotiations it would be an economic error of judgement, justifying the American journalist's anecdote that we were getting ready to "sink without ripple into the North Sea" '.[92] In this broader context, the attitude of the Prime Minister was crucial. Heath was certainly lobbied, for example in December 1970 by Lord Cromer, Senior Partner in Barings and a former Governor of the Bank of England, who passed on Louis Armand's 'grave misgivings at the seeming British apathy' and underlined the risks of alienating the French.[93] Peyton has recalled that ministerial opposition abated after he had a private meeting with Heath, who having asked, 'Well, do we want the bloody thing?', had decided that the answer was yes. The date of this defining moment in the Tunnel's history is uncertain, but it seems likely that the impasse was finally broken in March 1971.[94] This did not mean that the garden became instantly rosier, however. RTZ, who had been criticised in some Whitehall circles for their abrasive style and lack of tact, brought an 'emperor's suit of clothes' attitude to the proceedings as novices. One of their first reactions was, revealingly: 'if 18 banks, 2 governments, and 2 railways are involved, to say nothing of 2 construction companies, then the pace of progress will be very slow, and may stop altogether'.[95] Nevertheless, at least the show appeared to be on the road at last, five years after the optimism of the Castle-Pisani communiqué.

3. The 'interim' studies and their results, 1971–2

With RTZ Development Enterprises [RTZDE] installed as the British project managers and SITUMER in the lead on the French side, work on the new set of studies commenced in April 1971. Rio Tinto was supported by four specialist firms: two engineers, Mott, Hay and Anderson, and Sir William Halcrow; the architects Building Design Partnership; and the accountants Cooper Brothers (subsequently Coopers & Lybrand). On the French side SETEC-Economie was retained to handle the economic studies. Although it was anticipated that the final study period would take some 2–3 years to complete, a set of interim results was to be produced no later than 1 May 1972, the date by which the Preliminary Agreement was to be signed. The schedule of tasks, included in the 'studies agreement', covered two primary aspects. First, there was the question of technical feasibility and the preparation of a new estimate of construction costs. Second, there was to be a further series of economic studies, including traffic studies, a revised assessment of financial viability and a cost-benefit analysis. Expenditure on this work, estimated at £647,500 and with the British Government underwriting £340,000,[96] was to be added to the total study costs upon signature of the Preliminary Agreement. If no agreement were concluded then the two governments were obliged to purchase the studies at cost plus interest, limited on the British side to a maximum of £500,000 as authorised by the Cabinet.[97] In fact, as the May deadline approached, negotiations over the Preliminary Agreement were far from complete (see below). In order to avoid serious disturbance to the 'rhythm' of the project, the study period was extended to the end of July and the Treasury agreed to extend the Government's contingent liability by a further £350,000.[98]

The initial results from the studies, assembled in the form of draft volumes of a large report, began to reach London and Paris in the spring of 1972.[99] British officials created an inter-departmental working group, comprising the DOE, Treasury, DTI, FCO, CPRS, and Hambros Bank as consultants, to examine the findings and draw up a paper for consideration by ministers.[100] Early indications were somewhat mixed. Peter Kemp, Assistant Secretary in the Channel Tunnel Studies Unit and chairman of the working group, conceded on 24 April that the economic and commercial findings were 'by no means clear cut', the result of disagreements between the British and French project managers.[101] Peyton, on the other hand, adopted a more Panglossian approach when he briefed members of the EPC on the principal findings early in May. He pointed out that the Tunnel remained technically feasible, with construction costs now estimated at £366 million (in 1972 prices), together with an additional £50–100 million to cover road and rail access on the British side. He admitted that opinion differed as to the financial return. British project managers were more pessimistic in forecasting a 'central case' return of 8.2–11.8 per cent before tax, while their French counterparts estimated the return at about 14 per cent (in fact 14.3 per cent). Similarly, the British and French sides produced cost-benefit calculations which revealed community returns of 10 per cent and 17 per cent respectively, while the separate 'UK only' exercise suggested a figure of 12–13 per cent. Although Peyton enumerated these differences to his colleagues, and, with Chamant, called for a re-examination of the results, he somewhat glossed over their significance with the rather neutral statement that efforts were being made to reconcile them.[102] This attempt at reassurance did little to ease Treasury anxieties over the economic studies, which were made explicit by Patrick Jenkin, the Financial Secretary. His reply to Peyton drew attention to the 'serious discrepancies' in the results, found the position 'disquieting' and warned that 'we should resist any pressures from any quarter to take a more sanguine view of the results . . . At this stage of affairs we are bound to regard the project as a decidedly risky one'.[103] The inter-departmental working group completed its analysis of the studies with its 'Examination of the April 1972 Report' at the end of June. This paper, together with an accompanying memorandum from Peyton, was submitted to the EPC in the following month.[104]

Since the AF66 document (see above, pp. 60–1), there had been no British appraisal of the Tunnel and thus the 1972 report, together with a clearer indication of the likely financing arrangements, offered the opportunity for a fresh dialogue on the economics of the project, particularly within the Treasury. The project managers confirmed the previous findings on technical feasibility and estimated that the Tunnel could be completed and earning revenue by May 1980. Given the existing knowledge of geological conditions and proven tunnelling techniques, the working group considered that the estimated construction costs and the opening date were 'realistic and possibly even prudent'.[105] Nevertheless, the Treasury remained cautious about the likely capital outlay and returned to its familiar position that the project was 'marginal' (see above, pp. 38, 53). John Slater, an Under-Secretary, criticised the 'unwarrantable 'optimism' of the paper'; another official noted, 'one can confidently bet on cost escalation', while another raised the abiding issue of the Tunnel within the context of overall public expenditure plans.[106] The required level of investment in associated railway infrastructure was also extremely uncertain, with concerns about financial viability and the inadequate integration of the specifically *railway* elements within the project appraisal.[107] However, the most worrying aspect of the 1972 studies was the divergence between RTZ/Coopers and SITUMER/SETEC over assumptions and methodology. An early meeting of the working group was informed that the French and British documents appeared to differ on 'every meaningful point'.[108] These differences were most pronounced in the approach to the traffic and revenue studies. 'High' and 'low' toll scenarios were constructed, the former, favoured by SETEC, adopting charges based on the sea ferries' current rates (in real terms), the latter, advanced by RTZ/Cooper Brothers, envisaging that competition would force prices down. Critically, the French project managers argued that low tolls would virtually eliminate shipping and thus the diversion of traffic to the Tunnel would be greater. British officials thought that neither option could be said to represent the likely state of affairs if the Tunnel were built. They regarded the high toll option as unrealistic – the CTSU used the term 'inflammable' – since the current high tolls were the product of a car ferry cartel which was already under investigation by the DTI (and was subsequently referred to the Monopolies Commission in September 1972).[109] On the other hand, further work was required on the competitive reaction of operators in order to validate the low toll model. Traffic assumptions also varied, the British consultants being more sceptical about the extent of holiday traffic. The link between likely technological developments and the future modal split of cross-channel traffic was something of a perennial and the Treasury was quick to flag the issue once again. A special adviser's note for Chancellor Barber asked whether proper account had been taken of possible improvements in the efficiency of ferries, hovercraft and airbuses.[110] Overall, the officials' view was that the project was 'marginal' and the cost-benefit analysis far from satisfactory.[111]

If the revised financial data did little to comfort the Treasury, neither did the proposed financing arrangements. The two were linked because any reduction in the anticipated financial return would make it more difficult for the Anglo-French Group to raise its 'equity capital', and therefore would involve a transfer of the risk from the private to the public sector via the debt guarantee. The Treasury was quite clear that 'the willingness of the private groups does not necessarily imply either that the financial return is satisfactory or that the Government would receive an adequate return on their capital' and that the project remained basically a public sector one. Of course, there was scarcely anything new in these arguments, many of which had been fully rehearsed in the 1960s. Neither was it a surprise to find the Treasury pressing for another internal reassessment of the merits of the Tunnel. Yet, for all the scepticism about a project which 'comes pretty close to the margin of what is acceptable', it was conceded that the evidence was not sufficiently compelling to justify abandonment. Moreover, the decision was essentially a political one that no amount of expert advice or refined methodology could resolve.[112] Certainly, ministers received an equivocal view from the inter-departmental working group. Its conclusions were distinctly wary in stating that 'on balance' the central estimates of cost and financial return were 'useable, and, in some respects, prudent, as a basis on which the present decision could be taken'.[113]

This report, together with a memorandum from Peyton, was considered by the EPC on 24 July 1972. The Minister first set out the intended milestones. In Phase I, to June 1973, the studies would be completed. Phase II, from June 1973 to February 1975, would see construction on a trial basis. In Phase III, construction proper would begin, with completion in 1980. At this stage it was necessary for the government to decide whether it wished to support completion of the Phase I studies. Peyton's commentary on the interim results was broadly in line with his brief to colleagues in May, but some adjustments to the data were made. The estimate of ancillary road and rail investment was now lower at £40–80 million, the 'central' financial return was put at 8.3–12.1 per cent and the 'UK only' cost-benefit placed in the range 10–13 per cent.[114] Peyton noted that while the anticipated returns were not as favourable as those contained in the last two sets of studies (AF66 and SETEC-Economie 1969), they were close to those of 1962 (AF63) (see Table 4.2), and he was clear that the current studies should be completed. Authority was sought to finish the work, conclude the negotiations with the Anglo-French Group and to continue to underwrite expenditure until signature of the Preliminary Agreement. In line with Treasury wishes, Peyton also proposed that an inter-departmental committee of senior officials meet to undertake a thorough review of the tunnel project and to advise ministers on their future course of action. The EPC expressed some apprehension lest the Government be drawn into an irrevocable commitment to an expensive project, but Peyton argued that the summer of 1973 represented a natural break point at which to consider the project and a further review could be made before construction proper started. Peyton's intended course of action was then approved.[115]

4. Negotiating 'Agreement No.1': the Lancaster House agreement, March 1972

While the studies proceeded, discussions between the two governments and the Anglo-French Group continued with the objective of producing an acceptable version of the Preliminary Agreement. In spite of all the earlier work on the

Table 4.2 'Interim' study results, 1972, compared with 1963, 1966 and 1969

	1972	*1963*	*1966*	*1969*
Capital cost	£365.6 m.[a]	£143 m.	£171 m.	—
in 1972 prices	£365.6 m.[a]	£234 m.	£247 m.	
Outturn cost	£630 m.[b]	—	—	—
Financial return[c]	8.3–12.1%[d] RTZ	9.0–11.0%	14.0–20.0%	20.0%
(Central case)	14.3% SETEC			
Community cost-benefit	9–11% RTZ			
(Central case)	16.9% SETEC			
UK only cost-benefit	10–13%			

Sources: '1972 Studies – Background Notes', enclosed in Kemp-Creasy *et al.*, 1 June 1972, and supporting papers in Treasury file 2PE 91/199/01 Pt.M; British Channel Tunnel Co., Report, 9 June 1972, in Harcourt-Peyton, 9 June 1972, MT144/236, PRO. See also Morris and Hough, *Anatomy of Major Projects*, p. 28.

Notes

a Excludes interest, tax, inflation, and associated road/rail infrastructure of £40–80 million.

b Includes provision for 'escalation' (£168 million), interest (£85 million) and loan fees (£11 million), but excludes associated infrastructure.

c Test discount rate 10 per cent.

d Subsequently presented as 11.6 per cent.

'heads of terms', this became a prolonged task, characterised variously by periods of laborious drafting, argument and deadlock, ministerial intervention and apparent progress. As we have seen, the document, which quickly became known as 'Agreement No.1', had to be signed by 1 May 1972, but in the event this did not occur until October. The first step was for the Group to present a draft agreement to the British and French Governments by the end of January 1972. However, this proved to be a far from straightforward process. At a meeting with Peyton in early December 1971, Harcourt revealed that the two sides of the Group were experiencing difficulties in reaching a common position on financing and in drafting an agreement that would be consistent with the 'heads of terms'. He therefore asked the Minister to try to persuade his French counterpart to accept a more flexible interpretation of the heads.[116] Peyton duly raised the issue when he met Chamant in the following week and managed to extract a concession that variations to the September 1971 agreements would be entertained.[117] Otherwise, the portents were far from favourable. An unusually large amount of Anglo-French fencing, fuelled by suspicions in Paris about the project being 'RTZ-led', infected the proceedings. The production of a simple, four-point note for the Anglo-French Group referring to the timetable, and reiterating the Governments' determination that the tunnel operator would be a public sector institution, involved, in Kemp's words, 'a good deal of acrimonious and prolonged bickering'.[118] While Melville advised Peyton to steer clear of fundamentals in his meeting with Chamant, Scott-Malden, in a parting shot just before his move, advised the Minister to go further in order to crystallise thinking on the unresolved issues. If the Anglo-French Group was far from united, then the same could be said of the two Governments, who 'by no means understand each other's position fully yet'. Nor had the British Government's own position 'been completely thought through'. He advised Peyton to press for a programme of regular meetings with Chamant. Of course, the pessimistic observations of a senior official could have been made many times during the Tunnel's long history, but given the impending deadline they did not augur well.[119]

In early January 1972 the British and French Sub-Groups submitted separate drafts of Agreement No.1 to the two governments on an informal basis. British officials found much in their draft that was not acceptable but regarded the document as 'negotiable', provided that the French were thinking in the same way.[120] But in fact the submission of these drafts revealed yawning differences of position in London and Paris. Ten days before the end of January deadline, Chamant told Peyton that he could not conceal his 'serious apprehension' about the situation. Having met with members of the French Sub-Group in order to 'clarify matters', he understood that they would be able to submit proposals in line with the heads of terms; and he asked the British Minister to ensure that the British Sub-Group did the same.[121] When Peyton, who expressed some surprise at this development, took the matter up with Harcourt, a different picture emerged. Harcourt claimed that the French side seemed to have changed tack following an intervention from Chamant, and that in the circumstances he had no option but to submit a draft from the British side on the promised date. Général Maurin submitted a French draft to Chamant at the same time.[122] The two Transport Ministers then met in Paris on 7 February to consider the documentation. Neither was happy with the proposals. Peyton found the degree of French risk capital disappointingly low, while Chamant asserted that the British text had diverged some way from the heads of terms on finance, the timetable and operating control. Peyton's Panglossian side wore thin. 'What concerned him [about the French draft] was what was left out, not what was in it. He did not see much point in exchanging long lists of apparent discrepancies. Enough paper had been thrown around already'. Macé had not helped the atmosphere by referring to 'gamineries' (childishnesses) over textual points. Officials were asked to examine the texts and report to their respective ministers.[123]

A week later, Peyton and Chamant wrote formally and in uncompromising fashion to Harcourt and Maurin to point out their dissatisfaction with the submissions from the British and French Sub-Groups. A long list of required modifications was appended and the parties were instructed to submit revised proposals by the beginning of March.[124] Peyton's letter to Harcourt contrasted with his progress report to Heath on the following day. Prepared for the Prime Minister's meeting with Pompidou at Chequers on 19 February, this referred to the areas 'for further discussion' but expressed confidence that the negotiations would be concluded within the required timetable.[125] The British and French Sub-Groups produced a revised set of proposals on 9 March, and at the end of the month the 'quadripartite' team of Anglo-French ministers and officials returned to Lancaster House in an attempt to thrash out a solution. The discussions centred on the determination of specific stages for the project, which in turn affected the amount of risk money the Group would be asked to put up at each stage. Chamant adopted a strong line in seeking greater participation from the private sector.[126] Consequently, further Ministerial letters to the Anglo-French Group, sent in early April, asked for confirmation that Agreement No.2 would represent the decision by all parties to proceed with construction. The Group was also invited to consider raising the amount of 'risk' money it was to contribute to 50 per cent in Phase I (May 1972–June 1973) and 30 per cent in Phase II (June 1973–February 1975). In addition, and given the frequent references to the difficulties of handling financing in the two countries, the Governments undertook to examine a concept raised by both Sub-Groups, viz. that of separate, or 'split' financing (see below).[127]

5. Impasse: the points at issue, April–July 1972

By the time Harcourt was able to communicate the British Sub-Group's response to these Ministerial observations, the deadline for signing Agreement No.1 (1 May 1972) had just passed. What, then, were the fundamental points at issue? The level of financial contribution from the private sector was one of the long-standing matters, and it should have been no surprise that the temperature would become more heated when entrepreneurs were asked to turn promises into firm commitments. The British Sub-Group had accepted the idea, rather reluctantly it must be said, that the project should be divided into three phases instead of two, with 'break points' at June 1973 and February 1975. And in line with the Lancaster House agreement, it had suggested that the consortium would find £2 million (out of £5.1 million) in Phase I and £2 million (out of £20 million) in Phase II. Officials considered this to be too low. There was also disappointment with the modest nature of the French proposals, which were held to be 'almost devoid of any meaningful private commitment', since they had made no offer of money beyond their share of the first £2 million.[128] As we have seen, in April 1972 the Governments considered that sums of £2.5 million (or 50 per cent for Phase I) and £6 million (or 30 per cent for Phase II) would offer a better measure of private sector resolution.[129] The extent of private financing was one thing; the precise nature of the risk money was another. What did and did not constitute private capital in the two countries was another frequently rehearsed argument (see above, p. 51), as was the differing nature of the capital markets, and these continued to give rise to significant differences of position within the British and French Sub-Groups. While the British financiers, encouraged by RTZDE, favoured 'true' equity, the French were happy with the existing concept of 'participating preference' shares with a guaranteed return.[130] The two sides also differed in their ideas for the phasing of the risk capital. In January 1972, for example, initial financing plans contemplated expenditure of about £25 million to 1975, with £4 million in the form of founders' shares to be made available in the period May 1972–June 1973. The British, who had to go to the market for their funds, lacked the resources to provide their portion of the founders' shares immediately. This compromised the intentions of the French, who with their access to 'in-house' resources were prepared to put up the founders' capital immediately. However, they were unwilling to commit themselves to the rest before agreement in June 1973, which prejudiced the chances of the British raising money on the London market. As Dewdney observed, these plans were 'mutually inconvenient'.[131] Another bone of contention, at least on the British side, was the Governments' insistence on operation by a public authority, which, RTZ claimed, would make the task of raising capital much harder.[132]

A possible solution to the impasse, was the concept of split financing, whereby each side would be free to determine the preferred method of financing and remuneration for its half of the project. Difficulties over the nature of equity, the private-public composition of capital and the timing of investment could be eliminated, while the existing proposals for construction and operation of the Tunnel would be unaffected. At first sight, the concept was simple and transparent.[133] Having been discussed informally for some months the idea was raised formally in March 1972 when Harcourt suggested that if no acceptable solution were found then both sides of the Group would be happy to examine separate financing plans.[134] Enthusiasm for the idea quickly evaporated, however, particularly in Whitehall. The problems of guaranteeing both halves of the construction finance, and the impact on already complex contractual arrangements were seen as serious stumbling blocks. The DOE's advisers, Hambros, also argued cogently that split financing would neither resolve potential conflicts over the respective claims of classes of capital nor help the French to raise their share on the 'deficient' Paris market.[135] In fact, there was only limited support for split financing from Maurin on the French side. By the end of April this alternative appeared to have been ditched.[136]

The Anglo-French Group also asked for a number of government 'assurances' to assist them in capital raising and to mitigate risks. These embraced such matters as taxation, tariff policy and the supporting railway infrastructure, but the most important referred to the future operating body. If it were to be a public authority, then the British side sought guarantees that it would behave in a commercial manner, particularly in its relations with the two state-owned railway corporations.[137] This the civil servants at least were ready to concede in principle. A joint note produced by British and French officials in March 1972 stated that the body should have the 'freedom to manage', and that 'any external Governmental supervision must be exercised lightly'. It also promised that the construction companies would have representation on the board. Nevertheless, there remained some doubts about how 'commercial' the operating authority would actually be in practice, particularly since it was made clear that the Ministers would reserve the right to give the body non-commercial directives if 'national interests' demanded it.[138] Nor were the Governments prepared to accept the notion, advanced by Dewdney and Allen Sykes, that the Group should have a majority control in it. And from the government perspective, the granting of assurances required a quid pro quo from the private sector, that it would maximise its share of the capital investment.[139]

As these discussions went on, the Tunnel studies proceeded in tandem. Given the intended timetable for signing Agreement No.1, DOE officials expressed anxiety that since RTZ was both project manager and consortium member, the British Sub-Group would be in possession of useful 'signals' from the studies before the Government knew the contents. Although this position of information asymmetry did not arise, since the original May deadline had already passed when the British Sub-Group responded, on 3 May, to the Minister's April letter, the study findings remained a critical component in bargaining. It was thus no surprise when Harcourt's response to Peyton included the observation that the results had made it essential for the British banks to re-examine the financing plan for the project. While the Anglo-French Group was prepared to put up 50 per cent or £2.5 million for Phase I, it could commit no more than 10 per cent or £2 million for Phase II. However, if circumstances allowed, it would use its 'best endeavours' to raise finance up to the figure of 30 per cent (£6 million).[140] This 'offer' proved unacceptable to Chamant, who insisted that a commitment of 30 per cent be made. The Ministers then conveyed this view to the Group and offered to extend the deadline to 30 June provided that a satisfactory response were received.[141] The size of the commitment was psychological as well as real. Melville, in briefing Peyton, emphasised that if the private sector were unwilling to take a meaningful stake then 'some of your ministerial colleagues may wonder whether the game of mixing private with public money is worth the candle'.[142] After some arm-twisting by Peyton and much behind-the-scenes manoeuvring, the British and French Sub-Groups produced a formal reply at the end of May committing themselves to find the necessary £6 million in risk capital. Although there was something in the Group's argument that future market conditions might frustrate the investment, the private sector's reticence over a relatively modest sum (in comparison with the total investment required) confirmed Melville's frank analysis of the prospects of public-private partnership.[143]

In June the chances of reaching an agreement improved a little, although the Group began to upset the delicate negotiating balance by seeking to use the study results to 'hedge' its risk. In this context it increased the number of 'crunch points' on which specific assurances were required to more than a dozen. Officials found that some were capable of compromise, but others, for example, compensation arrangements and shareholders' rewards, including the request for some kind of income guarantee during the early years of operation, were more intractable. There was thus a very real chance of breakdown at what was expected to be the final round of quadripartite drafting talks in Paris at the end of the month. Melville suggested that a good negotiating tactic would be for the Governments to offer to underwrite the cost of the study programme until a decision to proceed were made. This would help the Group to defer its commitment until the results of the final studies, which he thought would prove more positive, were made known in 1973.[144] In fact, the meeting, on 26 June, confounded Melville's expectations. The British delegation, led by Kemp, was left in some disarray when French officials, having failed to persuade the Group to accept nine fundamental points, abruptly terminated the discussions. Their behaviour both perplexed and exasperated the DOE. Macé attended the meeting for only a few minutes. It was left to the senior negotiator on the French side, Roger Callou, to point out that the French Government, expecting to resolve matters by the 30 June deadline, 'felt that things had dragged on long enough, and that M. Chamant in particular "en ar [sic] marre" (is fed up with it).' Melville was sufficiently worried to warn the British Embassy in Paris that 'there are storms in the offing'.[145] Talks resumed in London on 5–6 July, with another deadline past. Despite genuine efforts to resolve differences at the level of officials, government intentions seemed to differ. The British wanted first and foremost to see the studies completed; the French, on the other hand, were intent on bringing the Anglo-French Group to heel, even if this interrupted the work. In any event, they were only prepared to extend the deadline for signing Agreement No.1 by a month (i.e. to 31 July). As Melville noted, there was a risk that the British Sub-Group might withdraw, 'a prospect which the French might not dislike (especially if it removed RTZ)'.[146] Given the dispute, separate financing was resurrected by Macé and Melville, though this was not included in the paper for EPC in July (see above, p. 95). From the French perspective, the option appeared preferable to attempts to find a joint solution in circumstances where the British Sub-Group kept raising the stakes and the British Government kept insisting on further studies.[147] The British saw things differently. As Peyton told Treasury Secretary Jenkin, the French Government was being 'dirigiste', while the French banks 'will do what their Government tells them; for our merchant banks such docility is just not possible'. With the extended deadline of 31 July only three weeks away and no sign of a uniform view from the Anglo-French Group, Peyton's admission that 'at best… we shall be in a position of some negotiating difficulty' was clearly an understatement.[148]

By this time Chamant, who had become frustrated with the lack of progress, had been replaced (on 6 July) by Robert Galley as French Minister of Transport. Galley, a Gaullist reputed to be both capable and ambitious, was an open-minded man and something of an Anglophile.[149] But he had been fully briefed by Chamant, who was a personal friend, and his appointment did nothing to change the French view that the Anglo-French Group was failing to face up to its responsibilities in accepting risk. Further correspondence with the Group had merely reiterated points for resolution. At a meeting with Peyton in London on 20 July he wanted to force the issue by stopping the clock at 30 June and refusing to extend financial support until Agreement No.1 were signed. He suggested that officials prepare an agreed text within a week and require the Group to sign it. Peyton, however, proposed a more conciliatory approach, given the fact that the Governments were responsible for some of the delays. The Ministers agreed that their officials would produce a final text of the agreement to transmit to the Group; the insistence on having it signed straightaway was dropped.[150]

This further drafting effort left the Governments with two outstanding matters: the date for the signature of Agreement No.2, and the concept of 'negotiating risk'. The first revealed a difference over timing. The British felt that there might be insufficient time for officials to analyse the results of the completed studies between their receipt, probably in April 1973 (with the final report in May), and the proposed date for signature of Agreement No.2 of 1 June. Consequently, they suggested 1 October as a more realistic alternative, but the French were reluctant to move away from June, and were less worried about the studies since their Government had 'already taken its decision on the Tunnel' and only required them for bargaining purposes. The dates finally agreed left only a short period for analysis. The final report on Phase I was to be submitted by 1 July 1973, with Agreement No.2 signed by 31 July.[151] The concept of 'negotiating risk' followed on from the acceptance that some points would be deliberately left out of Agreement No.1, but would be resolved in Agreement No.2. If the latter were not signed because it proved impossible to settle these points, then joint abandonment would be deemed to have occurred. At issue here were what items should be included in the risk and what consequences would follow from abandonment. British officials thought that the Group should recover 100 per cent of its risk money but lose its 'chosen instrument' status. On the other hand, the French, and their Treasury in particular, preferred the Group to retain its status but be paid less money. This proved to be one of the more intractable points and indeed was the last to be settled before Agreement No.1 was signed.[152] Another remaining area of difficulty, this time raised by the Group, was the demand for 'financing flexibility'. Given anticipated lower returns, there was particular anxiety about profitability in the early years of operation, and some amelioration was sought. Two ideas were floated: first, that relief might be provided by deferring the amortisation of government debt for the first five years; and second, that losses in the early years might be charged to capital. While the first point was conceded and included as an option in Agreement No.1, the latter was excluded, although a promise was made to consider it in subsequent negotiations.[153]

6. Concluding 'Agreement No.1', August–October 1972

August proved to be an unusually busy month. An apparently firm date for the signature of Agreement No.1 – 30 September – was agreed, and the four parties each undertook to meet one-quarter of the additional study costs. Both Peyton and Galley encouraged their officials and the Group to meet in permanent drafting session in order to adhere to the timetable.[154] Peyton, under some pressure from the French to make a public statement, was unable to do so before the Commons' summer recess, but a DOE press notice issued, somewhat reluctantly, on the 16th and intended to be 'as short and laconic as possible',[155] expressed the hope that a formal agreement would be signed by 30 September.[156] Indeed, as holidays beckoned, it was confidently expected that when the two Transport Ministers met in Paris on 21 September the matter would be settled within the deadline, though the civil servants would have to work flat out to achieve it.[157]

It will not be a surprise for readers to learn that last-minute hitches delayed matters for a further month. This time there were three main stumbling blocks: the project management agreements, the handling of the bond issue, and negotiating risk.[158] Turning to the first of these, the project managers' agreements were not to be included in Agreement No.1, but the Anglo-French Group wished to sign them contemporaneously, and the British Government took a close interest in the negotiations between RTZDE, SITUMER and the British and French companies. The size of the fees was the central area of concern. Here the key element was that the thinking of RTZDE changed substantially between the time of its first involvement and the summer of 1972. At first, it felt that £25,000 a month for 100 months might be appropriate as a fee for both the British and French managers. This amounted to £5 million, or 1.4 per cent of capital cost.[159] Later on, it insisted that the investment opportunity was now 'much less rosy'. The company had given up all hopes of a genuine equity investment, while the likely return on its so-called 'equity' was unlikely to be attractive.[160] Consequently, Duncan encouraged Frame to increase the level of management fees, and in July a draft management agreement was sent to the DOE which proposed a much higher remuneration for RTZDE. There was to be a two-tier structure comprising a fixed element of £5 million, and a variable, performance-related, element, dependent on the difference between outturn and forecast costs. If the actual cost of the Tunnel matched the forecast, the payment would be £7.5 million. If the French project managers were rewarded on the same basis, the fees would amount to £10 million fixed (2.7 per cent) and £15 million variable (4.1 per cent).[161] This demand not only provoked Peyton, who warned Duncan that he would have to defend the fees in Parliament, but also upset the French, who felt fees should be lower.[162]

On 25 September 1972, only days before Agreement No.1 was due to be signed, a substantially revised proposal was put to the DOE, and it was followed by a formal letter from Harcourt to Peyton asking that the sums to be paid to RTZDE be agreed before signature. This envisaged a fixed element of £3.8 million (£38,000 a month for 100 months), and a variable element, to be shared with the French, of £5.5 million, if the forecast cost was attained. Assuming the French were paid the same fixed fee, the total would be £13.1 million or 3.6 per cent. In addition, Mott, Hay and Anderson and SITUMER would be paid £4 million in engineering fees. The grand total of £17.1 million or 4.7 per cent was justified as lying within the 4–6 per cent range deemed appropriate for major projects of this type.[163] This still evoked unease in Whitehall. Len Creasy, the DOE's Director of Civil Engineering Development, conceded that the fees, which did not include staff costs, remained high by 'any "normal" standards', while Sir William Harris, the Director-General, Highways, was more forthright, referring to 'daylight robbery'.[164] Since there was no time to give the proposal the necessary 'detailed study', and the French had their own ideas about fees, it was suggested that in order to allow Agreement No.1 to be signed the general framework would be accepted as the basis for further negotiations. There were fears that RTZ might withdraw if not accommodated, and Peyton even wrote to Galley on Duncan's prompting to make an appeal for 'unified project management'.[165] Nevertheless, the British Government insisted that the timetable be followed. Although RTZDE submitted yet another schedule of fees in mid-October, Agreement No.1 was signed without project management contracts in place.[166]

The second stumbling block also surfaced at a relatively late stage. As we have seen, the banking interests in the Anglo-French Group had always assumed that they would handle the management and broking of the government-guaranteed tunnel bonds, a business which would be both prestigious and profitable, with commissions estimated at £1 million a year for 5–6 years. The British Treasury, on the other hand, took the view that the Bank of England should manage the issues, and the government broker, Mullens, should act as brokers. Not only was this established practice, but given the potential size of the issues and their virtual gilt-edged status, it was considered vital that the monetary authorities should exercise some control in the market.[167] The DOE was rightly irritated that the difficulty had first been raised in detailed correspondence between officials on 28 September.[168] It pointed out that the private group had a long-standing right to this work and would withdraw from the project if not given it. Under-Secretaries then locked horns, and Geoffrey Wardale from the DOE was moved to remind the Treasury's Peter Lazarus of the assumption in all the negotiations since 1967 that the tunnel companies would be entrusted with raising all the money needed for construction.[169] In this rather charged atmosphere, both the Bank of England and the Treasury quickly accepted that a commitment had been entered into and decided not to press the matter further.[170] The third and final problem was an old friend, 'negotiating risk', latterly known as 'special joint abandonment'. The terms under which the Group would have a case for compensation under this heading were thrashed out in meetings in October. The Governments also persuaded the Group to accept less than an immediate 100 per cent repayment of their expenditure – in fact 85 per cent, payable after $2\frac{1}{2}$ years. This, the final point to be settled, required the formal endorsement of the French Finance Minister, Valéry Giscard d'Estaing, before it was finally resolved.[171]

Agreement No.1 was finally concluded on 20 October 1972. There were in fact two parallel agreements, one signed by the British, the other by the French. At the same time, the respective obligations of the two Governments, particularly in regard to the sharing of costs if the project were abandoned, were set out in an official exchange of notes.[172] We have already noted the way in which the Channel Tunnel was often linked with negotiations about Britain's application to join the European Community. There was some symmetry in the fact that only three days earlier the European Community Act had received the Royal Assent, and the date of signature coincided with the end of a European Summit in Paris which was judged a success for Pompidou and Heath.[173] The agreement, in the British version a 'formidable' 76-page piece of 'complicated legal drafting',[174] provided for the completion of the Phase I studies by 1 July 1973. Although there was no obligation to proceed beyond this date, 'agreements to agree' on Phases II and III were outlined. It was estimated that expenditure on Phase I would amount to £5.4 million, about half of which would come from risk capital put up by the Group and the remainder from Government guaranteed loans. Phase II would

Table 4.3 Participation in the private consortium, October 1972

British Sub-group: British Channel Tunnel Co. Ltd	*Participation in Phase I (%)*	*French Sub-group: Société Française du Tunnel sous la Manche*	*Participation in Phase I (%)*
Channel Tunnel Investments Ltd[a]	25.00	Banque Louis-Dreyfus	13.0
Rio Tinto-Zinc Corporation Ltd	20.00	Compagnie Financière de Suez	13.0
Morgan Grenfell & Co. Ltd	10.50	Compagnie du Nord	13.0
Robert Fleming & Co. Ltd	10.50	Société Nationale des Chemins de fer Français	13.0
Hill, Samuel & Co. Ltd	10.50	Banque Nationale de Paris	8.0
Kleinwort, Benson Ltd	10.50	Banque de Paris et des Pays Bas	8.0
S.G. Warburg & Co. Ltd	5.50	Banque de l'Union Européenne	8.0
British Railways Board	4.74	Crédit Commercial de France	8.0
Morgan Stanley & Co. Inc. (USA)	0.92	Crédit Lyonnais	8.0
First Boston Corporation (USA)	0.92	Société Générale	8.0
White, Weld & Co. (USA)	0.92		
	100.00		100.0

Source: Agreement No.1, 20 October 1972, 2.3.1, also reproduced in Bonavia, *Channel Tunnel Story*, p. 100.

Note

a Before June 1971 the 'Channel Tunnel Co.'

commence with the signature of Agreement No.2 and an Anglo-French Treaty confirming the decision to proceed to construction of the Tunnel. During Phase II, to last until February 1975, shafts would be sunk and boring of the service tunnel would start. The Group would contribute 10–30 per cent of the envisaged £20 million cost. It was asked to raise £6 million within nine months of Agreement No.2 (or three months after the Treaty was ratified), but there was provision for this to be reduced by agreement to £2 million. Full construction would begin in Phase III, and upon completion in 1980 the Tunnel would be handed over to the public operating authority. A minimum of 10 per cent of the forecast cost was to be provided by private sector risk money. The Group would receive a free issue of shares on the basis of the 2.8 multiplier originally agreed (see p. 415, n.12), in addition to the issuing and management fees. Detailed terms for abandonment, varied according to circumstances, by any of the parties were also specified. The agreement also revealed the members of the Group, together with the extent of their financial contribution to Phase I (see Table 4.3). The companies' £3 million commitment to the members of the old CTSG, the subject of a separate agreement signed on the same day, was confirmed as part of the Tunnel's Phase III costs.[175]

After all the protracted wrangling, over 18 months since the proposals of March 1971, it was difficult to see Agreement No.1 as a major landmark. It is true that the studies had been itemised and fully costed. The circumstances in which abandonment might take place, and the parties' responsibility for costs incurred, were defined much more tightly. In particular, an 'anti-Concorde' clause was inserted, designed to discourage one of the parties from trying to manoeuvre the others into unilateral abandonment if costs escalated and/or the project's viability was threatened.[176] Provision had been made for the companies to stake more 'risk' capital at an earlier stage, viz. in phase II, July 1973–February 1975. Furthermore, for the first time the Group was putting up money that might be lost. Some concessions had been extracted from the Governments, notably in relation to negotiating risk, amortisation, and the setting of tunnel tariffs and tolls (where the construction companies were given the right to challenge pricing and invoke arbitration). On the other hand, many elements had still been left rather vague and/or to be determined later, notably the remuneration formula, taxation, and the infrastructure for road/rail access on the British side (details on the French side had been identified). All in all, the Agreement had exposed: 'the sheer difficulty of negotiations between four parties with very different interests'; the danger of judging and managing the project by reference to 'financiability' (whether the private capital could be raised) rather than viability; and 'the fundamental dilemma of control over a public/private enterprise'.[177] For better or worse the project had begun, and much was owed to the efforts of the principal officials, Melville, Kemp, Macé and Callou. Nevertheless, their efforts had frequently exposed the shortcomings of the public-private scheme which Peyton had inherited from the previous government, and about which he and Walker had nursed reservations.

5

THE HEATH GOVERNMENT AND THE TUNNEL

Taking the project forward, 1972–4

1. The 'final' studies, October 1972–June 1973: review and consultation processes

Following the October 1972 agreement to complete the study period (Phase I), Whitehall turned its attention to the preparation of the next stage of the required documentation, viz. Agreement No.2, and the Anglo-French Treaty, which in turn demanded consultative and legislative processes. As Peyton had promised in his submission to the Cabinet EPC in July 1972 (see above, p. 95), an Interdepartmental Committee of senior officials was established to undertake a fundamental review of the project prior to the critical decision-making required in July 1973 and to ensure that ministers received the best possible advice. Chaired by Sir Idwal Pugh, Second Permanent Secretary of the DOE, it was staffed, *inter alia*, by Peter Lazarus from the Treasury and Peter Carey from the DTI, together with representatives from the FCO and CPRS. However, senior officials from the DOE dominated its membership: Harris, Wardale, Tom Beagley, Humphrey Cole, John Rosenfeld, Bill Sharp and Henry Woodhouse, in addition to officials from the CTSU, Melville, Kemp, and a newcomer, Susan Fogarty, who joined the Unit as an Assistant Secretary and took charge of its work. When the Committee first met on 12 October 1972, the Chairman noted that its task was 'stiff'. First, it was to review the work undertaken by the Anglo-French Group and its project managers in producing the final assessments of the Tunnel's economic, financial and engineering viability. Second, it was to determine the 'total impact... on the economy and environment of the United Kingdom', including 'the commitment of physical resources, UK planning policies and the role of the project, with its associated road and rail investment', the economic and social impact on South-east Kent, and the effect on the balance of payments. Last, and certainly not least, the Committee was also to be the forum for ensuring that, if endorsed, the project could go ahead smoothly. This required it to determine the content and timing of the parliamentary programme, embracing consultative documents, bills and debates.[1] While this package of duties was onerous, officials were particularly concerned about the parliamentary timetable, which was very tight. A short 'money' Bill was required in the 1972/3 session, to give the Secretary of State authority to incur the limited financial obligations in Phase II. This was to be followed in 1973/4 by a comprehensive 'hybrid' Bill granting the full powers necessary for completion. And since no substantive public information had been provided since the White Paper of 1963, it was also necessary to inform both parliament and the public of what was proposed, by means of 'take-note' debates in the Commons and Lords, and a White Paper setting out the results of the final studies and financial negotiations. The obligations in Agreement No.1 clearly put such requirements under considerable pressure. The Anglo-French Group was not required to produce its financial proposals until 7 June 1973, and the deadline for the final report on the studies was 1 July, but Agreement No.2 had to be signed by 31 July (though there was provision, with some financial risks, for a delay until 15 November).[2] An organisational change was made within the CTSU in early 1973 to handle these complexities. Fogarty, who became an Under-Secretary, took responsibility for the economic studies, railway investment, and the parliamentary papers. This left Melville and Kemp free to concentrate on negotiating the Agreement and Treaty.[3]

The problem was that expediting the timetable would mean cutting down the consultative process, which might play into the hands of opponents, notably the shipping interests and environmental objectors in Kent. Signs that this would be a difficulty emerged in the autumn of 1972 when Peyton announced that he would not publish the results of the interim studies, but would merely place a copy of Agreement No.1 in the House of Commons Library. There was little overt criticism of this procedure, but anxieties within Whitehall about the need to allow debate and release more information led to the suggestion that a consultative 'Green Paper' be published in the New Year. The Committee accepted that there were risks in this course of action, since such a document, lacking 'economic arguments or financing proposals would be of slight value'. However, the advantages of facilitating a public discussion overrode this concern.[4] The Committee's unease was soon confirmed. The Green Paper was drafted by the CTSU, with the help of the Treasury.[5] When it was presented for consideration by the EPC in February 1973, ministers agreed that it should be published, but in debate it became clear that publication would be a tricky public relations exercise. If the document were too non-committal, as the Treasury had wanted,[6] it would be open to attack from opponents of the Tunnel; if it were too positive, the Government would be exposed to the criticism that it was seeking to push through a large project without having released any detailed supporting information for nine years. Ministers also had qualms about sponsoring such a large project at a time when the Government was determinedly pursuing counter-inflation measures by means of statutory controls of prices and incomes. Finally, doubts were expressed about the adequacy of the proposed parliamentary timetable (Green Paper in March, White Paper in July, assent to the Money Bill in October), given existing feeling about large projects in general.[7] The cost of supporting Concorde continued to rankle with many, and there was also opposition to a contemporaneous proposal to build the third London airport at Maplin Sands in Essex.[8] Jim Prior, the

Lord President, was particularly concerned. As he told Heath, 'some of our supporters are at present in a mood to criticise any proposal to tie up large resources in a project of this kind: even though there is no significant public expenditure involved, there are those who will see analogies with Maplin, Concorde, etc.'.[9] Heath responded by asking that those making the public presentation should emphasise that little government expenditure would be incurred until the second half of the decade.[10]

Such anxieties were clearly emasculating. When the Green Paper, *The Channel Tunnel Project*, was duly published on 21 March 1973, it gave very little away. A slim, 33-page document costing 36½p, it was a rather bland affair, outlining the history of the current project (illustrated in Figure 5.1) and the study programme, and reassuring the reader that the venture would 'only be undertaken if... shown by the current... studies to be a sound business proposition' and that the main results from the studies would be published before any further commitment was made. It also sought to mollify opinion in Kent by promising to publish the work on the economic and social implications for South-east Kent which had been commissioned from Economic Consultants Ltd.[11] The Green Paper suggested that the case for a tunnel had been strengthened by the 'immense' growth in cross-channel traffic in recent years, and that this traffic had assumed greater importance since Britain had joined the EEC (on 1 January 1973). The current estimate of construction cost – £366 million, first made public in July 1972 – was repeated.[12] However, the response from the media was scarcely ecstatic. In France, there was very little comment; in Britain, as the French noted, the reaction was 'dans l'ensemble peu enthousiaste' [on the whole not very enthusiastic].[13] Some newspapers were more critical. The *Times*, in a leader entitled 'Very Probably A Mistake', attacked both the Tunnel and the Green Paper. Numerous spanners were thrown into the works: 'The Channel Tunnel shows every sign of being the next large and costly public work to be foisted by the Government on the country without proper debate... and yesterday's Green Paper takes us little further'. The timetable would stifle debate, the Tunnel, which would funnel traffic 'from all parts of the country... into a corner of Kent', would have 'highly undesirable' planning implications. France would gain far more than Britain, and the 'over-simplified choice between development of existing modes with a Tunnel or without it', neglecting the advent of 'worldwide air transport', hovercraft, roll-on roll-off ships, 'the moonshot and magnetic levitation', was 'another grave defect'.[14] Oxford historian A.J.P. Taylor, writing for the *Sunday Express*, had no doubt that if there was an 'honest inquiry, the Channel Tunnel will be exposed as the Greatest White Elephant of all time'.[15] The *Economist* was less scathing, but condemned the document for failing to refer to what it saw as the critical issue on which the success or failure of the Tunnel hinged: the extent of the investment in high-speed railways from the capital cities.[16] And in spite of the Green Paper's efforts to treat the Tunnel and Maplin Airport as complementary and non-competing projects, there were those who were anxious to debate the two ventures together, since the Maplin Development Bill was at the committee stage, and

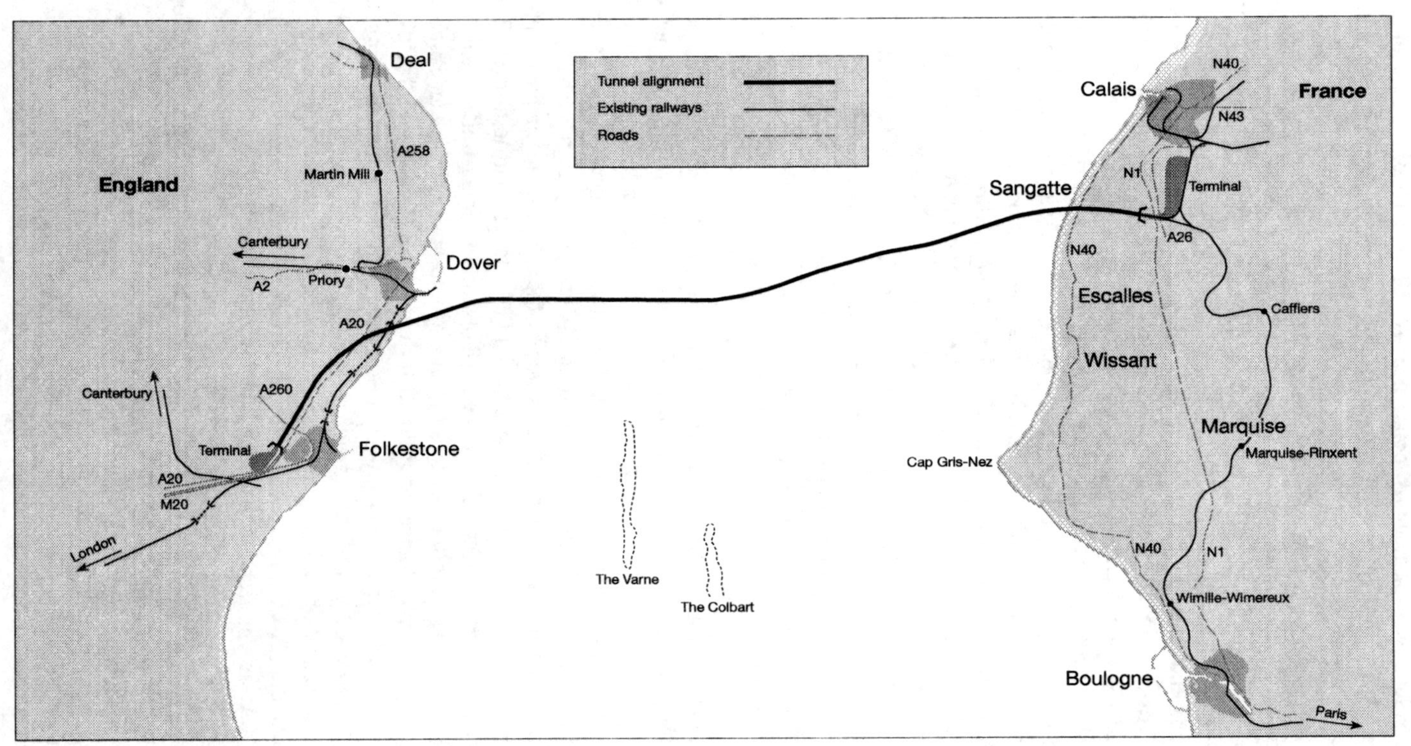

Figure 5.1 The 1970s Tunnel.

there were those who were arguing that at least one, if not both, of the projects was unnecessary.[17] Some vested interests were also moved to respond. Keith Wickenden, Chairman of European Ferries Ltd, which had built up a sizeable cross-channel fleet, produced a 'green paper' of his own. Entitled *The Channel Tunnel Project: an objective appraisal*, this cleverly presented document sought to use the Green Paper's slim database, and notably its cautious estimates of tunnel revenue, to challenge the project's viability and the Government's impartiality. All in all, the public relations exercise provided by the publication must be judged a failure.[18]

Meanwhile the study programme proceeded, in tandem with the preparations for Agreement No.2 and the Anglo-French Treaty. The studies, which were outlined in the Green Paper, included both technical and economic work.[19] On the technical side, further refinements were made to the reference design for the Tunnel and its associated infrastructure (e.g. terminals) and equipment. The findings were fed into a revised estimate of construction cost. Joint economic studies undertaken by Cooper Brothers and SETEC-Economie, under the direction of the British and French project managers and governments, were concerned with forecasting traffic and revenue streams. Taken together, the work would produce an up-to-date assessment of the project's financial viability and give a much clearer indication of the likely profits available to remunerate the Anglo-French Group (BCTC, SFTM) and the two governments. A further component of the economic studies was a new cost-benefit analysis for the United Kingdom produced by Coopers. Officials in both Britain and France had concluded that a broader, community-based calculation would be of limited value and should not be pursued.[20] As already noted, studies were also made of the environmental and regional impact, options for a new, dedicated rail link to central London, and the effect on the balance of payments.[21] One question that was answered quickly was that concerning alternative forms of cross-channel fixed link, an issue that had not been entirely resolved in either the 1963 or 1966 exercises. A detailed examination of the best alternative to a bored tunnel, the immersed tube, was conducted in France by the Inspecteur Général des Ponts et Chaussées, J. Mathieu, in 1968. He concluded that the tube technology remained uncertain and unproven in deeper, channel conditions. Likely costs were therefore highly speculative, and there was also the danger to shipping during construction.[22] Although an immersed tube tunnel was completed in Hong Kong in 1972, and alternatives such as bridges or hybrids on the Chesapeake Bay model were canvassed from time to time, official opinion in Britain also came down firmly in favour of the bored tunnel as the favoured method, as the Japanese had done for their Hokkaido-Honshu [Seikan] Tunnel, started in 1969.[23] The choice was confirmed in a CTSU paper considered by Pugh's Interdepartmental Committee in January 1973. The arguments were set out in both the Green and White papers, and confirmed by Peyton in his Commons statement in June.[24]

After an initial flurry of meetings, Pugh's Committee did not convene between the end of January and early May 1973, while output from the studies was awaited. Of course, preparatory work continued at a lower level, by means of six working parties with interdepartmental representation.[25] The first material to become available was the study of the economic and social implications in South-east Kent. Published in May, the consultants' report was primarily concerned with the employment effects in Dover and Folkestone. It produced the reassuring conclusion that the impact on job losses and pressure on land would be relatively small.[26] Officials therefore considered it unlikely that these factors would impinge on the decision whether or not to build the Tunnel.[27] Of far greater significance in the decision-making process were the emerging results from the economic studies. At the beginning of May, as required under Agreement No.1, the companies provided their forecast of the construction cost, viz. £464 million in January 1973 prices, or £846 million in outturn costs (allowing for interest and inflation at 8 per cent [6 per cent in France]), together with estimated gross and net receipts.[28] By this time, attempts to control the flow of information on the Tunnel were becoming increasingly difficult to sustain, particularly in view of some sensationalist reports in the press.[29] Harcourt, the Chairman of BCTC, was therefore authorised to reveal the new cost estimate during a debate on the Tunnel in the Lords.[30] Likewise, the two Governments had to agree that the companies could make details of the studies public, Peyton warning Pierre Billecocq, the Minister now responsible for the Tunnel in France, that 'Any other course would awaken the gravest suspicion and jeopardise the project'.[31] Thus, on 15 May, only a week after the companies had sent their consultants' findings to the Governments, the BCTC issued a brief statement summarising the main elements. This provided details of estimated traffic and revenue and put operating profits in outturn prices at £95 million in 1981, the first full year of operation, and £252 million in 1990. It also sought to be reassuring on costs. Most (83 per cent) of the increase from £366 million in 1972 to £468 million a year later was explained by inflation, exchange rate movements and French VAT. The document's bullish remarks about the extent of private sector risk clearly irritated Whitehall. It may have been, as Treasury official Margaret Elliott-Binns noted, 'an unashamed statement of the case for the Tunnel'. Nevertheless, the financial and statistical information offered was essentially what was made public in more detail in subsequent months (cf. financial return and traffic data in Tables 5.1 and 5.3). And the private sector companies were scarcely over-optimistic in forecasting that only about 25 per cent of the non-vehicle passenger market would be captured by the Tunnel, or in presenting forecasts of economic growth which were 20 per cent below existing OECD estimates.[32]

The pressure in London and Paris to process these results quickly in order to meet an already tight timetable was further increased by a commitment given by Heath to Pompidou when the two leaders met on 22 May. Officials had asked Heath not to mention the Tunnel because he would not be in a position to indicate the British Government's view. However, the subject was raised by the French Prime Minister, Pierre Messmer, who noted that a decision would be required by the middle of July, after which the project would enter 'a virtually irreversible phase'. Heath agreed,

Table 5.1 The 1973 studies: estimated financial return

	Low forecast (OECD growth rates minus 20%) (%)	*Central forecast (OECD growth rates) (%)*
Real return (as presented to Cabinet EPC, May 1973)	14.5	16.5
Real return (as published in Companies' Summary Report, June 1973)	14	17

Source: CTIC, Report on 'The Channel Tunnel Project: Outcome of Phase One Studies', in Rippon, Memo. to Cabinet EPC, EPC (73)30, 6 June 1973, CAB134/3599, PRO; BCTC and SFTM, *The Channel Tunnel Economic and Financial Studies: A Report* (June 1973), pp. 62–3; DOE, *The Channel Tunnel*, September 1973, pp. 12–14.

Table 5.2 Channel Tunnel, 1973: cost-benefit analysis for the United Kingdom (£m.)

	Costs (−) and benefits (+) in 1973 prices discounted at 10%	
	Low forecast	*Central forecast*
Capital: Tunnel	−158.4	−159.5
Rail	−98.5	−101.3
Total	−256.9	−260.8
Deducting capital costs avoided	+129.9	+156.1
= Net capital investment	−127.0	−104.7
User benefits and transport operators' net benefits/costs	+274.9	+396.5
NPV	+147.9	+291.8
Internal rate of return	14.6%[a]	17.6%[a]

Source: Coopers & Lybrand, *The Channel Tunnel: A United Kingdom transport cost benefit study* (June 1973), pp. 43–4, and DOE, *The Channel Tunnel*, September 1973, p. 16.

Note

a Earlier, provisional estimate (given to Pugh Committee): 14.4% and 17.4%.

but, following his DOE brief, stated that he was not sure when exactly his Government would be able to make its decision. He added as an aside that personally he favoured a bridge, since this would have allowed him to drive over to France for dinner, although he accepted that experts had now ruled out this option. The acceptance that there was a commitment to decide the matter by the end of July was repeated in a television interview with Heath immediately after the meeting.[33] This was not all. The Commons was due to debate the Green Paper

Table 5.3 Traffic forecasts, 1973, compared with those in 1963 and 1966

Traffic	*Lower estimate: 1973 White paper*		*Comparison with lower estimate: 1963 White paper*		*1966 Report*		*Central estimate: 1973 White paper*		*Comparison with upper estimate: 1963 White paper*		*1966 Report*	
	1980	*1990*	*1980*	*1990*	*1980*	*1990*	*1980*	*1990*	*1980*	*1990*	*1980*	*1990*
Passengers with vehicles ('000s)												
Leisure	5,368	10,074					5,987	13,164				
Business	461	930					557	1,364				
Total	5,829	11,004	2,600[a]	2,900[a]	5,700[a]	6,600[a]	6,544	14,528	3,800[a]	4,200[a]	7,600[a]	9,300[a]
Classic passengers ('000s)												
Leisure	6,897	10,496					7,255	11,889				
Business	1,865	2,683					2,048	3,099				
Total	8,762	13,179	3,000	3,040	3,230	3,490	9,303	14,988	3,700	3,800	3,810	4,180
Total passengers ('000s)	14,591	24,183	5,600[a]	5,940[a]	8,930[a]	10,090[a]	15,847	29,516	7,500[a]	8,000[a]	11,410[a]	13,480[a]
Freight ('000 tons)	4,660	8,220	3,000	3,400	5,200	7,550	5,407	11,269	4,000	4,500	6,010	9,570

Source: DOE, *The Channel Tunnel*, September 1973, p. 49; MT, *Proposal for a Fixed Channel Link*, September 1963, MT, Joint Report, August 1966, PREM13/1244, PRO.

Note

a Estimate based on 3.0 passengers per vehicle, est. rounded to nearest 100,000. Passenger:vehicle-unit ratio derived from data in BCTC AND SFTM, Channel Tunnel. Economic Report, June 1973, Part 1 (Main Summary), p. 35, MT179/28, PRO.

in mid-June, when Peyton would be required to make a statement to the House on the latest findings. Officials serving on Pugh's Interdepartmental Committee were therefore placed under intense pressure to produce a report to ministers within an extremely compressed timescale. On 21 May the Committee received a progress report on economic viability, and two days later the provisional results of the UK cost-benefit study were made available. By the end of the month a first draft of the officials' report had been prepared, and this was reworked at subsequent meetings, in time for the meeting of the Cabinet EPC on 11 June.

The drafting of the report, which in its final form ran to 41 pages plus 8 annexes, was not an easy exercise. The Treasury expressed doubts about DOE enthusiasm for the Tunnel. Tony Phelps challenged the document's 'flavour of commitment'. He preferred an 'agnostic' report, which would avoid making specific recommendations to ministers. Yet he was also anxious to see clear references to 'areas of substantial uncertainty particularly where the outcome might be less rather than more favourable'.[34] Such sentiments were a reflection of the continuing scepticism in some quarters about the project. Indeed, only a few months earlier, there had been talk in the Treasury of mounting an 'attack' on the Tunnel with the specific intention of bringing about its cancellation or deferment.[35] Critics had also been worried that Pugh's DOE-dominated Committee, which had been established thanks to the Treasury's insistence on taking a long, hard look at the project, would evolve into a body closely associated with the case for going ahead. They found some evidence for this in the fact that DOE officials tended to regard the companies' estimates as unduly cautious. But the main concern was with the wide margins of uncertainty in the calculations and the fact that evaluation of the data had had to be 'incredibly rushed and incomplete'.[36] In these circumstances, political considerations tended to mask the purely economic. With a strongly pro-European Prime Minister and a Transport Minister who had become an enthusiastic tunneller, the doubters faced some difficulty in applying the brakes. And the study results analysed in the Pugh Report, whether fragile or not, were more optimistic than the interim data in 1972 (Table 4.2). According to the central forecast, which applied OECD growth estimates, the cross-channel passenger market would double between 1971 and 1980 and double again in the following decade, by which time Tunnel traffic would reach 30 million passengers (1990). About 50 per cent of this traffic would be in the form of persons travelling with their vehicles. Eleven million tons of freight would be carried by 1990, 60 per cent of it on through rail services. Tourist traffic would account for two-thirds of Tunnel revenue, which was expected to grow rapidly, trebling in the period 1981–90. The central forecast put the financial return at 16.5 per cent, while the lower-bound estimate, derived from the companies' more cautious estimate of growth (OECD–20 per cent), amounted to 14.5 per cent. The UK cost-benefit exercise indicated returns of 17.4 per cent (central) and 14.4 per cent (low) respectively. These figures were confirmed, with minor adjustments, in the final documentation, published in June, and repeated in the September White Paper (Tables 5.1–5.3).[37]

2. Drafting 'Agreement No.2': initial problems, March–June 1973

Positive study results were necessary for the project to progress, but were of course insufficient in themselves. The finalisation of the arrangements with the private sector was the critical factor, and thus the drafting of Agreement No.2 and the Treaty, together with the resolution of the protracted negotiation of the financial terms, remained significant hurdles. In March 1973 the companies presented, as agreed, a draft of Agreement No.2. Its joint examination by British and French officials inevitably produced some tense exchanges, notably with the volatile Macé, and a long list of detailed points (initially over sixty). Among the more substantive of these was the need to specify the nature of the operating authority, and to ensure that the wording of the Agreement squared with intended government commitments.[38] In April Melville and Kemp began work on the Treaty in earnest. They were assisted by Sir James McPetrie, formerly legal adviser at the Foreign and Commonwealth Office, who had joined the team in 1972.[39] Kemp informed the Pugh Committee that three principal difficulties had emerged. Two were familiar: the structure of the operating authority, and the terms of abandonment. The third related to the executive status of the Treaty.[40]

The British Government and the private companies wanted the operating authority to be a single entity with dual nationality. The French, on the other hand, argued that there would be legal complications with this arrangement. Instead they advocated a 'pyramid' structure, comprising a joint body for decision-making, with separately-constituted British and French executive arms. A third suggestion, proposed by British officials, was the so-called 'mirror-image' solution, where national bodies would have separate identities but a common membership.[41] The provision for cost-sharing in the event of abandonment during Phase I of the project had been set out in an exchange of notes in October 1972, in which the two governments agreed to share any liabilities on a 50–50 basis irrespective of which party had initiated the process. There was a strong preference by the British for applying this formula to liabilities in the subsequent phases, but the French, clearly distrustful of British intentions, were not keen to do so, particularly where one government took unilateral action to withdraw. For this eventuality other options were considered, in which the defaulting government would bear a greater share of the costs. When members of the Cabinet EPC were informed of the debate, the Treasury expressed a strong preference for the 50–50 arrangement. It was agreed that EPC would be consulted if an alternative formula were negotiated.[42] With the Treaty, the two governments could not agree initially on what its precise function should be. The British envisaged that it would give effect to the Agreements and regulate matters not covered in these documents. The French, on the other hand regarded the Treaty as the definitive instrument for proceeding with the project. The British Government was keen to stress the primacy of the Agreements and to avoid any Treaty commitment reminiscent of the Concorde experience.[43] Difficult as these matters were, Peyton and Billecocq made a genuine effort to resolve them when they met for the first time in Paris on

17 May. Both were anxious to reassure the other that they were working on the same lines. They agreed to adopt a compromise solution for the operating authority. There would be two separate executive bodies, one British and one French, but the membership of each would convene as a single and supreme international authority. On the other matters, the French gave ground. In all cases of abandonment, the 50–50 principle would be applied to government liabilities. It was also agreed that the Treaty should reflect the fact that the project would proceed on the basis of the Agreements with the companies and that if these arrangements were abandoned, then the Treaty would lapse. The Interdepartmental Committee was informed that these outcomes from a cordial Anglo-French meeting were 'extremely satisfactory'.[44]

With little now standing in the way of a decision on the Tunnel, it only remained for the companies to submit their financial proposals. The critical element here was the extent to which their risk capital would be remunerated, which, in turn, reflected their view of the extent of the risk-sharing between the private and the public sectors. The remuneration formula, which had been discussed at some length in earlier negotiations, was to be based on a proportion of gross receipts ('*x*') and a proportion of net receipts ('*y*'). In addition, private money raised in Phase II was to be rewarded with a multiplier element ('*n*'). In earlier talks precision had been avoided, but now the companies were armed with the study results, though there was some suspicion within government circles that this information, and in particular, estimates of revenue growth, might be manipulated to the private sector's advantage.[45] As required, the companies submitted their proposals to the two governments on 7 June, and four days later the project was discussed at the Cabinet EPC, where ministers received a report from the Pugh Committee on the study results, together with an independent assessment from the Central Policy Review Staff. There were also memoranda from Peyton on the issues for decision, and from Lady Tweedsmuir, Minister of State for Foreign and Commonwealth Affairs, on the implications for Anglo-French relations. Peyton informed ministers that the time had come to make the 'substantive decision' on whether or not to proceed with construction. The studies appeared to give 'a reasonable assurance' about profitability and the benefit to the United Kingdom, though the Pugh report did not address the 'wider political issues which my colleagues may well consider to be, in the end, the determining factors'. For his part the Minister was convinced that the Government should go ahead with the tunnel and that a publicly-funded high-speed rail link was an integral part of the project. However, a decision could not be made at this stage. There had been no time to evaluate the companies' suggested remuneration package, but in any case, preliminary indications were that their proposals would be unacceptable to the two governments in their present form (see below) and that therefore the timetable would slip. This 'hurdle' in turn produced another, more immediate, concern: what Peyton should reveal in the Commons when the Green Paper was debated on 15 June.[46] The long Pugh report, with its mass of statistical information, did not receive a detailed examination in the Committee.[47] Neither did the paper from

Tweedsmuir, which repeated familiar Foreign Office concerns that Britain's wider interests with Europe and France were relevant when discussing major projects,[48] nor the limited, equivocal report from the CPRS, which endeavoured to pour cold water on the study results.[49] Some negative views did surface, for example, about the Tunnel's reliance on tourist traffic, and the opinion of Hambros that much higher returns would be needed if the project were to be funded entirely by the private sector was also picked up.[50] But the main focus of the discussion was upon parliamentary tactics given the compressed timetable. Peyton's intention to publish a White Paper in July and secure the second reading of a Money Bill before the summer recess was ruled out on the grounds that the Government would be heavily criticised for pre-empting public debate. The Minister was therefore advised to adopt as 'neutral a stance as possible' in the forthcoming debate and make no commitments before the summer recess.[51] A straight bat was duly played in the Commons in June. Peyton referred to the broadly encouraging results of the studies but little else. Anthony Crosland, replying for the Opposition, welcomed the fact that more time would be taken to consider the project. Impressed by the prima facie case for commercial viability, he was more favourably disposed to the Tunnel than to Maplin Airport. However, more information would need to be assessed, and consequently he was only 'halfway along the road to Damascus'. Indeed, the rather desultory debate that followed was clearly influenced by the fact that much of the voluminous study material had only just become available to members. In general, the Tunnel was considered to be an economic asset, but there were demands for sufficient time to debate it, and anxieties about specific aspects.[52]

3. The 'remuneration formula', June–July 1973: the timetable slips

In anticipation of the companies' terms, Hambros had already undertaken some preparatory analysis on financial viability, indicating the rate of return which investors might expect from a project of this kind. Its view was that a fair return would be 14 per cent before tax in the first year of operation, 1981. This implied a requirement of 10 per cent share of gross revenue ('*x*') and 5 per cent of net revenue ('*y*'). However, there were complications. Informal contact with the companies had suggested that their proposals would fix '*x*' and '*y*' at 30 and 10 per cent respectively. While British officials had fully expected the companies to submit excessive rates in the first instance, values of this magnitude came as something of a surprise. Melville noted that if this was 'even approximately what the market needs, then the viability of the project on the present financing plan must be in doubt'.[53] In fact, the companies' proposals of 7 June referred to an '*x*' element of 32 per cent (contributing 98 per cent of their total remuneration over the first five years) and a '*y*' element of 10 per cent, to service a share capital of £106 million. The companies also proposed that the multiplier for Phase II shares be 1.8, and that if additional risk capital were raised, then '*y*' should be increased on a straight-line basis such that by raising 30 per cent in risk capital the companies would take 90 per cent of the net revenue.[54]

The initial reaction of British officials, who with their French colleagues had a month to frame a response, was sceptical. Within the CTSU Kemp felt that either what the companies wanted was justifiable, in which case the project could not proceed, or 'they are trying something on to an unacceptable degree'.[55] More detailed deliberations, including a further assessment by Hambros and advice from the stockbrokers Rowe and Pitman, did nothing to dispel concerns. The proposed '*x*' and '*y*' formula would give investors a gross return of about 34 per cent, far in excess of what was considered reasonable and three times higher than the figure of 12 per cent envisaged in the 1971 Heads of Terms (see above, pp. 83, 91). Furthermore, the formula would produce an opening yield of 18 per cent, rising to 46 per cent in 1985 and 72 per cent in 1990, but the two governments would receive no return before 1985 and only a third of the profits in 1990 (Table 5.4). It should also be emphasised that these calculations were based on the companies' more pessimistic assessment of future economic growth.[56] While the values of '*x*' and '*y*' were foremost in the debate, other elements of the companies' proposals were also unpalatable. British officials challenged the suggested multiplier of 1.8; their own calculations had led them to a figure of 1.2. There was also some disquiet at the companies' suggestion that the interim rate of interest payable to shareholders during the construction period should be 7 per cent instead of the 6 per cent referred to earlier, though Rowe & Pitman thought the figure 'reasonable'.[57]

The British and French Transport Ministers were due to meet in London on 3 July to agree a response. Peyton, preparing the ground, told Billecocq that the companies' proposals were 'quite unacceptable' and 'not even a basis for negotiation'. The two quickly agreed that the companies should be asked to explain the basis for their scheme.[58] Early indications from Paris were that an acceptable return would be about half of the 34 per cent demanded. However, the interest of French officials in '*x*' and '*y*' was primarily in setting conditions which would encourage capital to be raised, rather than in producing equitable profit-sharing arrangements between the private and public sectors. This view had some weight given that a substantial part of the French 'private group' was in fact made up of nationalised bodies.[59] When officials met company representatives in Paris on the familiar quadripartite basis to discuss the proposals, it emerged that the methodological approach of the British and French companies was quite different. The BCTC had analysed the market in much the same way as Hambros and concluded initially that '*x*' should be 25 per cent and '*y*' 10 per cent. On the other hand, SFTM insisted that '*x*' must be 32 per cent, although they conceded that the figure was 'largely intuitive'. Both companies accepted that high profits in later years might tempt the governments to consider nationalisation, and they offered the suggestion that '*x*' and '*y*' might be tapered in some way to prevent their share of profits from becoming too great.[60] But with French officials showing no sign of resisting '*x*' at 32, the outlook remained bleak. Nor was it improved when John Page, Chief Cashier at the Bank of England, provided the Bank's views on the

Table 5.4 Suggested remuneration proposals (based on lower growth estimate), July 1973

		1981	*1985*	*1990*
Companies' proposal	Companies' return %	18	43[a]	72
$x = 32, y = 10$	Profit shares:			
	Companies	100%	84%	66%
	Governments	nil	16%	34%
Governments' offer	Companies' return %	7	10	18
$x = 8.0, y = 2.6$	Profit shares:			
	Companies	38%	20%	17%
	Governments	62%	80%	83%
Proposal with government dividend in 1981	Companies' return %	15	21	37
$x = 15.1, y = 7.1$	Profit shares:			
	Companies	86%	41%	34%
	Governments	14%	59%	66%

Source: Melville-Peyton, 2 July 1973, MT144/272, PRO. Data rounded to nearest whole number.

Note

a Figure shown as 46% in earlier calculations.

advice received from Hambros. While endorsing that advice, he added the observation that the Bank had 'always doubted the wisdom of seeking private risk capital for the Tunnel' and suggested that the possibility of removing equity participation from British financing should be carefully considered.[61]

When the Cabinet EPC resumed its consideration of the Tunnel on 28 June, Peyton provided ministers with details of the financial negotiations. He informed the Committee that the returns envisaged by the companies (see Table 5.4) were 'at least twice what should be needed to sell the shares in the British market', and that the proposed division of profits was 'indefensible'. Since the companies would also receive about £4.5 million in bonus shares and obtain commissions for issuing the shares and bonds, the package was 'quite unacceptable'. Ministers supported this assessment. Until a satisfactory formula was agreed, the Government could not make a public commitment to proceed. Another complication was the prospective rail link to London. Peyton repeated his view that 'a high quality rail link to London should be provided from the start'. Drawing on the Pugh Report, he told ministers that the low-cost option, costing about £40 million, would involve running the Tunnel traffic on the existing lines of British Rail's Southern Region. However, this would put commuter services at risk and seriously hobble the continental services. The only practicable alternative was a new line, built to continental loading gauge, which, according to a British Rail estimate, would cost about £120 million. The overall economic benefits of the Tunnel scheme would be greater if the rail link were included at the outset, and the rail investment alone was expected to produce a financial return of 17 per cent. The Committee, supporting the Minister, noted a growing public concern about the under-utilisation of the railways and believed that an effective link between the Tunnel and the rest of the rail network would do much to secure support for the project. However, as we have already observed, by no means all of Peyton's colleagues shared his evident enthusiasm. Some familiar concerns were aired, notably about skewed economic benefits, the impact on public expenditure, and regional opposition, and it was minuted that in Scotland the Tunnel 'would be seen as another massive injection of capital into the most favoured quarter of the country'.[62] On top of this, there remained the pressing, and at times confusing, matter of the timetable for decision-making. After the EPC had advised Peyton to be non-committal in the Commons debate, he had been encouraged by Heath and Prior to be more forthcoming about the Money Bill. Consequently, during the debate he had announced that in the event of a favourable decision a Bill would be introduced by the end of July.[63] On his return to EPC on 28 June the Minister asked once again for agreement to the publication of a White Paper and Bill in July if circumstances allowed. All this was baffling to the Treasury, where officials had assumed that ministers were moving towards a postponement of the decision until the autumn.[64] In the circumstances the EPC resolved that the Cabinet should be invited to examine the issues involved at the earliest opportunity.[65]

Peyton and Billecocq met in London on 3 July with the aim of producing an agreed response to the companies. The intention was to select values of '*x*' and '*y*' which would satisfy all requirements: they would enable the private sector to raise the equity capital; provide the two governments with profits from the first full year of operation; and prevent the companies from making excess profits in later years. Hard bargaining was required. The governments would have to 'beat the Companies down' to something more acceptable, and Kemp observed that 'if we are all going to play at being in the Egyptian market place, we might as well start at 10/5'.[66] In fact, Hambros' advice was that the two governments should make a counter offer of '*x*' = 7.6 and '*y*' = 2.6, with interest of 7 per cent paid during construction. Their suggested fall-back position was '*x*' = 12 and '*y*' = 5. Both sets of values would produce a significant share of Tunnel profits for the governments. In fact, the highest values of '*x*' and '*y*' which would ensure that the governments received *some* profit in the first year of operation were 15.1 and 7.1 per cent (Table 5.4). Hambros' negotiating strategy was endorsed by both the Treasury and the Bank of England, and Peyton was briefed to start with 8.0 and 2.6, with interest at 6 per cent.[67] At the London meeting, Billecocq began by stating that he felt '*x*' = 12 and 'y' = 4 'might be reasonable', with interest at 7 per cent. However, he quickly agreed that negotiations should start at the lower British figures, with a multiplier of 1.2, and this information was passed to the companies on 5 July. In these circumstances, Peyton's view was that it would not be possible to sign Agreement No.2 and the Treaty by the end of the month, as originally intended. However, he was eager to reassure the French Minister that the British were becoming more enthusiastic about the project and that the delay could be managed successfully. Billecocq's response was non-committal.[68]

Two days later, on 5 July, the Cabinet discussed the project. The only new element in a DOE memorandum rehearsing the now familiar arguments about pros and cons was the assertion that 'The full benefits of the Tunnel are only obtainable if a new high-quality rail link is provided'.[69] Peyton informed the Cabinet about the state of the financial negotiations, adding further information about procedure and presentation. He reaffirmed his intention to publish a White Paper before the recess and to secure the Money Bill before the end of the session. Familiar tenets of opposition re-emerged (dependence on tourist traffic, Scottish opposition, etc.), but Heath threw his weight behind letting the project proceed to the next stage on acceptable financial terms. And, accepting the argument that the transport effects of the Tunnel should be more widely diffused, the Cabinet also agreed that a high-quality rail link should be provided as an integral part of the project. Although a White Paper could not be published until the terms were settled, the Cabinet felt there was advantage in publishing in July if at all possible, and it asked for a draft to be circulated in order to facilitate this remote prospect.[70] A fortnight later the prospects had become gloomier. Peyton told Heath that 'some distance' still separated the Governments and the private companies, and it was therefore certain that agreement would not be reached in time to make a decision and announcement before the House rose. It looked increasingly likely that the White Paper would have to be published during the recess, and Peyton proposed making a holding statement to this effect.[71] Prior, the Lord President, who had been anxious about the project throughout the period, expressed characteristic unease that publication immediately after the House had risen might be interpreted as a deliberate attempt to stifle debate.[72] However, as Peyton emphasised, once financial terms were settled then it would be difficult to prevent them from becoming public. There was no alternative but for Peyton to play another straight bat in the Commons. Here, on 24 July, he stated that the Government was not yet in a position to make an announcement, but assured members that he would make one as soon as a decision had been reached.[73] On 26 July the Cabinet returned to the subject, this time to consider a draft of the White Paper, minus the section on financial arrangements. Once again misgivings surfaced, given additional impetus by an intervention from the UK Chamber of Shipping, which had challenged the conclusions of Coopers' cost-benefit study.[74] Nevertheless, as Heath reminded his colleagues, the Cabinet had already decided to allow the project to proceed to the next stage, and the emphasis should be on reassuring public opinion by presenting the case for the Tunnel with conviction. It was agreed that negotiations with the French Government and the companies should continue. The Lord President and relevant ministers, and notably the Treasury Chief Secretary, were asked to examine the text of the White Paper and arrange for publication as soon as practicable. But there was no escaping the fact that the timetable had slipped badly. Agreement No.2 had not been signed, the financial impasse had not been resolved, and the parliamentary process had not begun.[75]

4. Breaking the deadlock, July–September 1973

The reaction of the companies to the Governments' counter-proposal was far from encouraging. At a British meeting on 10 July, intended to allow the respective professional advisers to 'confront' each other, Harcourt told Peyton that the two companies were united in their rejection of the figures (lower GDP growth; 6 per cent interest; '*x*' = 8; '*y*' = 2.6; '*n*' = 1.2), which were 'totally unacceptable'. On these terms the companies would be unable to raise any equity, even with the most optimistic view of the market. Furthermore, the offered rate of return was lower than that envisaged in the Heads of Terms, when there were good arguments for raising it to take account of depressed market conditions, higher inflation, and the doubling of risk capital.[76] A quadripartite meeting at Lancaster House on 31 July, with both Ministers present, ended with strong words from Billecocq, who warned the companies that their continuing intransigence might well encourage the French Government to 'carry the project forward by other means'.[77] When Harcourt saw Peyton privately on 2 August, he expressed his disappointment with the outcome of the Lancaster House meeting, and reported that the RTZ project management team were 'becoming very unsettled' as a result of the failure to agree terms. Peyton conceded that 'if there was no agreement then the project seemed to be very near the point of breakdown'.[78]

In fact, considerable ingenuity was required to break the deadlock. It became increasingly evident that the apparently simple '*x*' and '*y*' formula was too crude to reconcile the competing objectives of the companies and the Governments.[79] The initial response of the companies had been to reduce '*x*' and '*y*' to 25 and 10, and incorporate a long taper for '*x*' from 1986, such that by 2000 the values would be reduced to 15 and 5. Their more considered reply suggested setting '*x*' and '*y*' at 25 and 10 until a specified cumulative return (23 per cent before tax) had been received. Thereafter, profits derived from 'x' would be limited to a fixed element, 25 per cent of gross revenue in the year in which the return was achieved, plus a proportion of the additional revenue earned. The alteration was designed to address the Governments' concern about high returns in later years, but the companies saw no justification for the demand that the Governments should receive a remuneration from the first year of operation.[80]

However, officials in both London and Paris were sceptical about the use of tapers, since these devices were invariably complex and might deter investors. On the other hand, the possibility of introducing some form of fixed element appeared more attractive. Dennis Cross of Hambros had initially floated the idea of adding an extra component, fixed in money terms, into the remuneration formula, and this idea quickly gained the acceptance of Peyton and Jenkin. Under this model, a relatively high fixed element – '*f*' – based on initial share value, would be paid to the companies each year, together with smaller amounts based on the '*x*' and '*y*' variables. The fixed component had the advantage of reducing the reliance on unpredictable factors and limiting the growth in the overall return on shares.[81] By mid-July the two Governments, at least, had reached a common understanding on the remuneration formula, although, as Melville conceded to Pugh, 'there is still some head bashing to be done on the Companies'.[82] British officials thought that acceptable values, based on the central growth forecasts and a risk capital of £104 million, might be as follows: '*f*' = 8½ per cent on the issue price, that is, £12.5 million; 'x' = 6.6 and 'y' = 3.0. This would give the companies 52 per cent of net revenue in 1981, but by 1990 the amount would fall to 18 per cent.[83]

Of course, for negotiating purposes these figures were pared down, and when Melville and Macé presented official notes to BCTC and SFTM, the companies were offered a fixed sum of £10.6 million ['f' = $7\frac{1}{4}$per cent], with 'x' at 5.5 and 'y' at 2.6.[84] The quadripartite meeting on 31 July was able to agree on the use of a three-part formula to achieve an initial dividend for shareholders – 22.4 per cent gross (SFTM), or 16 per cent net (BCTC) – and an acceptable real rate of growth – 3 per cent per annum. Although the exact figures were to be determined in 1975, in order to place the Phase II shares and as a necessary reference point, it was necessary to define 'f', 'x' and 'y' against an identified case. But in order to do so the parties had to agree on the most appropriate traffic and revenue projections, and here, as we have seen, there was a fundamental disagreement. The companies were adamant that the 'lower case' or 'most expected' data should be used. However, the formula which met the objectives under this case would give them too much under the 'central case' preferred by the two Governments. The latter would experience severe embarrassment if, were they to accept the lower estimates, actual revenues were closer to the higher estimates. And, in any case, if the project were to be defended satisfactorily in the British parliament and elsewhere, the higher estimates would be required.[85] It was the failure to agree on this fundamental point that explained the disappointing end to the meeting and Billecocq's outburst (see above, p. 123), but as so often with Channel Tunnel finance, an evident collapse in the negotiations was quickly followed by a compromise. Two days later in Paris, and after making various suggestions, involving the design of alternative reference cases and the setting of bands for 'f', 'x' and 'y', the two sides finally took refuge in an arithmetic average of the low and central forecasts.[86] Other outstanding matters, for example the size of the multiplier ('n') and the level of issuing fees, had also to be settled, but Melville doubted whether any of these would prove to be 'wreckers'.[87]

The intention was that a final round of negotiations at the end of August would resolve the financing issue in time for members of the Cabinet to endorse the project in the first week of September. Attempts by the French company, SFTM, to introduce an elaborate modification to the remuneration formula by setting a minimum 'floor' were rebutted by the British side, although as a concession the Governments agreed that the 'f' element should be adjusted in 1980 to take account of inflation during the construction period.[88] With a substantial measure of agreement now evident, Peyton presented the financial proposals to Cabinet members meeting as an ad hoc group on 5 September. Having explained that the negotiations had been 'arduous and complex', he set out the proposed terms to be used as the template for final settlement in 1975. With an opening shareholders' return of 16 per cent net in 1980, the values of 'f', 'x', and 'y' were provisionally set at 11.0 (7.8 after Corporation tax), 8.7 and 3.0 (Table 5.5). Interim interest would be paid at 7 per cent, and the hotly-contested multiplier, for shares raised to 1975, would be based on a compromise involving a sliding scale from 1.4 to 1.2, the actual value dependent on when the money was subscribed.[89] Melville's 'Score Card' on the negotiations outlined the satisfactory outcome for the Governments, who now expected to receive an adequate share of the profits: taking the pessimistic estimate, 19 per cent in 1981, rising to 75 per cent by 1990; with the central estimate, 44 per cent, rising to 79 per cent (see Table 5.5).[90] Although the question of issuing fees remained outstanding, Cabinet members were happy to approve the proposals, and Peyton was 'warmly congratulated' by Heath for his efforts. An amended text of the White Paper, declared to be 'sober and workmanlike', was cleared for publication on 12 September.[91] The final consideration was to manage the project in conjunction with that for Maplin Airport, which as we have seen, was also a parliamentary matter. MPs had already expressed concerns that the cost of the two projects would place an excessive strain on public expenditure, and the Maplin Development Bill experienced a rough passage at the committee stage and on its third reading in June.[92] However, the main problem was that owing to the difficulty in relocating the defence establishment at Shoeburyness the airport would not be ready to open in 1980. Ministers were worried that if they announced a delay to Maplin, which would ease the pressure on public expenditure, it would encourage accusations that the Tunnel was being given priority over the airport and encourage opponents to press for the abandonment of either or both projects. In the event, it was decided that an announcement about Maplin would be made on the same day as the Channel Tunnel White Paper was published.[93] On 12 September Peyton duly announced the Government's decision that the Tunnel would be built and the White Paper was published. Later that day, on a visit to Newcastle, Environment Secretary Geoffrey Rippon made a statement concerning the Tunnel and national resources in which he confirmed that it would not be possible to open Maplin Airport before 1982.[94] Meanwhile in Paris, Billecocq enthused that the 'project of the century' was now close to a 'practically certain send-off'.[95]

The long-awaited White Paper announced that Phase I had been completed under budget.[96] In 75 pages it set out the justification for the Government's view that a tunnel was in the public interest, being the 'cheapest and most satisfactory way' to cater for the 'dramatic' increase in cross-channel traffic. There was a soothing emphasis on taking freight off the roads and providing wider, regional benefits, and it was pointed out that full exploitation depended on a high-quality rail link to London, expected to cost £120 million in 1973 prices. There would also be a train ferry service between Cheriton and Fréthun, linking into the motorway system. The arguments in favour were supported by chapters dealing with technical feasibility, safety and cost, profitability, cost-benefit, environmental and regional implications, finance and organisation, plus annexes providing salient material from the Phase I studies, including detailed traffic forecasts (summarised in Table 5.3).[97]

The delay in producing the White Paper truncated the time available for debate before the Government introduced its Money Bill, on 31 October, and therefore

Table 5.5 Agreed remuneration package, September 1973, compared with the companies' original proposal

		With lower growth estimate			*With central estimate*		
		1981	*1985*	*1990*	*1981*	*1985*	*1990*
Companies' original proposal	Companies' return %	19	44	76	30	55	102
$x = 32$, $y = 10$	Profit shares:						
Interim interest 7%	Companies	100%	—	66%	100%	—	59%
	Governments	nil	—	34%	nil	—	41%
Agreed package							
$f = 7.8$ (11.0 before tax)	Companies' return %	15	20	29	17	23	36
$x = 8.7$	Profit shares:						
$y = 3.0$	Companies	81%	37%	25%	56%	30%	21%
Interim interest 7%	Governments	19%	63%	75%	44%	70%	79%
Payments	f	£10.99 m	£10.99 m	£10.99 m	£10.99 m	£10.99 m	£10.99 m
	x	£9.76 m	£14.80 m	£24.88 m	£11.15 m	£17.89 m	£32.31 m
	y	£0.80 m	£2.55 m	£4.86 m	£1.26 m	£3.26 m	£7.28 m

Source: Melville-Peyton, 5 September 1973, with supporting calculations, MT144/274, PRO.

Notes
x = % share of gross revenue.
y = % share of net revenue.
f = fixed payment.

provided an opportunity for opposition to the project to surface. Press opinion was mixed. The *Times*, a long-standing critic, thought the Paper only 'slightly less unsatisfactory' than previous statements and dismissed the project as a 'costly sunken car ferry'. However, leader columns in other papers, for example the *Daily Telegraph* and *Daily Mail*, were more enthusiastic, emphasising that the Tunnel would bring benefits to the country. There was little new argument.[98] The Channel Tunnel Opposition Association, which had been attacking the project for some time, went onto the offensive. A diverse but active body which included among its patrons Lord Brabourne, the film producer, and the Seamen's union MP, John Prescott, it published a number of hostile pamphlets with the help of Alan Cornish of Afco Associates.[99] A more authoritative threat to the project was provided by the *New Scientist*, which devoted 20 pages to a sceptical appraisal. In an article entitled 'Channel tunnel: bore of the century?', the periodical counselled caution, expressed anxieties about 'massive and unacceptable social costs', and poured cold water on the value of traffic and revenue forecasts. More significantly, it endorsed the argument raised by the Channel Tunnel Opposition Association, Peter Bromhead of Bristol University and opposition spokesman Tony Crosland, that a more environmentally-friendly, rail-only tunnel should be given serious evaluation. The piece, which concluded that several key questions had still to be answered, was considered sufficiently important to be passed to the Prime Minister.[100] Critics within Parliament had their chance when the White Paper was debated at the end of October. The five hours of discussion were dominated by an opposition amendment to the effect that the House,

> whilst not opposed in principle to a Channel Tunnel, declines to approve a 'rolling motorway' scheme which threatens both regional and environmental objectives, pre-empts scarce resources, lacks the support of a fully integrated transport strategy, and in its financial arrangements subordinates the interests of the taxpayer to those of private capital; and demands an independent inquiry into alternative transport strategies, including a rail-only tunnel.[101]

Certainly, the evidence suggests that several Labour front-benchers were hostile, including Tony Benn, Michael Foot and Peter Shore, and fears were expressed in Cabinet that the government might lose the vote.[102] But while Crosland was now apparently convinced that 'this tunnel is the wrong tunnel at the wrong place at the wrong time', he thought a fixed link would be necessary 'at some point', and gave the rail link his positive endorsement. And Eric Ogden, Labour MP for Liverpool (West Derby) and joint secretary of the all-party Channel Tunnel Group, swung the debate round when he attacked his party's amendment as 'ill-informed, illogical and appallingly pessimistic'. The Government then won the day by a surprisingly large margin – 250 votes to 181, thanks to the absence of several unpaired Labour members.[103]

5. Agreement and Treaty: 'devil in the detail', October–November 1973

Attention was now focussed on the final preparation of the Anglo-French Treaty and Agreement No.2, due for signature by 15 November. The first step was to secure the passage of the short 'money' Bill in order to obtain the financial authority for Stage II. The Channel Tunnel (Initial Finance) Bill, a draft of which was included in the White Paper, allowed the Government to guarantee loans of up to £30 million (with powers to raise to £35 million if required). Of course, if the French met their obligations, the net liability of the British Government would not exceed £17.5 million. The Bill was quickly enacted, receiving its first reading on 31 October and gaining Royal Assent on 13 November.[104] However, opposition to the project continued to surface, both at the committee stage and on second reading. Opposition spokesman Fred Mulley challenged the need for generous government guarantees, Roger Moate, MP for Faversham, demanded that there should be a public inquiry, and there was further sniping and nimbyism from such as Robert Sheldon (Ashton–under–Lyne), Sir Richard Thompson (Croydon, South), Frank Twomey (Hammersmith) and Renée Short (Wolverhampton, North-East). Their efforts were defeated, but the debates provided further evidence of the political hostility directed at large and complex projects in the UK.[105]

There were also associated matters to be handled: British Rail's provision of the rail link between London and the Tunnel portal (see Chapter 6); the project management contract between BCTC and RTZDE; and the issuing fees to be paid to the banks.[106] The second and third of these caused some anxiety. On the contract with RTZDE, we have already noted (above pp. 90, 103) that the negotiations over the project management fee were protracted. In October 1972 RTZDE were asking BCTC for £3.8 million as a fixed amount, plus £2.75 million as a variable, performance-related element. The French managers, SITUMER, were expected to receive £1.74 and £2.75 million, all in 1972 prices.[107] Both governments considered the fee structure proposed by RTZDE to be too high, and the difficulties were such that the DOE gave serious consideration to dumping RTZDE at the end of Phase I. On the other hand, the rather exceptional circumstances made it hard for officials to assess what a 'fair' fee should be.[108] After intensive negotiations in December 1972 the basis for an agreement was reached early in the following month. RTZDE accepted a reduction in the fixed fee – to £3 million – and payment of a higher, performance-related element of £3.25 million (if there was no overrun in construction costs), but in BCTC equity instead of cash.[109]

There was little satisfaction with the outcome. The Treasury, which had expressed considerable doubts about the deal, only gave it its blessing when Peyton said that otherwise the project would be compromised.[110] Further complications emerged over the course of 1973. The undertaking to adjust the payments for post-1972 inflation produced a considerable amount of squabbling over the methods of calculation, much of it directed at the variable fee, which was to be paid in shares. The project managers also demanded insulation from circumstances beyond their control. But the main difficulty was caused by the discovery that the proposed indexation would conflict with the Government's counter-inflation legislation, to be applied in November.[111] In these circumstances it was scarcely surprising that the British Government was unable to endorse a draft agreement until 17 November, the day on which the main documentation was signed (see below). This circumvented the Counter-Inflation Act by forecasting future inflation rates and referring only to cash sums.[112] Even then, this was not the end of the story, which proved once again that the devil was in the detail. All along, there had been problems in obtaining the agreement of the French to the proposed arrangement with RTZDE. Successive Transport Ministers expressed concerns. Galley wanted a greater proportion of the payment to be performance-related, and foresaw difficulties in paying the variable element in shares to SITUMER, which was expected to wind itself up after the construction period.[113] Billecocq, like his predecessor, was unhappy with the disparity in the fee structure, a departure from the 'moitié-moitié' principle. At the eleventh hour he rocked the boat by revealing that the French side proposed to strengthen its project management team by hiring Compagnie Génerale d'Électricité, indicating that this would lead to a demand for equality of fee payments. It was not until 1 February 1974 that he was able to express consent to the British contract, which was signed on the 5th.[114]

Government opposition to the private companies' demand that they should handle the share and bond issues had threatened the signature of Agreement No.1 (above p. 104). In negotiating Agreement No.2, there was now an argument over the level of fees that the companies' banking members should receive for this work. For Phase II issuing BCTC claimed that a reasonable figure was 4 per cent of the sums raised, while SFTM sought $4\frac{1}{2}$ per cent, the higher rate justified by the more difficult market conditions in France. Officials in both countries regarded these fees as too high when judged by ordinary standards, and the French Treasury proposed that the French rate should be reduced to four per cent.[115] The companies argued that there were good reasons for higher charges. For example, on the British side the fees would have to be shared by five banks rather than the single institution usually involved in an issue. The British banks also regarded the fees as a recompense for the substantial preparatory work and financial advice which they had provided in connexion with the Agreements. In September Cabinet members had hoped that the Governor of the Bank of England might bring pressure on the banks to be more accommodating, but wider consultations proved inconclusive. Both Hambros and the Bank of England elected to sit squarely on the fence. The Bank agreed that 'on a strict analysis' the fees were 'rather high', but its advice was that in the light of the project's special circumstances, it was for the Government to judge what might be considered reasonable. As Melville told Peyton, 'this passes the buck right back to us'.[116] This did not help the Minister, who, while sympathetic to the bankers' case, required a more positive statement from the Bank of England in order to defend any settlement in public. Asked to think again, the Bank relented, and after a meeting between Melville, William Merton (Robert Fleming & Co. and BCTC), and the Chief Cashier, Page, on 30 October, a solution was thrashed out. BCTC agreed to trim the fees and commission in Phase III, and the Governor of the Bank pronounced that given the fact that the issues had 'certain features peculiar to themselves' the revised fees were 'reasonable'.[117] The issuing fees were then set at 4 per cent for the Phase II and Phase III shares, and for the Phase III loan capital $1\frac{1}{2}$ per cent for an offer for sale or $\frac{1}{2}$ per cent for a placing, plus expenses. At the same time the French also settled for 4 per cent.[118]

The Treaty was finalised after a series of Anglo-French meetings. The final document, with its 18 articles, provided the basis for the two Governments to mutually ensure the construction, operation, maintenance and development of the Tunnel in accordance with the agreements with the tunnel companies, BCTC and SFTM. Their commitments also embraced the associated road and rail infrastructure in each country. As agreed in May, the Treaty established a Channel Tunnel Authority to undertake operating and management functions on a commercial basis. These functions were to be exercised through two, equally-constituted, national boards.[119] Provision was also made for a bi-national Consultative Committee and a Safety Commission. The frontier was set at the median line between the two coasts. The sharing of liabilities on a 50–50 basis was confirmed. The Treaty was subject to ratification in Paris, which would take place once the two governments had acquired the necessary parliamentary powers for the project. In the British case the instrument was the hybrid Channel Tunnel Bill.[120]

Agreement No.2, once again comprising parallel British and French agreements,[121] entrusted construction to the companies, who were to carry out the Phase II work, including about 3.5 kilometres of pilot tunnel, at an estimated cost of £30.8 million.[122] Of this sum £8 million was to be raised by the two companies as risk capital. The companies were also required to submit a draft of 'Agreement No.3' by 1 April 1975, and this final document was to be signed by 1 July 1975 (or later by agreement). Despite understandable anxieties over the numerous British and French drafts,[123] much of this 96-page document had been rehearsed many times and agreed months before, for example, on the details surrounding construction, the relationship between the private and public sectors, the management structure, safety specifications, and operation. However, the budget details and the provisional remuneration plan were subject to last-minute adjustments. Although Melville had announced in September that stumps had been drawn on the financing matter, play continued. There was a complication surrounding payment of the 7 per cent interest during construction under Section 65 of the 1948 Companies Act, and the formula was finally re-expressed in relation to a share issue price finally set at £1.15.[124] It was also evident that the provision for possible abandonment had been given much thought. Prominent in a long list of possible scenarios was the stipulation that the project would be regarded as having been abandoned if the Treaty had not been ratified before 1 January 1975.[125]

Thoughts now turned to the signature of the documents. Heath was keen that this should coincide with Pompidou's visit to Britain and suggested that a formal ceremony might be held in a suitable and historic place such as Dover Castle. However, Peyton pointed out that it would be best to avoid Dover since there might be only 'muted enthusiasm' in the town and an event there might be a focal point for opposition. His preference was for Lancaster House, because it could cater for a large attendance and in any case had important associations with the project. But this idea did not suit the arrangements for Pompidou's visit, and Lord Bridges, one of Heath's Private Secretaries, suggested that the Treaty might be signed at Chequers. Choice of venue aside, Prior was worried that presenting the signature as a major national occasion might prejudice the passage of the Initial Finance Bill. Heath's scheme received a further setback when it was realised, at a rather late stage, that protocol did not allow the French President to sign international treaties.[126] Unsurprisingly, given the tortuous history of the project, the final arrangements for the ceremony were a compromise. On the morning of 17 November, Peyton, Billecocq, Harcourt, and Maurin went to Lancaster House to sign British and French versions of Agreement No.2. They then travelled to Chequers to witness the British Foreign Secretary, Douglas-Home and the French Minister for Foreign Affairs, Michel Jobert, sign the Treaty in the presence of Heath and Pompidou. Upon reaching Chequers, the two Transport Ministers and the Chairmen of the private groups were required to wait for a lunch to finish, leaving Peyton to explain the 'tinkles of merry laughter' to the surprised Frenchmen and a furious Harcourt.[127]

Three days after the signing ceremonies, the hybrid Channel Tunnel Bill received its first reading in the Commons. The second reading followed two weeks later, on 5 December, after which the Bill was passed to a select committee for examination. The debate on second reading, introduced by Keith Speed, the Under-Secretary of State for the Environment, revealed little that was new. But economic storm clouds were gathering in the wake of the Yom Kippur War between Egypt, Syria and Israel. OPEC's 70 per cent increase in the oil price in mid-October, followed by a cutback in supplies, had already challenged the Government's attempts to curb inflation. The crisis, exacerbated by 'overheating' in the economy and industrial action in the electricity supply and coal industries, led to the declaration of a state of emergency on 13 November.[128] Some MPs were able to use the economic difficulties to raise doubts about the accuracy of the economic case for the Tunnel. Thus, Fred Mulley, replying for the opposition in Crosland's absence through ill-health, argued that higher inflation rates, the rise in oil prices and the prospect of lower economic growth raised doubts about the validity of the calculations. He also publicised Alan Cornish's criticisms of the assumptions about train frequency built into the revenue forecasts. Similar anxieties were expressed by John Sutcliffe (Middlesbrough), Leslie Huckfield (Nuneaton), and Graham Tope (Sutton and Cheam), the latter moving a Liberal amendment to oppose the Bill. But hostility was counterbalanced by support. Speed's view that the oil crisis actually strengthened the case for the Tunnel was taken up by Albert Costain (Folkestone & Hythe), Sir Douglas Dodds-Parker (Cheltenham) and John Wells (Maidstone). And, in contrast to earlier reactions from north of the Border, both Alexander Fletcher, MP for Edinburgh (North), in a maiden speech, and Tam Dalyell (West Lothian) welcomed the Tunnel as beneficial to Scotland and regional development. Peyton, closing the debate, was in buoyant mood. He ignored the references to inflation and economic crisis, dismissed his critics with a flourish, and poked fun at Mulley and Huckfield on the opposition front bench and at the Liberals, including the heavyweight Cyril Smith. The amendment was defeated by 207 votes to 182, and the second reading was carried by 203 votes to 185.[129]

At the project level, the DOE reorganised its Channel Tunnel organisation to reflect entry to the next Phase. With the Treaty and Agreement signed, Melville retired, and Kemp moved to the Treasury. Shortly afterwards, the Channel Tunnel Study Unit dropped the word 'Study' from its name. Susan Fogarty, by this time clearly identifiable as one of the Tunnel's staunchest supporters, led the British officials in Phase II (1973–5), with a Deputy Secretary, Tom Shearer, holding a watching brief. Fogarty was supported by John Williams, an Assistant Secretary who came from the Northern Ireland Office, and by Harry Gould, as Superintending Engineer.[130] At the company level, no time was lost. On 19 November 1973 Harcourt and Frame of the BCTC entered into a £6 million contract with Cross-Channel Contractors (Guy Atkinson, Balfour Beatty, Edmund Nuttall and Taylor Woodrow) for the trial borings, and in France Maurin signed a similar contract with l'Entreprise Industrielle. The next day work began at the sites at Shakespeare Cliff and Sangatte.[131] However, progress was soon to be threatened by the wider economic and political events that hit Heath's Government during the early weeks of 1974, culminating in a general election on 28 February. The state of emergency continued into the New Year. The train drivers' union, ASLEF, began industrial action on 12 December, joining the miners and electricity workers in their attempt to break Stage 3 of the Counter-Inflation Policy. In order to conserve fuel supplies a three-day industrial week was announced on the following day, taking effect from 31 December in England and Wales, and from 7 January in Scotland. That was not the end of the misery. OPEC raised oil prices again on 1 January, the new price of crude per barrel – $11.65 – producing an increase of 287 per cent in only three months. With a full-scale coal strike looming – it began on 9 February – Cabinet members met on 5 February to discuss the crisis. Their deliberations, led by Lord Hailsham, the Lord Chancellor, and Heath, soon turned to the option of going to the country. Two days later the Prime Minister announced that a general election would be held on 28 February, on the issue 'Who Governs Britain?' One of the shortest parliaments of the twentieth century came abruptly to a close, with the Channel Tunnel Bill at the select committee stage, and the Treaty still to be ratified.[132]

6. Conclusion: 'Peyton's Tunnel'

Peyton had every reason to be satisfied with what he had achieved in his comparatively long period as Minister of Transport Industries. Sidestepping the numerous doubters, the Heath Government had taken up Labour's baton in 1970 and turned the Channel Tunnel into a tangible project on the brink of construction. The French under Pompidou had maintained their enthusiasm, and officials in both countries deserved credit for sustaining the project – in London, Melville, Kemp and Fogarty, in Paris, Macé and Callou. While many of Peyton's ministerial colleagues had reservations about the Tunnel, the project represented a groundbreaking attempt at public-private financing which some, and notably Patrick Jenkin, found fascinating.[133] However, both sides had their pessimistic moments. In Britain the strain of several years of complex negotiation with France and intense bargaining with the private sector interests left its mark. The major lesson to be drawn was that the private-public character of the existing scheme contained as many deficiencies as advantages. Officials were disappointed with the behaviour of the British private company in attempting to maximise profits while at the same time shifting most of the risk onto the taxpayer, something that has become a familiar complaint in more recent examples of 'public-private partnership'. The BCTC's insistence that its return on investment should be based on pessimistic assumptions about traffic growth was particularly exasperating, and in meeting after meeting, Harcourt, Frame and G.F. Naylor whittled away at the risk element.[134] By November 1973 it was being argued in Whitehall that although the original intention had been to maximise the private equity stake in the Tunnel, it was better to limit the private sector to the specified minimum of 10 per cent, since a higher level of participation would only serve to reduce the governments' share of the eventual profits.[135] However, such a stance was in itself risky, since by making the Tunnel more of a public sector undertaking, it would become vulnerable to the vicissitudes of the Government's macro-economic management.

The private sector's experience of Whitehall was equally frustrating. The difficulty in getting the two governments to pledge unequivocal support for the project tried the patience of businessmen used to a more straightforward environment. At times the civil servants made something of a meal of abstruse points of detail, their behaviour all the more galling to RTZ and the merchant banks when negotiations were still necessarily at a provisional stage. Treasury officials were guilty of sophistry when they poured cold water on the prospects of an adequate return on the project, then complained about the prospect of the private sector earning 'scandalously high profits'.[136] The private sector claimed that it required higher returns, first because it had borne substantial costs arising from the British Government's 'on-off', 'stop-go' attitude to the project since 1960, and second, because there was every reason to doubt the Government's ability to organise a commercial enterprise. Thus, the difficulty of progressing the project on terms acceptable to both the public and private sectors was a major lesson of the period 1970–4. It may be too much to assert, with Michael Bonavia, that the Tunnel was prejudiced from the moment it became a public-private partnership in 1966. But there is no escaping the fact that there were substantial problems connected with the 'tartan quilt' of 'quadripartite negotiations'.[137] The work of the Heath Government was important because it anticipated all the elements, both of principle and of detail, of Anglo-French tunnel-building. We have chronicled the numerous difficulties at this interface, which not only delayed progress but also gave opponents ample time to sharpen their knives. It was left to a Labour Government to take the difficult decisions in the heated circumstances of 1974–5.

6

ABANDONMENT, 1974–5

1. Political crisis and a new government, February 1974

Edward Heath's decision to fight an election in February 1974 on the issue 'Who Governs Britain?' was not, with hindsight, a success. The Conservatives' manifesto, 'Firm action for a fair Britain', had a rather hollow ring, and Labour fought a subdued campaign, its main pledge being to renegotiate the terms of Britain's membership of the European Community. The balance was probably tilted by Labour's promise to be more adept at handling the unions and industrial unrest, Enoch Powell's exhortation to vote Labour in order to get out of the European Community, and by the publication, three days before polling, of the largest ever recorded trade deficit (£383 million). There was a pervading air of disillusionment with the two main parties, and both lost ground. An extremely close contest produced the first inconclusive result since 1929. Labour secured 301 seats to the Conservatives' 297; the Liberals polled 19 per cent of the vote, and with 14 seats held the ring. When Heath failed to obtain Liberal support, it was Harold Wilson who accepted the task of presiding over a minority government.[1] In fact, winning the election was something of a poisoned chalice. As we have seen, the economic and political circumstances inherited from the Conservatives were very bleak indeed. Inflation and unemployment were soaring, public expenditure appeared to be out of control, there was a serious deficit in the balance of payments, and the industrial workforce was in a state of heightened tension following the three-day week and a coal strike. As the *National Institute Economic Review* observed, 'it is not often that a government finds itself confronted with a possibility of a simultaneous failure to achieve all four main policy objectives – of adequate economic growth, full employment, a satisfactory balance of payments and reasonably stable prices'.[2] There was therefore much to sort out, and it is unsurprising to find that the prevailing mood was one of profound caution rather than adventure, or that references to major projects such as the Tunnel, Maplin and Concorde, were limited. The Tunnel had not been mentioned in either of the main parties' election manifestos, although the Conservatives had made dark hints about not making promises 'beyond what the country can at present afford'. Hunt asserts that both the Labour and Liberal leaders made rude noises about the project in their electioneering.[3] However, the only published reference was in the Liberals' document, a wholly negative statement that it was 'not acceptable to press on with the £3,000 million projected expenditure on Concorde, Maplin and the Channel Tunnel simultaneously', accompanied by the rider that the Tunnel 'should be rail only, saving £240 million'.[4]

2. Wilson's government and the Tunnel, March–September 1974

Taking up the reins on 4 March, the third, and last, of Wilson's governments was extremely weak politically. Consequently, it was all the more essential to balance left and right in the new Cabinet. In positions of relevance to projects such as the Tunnel, the right wing was in the ascendant, with Denis Healey as Chancellor of the Exchequer, Tony Crosland as Secretary of State for the Environment, and Fred Mulley as Minister for Transport. However, this was no guarantee of support. And with leading left-wingers such as Michael Foot (Employment), Tony Benn (Industry) and Barbara Castle (Health & Social Security) in important positions, Wilson could not be as assertive as he had been in the 1960s. Rather, as he himself admitted, he took up the role of 'deep-lying centre-half... concentrating on defence'.[5] The new Government's main concern was to avoid rocking a leaky boat. As one historian has observed, 'issue after issue was delayed or diffused'.[6] In such difficult and distracting circumstances, the prospects for major projects were rather depressing, notwithstanding any existing contractual obligations entered into by the previous administration.

What, then, was done about the Tunnel? Of course, with a change of government it was likely that the incoming Cabinet would review its commitments, and the Tunnel was no exception. In the Queen's Speech of 12 March, it was announced that ministers, while working for the 'protection and improvement of the environment, including the improvement of public transport', would 'reappraise accordingly the value of certain major development projects'.[7] There then followed a flurry of activity, embracing discussions at three Cabinet meetings, and two Commons statements. Given the economic situation, probably 'the worst which had ever been faced in peacetime', the new Chancellor was naturally anxious to make 'appreciable' cuts in public expenditure. In a memorandum considered by the Cabinet on 14 March, Healey indicated that defence expenditure and Concorde were clearly in his sights. Indeed, he thought that Concorde should be cancelled. Maplin Airport and the Channel Tunnel were also within view, though here the immediate demands on expenditure were less pressing.[8] Nevertheless, the two projects were treated differently. Healey had already asked Crosland, on 13 March, to suspend all expenditure on Maplin, but while he also wanted the Tunnel to be included in his Budget statement, he conceded that in this instance the situation was 'more complex and a judgement finely balanced'.[9] The Cabinet then asked for more information to help it reach a position on the two projects.[10] It is clear from Crosland's reply to Healey on 15 March that both Crosland and

Peter Shore, the Secretary of State for Trade, had come to the conclusion that spending on Maplin should be halted, the intention being to abandon the project after a further review. On the Tunnel Crosland was more equivocal. He was minded to continue with Phase II, costing £30 million (£22 million of which was being guaranteed by the two governments). The substantive decisions would be taken in 1975.[11] Wilson was in no doubt about Maplin too, annotating Crosland's letter with the terse observation: 'Can we not be more negative more early?'[12] Crosland quickly made the decision to halt work on Maplin public by means of a written answer on 20 March, and it was followed by Shore's Commons statement the next day.[13] The scheme was eventually abandoned in July.[14]

The Channel Tunnel was subjected to further scrutiny by the Cabinet on 21 and 28 March. At the first of these meetings Crosland reaffirmed Labour's approach when in opposition. He was not hostile to the Tunnel as such. However, he was concerned about the existing scheme's emphasis on road transport with its 'rolling motorway' ferry services from the Cheriton terminal, and he preferred to see a stronger focus on through rail services. He was also anxious to examine the existing financial arrangements with the private sector. In proposing that Phase II should be allowed to continue, he argued that the review of traffic, revenue and financial arrangements, already provided for in the Phase II budget, should be enhanced. A more fundamental reappraisal would be undertaken, a task which would be delegated to Mulley. To cancel the project at the end of Phase II, he argued, would cost the Government little more than terminating it immediately – about £4.5–13.5 million. And, of course, there were political considerations. An abrupt decision 'would create a major crisis with the French Government at a time when we may want to keep our powder dry for a battle over Concorde'. British Rail's prospects would be adversely affected, and the rail unions would be 'bitterly angry'. Ideally he wanted more time to introduce legislation, but his hands were tied by Phase II. If the Treaty were not ratified by 1 January 1975, then the governments would be deemed to have abandoned the project unilaterally. He therefore proposed to introduce a Bill by May at the latest, and in the circumstances the best option was to reintroduce the Conservatives' hybrid Bill, which would also have the advantage of saving petitioners' costs.[15] Ministers also had before them a short comment by the CPRS. This supported Crosland's position, adding the observation that it would be 'inopportune' to annoy the French at a time when EEC renegotiations were about to start. However, as in the past (above, p. 118), the CPRS took a more hawkish line on the Tunnel. Because the project was so dependent on tourist traffic for the bulk (68 per cent) of its revenue, it was sensitive to shifts in holiday patterns and car use, elements which might change radically with the surge in oil prices. Alternative investments in ships, ports and aircraft could be introduced gradually as the traffic built up, and there was scope for 'substantial reductions' in fares, something which was about to be revealed in the Monopolies Commission's report on cross-channel ferries. Finally, the rail link, which would cost at least £120 million, would be a direct claim on public expenditure. The CPRS therefore wanted a more 'thorough and radical' review, and criticised the reliance on a single firm of consultants, Coopers & Lybrand, for the British study programme. Here, then, was the origin of the Cairncross review (see below, pp. 140, 175–85).[16]

Armed with this information, Ministers indulged in a fair amount of soul-searching. They repeated many of the objections raised by their Tory counterparts over the period 1970–4: the economic case had not been established; the regional benefits were questionable; and more productive investment should be given priority. There were those who were firmly in favour of immediate abandonment, among them Shore, Foot, Harold Lever, Robert Mellish and Willie Ross.[17] Others had qualms over particular aspects. Roy Jenkins, Barbara Castle and Reg Prentice expressed worries about road transport and the environment.[18] Jim Griffiths, the Welsh Secretary, was particularly concerned about Crosland's rather unwise statement that it would only be possible to make relatively minor modifications to the existing scheme. Healey was inclined to treat the project like Maplin and freeze the work on Phase II until the Government had the information to reach a decision. His own view was that it should be publicly financed. Wilson, summing up, observed that the arguments were evenly divided, and the Environment Secretary was asked to return with a further memorandum responding to the objections raised.[19] This he did on 28 March. He rejected the idea that the current work could be put into cold storage as Healey had suggested, since the option of proceeding would be closed off. But by continuing with Phase II all options would be left open for a decision in mid-1975, a situation differing significantly from that facing the Concorde project. He made soothing noises about the Government's ability to alter the Tunnel's road-rail balance, and promised to examine the work of the consultants with the help of 'an outside economist'. But the main thrust of his argument was that the Government could not do nothing: continental traffic was growing, and the investment to cater for it had to be made.[20] In debate some of Crosland's colleagues expressed the belief that if they allowed Phase II to continue the momentum for going beyond might be irresistible. But while a few more dissenting voices were raised, for example that of Fred Peart, there was more support for proceeding with Phase II, notably from Eric Varley and Shirley Williams.[21] Consequently, the Cabinet endorsed the Secretary of State's strategy, but the Tunnel would be 'subject to a most searching reappraisal of all aspects of the scheme'. Crosland, consulting with Healey and the CPRS, was to arrange for 'an independent outside assessment to be made of the assumptions and judgments put forward by the consultants to the project'. The Minister was also asked to ensure that the legislation provided for parliamentary approval of any further commitment to the project.[22] A Commons statement conveying the decision was made on 3 April, the day after the death of a leading tunnel enthusiast, President Georges Pompidou. Crosland told the House that the Government had decided to make a 'full and searching reassessment of the project', embracing railway-orientation, and an examination of 'alternative transport strategies'. However, he confirmed that Phase II would continue, and the Conservatives' Bill would be reintroduced. This course of action was welcomed from the opposition benches by the Shadow

Environment Secretary, Margaret Thatcher, who had set aside her earlier opposition (in 1971), and by John Peyton.[23]

The Channel Tunnel Bill was duly reintroduced, on 10 April 1974, and given a second reading on 30 April. It then entered the Select Committee stage in May, and was recommitted to Standing Committee in June. The initial expectation was that a third reading would be obtained by the time of the summer recess.[24] This was not to be, however. Although the parliamentary process was somewhat low-key, it could not be hurried. During the Second Reading, the fourth debate on the subject in 12 months, there were distinct signs of ennui. Mulley promised that a 'small high-powered group of independent advisers' would undertake the promised reassessment. Margaret Thatcher pledged the Opposition's support for the Bill, and was in no doubt that the Tunnel was 'one of the exciting big projects on the political agenda', though she was anxious to see that those affected by the works and the rail link should receive adequate compensation. Opponents expressed concern about escalating costs, yet sought to add to the process by raising environmental objections to the rail link and demanding additional tunnelling. Nevertheless, the Bill was given a comfortable passage, by a margin of 287 votes to 63.[25] The Select Committee, which was chaired by Dr Edmund Marshall and included bright newcomers such as Robin Cook and Peter Snape among its members, reported in June, with relatively minor concerns.[26] After the report stage, an amended Bill was produced on 23 July, just before the summer recess, but further progress was halted by the dissolution on 20 September of the shortest parliament since 1681. The Bill was suspended for a second time, and another general election was held on 10 October.[27]

Meanwhile, in the private sector the British and French companies issued their prospectuses and placed the Phase II equity. On 18 February 1974, in the middle of the election campaign, the BCTC published a prospectus for 3,652,174 'A' Ordinary £1 shares at £1.15. Construction was now estimated to cost £970 million instead of £846 million, owing to higher rates of inflation, and although there was some anxiety about the intentions of the new Government, the allotment process was successfully completed on 29 March. A total of 55 institutional investors, 40 of them from the City of London, took up the £4.2 million issue. The French company, SFTM, raised a similar amount.[28] The contractors began work on the sites at Shakespeare Cliff and Sangatte, in preparation for the driving of service tunnels. In Kent, the excavation of access tunnels began in March. At the project management level, RTZDE's responsibilities increased when it took over the management functions of BCTC, also in March. On the French side CGE-Développement, a subsidiary of Compagnie Générale d'Électricité, joined the French project management team in a lead capacity in April, though the contract was not formally approved until September, due to Anglo-French wrangling over the proposed remuneration.[29] Nevertheless, there were signs that relations between the British and French teams were improving thanks to the rapport between Alistair Frame and Jean Gabriel. And in construction terms there were evident signs of progress, not least the decision to shorten the alignment on the British side, and the procurement of tunnelling machines. In Britain a boring machine built by Robert L. Priestley of Gravesend was erected on site; in France, an American machine was preferred, built by Robbins of Seattle. However, the main thrust of Phase II, set out in a side letter of 17 November 1973, was to enhance the Tunnel design and to review the project's economics.[30]

At the same time, dealings with the French were affected by numerous political considerations which helped to muddy the waters. The renegotiation of Britain's entry to the EEC began on 1 April 1974, dominating British discussions with the French for more than a year.[31] And French governments proved to be just as precarious as those in Britain in 1974. The restructuring of Pierre Messmer's administration in March was accompanied by a return to pre-1967 arrangements, transport being combined with regional development and housing under Olivier Guichard. Aymar Achille-Fould became Secretary of State for Transport, but he had little time to take up his responsibility for the Tunnel.[32] With Pompidou's death there was a change of regime following elections in May, which produced an uneasy alliance between the centrist President, Valéry Giscard d'Estaing, who had narrowly defeated François Mitterand, and the Gaullist Prime Minister, Jacques Chirac. Marcel Cavaillé became Transport Minister, and as an autonomous Secretary of State wielded more authority than Achille-Fould had done. However, as deputy mayor of Toulouse, the French counterpart of Bristol in aircraft production, he was naturally more concerned with the Concorde project. Indeed, in the summer of 1974 there were distinct signs that the distractions of Community renegotiation and Concorde, not to speak of the dispute over oil exploration in the continental shelf, were threatening to eclipse the Tunnel at the highest level of government. This was evident, for example, during the plans made for Wilson's meeting with President Giscard in July.[33] Concorde had been battered by rising oil prices, environmental objections from the United States and, above all, by escalating costs. But when Wilson met Chirac informally on 26 June, during the celebrations in Brussels of NATO's twenty-fifth anniversary, the French Prime Minister caused some consternation with his intransigent position. Wilson reported that he had responded to all suggestions of cancellation in the negative, recalling later that he had expressed the desire to build 200 planes.[34] All this made Concorde difficult to halt, and after the meeting with Giscard on 19 July, the decision was taken to continue with the authorised production of 16 aircraft, notwithstanding the losses that these would incur.[35]

Equally important, and certainly disconcerting for Susan Fogarty and her team at the DOE, were Chirac's remarks about the Channel Tunnel. Wilson was told that the French Government was seeking to scale down its expenditure in the coming financial year. Chirac 'did not challenge the principle of the Tunnel, but in view of current budgetary difficulties on both sides of the Channel, would be open to discussion of means of slowing down the project'. Wilson referred to the project's 'economic strain', and to his Government's interest in a more rail-oriented approach. Chirac replied that his Government 'was entirely open to discussion both on financial and technical aspects'. Whether rightly or wrongly, Wilson took this as an expression of French anxiety to defer the project, and told the Cabinet so on the following day.[36] Similar concerns surfaced when Wilson met Giscard on 19 July, where the President apparently indicated that deferment might be for a year. Whether putting a spin on the talks or not, Wilson noted: 'I got the impression that he might like at least further deferment, and possibly, in due course, cancellation'. French officials moved quickly in an attempt to dispel the impression given by their politicians, and Roger Macé even suggested that the initiative for the suggested slowing down had been taken by the 'English' (*sic*). And in response to British anxieties in fielding parliamentary questions at the end of July, where Lord de L'Isle asked whether the Tunnel was to be 'postponed sine die or abandoned', Cavaillé was quick to reassure Mulley about French intentions. His Government would complete Phase II and the economic studies, 'afin de ratifier le Traité et de signer la Convention n° 3 dans les délais convenus' [with a view to ratifying the Treaty and signing Agreement No. 3 in accordance with the agreed programme].[37] It is clear that the DOE was strongly opposed to deferment, and while the Treasury was prepared to consider it, officials in both countries quickly accepted that the process would actually add to project costs.[38] However, the events of June–July encouraged Whitehall sceptics to believe that the French nursed reservations about the Tunnel which were equal to their own.[39]

On the British side of the Channel, officials proceeded to the appointment of the independent review team, with the help of Christopher Foster of the London School of Economics, who had been appointed as a special adviser to the DOE.[40] In June it had been agreed that the chair should be offered to Sir Alec Cairncross, the Master of St Peter's College Oxford and former head of the Government Economic Service (1964–9). He took a little persuading before agreeing to serve, and his appointment was announced on 1 August, after the conclusion of the Wilson-Giscard talks.[41] Meanwhile, Phase II proceeded, with the attention of officials focusing on the minutiae of the economic and financial studies, amidst growing concern about the cost and environmental implications of the rail link to London. The study process was hampered by the difficulties which the British Government and the tunnel companies had in convincing the French Government to abandon some rather paranoid notions that the economic studies were being shaped to advantage the tunnel companies and the cross-channel ferry operators.[42] Thus, although BCTC and SFTM produced a draft agreement with the consultants, Coopers & Lybrand and SETEC-Economie, as early as 13 February 1974, it was not until 29 July that the four parties were finally able to sign the contract, which was modified to meet French objections.[43] The delay, which proved frustrating to the DOE and was the subject of complaint from both Alistair Frame of RTZDE/BCTC and General Maurin of SFTM, also affected the timetable for the other studies, viz. the financial study and a revised British cost-benefit analysis. Both needed to draw on the new estimates of tunnel revenue and on fresh assumptions about economic growth, the latter a thorny political issue.[44] The problems of the rail link are examined in the next section. Suffice it to say here that the revelation in June that the line would cost much more than originally envisaged – £375 million at May 1974 prices, instead of £123 million at February 1973 prices – became a dominant preoccupation in Whitehall, and was one of the main items on the agenda of the newly-formed Channel Tunnel

Reassessment Steering Committee. However, before the matter could be considered in detail, there was the distraction of a second general election.[45]

3. British Rail and the rail link complication: origins, 1969–72

British Rail was involved in the Channel Tunnel project in three ways. First of all, it was an investor. The Board had inherited a significant stake (26.1 per cent) in the old Channel Tunnel Co., which gave it an indirect interest in the financing group formed in July 1970, and it had retained this investment when the company was renamed Channel Tunnel Investments in June 1971. British Rail also decided to seek a direct shareholding in the consortium. Its primary motivation was to match the stake which the French railways, SNCF, had in the French group and thereby secure an influence during the planning of the project. A further reason was the 'purely mercenary' one of participating in the profits should the venture prove to be a success.[46] Thus, when the BCTC raised an initial share capital of £140,000 in June 1971, British Rail subscribed 5 per cent, and this, together with its indirect holding via Channel Tunnel Investments (5.2%), gave it a total participation of 10.2 per cent, which was not far short of SNCF's 13 per cent stake. When additional capital was raised prior to the signature of Agreement No.1 in 1972, British Rail's direct stake fell to 4.74 per cent, but its indirect participation was increased to 6.52 per cent, producing a total of 11.26 per cent.[47]

The second involvement came through British Rail's continuing input into the technical, commercial and operating considerations affecting the Tunnel. Of course, this was of long vintage, but such matters assumed a greater importance from 1971 as it became increasingly likely that the Tunnel would actually be constructed. In spite of the elaborate machinery of joint committees and working groups, the views of the British and French railway authorities had not always coincided, and a new factor was introduced into this potential minefield with the emergence of RTZ as a key player in the project. It is clear that there was an element of mistrust on both sides, and on occasions an uneasy relationship existed between the established railway interests on the one hand, and the project managers on the other. When the preliminary economic study was produced in 1972 David McKenna and Michael Bonavia, the senior British Rail managers responsible for the Tunnel, complained vigorously about the use RTZ had made of the railways' traffic and revenue estimates to produce a more pessimistic case. They also expressed exasperation that RTZ would not always accept the professional advice of British Rail on matters railway. Arguments about signalling and rolling stock revealed RTZ acting as 'amateur railwaymen'. RTZ, for its part, was bewildered by the extent of the disagreement between BRB and SNCF on technical questions, and was far from impressed with BRB's tardy response to its request for comments on its report. There was even a suggestion that Bonavia *et al.* had supplied RTZ with 'confusing and contradictory information'.[48] The third element of relevance to British Rail was the provision of train services between London, the Tunnel and beyond. In the form of the new rail link, this question became fundamental to the entire project. Indeed, by May 1972, as one official observed, 'the railway tail [was] beginning to wag the whole dog'.[49] Consequently, this element of Channel Tunnel history demands close inspection.

In the 1960s British Rail had no plans to construct a dedicated rail link between London and the Tunnel, since it was assumed that trains would use the existing infrastructure. However, there was a problem in that the British loading gauge, that is the maximum permissible height and width of the rolling stock, was more restricted than the standard UIC or 'Berne' gauge used on the continent.[50] In consequence, passengers would either have to transfer from one train to another at Saltwood terminal, on the British side of the Tunnel, or an investment in special rolling stock, compatible with both the British and continental gauges, would be needed. There were advantages and disadvantages in these alternatives. The 'all change' option was clearly the cheapest, but was unlikely to attract passengers from competing modes of transport (sea, air). Dual-purpose rolling stock would allow the running of through services between London and the continent, and, indeed, there was a long-established precedent in the vehicles used on the 'Night Ferry' services between London and Paris/Brussels. But there were some technical difficulties in operating these vehicles and a critical limitation was that of finding sufficient paths to run Channel Tunnel trains over the busy commuter lines of British Rail's Southern Region. Despite these drawbacks, the provision of special stock was the Board's preferred solution. However, by 1969 it became apparent that, notwithstanding the existence of train ferry vehicles, the continental railway administrations were emphatically opposed to the use of non-standard passenger stock, and did not wish to make a financial contribution towards its construction. British Rail was therefore pressed to accommodate standard UIC vehicles, either by upgrading an existing line, or by constructing an entirely new route.[51] The latter solution then became linked to wider aspirations for a European high-speed railway network which would compete with the airlines. This concept was predicated on advances in railway technology allowing speeds substantially in excess of 100 mph, as had already been proven with the Japanese 'Shinkansen' services, first introduced in 1964. The SNCF was pressing ahead with its plans for a turbotrain and 'Europolitain' network, later given the name 'Train à Grande Vitesse' [TGV]. British Rail itself was developing an ambitious Advanced Passenger Train [APT], with a tilting mechanism to facilitate its use over existing infrastructure at speeds of up to 155 mph.[52] Accepting the strength of feeling of its colleagues in continental Europe, the British Railways Board alerted the Ministry of Transport to these developments in June 1969. Officials responded by requesting that a more thorough assessment be carried out.[53]

A reassessment of rail passenger traffic forecasts, undertaken jointly by British Rail, the SNCF and Belgian railways, highlighted the potential benefits of high-speed working on both sides of the Channel. This 'tripartite' study, completed in January 1971, noted that at conventional speeds the journey time between London and Paris was expected to be 3 hours 40 minutes. High-speed running (at up to 300 kph [186 mph]) would reduce this to $2\frac{1}{2}$ hours, which would not only generate additional traffic but also produce a 'massive' diversion from the airlines.

The faster option was expected to attract over 10 million passengers in the first year, compared with 6 million at normal operating speeds. Gross receipts would also rise, to £9 million compared with £4 million.[54] British Rail then commissioned Livesey and Henderson, a firm of consulting engineers, to produce a feasibility study for a high-speed route.[55] Their report, considered by the British Railways Board in February 1971, identified four alternatives, with a civil engineering component of £44–61 million. Three of the routes were completely new alignments, and were expected to provoke environmental objections; the fourth, route 'D', involved an adaptation of the Ashford-Redhill line, together with some new tunnelling and upgrading work. British Rail put the total 'notional cost' of such a line at £100 million.[56] Containing the cost was clearly an important consideration for British Rail, which was already experiencing severe investment constraints in its core business.[57] A new line would cost much more than either 'ferry gauge' vehicles (£15–20 million) or widening the loading gauge of an existing line (£25–30 million). The Board noted McKenna's interest in adapting the Ashford-Redhill on cost grounds, and asked him to explore the feasibility of a 'minimum cost route employing the A.P.T. potential'. At the same time an internal evaluation was made of upgrading one of the four existing routes to accommodate UIC stock. On the other hand, there was also support for a high-speed line from the private consortium offering to build the Tunnel, and Alastair Frame of RTZ had raised the enticing prospect that it might be financed by a sizeable slab of equity capital.[58] The balance of opinion in British Rail then began to tilt in favour of a new line, encouraged by the realisation that a mere upgrading would cost several million pounds but would not produce a very dramatic change. Thus, at a meeting with the DOE in June 1971 British Rail explained that to upgrade would involve a 'substantial outlay' – about £25–40 million – and by operating at conventional speeds would be unable to exploit fully the city centre-city centre potential of the Tunnel and do nothing to alleviate existing capacity constraints.[59]

The discussions about potential routes were also affected by the need to determine the location of the London terminal for Channel Tunnel traffic. It had long been assumed that this would be at Victoria, the station then used by the Boat Trains. However, early in 1971 the DOE became concerned by rumours that British Rail wished to develop a site at White City in west London. When Barber inquired about the 'state of play', Bonavia confirmed that operational and planning difficulties at Victoria had compelled them to take a fresh look at the question. They had clearly been disappointed by opposition to their ambitious plans to make Victoria an international traffic centre with rail links to Gatwick and Heathrow airports, as well as to the Tunnel. By 1971 the projected Heathrow link was apparently out of favour, while Westminster City Council had raised serious objections to further development in the area. Attention had therefore been directed to a site on the under-utilised West London line (Clapham Jnc.–Willesden Jnc.). Initial evaluations had ruled out Olympia and West Brompton, but the White City/ Shepherds Bush area appeared more promising. There was plenty of railway-owned land, and the West London line offered the opportunity to provide services north and west of London.[60] DOE officials were somewhat dismayed by this news. They felt that to contemplate a terminal other than at one of the main centrally-located railway stations 'could undermine the whole attractiveness of the Tunnel'.[61] Nevertheless, British Rail was allowed to continue its discussions with Hammersmith Borough Council and the Greater London Council (GLC), and by May additional sites had surfaced: Bricklayers Arms in Battersea, on British Rail's initiative; and further east, Surrey Docks, Lewisham and New Cross, after prompting from the GLC.[62] However, by the end of 1971 it was evident that for British Rail White City was very much a first choice, and the preference became public after an unauthorised leak to the *Evening Standard*.[63]

As we have seen (Chapter 3, above, pp. 71–3), the attitude of senior railway managers to the Tunnel was often ambivalent in the 1960s, but senior appointments made in the early 1970s promised a change of heart. In 1970 David McKenna, an enthusiastic supporter of the project, succeeded John Ratter as the Board Member responsible for the project, and in the following year Richard Marsh became Chairman in place of Sir Henry Johnson. When Transport Secretary in the second Wilson Government, Marsh had made a contribution towards advancing the project, and he was generally regarded as a pro-tunneller.[64] Nevertheless, the initial development of the route strategy exposed tensions and frustrations both within British Rail and between the railways and the Department. The strained atmosphere created between the two, which proved to be long-lasting, was symptomatic of the fact that overall relations between the railways and the Government were at a particularly low ebb, principally because the operational requirements of a loss-making business were being challenged by investment constraints.[65] Opinions on the Tunnel within the railway industry also remained divided. After all, there was no certainty that it would proceed, and it did not form part of the core business. With resources severely constrained the opportunity costs of investment in a rail link were very evident. In these circumstances the Southern Region, led by its General Manager, Lance Ibbotson, was understandably reluctant to commit scarce resources.[66] At the same time, DOE officials harboured suspicions about British Rail's handling of the rail link issue. Peter Kemp noted that the Board was being 'a little reticent' in revealing details. Sir Eugene Melville was anxious to warn McKenna that 'you will, in preparing your various options, consult only your own commercial interests'.[67] Others were more forthright in questioning British Rail's motives, dismissing the link as 'a bit of extra flummery added in to pique the airlines'. It is clear that opinions were as divided in the DOE as in railway circles, with Marsh finding senior civil servants expressing 'considerable scepticism' about the need for a new line.[68] There was also the question of the basis on which the rail link expenditure should be undertaken within the wider context of British Rail's investment allocation and in relation to the Tunnel project proper. Certainly, at the end of 1971 officials wished to keep the two as entirely separate projects, with the latter to be justified as an investment on its own merits. Yet there was little that could be done until British Rail presented fully-costed options.[69]

By January 1972 sufficient work had been done for the Board to submit a more considered report to the Department. British Rail announced that after evaluating no fewer than seven schemes, they had concluded that the optimal route was via Ashford, Tonbridge, Edenbridge, Oxted and Croydon, with the terminal at White City. New sections of line would be constructed through the congested area of South London (mainly in tunnel), between South Croydon and Edenbridge, and from Tonbridge to Ashford (Figure 6.1). The product of considerable soul-searching, not all of which was revealed to the DOE, the outcome was very much a compromise between a new line and upgrading, and between high-speed and cost. Although calculations were necessarily tentative at this stage, British Rail suggested that the cost, assuming the provision of UIC gauge, would be about £77 million for speeds of 125 mph and a London-Paris journey time of 3 hours 40 minutes. The initial return was expected to be of the order of 12 per cent.[70] The Department was reassured that the selected route was suitable for later upgrading to achieve 'Europolitain' standards of 185 mph and journey times of $2\frac{1}{2}$ hours, should this be required.[71] However, the pressure for this was not immediate, since SNCF ambitions, which in any case were focussed primarily on a new line from Paris to Lyon, had been put on hold by a cautious French Government.[72] The railways' submission, together with the appointment of a new chairman, did nothing to dispel the strained relations with their sponsoring department. A lengthy period of fencing ensued, during which time the suspicions harboured by civil servants developed into more specific complaints that British Rail was being evasive and unhelpful. Consequently, little progress was made, and when Agreement No. 1 was signed in October 1972, the French were able to include an outline description of road and rail access on their side of the tunnel, but details of British commitments were held over until the signature of Agreement No.2.[73]

The plain fact was that DOE officials were not prepared to accept the decision-making of senior railway managers without further scrutiny. This immediately became clear when McKenna, on presenting the submission, had sought permission to make an early public announcement about the choice of White City for the terminal. Although officials were not entirely happy with the Board's apparent attempt to 'bounce' them into allowing a statement, they agreed that something 'low key' would be acceptable. A British Rail press release in early February confirmed that White City was being considered, but the DOE continued to challenge the broader wisdom of such a choice. The railways were obviously attracted by the development potential of one of their larger neglected sites, but a fundamental weakness was their admission that Tunnel traffic would be lower than with a terminal in central London.[74] As one junior official observed, 'White City has all the makings of a horse designed by a Committee that turned out to be a camel'.[75] Furthermore, the Department's initial reactions to the choice of route were far from favourable. The document was dismissed as unimpressive, with a 'tendentious air', while the approach to traffic generation was regarded as 'half-hearted'.[76] On the other hand, from a railway perspective the DOE appeared to be making rather a meal of what was only a policy paper, rather than a formal investment submission.[77] After exploratory talks with British Rail, Kemp, together with his colleague from the Railways 'A' Division, Andrew Lyall, undertook to produce an official response to the route strategy. While Kemp thought that 'inside BRB's rather poor submission was probably a good idea trying to get out', the Department was in no mood to endorse the Board's preferred option without detailed analysis, and the promised formal reply, sent in mid-April 1972, was deliberately cool and 'fairly unhelpful' in tone. At a time when the received view in Whitehall was that British Rail investment submissions were invariably unsatisfactory, the Department asked for a refinement of the financial case, both for the preferred and alternative options. It also required further work to justify the claim that additional railway capacity was needed, and an examination of terminals other than White City. British Rail was asked to respond with some urgency, given the imminent appearance of revised traffic studies from the Tunnel consultants and the timetable for reaching agreement with the private sector consortium.[78] But only frustration and annoyance were evident in Bonavia's 'personal' reply. It had taken the DOE three months of deliberation to produce a plea for further work, and exception was taken to the doubts cast on the railways' need for additional capacity. Bonavia also strongly refuted the suggestion that British Rail had a leisurely timetable, given the challenge of gearing a project of the anticipated magnitude to the Tunnel timetable. What he wished to impress upon Kemp was that British Rail wanted 'some indication of whether this scheme . . . is in general harmony with the Department's attitude to the Tunnel project as a whole'. Only then would a full financial evaluation be merited. 'Progressively firmer physical proposals' required 'progressive firmer conclusions' from government.[79] Relations were further soured by disclosures made by British Rail to the South East Regional Planning Council and to *Modern Railways* magazine about their preferred high-speed route. The revelation caused consternation in Kent and Melville was forced to endure an awkward meeting with local councillors in Folkestone as a consequence. McKenna and Bonavia had their knuckles rapped over the incident, their attempts to explain the circumstances falling on stony ground.[80]

Evaluations of route strategies were of course inextricably linked with traffic forecasts. Such forecasts posed problems since the causal effects ran both ways. Higher figures for 'classic', that is, rail passengers could be used to justify higher spending on railway infrastructure. On the other hand, a new rail link would itself attract custom and could be used to justify higher forecasts. It was the latter argument, highlighted in the 'tripartite' railway study (see above, pp. 142–3), that had underpinned the high-speed strategy. Unfortunately, the use of differing assumptions and methodologies ensured that the data contained in the Channel Tunnel project managers' preliminary reports of spring 1972 were at odds with the railways' own figures. While the railway estimates were based on the Anglo-French report of 1966 (AF66), updated with projections based on alternative service levels, the RTZDE/Coopers estimates were derived from their new traffic survey. Consequently, the two sets of data could not be reconciled. From a political perspective the most important observation was that the RTZDE/Coopers forecasts were more pessimistic, putting the number of rail passengers at about 4.1–5.8 million in 1980, compared with the railways' 6.8 million.[81] DOE officials responded to the situation by pressing British Rail to undertake an assessment, in discounted terms, of their preferred option, but using the RTZDE traffic estimates instead.[82] However, further inquiries revealed numerous complexities, and in particular evidence of 'negligence on the part of RTZDE in failing to base their study on sensible and consistent foundations'; consequently, their rail figures were 'quite simply a mess'.[83] The DOE was also anxious to see details of alternative options and, in particular, a low-investment route strategy which they discovered British Rail had prepared for RTZDE. Neither Bonavia nor Frame was keen on parting with this document, but it was passed onto Kemp by an unofficial route. It envisaged a very limited investment in infrastructure improvements, costed at £3.7 million, and the use of BR/UIC gauge stock costing £44 million. Journey times would be four hours-plus, and passenger demand under this option was put at 5 million in the first year.[84]

In May and June 1972 Melville and McKenna were involved in a series of meetings which resembled many of the Anglo-French Tunnel exchanges in the lack of progress made. There was no significant thaw in relations between the nationalised industry and its sponsoring ministry, and it is clear that personalities were a barrier to progress. The stakes were raised when Melville warned McKenna that the associated railway investment was becoming critical: 'indeed, I would not rule out the possibility that it could in the end turn the scale as to whether or not there were a Tunnel at all'. For this reason he insisted that they talk seriously about less expensive alternatives to the Board's preferred option.[85] Later on, McKenna responded, by his own admission, in 'slightly petulant mood', stating that he was puzzled by the suggestion that the choice of investment option was 'really the absolutely critical issue between tunnel or no tunnel'. Like Bonavia before him, McKenna sought 'some indication of a more strategic view of tunnel thinking', adding that 'Maybe we are not thought sufficiently reliable to be entrusted with strategic views and that we had better be kept on a very tight rein'.[86] Whether intended to be serious or not, McKenna's final comment was much nearer the mark than he realised, as the DOE papers indicate.[87] Further contact in July included a top-level meeting between Peyton and Marsh, where the rail link was raised at the Minister's insistence. In reply Marsh lent his support to the preferred option in characteristically emotive terms, asserting that the choice lay between a 'bodged job done reluctantly on the cheap or a first-class railway; he would hope that no-one would opt for the former'.[88] But beyond the rhetoric, there were indications that the Board was beginning to realise that comparative work on route strategies was unavoidable. At the Marsh–Peyton meeting reference was made to an appraisal of two broad alternatives to a new line: the use of special dual-gauge stock; and a rail link, with 'much new infrastructure', built to UIC standards. British Rail's undertaking to produce a detailed examination of the low-investment option was accompanied by an agreement to establish a joint DOE-BRB working party to co-ordinate the necessary work.[89]

Although there was clearly some urgency, the first meeting of the working party did not take place for three months. In the meantime, British Rail gave the DOE an expurgated version of the Livesey and Henderson report, which was taken to raise a fundamental question about the route strategy. There appeared to be little justification for spending large sums of money to build a high-speed link on the British side of the Tunnel when SNCF, which had spare track capacity, had no immediate plans to adopt a similar policy on the French side. Anticipating later arguments in the 1990s, officials observed that 'unilateral spending by BRB on route D of more than £57 m could not be justified by the resultant 11 minute reduction in a 3 hour 40 minute journey'. In these circumstances, they argued that the choice of route might rest on the potential benefits to London commuters, which would also influence the choice of terminal.[90] The working party, which met for the first time in October 1972, did not enjoy an auspicious start. In a telephone conversation on 9 November McKenna told Melville that the parties appeared to be moving backwards from the agreed position in July, and complained that the Department had introduced new elements. Melville countered by blaming Bonavia for not putting his cards on the table.[91] Bonavia complained that the small working party had been augmented by a much larger number of DOE officials, eight of whom had attended the second meeting on 1 November.[92] In fact, by this time the DOE's impatience with British Rail, and its disappointment at a senior level with the breakdown in relations between the CTSU and BR's Channel Tunnel Department, had led to a strengthening of personnel at the former. Susan Fogarty joined the team (see above, p. 107), and immediately took over responsibility for the rail link.[93] She inherited a challenging brief, as was emphasised by the tone of her Minister's letter to Marsh at the end of the month. Peyton agreed that 'We need attractive main line services for the passengers using the Tunnel route', but warned that 'if the rail investment is too expensive it could wreck the project. We must get this right and time is short'.[94]

4. The rail link: defining the route strategy, 1973–4

In December 1972 British Rail made a firm commitment to the Department that it would produce papers on the London terminal and route strategy in January 1973.[95] Although this timetable slipped, by the end of the month Fogarty was able to tell her Permanent Secretary, Idwal Pugh, that matters were 'looking up', although she added that it 'may not be saying all that much given the state they were in'. Apparently, 'the series of demarches has had an effect'.[96] Unfortunately, this optimism was to prove short-lived, and it was not long before friction between the parties returned.

The first paper to arrive, on 25 January, was British Rail's terminals document. This reported on its work in conducting feasibility studies of four options: Surrey Docks, the preferred site of the GLC; White City; Victoria; and a combination of Victoria and White City. Surrey Docks was quickly dismissed as impractical and costly, and the idea of constructing a high-level station at Victoria was also rejected. White City emerged as the best operational site and, with a notional cost of £15.5 million, was the cheapest option. However, the possibility of running some trains into Victoria, which would have commercial advantages, was not ruled out.[97] Although White City appeared to have won the day, unanimity was elusive. The DOE's attempt to encourage the GLC and British Rail to produce a joint consultation document had foundered in the autumn of 1972, leaving the Council to pursue its own agenda.[98] Having evaluated no fewer than 11 options, it had published a consultation paper in November 1972 that narrowed the choice down to three: Victoria; White City; and Surrey Docks. However, for all the talk of stimulating discussion the GLC appeared to have made up its mind. Attracted by the potential regenerative effects in London's Docklands, it came down firmly in favour of Surrey Docks.[99] With the DOE known to favour the locational advantages of Victoria, as did senior managers such as Tony Griffiths in British Rail's passenger department,[100] the selection of a terminal clearly could not satisfy everyone.[101] From the perspective of the DOE, the worst scenario had emerged. Each of the three major players preferred a different location, and it is quite clear that each had reached its conclusion without conducting sophisticated assessment and costing exercises.[102] The three outstanding options were inserted into the DOE's Green Paper in March 1973,[103] but it was not long before the matter was resolved. By the time the White Paper was published in September, White City had emerged as the clear winner.[104] It was accepted that the Victoria site was too constricted, while Surrey Docks presented a considerable environmental challenge and there was opposition from both British Rail and London Transport. As early as May, Sir Reginald Goodwin, the newly-installed Labour leader of the GLC, had told Marsh that the idea was 'pure bloody nonsense'.[105] Pugh's Inter-departmental Committee (CTIC) endorsed this view in its report to Cabinet EPC in June.[106] White City thus remained the only practicable choice, though the GLC continued to grumble about it, and there were repeated calls for a public inquiry.[107]

British Rail's terminals paper was rather like 'Hamlet without the Prince';[108] more important was the Board's paper on the route strategy, which arrived in Whitehall in draft form on 21 February.[109] This slim report contained further work on the preferred route, together with a new estimate of cost and, despite the Board's obvious dislike of the scheme, a more detailed consideration of the 'low-investment' option. The preferred route was refined. The earlier suggestion of upgrading the Oxted line as a cheaper alternative to a new line to Edenbridge was now ruled out. At the same time the physical constraints at Ashford station produced the suggestion of an additional stretch of new line, between Pluckley and Smeeth (see Figure 6.1). These elements, together with an unspecified adjustment for inflation, increased the infrastructure costs to £93.5 million. With somewhat conservative estimates for the London terminal (only £8.5 million) and rolling stock (£9 million for BRB continental stock), the total cost of the scheme, providing train speeds of 125 mph, was now put at £111 million.[110] The 'so-called' low-investment alternative, running into Victoria over an existing 'boat train' route at up to 90 mph, was now costed at £39 million, but British Rail was still unable to find any merit in this scheme, its sole advantage being to reduce the infrastructure investment to £10 million. Thus the Board remained adamant that its recommended route was the only one worth pursuing. It justified its choice by

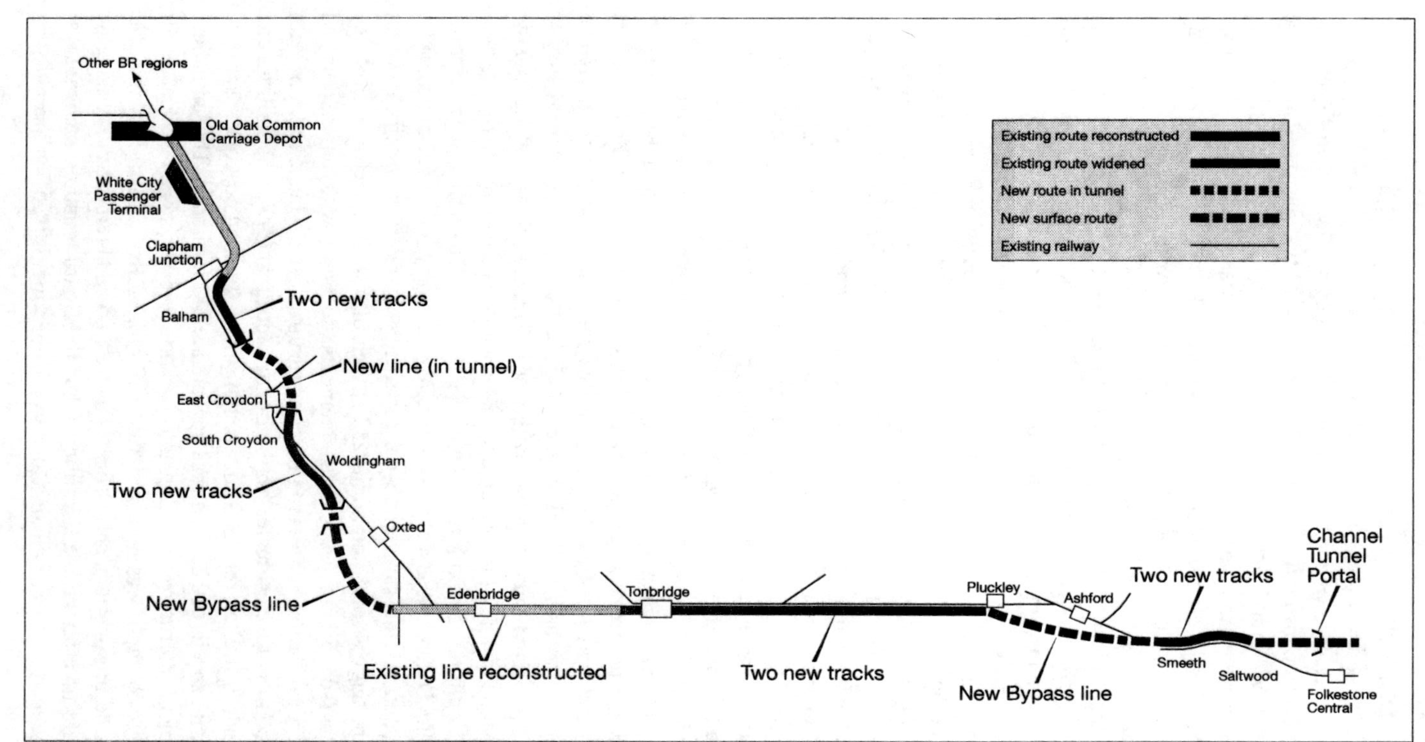

Figure 6.1 Route of proposed Channel Tunnel Rail Link, 1973.

reference to DCF calculations, confined to the passenger business, which produced NPVs of £29 million (preferred route) and £21 million (low-investment). The difference of £8 million produced a return of about 12 per cent [in fact 11.1%] on the additional investment of £72 million.[111]

Apart from the difficulties in reconciling the data with earlier estimates, the DOE's initial response was to complain that the preferred option had been presented 'complete', and did not, as the Department wanted, provide a detailed breakdown of the cost of, and justification for, individual elements. The intention behind this response was to draw British Rail into revealing the cost of a range of options between 'low' and 'preferred'.[112] However, Bonavia deftly sidestepped the request by stating that the recommended route needed capacity, gauge clearance and electrification throughout. 'If there is a discontinuity at any point the strategy is weakened to a situation little better than the low investment alternative.' As for costing the various components, 'simple back-of-envelope figuring should establish that they would be non-starters from your point of view and not just ours'.[113] Wider consideration within the DOE produced a familiar litany of criticism regarding the inadequacy of the submission, the expense of the link given the constraints on public expenditure and doubts over British Rail's calculation of the rate of return. Some within the Department thought that the actual return might be half that claimed in the strategy paper.[114] But above all it was the lack of alternatives that rankled. As Fogarty told Pugh, 'we cannot believe that there is no scheme which would provide a useful improvement between the two... Bluntly, if there are no options other than the "preferred" and the current "low" option, we may well end up with no Tunnel'.[115]

A complicating factor in the deliberations was the attitude of the French Government and railways and the two Tunnel companies, who were deep in negotiations over Agreement No.2. When Melville pressed for an assessment of the low-investment proposals to be included in the programme of joint studies, French officials had not unnaturally requested a note on the rail link assumptions. The DOE paper, provided without consulting British Rail, apparently provoked 'une certaine émotion' among the French and, at the same time, annoyed McKenna.[116] Peyton was informed by the French Transport Minister, Robert Galley, that his Government could not accept the low-investment proposal since it introduced capacity constraints and would be contrary to the Seventh Schedule of Agreement No.1, where a commitment was made to the provision of the 'necessary road and rail access'.[117] There was clearly a risk that 'necessary' would come to be interpreted as British Rail's preferred route. Indeed, in March it was reported that the Tunnel companies had inserted this option into their draft of Agreement No.2.[118] When DOE and BRB representatives met at the end of March, Fogarty emphasised the seriousness of the situation. There was no question of the Government financing a rail link that was not viable. The preferred route appeared to be 'just viable', but it was 'extremely expensive' and in the existing economic climate, this created difficulties. In addition, the high cost of the preferred option might 'wreck the finances of the Tunnel/rail combination', while the Companies and the French might find the low-investment alternative totally unacceptable and refuse to sign Agreement No.2. Thus, with only two options on the table, the whole Tunnel project was in danger, and Fogarty argued that 'it was essential that work be put in hand immediately on identifying a realistic intermediate option'. The parties agreed that Kemp would chair a joint working group to identify the minimum investment necessary to ensure the appropriate capacity, and Bonavia promised his full co-operation.[119]

A first meeting of the group was encouraging, but relations quickly deteriorated again. At the second meeting on 10 April, the two British Rail representatives revealed that they had been instructed not to work on any alternative options. Some that had been raised earlier were perfunctorily dismissed in a discussion terminated after only 20 minutes.[120] Fogarty and Kemp were furious, blaming Bonavia and McKenna for an 'intolerable' position, and Pugh was urged to have the matter raised at the highest level.[121] From the British Rail perspective, things were very different. Bonavia thought that the DOE were 'floundering, and do not know how to present the route strategy proposals to Ministers'.[122] It is also evident that he and his colleagues were working on the assumption that the Department was 'bluffing' and in the end would give way rather than recommend that the project should be abandoned. This was a somewhat dangerous strategy but one that was supported at higher levels, for example by the Chief Executive, David Bowick.[123] There was also something in the argument that the DOE had sat on British Rail's original submission for much of 1972 and had failed to offer a constructive alternative.[124] Three factors were to work in the Board's favour: (1) Peyton's personal enthusiasm for the project; (2) the extremely tight timetable for decision-making; and (3) better than expected results from the Tunnel studies. Thus, after the impasse in April 1973, events moved rapidly such that by June Ministers had accepted the case for the Board's recommended route.

Peyton undoubtedly played a critical role in breaking the deadlock over the rail link. When he met Marsh at the end of April the Tunnel was at the top of the agenda. The Minister immediately expressed his concern over the stance adopted by British Rail officials, but Marsh reiterated his Board's view that 'there was no practical intermediate option', a position which '15 months of further study had confirmed'. On a more conciliatory tack Peyton then said that if this were true then he would need to be clear precisely why in order to explain it to colleagues and later to the French. He therefore asked the Board to produce short notes, setting out the disadvantages of the low-investment option and the reasons why intermediate options did not exist. He also asked the Board to co-operate with the DOE in considering how the high-cost option might be justified.[125] This intervention by the Minister represented a significant shift in the Government's approach and McKenna responded by submitting the necessary papers the day after the meeting.[126] There were further meetings between Peyton and Marsh in early May, for which British Rail produced papers on the environmental impact and rate of return of the high-cost route, and a further justification for failing to produce an intermediate option.[127] By 10 May Peyton had accepted the merits of the Board's position and so, only a month after the abortive working party had reached a stalemate, British Rail was given the green light to make a full investment or 'new works' submission for its high-cost route. McKenna was able to tell Bowick that their resistance to the compromise strategy 'had produced the desired effect'.[128]

Given the need for CTIC to produce a report for Ministers (see above, p. 115), time was short, and British Rail had only a week to compile the documentation. A 17-page proposal was sent to Pugh by the Deputy Chairman, Michael Bosworth on 17 May, before there was time to obtain its endorsement by either the Investment Committee or the Board.[129] Discussions in CTIC then took place on 23 and 30 May, providing the first significant opportunity for a wider audience in Whitehall, including the Treasury, to examine the scheme, together with the arguments underpinning it.[130] Fogarty's CTSU memorandum, discussed on 23 May, included the documentation from British Rail. Annex A explained why the Board had found it impossible to identify an 'intermediate' strategy as a worthwhile investment. Modification of the recommended route would save only a small amount of capital and would greatly reduce revenue. Timetabling exercises had shown that any improvements to the low-investment option would be thwarted by capacity limitations. Waiting for the development of very high-speed (APT/TGV) trains in the 1980s was also raised, but though 'superficially attractive', was held to have 'major disadvantages'.[131] Annex B provided the reasons for rejecting a low-investment solution. By relying on the existing Southern Region infrastructure both revenue and profits would be severely constrained. Furthermore, an 'extremely poor public image' would result, while the effect on commuter services 'would be at best serious, and at worst disastrous'.[132] Finally, the Board's investment submission was included (at Annex C). The principal change from early drafts was an increase in infrastructure costs, bringing the total cost to £121 million. However, this increase was eclipsed by the Board's ability to draw on much more favourable traffic estimates emerging from the consultants' studies. With rail passengers now expected to total 8.4 million in 1980 and 12.9 million in 1990,[133] higher rates of return could be calculated. The Board put these in the range 13–20 per cent over a 20-year period from 1980, but clearly favoured 17 per cent as the 'most expected' scenario.[134] Fogarty presented CTIC with the three options: British Rail's preferred investment; the low-investment alternative; and the low-investment alternative as a holding device until the introduction of APT/TGV trains in the late 1980s. Work done by the DOE's economists had confirmed that the low-investment option was 'decidedly unattractive', and the 'low-holding' alternative, although requiring further assessment, was thought unlikely to prove more attractive than the high-investment scheme, which therefore 'appeared to offer the best all-round solution'. After discussion it was agreed that only the 'preferred' and 'low-holding' options should be incorporated into CTIC's report to Ministers. At the meeting on 30 May officials also agreed that the report should state that 'on the figures available' the former offered the better rate of return.[135] The documentation was then incorporated in the CTIC or Pugh Report on the Tunnel, which was discussed at the Cabinet EPC on 11 and 28 June and considered by the full Cabinet on 5 July (see Chapter 5 above, pp. 120–2). The Report contained an annex on the rail link, which passed on the information provided by British Rail, though not its full submission.[136] There were clearly some uncertainties, not least about the ability of British Rail to negotiate a more advantageous division of fares between itself and the French and Belgian railways, an element which had worried the DOE.[137] However, officials were now more confident about the prospects, and the main part of the Pugh Report indicated that the 17 per cent return was 'achievable'.[138] By this time, as we have seen, Peyton was adamant that the high-quality rail link formed an integral part of the Tunnel project and he was able to secure the agreement of his colleagues to this view (Chapter 5 above, p. 122). Shortly after the Cabinet decision, the British Railways Board also approved the scheme, the cost of which had been further adjusted, to £123 million.[139]

Having agreed the nature of the rail infrastructure, it was necessary to incorporate these commitments into Agreement No.2. The Third Schedule of the Agreement, signed in November 1973, outlined the general characteristics of the route, which was to be built to continental gauge with overhead 25kV electrification, suitable for speeds of up to 300 kph. Reference to the London terminal was less specific. It was to be 'within five miles of Charing Cross' and 'may be in the neighbourhood of White City'.[140] The Anglo-French Treaty stated that the road and rail systems would be adequate to meet the requirements of Tunnel traffic. The details were set out in a contemporaneous exchange of letters, which noted, *inter alia*, that the railway administrations had reached an agreement on the sharing of fares.[141] Also important was the 'Procedure Memorandum' agreed between British Rail and the DOE shortly before the signature of Agreement No.2. Without full Board commitment, the British Government could not sign the Agreement and Treaty, a fact of which the Board was well aware.[142] The Board accordingly asked for, and was granted, the Secretary of State's authority to seek the necessary powers to construct the rail link, for which a Bill was to be promoted in November 1974. The cost was estimated at 'about £123 million at February 1973 prices without interest'. It was stipulated that British Rail would make a further investment submission by the end of September 1974. The Secretary of State would then confirm authority for the scheme to proceed, but, critically in view of later events, confirmation was subject to the proviso that the new submission did not 'significantly vary the basis on which the scheme was put forward on 15 June, 1973'. As regards funding, the link was to be treated separately from the rest of British Rail's capital investment. Finally, the Secretary of State could stop work on the rail link 'in the event of any major change of circumstances'.[143]

Public consultation was another critical aspect of the work on the rail link. In July 1973 British Rail published *Express Link with Europe*, a short pamphlet which included a diagrammatic map of the proposed line. This was then reproduced in the Government's White Paper in September (see Figure 6.1).[144] While not showing the precise alignment of the new route, the map was sufficient to cause alarm in certain areas, and in particular the North Downs/Woldingham Valley area of Surrey, and MPs such as Sir John Rodgers and Sir Geoffrey Howe began to mobilise opinion.[145] A wide-ranging consultation exercise was inevitable, but Peyton was anxious to avoid a time-consuming public inquiry, and he sought to convince Kent and Surrey

County Councils that the Private Bill procedure would be sufficient to allow objections to be made.[146] The DOE then asked British Rail to prepare a more substantive consultative document, with alignment options for the new stretches of line, and in February 1974 *Channel Tunnel: London-Tunnel New Rail Link* was circulated to interested parties.[147] This more substantial booklet included 12 folded plates, and though not showing specific land requirements, gave a much better indication of a route which, at 80 miles, promised to be the first significant length of new railway to be constructed in Britain since the Great Central Railway's London extension of 1899. British Rail argued that any other general line of route would create much greater environmental damage, particularly in Kent. It was keen to confine the debate to the 25 miles of entirely new line and, in particular, the Woldingham-Edenbridge and Smeeth-Pluckley sections, for each of which four alternative alignments were presented. With the approval of the DOE, British Rail also floated possible enhancements to the existing sections of the route. Higher traffic forecasts and greater expectations for freight meant that a widening to four tracks (instead of two) was now envisaged for the West London line and Edenbridge-Tonbridge. More significant was the proposal for a 'long tunnel' between Chelsea Basin and South Croydon. In its original form, the alignment presented a number of challenges to the existing infrastructure, but the problems would of course be eliminated if the entire section were built in tunnel.[148] The consultants Mott, Hay and Anderson were therefore appointed to assess the cost and feasibility of the long tunnel concept. The study had yet to be completed at the time of publication, and at the insistence of the DOE the consultation document expressed considerable caution about the idea.[149] However, when the consultants reported in March, they confirmed that the 'long tunnel' was a distinct engineering possibility. Nor did the additional costs seem to be prohibitive. Mott, Hay and Anderson estimated the construction costs (excluding track and signalling) of the original 16.6 km 'East' route at £55.8 million; the 15 km 'West' route ('long tunnel') was expected to cost about £10 million more, at £65.2 million. Given the difficulties posed by the East route, the consultants recommended that the more direct West route should be adopted, and British Rail endorsed this conclusion. Indeed, in a memorandum forwarded to Fogarty, Ian Campbell, the Executive Director (Systems & Operations) noted that with the additional elements the East and West routes would cost almost the same – £71.5 and £72.65 million respectively.[150] On receiving the report Fogarty's first reaction was: 'I am sure that we must go for this route', and this view was supported by her DOE colleagues.[151] With such unanimity on all sides, including the Treasury, work on the East route was abandoned.[152]

As we have seen, in April 1974 Crosland informed the Commons that the new Labour Government wished to orient the Tunnel project more towards rail. Shortly after this statement, Marsh told Transport Minister Mulley that British Rail's current plans catered for the maximum amount of railway traffic which could be justified commercially. However, later on he provided a list of possible options to increase the railways' share of freight traffic, including the provision of a larger loading gauge to allow 'piggy-back' operations (the carrying of lorry trailers on rail wagons). Such enhancements would, as Marsh admitted, 'require the injection of additional capital', but by this time this was something of a hostage to fortune, since officials were now more than a little concerned about the likely real cost of the rail link.[153] Distrust of British Rail estimates was, of course, endemic in the DOE. The Department had already ignored British Rail objections and taken the precaution of raising the estimated cost from £123 to £145 million, thereby creating a £22 million 'contingency' which was incorporated in the economic assessment. It was the figure of £145 million which was published in both the Cost Benefit Study and White Paper of 1973.[154] However, officials were scarcely prepared for what was to follow. In 1974 concern increased when Mott, Hay and Anderson's 'long tunnel' report was received, and the consultants' estimates for the Chelsea-Croydon section were compared with those contained in the Board's 1973 submission. Alarm bells sounded when it emerged that these costs could be up to 40 per cent higher. While high levels of inflation were clearly at work, there were strong suspicions that a significant proportion of the increase was the product of omission and underestimation. As Fogarty noted, the disparity for this one section of the route had 'used up' the £22 million contingency.[155] The Treasury was also worried by these developments and emphasised that the rail link should pass commercial tests: there was no question of subsidising it.[156]

Within British Rail, Bonavia was well aware of the seriousness of the situation, and drew the attention of senior managers to the implications of spiralling costs. In an internal memorandum entitled 'The slippery slope', written shortly before he handed over his brief to Peter Keen,[157] he observed that the single factor most likely to kill the project was a 'Concorde-like escalation' of investment expenditure. He noted that a combination of enhancements, environmental improvements and over-cautious estimating was threatening to increase the costs to an unacceptable £410 million and suggested that efforts be made to scale down the project. His remarks were made in the knowledge that the Department had pressed for a revised estimate of cost for the entire route and that officials would certainly find the results unpalatable.[158] At the end of April, the DOE was told that the basic infrastructure cost of the rail link had risen from £114 million (1973 scheme) to £168 million, most of the increase (£49 million) being attributed to inflation. On top of this the redesign of the White City terminal, provision of quadruple tracks and the 'long tunnel' would cost a further £40 million. With additional sums required for freight traffic (£25 million), more tunnelling to meet environmental objections (£42 million), and full exploitation of the link, for example access to Victoria, upgrading to the UIC gauge, etc. (£62 million), the grand total was £337 million.[159] Fogarty was exasperated, if not dismayed, by these revelations and felt that the material provided by British Rail was 'sadly defective'. She was critical of both the choice of inflation rate and the entangling of inflation and underestimation. In particular, she was annoyed that the increased cost of the Chelsea-Croydon section was now attributed to the 'long tunnel' decision, when the earlier work had revealed clearly that there was little difference in cost between the old and revised schemes. British Rail's latest figures she argued, confused costs attributable to the basic link, costs required to cater for higher levels of traffic, and 'optional extras'. The DOE's own reckoning was that the cost of the basic link, including unavoidable environmental options, was of the order of £200–210 million.[160] At the end of May Fogarty pressed Keen for clarification of a number of points relating to a calculation which was now looking distinctly fragile.[161]

Another complication was the pressure to obtain parliamentary powers for the new line. Naturally, there were concerns over the proposed timetable, which was extremely tight. But it was also uncertain whether the Bill should be 'hybrid' and introduced by the Government, or 'private' and promoted by the British Railways Board. The prospects were scarcely improved by internal legal opinion that a time-consuming planning inquiry might be necessary. All in all, it would be a 'huge task'.[162] The Minister's own position was critical. Mulley firmly believed that 'if we want it to be passed, it must be a Govt. [i.e. hybrid] Bill', despite the difficulties that this would give the DOE, which lacked the necessary engineering expertise.[163] The intention had been to present the Bill in November 1974, with Royal Assent in July 1975, but by June 1974 Mulley had come to the conclusion that a deferment was necessary. Conscious of public pressure for further consultation, he was worried about the difficulties of presenting the Bill in the next session before a decision had been made on the Tunnel itself. He therefore urged officials to defer a decision on the route until the end of the year, which would facilitate an extension of the consultation period to October, and provide a further two months for Government deliberations. Confidentially, the expectation was that the Bill would not be presented before July 1975.[164] When the deferral was communicated to Marsh, the British Rail Chairman expressed fears about the implications this would have for meeting the construction deadline, but he could only fall in line with Government intentions.[165] The change of policy, which was made public on 1 July, may have been unavoidable given the existing uncertainties about the rail link. However, far from tempering the 'rising political temperature', it gave further time for local opposition to exploit the critical opinion then emerging, for example from the Royal Institute of British Architects, and for press speculation to mount.[166]

In the same month (June 1974), British Rail submitted revised estimates for the rail link. Those of June 1973 had been produced on a general basis, applying percentage adjustments and amendments to the Livesey and Henderson report of 1970. This time, the figures were derived from the work of Rendel Palmer & Tritton, consulting civil engineers equipped with detailed plans of the route, and the use of quantity surveyors. The exercise confirmed all the worst fears about escalating costs and falling returns. Bowick, British Rail's Chief Executive, informed his Chairman that the Board would be unable to recommend proceeding with the link as a commercial venture.[167] Marsh then rang Sir Robert Marshall, who had succeeded Pugh as the DOE Second Permanent Secretary with responsibility for the Tunnel, to warn him that the latest estimates showed a 'devastating increase'.[168] The offending 'report on estimates', sent on a confidential basis, reached the Department at the end of the month. It did not make for comfortable reading. Fogarty's initial reaction was that the difference between the estimates was 'startling – and far more startling than the figures we thought we were dealing with even a few weeks ago'.[169] British Rail now thought that the infrastructure would cost £352.5 million and the grand total, including £22.5 million for rolling stock, was £375 million. The financial return was put at $9\frac{1}{2}$ per cent for the passenger investment, $10\frac{1}{2}$ per cent if freight were included. The dramatic increase in cost was attributed to a host of factors: inflation, additional facilities, freight provision, design development, environmental factors, design costs and under-estimation.[170] Marsh asserted that one of the main reasons for cost escalation was the need to meet environmental objections, but at £34.4 million this element accounted for only 14 per cent of the increase.[171] The DOE's own analysis, on the other hand, concluded that environmental requirements had added a mere £17.8 million. It claimed that under-estimation was of the order of £100 million, three times the figure produced by British Rail.[172] But however attribution was contested, the Department conceded that the revised costings at least had been undertaken on a sensible basis.[173] After two rather tense DOE-British Rail meetings in July, British Rail undertook to make a formal submission as quickly as possible.[174] Meanwhile, the political pressure mounted. Mulley was able to fend off a parliamentary question, on 31 July, about escalating costs by maintaining that no revised estimate had yet been formally submitted to him.[175] He also met a deputation of MPs, led by Howe, where he heard allegations of poor communication between British Rail and the public, especially over the land referencing process, and was pressed to extend compensation to those affected by blight.[176] In an attempt to diffuse some of the clamour, Mulley announced that steps would be taken to reduce uncertainty by an early indication of route options no longer under active consideration, and on 6 August British Rail revealed its intentions for the Surrey section by identifying four options.[177]

At the beginning of September Marsh sent Mulley an interim report on the revised estimates. Since the consultation period had been extended, the precise route had not yet been fixed, and so the estimates could not be regarded as a final investment submission. Nevertheless, Marsh admitted that the report raised 'extremely serious problems'.[178] This refined estimate totalled £373 million in May 1974 prices. Expressed in 1973 prices, it amounted to £266 million, an increase of 116 per cent on the original figure of £123 million. British Rail's analysis of the causes of the escalation is shown in Table 6.1. The largest single factor (£108.3 million) was the product of additions to the original scheme, and the remaining elements were inflation (£50.1 million), design development (£47.0 million) and 'omissions and under-estimation' (£44.0 million). Of course, the interpretation of these cost increases was somewhat imprecise. Thus, British Rail could justifiably point out that freight had not been included originally, and defended its additions to each of the eleven sections of route. Fogarty, on the other hand, was adamant that 'the bulk of the additional costs appear to us to be culpable under-estimation'.[179] But for whatever reason, it was evident that the estimate of the rail link sold to Peyton in 1973 was patently flawed. Even the new estimates had to be treated with caution since they omitted three significant items: additional environmental adjustments, including noise reduction; fuller provision for freight (including rolling stock), amounting to £44 million;

Table 6.1 Channel Tunnel Rail Link: analysis of increases in cost between June 1973 and August 1974 (£m., in June 1973 prices, uplifted to May 1974 prices)

	June 1973	*Inflation to May 1974*	*Additions*			*Total Additions*	*Dev. of design*	*Omissions and underestimation*	*August 1974*
			Pass.	*Freight*	*Env/LA*				
Route									
Civil engineering	79.9	32.1	21.9	12.1	23.1	57.1	27.0	16.9	213.0
Other works including signalling/electrification	19.9	10.1	3.5	2.9	6.2	12.6	9.8	8.5	60.9
Total for route	99.8	42.2	25.4	15.0	29.3	69.7	36.8	25.4	273.9
White City terminal	8.7	2.9	1.2	—	19.8	21.0	2.5	3.0	38.1
North Pole depot	6.2	2.5	—	—	—	—	3.3	0.5	12.5
Design/supervision costs	—	—	2.3	1.1	4.6	8.0	2.8	15.1	25.9
Total infrastructure	114.7	47.6	28.9	16.1	53.7	98.7	45.4	44.0	350.4
Rolling stock	8.8	2.5	9.6	—	—	9.6	1.6	—	22.5
Grand total	123.5	50.1	38.5	16.1	53.7	108.3	47.0	44.0	372.9

Source: BRB, 'Channel Tunnel Rail Link: Interim report of revised cost estimates and expected financial return', 30 August 1974, Appendix B, MT144/392, PRO.

and some of the compensation costs imposed by the Land Compensation Act of 1973.[180] Marsh had only two proposals to offer, and fairly lame ones at that. First, he suggested that the link might be financed on a 'European' basis, with a sharing of capital costs among the various railway administrations. Second, he offered to return to the examination of low-investment alternatives, a strategy he had so vigorously opposed only a year earlier. In fact, DOE officials had already begun to look at cheaper options, and had asked a former consultant with World Bank experience to assist them.[181] While the civil servants met British Rail managers to explore the possibilities, Mulley encouraged Marsh to work on both his suggested courses of action. He then briefed Wilson, Callaghan and Healey on the situation, noting that the increase in the cost of the rail link was 'clearly going to be a very important factor in the re-assessment of the case for the Channel Tunnel'.[182]

5. A second election and Labour doubts, October 1974–January 1975

With so much of the project in the air in the early autumn of 1974 – the Channel Tunnel Bill, the rail link, the final studies, reassessment by the Cairncross advisory group, and the prospects for private sector financing in a worsening economic environment – matters were hardly helped by Wilson's decision to go to the country again on 10 October. Announced on 18 September, the election was dominated by Britain's economic difficulties – inflation, the balance of payments and the collapse of the stock market – together with an intensification of the IRA's bombing activities on the mainland. But in general this was a subdued campaign for a somewhat disillusioned electorate. Enlivened only by some defections, a resignation, and some injudicious muscle-flexing by the Tory right-wing, the results were little different from those in February, and once again there was no clear-cut winner. Labour's 319 seats may have exceeded the Conservatives' 277, but the Party secured an overall majority of only three, with a reduced vote and indeed the lowest share of the poll for a majority government since 1922.[183] As far as the Tunnel was concerned, ministerial personnel remained unchanged, but there were no signs that the re-elected administration was any more confident about taking risks with large projects in the prevailing economic climate. The escalating costs of the rail link provided an opportunity for critics to make their views known. The CPRS, a consistent opponent of the Tunnel, had already informed the Cabinet in September that the project 'must be a very strong candidate for cancellation'.[184] The Chancellor, Denis Healey, being drawn more and more into a deflationary approach, told Wilson, on 24 October: 'I am sure that rail costs of £400 million would by themselves be fatal to the project. This apart, the Tunnel could hardly have been classed as a priority project at the time of the last major decisions, and with our prospective serious problems in allocating our resources it must surely rank lower now'. He went on to ask for 'fully adequate time' to reassess the project.[185]

The main effect of the October election was to provide a further interruption to an already overstretched parliamentary timetable for the Tunnel, encouraging press speculation about postponement or abandonment.[186] It was 11 November before the Commons debated a procedural motion to allow the Bill to be reintroduced at the stage it had reached in the previous parliament. While the motion was carried by 168 votes to 115, there was a significant opposition, and the Cabinet was somewhat unnerved by the fact that some Labour backbenchers had voted against the Government. Three days later it resolved that Environment Secretary Crosland should make a reassuring statement to the effect that while the Bill would be reintroduced, any decision whether or not to go ahead with the Tunnel would be postponed until full account could be taken of the Cairncross report, which was expected in the spring.[187] The Cabinet returned to the subject at a meeting on 21 November, chaired in Wilson's absence by the Lord President, Edward Short. At this critical stage Crosland informed colleagues about the escalation in the cost of the proposed rail link, but asserted that he was strongly opposed to abandoning the project at this stage. Instead he argued that the Government should: (1) investigate with British Rail the feasibility of a lower-cost option for the high-speed rail link; (2) approach the French to seek a delay of at least a year before a commitment to go ahead with Phase III; and (3) bring the matter back to Cabinet in 1975, when more information, including the Cairncross report, was available. This policy was justified, somewhat speciously, on the grounds that 'British Governments in the past have taken decisions on major investment projects in a frivolous and insouciant spirit (for example Concorde and Maplin). I hope and propose that we should do better in the case of the Tunnel'.[188] In discussion Crosland was up-beat, emphasising that the Tunnel 'might well prove more cost-effective than any other option'. He secured Healey's 'reluctant' agreement that it was difficult to justify immediate cancellation in advance of Cairncross, but other colleagues were more difficult, notably the Tunnel-sceptics (Michael Foot, Tony Benn, Harold Lever, Reg Prentice, John Morris and Willie Ross). There were complaints about the cost escalation and more familiar gripes about 'regional imbalance'. However, the weight of opinion lay with Crosland. The Cabinet, in approving his recommendations, invited him to seek French agreement to a postponement, arrange for the reintroduction of the Bill on report, prefacing this by a parliamentary statement on the rail link and the outcome of his negotiations with the French. It was also agreed that a small Ministerial Committee be established to 'keep an eye on developments'.[189] This was set up under the chairmanship of the Lord Chancellor, Lord Elwyn-Jones, in December.[190]

The Government's decision was made known on 26 November, though by this time the press had predicted the outcome.[191] Crosland wrote to the French Minister, Cavaillé, and the Chairmen of the Tunnel companies, Harcourt and Maurin, to inform them of the British Government's anxieties about the rail link, now expected to cost as much as £500 million, and its intention to seek a year's standstill. With no prospect of the link paying its way, Crosland observed, 'the Government views with dismay the prospect of bearing sums of this magnitude on the Exchequer for the foreseeable future. Indeed, unless very substantial capital assistance were forthcoming from, for instance, the Continental railway administrations...there is frankly no hope whatsoever of investment on this scale'.[192] Time should therefore be given to exploring cheaper alternatives. Delay was also justified by the state of the world economy and money markets, which raised at least a question as to whether the Tunnel companies 'could readily contemplate embarking on a financial enterprise of the magnitude of Phase III in the summer of next year'.[193] At the same time Crosland addressed the Commons in similar vein. He told MPs that financing the rail link at a cost of £373 million plus was 'out of the question', confirming, in reply to questions, that his statement was 'a formal Government decision to abandon the construction of a high-speed rail link'.[194] British Rail was informed that 'For practical purposes…we must regard the link as previously envisaged as abandoned'.[195] But by this stage British Rail had completely reversed its earlier stance, and had conceded that cheaper alternatives could be pursued.[196]

Crosland had promised the House that the Channel Tunnel Bill would be reintroduced once he had received a positive reply to his request for a deferment from the French Government and the Tunnel companies. But this was not a simple matter. The French Government's initial response to the news had been to seek to protect its position by insisting that Crosland include in his statement a reference to French determination to complete Phase II and the studies, with a view to signing Agreement No.3 'within the agreed time schedule'. This was confirmed when Wilson met Giscard d'Estaing and Chirac on 3 December.[197] However, a more supportive response was given in discussions between Cavaillé and Mulley on the same day,[198] and on 9 December the French Minister's formal agreement to the delay was conveyed to Crosland. Nevertheless, the French continued to nurse suspicions that the British were using the cost of the rail link as a way of extricating themselves from the project without questioning the merits of the scheme itself. In Cavaillé's formal response there was a complaint about the lack of consultation, and an insistence that a new agreement, setting out the modifications and protecting the interests of all parties, be included in a Protocol to be signed before 31 December 1974.[199] While there was support, if rather grudging, from the French Government, the reaction of the private companies on 10 December was more hostile. They were understandably anxious to protect the interests of their institutional shareholders. As Harcourt observed, since March the companies had viewed 'with growing concern various statements by H.M. Government that they are not committed to the Project. These statements are contrary to the spirit of the agreements made last year, and they do not give confidence that it will be possible to negotiate Agreement No.3 in the middle of next year'. Harcourt emphasised that the further delay would 'certainly make the task of…management and financing even more difficult.' He added: 'The conclusion which we reach is that your proposals constitute a breach of the agreements entered into in 1973 and involve a fundamental change in the entire basis upon which the Phase II share capital was subscribed'. In the circumstances, therefore, they could only be non-committal, though they 'welcomed' the opportunity to explore options.[200] Fogarty remained calm in the face of the storm. She found the letters 'predictable' and 'for the record', and was sanguine about the companies' tactic of letting the date for ratification of the Treaty (1 January) 'hang like a sword of Damocles over subsequent negotiations'.[201] More problematic, however, was the French Government's request for a protocol by the end of the year. Fogarty thought it unlikely that one of the elements required in it – approval of 'the essential characteristics of the new rail link – gauge, speed and capacity' – could be defined by then. She observed: 'It is simply not clear to us whether the French Minister realises the implications of this, and is trying to ensure breakdown while appearing reasonable, or does not understand the implications; I believe the latter to be the true situation'.[202] Nevertheless, work began on a draft protocol, in line with French intentions.[203] Meanwhile, the draft law enabling the French to ratify the Treaty was passed by the French Senate on 19 November, and was then adopted by the National Assembly on 16 December.[204]

There was no resolution of the seeming impasse as Christmas approached. The British and French Governments were unable to agree on a new date for British ratification, the British offering 16 May, the French insisting on 1 April.[205] A meeting of the Channel Tunnel Reassessment Steering Committee (DOE, Treasury and CPRS) on 20 December, held on the day the Tunnel Bill was formally presented in the Commons, learned that the companies had expressed their unwillingness to sign the protocol, but had made no positive suggestions to resolve the crisis.[206] Indeed, it was known that the French company in particular was suspicious of British intentions.[207] Efforts to move forward on the basis of an exchange of letters were overtaken by further correspondence from the companies, received on Christmas Eve, which affirmed their refusal to sign the protocol and indicated that they would serve a notice of abandonment after 1 January.[208] On the other hand, Agreement No.2 provided for a further 60-day period before compensation payments were due, and the companies suggested that this offered a final opportunity for renegotiation.[209] A period of heightened activity early in the New Year, involving Tom Shearer, the relevant Deputy Secretary, and Fogarty from the DOE, and Macé and Callou on the French side, failed to achieve very much. On 2 January the companies duly served a formal notice that unless the Treaty were ratified by 20 January the project would be deemed to have been abandoned by the Governments.[210] By this time Mulley had come to the view that it would be best to accept the companies' claim of abandonment and 'terminate the arrangements as tidily as possible'.[211] British officials, led by Sir Robert Marshall, were prepared to consider any proposals which might keep the project alive. Meanwhile in Paris, the British Ambassador, Sir Edward Tomkins, argued that everything should be done to keep the companies in play for a little longer so as not to compromise the delicate discussions with the French on Britain's renegotiated membership of the EEC. It was even suggested that the two governments might fund the project with recycled Arab petro-dollars.[212] However, as Fogarty conceded, it would only be worth hanging on if there were a real chance of building the Tunnel. She was far from optimistic: 'it does not look as though it is politically practicable in face of the sort of qualified rapture the Phase II figuring and Cairncross are likely to produce'.[213]

A final 'quadripartite' meeting was held in London on 9 January 1975. It was attended by all the protagonists below ministerial level, including Shearer and

Fogarty; Macé and Callou; Harcourt and Maurin; and Merton, Frame and Gabriel. Harcourt, for the companies, advanced a rather ill-defined set of proposals for a possible continuation in a distinctly half-hearted fashion. A range of 'work programmes' was presented, the gist of which was that the companies were prepared to agree to a moratorium until 15 March, but expected the time to be used to prepare a new agreement, to be concluded by 31 October 1975. The enactment of legislation and Treaty ratification would be achieved by 31 July 1976, and authorisation to proceed by 31 December. The timetable was not in itself unreasonable, but the companies added three demands: (1) that Phase II shareholders should have the right to take their money out at a premium (via the multipliers formulae); (2) that the remaining shareholders could do the same if for any reason the project were abandoned before construction started; and (3) that the interim interest rate be raised to a commercial level.[214] DOE officials felt that there was little chance of getting such a package accepted by the British Government. Quite apart from the enormous advantage the new arrangements would give the companies, it would not be possible to complete the reassessment of the rail link before the October 1975 deadline, since Marsh had just confirmed that a 'fully elaborated' low-cost option would not be ready until February 1976.[215] There was also every expectation that the Phase II shareholders would withdraw their investment. In the circumstances, it was felt that the only option was to allow the project to fail.[216] At the eleventh hour Marsh and Keen telephoned the Department to say that an adequate rail link could be provided for 'at least £100 million' less than originally proposed. But this was a case of too little, much too late.[217] Abandonment was then discussed by the Cabinet on 14 January and by the Ministerial Committee on the evening of the same day. At Cabinet Crosland told his colleagues that the companies' counter-proposals were 'completely unacceptable', and that the present project should be abandoned. After a brief discussion it was resolved that subject to the agreement of the Ministerial Committee, Crosland should inform the French Government of Britain's acceptance of abandonment.[218]

The Ministerial Committee was left to consider the consequences of the decision with the aid of a memorandum from Crosland, which put the cost of buying up the companies at about £40 million and set out the options available to the Government. There were four of these: (a) continue with the Tunnel as a public sector project; (b) place the project on a 'care and maintenance' basis to allow the two governments time to reconsider; (c) terminate the project, but keep open the possibility of reviving it 'in a few years' time'; and (d) close the project down with no prospect of revival for the rest of the century. Of these the DOE expressed a strong preference for option (c).[219] In discussion Roy Hattersley, Minister of State for Foreign Affairs, mounted a vigorous campaign for option (b), conveying the Foreign Office's belief that a peremptory abandonment would be 'deeply prejudicial' to Britain's negotiations with the EEC. However, this tactic was thought unlikely to impress the French, and the balance of opinion in the Committee was in Crosland's favour.[220] His decision was communicated to the French via the French Ambassador, Jacques de Beaumarchais, and via Tomkins in Paris on 15 January,[221] and the next day the Cabinet was informed of events. The rejection of the option to continue negotiating, about which Callaghan, Elwyn-Jones and Jenkins expressed concern, was firmly defended. As Crosland noted, 'Let Albion not be perfidious on this occasion'. The project was to be closed down in an orderly fashion, 'to keep open the possibility, *at modest expense*, (my italics) of taking it up again in five or ten years' time'. There were no Tunnel defenders, and very little discussion.[222] Barbara Castle had completely reversed her earlier enthusiasm in 1966, recounting in her diary that she nursed 'a kind of earthy feeling that an island is an island and should not be violated. Certainly I am convinced that the building of a tunnel would do something profound to the national attitude – and not certainly for the better'. Benn's response to the news that 'the whole thing would be abandoned' was the terse observation, 'Very good news'.[223] The emphasis in Crosland's Commons statement on 20 January was that while the origin of the difficulty lay in the cost of the rail link and the failure to ratify the Treaty, the Government had been placed in an impossible position by the actions of the private companies.[224]

The French made predictable noises of complaint. When de Beaumarchais was given the news he was reported to have been 'visibly taken aback. He said his Government would be dismayed'. Cavaillé's letter to Crosland expressed surprise at the decision and reiterated the French Government's deep attachment to the project.[225] Chirac went much further. Lecturing Tomkins for half an hour on the day of Crosland's statement, he complained about Britain's 'unilateral action' and claimed that there had been no proper consultation. Since the British had played a 'dirty trick' on the French, he challenged the idea that the costs of abandonment should be shared 50–50, as provided for in Agreement No.2. Fortunately, he was prepared to detach the issue from other aspects of Anglo-French relations, including EEC membership.[226] In France and Belgium press reaction was generally shrill. Although there was little regret about the lost infrastructure outside the Nord-Pas de Calais region, the cancellation was taken to be an example of Britain's 'atavistic insularity' and 'anti-European' stance; some attempted to link the matter with Britain's decision, reached on 21 January and announced two days later, to have a referendum on her continued membership of the EEC.[227] In the UK, the media's response was muted, unsurprisingly so in view of all the earlier leaks and speculations. The *Times* revealed the news on Saturday 18 January, and most of the comment came next day in the Sunday newspapers. Although they expected a storm of protest from the French and from MPs, and criticised a conclusion reached before further reports from British Rail and the Cairncross committee, the period of protest was brief. Neither backbench MPs, nor the press, nor wider opinion appeared unduly concerned about the potential loss of an important transport facility. On the contrary, many welcomed the fact that it had been sidelined.[228]

6. Abandonment

Why was the project abandoned? After the decision, inquests were conducted by the DOE, FCO and RTZ, so that the appropriate lessons might be learned. The DOE's

Cartoon 4 Abandonment in 1975, as seen by Derek Alder, *Sunday Times*, 19 January 1975.

document, much the largest, also served as a set of confidential notes for successor officials, should the project be revived.[229] Published accounts, some of them from active players like Michael Bonavia and Donald Hunt,[230] also sought ways through the explanatory minefield. Bonavia defended the actions of both British Rail and the private companies and blamed political factors for the Tunnel's demise: the disruption of the two elections; Labour's lack of support; and the 'uncertain world of politics where one year's enthusiasm becomes next year's scepticism'.[231] Hunt noted that 'political storm clouds precipitated by world events' cast a shadow over the project. The death of Pompidou, the change of government in Britain, and a lukewarm attitude from British Rail, all played their part. But observing that Wilson promised to cancel expensive 'white elephants' in order to win support from the TUC, he identified the principal reason to be the fact that the Tunnel, like Maplin, Concorde and the London Ringway (M25), was a 'political football, vulnerable to trade off in return for short–term gain elsewhere'.[232] More impartial observers, such as Peter Morris and George Hough, and Ian Holliday *et al.*, highlighted the lack of an effective project champion on the British side. The project died because of 'political indifference', together with the ability of the private sector to utilise favourable escape clauses.[233] Finally, Richard Gibb, Laurent Bonnaud and Roxanne Powell gave more importance to the escalating cost of the rail link, which, according to leading planner Peter Hall, was one of the great negative planning disasters. However, they too found 'the changing political environment' to be the most important in 'a wide range of policies and problems'.[234]

To these factors we may add our own. First, the psychological impact of the economic crises of 1974–6 must not be underestimated. For many observers, Britain appeared to be on the brink of an economic and financial collapse, and the Treasury's underestimation of Britain's Public Sector Borrowing Requirement in 1974–5 scarcely created a climate in which the rail link – a new and large public sector scheme – could be presented with confidence.[235] Furthermore, a lack of enthusiasm for large projects such as the Tunnel could be found all over Whitehall, not only in the Treasury, where concern concentrated on the implications of such a large bond issue, but also in the DOE.[236] Second, there was the patent inexperience of the DOE and British Rail in mounting a major railway project, the rail link at £373 million being equivalent to more than double the total railway investment in 1974.[237] Third, the French should not escape censure. It is clear that after Pompidou's death Chirac gave the British misleading signals in the summer of 1974, which suggested that France too was half-hearted about the venture, though of course this was strenuously denied later on.[238] And there were concerns on *both* sides of the channel about the prospects given the state of world money markets. Finally, the companies were also implicated in the decision. They were suspicious of Crosland's wish to renegotiate the timetable, on the grounds that this might weaken their entitlement to compensation. Indeed, at an informal meeting of BCTC directors in December 1974 Naylor had revealed that Shearer had advised him that the companies should get out, saying: 'there was no political will to proceed with the tunnel'.[239] As William Merton of Flemings noted, if they consented to an extension and the Cairncross report indicated that the project was not viable, it might not be possible to demonstrate unilateral abandonment. More significantly, they were privately worried about their ability to raise the equity portion of the investment needed to construct the Tunnel, and there were also signs that some of the partners in the consortium were getting cold feet. Kleinwort Benson in particular was reported to be in favour of quitting.[240] In fact, there is a sense in which, as in Agatha Christie's *Murder on the Orient Express*, all the parties were culpable. In the prevailing atmosphere of bluff and counterbluff, cynicism about the Tunnel's prospects was widespread.

Nevertheless, the official documentation, confusing and self-serving as it sometimes is, enables us to advance further along the trail of causation. The emphasis that appears most convincing is that, in an unpromising environment of vacillation, the escalating cost of the rail link provided the doubters and opponents with all the ammunition they required to jettison the Tunnel. Two fundamental misjudgements were made. The first, by Peyton, was to tie in the rail link so closely with the Tunnel, without prior development work; the second, by British Rail, was to nail its colours so inflexibly to a high-cost option. By making a high-quality rail link a *sine qua non* of the Tunnel, the Conservative Minister created the circumstances in which his successors could use it to challenge the validity of the project as a whole, although he could not have anticipated that with a final estimate of £373 million the supporting infrastructure promised to cost the Exchequer as much as its obligations to the Tunnel proper. British Rail, while having justification for some of its whingeing, must bear a considerable proportion of the blame for letting things get out of control as much as it did. Of course it is true that the Board did not accord the project a high priority in the early 1970s, and justifiably so in view of its highly speculative nature. Equally true is the observation that the team at Bonavia's disposal was a rather meagre one, housed in a post-McKinsey 'corporate' department, away from the railway business.[241] Indeed, the Board, by appointing Bonavia from the railways' Staff College at Woking, instead of choosing someone more used to the hurly-burly of 'real' operating management, gave a clear sign, whether wittingly or not, to the Southern Region, the HQ Passenger Department and the railway engineers, as to where the Tunnel came in the railway pecking order. In any case there were more pressing issues, for example the problems caused by investment constraints, and the widespread demoralisation felt by regional railway managers as a result of the Board's attempt to introduce the 'field organisation', a further and unwelcome piece of McKinsey-inspired change which, like the Tunnel, was abandoned in 1975.[242] After Agreement No.2 was signed the Board did recognise the greater importance of the project. It established multi-functional policy and technical steering groups, made BR's Channel Tunnel Unit a responsibility of the railway business, and appointed Keen to first support and then succeed Bonavia.[243] But all this said, it is perfectly reasonable to argue that if British Rail had drawn up a more considered and flexible strategy in the early stages, including a more reasonable attitude to low-cost options, there would have been very much less ammunition for a sceptical Labour administration to use to subvert the project. Bonavia may have claimed that British Rail had no fewer than eight options in its cupboards,[244] but in the period 1972–4 railway managers were extremely reluctant to reveal any of them.[245] Indeed, their dealings with their political masters often left something to be desired. There is plenty of evidence that the DOE had no confidence in either the 'egregious' McKenna or Bonavia, as the appointment of an independent railway consultant made clear. Indeed, by December 1974 Mulley was openly calling for McKenna's head.[246] Bonavia was the author of a book on the economics of transport, but as the records indicate, his mastery of investment appraisal techniques was far from perfect. It is quite clear that there was a failure to appreciate how much of a difference additional costs (on top of the initial, back-of-envelope calculation) were making to the overall estimate.[247] Moreover, there was something capricious in British Rail's insistence that 'Mother Railway' knew best.[248] And with the benefit of hindsight one might be puzzled at the inflexibility of railway planning – why no Waterloo terminal, for example? – while the notion that the Southern Region would be clogged up by Channel Tunnel trains sits uneasily with the knowledge that today's Eurostar trains require only seven paths for London-Paris/Brussels trains in the morning rush hour.[249] Susan Fogarty's recollection of events, at a seminar convened by the Major Projects Association in 1981, is also instructive. While accepting a multi-causal analysis, she regretted the fact that British Rail had not been properly integrated into the project. 'The Board should have demanded action by their Southern Region and their Civil Engineering Department. If that had been done sufficiently early, the later surprises on costs could have been avoided'.[250] The DOE's private thoughts were much more acerbic. Its inquest had concluded that British Rail lacked the necessary management talent to construct a tunnel, or operate tunnel services: 'Unless there have been major improvements in the management of the railways, we would strongly advise against entrusting them with the operation of a multi-purpose Tunnel, or with the construction of any type of one'.[251]

The Department's stance was rather unfair, however. Responsibility for some of these difficulties was shared. During the inquest into abandonment held by the Department, Henry Woodhouse, its transport solicitor, was particularly critical of the Department's role in the debacle. He noted that 'A fatal mistake was made by the planners in the 1960s when they decided to put on one side the question of the Rail Link. The result... was that by the early 1970s the Tunnel project itself had been developed very fully and adequately but, when it was decided to undertake the Rail Link as well, the scheme for this came along in an exceedingly half-baked condition... The Department ought to have seen that the Rail Link project, as put forward by British Rail, was a non-starter... It still amazes me that the basic unsoundness of this scheme was not perceived by everyone as soon as it was put before the Department'.[252] However, 'figuring' was no better in the DOE, and there was clearly something in Bonavia's complaint that the Department was inconsistent, 'at times insisting that the demand for an independent rail link would imperil and probably frustrate the total Channel Tunnel project, at times insisting that a compromise or low-investment must be practicable'. In the critical period of policy formation in 1972–3, Bonavia was able to claim that 'not a single constructive or sensible suggestion has come from their side'.[253] Given the situation, a greater input from the Treasury might have helped, but the DOE's Channel Tunnel Unit was only too aware that senior Treasury officials, characteristically captious, were 'lukewarm' and indeed were talking about abandonment before it had become a major agenda item.[254]

Peter Snape, the NUR-supported MP and tunnelliste, was characteristically trenchant when he attacked the ministerial team for approaching the project 'with the enthusiasm of a couple of Trappist monks advocating birth control'.[255] It was common knowledge that Mulley, the Transport Minister, was a sceptic who was eager to axe the Tunnel. After the Commons vote on 11 November 1974 his was the first voice to suggest that the project should be abandoned, and significantly, 'in the light of the effect of the revised rail link estimate'.[256] However, his Secretary of State, though lacking Peyton's zeal, was much more of a supporter. Furthermore, Crosland might have been able to keep the project alive had not the escalating rail link, coupled with the delay in producing properly costed low-cost alternatives, made it extremely difficult for him to do so. Had he had more to work with, the Tunnel could have survived on to an evaluation by the Cairncross Group and not suffered the charade of the sentence being imposed before the jury had announced its verdict. The companies were certainly complicit in the decision to the extent that they had found it hard to raise money, appreciated that the new economic situation had made the project more risky, and were anxious to avoid a situation where they lost their compensation. On the other hand, the evidence shows that the British and French project managers were keen to continue, tunnelling had just started, and there is every reason to believe that with more backing from the British Government the project would have gone ahead. It was the escalating cost of the rail link cost, and the pantomime surrounding it, which provided the catalyst for abandonment. The lesson drawn by both RTZDE and the DOE was that the Tunnel should have been a public sector project from the start with private sector project management.[257] The DOE concluded: 'Our advice on the inclusion of private risk capital is "DON'T" '.[258] While the argument is superficially convincing, the 1970–5 project was very much a public sector project with its high proportion of government-guaranteed bonds. Abandonment occurred when a conflict of interest emerged, and the rail link escalation was the catalyst. As the DOE conceded, 'In the end we came unstuck because the shared interest of most of those concerned with an adequate review of the rail link in the UK, and in a complete assessment of the changes in the world economic situation, conflicted with the interest of some of the shareholders… we came unstuck because we had inadvertently built in a major financial incentive to two parties to withdraw in circumstances which arose accidentally'.[259] British Rail's belated realisation that cheaper rail link options were required merely indicates that if railway managers had come round to this view earlier, and if the DOE had demonstrated more expertise in handling the first major piece of railway infrastructure for over 70 years, we might have been spared another decade or so of delay.

7

KEEPING HOPES ALIVE, 1975–81

1. Loose ends, 1975: compensation and protecting the infrastructure

The abandonment of the Channel Tunnel in 1975 left several messy loose ends, not least the revised studies, the alternative rail link options, and the deliberations of the Cairncross Group, all of which remained in limbo. More pressing was the strict timetable, imposed by the abandonment rules, for the Governments' buyout of the two companies and their assets. It was also necessary to protect the existing works and wind the project down in an orderly fashion. Much of this was essentially administrative, and the exercise marked the end of the Labour Government's active promotion of the Tunnel.

The detailed provisions for abandonment were contained in Agreement No.2 and the Exchange of Notes dated 17 November 1973. If the project were abandoned by one or both of the Governments, they were required to repay any outstanding guaranteed loans within six months and acquire all the shareholdings in the companies within 60 days, that is by 22 March 1975. As we have seen, in these circumstances the costs up to the date of abandonment were to be shared between the Governments on a 50–50 basis.[1] To cover the immediate post-abandonment position, the two governments and the two companies, BCTC and SFTM, signed a quadripartite holding agreement. Lasting for a period of seven days, this allowed the companies to maintain existing contracts and carry out any necessary maintenance and safety work.[2] At the same time, officials commenced the urgent task of drafting a new Exchange of Notes setting out the principles guiding the closing down of the project and, in particular, those relating to the treatment of costs and the acquisition of the companies. At first, negotiations proceeded satisfactorily. There was agreement with French officials that the costs of running down the project, i.e. expenditure incurred after abandonment, would also be shared on a 50–50 basis, and some acceptance of the British preference for each country to acquire the assets of its own company rather than taking a joint share in both.[3] However, by the end of January, the French Government had declared that it would not now proceed on the lines envisaged thus far; on post-abandonment costs each government should go its own way. The French also refused to sign a further quadripartite agreement and so a bipartite one, between the British Government and the BCTC, had to be hastily arranged. This new holding agreement, again lasting for seven days, repeated the authority for the BCTC to continue its operations. Two further agreements were necessary to cover the period to the Government's acquisition of BCTC.[4] The attitude of the French was unsurprising given that many in Paris were still smarting from the shock of abandonment. DOE officials suspected that the move was a political one designed to re-open the issue of 50–50 sharing of the pre-abandonment costs. Certainly, the subject was an extremely sensitive one and the Foreign Office was concerned that the issue should not become enmeshed in the wider negotiations over Britain's membership of the EEC.[5]

On 3 March, after a period of prevarication, French officials eventually assented to the proposal that each Government would purchase its own company. By this time, both sides had appointed accountants to examine the companies, and on the same day a satisfactory report from Touche Ross on the British company was received. Fogarty was thus able to tell Harcourt that the Government would purchase BCTC for the sum of £8.505 million.[6] Nationalisation of the British Channel Tunnel Company was effected on 21 March when the existing board members approved the transfer of shares to the Secretary of State and six DOE nominees. Then, with the exception of Frame and Naylor, the directors resigned and were replaced by Shearer (chairman), Fogarty and Rosenfeld. Responsibility for running down the activities was delegated to a specially established project management committee, while the services of RTZDE were retained by means of a new management agreement, but with a much reduced level of fees.[7] Little publicity was given to these events, which were followed by a small gathering held at the offices of Hill Samuel. The occasion was apparently conducted in a friendly if rather depressed atmosphere. It marked the departure of two long-standing tunnelistes, Leo d'Erlanger and Lord Harcourt. Founder members of the CTSG in 1957, their aspirations ended with the effective demise of the BCTC.[8]

There were two other issues to settle. The first concerned the payment for the studies owned by the CTSG. Under the Channel Tunnel Studies Group Agreement of October 1972, the British and French companies undertook to pay £3 million for the assets of the CTSG; payment was to be made after the issue of the Phase II shares. The termination of the project rendered the agreement inoperative, but the abandonment provisions of Agreement No.2 gave the Governments the right to substitute themselves for the two companies in order to buy the CTSG studies. Officials, asked to decide whether to exercise this option, felt that the material was now of 'purely historic interest' and was certainly not worth £3 million. It was also argued that members of the CTSG had in any case received recompense by means of the multipliers applied to their direct investment.[9] This was a slight misrepresentation, for while true of Channel Tunnel Investments on the British side, it did not apply to the American interests represented by Technical Studies Inc., who had left in 1971 and thus remained without reward for their efforts and expenditure.[10] After some fishing the CTSG made a formal approach in October 1975, asking the two governments whether they wished to take up the right to purchase the studies. This request was declined, however.[11] A similar fate befell the request by Channel Tunnel Investments to regain its former name of British Channel Tunnel Company. There was an element of opportunism behind this apparently innocent approach, since as David Burr of the CTU observed, it would 'reestablish in the collective consciousness exactly those historical claims to favour which it has just cost us so dear to buy out'. With this in mind Fogarty informed Merton that 'you can't have your ball back just now, and it may have been permanently confiscated!'[12]

Work on the Exchange of Notes continued amid some uncertainty as to the French response to the sharing of costs. While British and French officials were able to reach broad agreement on the terms on 6 February, and indeed had produced a detailed draft by mid-March, it was not clear whether French ministers would concur. Officials in Paris were clearly worried that some of them 'would not be averse to picking a quarrel'. The basic premise was that the cost of the work done to 27 January 1975, when the Governments elected to go their own way, must be shared. The net effect of avoiding the wider application of the 50–50 rule was held to be financially advantageous to the British Government.[13] Unfortunately, it proved difficult to settle the matter because discrepancies were discovered in the accounts of the French company, SFTM, which delayed its acquisition by the French Government. A 'non-contractual' two million franc interest-free loan from SFTM to SITUMER was revealed by the French accountants, La Fiduciaire, together with significant overspending by SITUMER. Assurances from the French were produced, but there were also other items, notably cancellation charges claimed by sub-contractors Pont-à-Mousson on an unauthorised contract.[14] However, the British Government's liability, put at a half-share of about £250,000, was held to be too small to warrant delaying the overall settlement. Nevertheless, these investigations, which were exploited by members of Jean-Pierre Fourcade's Finance Ministry, and some 'toing and froing between the Embassy and the Quai d'Orsay' about the precise language, had the effect of delaying the signing of the Exchange of Notes until 24 June, three months after the stipulated date.[15] The short 16-page document confirmed that each Government would buy the equity in its own company but share the aggregate costs of the two transactions. Each Government would also repay the loan capital raised by its company. The abandonment costs qualifying for inclusion under the 50–50 arrangement were closely defined, with a schedule itemising the payments under the specified contracts – primarily cancellation charges and the costs of reports – prior to 28 January 1975. Provision was made for the free exchange of documents and information between the two parties. Finally, both Governments undertook to maintain their Tunnel works in a condition that would enable them to be brought back into use if the project were revived.[16] Six days later the belated acquisition of SFTM was completed. The winding-up once again revealed all the difficulties in trying to secure a common approach by both countries to a complex project.[17]

At the time of the abandonment, a significant amount of preparatory civil engineering work had been undertaken. On the British side, a road access tunnel between the upper and lower Shakespeare Cliff sites had been completed, as had tunnelling (the 'conveyor adit' and the 'marshalling tunnel') to a forward area where the Priestley boring machine was installed. In addition to the work on site, thousands of lining segments, in precast concrete and cast iron, had been manufactured.[18] At Sangatte, where the ground was known to be more difficult, the plan had been to sink a cylindrical 'descenderie' to a point below sea level, from where the Robbins boring machine would excavate a trial section of service tunnel.[19] However, conditions proved to be far worse than expected, and a fall of fissured chalk rendered this method impracticable and unsafe. A new approach, involving partial tunnelling, had to be adopted.[20] The Robbins machine was still above ground when the project was aborted.[21] According to RTZDE, the British tunnelling machine was ready to commence work on 20 January, the day on which Crosland announced the abandonment, though both Donald Hunt and Drew Fetherston assert that boring operations actually took place on that day. In fact, the Priestley machine was to enjoy a real moment of glory since it was used subsequently to bore a short section of tunnel for experimental purposes. The DOE argued that the experience of tunnelling was likely to benefit a future Tunnel project, as well as being of interest to the Department's Transport and Road Research Laboratory [TRRL]. In addition, Fogarty contended that running the machine would improve the morale of the workforce, whose co-operation was required in the shutdown.[22] These arguments were sufficient to persuade the Treasury to agree to a gross expenditure of £350,000 for the work, although it insisted that a proportion of the money be found from other research budgets. In fact, the net cost proved to be substantially less than £350,000 due to offsetting savings from lower cancellation charges, virement of DOE research funds, and contributions from the TRRL and the DTI.[23] A short drive of 250 metres was completed in April 1975, thus creating a section of Channel Tunnel financed by the public sector. Thereafter the machine was maintained until 1976, after which it was sold for scrap.[24] It was also necessary to protect the Tunnel and associated site works, a task which was completed by Christmas 1975, when the site was handed over to the Property Services Agency. The level of administrative support was gradually reduced. Crosland told the Commons in July 1975 that the number of Channel Tunnel Unit staff had fallen from 28 to 13, and explained that the Unit would be completely disbanded once all the loose ends had been tied.[25] At the end of August Fogarty left to take up a new appointment as DOE Regional Director, West Midlands, leaving Gould to oversee Tunnel affairs, with the assistance of John Noulton, who was at the beginning of what proved to be a long association with the Tunnel. With the site works completed, the Project Management Committee held its last meeting in December 1975.[26] Before Fogarty's departure, the remaining staff devoted considerable time to the preparation of a substantive document entitled 'Experience of Project Abandoned January 1975: Notes for our Successors'. Work on the Notes, which continued under Gould, was intended to guide future administrators should the project be revived.[27]

How much did the British Government have to find to end the project? In January 1975 Crosland told the Commons that the cost of abandonment would be about £20 million, while in the following month, Mulley thought total obligations would be of the order of £16 million.[28] The calculation was made up of several elements and was complicated by the 50–50 arrangement with the French, final settlement of which was not completed until August 1977.[29] Taking the British side only, the Government spent £8.505 million in acquiring the BCTC, and on top of this the repayment of government guaranteed loans amounted to approximately £7 million. Then came the adjustments relating to the 50–50 undertaking. Payments equivalent to £1.6 million were made to the French, comprising £877,000 to balance the costs of purchasing the companies, and £686,000 to cover the qualifying joint expenditure.[30] Finally, a figure of approximately £4.3 million was incurred by the British Government alone in winding up the project in Kent.[31] These elements totalled £21.4 million, in line with the estimate given by Crosland. Assuming that the costs on the French side were of a similar magnitude, then altogether the aborted Channel Tunnel project had cost the two governments in the region of £44 million.[32]

2. Loose ends, 1975: the Cairncross Report

As we have seen, it was not until August 1974 that the British Government was able to announce the appointment of Sir Alec Cairncross as Chairman of the Channel Tunnel Advisory Group (CTAG). Further time elapsed while the other members were assembled and the first meeting did not take place until 7 October.[33] Civil servants experienced great difficulty in finding 'people of standing who have not committed themselves publicly in respect of the Channel Tunnel – or become too deeply involved in the Government's assessment of it'.[34] Plans to add a merchant banker were unsuccessful, and it was December before an industrialist, Arthur Knight, was found to complete the Advisory Group, by which time it was evident that the project was in some difficulty.[35] A banker, an academic, an industrialist and a trade union official joined Cairncross. This apparently heterogeneous band in fact shared a common intellectual background. J.R. (Dick) Sargent, Group Economic Adviser at the Midland Bank, had been Professor of Economics at Warwick University and an economic adviser to the Treasury and DEA in the 1960s. Alan Wilson, Professor of Urban and Regional Geography at Leeds University, had served as Mathematical Adviser to the Ministry of Transport in 1966–8. Arthur Knight, an experienced businessman and Deputy Chairman of Courtaulds, had been a member of the Economic Committee of the CBI and had sat on the Roskill Commission on the Third London Airport, while the Group's secretary, David Lea, was Secretary to the TUC's Economic Department. Since Cairncross was himself an economist, the Advisory Group's primary focus was in matters economic. This was no disadvantage, however. The membership reflected the narrower instructions given the Group following interdepartmental discussions, in which the Channel Tunnel Reassessment Steering

Committee had decided that engineering and environmental issues should be excluded. While Cairncross was given no formal terms of reference, his remit was essentially to assess the adequacy of the consultants' Phase II studies, with the aim of determining whether the material 'provided an adequate and appropriate base for the Government to decide whether the Tunnel is in broad and economic terms more advantageous to the UK than reliance on sea and air services'. This was a more modest task than the searching reassessment promised by Crosland in April 1974 (above, p. 137).[36] But by the time Knight completed the Group in December, even this remit seemed in doubt, since members were now aware that Crosland was seeking to delay the project for a year. Nevertheless, despite the bleak outlook for the Tunnel, the Group was reassured at successive meetings that the Secretary of State remained anxious to hear their views.[37] After the British Government had lurched towards abandonment and the cancellation of the Phase II studies in January 1975, Crosland asked Cairncross to submit a brief report as soon as possible. This was to cover the project as originally conceived and also consider the methods of assessment to be used if it were revived in the future. Cairncross, while assenting to this request, observed that public attention would 'evaporate quite rapidly' and warned that his Group would 'not be altogether immune from this waning of interest'.[38]

Despite Crosland's assurances the cancellation of the project created difficulties for the Advisory Group, not least because the programme of studies was terminated before its completion. But in any case, the economic studies, for which Coopers & Lybrand had been re-engaged on the British side, had been subject to considerable delay. First, British and French civil servants had disagreed over the inclusion of certain elements such as peak pricing (see above, p. 140 and n.42); second, the British Treasury had expressed reservations about the macroeconomic assumptions which the British consultants wished to apply. As with the Phase I studies, officials were concerned that the use of more pessimistic GNP growth forecasts would be taken to represent the Government's view of economic prospects. To meet the timetable for completion of Phase II, officials were required to endorse the assumptions needed to establish a 'central case' by the end of October 1974, but it was not until 11 December that the Treasury was able to sanction, with some reluctance, the revised estimates offered by Coopers & Lybrand. The endorsement of the French Government had still to be obtained.[39] While indicative of continuing tensions between the Treasury and the consultants, the delay did not have dramatic consequences, since sufficient work had been undertaken at the time of abandonment to enable Coopers & Lybrand to produce a limited report for use by Cairncross and the CTAG. The cost-benefit study had not proceeded as far, however. The contract for this work was not authorised until October 1974, which delayed the refinement of the model, and the cancellation of the rail link in the following month left the consultants completely 'in the dark' about the appropriate figures to use for rail investment.[40] With the slippage in the work on the economic studies, the results of which were of course to be fed into the cost-benefit analysis, Cairncross could only be given a set of provisional results. Nevertheless, he was fairly sanguine about the database, defective as it may have appeared when judged against the ideal.[41] His Report noted that the work of Coopers and SETEC had provided an 'indispensable starting-point' for his inquiry and that the original cost-benefit study, together with its incomplete revision, provided the main underpinnings of his evaluation.[42]

When the decision was taken to cancel the studies in January 1975, Mulley directed the British Railways Board to suspend all work on the Channel Tunnel and the rail link studies, other than that required to assist Cairncross and RTZDE in completing their now more modest tasks.[43] In fact, an initial examination of lower-cost options for the rail link had already been completed, and a copy of the report was sent to the DOE and the Cairncross Group in February.[44] This was yet another provisional and preliminary effort, as Marsh was anxious to make clear. It was intended to 'give an outline' of the physical alternatives, with their advantages and constraints, and the capital costs quoted were 'orders of magnitude only'. Even so, the document was somewhat disappointing, simply rehearsing once more many of the familiar arguments concerning capacity limitations, and the impact on traffic levels. Two options had been studied: a 'low' investment option sharing the Southern Region's tracks (boat train route No.1) to Victoria and costing £164 million (in January 1975 prices); and an 'intermediate' option, via Oxted to White City, the final portion of which would be new tunnel, costing £303 million. For purposes of comparison the cost of the now discarded route was put at £423 million. The low-cost option was something of a straw man. With its longer journey times, insufficient capacity, and serious repercussions for Southern Region, it was easy to reject. There was a germ of new thinking in the 'intermediate' option, which suggested that through running of passenger trains could be effected by upgrading existing lines to cater for continental '*X*' and '*Y*' passenger coaches rather than introducing the full UIC 'Berne' gauge, as had been originally envisaged. Nevertheless, £303 million remained a substantial investment, and the figure did not include any expenditure either for freight or to mitigate environmental impact. There was little new in all this, and although the DOE did not give British Rail's report detailed consideration, officials expressed misgivings, not least that the low-cost option bore a 'disagreeable resemblance to one which was reputed to cost next to nothing when it was dismissed in 1973'.[45] Greater attention was given to the issue as to whether or not to publish the document. Mulley, whose relations with British Rail had deteriorated badly by this time,[46] was understandably forthright. He had clearly been stung by press reports, leaked by Keen, that British Rail had had a satisfactory and significantly cheaper rail link proposal 'almost ready' when the project was abandoned and he was also annoyed by an associated debate that was taking place within the European Parliament. Mulley felt that publication would set the record straight, moderate the implied criticism of the Government and deflate the renewed interest in Europe.[47] DOE officials counselled caution, however. Fogarty felt that revelation of the three cost estimates would 'do nothing but scare everyone rigid', and British Rail's blushes were spared when Crosland announced in the

Commons that the project was abandoned before the new proposals were ready for publication.[48]

In addition to consideration of material from the consultants and British Rail, the Advisory Group also received submitted evidence and correspondence from over 30 organisations and individuals. A limited number of hearings was held to clarify written material. Familiar names from past tunnel jousts put themselves forward: Peter Bromhead, Alan Cornish, Keith Wickenden and the Channel Tunnel Opposition Association (see above, p. 99), and environmental lobby groups such as The Defenders of Kent and the Conservation Society. Here, the alternative of a 'rail-only' tunnel was canvassed. Shipping and hovercraft interests were represented, including British Rail's Shipping and International Services division. Among the academics questioned were two Professors of Economics, Ralph Turvey from the LSE, and Gordon Mills from Kent, and information was provided by a well-known transport economist, Denys Munby, Fellow of Nuffield College Oxford. Both Turvey and Munby had worked on the Tunnel in the 1960s when respectively advising the Treasury and the DEA. Submissions were also provided by Arthur Baker, Professor of Concrete Structures and Technology at Imperial College London, who had helped to build the Mersey Tunnel in the 1920s and had written articles on his favoured solution to the channel crossing, a road/rail immersed tube. Officials in the DOE, notably Alastair Balls and Jenny Williams, both of whom were singled out for special praise by Cairncross, prepared a number of working papers covering the various technical and statistical aspects.[49]

Although the Cairncross Group had largely completed its task in February, it took some time to finalise the text, although there was little that was contentious and the successive drafts sent to the Department produced no serious reactions.[50] As to publication, Mulley again flexed his muscles, on this occasion arguing *against*, but Crosland had already promised the Commons that it was his 'strong preference' that the report be published.[51] Timing was another matter, however. Both Westminster and Whitehall saw advantage in delaying publication until interest in the Tunnel had waned. A further consideration was the referendum on Britain's membership of the EEC, and here the DOE was well aware that the Cairncross Report might not be the kind of document to publish in the heat of the campaign leading up to the vote on 5 June. However, there is no evidence of any deliberate obstruction, and once Cairncross had formally submitted his complete report at the beginning of June, officials put in hand arrangements for its publication on 23 July, just before the summer recess.[52] Fogarty, when briefing Crosland, noted that the Group had 'made a good job in difficult circumstances'. However, there were some potential minefields, not least the strong criticisms of British Rail, which would not reflect well on its sponsoring Department.[53] Nevertheless, the report was not deemed to be controversial, and Crosland did not think it necessary to pass it to Elwyn Jones's ministerial committee for consideration prior to publication.[54] The actual publication was a deliberately low-key affair, with no Commons statement or press conference. The danger that British Rail might take public exception to some of the revelations was a real one.

McKenna had already warned that the Board, which had been sent an advance copy, would have 'some fairly vigorous things to say'. But, as Fogarty observed, 'if they get rough then others will get rougher and they would not come out of it well', and she went on to advise McKenna to play a straight bat, which he duly did.[55] Six months after the abandonment, the publication of the Cairncross Report was announced by Crosland, in reply to a parliamentary question from Albert Costain on 23 July.[56]

The Report itself, entitled *The Channel Tunnel and alternative cross Channel services*, was a rather academic effort, printed in two-column format with a small font and stretching to about 40,000 words. With its 54 pages, 35 tables and 6 annexes, it was sometimes difficult to identify the wood of conclusions for the trees of detailed analysis, which culminated in a series of illustrative cost-benefit calculations. A largely technical document, it devoted considerable attention to the patterns of cross-channel traffic, with sections on the size of the ferry fleet, the prospects for hovercraft, and the interaction of these elements with the Tunnel and rail link. As we have seen, the Advisory Group's basic task had been to determine whether the programme of studies provided an adequate basis for deciding whether the Tunnel was a more advantageous investment for Britain than continued reliance on air and sea transport. Although qualms were expressed about some aspects of the consultants' presentation and methodology – SETEC in particular was criticised for its 'narrowly conceived' model – the Report's overall assessment was that the studies had been 'thorough, balanced and comprehensive'.[57] While the Group had little doubt that cross-channel traffic would continue to increase, they elected to adopt the 'low' Phase I forecast, instead of the Government's preferred 'central' case, which was now felt to be too optimistic. Use was also made of Phase II provisional figures. These took account of higher fuel costs and lower GNP growth in the wake of the 1973 oil crisis, and consequently reduced the forecast of passenger demand by about 10 per cent. On the other hand, the estimates for freight traffic, where the growth of the roll-on roll-off business in 1970–3 had been spectacular, were raised (see Table 7.1). Consideration was then given to how this expected growth could best be handled. Four main options were examined: Tunnel plus rail link to London; Tunnel only; ferries and aircraft; ferries, aircraft and additional hovercraft. Costings of these options indicated that even with differing assumptions about the efficiency of ferry operations, for Britain the Tunnel was 'almost certainly not more expensive than other means…[and] would also provide a faster and more comfortable service'.[58] Environmental, social and regional factors lay outside the Group's concerns, but the opportunity was taken to make some pertinent contributions to the debate. Particular attention was drawn to the claim that by not building the Tunnel millions of pounds would be released for schools and hospitals. This hoary old chestnut was based on a patent 'misconception', since unless demand for cross-channel travel were curbed, the investment 'released' would merely be consumed in spending on other modes, which as the Report observed, would consume more resources than would the Tunnel. Neither regional nor distributional effects were felt to be significant elements in the equation. As to the environment, the arguments

Table 7.1 Cross-channel passenger and freight traffic: actual, 1962–73, and Cairncross Report forecast, 1980–90

	Actual			*Forecast*			
Passengers with vehicles	*1962*	*1971*	*1973*	*1980*		*1990*	
				Phase II provisional	*Phase I low*	*Phase II provisional*	*Phase I low*
('000 crossings)							
Surface							
Passengers with vehicles	1,390	4,088	4,831	7,480	8,693	13,620	15,603
Classic passengers	2,926	4,812	5,239	7,000	7,116	9,700	8,426
Total surface	4,316	8,900	10,070	14,480	15,809	23,320	24,029
Air	5,336	16,031	19,621	23,670	26,513	41,540	47,985
Total passenger traffic	9,652[a]	24,931	29,691	38,150	42,322	64,860	72,014
Freight (unitisable, m. tons)		5.7[b]		15.1	12.9	25.2	20.2

Source: CTAG Report, 1975, tables 2.10–11.

Notes

a Appears as 9,552 in the Report.
b 1970.

were found to be 'fairly evenly balanced', and the issue was held to be something for the Government to determine. However, the Group did observe that 'great emphasis was placed on these factors, often without quantification of any kind, by people holding very different views'.[59]

Turning to the financial return, the consultants had estimated that the project would achieve a rate of 14 per cent, using the Phase I low traffic forecast and assuming that the high-speed rail link were built. With the low-cost rail option, the return would fall to 12 per cent. Consideration of rail investment options was of course hampered by the failure of British Rail to provide sufficient information, but the Advisory Group was able to estimate that the return on the high-speed option rejected by the Government would be less than 5 per cent. This highlighted a serious problem. The return on the Tunnel with the high-speed link was a respectable 14 per cent, while that for the link itself was far too low. The difference was largely explained by assumptions about how the revenue from 'classic' passengers would be shared between the Tunnel Authority and British Rail, with the former gaining revenue at virtually no cost to itself. Treating the Tunnel and the link as a single joint project offered a prospective return of 10 per cent, but this was still problematic because 12 per cent could be achieved with the Tunnel alone. Even if the incremental revenue were applied to the rail investment alone the return would only be 7 per cent. As Crosland conceded, the more rail-oriented the project became, the less profitable it was.[60] A range of cost-benefit scenarios was then examined (Tables 7.2–7.3). The first took the expansion of ferry services as the 'base case', and compared it to the Tunnel without additional rail investment. Here the much greater capital costs of the Tunnel were compensated for by lower operating costs. Revenue streams to operators were broadly similar, as were fares, but significant benefits were derived from time savings. Investing in the Tunnel would therefore produce a positive net present value (NPV) of £106 million in 1973 prices, equivalent to an internal rate of return of 16 per cent (Table 7.2). Two further calculations compared the Tunnel and two levels of rail investment ('intermediate' and 'low') with the expansion of ferry and air services. Again, lower operating costs offset the Tunnel's high capital cost. While there were large revenue losses for UK operators, these were partly compensated for by benefits from lower fares and time savings. Positive NPVs for the Tunnel were £84 and £113 million for intermediate and low rail investment respectively, producing returns of 12 and 14 per cent (Table 7.2). Nevertheless, the economics of the rail link on its own remained questionable. Separate calculations for associated railway investment showed that the low-cost option produced a positive NPV of £10 million and the intermediate alternative a negative figure of £29 million. Rates of return were a disappointing 11 and 8 per cent respectively (Table 7.3). The conclusion was that the economic case for the more expensive rail options was 'very poor'.[61]

What, then, were the main conclusions that Cairncross and his colleagues derived from their work? Aside from the frustration of being asked to give an opinion after a decision had already been taken, the Group was in general optimistic

Table 7.2 Cairncross Report estimate of Tunnel costs and benefits (UK share), 1975–2030 (discounted costs to 1973, £m in 1973 prices, 1975–2030) in carrying Phase I low traffic

	[1] Tunnel (A1) compared with Ferries (B1)[a]			*[2] Tunnel plus intermediate rail (A2) compared with ferries, existing rail and aircraft (B2)*			*[3] Tunnel and low rail (A3) compared with ferries, existing rail and aircraft (B3)*		
	A1	*B1*	*Benefits (+) and costs (−) of A1 over B1*	*A2*	*B2*	*Benefits (+) and costs (−) of A2 over B2*	*A3*	*B3*	*Benefits (+) and costs (−) of A3 over B3*
Capital investment	145	89	−56	322	136	−186	200	123	−77
Operating costs	41	145	+104	117	589	+472	96	369	+273
Revenue to UK operators	235	247	−12	450	783	−333	368	545	−177
Fares paid by UK consumers	255	265	+10	553	620	+67	438	484	+46
Time saving	60		+60	64		+64	48		+48
Net present value			+106			+84			+113
Internal rate of return			16%			12%			14%

Source: CTAG Report, tables 2.17, 4.6, 4.7.

Note

a 80 per cent diversion of traffic to the Tunnel assumed.

Table 7.3 Cairncross Report estimate of rail investment costs and benefits (UK share), 1975–2030 (discounted costs to 1973, £m. in 1973 prices, 1975–2030), in carrying Phase I low traffic

	Low cost rail (A1) compared with existing rail and air (B1)			*Intermediate rail (A2) compared with low cost rail and air (B2)*		
	A1	*B1*	*Benefits (+) and costs (−) of A1 over B1*	*A2*	*B2*	*Benefits (+) and costs (−) of A2 over B2*
Capital investment	55	10	−45	122	13	−109
Operating costs	20	180	+160	21	220	+199
Revenue to UK operators	83	195	−112	82	238	−156
Fares paid by UK consumers	105	124	+19	115	136	+21
Time saving	−12		−12	16		+16
Net present value			+10			−29
Internal rate of return			11%			8%

Source: CTAG Report, tables 4.8 and 4.9, and corrections, p. ii.

about the prospects for a Tunnel, though there was a fair amount of equivocation in the language used. 'Had the issue been one relating to the Tunnel alone', the Report stated, 'and had the Government been able to contemplate the allotment of large additional sums on its own credit, we think that a good but not overwhelming case for going ahead could have been put'. Of course, there was 'considerable doubt' about the second of these conditions, while the first had been 'called into question' because the project had become inextricably bound up with the rail link, the viability of which was, to say the least, uncertain. Indeed, much was made of the fact that the rail components, both in Britain and on the continent, had been imperfectly developed, which made it 'impossible' to evaluate the project with which the Group had been presented.[62] Drawing together the various 'tentative' analytical strands, the Report was able to conclude that 'total UK operators' costs (capital and operating) would be less if the Tunnel were built than if ferries and air services were expanded'. While dependent on the assumption that cross-channel traffic would continue to grow rapidly, the estimates were held to be 'fairly robust', though this did *not* mean that the Tunnel was 'indisputably better than the expansion of existing services'. The cost-benefit calculations suggested that the Tunnel would produce an 'acceptable' return, but this was not the case with the 'additional investment in any of the rail links so far proposed'.[63] British Rail attracted a good deal of criticism, not only because of its inability to provide the Advisory Group with answers on the rail link, but also for its inconsistent attitude to, and management of, the cross-channel traffic. Its managers were criticised for hailing the rail link as a major opportunity while at the same time making 'virtually no attempt' to develop a premium ferry or hovercraft service. Nor was the Group impressed by the railways' arguments about lack of capacity. Little imagination or effort appeared to have been directed towards easing congestion on commuter services, and there had been insufficient investigation of peak pricing to spread demand and effectively increase capacity.[64] Finally the Group raised a number of wider issues to be considered in the wake of abandonment. They included: the need for British Rail and SNCF to review improvements to cross-channel services, together with government supervision of British Rail's shipping, rail and hovercraft investment programme; the role of peak pricing in managing shipping capacity; the desirability of monitoring international traffic; and the need for greater co-ordination in transport planning.[65]

The subdued appearance of an academic report on a project that had been abandoned was unsurprisingly followed by a low-key response. British press reports gave more attention to the criticisms of British Rail than to the findings on the Tunnel itself.[66] And the reaction in France, aside from official displeasure about the attacks on SETEC, was similarly muted.[67] Whitehall focussed on the broader issues raised about government management of large-scale projects. On the question of transport co-ordination, for example, Shearer conceded, in a note to Cairncross, that 'the Department had tended to treat the Tunnel too much as a thing in itself, rather than part of a general transport problem'.[68] The CPRS, long-standing Tunnel sceptics, chose to highlight British Rail's failings in its cross-channel operations.

After an informal discussion with Cairncross, Sir Kenneth Berrill, head of the CPRS, informed Pugh that the Group had been 'amazed' to find that the Tunnel plus high-speed rail link was British Rail's only strategy for dealing with cross-channel traffic. Pugh chose to defend British Rail against this charge. He found the criticism 'rather severe' and argued that since successive administrations had shown a strong commitment to the Tunnel British Rail had been 'quite justified in devoting their energies to implementing that policy without doing any contingency planning on the basis of a different policy'. The key failure, in Pugh's opinion, was that this planning was 'patchy and inadequate and in the end unrealistic'.[69] For its part British Rail merely nursed its wounds, at a time when there were severe disagreements with the Government over other elements of railway management. McKenna did send a series of comments to the DOE on the day after publication, but this contained nothing new and was not well received, Fogarty noting that it gave 'the impression of closed minds who have not learnt, and are unwilling to learn, anything'. After a three-year involvement with the frustrations of the project, she was happy to let the Board have the last word. Just before leaving to take up her new post, she concluded that there was 'no purpose' in replying to McKenna's letter since it would only 'lead to endless recriminations'.[70] Aside from reacting to some private contributions from Bonavia and Cornish,[71] there remained the last rites of the Ministerial Committee on the Channel Tunnel. When Crosland eventually got round to sending his promised memorandum in October 1975, he noted that expectations were that the project would not be revived before 1980, and consequently, 'no Tunnel will be in operation before the later 1980s'.[72]

The longer-term significance of the Cairncross Report lay more in what it ruled in, than what it ruled out. With its limited outlook and modest pretensions, the Report certainly did not provide the unequivocal rejection of the project that the proponents of a thorough independent review had anticipated. Neither did it address two of the most contested issues which had dogged the Tunnel since 1970: financing arrangements; and environmental concerns. However, its focussed economic analysis had concluded that the Tunnel was a worthwhile proposition, or at least not an uneconomic one. Ironically, for someone who had argued, albeit in 1949, that the idea had 'about as much relevance to current economic policy as a project to re-erect the pyramids in the Scottish Highlands', Cairncross had left the way open for those who wished to make a renewed effort.[73]

3. The origins of the 'Mousehole', 1975–9

No sooner had the British Government announced its decision to abandon the Tunnel, than enthusiasts in the private sector produced plans to revive the scheme. Notwithstanding the poor reception given by the Cairncross Report to 'rail-only' tunnels of the type advocated by Professor Bromhead, interest focussed on schemes for a much cheaper alternative to the three-bore scheme (twin tunnels plus a service tunnel).[74] In the United States, Frank Davidson, disappointed with Technical Studies Inc.'s failure to gain any reward for its investment in the Tunnel while a member of the CTSG (above, pp. 81–2), gave his encouragement to the idea of a small, single-bore, using the dimensions of the abandoned service tunnel. More inventor than entrepreneur, he was attracted by the work of an MIT Professor, Gordon Wilson, on an automated, palletised transport system for containers and automobiles. Davidson commissioned De Leuw, Cather & Co. to explore the notion of a pallet-carrying, 4.5 metre tunnel, as the first stage of a Tunnel project. Reporting in June 1975, De Leuw, Cather believed the idea had 'merit', though the firm also made the pertinent observation that consideration be given to the alternative of a single-track rail line. The report was not without its comic side. The project was intended to be freight-only, but the consultants attempted to beef up the financial case by making the assumption that revenue would be gained by carrying cars on pallets while their drivers made the journey by sea.[75] Nevertheless, the efforts of Frank Davidson and his French-based brother, Al, awakened interest in both Britain and France about the possibility of reviving the Tunnel. RTZDE responded to the situation by producing a report of its own. Ruling out the Davidsons' single-bore without service tunnel on safety grounds, it looked at a number of two-bore options, though the financial attractions appeared to be limited.[76] Meanwhile French interests had also been stimulated to examine cheaper alternatives, that is a tunnel 'beaucoup plus modeste'.[77] In August 1975 an initial study was made by the project managers, CGE-Développement [CGE-DE], in association with SNCF. Taking up the Davidsons' initiative, this examined the feasibility of a rail tunnel limited to a 'simple galerie' [single-bore] and 'voie unique' [single track]. However, the French also thought its diameter should be greater, and after evaluating a series of options, they concluded that an increase of 10 per cent in diameter, that is to 4.8 metres, would allow through rail traffic.[78] The Davidsons made efforts to reconvene the old Channel Tunnel Study Group, but the response to their efforts was rather chilly, and they soon dropped out of serious contention.[79] The Americans subsequently pursued other imaginative flights of fancy, notably a tunnel construction system based on submerged caissons.[80] RTZDE was also rather lukewarm about taking an active interest, though it agreed to work with CGE-DE in developing an evaluation of a single-bore system.[81]

While government officials maintained a watching brief, none of this effort reached the upper echelons of government.[82] For example, when a draft report prepared by CGE-DE and RTZDE on the single-bore was sent by Frame to Marsh of British Rail and Marshall at the DOE, it fell on deaf ears. Marsh, in particular, felt that the scheme had little chance of success.[83] On the other hand, an idea from a completely different direction *did* reach the Prime Minister's desk. In March 1976, just after Wilson had announced his resignation as Prime Minister, Sir Douglas Wass, the Treasury Permanent Secretary, was canvassed by Sir Maurice Laing. John Laing Construction, acting with French and German construction companies (Grands Travaux de Marseille, Hochtief), proposed employing immersed tube technology to carry road traffic. The possibility that this new tunnel scheme might be raised by either President Giscard or Chancellor Schmidt at a meeting of the European Council was sufficient for the matter to be drawn to the attention of No.10.[84] However, the DOE quickly dismissed the approach. In its last pronouncement on the Tunnel before the establishment of a separate Department of Transport (DTp) in September, it produced an extremely defensive brief for the European Council meeting in early April. The Laing proposal, it noted, was only in outline form. There was nothing to suggest that either the technical or the financial uncertainties had been resolved; the promoters were even suggesting, somewhat unwisely in view of the fate of the failed project, to raise 90 per cent of the capital in the form of government-guaranteed bonds.[85] In the event, the brief was not required, since no reference was made to the Tunnel in the European Council's deliberations. Nevertheless, Laing continued to lobby the Prime Minister, now Jim Callaghan, who had succeeded Wilson on 5 April. Giscard's impending state visit to London in June, it was claimed, provided another opportunity to advance the matter. But once again the subject was not raised by the French, and in Britain, Environment Secretaries, old (Crosland) and new (Peter Shore), and the Treasury Chief Secretary expressed strong reservations about the Laing proposal. By this time, its estimated cost had been revealed, which, at £1,350 million in January 1976 prices, was considered to be prohibitive.[86]

Despite the lack of encouragement from the Government, CGE-DE and RTZDE continued work on the single-bore concept. In February 1977 a preliminary note on the feasibility of such an approach was produced. In its basic form a 5-metre tunnel was envisaged, with a single-track railway line, suitable for British Rail stock and third-rail electrification. Two variants were also considered: with diameters of 5.685 and 6.03 metres there would be room for 25kV overhead electrification and for British Rail and UIC gauges respectively. Given earlier safety concerns, the report considered in some detail the risk of fire and the means of evacuating the single-bore in the event of an emergency. The estimated cost of the preferred 5-metre option was a modest £237 million in mid-1976 prices, and the internal return was put at 13 per cent in real terms.[87] At this point British Rail came back into the picture. Although somewhat disillusioned about events in 1975, the Board had never removed the Tunnel from its agenda because of the requirement to formulate a strategy for meeting the growing cross-channel traffic. Yet, at the top, views were clearly mixed. In December 1976, for example, Bosworth, who was Chairman of the Board's Shipping Division, expressed surprise that the railways' chief executive, Bowick, should be keen to resuscitate the Tunnel 'at the earliest opportunity'.[88] However, the latter found a strong ally in his new Chairman, Peter Parker. Having succeeded Marsh in September 1976, he soon proved far more proactive towards the Tunnel than his predecessor had been after the abandonment. Another key figure was Bob Barron, the Director of Planning and Investment before he joined the Board as a part-time member and took on McKenna's Tunnel brief.[89] Although railway managers had been unimpressed with the earlier versions of the single-bore, with Barron and Parker showing more interest the new proposal was deemed worthy of further consideration.[90]

The so-called mini-tunnel possessed a number of advantages. It was cheaper to construct, and required only a 'modest investment' in British Rail's existing infrastructure, while the absence of a high-speed rail link would lessen the environmental impact. Moreover, in contrast to the previous notion of an independent Channel Tunnel Authority, the single rail tunnel gave British Rail and SNCF the opportunity to manage the fixed link themselves. This would also prevent the project from being fragmented into 'tunnel proper' and 'supporting infrastructure', an element which had condemned the earlier proposal in 1974–5. Though the traffic was expected to be modest, both Barron and Bowick felt that the proposal would offer a 'handsome monopoly' for the two railways, which 'might well make it the optimal solution'. As to the effects on the Shipping Division, a rail-only tunnel might well prove to be a 'blessing in disguise', since it would allow shipping resources to be concentrated on accompanied car traffic and roll-on roll-off services.[91] A speedy decision on the mini-tunnel was required in order to avoid a blight on further shipping investment, a situation which had occurred while the earlier scheme was being developed. In the light of these arguments the Board's Railway Executive Committee agreed, in August 1977, that a comprehensive study should be undertaken into the practicality of the single-bore.[92]

British Rail wished to keep its study of the mini-tunnel confidential, but there was the delicate question of how to handle matters with outside bodies. The intention was to maintain a low-key approach while portraying some 'controlled enthusiasm', but given the multiplicity of interests, this strategy proved difficult to follow.[93] First, it would be impossible to exclude both central and local governments, since the scheme was conceived as a public sector investment, and local fears about its impact would need to be allayed if the Tunnel were to be revived. Second, collaboration with both SNCF and the Belgian railways, SNCB, would be necessary, although during informal discussions it became evident that the French were also interested in the single-track proposal and were keen to participate more fully.[94] Third, there were the former project managers. Here, British Rail was opposed to their involvement in the planning stage. Its senior managers, clearly bruised by past experiences of being 'tail-end charlies', 'cast as the fall guys for the escalation of costs', were keen to keep the studies in-house. Senior engineers, unaware of Whitehall's criticisms of their earlier efforts, thought that, tunnelling issues aside, British Rail possessed sufficient expertise to undertake the assessment itself. Officers at SNCF adopted the same stance in France.[95] Naturally, the old Tunnel backers, while not anxious to take the lead, did not want to miss an opportunity to assert their rights in any new project. This presented some problems for British Rail, which did not wish to see its cautious stance undermined. While both RTZDE and CGE-DE had no copyright of the single-bore idea, their earlier work established a 'moral' right to be involved. Moreover, both possessed an influence with their respective governments and had undoubted experience of tunnelling.[96] Diplomacy was clearly required when Barron and Parker met the Davidson brothers in October 1977. The Davidsons were continuing their lobbying activities, with the intention of obtaining compensation for Technical Studies' past endeavours, and had close links with CGE-DE. There were fears that if Parker was at all positive the brothers would 'put it around' that

British Rail supported the project.[97] At the same time Alistair Frame, while privately expressing scepticism to his colleagues, was pressing for RTZ to be associated with the project, and this also put pressure on the Board to reveal its intentions.[98] Fourth, there was a European dimension. The European Parliament had been making supportive noises about the Tunnel ever since abandonment.[99] The prospect that European financing might be made available gained ground after July 1976, when the Commission drew up a draft regulation for an aid programme for transport infrastructure projects of Community interest.[100] Certainly, Peter Parker was aware of the possibilities, and in December 1976 he had sought to influence Roy Jenkins, on the eve of his appointment as President of the European Commission, by emphasising the attractions for the Community of reviving the scheme.[101] The subject was also raised in the summer of 1977 when Parker and Bowick briefed Sir Nicholas Henderson, Tomkins's successor as British Ambassador in Paris, about the mini-tunnel project.[102] Newspaper stories reporting further support from the European Parliament for infrastructure aid and the Tunnel appeared, requiring William Rodgers, now the Secretary of State for Transport, to field questions in the Commons. Rodgers was able to reassure his colleagues that there had been no change in the Government's position since Crosland's statement two and a half years earlier. But although he found it easy to point out that the EEC was a long way from producing concrete proposals, the rumours persisted.[103] Finally, within British Rail itself it was 'fairly common knowledge amongst the staff' that new initiatives were taking shape, and leaks to media contacts began to occur. All this made it increasingly difficult to keep the work on the single-bore Tunnel under wraps, and at the end of 1977 Barron was forced to draw the attention of Board members to the developing 'public relations problem'.[104]

Interest in the possibility of reviving the project continued in 1978. Both the European Commission and the Parliament continued to debate the infrastructure aid issue, and a Committee on Transport Infrastructure was established. Encouraged by the European Transport Commissioner, Richard Burke, the Channel Tunnel was being put forward as a suitable candidate for funding if the regulation were ever approved.[105] In April the *Times* reported leaked details of the single-track scheme being 'planned' by British Rail and SNCF, putting the cost at £500 million. The revelation produced non-committal reactions from the European Commission, the British Government and the railway administrations, but the share price of Channel Tunnel Investments shot up from 16 to 59 pence at the news.[106] The story also drew Cairncross into the debate. Writing to the *Times* in his capacity as former chairman of the CTAG he observed that the single-track tunnel appeared to offer many of the advantages of the earlier scheme but at much less cost. Moreover, economic circumstances had changed: the scheme would provide a much-needed boost to investment and employment, and therefore demanded 'urgent consideration'.[107] Rodgers was also questioned further in the Commons, but MPs were unable to tease anything very significant out of the Minister. He conceded that a fixed link would probably be in the interests of the British and French railways, but such a large public expenditure could not be contemplated in present circumstances. He went on: 'I could not argue that a Channel Tunnel should be at the top of the present list of priorities'.[108] Nevertheless, he did see fit to minute Callaghan that the joint railway study was expected shortly, and referred to the lobbying in Europe, notably by Sid Weighell, General Secretary of the National Union of Railwaymen. The subject had also been raised during a visit to the London by the West German Transport Minister, Kurt Gscheidle, who was interested in improving the freight prospects of European railways. Whatever the merits of any scheme, Rodgers's firm line was that there was no question of Ministers considering the issue during the present parliament, given the country's economic difficulties and the necessary constraints on public sector spending.[109]

British Rail and SNCF completed their preliminary report in August 1978. This estimated that on the basis of a London-Paris journey time of $4\frac{1}{2}$ hours [London-Brussels in $4\frac{1}{4}$ hours] six million 'classic' passengers would use the service in 1988, the first year of operation. Freight traffic was forecast at 5.5 million tonnes. Unlike the abandoned project of 1975, the scheme made no provision for shuttle services. The single-track Tunnel would be operated by alternate 'flights' of ten trains in each direction. A departure from the RTZDE–CGE-DE scheme was that, for technical and economic reasons, the two railways could not accept the use of third-rail electrification. Their decision to adopt the 25 kV overhead standard meant that the Tunnel bore would have to be slightly larger than five metres, although the report made no direct reference to dimensions. Railway managers were able to accept the concept of a single-bore, but at the same time did not rule out the possibility of adding a service tunnel. Thus three options were presented: British Rail gauge without a service tunnel; UIC gauge without a service tunnel; and UIC gauge with a service tunnel. The total cost was estimated at £518–650 million with an internal rate of return of 13.5–15 per cent (Table 7.4). The report concluded that the single-track Tunnel was a 'viable solution' to the provision of a fixed link. Further work would focus on the UIC gauge option, since the BR alternative was felt to be too restrictive, and on the merits of a service tunnel.[110] British Rail's Board considered the report in September and approved a recommendation that the reaction of the two governments should be sought. It was also agreed that not more than £500,000 would be spent in drawing up a specific scheme. Studies would also be made of the appropriate financial and institutional framework, in conjunction with SNCF, and the Board also endorsed the launching of an active market research and public relations effort.[111]

Before the Board met in September Barron sent a copy of the report to Peter Lazarus, now Deputy Secretary, Transport Industries and International Policy, in the Department of Transport. Lazarus immediately sent a copy to the Treasury, noting that the figures looked 'sufficiently interesting for it to be quite clear that there is no possibility of simply sweeping the issue under the carpet'.[112] British Rail had sent the paper in anticipation of Rodgers's meeting with his French counterpart, Joel Le Theule, in early September. Here the two Ministers agreed

Table 7.4 BRB and SNCF single-track rail tunnel: estimate of capital investment, 1978 (£m. in Jan 1978 prices)

	BR gauge without service tunnel	*UIC gauge without service tunnel*	*UIC gauge with service tunnel*
Tunnel	340	360	450
Installations at or near portals	28	56	56
Modification to existing railway infrastructure			
United Kingdom (including London terminal)	25	25	25
France (Calais-Hazebrouck electrification)	15	15	15
Rolling stock and locomotives	110	104	104
Total	518	560	650
Internal rate of return	15%	14%	13.5%

Source: BRB and SNCF, 'Channel Tunnel Joint Report', August 1978, AN191/306, PRO.

that British Rail and SNCF should be encouraged to continue with the studies, and affirmed that if the project were started, a second failure of the Tunnel project could not be countenanced.[113] In the following month Lazarus sought guidance from his Minister on the appropriate tactics to adopt in meeting with French officials. Rodgers's reply called for a familiar approach, redolent of contacts in the 1960s and 1970s: 'Let the French to [sic] seen to be dragging their feet, although without precise commitment on our part'.[114] In fact, there was delay on the French side, notably in having the joint report accepted by the SNCF Board. Given the SNCF's greater dependence on the French Government, joint publication would be taken to imply official support for the proposal, whereas the attitude was distinctly cautious, even cool. However, French officials had no objection to unilateral publication by British Rail.[115] In the circumstances, a report in British Rail's name was sent as a formal document to Rodgers on 1 February 1979, and subsequently published as a popular brochure.[116] Callaghan was informed and warned that publication would lead to a resurgence of interest in fixed links between Britain and France.[117] But in the midst of the infamous 'winter of discontent', with pay bargaining in disarray and with the date of a general election to consider, there was no prospect of a renewed discussion of the Tunnel within senior government circles.[118] In the Commons, Rodgers promised that British Rail's report would receive 'careful consideration', but he repeated his view that the Government's position remained unchanged.[119] Shortly after this, the Callaghan Government came to an abrupt end. A vote of confidence was lost on 28 March – the first since 1924 – and a general election was announced for 3 May. Callaghan had shown little enthusiasm for either Europe or the Channel Tunnel, and his Government did little to advance the cause of either.[120] Rodgers was more open-minded about the Tunnel, though he could see no immediate prospect of taking it up, especially given the lukewarm attitude of European member states to the infrastructure aid proposals.[121] Nevertheless, in the four years since abandonment, advocates of the project, by formulating and lobbying for a cheaper scheme, later dubbed the 'Mousehole', had managed to keep the concept alive.

4. The Thatcher Government and the 'Mousehole', May 1979–October 1980

Margaret Thatcher's victory in the general election of May 1979 was scarcely a surprise. With the Conservatives well ahead in the polls, Callaghan expected to lose. Given Labour's poor record on unemployment and prices and the failure of its pay and devolution policies, a return to Conservative government seemed inevitable. Thatcher played down the radicalism of the right, and the result 'turned more on the losers' failings than on the victors' strengths'. In the event the Conservatives were returned with 339 seats to Labour's 269, and an overall majority of 43.[122] At the hustings there had of course been much more to debate than a single piece of transport infrastructure and, in any case, the scheme presented by British Rail and SNCF had not been developed fully. As in previous campaigns the manifestos of the two main parties had been silent on the Tunnel. Only the Liberals referred to it, pledging to 'support a rail-only Channel Tunnel financed with the aid of EEC finances', an undertaking which essentially restated the stance they had adopted in 1974.[123]

The new Transport Minister, Norman Fowler, was an inexperienced minister – this was his first appointment and until January 1981 he remained outside the Cabinet. However, he was enthusiastic about the idea of a fixed link between Britain and France.[124] When briefed on the state of play with the British Rail/SNCF proposal, he was informed that his predecessor, Rodgers, had promised Parker that the Government would provide at least a preliminary response by the end of 1979. This, he was told, should be as 'creative' as possible, and the scheme, together with alternatives, should not be dismissed out of hand.[125] Fowler subsequently informed Thatcher that there had been renewed interest in the Channel Tunnel and he was being pressed to reveal the Government's attitude. He pointed out that in the prevailing economic climate even a cheaper scheme was 'far too expensive', but was anxious to emphasise that 'it could be a mistake to rule it out entirely on those grounds'. The railways' single-track proposal appeared to be viable and therefore had a real chance of attracting finance from the private sector, and there was also the prospect of support from the EEC. He therefore intended to 'do some further work' and suggested that Cairncross be appointed to advise him on the merits of the scheme. The Prime Minister, in assenting to this course of action, minuted: 'I should like the study to go ahead'.[126] In October Cairncross was duly appointed to advise the Minister. However, his involvement for a second time was not a new initiative by a new government. Officials had been planning some form of independent assessment during the Labour administration, with a preference for reconstituting the Cairncross Group, and Sir Alec had been approached informally by the Permanent Secretary, Peter Baldwin, before the 1979 election.[127]

In the meantime the DTp was busy evaluating the British Rail/SNCF proposals. The work was undertaken by a new Channel Tunnel Unit, which had been reconstituted in April 1979 as part of the Department's International Transport Division, led by Tony Fairclough, an Under-Secretary. Initially staffed in a modest way, it was strengthened in the following year with the establishment of two divisions, headed by Peter McIntosh, and Brian Payne.[128] British Rail also decided to build up its own Tunnel organisation. In addition to the existing planning group, headed by David Williams, Barron established a steering committee of heavyweight railway managers to ensure co-ordination. Liaison with SNCF was strengthened following the French Government's decision in March 1979 to allow its railways to take part in the development work required to produce a definitive proposal. For this purpose a typically elaborate structure of joint directing group and working groups was erected, reminiscent of the position in 1964 (above, p. 46).[129] Here, the path was far from smooth, however. Difficulties of the now familiar Anglo-French type were encountered with methods of financial evaluation, financing options, and methods of train working. On the last issue, SNCF was implacably opposed to dual-voltage traction, and the disagreements even extended to the choice of toilets. At the end of 1979 Barron predicted 'tough negotiations ahead' with Louis Lacoste and his team.[130] British Rail also revisited the question of the London terminal. A site in West London – either West Brompton or Olympia – remained the preferred option, with some trains running into Victoria. However, there was no clear consensus about these 'split' arrangements, and at least one Board Member questioned whether the planners had been sufficiently imaginative.[131] Meanwhile lobbying continued at a high level. In Europe there were meetings in Brussels in October 1979, when Parker and Bowick, and from SNCF, Paul Gentil (the Director-General) and Lacoste met Jenkins and Burke, and in December a reception was organised for British MEPs in Strasbourg.[132] Exploratory talks were also held with representatives of other organisations seeking a possible involvement in a fixed link, whether as competitors, partners or putative project managers. Here the main protagonists were Sir David Nicolson, a leading British businessman, and Pierre Billecocq, the former French Minister who with Peyton had signed Agreement No.2. British engineers came up with a rather fanciful idea to produce a modern version of Mathieu-Favier's famous scheme of 1803. Submerged tubes would carry a double-track railway and a dual three-lane motorway, with the road emerging onto narrow islands reclaimed from the Varne and Le Colbert sandbanks. A consortium called the European Channel Tunnel Group was formed to develop the idea.[133] Finally, British Rail held meetings with the Government's adviser, Cairncross. Barron's initial assessment was that a good rapport had been developed with Sir Alec, and that 'in the end we shall get a fair report'. Yet there were warning signals too. Cairncross had made repeated references to the earlier scheme, and as Barron observed, 'he will want to show that his Committee were right'.[134]

Cairncross conveyed his preliminary views on the British Rail/SNCF project to Fowler in January 1980. In a short, ten-point minute he revealed that his first impressions were favourable in that the proposals required a modest capital expenditure, and if successful could incorporate an additional tunnel. Nevertheless, on further examination he expressed doubts about a scheme which elected to dispense with the bulk of cross-channel traffic, viz. car-accompanied passenger traffic and roll-on roll-off freight. The project would be unlikely to attract private capital unless it attracted more traffic, and the logical extension of this argument led to something like the original twin-tunnel scheme of 1975 for rail and shuttle traffic, but without the expensive high-speed rail link. Further study was needed, but these initial conclusions were scarcely a ringing endorsement of British Rail's plans.[135] Parker may have proclaimed the appointment of Cairncross as 'great news',[136] but it is clear that the Government's independent adviser was inherently unsympathetic to a rail-only tunnel based on classic passengers and rail freight. In February Fowler received the report of Channel Tunnel Unit officials on the single-track tunnel. A far more substantial document than Cairncross's note, it came to similar conclusions. Focusing on the UIC gauge option [six metres] with service tunnel [cost raised to £800 million in December 1979 prices], the estimated return of 13.5 per cent rested on traffic forecasts which were considered to be optimistic. The likelihood of airline deregulation would produce cheaper air fares, while the freight estimates seemed too high given the scheme's failure to cater for the fastest-growing segment of the market (roll-on roll-off). Furthermore, the return to British Rail itself would be lower still, since some of the traffic would be taken from its own cross-channel services. It was reckoned to lie within the distinctly modest range of 0–8 per cent, with 4 per cent as the best guess. A fixed link catering for larger traffic volumes would prove more attractive to the private sector, and a private venture would please both the Treasury and the Conservative Government. But the issue was not straightforward. Experience with private risk capital in the 1970–5 scheme suggested that a public venture would be administratively much simpler. Furthermore, if the Tunnel were constructed by a private company charging the railways tolls or a rental, it would be difficult to evade the issue of government guarantees, and the private company would be tied to the state-owned railways in a symbiotic relationship which would make it impossible to escape from the public sector. Allowing the private company to run shuttle traffic would increase the degree of private risk, but would inevitably lead in the direction of a different scheme. Thus, the economic limitations of the BR/SNCF Tunnel inevitably raised the question as to whether a more ambitious proposal would be preferable. One might increase the diameter of the single-bore to seven metres (as in the abandoned scheme) to accommodate shuttle services; revert to the original twin-bore plus service tunnel; or examine alternative schemes. The latter included immersed tubes, bridges, and bridge-tunnel combinations, which had all begun to materialise by the beginning of 1980 in spite of their rejection in earlier studies in the 1960s and 1970s. The exercise suggested, as Baldwin pointed out to Fowler, that 'there may be a sound Channel Tunnel project to be found... but (unless it were to be significantly modified) it seems unlikely to be the scheme that is before you'.[137]

Though critical of the British Rail/SNCF scheme, officials did not formally reject the plans, and at the end of February British Rail Board Members were therefore surprised to read a story to this effect in the *Financial Times*.[138] Undaunted, Parker and Barron continued to campaign with enthusiasm. In an address to the British Chamber of Commerce in Paris Parker extolled the virtues of the single-track Tunnel, and he repeated the dose in evidence before the newly-formed Commons Select Committee on Transport on 5 March.[139] On 12 March British Rail made a presentation to Fowler, his Parliamentary Secretary, Kenneth Clarke, and DTp officials. Barron felt it had been a success, noting that despite newspaper reports to the contrary, 'my overall impression is that there is now much more sympathy for our scheme in Marsham Street'.[140] In fact, the Department's preoccupation was with the need for a statement of government policy, though it was agreed that given the existing uncertainty this should be little more than a 'holding' one.[141] On 17 March Clarke replied for the Government in an adjournment debate on the Channel link. Discussion centred on the prospects for EEC funding of transport infrastructure, following the publication in November 1979 of a Commission Green Paper on the subject, which saw the

Tunnel as a prime candidate for support and had attracted the attention of the Transport Select Committee.[142] Clarke fended off Eric Ogden and other tunnelists, pointing out that EEC funds were not yet available, but he reminded them that his Minister would be making a statement on the Tunnel in two days' time.[143] On 19 March Fowler's statement took the form of an answer at question time. The first official view of the Thatcher Government on the subject, it was measured in tone, and unsurprisingly in view of the new Cabinet's macroeconomic intentions, shifted the debate from the public to the private sector. The Minister pointed out that he was waiting for British Rail/SNCF's full proposals, which were expected in the summer, and the decision to have a link would require the agreement of the French Government. However, the cost of *any* scheme would be large, and it was stressed that 'the Government cannot contemplate finding expenditure on this scale from public funds'. He therefore invited proposals, in addition to the railways' scheme, 'which would attract genuine risk capital'. Cairncross was asked to widen his remit to embrace a study of all schemes submitted to the Minister.[144] DTp officials, led by Lazarus, were aware that Parker would be disappointed by this news. However, British Rail cannot have been surprised at the shift of emphasis, since Fowler was known to be an enthusiastic privatiser, and railway managers were already responding to his wish to detach the Board's subsidiary businesses from the public sector.[145]

In April 1980 the Transport Select Committee announced that in the light of Fowler's statement it would undertake an inquiry into the Channel link.[146] This apparently fortuitous decision was in fact the result of a co-ordinated effort in Whitehall, since the inquiry was intended to serve a dual purpose. First, the newly-created Committee, one of 14 specialist bodies established in 1979 to make executive government more accountable, was keen to examine a policy of substance.[147] The Channel Tunnel offered such an opportunity, and indeed had some resonance with the Committee's first report, on the European Commission's Green Paper on transport infrastructure.[148] Second, DTp officials had been concerned for some time about the appropriate form of public consultation to adopt if the project were to be revived. The initial briefing that Fowler was given in May 1979 had discussed the possibility of recalling and expanding the Cairncross Group, and emphasised the need for the widest possible dissemination of evidence in the spirit of open government.[149] The consultation process for the abandoned scheme had been limited, being confined to the rail link and the location of the terminal in Kent, and Peyton had been insistent that there should not be a public inquiry (above, pp. 154–5). However, since then a number of high profile investigations, for example into motorways, nuclear power (Windscale) and coal mining (Vale of Belvoir) had changed expectations, and officials were convinced that some form of public consideration was unavoidable. On the other hand, the experience of the Roskill inquiry into the Third London Airport presented a strong argument against a lengthy and open-ended examination, with a larger number of options.[150] Fortunately, the positive interest in the Tunnel emanating from the Transport Select Committee appeared to offer a way forward. At its very first meeting in January 1980, Fowler was asked whether he would welcome an investigation by the Committee, and he had replied in the affirmative.[151] Baldwin then advised the Minister that the Committee should be sounded out, since 'there seems some virtue in inviting them to do a thorough job. This would, in part at least, meet the need for public consideration; it would buy time... and... might go at least some part of the way in ruling out of court some of the more unrealistic alternatives'.[152] The Committee took very little persuading to embark on the inquiry.[153]

The Committee's initial intention was to produce a fairly quick report, with all the evidence gathered before the summer recess.[154] However, this proved to be an optimistic target. The Committee, led by Tom Bradley, MP for Leicester East, amassed a considerable body of evidence between May and November 1980. Over 1,000 questions were asked of 22 witnesses, and there were 116 written submissions from a wide constituency, ranging from the Home Office and Customs & Excise to the Parish of Ash and the Folkestone Fishermen's Association. The Committee also visited Dover, Folkestone, Calais, Sangatte and Paris, and held informal discussions with the French Ministry, SNCF and other bodies. The published proceedings amounted to a monumental 643 pages, a major contribution to the debate, providing a contrast with events in 1973–4, when a select committee had not been considered necessary. All the major players were involved in the exercise: the Minister, Norman Fowler, and the Department; British Rail; and opponents of a fixed link, notably Dover Harbour Board and Keith Wickenden of European Ferries. Evidence was also taken from Cairncross, Professor Christopher Foster of Coopers & Lybrand, the GLC, Freight Transport Association, local authorities in Kent, and the major transport trade unions.[155]

Naturally, interest focussed on the evidence offered by the promoters of alternative schemes for a fixed link. Aside from British Rail/SNCF, 11 schemes were floated by seven groups, some more seriously than others and in varying degrees of development.[156] Some were little more than kite-flying affairs, others were 'pre-feasibility' and 'desk' studies giving an idea of costs. There was a fair amount of opportunism in these submissions, since they made use of information provided by the abandoned scheme of 1970–5 and the BR/SNCF proposal, the details of which had been widely circulated.[157] The European Channel Tunnel Group, an international consortium of Spie Batignolles Batiment, Costain Civil Engineering, Bos Kalis Westminster and Philipp Holzmann, put forward no fewer than five schemes. While their earlier and ambitious Island Project of 1978–9 (see above, p. 194) had been abandoned, the new portfolio ranged from an expensive immersed tube for a single-track railway and dual two-lane motorway, costed at £3,256 million, to something resembling the British Rail/SNCF Tunnel, costed at £539 million (January 1980 prices). Cross Channel Contractors were strong advocates of a scheme modelled on the abandoned Tunnel, for which they were the British contractors. Tarmac was also in favour of the 1970–5 scheme, but proposed to construct it in stages, beginning with a rail-only Tunnel on British Rail lines. The total cost was put at £1,730 million (1981 prices).

George Wimpey, in partnership with Royal Volker Stein of Holland, drew up plans for a submerged tube matching the facilities abandoned in 1975. Two bridge initiatives were launched. Linkintoeurope, established by old tunnel hands Freeman Fox & Partners (see Chapter 4, p. 85), and Redpath Dorman Long, a subsidiary of the British Steel Corporation, proposed a dual three-lane motorway carried over a 34-kilometre suspension bridge (£2,000 million in 1979 prices). The Euro-Bridge Studies Group, which included the engineering consultants Pell, Frischmann & Partners and Sir Frederick Snow & Partners, proposed a dual six-lane motorway carried over a 33-kilometre suspension bridge, plus a rail tunnel. Finally, Redpath Dorman Long proposed an extremely ambitious hybrid in the form of a submerged tube. The scheme combined a continuous rail section with a road section (dual two- or three-lane) carried on viaducts to artificial islands. The 19-kilometre section between the islands, straddling the shipping lanes, would be in submerged tube. This piece of extravaganza was reckoned to cost between £4,600 and £5,900 million (mid-1980 prices).[158] In parallel with this exercise in project making, the Transport Committee was able to draw on a report prepared for the European Commission by the consultants Coopers & Lybrand and SETEC-Economie. Overseen by Christopher Foster, the report examined the feasibility of a Channel link, and a summary was published in March 1980. Having examined four plans in detail the consultants concluded that all forms of link, from single-track rail tunnel to road-rail bridge, were likely to be profitable. However, a double-track tunnel appeared to be the most profitable and promised the highest economic return (though the single-track scheme indicated very similar returns and benefits). The bridge options showed much lower returns and were held to be unpromising in the short run (i.e. over a ten year life). Although the estimates of economic and financial returns were necessarily speculative, they found their way into the British press, where they were heralded as providing a strong boost to the prospects of a tunnel.[159] Finally, to add to the complications Thatcher, like Heath before her, had actually expressed interest in a bridge. In February 1980 she asked specifically whether a bridge had been entirely ruled out. She was told that it had not, but that the existing schemes were 'pretty unlikely runners'. The balance of technical opinion lay with a bored tunnel, but the Prime Minister continued to express the view that bridge options should not be discarded prematurely, and consequently the advocates of such alternatives could not at this stage be discounted.[160]

While these debates were taking place, the railways were unable to submit their definitive joint report on the single-track scheme in the summer of 1980 as promised. The Minister's disconcerting statement (to British Rail) that the investment should be funded with risk capital was one factor. But the main reason for the delay was a deterioration in the relationship between British Rail and SNCF. There had been strong disagreements over the scope of the study, and specific aspects of the work could not be resolved, notably the issue of dual- v. single-voltage traction, where a position of deadlock had been reached. The blockage was partially cleared in September when the two sides agreed to conduct a joint study into the practicality of dual-voltage.[161] However, the differences had not been resolved by the end of 1980, though they were not considered fundamental to the financial viability of the scheme.[162] Closer to home, British Rail began to encounter problems with both the Department and its adviser, Cairncross. Relations with the DTp were scarcely helped by the rather begrudging manner in which the CTU's February report on the scheme was passed to the Board. Barron was forced to make several requests before Fowler finally sent Parker a copy in early April. This version of the report, though sanitised to remove elements of a politically sensitive nature, included a new foreword by Cairncross which essentially revealed the Department's verdict on the BRB/SNCF Tunnel. British Rail, he observed, had 'swung from a scheme that failed because it was too ambitious in 1974 to one that may now be too modest in 1980'.[163] While Parker welcomed the document as one that added 'substantially to our knowledge and understanding', he also raised some objections with Fowler, and Board members were later reminded that there had been no dialogue with the Department and that the verdict was far from positive.[164] If British Rail found the attitude of officials 'disappointing', they conceded that Cairncross showed a greater preparedness to debate the issue, though he was a 'formidable and tenacious questioner'.[165]

An enduring source of conflict between Department and Board was the size of the proposed Tunnel; a larger diameter was attractive to the former because it would accommodate an additional shuttle service for road vehicles. Barron observed that the modification had originated with Cairncross and that officials had 'battened on to Sir Alec's idea'.[166] The Department then worked up a variant of the British Rail/SNCF scheme. Preliminary work completed in January 1980 suggested that a modification of the train timetable would allow for greatly increased capacity, viz. 114 trains in each direction instead of 60 under the railways' proposal. This opened up the possibility of a mixed-use tunnel with shuttle services, and in order to cater for lorries the suggested diameter was increased from six to seven metres. If required the variant could be expanded into a two-bore tunnel, thus effectively returning to the scheme abandoned in 1975. The cost of this mixed-use variant was estimated at £300 million on top of the £800 million for the six-metre bore.[167] British Rail was asked to consider this variant, but it was steadfastly opposed to such a development. Parker had already told Fowler in April that a hybrid single tunnel was 'unattractive' to the Board, and Barron made it clear to officials that additional studies would set the whole project back 'by a year or two'.[168] Fowler did not give ground. He asked Parker about the prospects of raising private capital for the Board's preferred option. He added: 'On the face of it a variant attracting a wider range of traffic and working nearer to capacity might be easier from this point of view'.[169] Reluctantly British Rail agreed to undertake a separate assessment of the seven-metre variant on the completion of the current studies. But Parker retained 'strong reservations about the wisdom of departing from the essential simplicity of the scheme', and in a written submission to the Transport Committee in October the Board concluded that a six-metre tunnel was all that was necessary to 'meet the declared objectives of BR/SNCF'.[170] Privately, Barron was prepared to concede that a larger bore would have political attractions and 'provide the best insurance for all future Cross-Channel options', but the argument that private sector money would be attracted more easily if the Tunnel incorporated a road shuttle was dismissed as 'a convenient invention'. Nonetheless, it is evident that for the Tunnel, form was becoming increasingly tied to the financing question, and this was progressively diminishing the attractiveness of the rail-only scheme.[171]

At the Transport Committee Barron was asked whether British Rail's 'mousehole' scheme had not been pitched too low. Indeed, this criticism was implicit in the use of the word 'mousehole', which had been coined as a shorthand for the single-track proposal, but was rapidly becoming a pejorative term in the hands of critics.[172] And the Committee recognised that the proposal, conceived as a low-cost, public sector scheme, had been largely overtaken by Fowler's declaration about private funding.[173] In its evidence to the Committee, British Rail maintained that its scheme was robust and it should be possible to find sources of private capital. However, behind the scenes Barron and his colleagues accepted that the Minister's edict had created a 'whole new ball-game'.[174] Exploratory talks were therefore held with the Davidsons, the European Channel Tunnel Group and Tarmac, while S.G. Warburg was employed to act as the Board's advisers. Only limited progress was made, primarily because the Board wished to complete the definitive studies before considering potential financial packages.[175] But the main stumbling block was governmental. Locating private money was one thing; securing it on terms acceptable to the Department and, more particularly, the Treasury, was quite another. Here, the doctrine of 'symbiosis', highlighted in the CTU's report (above, pp. 194–5), loomed large. First elaborated by the Treasury in November 1979, the notion was clarified in June 1980, and in uncompromising terms. The scope for a private rail-only tunnel company to fulfil the risk criterion, by exploiting the facility independently of British Rail/SNCF, was felt to be 'vanishingly small'. Any prior agreement on guaranteed minimum rentals was ruled out, although the Treasury conceded that it was 'inconceivable that a company would construct a rail-only tunnel without some guarantee of rental from the sole potential user'. To qualify for private sector status, free of the PSBR, a company could not expect an agreed rental from the railways to cover its full cost. Its return would then be dependent on the ability to exploit the Tunnel in other ways: suggestions ranged from the sale of duty-free goods and advertising space to train catering and the running of excursions. In conclusion, the Treasury asked: 'Given the inherent difficulties in involving private capital in the BRB scheme, has the time not come to widen our horizons somewhat and focus more on alternative schemes?'[176] However, because most of the other options contained a rail element, the problem of 'symbiosis' did not disappear entirely. DTp officials pressed for a relaxation of the doctrine, but the Treasury insisted that any arrangement in which the railways were the main users of the Tunnel would be symbiotic and therefore rank as a public sector venture.[177] When Clarke met Cairncross in September 1980, he confirmed that the Treasury doctrine was a 'major obstacle' for the British Rail scheme, and suggested that there was 'a case for attempting to detach Government somewhat publicly from BRB, without at the same time appearing to dismiss them'.[178]

5. Struggling to make a decision, November 1980–August 1981

When Fowler appeared before the Transport Committee in November 1980 he was naturally asked about the prospects for raising private finance. There were of course many problems in attracting genuine risk capital, as had been evident in the protracted negotiations of 1970–3, and it was impossible for the Government to resolve these before the detailed schemes were submitted. First, there was the thorny question of government guarantees. At the time of his March statement Fowler had stated that he did not 'preclude consideration of guarantees in the wider area', essentially to cover cancellation or interruption through political action.[179] However, later in the year he suggested to the Transport Committee that the concept might be extended to embrace a usage agreement with the railways.[180] Second, an element of public expenditure was required to provide the associated transport infrastructure. Third, after all the difficulties with the abandoned scheme, the banking sector was reported to be wary about the use of equity capital in a project such as this. The Select Committee certainly found little hard evidence that private finance would be forthcoming, a view shared in private by Treasury officials.[181] Of the backers associated with the Tunnel in the past, the Davidson brothers re-emerged in the summer of 1980 with a plan to reconstitute the Channel Tunnel Study Group and finance either a single- or double-track tunnel. The railways would be the contractors and operators, but would bear the risk of any overruns. This was typical Davidson bravura. In the manner of Osborne O'Hagan, the great nineteenth-century company promoter, the Americans proposed 'a masterpiece in dodging risk and cornering profit'. However, the Davidsons, who were still primarily concerned to obtain compensation for past endeavours, were quickly 'sidelined' when Technical Studies Inc. and the British banking interests, led by William Merton of Robert Fleming, parted company.[182] Merton then promptly reappeared as a representative of the five British merchant banks – Flemings, Hill Samuel, Kleinwort Benson, Morgan Grenfell and Warburgs – which had been involved in the aborted project and which were busy advising the several promoting parties.[183] These banks offered to carry out a staged evaluation of the fixed link project for the Government, something that was welcomed by Fowler when he met them in November.[184] Significantly, a notable absentee from the list of hopeful promoters was RTZ. The company had adopted a low profile on tunnel matters since its joint work with CGE, and had no further interest in the project. When Frame met Barron in August 1980, he explained that in the previous scheme his company had been 'thwarted' by government interference, and in spite of Fowler's pronouncements, he did not consider the climate to have changed. Frame's opinion was that it was 'virtually impossible' to finance the project on an 'honest equity basis'.[185]

A further problem was the fact that the attitude of the French to a private finance initiative, which had been rather disconcerting in the past, was uncertain. Aside from simmering resentment over the 1975 abandonment, relations between the two countries had also become strained by Britain's efforts to renegotiate her contribution to the EEC budget in 1979–80.[186] Here the Foreign Office, ever anxious to improve Anglo-French relations and suffering, according to the Treasury, from 'a virulent bout of "tunnelitis" ', had suggested that the Tunnel be included as an item of offsetting expenditure, though the arguments in favour of introducing the project into budgetary discussions were rather weak, and the idea was quickly dropped.[187] After the budget issue had been settled, the Transport Ministers met informally on 9 June. Le Theule told Fowler that finance was one of the three factors worrying the French. Clearly thinking in terms of *public* funding, he remarked that with an austerity budget in prospect, this was an inauspicious time to be contemplating a large-scale project. The British Minister responded by tentatively raising the prospect of private financing.[188] Fielding questions from the Transport Committee in November, Fowler admitted that 'the French take the view that the ball is very much in our court and historically I do not think anyone can blame them for taking that particular view'.[189] There had still been no formal contact between the two sides, but another informal meeting took place with Le Theule's successor, Daniel Hoeffel in December. Here the French welcomed the work of British Rail and SNCF, and gave a more positive response to the idea of private financing. Further discussions were promised after the French presidential elections in May 1981.[190] Reporting to Thatcher, Fowler said that the discussions had been 'fairly encouraging', with Hoeffel giving the impression that the French were interested in reviving the project. Once the Minister had received the railways' detailed submission, the proposals from other parties, advice from the merchant banks, and the report of the Transport Committee, all expected in January 1981, he would be in a position to formulate a view on the commercial prospects. Some joint study by the British and French 'would obviously be essential'.[191]

At the end of January 1981 Parker sent Fowler a confidential report on the six-metre single-track tunnel, together with a financing paper from Warburgs. This was a 'BR commentary on the results', since, as in 1979, it had not been possible to secure French agreement to a joint document. Parker was nevertheless bullish about the conclusions of a rather thin document. Arguing with little detailed support for a 9.5 per cent return on the investment, he maintained that private sector funding, while presenting a challenge, could be found for the scheme.[192] Fowler, who by this time had been elevated to the Cabinet as Secretary of State, was not very encouraging in return. His reply focussed on the need to evaluate the alternative, seven-metre tunnel with a road vehicle shuttle.[193] Between October 1980 and March 1981 the initial proposals of competing promoters were submitted to the Department, and the CTU began its assessment work. In March 1981 the Department also received the financing survey undertaken by the five merchant banks. Unsurprisingly, this was a cautious document which contended that the prospects for raising equity were slim and emphasised the need for a minimum revenue agreement and government guarantees on the loan capital to cover overruns and political risks.[194]

The Transport Committee's report was also published in March 1981. Despite its length, and the wealth of evidence collected, it had limited aims and a limited impact. The Committee, while in favour of proceeding with the project, made it clear that it had not been its intention to 'endorse a single proposal by a single promoting group'. Nor could it do so, since much of the information on alternatives appeared after its deliberations had ended, and, in any case, the choice of option was dependent upon the determination of financing arrangements. Nevertheless, to the Department's surprise, the Committee produced a 'preferred option'. Apparently the result of a compromise designed to secure unanimity, its recommended scheme was a bored tunnel for a single-track railway, built to dimensions that would permit the expansion of services at a later date. This would mean an initial 6.85-metre tunnel capable of providing for road shuttle traffic.[195] Fowler responded by promising to reach 'decisions in principle' by the end of 1981, but it was a full year before his successor appeared before the Committee.[196] However, British Rail put a positive gloss on the report. A press release, a Parker speech, and another popular brochure all claimed that the Committee's preferred option corresponded very closely with the Board's scheme.[197] Nevertheless, the issue of the tunnel diameter remained an open one. The Board was advised to stick publicly to six metres, though, as Barron noted, it might 'confidently expect to be directed to accept 7 metres'. One thing was evident: British Rail remained firmly opposed to the idea of accepting shuttle services.[198]

At long last the text of a joint British Rail/SNCF report was completed, and in May 1981 Parker and two of his senior Board colleagues travelled to Dijon to inform Gentil and Lacoste of SNCF about the arrangements to submit the report to the British Government. However, by this time a new complication had arisen. The unexpected victory of the socialist leader François Mitterand in the second round of the French presidential election on 10 May had created a further uncertainty. Gentil thought that the socialists were likely to favour a Tunnel, but the change of government itself could slow down the decision-making process.[199] Undaunted, Parker sent Fowler the full submission three days after the meeting, describing it as a 'complete, well-researched scheme which is commercially attractive and robust'. This was Panglossian. Though strengthened by a detailed assessment of financial feasibility from Warburgs, the main report was scarcely fuller than earlier versions.[200] In June British Rail sent the Department its promised paper on the seven-metre variant. This 'broad-brush' exercise produced no enthusiasm at all for the concept. The return on an investment which would cost £216 million more than the six-metre project [£742 million] was put at 8.0 per cent [cf. 9.5%]. Barron told Fairclough that 'the economics of a 6 metre tunnel are superior to those of a 7 metre tunnel, with or without a road shuttle', and that if a seven-metre tunnel were constructed, 'it would be better to limit its usage to the passage of conventional traffic'.[201] In fact, British Rail put more effort into its concurrent deliberations on the location of a London terminal. Doubts about the plan to construct the West London Relief Road, an integral part of the transport links necessary for a terminal at West Brompton or Olympia, had re-opened the matter. Detailed study showed that the Tunnel traffic could instead be accommodated at Waterloo, thus obviating the need for a West London/Victoria split. The Waterloo option, which had first been raised by the London Boroughs Association in 1973, was now enthusiastically taken up by British Rail managers, in marked contrast with their stance before the Transport Committee only eight months before. The station would be provided with additional platforms, while a new flyover at Stewart's Lane would give access to the existing boat train route. There was evidently more agreement here than with the Tunnel's diameter.[202]

DTp officials clearly had it in mind to use the conclusions of the Transport Committee to advance the project, and it was envisaged that a response to the report would be made in the form of a Commons statement. The Transport Secretary would announce that bridge and immersed tube options should now be eliminated, and that work would now concentrate on a seven-metre bored tunnel. On 24 April both Fowler and Clarke accepted this strategy, and civil servants began to draft three papers: a minute to the Prime Minister; a statement to the House; and a possible Cabinet paper.[203] However, by early June, Fowler had had a change of heart. Having consulted with Cairncross, he now argued that it would be premature to rule out completely the bridge and tube options, and consequently, the draft documents were rewritten to convey this more tentative position.[204] At the same time, concerns were expressed within the Department about the timing and content of the proposed papers, given that evaluation work and meetings with promoters were still proceeding, and no satisfactory financing proposals had been received.[205] These factors, together with the change of government in France, led Rosenfeld to advise Fowler that the proposed minute to Thatcher be postponed until the autumn.[206] The lack of a response certainly gave the impression that the Department, having invited expressions of interest from entrepreneurs, was finding it difficult, with limited resources, to sort out the various proposals. It was also apparent that it would welcome some merger activity among the promoting groups.[207] In fact, this was already happening, since Tarmac and Wimpey had joined forces and Channel Tunnel Developments (1981) Ltd (CTD) was formed to progress their plan to construct the 1975 Tunnel in stages.[208] British Rail also responded to the call for private finance by attempting to find a suitable partner. For some time rival groups had been courting railway managers as well as departmental officials. With the encouragement of the Minister British Rail held meetings with the European Channel Tunnel Group (ECTG), Tarmac/Wimpey, Cross Channel Contractors, and the British Steel subsidiary, Redpath Dorman Long.[209] Of these, ECTG, with ambitions limited to project management, appeared to have most to offer, but at the end of the summer it had not been possible to reach a formal agreement with the consortium.[210]

Thus, by the summer of 1981, a mass of evidence, reports and other documentation had been generated on the fixed link. Indeed, the wealth of information and the range of possibilities were arguably greater than at any time in the Channel Tunnel's long history. The Department had received proposals from eight groups, including a revival of John Laing's submerged tube proposal, which came too late for consideration by the Select Committee. There was also a further report from the Dover Harbour Board presenting the 'do nothing' option of shipping interests, under the banner of the 'Channel Tunnel Study Working Party'.[211] Ministers and officials had now to decide what to do and, critically, how matters should be taken forward with the French Government. But in many ways the prospects seemed dimmer than before. The vexed issue of financing revealed once again that there appeared little sign of escaping from the circularity of what we may call 'Tunnel realpolitik': the interface of private v. public funding, and risk v. guarantee (see Figure 7.1). Similar issues had arisen with other projects, notably the gas-gathering pipeline, and attempts to bring private money into the railways.[212] The DTp accepted that it needed to 'winkle the promoters out of their defensive positions on financial guarantees', but a letter sent to all the parties on 5 August in order to evoke a more satisfactory response failed to produce much of an improvement.[213] Further, the most ardent and enduring supporters of the project had had their optimism dented. The two railways, having revived the idea in 1975, had gone from a position of being the only scheme to being merely one of many, and no longer a favourite at that. Ex-post rationalisation encouraged by Parker *et al.* suggested that the smaller single-bore or 'mousehole' had been little more than a device to keep the project alive with sceptical governments until a more considered scheme could merge. In Parker's words, 'Our "mousehole" was for starters'.[214] The archives do not support this contention, however. British Rail made strenuous efforts to advance the concept of a rail-only tunnel under its control. But by

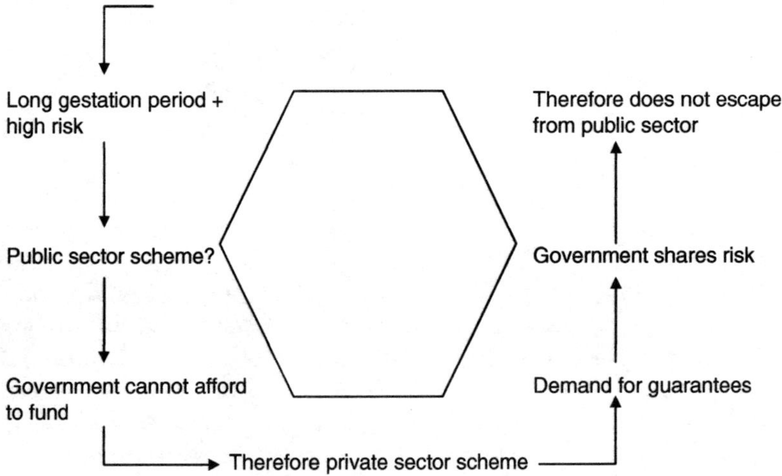

Figure 7.1 The Channel Tunnel circle.

August 1981 it was evident that it had made little headway in persuading the Government to back its scheme unilaterally. Moreover, the Department's adviser, Cairncross, was arguing that a twin-track seven-metre tunnel must be the 'front runner'.[215]

How fair had Whitehall been to British Rail? Officials had condemned its scheme before it had been fully worked up, and by the time the full report was ready, it was too late. The 'Mousehole' was the victim of another shift in emphasis, this time from the public to the private sector, forgetting all the problems chronicled by Fogarty and her DTp colleagues in relation to the scheme abandoned in 1975. One might also question the wisdom in reopening the can of worms containing tunnels, immersed tubes and bridges, when successive investigations – the White Paper of 1973, the Cairncross report of 1975 and the Transport Committee Report of 1981 – had pronounced firmly in favour of a bored tunnel. In defence of the Marsham Street approach, the chances of public sector funding were remote, both domestically and further afield. However hard British Rail lobbied, and whatever the Government may have said publicly about the possibilities of EEC funding, it was evident that the United Kingdom would not be a net beneficiary of any Community-wide infrastructure aid programme, and was therefore unlikely to support it in the European Council.[216] Nor were the French any more enthusiastic about the putative aid programme, and fully committed as they were to nuclear power, they were not in a position to contribute to a Tunnel from public funds.[217] And yet none of the private promoting groups had come up with a promise of venture capital. It would require a firmer resolve, improved financial arrangement, and more impressive planning from would-be promoters, to break the deadlock.

8

THE THATCHER GOVERNMENTS AND THE TUNNEL

From hope to eternity, 1981–4

1. Anglo-French talks and their aftermath, September–December 1981

In September 1981 there was a rather surprising development when the subject of the Fixed Channel Link was raised at a high level during an Anglo-French summit in London. The change of direction began with a considerable measure of disagreement within Whitehall. The Foreign Office had been anxious to include the Link on the bilateral relations agenda, but, having obtained Department of Transport support, had encountered strong opposition from the Treasury, which was keen to avoid this given the undeveloped state of the project.[1] There was also nervousness within the Cabinet Office. Following the Left's landslide victory in the French National Assembly elections in June, the caretaker Transport Minister, Louis Mermaz, had been replaced by the leading communist, Charles Fiterman. Efforts were therefore made to remove transport matters from the formal agenda in an attempt to exclude him from the talks.[2] While British departments continued to argue, it became evident that Mitterand was more sympathetic to the idea of a fixed link than his predecessor, Giscard, had been, and when at last the membership of the French delegation was revealed, on 28 August, Fiterman's name was included.[3] The agenda was hastily rewritten and Fowler's name was added to the British team. However, the Treasury continued to complain, seeking adjustments to the ministerial briefing and insisting that the Link be excluded from the formal record.[4] On 10 September Fowler had 'an extremely amicable' first meeting with Fiterman. Both Ministers adopted a bullish tone about the project. Fowler 'said that the British Government would be in favour of a fixed link if France also welcomed it', though they 'would want to be sure that the UK share could be financed privately'. Fiterman 'said that in principle the French Government would be in favour of a study which would allow a Link to be established in the best conditions', but they 'would expect public financial control of their share of the project…and they favoured a rail link'.[5] Officials then prepared a low-key statement about plans for further studies.[6] But events took a more positive turn at the highest level. The Channel Link did not figure in the minutes of the Thatcher-Mitterand talks later in the day, where the discussions embraced issues such as telecommunications, computing and aircraft engines. But in the evening the Elysée's Secretary-General, Pierre Bérégovoy, pressed Sir Robert Armstrong, the Cabinet Secretary, 'for some demonstration of practical bilateral co-operation' to emerge from the talks. As Armstrong noted, 'he suggested that the President and the Prime Minister should "relaunch" the idea of the Tunnel. They should make a definite statement of intention'.[7] At a plenary session on the following day, 11 September, Fowler referred to his 'useful discussion' with Fiterman on the Channel Link, and the latter announced that the 'French government approach was positive in principle' and that he 'welcomed the British desire for joint studies'. The ensuing press conference conveyed the fact that the talks had been conducted in a friendly and constructive atmosphere. On the Channel Link, Thatcher announced that the two sides proposed 'to go ahead immediately with joint studies' of the schemes being advanced. She announced that the British would wish it to be financed privately, while Mitterand observed that 'each of the

Cartoon 5 The illusive Tunnel dream: Varney, in *Building*, 20 November 1981.

two countries will have to carry out its own specific means of financing'.[8] The British press was surprised by this announcement, although three newspapers got wind of the decision on the previous day.[9] But the fact that the two leaders, with their very different perspectives, had suggested that political difficulties would not be allowed to obstruct the project represented the firmest expression of support since abandonment. The summit marked the beginning of a more intense period of debate in British government circles.

British Rail, who had kept up the pressure on ministers over the summer, also sensed that the pace had quickened as a result of the Thatcher-Mitterand talks. In August 1981 the Board had decided that it would seek a joint venture arrangement with one of the three other sponsors of a bored tunnel: Cross Channel Contractors, Channel Tunnel Developments (1981), and the European Channel Tunnel Group.[10] After the summit meeting British Rail acted quickly to choose a partner. In doing so on 21 September, rarely used emergency powers were invoked allowing the Chairman and four other Board members to act collectively if an urgent decision could not wait until the next Board meeting. After assessing factors such as project definition, organisational arrangements and financing, Board members accepted Barron's recommendation that British Rail should join with ECTG to take the project forward. The decision was in fact easy to reach since members were already in agreement that ECTG, which had been in discussions with British Rail for nearly two years, were potentially the best partners.[11] Following ratification by the full Board on 1 October, news of the informal alliance was communicated to David Howell, who had succeeded Fowler at Transport in a major Cabinet reshuffle in September.[12] Parker took the opportunity to emphasise the advantages of the British Rail/SNCF scheme, which he described as a 'glittering' initiative. It was 'in a quite different category' from the others, most of which were 'barely at the feasibility stage', and was the only one that could be prepared in time for inclusion in the 1982–3 legislative programme. With a characteristic flourish Parker recognised that the Board's objective was 'unashamedly commercial', but believed that 'it must be the best option too for U.K. Ltd.'[13] British Rail and ECTG now commenced work on a suitable financing package in association with their bankers, Warburgs, and N.M. Rothschild, but, as Howell had been warned, agreeing the terms of private sector funding proved to be a tough hurdle. In particular, the absence of a government guarantee of completion produced difficulties. An initial financing plan drawn up by Rothschilds on this basis was rejected because it imposed an 'intolerable burden' on British Rail in terms of the scale of traffic throughput payments it would have to make in a usage agreement lasting 40 years. Warburgs were then encouraged to work on an alternative, incorporating a completion guarantee. As Barron noted on 23 November: 'a brave but unsuccessful attempt has been made to relieve the Government of completion commitment... it was now necessary to move quickly and fundamentally to a different financing method'.[14] But time was short, since a joint presentation was to be made to Howell on 11 December. The hastily devised alternative envisaged lower usage payments over 30 years, and although this was trumpeted in a press release, it masked the fact that the details of a financing plan were far from being resolved when the presentation to Government was made. What British Rail and ECTG really required was some guidance as to the kind of financing package which would be acceptable and the extent to which the Government's stance on guarantees might be relaxed.[15]

Of all the various schemes for a fixed link, a bored tunnel remained the favourite, though this did not necessarily mean a six-metre, single-track rail tunnel. British Rail's selection of ECTG as its partner left the Tarmac/Wimpey alliance, CTD, as a serious rival. Not only did CTD advocate a seven-metre tunnel, but its interests lay predominantly in encouraging road transport, and the Chairman, Tony de Boer, had been President of the British Road Federation since 1972. Barron assessed the situation as 'virtually . . . a two-horse race'.[16] But, in fact, the most vigorous lobbying came from a complete outsider. Redpath Dorman Long's scheme, now known as EuroRoute, was an ambitious plan for a bridge/immersed tube/bridge for road traffic, together with a railway in tube. Fronting its campaign was Ian MacGregor, the uncompromising Chairman of the British Steel Corporation (BSC). MacGregor was able to use his influence to gain a meeting with Thatcher in order to explain EuroRoute's proposal.[17] Nor was the idea, expensive as it was, totally without merit. When MacGregor presented his scheme to the Prime Minister, Howell and Patrick Jenkin, the Secretary of State for Industry, in November 1981, he made much of the fact that the venture would be of advantage to the ailing British steel industry. In particular, the improvement in transport infrastructure would enable BSC to penetrate the European steel market more readily. Beyond seeking to advantage his own company, MacGregor has recalled that he was also looking for a 'symbolic "Queen Mary" gesture' to boost the country's economic recovery: 'What better way than with the long-dreamed-about Channel Tunnel crossing?'[18] Civil servants from the Departments of Transport and Industry were more sceptical, however. They conceded that the proposal had the support of some of the world's leading financial and engineering firms, including Lazards, Mott Hay and Anderson and Robert MacAlpine, but the analogy with the American Chesapeake Bay crossing was regarded as a weakness rather than a strength – this shallow-water scheme had already been damaged five times by shipping. And although the scheme would consume steel and help to protect jobs, the effects would not be dramatic.[19] Advised not to offer EuroRoute direct encouragement in view of doubts about practicality and cost, Thatcher adopted a non-committal position at the meeting. However, she did agree with MacGregor that the provision for car and lorry traffic was one of the scheme's attractions.[20] The Prime Minister was also careful to avoid being drawn into any implied association with EuroRoute by MacGregor's manoeuvrings. When in the following week MacGregor tried to pursue a request to see Mitterand, Thatcher commented: 'he cannot say that I endorse his particular plan', adding, 'He must not indicate that I am urging him to see the President'.[21] As for the other promoters, Howell saw representatives of all the groups and these presentations revealed that British Rail and ECTG were not alone in struggling to meet the Government's financing demands. Here was something of a 'Catch-22' situation. The promoters would not make proposals without guarantees; the Government wanted to see worked-up proposals before discussing the issue of guarantees.[22]

At the end of September 1981 officials from the British and French transport ministries met to discuss the arrangements for the new joint studies. The negotiations were led by Andrew Lyall, who became Fairclough's successor as head of the International Transport Division, and Fiterman's Chargé de Mission, Guy Braibant. A year at the Ecole Nationale d'Administration, and fluency in French helped Lyall to forge a good working relationship with his opposite number in Paris.[23] A programme of work was agreed covering technical, economic, social, financial and legal matters.[24] Given the wide-ranging nature of the proposed studies, together with an understandably cautious approach on the part of French officials, it quickly became evident that Fowler's stated objective of reaching a decision by the end of the year could not be met.[25] Indeed, the French Government was scarcely prepared for a revival of the project, having closed its files after the 1975 abandonment.[26] On 27 October, only a fortnight after Howell had promised the Conservative party conference that he would adhere to his predecessor's timetable, he had to inform Thatcher that it was likely to be February before the French, given their late start, would be able to narrow down the options for detailed study. This, he contended, would make it difficult to enact legislation over the projected life of the parliament, that is by the end of the 1982/3 session.[27] In fact, when Howell met Fiterman on the following day, French officials accepted the idea of producing a short study leading to a decision, by the end of February, on whether to proceed with a fixed link, and if so, in what manner. Howell was then able to tell the Prime Minister that he intended to raise the main issues at Cabinet level 'in the next few weeks'.[28]

Howell's commitment to present a paper was certainly welcomed by the Treasury, which for some time had been watching developments with unease. Earlier in the year the Chief Secretary, Leon Brittan, had expressed concerns about the economics and financing of a fixed link, concerns shared by the French Finance Minister, Jacques Delors, and we have already noted that officials were opposed to the inclusion of the subject on the agenda of the September summit.[29] The announcements of Thatcher and Mitterand only served to strengthen the Treasury's reservations that a heightened state of public expectation would create pressure for the Government to make a decision before major uncertainties had been resolved. Two fundamental and familiar points were identified: first, the conditions for financing the link with private risk capital; and second, the need for a complete economic appraisal. Fears were partially allayed at a meeting between Transport and Treasury permanent secretaries, Peter Baldwin and William Ryrie, where it was agreed that there should be greater co-operation between the two departments. Despite an undertaking to work together on an economic assessment and the promoters' financing proposals, anxieties persisted. The Treasury's private objective was thus 'to prevent joint talks reaching a publicised conclusion... before UK Ministers have been able to reach a clear detached decision about the economic merits of proceeding and the financing conditions for doing so'.[30]

As some elements of the picture became clearer, Treasury scepticism was apparently confirmed. The most recent figures on economic return were in the range 5.6–7.3 per cent, which compared unfavourably with the modest discount rate of 7 per cent expected of major transport investments in the public sector. Not for the first time in the Tunnel's history, a Treasury official was able to describe the project as 'extremely marginal'.[31] On top of this, there was the thorny problem of government guarantees. Promoters of tunnels had shown little inclination to budge from their demands for completion and/or throughput guarantees. Promoters of bridges continued to maintain that they could raise sufficient capital without guarantees, but there was no evidence that they could do so. The Treasury was also disturbed to learn that the French Government not only required some protection against abandonment (unsurprisingly in view of past events), but were also insistent that tariffs and timetables should be placed under government control. All this meant that there were clearly going to be 'considerable difficulties' in securing a genuinely private financing package.[32] Nor did a circulated draft of Howell's paper to the Ministerial Committee on Economic Strategy (E Committee) offer the Treasury any comfort. The paper, which assumed that the Channel Link was a 'good thing' and concentrated mainly on the choice of scheme and on timing, was regarded as doing little to clarify the issues, and in particular whether there should be a Fixed Link at all. The discussion of private finance was thought to have been obscured to such an extent that 'it is difficult even for those familiar with the issues to decipher what is intended'. Furthermore, the references to guarantees failed to address the fact that the project might be so transformed as to fall within the public sector, which would completely change the rules.[33] By this time, the Treasury was also aware that Sir Alec Cairncross, who was still advising the Department of Transport, was 'distinctly lukewarm' about the project. Officials therefore advised Brittan, much to the annoyance of the DTp, to present his own paper to E Committee.[34]

Cairncross had been busy working on the fixed link over the course of 1981. In a note to Fowler in June he had offered to prepare a report on the various schemes then emerging, which did not form part of his original remit, and had also suggested that the Channel Tunnel Advisory Group of 1974–5 might be reconvened. The DTp's Channel Tunnel Unit, while welcoming a report, resisted the reformation of CTAG, a move that was felt would duplicate the work being done and cause delay.[35] After the summit meeting in September the Secretary of State asked Cairncross to fulfil his earlier promise to submit a report by the end of October.[36] In fact, the delay was limited, and Cairncross managed to deliver his final draft, together with a minute to Howell, in November. Unfortunately his report did little to relieve a rather beleaguered ministry, which was having to deal with criticism of British Rail on a number of fronts. Like the 1975 report, 'Cairncross 2' was a dense and hefty document which by his own admission appeared to be 'rather inconclusive'.[37] Certainly, the adviser's attitude had changed somewhat in the intervening years, and cold water was poured on all sides. Cairncross could find no merit in either a tube or a bridge, which were ruled out by the capital costs and safety considerations. If a link were to be built, his preference was for a twin-bore tunnel seven metres in diameter, the choice resting on the assertion that this would produce a fourfold increase in capacity with only an additional 30 per cent in capital cost. But even here, the case was apparently less compelling than it had been in 1975, principally because the cross-channel ferries were becoming more efficient and were therefore eroding the cost differential between them and a tunnel. However, the picture was further muddied by the absence of a considered case by the 'do-nothing lobby' for the development of existing modes. All Cairncross could do was express the doubt that the ferries would be able to reduce costs by the 50 per cent claimed in the work co-ordinated by the Dover Harbour Board. The adviser's pessimism also extended to finance and the position of the Government. 'There was never much prospect', he observed, 'that equity capital could be found for a completely new undertaking requiring £1,500 m or more with no assets or profit record to offer to investors'. And the likelihood of private borrowing looked remote unless the Government relaxed some of its financial and commercial constraints. In general terms Cairncross found the Government at something of an 'impasse'. It was criticised for displaying a 'rather equivocal' attitude towards some of the fundamental issues, by seeking to 'wash its hands of any scheme', and at the same time being drawn inextricably into decision-making by the very nature of the project (given legislative and treaty requirements, planning responsibilities, ancillary public investment, etc.). With its numerous provisos and academic hedging the overall tone of 'Cairncross 2' was scarcely optimistic. 'What this comes to', he told Howell, 'is that there is a case, but not a conclusive case, for a tunnel'.[38] His belief that the case for a fixed link had been weakened since 1975 was repeated when he met the Secretary of State on 25 November, in what was 'effectively his swan-song'.[39] The DTp was stung by some of Cairncross's remarks, and at a policy level the report appeared to raise more questions than answers. Officials felt that their adviser had displayed excessive gloom about the project based on estimated rates of return which were higher than their own; his financial agnosticism was also felt to be misplaced. The Department warned the Treasury that the report should be 'treated with reserve', and, according to a CPRS source, it had 'gone down like a lead balloon' with Ministers.[40] Cairncross was keen to see his work published, but officials were far from enthusiastic about the idea. Publication *was* undertaken, but in a deliberately 'unobtrusive' manner by appending a modified version to evidence provided by Howell when he appeared before the Transport Select Committee in February 1982.[41]

On 3 December 1981 the Fixed Channel Link was considered by E Committee, in the first formal debate of the subject at ministerial level since the abandonment in 1975. There were memoranda from Howell and Brittan, and a note from the CPRS, which had renewed its interest after a long period of dormancy.[42]

The Transport Secretary set out the various alternatives of bored tunnels, bridges and immersed tubes (see Table 8.1), and identified the ranges of financial and economic returns. On financing he noted that there were 'certain facts of life which must be recognised', notably the inevitability of some measure of Government involvement. The complications were 'formidable', the permutations numerous. But it seemed likely that an element of guarantee was inevitable, and in the circumstances, the possibilities offered by 'hybrid' private-public financing arrangements, with appropriate risk adjustments, were articulated. Howell then sought support for the line to adopt with the French, presenting colleagues with three possible scenarios: (1) to go for a quick start on a rail tunnel; (2) to study bridges or tubes more thoroughly; or (3) to rely on existing shipping services. The Minister suggested that a bored tunnel was the 'most probable choice'. Although he conceded that the case, based on estimated returns, was 'not overwhelming', there was no hint of Cairncross's ambivalence towards the project.[43] Brittan's paper revealed a more realistic assessment of the prospects for a link financed entirely by private risk capital: 'it looks increasingly doubtful whether that will be possible'. The French insistence on a completion guarantee would take the project into the public sector, where 'hybrid' financing was a possibility, but the essential point was that decision-making should be based on an economic assessment of the project, which had already appeared 'at best… marginal'. Brittan doubted whether the Fixed Link should be pursued, but, in any case, was anxious that talks with the French should not lead the Government into a position of 'semi-commitment' before a considered view had emerged.[44] The CPRS questioned whether there was enough information to determine the choice of option at this stage, and, like the Treasury, was concerned about the need for a proper economic assessment.[45] In discussion, the Committee agreed that there should be no commitment to any particular course of action until a full risk assessment had been made. While the choice of option would have to be taken in the light of the economic appraisal, it was accepted that it would be a mistake to rule out the more imaginative schemes. Summing up, Thatcher asked Howell to continue with the studies and report further in the New Year. Discussions with the French should be on the basis that all options remained open. The stated aim was to fund any link with private sector capital and 'reduce any Government involvement and undertakings to a minimum'.[46]

These deliberations were regarded, in the Treasury at least, as being 'inconclusive', with the crucial issue of financing having been 'badly fudged' by the DTp.[47] The Foreign Office was also disappointed. Officials in the Western European Department gained the impression 'of a less than whole-hearted political commitment to the project'. Its Head was more trenchant: 'This is getting nowhere fast. What wd [*sic*] our Victorian ancestors make of this cowardly approach to risk?'[48] However, some progress was made with the French. A week after the Committee had deliberated, British and French officials met to consider the output from the study groups. It was evident that the two sides shared much common ground on technicalities, and it was agreed that a short interim report on

Table 8.1. Channel Fixed Link options, December 1981

Group	*Proposal*	*Cost (£m., Jan.1981 prices) Link +portal facilities*[a]
Bored Tunnels		
British Rail/European Channel Tunnel Group (Costain etc.)	Single 6 m tunnel for through rail traffic	879
Channel Tunnel Developments 1981 (Tarmac/Wimpey)	Single 7 m tunnel for through rail traffic	982
	Above + shuttle	1,373
	Twin 7 m tunnels	
	Phased	1,785
	Unphased	1,682
Anglo-Channel Tunnel Group (Taylor Woodrow, Balfour Beatty, Nuttall)	6 m or 7 m tunnel	—
Immersed Tube		
Laing	Dual 2-lane road	2,345
	Dual 2-lane road + twin-track railway	3,391
Bridges		
Linkintoeurope (Freeman)	Multi-span suspension bridge for dual 3-lane motorway	1,952
	Above + single 6 m rail tunnel	2,831
Eurobridge	Multi-span road bridge	3,556
	Above + single 6 m rail tunnel	4,435
Viaducts and Tube		
EuroRoute (British Steel)	Inshore viaducts and central immersed tube for road; rail link in immersed tube throughout	4,056

Source: E(81) 121, 26 November 1981, Annex A.

Note

a Alternative estimates, including the cost of associated infrastructure, are given in Cairncross Report, Table 4.1, HC Transport Committee Report on *The Channel Link*, p.p. 1981, xxiv, HC207, and DTp, *Fixed Channel Link. Report of UK/French Study Group*, June 1982, P.P. 1981–2, liv, Cmnd.8561, Table K.1, and note para.K.12.

the findings would be released to Ministers in the New Year. As to the anticipated tone of the final report, there was a delicate decision to be made as to whether this should adopt a neutral stance or make firm recommendations. True to the form of previous Anglo-French tunnel negotiations, an element of political manoeuvring was present here. As one official conceded: 'each side is attempting to secure a position which would allow it to blame the other for an unsatisfactory result (whatever that might be)'.[49]

2. The Cabinet's rejection of guarantees, January–February 1982

The drafting of an interim report on the Anglo-French studies, required for Howell's reappearance at E Committee, was a straightforward matter and the document was largely complete by early January. But there were problems in relation to the timing and content of an interim public announcement on the Fixed Link, which was needed before Howell appeared before the Transport Committee to comment on the latter's own report.[50] Howell and Fiterman had agreed that there would be consultation before any statement and on 14 January Lyall and Braibant met in Paris to agree the text of the interim report and to discuss tactics. The main business was dispensed with quickly. Both sides agreed to restrict public comment, and a formal joint letter transmitting the report to the two Ministers was signed. Lyall was then introduced to Fiterman. This was more than purely a matter of courtesy, with the British official left in no doubt that the French Minister 'wants a tunnel…He wants a quick decision. He hopes it will be positive'.[51]

A complicating factor in the negotiations with the French was Braibant's revelation that the politics of the Fixed Link in the Nord-Pas de Calais region were far from simple. While the area would undoubtedly benefit from the project, attitudes were not entirely positive, particularly in the ports. Here, the British Rail/SNCF proposal for a six-metre, rail-only tunnel was perceived as a clear threat to jobs. However, there was greater acceptance of the seven-metre alternative with shuttle services, since this was believed to offer compensating employment opportunities. In addition, SNCF itself was not formally committed to the six-metre scheme, and its new President, André Chadeau, former Prefect of Nord-Pas de Calais, was expected to be sensitive to regional opinion.[52] On the other hand, there were also grounds for optimism in that northern France was the political base of Pierre Mauroy, Mayor of Lille from 1973 and now the French Prime Minister. Not only was he pro-European and a supporter of Britain's entry into Europe; he was also a long-term 'tunneliste', having raised the subject when he met the Chancellor, Denis Healey and Eric Varley, the Industry Secretary, in 1978.[53] In January 1982 Mauroy visited the Nord-Pas de Calais as part of a series of regional tours. The French press reported him to have been most enthusiastic about the Fixed Link, and the British Embassy even claimed that he had, in modern phraseology, 'sexed up' his brief in order to emphasise his support for the project.[54] The prospect of renewed speculation in the French media created a potential difficulty for Howell, who had been called to appear before the Transport Select Committee. In order to avoid any embarrassment during the weeks between Mauroy's visit to Calais and Howell's appearance in February, departmental officials recommended that a paper, summarising the main contents of the interim report, be sent in advance to Committee members.[55] The report itself, drafted by the French, was, as intended, fairly anodyne. It described the nature of the work that had been undertaken up to the end of 1981, and while refraining from too positive a position, did give an indication that a bored tunnel option – and officials were careful to distinguish between options and proposals – was favoured. After taking into account the legal, environmental and ecological issues, costs and timescale, the report concluded that if a Fixed Link were to be built quickly, then it could only be in the form of a bored tunnel. As so often before, time was short, and it was pointed out that for a decision to be taken in the life of the current British parliament a bill would have to be presented by November 1982. Other options would require further prolonged investigation and would only delay the start. The interim report was given only a limited circulation, but in any case the final version was expected by the end of February. While a low-key affair, it did highlight some potential stumbling blocks. The French insistence on a completion guarantee and its view that, at least on its side, the venture should be a public sector undertaking, were somewhat at odds with British aspirations since the change of government in 1979.[56]

While the joint study work proceeded, officials from the DTp and Treasury also undertook their own work on the economic appraisal of the Fixed Link. This incorporated familiar elements such as traffic forecasts, regional impact and the corporate effects on British Rail. A major area of concern was that the research was being hampered by the delay in receiving a final contribution from the working party led by the Dover Harbour Board on the potential for developing existing services (the 'no link' option).[57] The port authority had produced further information in December 1981, which challenged the case for a link. Its estimates, shrouded in technicalities as they were, indicated that the ferry companies would achieve considerable efficiency savings, largely through improved utilisation rates and the introduction of a new generation of larger ships, exemplified by Townsend Thoresen's 'Free Enterprise' and British Rail Sealink's 'Saint' vessels.[58] The Harbour Board's claim that the anticipated reduction in unit costs was now even greater than that estimated previously threatened to destroy the case for a Fixed Link.[59] But by no means all experts were convinced by this work. As we have seen, Cairncross had raised doubts about the earlier report, and the Department itself was sceptical about the findings, and in particular about the scope for rationalising the fleet. It went to some lengths to resolve the issue, appointing a specialist adviser to assist in its work.[60]

Officials also continued to deliberate on the financing arrangements for a Fixed Link. Particular attention was directed at the possibilities of a hybrid scheme, in which private sector finance would be used to fund a public sector activity. The idea, which had surfaced in a report from an NEDC working party on

Nationalised Industries' Investment in September 1981, came with fairly stringent requirements, however, and it was not at all clear that the Link would be able to meet these (later dubbed the 'Ryrie rules').[61] As ever, the sticking point remained the fact that guarantees and throughput agreements would offer a degree of investor security against risk. DTp officials were confident that suitable mechanisms *could* be constructed to meet the NEDC's criteria. For example, private equity shareholders might be made liable to financial penalties if a completion guarantee were called: for each £1 of government money provided, the promoting company would lose £1 of equity at par. Nevertheless, at this stage [January 1982] the hybrid concept was still in its infancy, and before it could be pursued properly in relation to the Fixed Link, Ministerial approval would be required.[62] In any case, the Treasury remained sceptical, and by no means everyone wished to see a complicated fix. Andrew Turnbull, head of the Monetary Policy Division, comparing the Link with the gas-gathering pipeline project, advocated a more straightforward approach: 'if the project passes the project appraisal criteria, build it, finance it and operate it as a public sector project. This would be cheaper and avoid an elaborate charade of trying to devise ways in which non-existent market pressures can be stimulated'.[63] Civil servants also debated the European Community aspects. As we have seen, both the Commission and the Parliament had taken a long-standing interest in the project as a key piece of transport infrastructure, and this was reconfirmed in May and September 1981.[64] Some EC involvement was inevitable under the 1978 consultation procedure, but beyond this there were a range of financial aid possibilities: grants, interest subsidies or rebates, loans and guarantees.[65] Officials were unsure about the degree of legitimate support that should be pursued for a project intended to be commercially viable, though it was conceded that some form of Community guarantee might be attractive to promoters. While discussion at the Official Committee on European Questions in February 1982 covered much ground, there was little that could be done until Ministers had delivered their verdict on the project's future.[66]

When Howell returned to the E Committee in early February he gave a brief report on the progress of the joint studies, noting that he hoped to return in the following month with a 'fully developed analysis'. However, before a final decision could be made the Minister required guidance on the vexed question of guarantees. As we have seen, the French had called for, and were prepared to reciprocate, a compensation guarantee from the British such that: 'all their costs would be reimbursed if work on the link was abandoned either as a result of a decision by the British Government or of failure of its chosen instrument'. Given the French insistence on this point Howell concluded that 'if we eventually decide to have a link we shall have to provide reciprocal guarantees'. In any case, the Department felt that by acceding to this demand it would create a useful bargaining counter to persuade the French to drop their 'instinctive wish' for government control of tariffs. Two key arguments flowed from the acceptance of such a guarantee. First, since the Government would assume ultimate responsibility for its chosen instrument, the finance raised would no longer be competing on equal terms with other private sector projects. Howell therefore concluded that 'genuine private risk capital is no longer an option' and hybrid financing arrangements would have to be employed. Second, given the contingent liability of the Government-Government guarantee, 'the prudent approach would be to reinforce the position of the UK promoter by issuing a completion guarantee'. This would take the form envisaged by officials whereby the promoter would lose all or part of his equity share in the Link if the guarantee were called. Howell argued that this would represent only a 'minimum departure from our original intentions'. The degree of risk remaining with the private sector 'was so substantial as to correctly motivate them', while the risk of government involvement would be 'kept to a minimum'.[67]

There was some stiff opposition to this strategy. The CPRS provided a second note which, while accepting the need for a reciprocal compensation guarantee, opposed the idea of a Government completion guarantee, which 'would give the promoter an open-ended right to require additional Government help'. In its view, a better solution would be to 'seek a completion guarantee <u>from</u> the promoter, backed by a charge on the promoter's business and assets'. If the promoter subsequently failed, the Government would be able to appoint a receiver and pursue a number of options in order to complete the project. The CPRS was attracted to this approach because it promised to reduce the Government's exposure to *commercial*, as opposed to political, risk.[68] Treasury officials adopted a similar line. They recommended that the Chancellor suggest to Howell that he look at hybrid financing on the basis of the promoter providing undertakings to the Government about completion.[69] DTp irritation with such opposition was clearly evident. Howell later recalled that 'there was a tremendous, almost Luddite hostility everywhere and the Treasury were terrified of getting involved with the financing'.[70] This may have been something of an exaggeration, but it is certainly true that the Department regarded a promoter completion guarantee as 'unrealistic' and the idea of putting in a receiver as 'nonsense'.[71]

The Treasury and CPRS were not the only ones wary of guarantees. The Department of Trade's Shipping Policy Division expressed the view that whoever gave the completion undertaking, it did little to remove the possibility that the Government would be left 'holding the baby'.[72] John Biffen, the Trade Secretary, informed Howell of his Department's opposition to reciprocal guarantees on 8 February, the day before the E Committee meeting. Repeating some of the arguments used during the early 1960s (see Chapter 2, pp. 30, 40), he warned that to go against the 'repeated pledges' that the Fixed Link would be a private sector project would be a breach of faith with the shipping industry, while there was also the spectre of an open-ended commitment 'of the kind which proved so expensive for Concorde'.[73] However, the most formidable and influential criticisms of Howell's intentions came from Alan Walters, the Prime Minister's personal economic adviser. In a note to Thatcher, Walters, a leading right-wing economist, expressed doubts about any form of guarantee. On the question of reciprocal guarantees, he argued that it was difficult to determine whether an action was political or commercial. There might be sound commercial reasons why the

British Government would wish to withdraw unilaterally, but such an action would be difficult to disengage from what the French would inevitably regard as a 'political' cancellation. He was also unconvinced that such a guarantee could really be used to persuade the French to drop their demands for tariff control. On the completion guarantee, Walters was also sceptical, pointing out that such a device had been rejected in connexion with the gas-gathering pipeline and that both EuroRoute and Eurobridge did not appear to be asking for one. He suggested that the concept 'seems to be the brain-child of the rail tunnel promoters'.[74] Nor was Walters enamoured with the CPRS's suggestion of a promoter guarantee, suspecting that it would cost something. Invoking another contemporary economic guru, Milton Friedman, he informed the Prime Minister that 'just as there is no free lunch, so there is no free guarantee'.[75] Walters had an almost pathological dislike of railways, and his influence had already been evident in the opposition to British Rail's electrification programme and the insistence that railway costs be put under the microscope. It was not therefore surprising that he opposed a rail-only tunnel, which he regarded as 'an act of faith in the resuscitation of rail', a project with monopoly implications which would also reinforce the unionised railways against the non-unionised road sector.[76]

At the E Committee itself on 9 February the Transport Secretary repeated his proposals for reciprocal and completion guarantees. But the meeting did not go well for Howell, since the Committee aligned itself according to what later became known as classic Thatcherite economic principles, with the majority of opinion opposed to the offering of any guarantees. In discussion it was agreed that such arrangements would entail an open-ended commitment to supplement funding, while being inconsistent with the Government's declared objective to leave both the costs and the risks with the private sector. It was also argued that if the Fixed Link were a viable commercial proposition then private sector promoters should be able to find the money without recourse to Government. The Prime Minister, drawing on Walters's advice, emphasised that although she was in favour of a Link, the French insistence on a reciprocal guarantee was something of a negotiating ploy and in the light of the experience with Concorde must not be accepted 'under any circumstances'.[77] The Committee therefore formally minuted that the Government 'should not undertake to enter into reciprocal compensation guarantees with the French Government' and 'should not offer completion guarantees to prospective United Kingdom promoters of the link'.[78]

The setback caused by the rejection of guarantees presented serious difficulties for Howell and his Department. The most immediate issue was to agree what the Minister might say to both the Transport Select Committee and French officials, whom he was due to meet in quick succession on 17 and 18 February. The project was clearly at a delicate stage. The view of DTp officials was that either the British should withdraw 'quickly and honestly' or proceed with the project on the basis of a completion guarantee, which would substantially modify the Cabinet's stance on financing.[79] A week after the E Committee meeting, Howell discussed tactics with the Foreign Secretary, Lord Carrington. Despite the seemingly unequivocal decision reached by the Committee there was some dispute as to what had actually been agreed. Howell felt that he had to tell the French quickly that there was no question of a reciprocal compensation guarantee, but he wanted to explore further with them the option of a political guarantee. However, Carrington, armed with a brief from the Lord Privy Seal, Humphrey Atkins, doubted whether the Committee's decision allowed for the possibility of a guarantee against cancellation for political reasons, though he conceded that there was 'some ambiguity' about guarantees to the British promoter. Howell chose to believe that the matter remained open.[80] Whatever the position, it was decided that something would have to be said to the French sufficient to 'keep them in play' and allow completion of the joint studies. A convenient neutral position was contained in a published letter to the Transport Committee from Fowler in November 1980, in which the Minister stated that he would be prepared to 'consider' a political guarantee. But this certainly did not mean, as Thatcher emphasised, that the Government was ready to give such a guarantee, an equivocal stance which the Treasury at least interpreted as 'sogginess at the edges'.[81] Howell's appearance before the Transport Committee on 17 February was his first. Essentially he presented a straight bat and gave little away. His memorandum was not intended to be a response to the Committee's report of March 1981, as originally envisaged. Instead, as we have seen, it summarised the joint study group's interim report, providing a resumé of developments, and revealed details about the work of the group, stating that the next steps were dependent upon the outcome of the group's final report.[82] A more critical meeting took place on the following day when Howell met Braibant to inform him about the stalled position on guarantees. Braibant repeated the French Government's view that there should be both political and completion guarantees, and Howell, while referring to his Government's 'special difficulties' in being asked to provide a guarantee to a private promoter, promised to undertake further work. The issue was therefore left unresolved.[83]

The rejection of guarantees was also awkward for the British officials who had to attend a meeting of the Anglo-French Directing Group held on the same day as Howell's meeting with Braibant. Lyall urged his colleagues to 'do everything necessary to convey the impression of "business as usual" '. Work was concentrated on sections of the final report, although this was mainly a 'tactical exercise', intended to deflect attention away from the guarantees issue.[84] After the meeting, Howell was briefed on the state of play. Lyall reported that French Ministers had already come down in favour of making an early start on a seven-metre tunnel, a decision which Braibant contended was 'to a large extent political'. Here the motivation was apparently to introduce a positive element into Anglo-French relations at a time when 'major rows' were expected over European Community issues. Lyall also reported that the French were disappointed by what Howell had said on guarantees, though they remained determined to find a mutually acceptable solution.[85] It had been agreed at the Directing Group that the British side would prepare the first complete draft of the Joint Report and Lyall outlined the likely contents to his Minister. While the interim report had suggested that a decision on the Fixed Link might be deferred pending further study of the non-bored tunnel options, Lyall and Braibant argued that given the technical risks and potential for monopoly 'we must advise Ministers that such schemes should be firmly ruled out'. The full economic assessment had not yet been completed, but Lyall expected to be able to make a case for a bored tunnel, and the recommendation was likely to be for a phased approach to a twin seven-metre tunnel with vehicle shuttle service. The Secretary of State was therefore asked if he was content to see a report that (1) 'for very fully argued reasons "kills" the non-tunnel schemes' and (2) recommended the adoption of a phased twin seven-metre tunnel.[86] Although Howell concurred with the latter, he was more hesitant about killing off the other schemes, preferring instead that they be put into 'deep freeze'.[87]

What of British Rail? By the beginning of 1982 the Channel Tunnel was scarcely a high priority for the Board. It had just taken the first steps in its most significant organisational change since nationalisation: the creation of business sectors under the banner of 'sector management'. But this was not all. Railway managers were locked in an acrimonious dialogue with both the Government and the trade unions. The arguments centred on the Board's deteriorating financial position during the recession, its demands for higher levels of investment (particularly for electrification), and the Government's insistence that more vigour be put into the reduction of costs and the reform of restrictive practices. The impasse had been such that Howell had accepted the need for a comprehensive policy review, which culminated in the Serpell Report of January 1983. At the same time, the Board was in the midst of a prolonged and highly damaging industrial relations dispute with ASLEF as it tried to extract the promised productivity gains from the workforce.[88] But even if the political environment facing Parker and his colleagues had been kinder, and there had been an opportunity to promote its tunnel more vigorously, it would have made little difference. As we have seen, the debate about the Fixed Link was now moving decisively against the Board's own ambitions. French opposition made acceptance of the British Rail/SNCF six-metre, rail-only design highly improbable, and it was now necessary to ensure that British Rail co-operated with the promoters of seven-metre rail/road shuttle tunnels on an 'arm's length' basis. The DTp therefore took the first steps to remove the railways from the promoting arena. As Lyall put it, the intention was to 'invite them…to break their connection with ECTG and to get out of the promotional game'.[89] The Department's position was conveyed to the Chief Executive, Bob Reid [I], in rather oblique fashion, at the end of January. Thus, three years after British Rail had first submitted its proposal to build a six-metre tunnel, it was now being asked to confine its role to that of co-operating over the rail aspects of a seven-metre scheme.[90]

Acquiescence was not immediate, however, and the Channel Tunnel Unit continued to experience frustration with British Rail's antipathy towards the seven-metre design, a subject on which there was felt to be 'no possibility of our having… a really objective discussion'.[91] And yet, with the assistance of informal contacts between Barron and Lyall, the Board was edged towards a basis for acceptance, since the DTp judged its co-operation to be essential if the project's timetable were to be met. Barron was given a confidential indication of the Study Group's likely recommendation in the form of an 'hypothesis': a single seven-metre tunnel would be built for classic rail traffic, with the possibility of (1) incorporating a road shuttle, and/or (2) constructing a second tunnel (with road shuttle), at a later stage.[92] In March Barron briefed the Board on the two Governments' emerging policy. The original intention to promote the six-metre tunnel would have to be abandoned due to the 'attitude of Government and the wider definition of the project'. It was thus necessary to take a fresh stance, designed to protect British Rail's interests, and put this formally to Government.[93] This meeting was Barron's last before retirement. In his five-year stint he had made a vital contribution to both the Tunnel's initial revival and its subsequent development. He was replaced as Director, Channel Tunnel by Peter Keen, former Chief Passenger Manager and a casualty of the Board's sector management revolution. Keen was no newcomer to this arena, having been associated with the development of the ill-fated rail link in the mid-1970s (above, pp. 156–7). However, it may have been indicative of British Rail's relative 'disengagement' with the Tunnel that the brief should be combined with that of International Marketing, with both jobs suggesting (for Keen at least) a degree of demotion.[94] Shortly after the Board meeting Parker informed Howell of the revised position. Taking the strong hints from Lyall and the Department, Parker admitted that it was no longer considered realistic for the Board to be a promoter. Nevertheless, he was determined to 'negotiate organisational and financial terms with the promoter which fairly reflect the very substantial contribution which the Board will be making to the enterprise'. He then listed six conditions or principles that were, in effect, demands for the Board's co-operation. These related primarily to the railways' technical and operating requirements, but included demands for an equity stake in the owning body and 'full public recognition to be given to BR's part in initiating and developing the Governments' preferred solution'.[95] Howell welcomed British Rail's willingness to co-operate and thought the approach 'constructive'.[96] But the fact remained that from this point in the story British Rail was effectively removed from high level policy formulation, and its role became more reactive than proactive.

The Department had also begun to reassess its attitude towards the other promoters, and in particular those advocating a bored tunnel. Barron had clearly sensed some shift in policy when he complained to Lyall that the Government appeared to be making the selection of the type of link and the choice of promoter into 'quite separate processes'. Barron found this notion 'baffling', but it was nonetheless the direction in which Departmental thinking was heading.[97] In fact, policy was moving away from the original concept of picking a winner from among the competing promoters and their proposals. In some ways this was the inevitable outcome of the Anglo-French joint study, with its emphasis on options rather than schemes, and the preference of officials for a tunnel. But it was also the product of discussions with the more opportunistic promoters, such as Cross Channel Contractors, now called the Anglo Channel Tunnel Group [ACTG], whose main objective was to secure the lucrative role of project manager rather than act as contractors.[98] Since the British Government were beginning to accept that they were essentially acting as proxy for the eventual owner/operator, it was recognised that 'in selecting a tunnel promoter, what we are in reality doing is selecting a project manager'. As Lyall put it, 'The idea that in selecting a particular promoter we are selecting the particular scheme he is identified with is illusory…The fact is that the two Governments will decide what they want and I do not think that decision, whatever it is, will limit our choice of "promoters" '.[99] The promoter-project manager issue was evidently complex, and the possibility of the Government acting as promoter by inviting bids for the government-owned British Channel Tunnel Co (BCTC) was also raised. After some debate, a Project Management Panel was established to assess the project management capability of the three bored tunnel promoters, ECTG, CTD and ACTG. Chaired by the Department's Chief Highway Engineer, Kanagaretnam Sriskandan, it was quickly overtaken by events. Nevertheless, its work epitomised the determination of DTp officials to assist the Secretary of State in finding the most appropriate vehicle to progress the bored tunnel option.[100]

3. The Anglo-French report, March–April 1982

In March 1982 British and French officials firmed up the Joint Study Group's report. They continued to wrestle with the stumbling block of guarantees, but the portents were not encouraging. Lyall and Braibant agreed that it would be difficult to reconcile perceived differences while these were discussed in a vacuum. Decisions on the type of link, its timescale, the choice of government instruments, and the inter-relationships between the British and French promoters would all have a bearing on the matter. One solution was to move forward with the submission of the Joint Report, leaving the guarantee question open. Of course, such a ploy had been used before, during the tortuous negotiations over financing in the early 1970s.[101] In addition, the selection of the British promoter had still to be resolved, and here there were two possibilities. The first was to make one of the competing consortia the Government's 'chosen instrument'. The second was to seek financial backers to take control of a promoting company, which would have overall responsibility for construction and operation of the Link, with the consortia treated as would-be project managers. The first was considered unsatisfactory because the companies' short-term interests as either project managers or contractors might prove incompatible with the long-term objectives of the promoter as owner and operator. With the second, there might be complaints that the Government was going back on Fowler's original invitation for complete packages, but the process would still leave the consortia free to act in their preferred role of project managers. The establishment of a Project Management Panel had already indicated that officials were moving towards the second option, which, significantly, had a further advantage. As Tony Rosenfeld, head of Licensing, Safety and International Policy at the DTp, observed, neither country had a promoter and there was thus an opportunity to create 'a single bi-national "owner" for the tunnel'. If this could be achieved, 'it would ease the problem of re-assuring the French about possible financial failure of the promoter'. Although Rosenfeld told Howell that he considered this 'a reserve possibility rather than one on which we ought to stake our chances of success',[102] the Minister was quick to express an interest, and asked officials to explore with the French the idea of a 'supra-national' construction/owning/operating authority.[103] One thing was agreed, however. On the method of financing, the French performed a U-turn. Ever since the Anglo-French summit of September 1981 they had argued that their portion of the capital investment would come from the public sector. Now they were saying that the French promoters would have to seek capital from the market, as the British were proposing on their side.[104] This change of stance came as something of a surprise to British officials. Lyall declared himself astonished when told by Braibant that the French were determined that the project should be financed on a normal commercial basis and without guarantees, other than political, from the two governments. The prospects were finely balanced. Lyall minuted: 'I cannot advise the Secretary of State on the prospects of a successful outcome. All I can say is that I am convinced of M. Braibant's determination . . . to explore all possibilities of finding a way through the problem'.[105]

Howell and Carrington held a further meeting on 10 March. Their talks were wide-ranging. For the Foreign Secretary the essential point was that, having encouraged the French, Britain should not now 'drag its feet'. At the summit Thatcher had given an 'enormous green light' to the idea of a Fixed Link and Mitterand now saw it as 'a touch stone of Anglo-French relations'. The discussion then moved on to embrace the nature of the Link – Carrington's personal preference was for one he could motor through – the strength of the Dover Harbour Board's case against, and the challenge of financing. Howell reported that he had sought to break the deadlock over promoter guarantees by proposing the 'radically new idea' of a bi-national company, 'which could not possibly be in default against itself'. Since this would take several weeks to explore, the report of the Joint Study Group could not yet be finalised. Carrington gave his support to the approach. Consonant with Conservative thinking on wider share ownership, he expressed the hope that the company be floated in such a way as to attract a large number of small investors. Howell ended the meeting by expressing two serious concerns. First, the Treasury might express opposition to such a 'jumbo' project, despite its private sector status; second, the Link might founder due to 'lack of warmth' from Cabinet colleagues. Carrington shared these concerns, and not for the first time in the Tunnel's lengthening history there was anxiety about a display of British coolness just at the moment when the French were displaying enthusiasm.[106]

The Ministers, in reporting to Thatcher, agreed that Carrington would emphasise the wider sensitivities of Anglo-French relations. These included the EC budget mandate, the Common Agricultural Policy, and other collaborative projects such as Concorde and the Airbus. In this broader context, Carrington warned the Prime Minister that nothing should bring the Fixed Link project to a 'grinding halt'. He added that even if ultimately a solution could not be found, 'I do strongly feel that we need to proceed very carefully if we are to avoid wrong-footing ourselves tactically and running the risk of undermin[in]g our other interests with the French'.[107] Howell focussed his briefing on finance, and in particular on his hopes for the bi-national company, but this meant that there would be an unavoidable delay in completing the Joint Report.[108] The delay played havoc with the DTp's decision-making timetable and the uncertainty about chosen instruments challenged a legislative programme that was already extremely tight.[109] On top of this there was the need to draft and circulate a White Paper which was to be published simultaneously with the announcement. At the beginning of March, officials were suggesting that a paper would go to E Committee on the 24th, and drafts of a memorandum and statement were prepared. But the delays put the E Committee timing back to late April and then into the first week in May.[110] It was now expected that the Government announcement about the Link would be made on 17 May, the date on which the British and French Prime Ministers were due to meet in London.[111]

With Howell's encouragement, British officials attempted to make something of the bi-national company. The original intention had been to establish separate British and French companies that would each undertake construction of half of the Link. But instead a single private company might be established by Treaty as the 'chosen instrument' of the two governments, with British and French institutions each holding 50 per cent of the shares. This body would appoint a single project manager and raise the necessary funds without government guarantee. It would therefore bear the risks of any construction problems, cost overruns or traffic shortfalls, and might be structured in such a way as to ensure that even if a crisis occurred most if not all of the works would be completed.[112] The concept had the distinct advantage of eliminating the French demand for protection against failure by a British company. There were also other benefits. The company would have a single project manager, an approach championed by RTZ at the time of the 1975 abandonment. It would be a major force in capital markets, would help remove the inherent antagonisms of dual structures, and provide the two governments with a single body with which to negotiate. Of course, the concept had its drawbacks, not least the immense legal challenge of creating 'this child of Marianne and John Bull'. But although there appeared to be no obvious precedent for such a body, the consensus of legal opinion in the DTp, Foreign Office and Lord Chancellor's Department was that it was feasible in law.[113] The idea now had to be sold in Paris, where there was interest and scepticism in equal measure. The British worked hard to make an effective case, and by the end of a meeting on 23 March Lyall thought Braibant 'more than half persuaded'.[114] Informal talks were also conducted with financial institutions which were invited to declare an interest in financing the company. The Midland Bank displayed 'considerable if qualified enthusiasm', and began to examine the proposal in conjunction with Crédit Lyonnais. The National

Westminster [NatWest] Bank was also reported to 'strongly favour' the idea. However, at this stage such contacts were little more than soundings out of the financial market. Moreover, for those who cared to look, there was evidence of banking caution and risk aversion of the kind that had dogged the project in the past.[115]

These discussions were overshadowed by international events. On 2 April Argentina invaded the Falkland Islands and three days later the British task-force set sail for the South Atlantic. The War also produced a major political casualty with the early resignation of Carrington.[116] On the day of the invasion Lyall was in Paris having further talks with Braibant on the bi-national company. After the meeting he found it difficult to give Howell a precise account of where matters stood. The French were by no means convinced that the bi-national device would be effective. In particular, they argued that unresolvable disputes might arise within the company that would have the same practical effect as a failure to perform by one of two companies. Lyall expressed matters thus: 'The French . . . have an obsessive fear of another British betrayal. Their intellect tells them that the bi-national idea is a good one from a practical and political point of view. But it is a British suggestion . . . They are therefore naturally suspicious'.[117] In this context an unexpected benefit was the rediscovery, by an assiduous Foreign Office official, of the 1965 Rigaud Report (see Chapter 3, p. 52) which had proposed just such a device. This find offered the tactical advantage that the idea could now be presented as something that had French origins, though the initiative does not appear to have tipped the balance.[118] Both Lyall and Braibant agreed that the bi-national approach was the most promising way of reconciling the differences between them, but they admitted that 'neither of us could think of anything better'. In an attempt to resolve the complexities, Lyall undertook to crystallise the outstanding issues in a position statement. Extending to 7 pages and 34 sections, it resembled some of the longer memoranda produced in the 1970s by an earlier generation of officials, such as Kemp and Melville. However, as Lyall acknowledged, 'one cannot boil down complex issues into a few sentences, particularly where the French are concerned'.[119]

The final report of the Anglo/French Joint Study Group [for convenience 'AF82'] was agreed in early April 1982 and then circulated among Whitehall departments. Running to more than 100 pages, including 11 appendices, the document was a further weighty contribution to the debate on a Channel Link. Like its predecessors in 1963, 1966, 1973, 1975 and 1981, it rehearsed all the familiar issues: the development of cross-channel traffic; types of link; existing transport modes; traffic forecasts; economic evaluation; and wider effects. Officials also received a separate note on the proposed bi-national company, a subject that was not discussed in the report itself.[120] On the traffic prospects, the Group pointed out that sea crossings had doubled in the 1970s, with Cairncross's 1975 projections for 1980 being comfortably exceeded. It was thought that some slowdown would occur, but since the increase in air traffic had been modest over the previous decade the surface passenger market was still forecast to grow by about 150 per cent, from 18 million in 1980 to 45 million by 2000. Freight traffic was also expected to increase by a similar amount, from 16 to 37 million tonnes (Table 8.2). The case for continuing to rely on existing shipping services was then evaluated with the help of the final report from the Dover Harbour Board. Although the Group conceded that significant improvements in ferry operating efficiency were likely, they did not accept the claim that ferry operators could carry the increased traffic at such a reduced cost as to destroy the case for a Fixed Link.[121] The arguments, raising concerns about the pace of technical change, the scope for reducing peaks of demand, and the ability to eliminate excess capacity, were set out in the Report with great care, and the language was measured. However, as we have already suggested, behind the text the DTp nursed a more hostile and less diplomatic attitude to the Harbour Board's case, which with the help of an independent consultant, Professor Richard Goss, was attacked as 'tendentious' and 'selective'. More cautious views were provided by the Department of Trade and the Treasury, but all were agreed that the Board had exaggerated shipping capabilities in a document that was in several places 'obscure' and 'impenetrable'.[122] The report's account of types of link and associated technical aspects contained little that was new, since the potential difficulties surrounding alternatives to a bored tunnel were by this time well-known. More important was the economic evaluation, which rested on the traffic estimates and the expected diversion from sea and air transport. Three calculations were offered: most favourable [Scenario A], central [B], and least favourable [C]. The report's central case [B], using UK time values, yielded internal rates of return in the range 4.0–8.4 per cent. Of the tunnels a double seven-metre rail tunnel with vehicle shuttle was found to give the best return (7.3 per cent). The highest return was given for the road bridge project – 8.4 per cent – though here there was more uncertainty (Table 8.3). Both the favoured tunnel and the bridge promised a return which just exceeded the target rate customarily used when evaluating public sector transport projects, though they were much lower than the 17 per cent return estimated for the earlier scheme in the 1973 White Paper (Chapter 5, p. 113).[123]

AF82 offered Ministers three options: (1) to rely on existing services; (2) to defer a decision until further studies were made of links 'other than bored tunnels'; and (3) to decide in principle that a bored tunnel was desirable. Option (1) was essentially ruled out. On option (2) officials hedged. There was much reference to uncertainties in the calculations and to margins of error. There was little doubt that a drive-through link would be attractive to users, and the Group was unable to advise Ministers that such schemes should be 'ruled out'. On the other hand, option (2) would involve 'prolonged study, at substantial cost', causing damaging uncertainty. It was for Ministers to 'weigh these considerations'. Turning to bored tunnels, the six-metre rail-only variant was given its final coup de grâce, and the report, as expected, came down in favour of a twin-bore seven-metre tunnel plus vehicle shuttle, with the construction to be phased. Ministers were advised that if they favoured a Fixed Link, the only decision that could be made immediately was one of principle subject to the 'ability of the designated instruments to raise market finance on terms acceptable to both Governments.'[124]

Table 8.2 Cross-channel traffic forecasts, 1980–2000 (April 1982)

	1971 Actual	*1980 Forecast (1975)*[a]	*1980 Actual*	*1990 Forecast*	*2000 Forecast*
('000 crossings)					
Surface					
Passengers with cars	4,088	7,480	6,100	10,200	14,100
Coach passengers	—	—	3,100	7,700	11,400
Classic passengers	4,812	7,000	9,000	14,900	19,400
Total	8,900	14,480	18,200	32,800	44,900
Air					
London-Paris/Brussels	—	—	2,400	2,900	3,500
Freight, unitised ('000 tons/tonnes[c])	5,700[b]	15,100	17,730/ 15,900[d]	27,300	37,200

Source: Table 7.1, Cairncross Report, 1975, Table 2.10a, and Report of Anglo/French Study Group, April 1982, Tables 2.1, 2.2, 7.1, 7.2, J.1, J.3, DTp file IT40/6/5 Pt.3 [rounded figures appear in the published report, DTp, *Report of UK/French Study Group*, June 1982].

Notes

a Cairncross Report, phase II provisional estimate.
b 1970 figure.
c Tons in 1975 estimate, metric tonnes thereafter.
d Two freight estimates given in the Report, the higher figure including bulk shipping.

Table 8.3 Channel Fixed Link: estimated rates of return and resource costs (in NPVs) with UK time values, April 1982

	Bored tunnels				*Road bridge*	*Road bridge/ rail tunnel*	*Composite scheme*
	Single 6 m	*Single 7 m*	*Single 7 m +shuttle*	*Double 7 m +shuttle*			
Central case Scenario B							
Rate of Return [%]	5.3[a]	4.9[a]	4.0	7.3	8.4	7.1	5.3
Resource Costs [£m.][b]	−201	−282	−474	+87	+341	+42	−820
Lower bound Scenario C							
Rate of Return [%]	1.3[a]	1.2[a]	1.0	2.4	0.3	0.0	0.0
Resource Costs [£m.]	−664	−757	−1,035	−1,057	−1,573	−2,237	−4,122
Upper bound Scenario A							
Rate of Return [%]	9.1	8.5	6.1	12.3	13.9	12.0	10.2
Resource Costs [£m.]	289	221	148	1,456	1,828	1,845	1,561

Source: Report of Anglo/French Study Group, Table 8.1, K10–11.

Notes

For time values, the British and French Transport Ministries assigned different estimates for types of traveller. The French values are higher in all instances, adding 1–1.5% to the rate of return and £84–617 m. to NPVs. See report, paras.K.42–3.

a Figures amended in published report: Scenario B: 5.4%, 5.0%; lower bound: 1.6%, 1.2%. DTp, *Report of UK/French Study Group*, June 1982, Table 8.1.

b Resource Cost Comparison with development of existing services, NPV discounted at 7% in January 1981 prices.

As with earlier reports, AF82 adopted a cautious tone. The road schemes were not 'killed off', as officials had wanted, but neither were they quite chilled enough to put into 'deep freeze', as Howell had requested. And given the rather equivocal nature of the economic analysis, the case for the preferred bored tunnel was far from impregnable. Consequently, in spite of another raft of information, the decision was once again to rest upon political rather than economic or technical considerations.

4. Grinding to a halt: April–May 1982

With the completion of AF82, DTp officials turned to the final preparations for Howell's appearance at E Committee in May. Unfortunately, the environment within which this occurred was difficult. At the international level, the French continued to display a reserved attitude to the notion of a bi-national company. In Britain, there were ill-timed press stories about the findings of the Dover Harbour Board and Cairncross reports. We have seen that officials had tried to lessen the impact of 'Cairncross 2' by having the Transport Select Committee publish it. The strategy backfired. While AF82 was being circulated, newspapers carried headlines such as 'Channel tunnel "doomed by efficient ferries"' and 'Report kills Channel hopes', while Cairncross's opinion that there was 'no overwhelming case for a fixed link' was unanimously quoted.[125] Whether influenced by the press or no, the Chancellor, Sir Geoffrey Howe, read 'Cairncross 2' for the first time and reportedly felt that the arguments were 'fairly conclusive against a fixed link'.[126] Howe's was not the only voice against. Awkward questions were asked at a large inter-departmental meeting on 21 April, chaired by Rosenfeld and attended by officials from, among others, the Treasury, FCO, Trade, Industry and the CPRS. Here too Cairncross's views were cited as throwing doubt on the Link, but the DTp countered this by claiming that he 'had in fact opted in favour of a twin rail tunnel... and was thus close to the Governments' position, save that he wanted public sector finance'.[127] In the defensive brief for E Committee, Howell's officials told him that 'Cairncross 2' was on balance helpful and that the newspapers had been selective in their criticisms.[128]

Another challenge emanated from EuroRoute's persistent and effective campaigning. The promoters lobbied the Government strongly and on a scale greater than any rival. Between February and April 1982 MacGregor, 'using all the force of his intimate position in Thatcherite circles', secured meetings with a number of Ministers, including Howell, Brittan, Biffen, Norman Tebbit (Employment), Michael Heseltine (Environment) and Nicholas Edwards (Wales).[129] This lobbying, which included claims that the scheme could be started as quickly as a bored tunnel, clearly generated some favourable impressions, causing Howell and his officials to seek to temper the enthusiasm.[130] In a 'round robin' letter to members of E Committee on 27 April, Howell referred to two 'extremely formidable' objections to EuroRoute: first, by 'knocking out the ferries' it would establish an 'effective monopoly'; second, the French would not accept it. For these reasons he felt there was no realistic prospect of such a link in the foreseeable future.[131] The arguments failed to convince some. Northern Ireland Secretary Jim Prior, unable to attend E Committee, made his views known in a note to Thatcher. He was emphatic that a link was required, but expressed serious doubts about relying on rail transport and thus favoured the EuroRoute scheme, readily admitting that he had been influenced by MacGregor, whom he saw as 'a man of vision and imagination'.[132] The British Steel Chairman continued to press the case in government circles and was quick to seek an appointment with the new Trade Secretary, Lord Cockfield. Although MacGregor did not know it, this meeting was arranged for 4 May, the day on which E Committee was due to consider the Fixed Link.[133]

Howell's further memorandum to E Committee, dated 27 April, provided a summary of AF82, and with five annexes gave, as promised, a more complete assessment of the Fixed Link. Much of the analysis was already familiar, and the paper concentrated on highlighting the Department's support for a twin-bore rail tunnel, which offered the 'best return of any tunnel scheme'. In doing so 'drive-through' alternatives were condemned by referring to monopoly power and French antipathy. In presenting the economic case, Howell skated over the Dover Harbour Board and Cairncross reports, resorting to a selective use of the latter in noting that his adviser had felt that 'the choice lay between a single or a double 7 metre tunnel'. A fully integrated bi-national company was offered as a solution to the 'guarantee problem', although political guarantees, as yet undefined, would still be required. In conclusion Howell recommended that 'we decide in principle in favour of twin rail tunnels, and let the market decide whether it can attract finance on acceptable terms'. He asked his colleagues to allow him to offer financial institutions the prospect of a guarantee against political cancellation.[134] The Committee also received a note from the CPRS. While endorsing the twin tunnel as the 'best choice', the CPRS raised two potential hares. First, it suggested that the private sector would show little interest unless tariffs were unregulated. Second, the creation of a bi-national company would not prevent the Government from becoming directly involved in the event of a private sector failure. It would then be difficult to resist pressure to complete and run the Tunnel as a public sector enterprise.[135]

Howell's approach had already been subjected to tough scrutiny within the Treasury, where all the predictable arguments were marshalled together by Richard Broadbent, in what amounted to a thorough demolition job. The tune may have been familiar, at least to those with long memories, but it was played fortissimo. On economic and financial grounds the Treasury was inclined to recommend 'against a decision in favour of a fixed link'. Cairncross was adduced as evidence that the Link was 'at best marginal'. AF82, though drawing 'more hopeful conclusions from slightly worse figures', had to be seen as a 'negotiated document'. And even with private financing, the sheer size of the project was such that it could not be ignored by macroeconomists. The Government would have to be satisfied that the scheme did not 'conflict with the national economic interest'. With the legislative and treaty requirements, the necessary involvement of British Rail and the potential for 'lock-in' offered by the bi-national company, it was 'unthinkable' for the Government 'not to pay serious regard to the economics of the project', which were clearly unattractive. The bi-national company was condemned as 'squaring the circle'. It would merely be a 'device to implement a decision reached by the Government (rather than the market)', and the scope for genuine initiative by private investors would be 'virtually nil'. If political considerations dictated that it was necessary to proceed, the Treasury urged caution; further consideration should be given to resolving the financing problems *before* enacting legislation.[136] Ryrie commended Broadbent's 'comprehensive' document to the Chancellor, and for good measure emphasised some of the criticisms. However, he also confessed that it had been his view all along that the Link was not the kind of project that could be 'genuinely financed as a private sector affair'. There was a case, 'although not a very strong one', for proceeding in the public sector, using a special form of borrowing such as 'Channel Tunnel bonds'. But even in these circumstances the prospects were remote because the anticipated return on the investment was so poor. This diversion aside, it was clear to Ryrie that Howell's proposals would 'not come near to meeting the criteria we have had in mind for involving private finance'.[137]

Before E Committee met, there was a further inter-departmental discussion on financing. Here the Treasury found an ally in the Department of Trade, whose lawyers described the bi-national company as 'novel, obscure and probably unworkable'. A more promising alternative was the organisational form adopted by multinational corporations, notably the joint company board structure of the Anglo-Dutch giant, Unilever.[138] However, these talks did nothing to dissuade the Treasury from its view that the financing arrangements were fraught with difficulties and would take a considerable time to resolve, with little prospect of success.[139]

Two special advisers also made interventions. At the Treasury, Adam Ridley, Howe's adviser, felt that discussion of the project was becoming 'rather surreal'. A road bridge was being ruled out in spite of a return which indicated that it was 'clearly the best thing to go for'. Ridley found it hard to view a rail tunnel with enthusiasm, since he could see little future for the railways as a major mode of transport. The danger of entering into irreversible commitments led him to conjure up a new take on an old theme, when he complained that the venture could 'quickly turn into a sort of aquatic Concorde'. Thus he saw a road bridge as the better choice, and went so far as to suggest that the additional research and trials should be financed from the public purse. 'After all', he argued, £30 million was a 'tiny sum when set alongside the negative NPV involved in proceeding with a doubtful rail project'.[140] A more significant contribution came in the shape of a further polemic from Alan Walters, who advised Thatcher that the DTp's case contained 'a number of flaws, many serious, some fatal'. He declared himself 'impressed' by the Dover Harbour Board case, and having been misled by Howell's rather thin presentation of the subject, criticised the Department's failure to evaluate the 'no link' option properly. He also expressed disappointment that the issue of government guarantee was still unresolved. He felt that the scope of the political guarantee needed to be defined and agreed before the Fixed Link could 'gather any more steam'. Walters, like Ridley, observed that the economic analysis showed the road bridge, and not the rail tunnel, to have the greater return. In fact, using net present values, the preferred method of comparison when examining mutually exclusive projects, the road bridge was 'far superior'. In his paper Howell had justified his choice by arguing that a bridge would remove the ferries and achieve a 'near monopoly', while a rail tunnel would leave the ferries with a 'healthy market share'. Walters was rightly incredulous about a suggestion that maintained 'that we should not build the road bridge because it is too efficient an option and will eliminate competition!' He also joined Ridley in opposing the rail tunnel because it would pre-empt contemporary decision-making about the future of British Rail. By this time railway industrial relations had deteriorated further, and hawks were suggesting that there would inevitably be a substantial contraction in the network – a 'son of Beeching'. He therefore advised the Prime Minister to reject the rail tunnel and inform the French that the Government's interest lay in a road bridge.[141]

The customary counterpoint of Foreign Office enthusiasm was missing on this occasion. Lord Bridges, a Deputy Under-Secretary, revealed that he was personally in favour, but, as he told the new British Ambassador in Paris, Sir John Fretwell, 'the project does not have many friends in Whitehall', and officials had already detected a 'cool undercurrent' from the leading departments. There was further disappointment with the realisation that the incoming Foreign Secretary, Francis Pym, was not a supporter.[142] The main argument for going ahead – that Anglo-French relations would be jeopardised if we did not – was certainly present. As in earlier exchanges diplomats were able to produce a sizeable list of 'sensitive areas': Airbus, Concorde, the fast breeder reactor, naval ground-to-air missile, European wind tunnel, and the Guandong Nuclear Power Station. The French were reported to be keen to secure agreement on at least one of these bilateral projects while broader relations were 'going through a rough patch'.[143] Nevertheless, Foreign Office officials were on this occasion unable to recommend that the Foreign Secretary endorse Howell's position. The Fixed Link was regarded as being of largely symbolic significance, and consequently a defensive brief was prepared which focussed on limiting the damage to Anglo-French relations in the event of a 'No'.[144]

It was scarcely a surprise when Howell encountered strong opposition at E Committee on 4 May. He said that the choice lay between a twin-tunnel or reliance on ferries, maintaining that he favoured the former. But Ministers argued that the economic case for a Fixed Link was weak; the Government would have to step in if the constructors ran into difficulties; the concept of the bi-national company required further work; and a rail-only link would extend the monopoly powers of British Rail and its trade unions. This was damaging enough for the Minister. What was more disconcerting was the fact that Committee sentiment moved positively in favour of MacGregor's EuroRoute, described as the only scheme 'which stood any chance of capturing the public imagination'. In her summing up Thatcher said that 'the Committee were agreed that no further work should be done on a rail-only link. The only type of project which might merit further study was one allowing the possibility of road transport, such as the

Euroroute proposal'. It was essential to 'avoid misleading the French Government... [and] a decision to withdraw would need careful handling'. The best tactic might be to indicate the British Government's preference for a road link, and if the French found this unpalatable, they might accept at least part of the responsibility for terminating the discussions.[145] This was obviously a major blow to the Channel Tunnel ambitions of Howell and his officials. Not only had work on a rail tunnel been stopped, but the road alternatives were very much in play. Howell might have had cause to regret the fact that he had not killed off the bridge options when given the opportunity.

It is often maintained in the secondary literature and among tunnelists that the Tunnel was dropped because consideration at Cabinet level was interrupted by the news of the attack on *HMS Sheffield* during the Falklands campaign. A subdued Cabinet, so the argument runs, was in no mood to make a favourable decision.[146] We find no evidence to suggest that the two events were linked directly, and, in fact, the War Cabinet was informed about *HMS Sheffield* after the E Committee meeting had finished.[147] Of course, the Falklands conflict provided a convenient excuse for saying no, but the build-up to the crucial meeting indicates that there was a clear force of argument against Howell's twin-bore scheme whatever was happening in the South Atlantic. Indeed, Lyall told Foreign Office colleagues on 21 April that it was unlikely that the Committee would agree to the project going ahead.[148] The decision was taken amidst straightforward concerns about the economics, financing and organisation, and in a climate of anti-railway feeling. If there was a 'Falklands factor', then it operated in the opposite direction. As we shall see, the project had to be kept alive in some way if French support for the War was to be retained.[149]

5. Keeping the French sweet, May–June 1982

The negative decision reached by E Committee necessitated some delicate diplomacy. It was known in Paris that British ministers had considered the Fixed Link, and French officials were pressing to be told the outcome. In the short-term the British response was to make use of events in the Falklands. The agreed line was to reveal that discussions had indeed commenced, but that no decision had been taken because discussions had been interrupted by the news of the plight of *HMS Sheffield*. This served as a stalling tactic, but still left British officials with the problem of precisely what to reveal about the verdict of E Committee. After consulting with the Foreign Office, it was agreed that DTp representatives would go to Paris on 10 May to explain the position to Braibant, while Fretwell would make an approach to Mauroy's Cabinet. These actions would prepare the ground for possible discussions between Howell and Fiterman, and thereafter between Thatcher and Mauroy, who were due to meet in mid-May.[150] The challenge was considerable. Fretwell initially informed London that the French were not disposed to question the contents of the Joint Report and confidently expected the project to go ahead. The Ambassador also contended that it would be difficult to draw the French into a study of road bridge alternatives.[151] The DTp was briefed to be 'fairly frank' in its meeting with Braibant, but should set E Committee's decision within the parameters of the September 1981 summit, emphasising the twin principles of economic viability and private financing. Thus, after the paper for E Committee had argued that AF82 supported the case for a rail tunnel, it was suggested that the same document should now be used to argue the opposite. Braibant should be told that British Ministers had found the economic case weak; a high degree of public sector involvement was likely, particularly for a rail tunnel; and the position on road links was less clear. Howell was prepared to discuss these concerns with Fiterman. The intention would be to publish AF82, together with a commentary by the two governments indicating that the rail tunnel would not be pursued, but that further studies might be carried out in order to clarify issues relating to the road-based alternatives. If, as expected, a road link proved unacceptable to the French, then it would be argued that the problems of such options were insurmountable, and that the two governments could only conclude that a Fixed Link was not feasible at present. This matched the line taken by E Committee, or in Foreign Office parlance, gave the French the opportunity of 'playing the game our way or coming up with some new game of their own devising'.[152]

On 10 May Braibant received the British delegation: Rosenfeld, Patrick Brown, an Assistant Secretary, and John Noulton (now returned to the CTU) from the DTp, together with John Gray, Head of the FCO's Maritime and Aviation Department, and Rosemary Spencer, a Counsellor from the British Embassy in Paris. The French official apparently expressed surprise and disappointment at the news, since he did not believe that AF82 provided grounds for a final decision at this stage, let alone a negative one. He said the French would have great difficulty in endorsing a joint statement expressing doubts about the project's economic viability. In any case, there was no requirement for the French Government to make a statement. He was certainly not attracted by the prospect of further work on bridge options, a position which was easy to reach, it seems, after DTp officials had made their scepticism about such options all too apparent. This allowed him to see the tactic for what it was, a means to delay an inevitably negative conclusion. Braibant undertook to make enquiries about a meeting between Fiterman and Howell, but on the next day the Embassy was informed that Fiterman entirely understood Howell's predicament and in the circumstances there was no need to meet.[153] In London, the outcome of the Rosenfeld-Braibant talks was carefully digested. At the Foreign Office, there was a sombre assessment of the implications for Anglo-French relations, and Gray contended that the Link was 'using up French goodwill at an alarming rate'.[154] On 12 May Howell informed Thatcher that in the light of French reactions, 'it might be wisest to consider playing matters rather more slowly', with the aim of eventually securing an agreed statement on the conclusions of AF82.[155] Quite how this was to be achieved was unclear, but Pym concurred in Howell's approach. He repeated the concerns expressed by his predecessor, adding that there was now the need to maintain French support for Britain's Falklands policy. 'We do not want another showdown now', he told the Prime Minister. The French had to be kept 'in play and out of mischief' pending an agreed response to the report.[156] The diplomatic manoeuvring left Howell exposed to potentially awkward questions in the Commons about the date of a statement on the Link. Although he was easily able to brush these aside, Tunnel opponents seized the opportunity to condemn the project as a 'white elephant', 'dead duck' and 'grandiose lunacy'.[157]

Top level exchanges now loomed. Prime Minister Mauroy was due to attend the conference of the Franco-British Council in Edinburgh over the weekend of 15–16 May, and although Thatcher was also speaking at the event, it had been agreed that the two would hold discussions in London on the 17th. However, the arrangements were overtaken by President Mitterand's last minute decision to visit London on the same day. With the meeting less than a week away, it was decided that time would be made for Thatcher and Mauroy to meet for an hour before dinner on 15 May.[158] When drawing up the original agenda for the talks, Thatcher had let it be known that she wished to 'keep off the "Channel Tunnel" item. We have nothing to say on this at present'.[159] However, in the aftermath of the E Committee decision the indications were that Mauroy, and possibly also Mitterand, would raise the subject, making discussion 'unavoidable'.[160] At the meeting Mauroy told Thatcher that he had a particular interest in the Channel Link, and as Mayor of Lille 'he had always had a dream which he wished to turn into reality'. Mauroy might have been expected to press the British Government on its stance, but instead he adopted a more conciliatory tone: 'He hoped that we could take the line publicly that, while the matter was not right for decision yet, studies would continue'. Thatcher responded by saying that 'she too harboured a dream of a fixed link', but beyond this was more cautious. She doubted that private finance would be available for a rail link alone, and did not know whether it would be possible to have a road link as well, though 'that would have more appeal'. Nevertheless, she 'was happy to continue with studies'.[161] With this somewhat messy rapprochement reached, the subject was not raised again when Mitterand met Thatcher two days later.[162] The compromise, intended to 'keep things simmering', was made possible because Mauroy's enthusiasm had been tempered by doubts expressed elsewhere within the French Government and in French banking circles about the prospects of raising finance.[163]

The recourse to further study, familiar in Channel Tunnel history, was thus a convenient device for both Governments. What exactly should be studied was another matter, however. In Whitehall there was no unanimity. At the Department of Transport Lyall took the optimistic view that the project, together with the favoured rail link, had been given a reprieve; indeed, the Thatcher-Mauroy 'accord' might even be interpreted as re-opening the decision of E Committee. The Foreign Office, on the other hand, was much more pessimistic. It was more a case of 'giving the corpse a decent burial', and all that remained was to use the moratorium to avoid a damaging clash with the French. For the Treasury, which had assumed that the Fixed Link had been killed off by E Committee, the acceptance of further studies came as 'something of a surprise'. In France, too, there were both enthusiasts and sceptics, and therefore reasons for playing things 'long'.[164] When British and French officials met to determine the basis and scope of the studies, they agreed that AF82 would be published in both countries on 16 June. The new studies would be carried out by the private sector, and in particular the major banks. It had already been ascertained that some institutions were willing to be involved.[165] The banks were expected to bear the costs of the exercise, the main purpose of which was to 'see whether organisational, legal and financing arrangements, satisfactory to both Governments, could be devised for the construction of any of the competing forms of link'. The French agreed that EuroRoute should be kept in play, but argued that all options, including the discredited six-metre rail-only tunnel, should be included in the assessment. The intention was to complete the studies in time for the next Anglo-French summit in November 1982.[166] Of course, there were risks in outsourcing the studies, notably the possibility that the banks might produce a conclusion at variance with that of ministers, for example by favouring a rail link. However, the need for damage limitation outweighed such concerns. As Gray put it: 'a negative decision by HMG now would still provoke a row with the French, whereas one in the Autumn might not'.[167]

On 7 June Howell informed Thatcher that progress was being made with the establishment of studies and revealed the plans for the simultaneous publication of AF82.[168] An agreed statement was then made in the House.[169] The process was not without some sniping from the Treasury and CPRS. An attempt was made to persuade Howell to tone down his interpretation of AF82, while Brittan warned him that his proposal for further studies might 'cause a lobby to build up in favour of a tunnel' and produce 'incompatible' conclusions. Nevertheless, he was prepared to support the policy provided that the participating banks were made fully aware of the framework of UK Government requirements.[170] Pym expressed similar reservations, and told Thatcher: 'I regard it as vital that the French are given no grounds for undue optimism about our position'.[171] Howell's low-key statement explained that further study would be made of 'organisational, legal and financial arrangements'. In Paris Fiterman's statement in the National Assembly was by contrast both lengthy and more upbeat.[172] The Foreign Office decided to keep a careful eye on such political manoeuvring, but their qualms were unnecessary. Following some months of hectic activity, the Channel Tunnel was about to enter one of its periods of slumber. The *Times* noted that the Tunnel had sunk 'further into the sand', and the *Economist*, in favour of a road scheme, castigated the parties for their timidity. It was not until May 1984 that the issue re-emerged in the upper echelons of government.[173]

6. The Banking Group studies, July 1982–May 1984

It will come as no surprise that it took some time to resolve the terms of reference for the studies. It was not until early August that the respective transport ministries were able to make a formal exchange of letters with the Franco/British Channel

Link Financing Group. This comprised five institutions: on the British side, the Midland and NatWest banks; on the French, the Banque National de Paris, Crédit Lyonnais and Banque Indosuez.[174] The involvement of two of the leading British clearing banks marked something of a departure since Tunnel financing had traditionally been the preserve of the merchant banking houses. Although diversification was rapidly breaking down City barriers, this 'usurpation' of old demarcations evidently ruffled feathers, producing a complaint to the DTp from CTD's bankers, Kleinwort Benson and Robert Fleming.[175] When Baldwin and Rosenfeld met their representatives, they made it clear that had the clearing banks not made their approach, the project would have stalled. This may have been unpalatable medicine for the merchant banks, which were experiencing difficulties of their own in the more competitive conditions of the early 1980s. But the bald fact was that by expressing an interest the clearers had reassured the French that the British 'instrument' was acting in good faith.[176] The Franco-British Group proposed to undertake their work in two stages. In the first the 'financeability' of all the proposed schemes would be examined; in the second the focus would be on specific options which appeared to warrant more detailed study. In this latter stage consideration would be given to the sources and scope of finance, the legal and fiscal framework, and the allocation of risks and responsibilities. The Group intended to produce a report in January 1983, a little later than previously envisaged.[177]

Although playing no direct part in the studies, the two Governments agreed to supply the banks with detailed information, and officials maintained a watching brief. However, there was no longer a requirement for the Department of Transport to maintain a fully staffed Channel Tunnel Unit, and this was gradually disbanded.[178] As for the existing promoters, they were each provided with a copy of AF82 and given details of the work to be undertaken by the banks.[179] British Rail, on receiving news that the Tunnel had fared badly in E Committee, worked hard behind the scenes with their French contacts in an effort to retrieve the situation. Then, in a characteristic search for consensus, Parker called a 'council of war', bringing together all the promoters of bored tunnels. This impromptu gathering agreed that attempts should be made to 'knock EuroRoute', and there followed a lively exchange of letters in the *Financial Times* between Tony Gueterbock of CTD and EuroRoute's Chief Executive, Ken Groves.[180] Alfred Davidson also entered the debate in his capacity as spokesman for the Mid Channel Access Corporation. This firm was another device inspired by the persistent brothers, who were now proposing to use submerged caissons to allow tunnelling from the middle of the Channel as well as at both ends. It was claimed that the technique would reduce the construction period by at least two years.[181] Meanwhile John Laing abandoned its scheme for an immersed tube link, choosing instead to emphasise the company's experience in setting up, financing and running road concessions. The prospect of an immersed tube had always been slim, and Laing's action served to seal its fate with the banking group.[182]

EuroRoute also continued to lobby, notwithstanding its competitors' brickbats and the conclusions of AF82. The company challenged the way in which the Joint

Report had handled some of the doubts surrounding the bridge-tunnel-bridge scheme, and in particular the judgements made on technical uncertainty and navigational problems. These concerns were made clear when MacGregor met Howell in June and then in prolonged correspondence.[183] When EuroRoute representatives met the Chancellor in September, MacGregor was clearly frustrated, complaining about the lack of drive from government and criticising both the transport and trade departments. Howe gave him no encouragement, and after the meeting confided to his officials that 'he had found it difficult to stop himself from saying just how ridiculous the whole project was'. Indeed, he had been opposed to the idea of a link ever since 1974, when his constituents had been threatened by the high-speed rail link.[184] EuroRoute also took the campaign to France, where the Transport Committee of the National Assembly was given a presentation, and there were attempts to construct alliances with leading industrialists.[185] In order to strengthen such connections, the promoters courted Lord Soames, former British Ambassador in Paris, with a suggestion that he meet MacGregor, and, surprisingly, Peter Parker. This was interpreted as a sign that EuroRoute and British Rail were trying to 'sink their differences', but when the two sides met, in early January 1983, Parker stated that his Board could not take a position on alternative schemes until the content of the banks' report was known.[186]

As so often with Anglo-French Channel Tunnel endeavours, it emerged that the studies would be subject to alteration and delay. In fact, the banking group was unable to make a clear separation between the two stages of work, while differences between the two sides resulted in timetable slippage.[187] The French bankers had tended to adopt a more pessimistic approach, and internal disagreements had also surfaced. Not only was the report late, but what tentative results were available at the end of 1982 suggested that only the twin seven-metre tunnel was capable of being financed on a basis consistent with the Governments' criteria. If this view persisted, Lyall observed, it would 'run smack up against the collective view of Ministers' at E Committee.[188] When Howell asked for a note on progress, he was advised that he might either keep open the possibilities of proceeding with a tunnel scheme, or consider the appropriate action to be to 'kill or put in limbo the whole idea, with minimum damage to Anglo/French relations'.[189] Howell, maintaining his enthusiasm for the project, opposed any killing off, and wanted the banks to produce 'a more open ended report from which the conclusion could be drawn that a Channel Link could be reconsidered, should market conditions improve'.[190] To that end he met the chairmen of the Midland and NatWest, Sir Donald Barron and Robin Leigh-Pemberton, in late December 1982.[191] At the same time Braibant and French officials made reference to the need to 'play things long' or put the project 'on the back burner'. They recognised that the French Government might have to follow the British lead and lean on its banks.[192] European complications also added to the delay. Although no progress had been made in securing the long-promised EEC transport infrastructure regulation, 10 million ECUs were set aside from the 1982 budget for transport projects, and under a 'mini' regulation, approved in December 1982, 0.5 million of this was allocated to the Fixed Link studies. The banks received 0.4 million ECUs [£200,000] to fund additional work on possible EEC financing, and the date for completion was extended by five months.[193] That the document was not produced in January 1983 certainly suited the DTp, since it was now busy dealing with the controversial fallout from the publication of the Serpell report on British Rail's finances.[194] In early May British officials met the banks to review progress. It was a gloomy affair. The banks had been unable to agree on a suitable financing plan and the French wanted to draw matters to a swift close.[195] But before the next moves could be determined, a general election was called.

The Conservatives' landslide victory in June 1983 – with 397 seats to Labour's 209 – certainly allowed for a more confident and radical government to emerge, although it was some time before these attributes were to benefit the Channel Fixed Link, which did not figure in any of the party manifestos.[196] While electioneering in Dover, Thatcher had met opponents, and apparently endorsed the view that the prospects were remote.[197] An introductory brief prepared for the new Transport Secretary, Tom King, confirmed that there was currently limited government activity on the project, and the DTp had 'taken a very low profile in Whitehall'. The substantially delayed banks' report was now expected in September.[198] Of course, the arrival of a new minister provoked a resurgence of interest. MacGregor, predictably, was quick to arrange a meeting with King, and the 'tunnellers' were said to be 'battering at the door'. There were questions in the Commons, including no fewer than six tabled by Howell, now a backbencher. Public interest was also awakened when several journals, among them the *Economist*, carried stories based on leaked sections of an interim report completed in July.[199] In advance of a meeting between King and his officials at the beginning of September, Lyall assembled a lengthier brief. He admitted that the banks' study had taken rather longer than expected. Although the final report was not likely to arrive before mid-October at the earliest, the Department had seen 'numerous' chapters in draft form, and was thus able to gauge the progress that had been made. Much had been agreed, but on the central issue of financing the Banking Group could not devise a single plan. Instead, two were offered, one British, the other French, and neither met the stated criteria on government guarantees. Lyall also offered observations on the stance of the French Government. Here, the impression was that interest in Paris was now fading as a result of the country's severe financial difficulties. Yet Mauroy had apparently reiterated his full support for the Tunnel and wanted to see it launched before the expiry of his term of office. Indeed, he had charged Senator Robert Pontillon, a close political ally and Chairman of the French section of the Franco-British Council, with the specific task of advancing the project. Pontillon was planning to visit London on 12 September. Finally, Lyall made an important observation in an attempt to place the conclusions of E Committee in context. He argued that the Committee had 'not fully appreciated' the nature of the twin rail tunnel scheme, and in particular the fact that the shuttle services did not need to be run by British Rail and SNCF. The Banking Group concurred with this, and officials were also exploring the scope for privatising through rail services. Evidently, the DTp still hankered after a twin rail tunnel and hoped that the use of private sector railway operators would temper fears of a British Rail monopoly, which, as we have seen, was one of the decisive arguments offered against Howell's preferred option in May 1982.[200] With all the information to hand, King expressed an open mind. All options were to be kept open, and there was no question of bringing the project to a quick end. He was also happy to see Pontillon during his visit.[201] When the meeting occurred, the conversation was polite, but hardly went beyond general expressions of intent, hedged with an acceptance that the Governments should wait to see what the banks had to say.[202] It was another case of *déjà vu* when King met Fiterman on an informal basis during a meeting of the European Council in Athens in early October. Without the report, purportedly imminent, there was little that the two ministers could say, aside from making the right kind of soothing diplomatic noises.[203]

In the event, King did not have the opportunity to develop an interest in the matter. On 16 October – ten days after the meeting with Fiterman – a scandal surrounding Cecil Parkinson, the Trade and Industry Secretary, forced an unplanned Cabinet reshuffle. King was switched to Employment and replaced by Nicholas Ridley. The new Minister, a civil engineer by background, was a highly effective political operator. He proved to be an admirable Transport Secretary, in particular as a result of the relationship he forged with Reid, Parker's successor as Chairman of British Rail.[204] The indefatigable MacGregor, now Chairman of the National Coal Board, immediately wrote to congratulate Ridley and extol the virtues of EuroRoute.[205] Barely one week into office, the Minister had to field questions in the Commons. He adopted the familiar Tunnel mantra that all options were open, and hoped to receive the banks' report 'very shortly'.[206] 'Very shortly' was rather longer, in fact. Latest indications were that the final version would be available by the end of November, making an announcement possible on 5 December.[207] However, continuing differences within the Franco-British Group meant that the banks were unable to adhere to this timetable, and when Ridley replied to a Commons question in December, all he could do was state that he expected the report in the New Year.[208] The DTp hoped that it would surface in January 1984, but on the 20th Colin Stannard of NatWest informed Lyall of further slippage. He was now promising that the summary and conclusions would be sent 'by latest 13 February', with the main report following by the end of the month.[209] Lyall hoped that British and French officials would be able to discuss the banks' conclusions before a meeting between Ridley and Fiterman on 20 February, but it immediately became apparent that there would be further delay.[210]

In fact, the Department had already received sufficient 'under the counter' provisional text to gain a reasonable indication of what was in the banks' report.[211] There had been considerable disappointment with both the style and the content of the interim report, and subsequent drafts did little to change the views of officials.[212] And yet some advances had clearly been made on earlier plans. On the initiative of the British banks, it was promised that equity instruments would finance a substantial slice – 20 per cent – of the project, and the banks were also ready to forego unconditional completion guarantees and accept a large measure of traffic and tariff risk. Nonetheless, the inescapable fact remained that these modified proposals failed to meet Government objectives. On top of this, the British banks took umbrage at the Department's intention to appoint a merchant bank – Schroders – to conduct a financial appraisal of the report, while the French partners in the Group were arguing that the document should be regarded as private and therefore remain unpublished. Further delay was likely because the French Transport Ministry felt that the draft summary and conclusions were weak in their handling of key material contained in the first three chapters, which reviewed the cross-channel market and analysed the Fixed Link options in detail.[213]

Lyall now produced a candid memorandum entitled 'Channel Fixed Link: Where do we go from here?' He conceded that the French complaint was valid. The early chapters formed the 'guts' of the report, and merited far more attention than the 'fascinating' subject of alternative financing plans. However, more delay would serve no purpose. A somewhat exasperated Lyall wanted the report 'delivered as soon as possible, warts and all'. Unimpressed with the banks' 'hypnotic concentration' on financing details, he suggested, that having produced recommendations which clearly contravened the criteria of both Governments they 'must be told tactfully that they are living in cloud-cuckoo land'. The only thing that would impress the Secretary of State was 'a fully coalesced group, raring and eager to go, demonstrably capable of carrying the project through and prepared to do so on a "no guarantee" basis'. Lyall was also contemptuous of the suggestion that the report should not be published, and of the banks' protests that the Government should not use a merchant bank to obtain independent advice.[214] On the French side Braibant also expressed concerns about the delay, and was inclined to blame the British banks, and behind them, the British Government, for holding things up. He was also disappointed that nothing would be produced for the Ridley-Fiterman talks on 20 February, since Fiterman was reportedly keen to see some progress before the end of the French presidency of the EC in June. Once again, the absence of the banks' report made discussions of substance impossible.[215]

Four days after seeing Fiterman, Ridley met representatives of the Midland and NatWest banks. His negotiating stance was by this time patently clear. As he had explained to another sceptic, Geoffrey Howe, now Foreign Secretary, if a private enterprise group wanted a fixed link, why should the Government try to stop them? His principal concern was therefore to 're-state clearly our commitment to no public finance or government financial guarantees'.[216] Armed with Lyall's brief, the Secretary of State was in no mood to beat around the bush. The bankers began by seeking to explain the delay in producing the report, referring to 'fundamental differences' between the British and French approaches. The British had insisted on private funding, while the French had preferred a public sector operation; the French wanted single finance, rather than two separately-financed schemes 'meeting in the middle'. But when the bankers attempted to outline their preferred solution, Ridley said that he did not wish to go into the details of the proposals at this stage. This did not prevent him from condemning aspects of the emerging conclusions. He warned the bankers that the type of guarantees they required might be difficult for the British Government to accept, saw little prospect of obtaining support from the European Community, and suggested that promoters would challenge the findings. He also made it clear that he expected the report to be published, and while agreeing not to appoint a merchant bank as an independent adviser, reserved the right to do so if circumstances warranted it. After the meeting, the Secretary of State told officials that he had 'serious doubts' about the extent of Government underwriting that the banks required.[217] On 27 February Ridley, together with his Parliamentary Under-Secretary, David Mitchell, met officials to consider how the banks' report should be handled. As to the various schemes, he was all for remaining neutral and letting the market decide, though civil servants were more nervous about the implications. It was agreed that Ridley would clear a holding statement with his colleagues. At this stage the outlook was bleak. If Howell had been a passionate supporter of the Tunnel and King had had insufficient time to take a view, Ridley was deeply sceptical.[218]

Drafts of the report started to receive wider circulation within Whitehall. Clarity was far from evident, and even the Treasury found the material 'very heavy going'.[219] At the Number Ten Policy Unit, which had replaced the CPRS, it was recognised that the report would 're-awaken public interest in the project after years of hibernation'. The Government's response would be tricky, but the issue was not thought to be a 'grade A banana skin'.[220] With publication imminent and leaks of the contents emerging at regular intervals, the promoting groups stepped up their campaigns. EuroRoute had remained active throughout and had recruited two major French industrial groups – Alsthom-Atlantique and Grands Travaux de Marseille – to its cause. On 25 January MacGregor had a meeting with Ridley where, as expected, he took exception to some of the leaked assertions of the banks, and in particular to the extent of the loan capital EuroRoute would require.[221] He also had another meeting with Thatcher, on 14 March, but this was brief and inconclusive.[222] Meanwhile his opponents had regrouped. Over the course of 1983 they had come to appreciate the value of a collaborative approach to the project. Thus, Balfour Beatty, Costain, Tarmac, Taylor Woodrow and Wimpey – the five construction companies which had lobbied for a bored tunnel via CTD, ECTG and ACTG – agreed to present the banks and the Secretary of State with a single set of cost estimates.[223] They then went further. In March 1984 they announced that they had joined forces under a single body known as the Channel Tunnel Group. The move was heralded as a major commitment by the British construction industry to the Channel Tunnel.[224] In France an Association Transmanche was formed to lobby for a Fixed Link. Inspired by Michel Delebarre, Mauroy's Directeur de Cabinet, it enjoyed broad support from central government, interested local authorities, SNCF, chambers of commerce and the banks, and held its inaugural meeting on 15 March.[225] The Association went on to press for French alternatives to the existing British projects, notably a large-diameter, drive-through tunnel scheme popularly known as the 'Pilon tunnel' after its advocate, Bernard Pilon.[226]

In early April, with the banks' report expected within a month, officials prepared a draft minute for Ridley to send to Thatcher. However, the Transport Secretary was not entirely happy with its tone. The draft had suggested that he point out that if the Government did not want a Link, then it should discourage the promoters and seek agreement with the French that the project should not be pursued. Ridley doubted the political wisdom of this approach. The Government would be criticised for retreating from its belief in the market and be accused of bad faith by the French and the promoters. However, he was prepared to say that the market itself was 'likely to kill the project' if the Government maintained its view that public financial guarantees would not be given.[227] David Holmes, Rosenfeld's successor at the DTp, agreed with the Secretary of State that it was unlikely that any promoter would be able to satisfy the Government's financial conditions, but he observed that the promoters would argue that if the Government were prepared to offer the Link real political backing, then finance would be made available. Certainly MacGregor took this view, and would not be persuaded otherwise. Ridley may have been hoping that the market would kill the project, but, as Holmes observed, 'all experience shows the project to be indestructible'.[228] At the beginning of May the timetable became firmer. The banks' report was to be published on the 22nd and a parliamentary statement was arranged for the same day.[229]

Ridley then briefed Thatcher and members of E Committee. The main conclusions of the Banking Group report were no surprise: (1) with costs of £2–6 billion and a long payback period, none of the schemes could be financed privately without some Government or EC commercial guarantees; (2) the best option was a twin rail tunnel with vehicle shuttle; and (3) commercial risks and higher costs precluded the private financing of bridge schemes and EuroRoute. Of course, these conclusions would be challenged, but for the time being Ridley proposed to say only that he was studying the report. For the benefit of his colleagues he went on to rehearse some of the main issues in the debate. While the country would 'probably be better off' with a Fixed Link, it was for the market to decide its value, and the Government should stick to its guns by refusing to interfere with the process by offering funding or guarantees. This approach was consonant with the Conservatives' aim of reducing state intervention in international transport through the privatisation of Sealink (effected in July 1984) and British Airways (February 1987) and the deregulation of air and road transport. Countering popular speculation, Ridley repeated his view that European Community assistance offered 'no way out'. Britain would have to contribute to any EC funding, and consequently such measures would not meet the condition of 'no taxpayer involvement'. In any case, the Minister was 'strongly opposed' to any substantial EC transport spending. As usual, relations with the French would require careful handling, given the enthusiasm of Fiterman and Mauroy. It was suggested that a non-committal stance be adopted until the end of the French Presidency and the European elections, both in June.[230]

There was comparatively little dissent from Ridley's ministerial colleagues, and none objected to his proposed statement.[231] The banks formally delivered the report to the two governments and the European Commission on 17 May and it was published five days later. Entitled *Finance for a Fixed Channel Link*, with a cover price of £125, and running to nearly 500 pages in a two-volume boxed set, it looked an impressive addition to the library of Fixed Link studies.[232] In response to a parliamentary question on the same day, Ridley announced its receipt and public availability. He noted that neither of the two suggested financing plans met the Government's criteria, and stated once again that the project would have to be financed without public funds or commercial guarantees. Both the Government and the promoters, he observed, would need time to digest the implications of the report.[233] The French, while also endorsing Ridley's statement, were not entirely happy with its rather negative tone. Fiterman's own statement was more optimistic, welcoming the Report as a 'positive contribution'. He was also more sanguine about guarantees. The French Government, said Fiterman, 'has affirmed that all guarantees and precautions should be taken so that, once begun, the project can be brought to a satisfactory conclusion, to avoid the disappointments of the past'.[234]

In the two and a half years from the Anglo-French summit in September 1981 to the publication of the banks' report in May 1984 little progress had been made in resolving the basic issues affecting the Fixed Link. But whatever differences Howell and Ridley had, they were both forced to confront the same realities. AF82 and the banks' report of May 1984 were clearly horses from the same stable. In his presentations to Ministers in December 1981 and May 1982 Howell had noted that a bored tunnel was the most likely option, that bridges and tubes would be too expensive, and that some element of government guarantee was required. After nearly two years of further study by the banks, Ridley had no alternative but to recognise the same essentials. Holmes had warned: 'we do not want to be in an endless loop of inviting proposals which we cannot adequately assess; then setting up a joint study with the French; and ending up exactly where we started'.[235] But that is essentially what happened in the period 1981–4. It is true that British Rail's 'mousehole' had been firmly rejected, and the leading banks from the two countries had been drawn into the debate. On the other hand, the fundamentals relating to the choice of crossing and the extent of private sector risk had been debated many times, but had not been resolved. In the familiar demarcation, enthusiasts – Howell, Lyall, Braibant – confronted sceptics – Howe, Walters, Broadbent. French goodwill, an essential component, had been stretched considerably. After the abandonment of 1975, the British Embassy in Paris and the DTp had been so anxious to avoid the 'negative effects of failure' that they tended to give the French a more enthusiastic impression of their position than was actually the case.[236] But this was another old tale. All in all, it had been a long way to travel to reach the starting point again.

9

THE THATCHER GOVERNMENTS AND THE TUNNEL

Choosing a promoter, 1984–6

1. From the Banking Group Report to the Anglo-French Summit, May–November 1984

The work of the Franco-British Channel Link Financing Group received a mixed reception. Journalists were sceptical. When they met DTp officials for an off the record briefing on 22 May they expressed the view that the report did not take the link any further forward. Many felt, with the *Financial Times* and *Le Figaro*, that Ridley's Commons statement had poured cold water on its conclusions and that the project was still at first base.[1] To be fair, the Channel Link was an entirely novel challenge from a banking perspective. As the report pointed out, its sheer size, the very long gestation period, the dependence for revenue on traffic growth, and the insistence that there should be no government aid 'put it outside the common experience of the private markets'. On top of this, the Link would be the longest crossing under or over water in the world, and the asset would have 'no intrinsic value except to the project'.[2] Beneath the almost impenetrable layers of detailed analysis, the banks presented revised traffic forecasts and costings, building upon the estimates provided for the Anglo/French Report (AF82) of 1982. A more conservative view was taken of contractors' estimates by adding 10 per cent to capital costs and assuming an eight-year construction period, with up to two years overrun. The cost of their favoured option, a dual-bore rail tunnel with a shuttle for road vehicles, was put at £2.0 billion in 1983 prices, and the maximum level of indebtedness was estimated to be £7.5 billion, £2.4 billion in 1983 prices. The real rate of return was given as 8.3 per cent, higher than that for the alternative tunnel options, and attractive when compared with the much higher capital cost and indebtedness for a bridge or composite scheme (Table 9.1). The impasse was created in the critical area of financing, where the bankers ignored the British Government's determination that there should be no government guarantees. Two financing plans were presented, both involving a mix of investment capital, bond issues (indexed or revenue) and loan facilities, and both assuming a measure of government support, including protection against political risks, and government and/or EEC financing of a two-year development stage costing £18 million [in 1983 prices]. In the first proposal, put up by the

Table 9.1 Evaluation of Channel Link options by Banking Report, 1984

Option	*Capital cost (excluding rolling stock) £bn 1983 prices*	*Maximum debt money terms £bn*	*1983 prices £bn*	*Real rate of return %*
Favoured				
Bored dual bored tunnel with shuttle – unphased	2.0	7.5	2.4	8.3
Other bored tunnels				
Single no shuttle	1.1	7.4	1.3	5.4
Single with shuttle	1.6	12.2	1.9	4.8
Dual phased	2.1	10.7	2.2	7.9
Others				
Road bridge	3.1	13.6	3.6	8.5
Composite (viaduct/ immersed tube)	6.1	54.0	7.2	5.1

Source: Franco-British Channel Link Group, *Finance for a Fixed Channel Link*, May 1984, Vol. I, p. 25.

British, all funds would be committed before construction began. There would be an investment capital of £540 million [£393 million in 1983 prices], mainly in the form of convertible loan stock, and the remainder – £5,398 million [£1,920 million in 1983 prices] – would be raised by the banks as non-recourse loans, to be converted after opening into revenue bonds. Governments would shoulder some responsibility in the event of a substantial cost overrun and share in the refinancing risks. In the second proposal, advanced by the French, there would be a progressive commitment of funds during the early construction period, and the Governments would therefore bear a higher degree of risk. Investment capital would be £540 million, with the remainder – £3,494 million [£1,242 million in 1983 prices] in bank loans – committed after the first two years of construction and progressively converted into non-recourse form – and indexed bonds. The banks would bear very limited risks until the service tunnel had been completed.[3]

Officials in Transport now had to consider the steps to be taken in the wake of the banks' report. There were, of course, three main constituents: the banks; the promoters and the French Government. At a follow-up meeting with the DTp in June the banks argued that the ball was firmly in the Government's court. Until the Government made some kind of commitment to a particular option, and gave some indication of the support it might provide, the private sector would find it impossible to obtain financing undertakings. The Government, for its part, was reluctant to make such commitments until it received firm financing proposals from promoters.[4] In July Colin Stannard and John Bennett of NatWest offered an alternative approach designed to break this 'Catch 22' deadlock. Adopting the role of self-appointed lead promoters rather than advisers, they concocted a 'stage by stage' approach to the project's development, in which the planning would be incremental. The process would begin, given Government encouragement, with a submission from NatWest.[5] However, this proposal left much to be determined, nor could it resolve the very different approaches to financing offered by the British and French banks. Furthermore, officials were reluctant to close off the choice of options for the Link. Discussions with the French at government level were clearly required. After further meetings in September and October both NatWest and the Midland expressed frustration with the lack of movement by the Government. But the fact was that officials had no alternative but to adopt a holding stance – reiterated in person by Peter Lazarus, Permanent Under-Secretary at the DTp – until meetings with French officials were held.[6]

Promoters were equally frustrated by the impasse. Most vocal was EuroRoute, which repeated its challenge to the conclusions in the banks' report and employed Coopers & Lybrand to contest the costings.[7] The promoter also complained when a NEDO technical committee made noises in favour of a tunnel.[8] The Davidsons put in another brief appearance with their ideas for tunnel construction, but otherwise the mood was subdued.[9] The Channel Tunnel Group (CTG), the bored tunnel promoter, was clearly in the pole position, and fully expected to take the project forward as the Governments' 'chosen instrument'. Sir Nicholas Henderson, former British Ambassador in Paris, was a recent recruit to the CTG who lobbied hard, organising a dinner for Peter Rees, the Treasury Financial Secretary in June, meeting with Ridley shortly afterwards, visiting the Foreign Office, and stirring up the All-Party Channel Tunnel Group. In the autumn he contended that CTG could complete construction in $4\frac{1}{2}$ years instead of six, which would strengthen its chances of attracting funding.[10] Henderson found a new adversary in Sir Nigel Broackes, Chairman of Trafalgar House, who succeeded MacGregor as Chairman of EuroRoute in December, following the latter's move from British Steel to the National Coal Board. Broackes, another feisty businessman, and MacGregor used the period of transition to press the Government once more about its intentions towards their scheme, and hints were dropped about substantial modifications to reduce the cost. These efforts culminated in a meeting with Nigel Lawson, the Chancellor of the Exchequer, and Rees on 19 November. The discussion did not proceed very far, but the ministerial tone was not as discouraging as it had been in Howe's time.[11]

Little substantive could be undertaken by any of the parties until official contacts with the French were resumed. Here, there was some 'soft pedalling' on both sides. The evidence suggests that Lyall was in no immediate hurry to resume a dialogue with Braibant.[12] Braibant was of like mind. In Paris, there was the distraction of Mitterand's declining popularity, demonstrated by the French elections to the European Parliament on 17 June, where the Left took a battering. In contrast, there were some more positive factors. Relations between Britain and France were excellent, and at the European summit in Fontainebleau a week later, Britain's contribution to the EC budget was finally resolved. The agreement created a more favourable environment for the settlement of bilateral matters, including the Fixed Link.[13] In early July Braibant enquired through the British Embassy whether talks might be resumed. But this intention was frustrated by the fall of the Mauroy Government soon afterwards, on 18 July. Fiterman and the Communists left office, and a new administration, led by Mitterand's young protégé, Laurent Fabius, was formed. Transport was incorporated in Housing and Town Planning under Paul Quilès, a former oil executive (Shell). With Fiterman's departure, Braibant's special responsibility for the Fixed Link ended.[14] It was some time before the British knew with whom to deal. Jean Auroux, a socialist from the Loire, was eventually appointed State Secretary (junior minister) for Transport, reporting to Quilès. A new administrative team was then appointed.[15] In early September, Auroux, who appeared to have taken on the Fixed Link brief, came to London to visit the Farnborough Air Show. Unexpectedly, he raised the matter in informal discussions with both Ridley and Norman Tebbit. At the Air Show he spoke briefly with Ridley, suggesting that the two meet after he had studied the dossier. Later, when visiting Tebbit at the DTI, he indicated that both Mitterand and Fabius were interested in the project and wished to pursue it further. He thought it likely that Mitterand would be briefed to raise the subject during his state visit to the UK at the end of October. Tebbit naturally referred him to Ridley, but indicated that he was personally in favour of a Link.[16] Ridley, though still firmly opposed to the project, accepted the need for further dialogue, and on 4 October he wrote to Auroux suggesting that they meet 'to make a preliminary assessment of the prospects'. With NatWest Bank and, to a lesser extent, the Midland, 'off the fence' and the promoters champing at the bit, something had to be done. As Lazarus argued, in a minute to Ridley: 'this affair has gone on long enough... we should try to decide for ourselves, before the State visit, whether and how we want to proceed. We should not leave the initiative to the French and we do not want to leave them room and opportunity to blame us for delay or inaction'.[17] Britain's readiness to resume talks was also passed to the press.[18] The intention was to consult Cabinet colleagues quickly, and arrange a meeting between Ridley and Auroux, so that the matter could be taken off the summit agenda.[19] In anticipation of the meeting of ministers, Lyall met Jean-Paul Paufique, Auroux's Directeur de Cabinet, on 18 October. These informal talks, which were held at the French Ministry of Transport, were 'cordial and frank'. Nothing new emerged. Paufique was more optimistic than Lyall about the prospects of EC involvement, and suggested that the British Government might join the French in specifying the type of link preferred. Lyall, on the other hand, repeated Ridley's position on guarantees and emphasised that the initiative lay with the private sector; it was for the market to decide on the choice of link. A spirit of pragmatism and co-operation was evident, and the two sides appeared ready to give ground on their earlier positions in relation to the nature of political guarantees and commercial controls. It was agreed that Ridley and Auroux should now meet to discuss outstanding issues and clarify the 'rules of the game' for promoters.[20] No formal talks on the subject took place during Mitterand's state visit on 23–6 October. However, the French President made a brief reference to the 'Channel Tunnel' at a dinner given by the Queen, then, at a concluding press conference, rather impishly suggested that he and Thatcher had discussed the Tunnel 'all the time', and claimed that for the Prime Minister 'it is an obsession'.[21]

More progress was made when Ridley met Quilès and Auroux in Paris on 14 November. The French were clearly taking things seriously, since the Transport Ministers were joined by Georges-Marie Chenu from the Quai d'Orsay and Jean-Phillippe Verret from Fabius's Cabinet.[22] It was accepted that the time had come for the two Governments to define their position more precisely. To that end Ridley suggested that a joint working group of officials be established to examine criteria and rules. There was a long list, including the nature of political guarantees, financing, technical acceptability, organisation, competition, taxation, customs, immigration and security. Auroux welcomed the idea as 'a useful step forward', and a three-month timescale was agreed. In a joint communiqué issued after the meeting the Ministers reaffirmed the willingness of the two Governments to facilitate a link on the clear understanding that it would be financed without support from public funds or government financial guarantees. The latter stipulation was conceded by the French after an abortive attempt, with EC possibilities in mind, to remove it from the communiqué. Promoting groups were invited to submit proposals to the two Governments jointly, drawing on guidance provided by the working group. With all the customary provisos about financing, competition, safety and the environment, the Link was firmly back upon the political agenda.[23] In fact, signs of a change of heart were evident within the British Cabinet. When Ridley sought the views of his colleagues prior to his meeting in France, the replies received were more positive than negative. Ridley himself had set aside his personal scepticism and put a more optimistic gloss on the prospects of a private sector success. He referred the Prime Minister to NatWest's encouraging approach, and suggested that the French were now ready to accept 'no guarantee' market financing.[24] Asked whether colleagues were ready to see a link authorised if the conditions were met, most, like Thatcher, replied in the affirmative.[25] Clearly there was now a more confident tone about British capitalism. The Link 'would be bound to be seen as a mark of private sector confidence in the economy', observed Lord Young, Minister without Portfolio. John Gummer, the Paymaster General, was more forthright: 'is it not time we cleared the way for some entrepreneurial achievement?'[26] The response of an inveterate opponent, Geoffrey Howe, now Foreign Secretary, was instructive. 'I have always been profoundly sceptical', he told Thatcher, 'about the possibility of such a large investment being carried through without the Government being drawn in financially at some stage . . . Nevertheless, I accept that we have probably come too far down the road . . . to leave much room for a fundamental change in position . . . I therefore agree with you that if a viable package can be put forward without a requirement for taxpayers' money, we should be prepared to look carefully at it'.[27]

The press reaction to the Ridley-Auroux talks was decidedly low-key, especially in France. In Britain both the *Times* and *Financial Times* welcomed the talks as a step forward, but little more.[28] With overtones of 1981, there was pressure from the French for the subject to be included on the formal agenda of the Anglo-French summit in Paris on 29–30 November. Indeed, at the inter-ministerial meeting Quilès had suggested that the event be used to reaffirm the move to a position of clear political commitment to the project. The British, as we have noted, were more cautious. Ridley argued that it was premature to make a major political declaration since it was by no means certain that the promoters would succeed in satisfying the Governments' criteria.[29] Nevertheless, the French persisted, and a week before the summit asked that Ridley attend in order to raise the profile and, more specifically, to take part in a meeting which would make public decisions on the composition and terms of reference of the joint working group. Reluctance was evident on the British side – Ridley commented, 'I see no point in going' – but the matter was eventually conceded after some encouragement from the Foreign Office.[30] As the summit approached, the French exerted further pressure by asking for a new communiqué on the Fixed Link to be issued by Mitterand and Thatcher after the talks. There was a flurry of diplomatic activity about this suggestion as British politicians and officials left for France.[31]

At the initial meeting between Mitterand and Thatcher on 29 November, there was only a brief reference to the Channel Fixed Link. Mitterand said that it was one of the bilateral matters which might be discussed over dinner later that day.[32] After the dinner British Ministers attended a debriefing at the British Ambassador's residence at 10.30 p.m. This session, which continued until well after midnight, was dominated by the Link and produced the frankest record of British thinking for some time. Thatcher and Ridley agreed that two French drafts of the proposed communiqué were unacceptable and a hastily concocted British alternative was discussed. On the Link itself Defence Secretary Michael Heseltine got the ball rolling by expressing 'the strong view that a Channel link should be proceeded with', though he felt that the private sector would be unable to finance it on its own. Thatcher and Ridley then exchanged personal views. The Prime Minister said that 'it would be nice to have something exciting getting under way'. The cancellation of the Channel Tunnel and of Maplin in 1975 'had been the end of everything exciting. If all that was possible was a rail link, she was not interested'. Her antipathy for a tunnel was manifest. She did not mind if a road link wiped out the ferries. Her position was clear: 'I don't want the rail tunnel, I want EuroRoute'.[33] In response Ridley was cast in the role of tunnel advocate. By this time he had conceded that the EuroRoute and Eurobridge schemes presented navigational difficulties and had also come round to the view that a road link could not be financed by the private sector alone. Furthermore, EuroRoute 'were not on the same start line' as the tunnel promoters, since it would take them some time to demonstrate that their impact on navigation would be acceptable. Consequently, he told Thatcher that the tunnel group, CTG, was the promoter most likely to come up with an acceptable scheme.[34] The Prime Minister felt that a decision might have to be delayed to enable EuroRoute to provide more detail, and she was even prepared to spend up to £20 million on the development work necessary to demonstrate the full acceptability of the scheme.[35] Ridley's note of realism did not disturb the optimism of the meeting, which broke up, as Lyall recalled, 'on the note that the (EuroRoute) project would be "unbelievably exciting" and "good for employment"'.[36]

Early the next morning Mitterand and Thatcher met for a second time. Mitterand suggested that they should say something encouraging about the Link at their press conference, and Thatcher agreed. The discussion resembled that with Mauroy in 1982 (above, p. 237). Once again Thatcher expressed her belief that the British people would greatly prefer a link which enabled them to drive directly to the Continent.[37] At the same time Ridley was conferring with Quilès and Auroux at the French Transport Ministry. Their 40-minute meeting was spent drafting the text of the joint statement to be used by the two leaders at their press conference, in place of a formal communiqué. Examining the third (British) draft, the French sought a more positive comment on technical and financial feasibility, and wanted the working group to 'pursue its work with real urgency'. The British, in contrast, argued for caution. With time pressing, a compromise was quickly reached.[38] The plenary session of the summit followed immediately afterwards at the Elysée. The Channel Fixed Link came towards the end of an agenda which included such matters as security and arms control, UNESCO, European Community issues, Africa and the United States and protectionism. Quilès, opening the debate on the Link, was bullish about the 14 November talks, making rather more of the commitments they represented than the British had wanted. 'Today', he said, 'it could be announced that the summit was giving the project a new push, that the project was important for Europe and that it appeared to be technically and financially feasible. It could also be announced that a Working Group was being set up to define the "cahier de charges" and to determine the nature of the government commitments that might be necessary and the forms they might take, such as a treaty'. To British surprise, he referred to 'the end of 1985' as the date by which promoters should have submitted proposals to the two governments. 'The group', he observed, 'should meet within a fortnight and submit a report within three months'. Ridley 'was pleased to confirm M. Quilès' account. Establishing a working group was clearly the correct next step'. The group, which would complete its work by the end of February, would define the requirements and undertakings necessary for the private sector to put forward proposals for any form of link. The successful scheme would be privately financed and independent of government. It would therefore compete with ferries and aircraft free of any accusation of unfair competition. 'The Summit', said Ridley, 'had succeeded in giving a new note of urgency'. He also 'detected a new optimism among the competing groups'. Thatcher commented: 'The news we have heard is exciting and I hope the work will go ahead because this, in the eyes of the public, is the obviously exciting thing we are doing... It should be clear soon whether the private sector really could finance the project'. Mitterand, in reply, said simply: 'I entirely share your views'.[39] At the ensuing press conference, Mitterand referred journalists to the text of the agreed statement. Thatcher said that one of the major areas of co-operation for the two governments was the 'Channel Tunnel' [*sic*]. She pronounced herself 'cautiously optimistic'. In the agreed statement the two leaders recognised 'the potential importance of a Channel Fixed Link as an element in the European transport network', endorsed the outcome of the 14 November talks, and noted that 'the time has come to take the next step'. The Franco-British working group 'should pursue its work with real urgency and submit its report within three months'.[40] Thus, three years after the 1981 summit, events had come full circle and fresh impetus had been given to start the ball rolling again.

Most commentators see the November 1984 summit as a defining moment in the history of the Channel Tunnel, though, in fact, the decisive steps had been taken in the earlier and less-publicised talks between Ridley and Auroux.[41] Nevertheless, the summit represented a clear change of mood. There was now a consensus among leading British ministers in favour of a Link, and for all the sloppy references to 'tunnels' a road scheme was the favourite. This was seen in Thatcher's positive remarks when interviewed by the British media in Paris on 30 November. She told John Simpson: 'many people have a great dream that they would like to get in their car at Dover and drive all the way through to Calais'. Interviewed by Philip Short, she concluded: 'It would be something which our generation could show, that we had added to the new technology, to the new spirit that is abroad in Europe, to linking the Continent of Europe to Britain . . . it would make us confident in the future and as forward-looking as some of those of our forbears who built the first industrial revolution'.[42]

2. Advancing the project, December 1984–April 1985

After Ridley's talks with Quilès and Auroux on 30 November, the British put forward dates in December for the first meeting of the joint working group. However, despite the French insistence on 'urgency' in the public statement, they were not able to adhere to this timetable. With their more bureaucratic approach to civil service initiatives of this kind – rather unkindly, they were reported to be organisationally 'at sixes and sevens' – they took some time to choose the officials and give attention to the agenda. Consequently, the first meeting of the group was not held until 10 January 1985. At this stage British officials feared that the undertaking to complete the work by the end of February might prove a tall order.[43] However, the French assembled a strong team, and a surprising degree of co-operation and speed was exhibited by the two sets of civil servants, led by Lyall and Raoul Rudeau, a senior engineer in the French Ministry.[44] This situation contrasted sharply with past experiences, notably in the early 1970s, where the same subject areas – financing, rail links, ownership and control, competition policy and tariff control, etc. – had taken officials months, even years, to resolve (above, pp. 88–102, 116–18).[45] Furthermore, attitudes across the Channel had clearly changed, with the French now adopting the 'hawkish' stance that there should be no financial guarantees, and taking a more 'relaxed' approach to the question of governmental tariff controls.[46] They were also able to respond positively to the

British insistence that the group, instead of reporting to ministers and drawing up the guidelines after this, should draft the guidelines themselves and put these to ministers by the end of February.[47]

Lyall, while in no doubt that 'we should have no great difficulty in agreeing guidelines with the French', was less certain about the prospects of 'reaching agreement within Whitehall'.[48] In fact, these worries proved unfounded, although the Treasury naturally took a renewed interest in the project, and was evidently anxious to avoid being pushed into a decision, as had appeared likely in 1981–2. Paradoxically in view of the French change of heart, the Treasury was now expressing fears that without tariff controls the Link might capture too much of the cross-channel market.[49] Early in the New Year Lawson's officials produced an assessment paper which the Chancellor was anxious to circulate to colleagues. However, the Department felt that such a move would be premature, and Lyall effectively defused the situation by persuading Treasury officials that Lawson should 'mark up his interest' in a more general way.[50] Consequently, at the end of January Lawson wrote to Ridley with a list of concerns, including tariff control and terrorism. He was anxious to avoid a situation where promoters made assurances, only for the Government to be drawn into a substantial measure of risk-taking. Perhaps for this reason, he indicated his support for a twin-tunnel scheme, which he felt was not only less risky but also looked 'less unattractive to motorists than appears at first sight'.[51] Partly in response to the Chancellor, but primarily to give British officials a 'broad steer' before they finalised the draft guidelines, Ridley canvassed his colleagues' views on the crunch points at issue.[52] Drawing on the ensuing correspondence, together with an officials' note, the Transport Secretary produced a memorandum for discussion at the meeting of the Cabinet Sub-Committee on Economic Affairs (E(A)) on 25 February.[53]

The documentation highlighted the several elements in the negotiation, encompassing, for example, the nature of the concession, the type of company organisation, the desirability (or otherwise) of duty free facilities, territorial and frontier questions, the prospects for EC finance, and the tax regime. But the two issues which provoked most discussion were the survival of the ferries and the funding of any associated railway infrastructure. Fears that a Fixed Link would quickly establish a dominant position in the cross-channel market and put the ferry companies out of business were nothing new. The arguments for maintaining ferry capacity rested largely on defence requirements and, specifically, the need to use merchant shipping to support a reinforcement of the British Army on the Rhine. In this context the Link's apparent vulnerability to industrial action, accident or sabotage was an obvious concern.[54] For these reasons Ridley wanted the guidelines to include a reference to the possibility of Government intervention to preserve some competition by ferries. He received a measure of support from Lawson and Howe.[55] On the other hand, Tebbit, the Trade and Industry Secretary, was adamant that the pattern of cross-channel services should be determined by market forces.[56] In any case, Heseltine, the Defence Secretary, was more sanguine about the prospects, and did not see why the ferries should be kept running in order to meet defence needs. His major concern still lay with financing. He did not believe the project would succeed unless there was a measure of public funding.[57] The French, on the other hand, were happy to leave the threat of monopoly to competition law.[58] The role of railways in the project once again provoked strong differences of view between the British and French. Both sides agreed that there was no need to insist that the Link should include a rail component. However, the British raised alarm bells when they insisted that British Rail should play no part in the Link itself (including any shuttle services) and that any infrastructure investment it might undertake in support of the project must be on a 'fully commercial basis'. The French, 'with memories of 1973 [*sic*] firmly in mind', suspected that Britain was 'seeking to prejudice the rules against a rail link' and in favour of schemes such as EuroRoute.[59] Furthermore, the process of funding the inland rail infrastructure on the British side, which was likely to cost some £200–300 million, presented serious difficulties. It was unlikely that the full cost of the works would meet the financial return demanded of British Rail (7 per cent DCF), and therefore a large (and possibly prohibitive) contribution from the promoters would be required. Officials therefore warned that if British Rail were unable to invest adequately for commercial reasons, it might rule out a link with through rail services, or indeed any scheme which depended on through rail traffic for part of its financing.[60]

Ridley's consultation process produced other concerns. Patrick Jenkin, the Environment Secretary, and Lord Gowrie, Chancellor of the Duchy of Lancaster, both questioned whether too many constraints were being imposed. Gowrie told Ridley that 'the more conditions we lay down at the start, the less ambitious and therefore potentially less worthwhile the proposals . . . will be'. He also feared that the key objective was being lost amidst the fixation with frontier controls, adding that if there was not free movement at either end of the Link, 'I seriously question whether the whole enterprise is worthwhile'.[61] The existence of a rather negative frame of mind was also observed by John Wybrew, the Policy Unit's representative on the joint working group. In a briefing note for the Prime Minister, he appealed to Thatcher's positive enthusiasm for the Link, noting that it offered more than merely the prospect of cheaper, more efficient Channel crossings: it could 'symbolise a new-found confidence and spirit of enterprise within Europe'. Unfortunately, he argued, there was a more negative attitude in Whitehall,

> which sees more pitfalls than opportunities – hence, as it were, the need for a man to walk in front of a train waving a red flag. The loss of our insularity is seen as threatening. Rabid dogs and terrorist attacks on the Link are given as much weight as the benefits to millions of users and British trade. This frame of mind worries about the demise of the ferries and the consequent threat to economic and military security (not apparently shared by the MoD). It fears the abuse of monopoly power and anti-competitive behaviour, and contemplates tariff regulation and the

> possible need for special taxes or levies. It expects the promoter to take all the technical and commercial risks, but feels uncomfortable about allowing him the possibility, if successful, of high reward.[62]

Wybrew also contrasted this negativity with the more positive attitude within the French team. They were now 'embracing the positive spirit of the Thatcherite private enterprise formula for construction and operation of the Link, with more inspiration and enthusiasm than the British'. All this was evidence that within government circles in 1985 there was a growing determination to be bolder in entrepreneurial responses, to arrest the 'decline' of Britain's 'entrepreneurial spirit', which some writers were suggesting had affected our economic performance since 1945.[63]

The meeting of E(A) Committee on 25 February was the first occasion on which the Channel Fixed Link had been discussed by a Cabinet committee since the unhappy experience in May 1982. This time there was a much more positive approach. Thatcher, in her summing up, welcomed the project and noted that it should be subjected to the minimum of regulation. In particular, 'there should be no question of imposing price control or other interference with free competition'. Matters such as security, the future of the ferries, duty-free and animal (rabies etc.) and plant controls, were left for future consideration.[64] The Committee agreed all of Ridley's recommendations save one. It felt that Eurobridge, which with its engineering and navigational problems looked an unlikely candidate, should not be ruled out of the competition.[65] On 27 February the final details of the guidelines to promoters were agreed by the joint working group and were delivered to the British and French Transport Ministers on the following day, the appointed deadline.[66] A remaining issue was the length of time that promoters should be given to submit their proposals. Tunnel supporters favoured a short period, while Ridley's own inclination was for something longer to ensure that EuroRoute was not disadvantaged. Initially, he had proposed a deadline of 31 December, but accepted the alternative of 31 October after receiving an assurance that EuroRoute would be happy with this.[67]

Ridley and his Parliamentary Under Secretary, David Mitchell, met Quilès and Auroux in London on 20 March. Lyall and Rudeau made a formal submission of the guidelines and the Ministers agreed to publish the document as soon as drafting amendments and printing allowed. As to the closing date for proposals, Quilès and Auroux were anxious to reach a final decision by the end of the year. The looming French elections were a major concern. These were likely to be held in March 1986, and all the indications were that Mitterand and the socialists would lose. In these circumstances, and with a suggested maximum of 100 days for government decision-making, a deadline of 31 October seemed too late.[68] However, the British successfully argued against these points. The 31 October date stood, but the 'Governments would make their best endeavours' to reach a decision by the end of the year. Attention was given to a range of additional items. There were a few irritations. The French again pressed for some reference to be made to the possibility of EC finance, specifically for inland infrastructure, and asked for a further redrafting to 'avoid the impression that unnecessary – and potentially ridiculous – prominence was being given to the need to exclude rodents'. Ridley, for his part, took the opportunity to 'tweak the French tail' by suggesting that the time had come to end quota restrictions on bilateral road haulage, which appeared incongruous given traffic expectations for the Link. But the overwhelming tone was positive. It was agreed that officials should begin work immediately on a Treaty, the further consideration of defence and security issues, border controls and duty-free facilities. The meeting concluded with Ministerial appreciation of the 'effective and successful' work of the civil servants.[69] This was more than mere *politesse*. On this occasion the passage of Anglo-French negotiations had not resulted in the familiar delays and backsliding. The progress made in little more than four months was, by Tunnel standards, positively rapid and there was certainly a sense of achievement within Whitehall.[70]

All this was conveyed to the Commons by Ridley on 2 April, the day on which the guidelines, entitled *Invitation to Promoters*, were published. The French did likewise via a simultaneous press conference in Paris. Ridley's statement made reference to the process of invitation, and sought to reassure the House that there would be 'adequate public consultation' and that 'environmental, social and employment impacts' would be fully assessed. He concluded: 'the private sector now has a unique opportunity.... I wish the promoters well in this great endeavour'.[71] Replying for Labour, Gwyneth Dunwoody welcomed the prospect of substantial infrastructure investment, but raised several issues, embracing safety, the environment, employment in the Dover area and support for British Rail investment. She also asked for a full opportunity to debate such matters. Some old hobby-horses reappeared. David Howell and Nicholas Winterton wanted the Government to first specify the type of Link it wanted. A number of MPs complained that the project would largely benefit the South-east, while those representing Kent, notably Michael Howard (Folkestone and Hythe), were worried about the impact on the county and the need for adequate consultation. Among the sceptics Jonathan Aitken felt that the *Invitation to Promoters* sounded 'suspiciously like a prospectus for a latter-day South Sea Bubble'.[72] Ridley had been worried about the tricky matter of consultation. His own view was that a 'full-blown public inquiry' would kill the project by discouraging promoters.[73] While not without its risks, the policy of relying on the debating of a hybrid Bill, together with informal local consultations, the approach adopted in the 1970s, was endorsed by Ridley's colleagues. Nevertheless, the short debate on the statement indicated that this method of consultation would not be without its traps and bunkers.[74]

3. The competition, April–December 1985

The *Invitation to Promoters* asked promoters to bid for the right to construct and operate a Fixed Link under a concession granted by the two governments, the length of which would be dependent on the type and financial profile of the successful scheme. The document laid down three basic conditions: responses had to be technically feasible, financially viable and accompanied by an Environmental Impact Analysis (EIA), undertaken in anticipation of an EC Directive adopted in June (85/337). The Governments made it clear that there would be no financial guarantees but pledged a political guarantee against termination, other than for reasons of national security and defence. They then listed the several legal, security, maritime, environmental and organisational requirements.[75] However, it was made clear that commercial policy and tariff levels would be not be subject to government interference. Similarly, inland rail infrastructure, to be provided by British Rail and SNCF, was to be on a strictly commercial basis. The organisational form was not specified, but the guidelines gave a strong steer towards a joint venture with one company incorporated in the UK, the other in France. In addition, independent project managers were to be appointed during the construction stage by each concessionaire. It was stated that preference would be given to promoters willing to invest their own funds, and bidders were also required to put up a refundable deposit of 300,000 ECUs (£176,000) with each Government, the intention being to deter 'mischievous or frivolous proposals'. Proposals were to be received by 31 October and remain valid for 100 days. The Governments would endeavour to reach a decision within three months.[76]

Cartoon 6 Margaret Thatcher and Nicholas Ridley encounter opposition to the Tunnel: Garland, *Daily Telegraph*, 11 December 1985 [Centre for the Study of Cartoons and Caricature].

The task of responding to the guidelines posed a huge challenge for promoters. As Henderson put it, this was 'an exam-paper of almost Chinese dimensions'.[77] For one thing, when the document was issued the respective groups were still far from being in a position to mount full, credible and compliant bids. There thus followed a hectic six-month period of intrigue and jockeying for position, in addition to technical work, as the various parties put their packages together. Evidently the initial manoeuvring took longer than expected, but by the summer both the CTG and EuroRoute had managed to reconstitute themselves as substantial Anglo-French consortia.[78] These groups also continued their lobbying activities. The CTG benefited by having installed Henderson as its Chairman in February 1985. With its leader's impeccable connections, it could no longer be dismissed as a mere group of contractors, and Henderson was able to secure an audience with both Thatcher and Quilès. At his meeting with Thatcher on 13 May, he asked whether the Prime Minister had not made up her mind in favour of EuroRoute, and she was anxious to assure him that she had no firm preference.[79] Indeed, British officials had apparently been so assiduous in maintaining an 'all options open' approach that, as Lyall observed, the French 'must be wondering whether the Prime Minister has changed her mind about her preferred scheme'.[80] In fact, and to some astonishment on the British side, the French were now warming to EuroRoute. As Pierre-Alain Mayer, a member of the joint working group, was keen to point out, the emerging French presence in the development of this project, the prospect of significant job creation, and concerns about the political power of SNCF, which might dominate a rail tunnel, were factors in this volte-face.[81] Meanwhile, Eurobridge, led by the engineer-industrialist Lord Layton, which as we have seen was lucky still to be in the contest, continued to adopt a low profile and made little headway. In contrast, the Dover Harbour Board repeated its activity of 1981–2, and Jonathan Sloggett, its Managing Director, ran a vigorous 'do nothing' campaign in association with shipping interests under the banner 'Flexilink'.[82]

At the same time there was plenty to occupy the minds of British and French officials: the preparatory work on the Treaty and concession; clarification of the guidelines and refinement of the outstanding issues; and the form that the assessment of the bids would take.[83] To advance the work a Channel Fixed Link Division, led by Dr Christopher Woodman, was reconstituted, then strengthened with the return of some old hands, such as Ian Jordan, Brian Webber and Ted Glover.[84] Negotiation of the draft Treaty was undertaken by a separately constituted and FCO-led Anglo-French working party.[85] By the end of October, good progress had been made and with only one point unresolved, that relating to commercial policy, Ridley was able to reassert that the Treaty would indeed be ready in February 1986, if required.[86] Signature of the Treaty was a key element in the extremely tight legislative timetable. So too, of course, was the necessary legislation, on the British side a hybrid Bill. Here, steps were taken to ensure that work was commenced in sufficient time.[87] Officials drafting the Treaty were able to make use of the 1973 precedent, and likewise work on the concession was able to draw on the experience of Agreement No.2 (above, pp. 116–18, 128–32), together with the Agreement for the eight-mile Fréjus road tunnel between France and Italy.[88] Since the final form of the concession would be largely dependent on negotiations with the eventual winner, developments at this stage were necessarily limited. As for the assessment exercise itself, it was agreed that it would be led by a 'jury' of officials which would test the submitted projects against the requirements of the *Invitation* document. However, it was recognised that the role of the jury was to be purely advisory, and would not pre-empt the decision of Ministers.[89] Specialist expertise would be provided by external consultants, and in August the British Government announced the appointment of its advisers on finance, engineering, project management, hydrology, environmental impact and assessment co-ordination.[90] The familiar disjunction between French and British administrative responses – the British able to respond flexibly at the Whitehall level, the French more attuned to regional and consultative processes – was again evident. British officials were able to advance the assessment process to their own satisfaction, and their appointment of consultants was decided unilaterally.[91] But in general terms both governments used the short time at their disposal well. While the promoters were finalising their bids, civil servants prepared the critical groundwork for assessing the competition, and made good progress in resolving the outstanding issues involved in the joint diplomatic and legislative processes. Lyall's successor was also chosen. In October John Noulton returned to Fixed Link duties as joint head of the DTp's International Transport Directorate. Until Lyall retired in January 1986, they split the work between them. Lyall retained responsibility for the assessment exercise and the briefing of Ministers, while Noulton handled the work on the Treaty, the concession agreement, preparation of the hybrid Bill, and public consultation. One highly effective civil servant succeeded another.[92]

On 31 October 1985 the promoters duly submitted their formal bids to the respective ministries. The British Department of Transport received 9 proposals, but 5 were immediately ruled out as non-compliant, leaving the 3 established projects of CTG, EuroRoute and Eurobridge, together with a late entrant, James Blair Sherwood's Channel Expressway (Table 9.2). The latter had been developed in some secrecy, and did not come to the attention of the Department until late September.[93] When Ridley briefed Thatcher on the assessment exercise, he conceded that the sheer size of the four serious submissions, together with the substantial differences between them, meant that the task would be difficult. Nevertheless, he aimed to produce a report by mid-December.[94] The promoters had clearly made some progress over the past six months. When the guidelines had been issued, the CTG comprised only five British construction companies. By the time its bid was submitted, the active involvement of Henderson, together with that of Jean Renault of Spie Batignolles and Jean-Paul Parayre of Dumez, had produced support from the five leading French construction companies, together with the backing of all the five banks involved in the May 1984 report. After dealing with the tricky matter of getting Francis Bouygues on board (he preferred a bridge), CTG's partnership with the French was announced in July. The French element of the consortium, calling itself France-Manche (FM), was an

Table 9.2 Competing bids for the Channel Fixed Link concession, October 1985

		Promoter (UK)	*Promoter (France)*	*Link specification*	*Capital cost (£bn)*
1	Channel Expressway	*British Ferries* [Sea Containers] added later:	 Crédit du Nord (Nov. 1985) SCREG (Dec. 1985)	Twin 11.3-metre bored drive-through tunnels for combined road and rail traffic	2.1
2	Channel Tunnel Group/ France-Manche	*CTG*	*France-Manche*	Twin 7.3-metre bored rail tunnel for rail and shuttle traffic	2.5
		Construction companies Balfour Beatty Costain Tarmac Taylor Woodrow Geo. Wimpey	 Bouygues Dumez Spie Batignolles Société Auxiliare d'Entreprises Société Générale d'Entreprises		
		Banks Midland National Westminster	 Banque Nationale de Paris Crédit Lyonnais Banque Indosuez		
		Associates Granada Mobil Oil			
3	Eurobridge Studies Group	*ESG*	*Europont*	Multispan suspension 12-lane road bridge; optional rail link	5.9
		Named associates Arbuthnot Latham Bank, BCCI, IBM, ICI Fibres Sir John Laing Group Brown & Root (UK)			

4	EuroRoute	*EuroRoute UK*	*EuroRoute France*	Combined road bridge/ immersed tube, with separate tube rail tunnel	5.2
					3.7*
		Concession companies			
		Assoc. British Ports	Alsthom		
		Barclays Bank	Banque Paribas		
		British Steel Corp.	Compagnie Générale d'Electricité		
		British Telecom	GTM-Entrepose		
		Kleinwort Benson	Société Générale		
		Trafalgar House	Usinor		
		Construction companies			
		EuroRoute Construction	*Scoltram*		
		British Shipbuilders	Alsthom		
		British Steel Corp.	GTM-Entrepose		
		GEC	Usinor (CFEM)		
		John Howard			
		Trafalgar House			

Source: DTp, Submission documentation, 1985.

Note

* Capital cost without a separate tube rail tunnel.

impressive partner for the British side.[95] At the same time the EuroRoute project had also strengthened its industrial and financial support in the two countries, with the addition of CGE, Usinor, Associated British Ports, British Telecom and Barclays Bank.[96] Eurobridge, on the other hand, had made less headway. While it was able to produce superficially impressive lists of potential backers, such as Arbuthnot Latham, ICI Fibres and John Laing, officials could find precious little evidence of any genuine financial commitment. The unexpected proposition came from Channel Expressway. Sherwood, an entrepreneurial American, was President and CEO of the Bermuda-based Sea Containers, which had purchased Sealink, British Rail's cross-channel ferries, in July 1984. He used his British subsidiary to promote a twin 11.3 metre tunnel scheme for combined drive-through road and rail traffic. The idea of a large diameter tunnel was not entirely new (cf. the short-lived Pilon scheme of 1984, pp. 244–5).[97] But the Expressway bid came as something of a surprise to everyone, not least the other shipping interests, since Sherwood had been an opponent of the Fixed Link and strong supporter of Flexilink. His proposal was not fully developed on submission, and because he admitted that there might be no case for a Channel Tunnel, it was suspected of a being a decoy bid or delaying tactic. Nevertheless, it was to prove a major complication in the decision-making process.[98]

The Fixed Link was the most important item of business at the Anglo-French summit held in London on 18 November. Eager to have the matter resolved before the March 1986 elections, the Elysée wanted the announcement of the decision and signature of the Treaty to occur on the same day. For British officials, this was 'unrealistic'; an alternative, proposing that the Treaty be signed two or three weeks after the announcement, was felt to be 'only a little less impossible'.[99] Nevertheless, it was agreed that Thatcher and Mitterand would make the announcement in France in January and then sign the Treaty in the following month. This decision was immediately made public.[100] The quid pro quo was to be a relaxation by the French of lorry quotas, an awkward question that had already been the subject of tough negotiations at both ministerial and official level. Under the UK/France bilateral road haulage agreement, mutual quotas were placed on the number of return trips by accompanied vehicles. If such an agreement remained in place when the Fixed Link opened, it would act as a significant restriction on trade. Consequently, the British Government pressed for a complete liberalisation. During discussions in the summer the French had raised a 'smokescreen of objections', and attempted to bring other elements into the equation, notably the demand that Britain accept heavier, 40-tonne lorries and allow high-speed TGV trains to run through to London. Nevertheless, they subsequently agreed to raise the quotas by a substantial 17 per cent.[101] At the summit, a confidential undertaking was signed which ensured that although bilateral quotas would be retained pending Community-wide liberalisation, they would be regularly set at levels which imposed no quantitative limitations on Anglo-French traffic. Transit traffic would be unrestricted.[102] At the same time, confidential undertakings were made in relation to road and rail infrastructures.

The United Kingdom promised, in somewhat vague terms, to improve the road network in the South-east, and both Governments declared themselves to be in favour of a high-speed rail link between Paris and London. If the choice of scheme permitted it, the two railway authorities would be encouraged to develop a special fleet of new trains to operate between the two capitals.[103]

In the same month the Commons Select Committee on Transport decided to undertake a further examination of the Fixed Link, adding to its substantial contribution of 1981. This was necessarily a hurried affair. The Committee wished to reach a view in order to assist the Secretary of State with his decision, and report before the subject was debated in the House on 9 December. Taking evidence from the four promoters and Flexilink on 13–14 November, the report was agreed on 2 December and published three days later.[104] The process was not without its difficulties, however. The Committee was fiercely divided, and some members saw 'no economic or special necessity for such a link'. As to the competing schemes, there was agreement that the main contenders were CTG and EuroRoute, but no clear majority in favour of one or the other. Thus, the Committee's principal recommendation, in favour of CTG's rail tunnel scheme, was only carried after an alternative resolution, supporting EuroRoute, was defeated on the casting vote of the Chairman, Gordon Bagier.[105] Concerns about the Fixed Link among the broader constituency of MPs were also evident during a six-hour adjournment debate on 9 December. As we have seen, Ridley was anxious to avoid the complications of a public inquiry. He had allowed the decision to emerge by default after his press conference on 31 October, but made his position clear in introducing the debate. The Transport Select Committee had reached a similar conclusion.[106] However, many MPs pressed for adequate consultation procedures, including a public inquiry, among them Robert Hughes, John Silkin, Gwyneth Dunwoody and Jonathan Aitken.[107] And supporters of the Link, who were in the majority, fully realised the importance of portraying the project in a more positive light, notably when they encountered trenchant opposition in the debate. Aitken, for example, attacked the Government's '100 days of secret political decision-making' as pure Alice in Wonderland: 'Sentence first – verdict afterwards'; and Sir David Price quoted Voltaire in opposing the project: 'Je n'en vois [pas] la nécessité'.[108] But after the clamour the Government won the day, by 277 votes to 181. Once again, the marked contrast between British and French procedures was evident. A British public inquiry was necessarily a lengthy affair, and with an equally time-consuming hybrid Bill would have made it difficult to progress the project within the life of the existing parliament. In contrast, the French, whose regional interests were far more integrated into the planning and assessment processes, would be able to obtain the necessary 'declaration d'utilité publique', a process which provided for a public inquiry, in a relatively short period of time.[109]

On 7 November, a week after the bids had been submitted, Ridley had a brief discussion with Thatcher on his first impressions of the proposals. Guided in large measure by his civil servants, the Transport Secretary pointed out that the Eurobridge project was likely to be ruled out on technical grounds, and there were a number of important objections to EuroRoute, notably its vulnerability to terrorist attack, and the absence of a rail link. The two bored tunnel schemes were therefore the most promising. Although a late entrant, Sherwood's Channel Expressway [CE], with its drive-through road and rail combination, offered some important advantages over CTG-FM, and Ridley hoped to resist any attempts by the French to knock it out of contention. At this stage, he offered a balanced appraisal. While clearly attracted to a drive-through element, he also noted that a rail link would offer 'enormous possibilities'.[110] The assessment process itself was undertaken by parallel teams of British and French officials and overseen by a joint co-ordinating group. The time allowed was limited: barely six weeks.[111] Indeed, Thatcher had raised the issue with Ridley, asking whether it might not attract criticism, but she was assured that a proper assessment could be made.[112] When the results of the initial British sifting were discussed at a meeting of officials on the following day, it was concluded that further work on Eurobridge should cease, since the submission was found to be 'almost totally deficient' on all the main criteria. CTG's bid presented no serious difficulties, but the rail elements of both the EuroRoute and CE schemes required further clarification.[113] When the British and French plenary group met on 12 and 19 November there was unanimity about the treatment of Eurobridge, though it was agreed that the decision should remain confidential. But, as Ridley had foreseen, the French also wanted to eliminate CE.[114] While Sherwood's uncompromising manner plainly grated on the equally uncompromising leader of the French team, Rudeau, the scheme's lack of French partners was politically unacceptable to Mitterand, and there were also strong and defensible objections to the scheme as it stood. Its unorthodox proposal for trains to share the road carriageways was ruled out on safety grounds, a point supported by the railway inspectorates in both countries. Furthermore, the French, mindful of the difficulties they had encountered in attempting trial borings in 1974–5 (see above, p. 174) were sceptical about the cost and feasibility of boring large diameter tunnels in chalk.[115] With Rudeau inclined to treat the promoters' guidelines as 'tablets of stone', the British had to work hard to keep CE in play.[116] In order to defuse concerns about the rail element, David Bray quickly offered to add a conventional bored rail tunnel, either single- or twin-bore, an option that he claimed was 'fully developed' and 'on the shelf'.[117] But this did not appear to be true, thus reinforcing French demands that the project be ruled inadmissible. And antagonism towards the latecomer was scarcely diminished by CE's delay in making copies of its new plan available to the French.[118] Fortuitously for Sherwood, EuroRoute, which was thought to be the favoured scheme in Paris, also changed its rail proposals. The October submission had provided for a railway carried in a submerged tube, but the British and French assessment teams rejected the idea, again on the grounds of safety, and they were also unhappy with the plan to open this part of the scheme two years after the road bridge had been completed. Faced with this opposition, EuroRoute, like CE, quickly changed tack. They offered instead a twin-bore rail tunnel, to be constructed in stages, and also claimed that this variant was a developed option.[119]

The assessment teams were disconcerted by these manoeuvres. Time was short, but the goalposts seemed to be constantly moving. Ideally, a longer period of assessment was required to take account of the new rail proposals, but the decision-making timetable imposed by Thatcher and Mitterand, subsequently tied to a meeting in Lille on 20 January, was immutable.[120] It was now becoming clear that the modified plans could not be fully appraised in the time available.[121] The position would have been eased had it been possible to evaluate CE and EuroRoute as drive-through road schemes only. However, these promoters wished to hedge their bets by incorporating a railway, and, in any case, British officials were convinced that for all the French denials, a rail element was a non-negotiable issue in Paris.[122] A related stumbling block was the difficulty which the promoters had in agreeing financial terms with British Rail and SNCF for through traffic. These negotiations had not been completed by the time the final assessment report was completed, but by 5 December Ridley had been informed by his officials that since the Government had instructed British Rail to adopt a tough stance the promoters were unlikely to receive the rail revenue which they were seeking. A further complication was the nature of the concession agreement. Under the guidelines promoters could specify the length of the concession period, but they had also gone further than this, for example in suggesting that the Governments make an undertaking that a second Fixed Link would not be built during the concession period. This would not have mattered had it not been for the fact that both CTG and EuroRoute had obtained financial support on the basis of these assumed terms.[123]

While the assessment was being undertaken in November and December 1985, the promoters continued to lobby and intrigue. Channel Expressway attempted to address its lack of French representation by bringing on board the bank Crédit du Nord, together with Société Chimique Routière et d'Entreprise Générale [SCREG], the largest road construction firm in France. These moves were not entirely convincing. Crédit du Nord was a subsidiary of Banque Paribas, which was supporting EuroRoute. It also emerged that Bouygues, a member of CTG-FM, had acquired a 9 per cent shareholding in SCREG, with an option to take a further 17 per cent, and was thus in a position to take effective control.[124] Undaunted, Sherwood made further efforts to raise his standing by promising that French companies would be guaranteed a significant share of the construction work. He promised them 70 per cent.[125] Unsurprisingly, the Board of CTG was annoyed by reports that major modifications had been made to the bids of their rivals after the apparent deadline. The *Invitation to Promoters* had stated that 'in the case of variants, each variant must be spelt out in full', and in September CTG had been assured that new proposals could not be made.[126] Lyall was able to mollify Henderson, but there were fears that a charge of maladministration might result if the CTG bid proved unsuccessful.[127] Henderson was also perturbed by reports that the British Government fully expected any successful bidder to associate with Sherwood. Lyall quickly dismissed this as 'ridiculous'. However, there was some substance in the rumour, since it was not long before Wybrew from the Number Ten Policy

Unit suggested to Thatcher that she should exploit the synergies between the constructor-driven CTG and the operator-driven Expressway and invite Ridley to encourage a merger between the two. Thatcher refused to intervene, although she had no objection to Wybrew feeding his ideas to the Department.[128] EuroRoute also complained about the manner in which the assessment was being carried out, describing it as 'fragmented and confusing'. Amidst growing tension it went further, breaking ranks by attacking its competitors rather than justifying its own scheme.[129] In the circumstances, it was imperative to handle the adversaries with due process. The plenary group thus held formal meetings with all four promoters in London on 11 December. These were intended to clarify aspects of their bids, warn each promoter of the areas which were deemed unsatisfactory, and, above all, to ensure that, once selected, the winner could not subsequently reject the Governments' conditions.[130]

At a two-day plenary session in Paris on 18 and 19 December the text of the assessment document was agreed. Whereas earlier Anglo-French reports on the Fixed Link, in 1963, 1966 and 1982, had reached firm recommendations, this one was more neutral. The 87-page main report (together with a 16-page summary) recorded the British and French positions, both agreed and disagreed. A substantial body of secondary annexes set out the work undertaken by the national teams, which was not generally exchanged between the two countries. These dealt with no fewer than seventeen separate areas, ranging from finance and insurance and traffic and revenue to frontier controls, hydrology and the marine environment.[131] However, for all the hard work of the officials on both sides, the documentation, a masterpiece of equivocation, was not considered an adequate basis for a decision by British ministers. Thus, a separate note was produced, together with a report from the Government's financial advisers, Schroder Wagg. Just before Christmas Ridley circulated the main report and officials' note to Thatcher and her senior Cabinet colleagues, promising that he would consider the issues and prepare a memorandum for a meeting of E(A) Committee in early January.[132] Ministers now had to decide which project, if any, to select. Assuming that they would elect to take their responsibilities seriously, it promised to be a distracting Christmas.[133]

4. Selection of a promoter, December 1985–January 1986

The report of the assessment group set out the strengths and weaknesses of the four competing bids. Unsurprisingly, given its longer gestation period, the submission of CTG-FM was considered to be the most technically comprehensive. EuroRoute's provided less detail and Channel Expressway's was 'considerably less well worked up'.[134] The negative aspects of Eurobridge were so clearly evident that both countries were able to dismiss the project. However, consensus was much harder to reach over the other schemes, particularly in the critical areas of costs and revenues. The assessors felt that the promoters had underestimated the former and overestimated the latter, but there was disagreement about the extent to which this had occurred, and thus the report presented alternative sets of

Table 9.3 Comparison of promoters' capital cost and revenue estimates, December 1985

Promoter	*Capital costs (£bn 1985 prices)*		*Revenue (£m 1985 prices)*					
			1993		*2003*		*2013*	
CTG-FM	2.55		385		438		483	
British assessment	2.7	+5%	335	−13%	420	−4%	520	+8%
French assessment	2.6	—	282	−27%	391	−11%	494	+2%
EuroRoute	4.61–5.11[a]		437		608		800	
British assessment	5.3–5.9	+15%	367	−16%	439	−28%	550	−31%
French assessment	4.8–5.4	+5%	363	−17%	498	−18%	628	−21%
Channel Expressway	2.87[b]		474		640		778	
British assessment	3.9	+35%	367	−23%	439	−31%	533	−31%
French assessment	5.0	+75%	329	−31%	453	−29%	521	−33%
Eurobridge	5.9		—		—		—	

Source: 'Assessment Report on Proposals for a Channel Fixed Link', Detailed Report, December 1985, pp. II/6, III/23 (capital cost %s were rounded). British revenue assessment assumes TGV trains running from 1993; French assessment assumes TGV trains from 1998.

Notes

a Road and rail (1 or 2 tunnels).

b Separate road and rail tunnels.

data (see Table 9.3). On capital costs, the estimate provided by CTG-FM was broadly accepted. But British assessors thought that EuroRoute's costs would be 15 per cent higher, and those of CE 35 per cent higher. The French were also sceptical about CE and raised its costs by 75 per cent, a reflection of their opposition to the scheme. On expected revenue, most of the promoters' estimates were considered to be optimistic to a greater or lesser degree, and again the views of the British and French assessment teams differed (Table 9.3). Over the long run, i.e. to 2013, the projections of CTG-FM exhibited the greatest convergence with the assessors' figures. The estimates of EuroRoute appeared increasingly unrealistic, particularly against the British assessment, while both teams reduced CE's forecasts by a third. Such assumptions were critical to the assessment of financial viability. Under pessimistic scenarios, the assessment teams agreed that none of the schemes was financeable. With costs and revenues closest to those of the assessors CTG-FM was the most credible of the three options. CE looked attractive, but only if the promoter's own data were accepted. The British team felt that the fragility of Sherwood's cost and revenue projections should not be regarded as necessarily fatal to the prospects for financing, but the French remained profoundly unconvinced. In contrast, it was the British who thought that EuroRoute was scarcely viable, while the French appeared more sanguine about its alleged shortcomings.[135] These manoeuvres, which bore some resemblance to Anglo-French arguments about the choice of promoter in 1967–8 (pp. 60–70), ensured that the joint report could be no more than a cautious balancing of complex issues, and the equivocation was repeated across the full range of the assessment. And yet, concealed behind the careful wording was the essence of the debate. On virtually all criteria, the CTG-FM scheme appeared to be ahead of its rivals, though it was not sufficiently in front to be the clear choice. Nor was it possible to put up a single challenger, since the two countries were fundamentally divided about the relative merits of the two drive-through options.

Introducing British Ministers to the contents of the joint report, officials sharpened up the debate. They observed that CTG was the most 'thoroughly developed' project with the 'fewest risks'. But doubts about the assumed traffic and revenue levels meant that the financing of even this project could not be assured. Although EuroRoute met the apparent public preference for a drive-through link, it did not appear to be financeable, 'even on the promoters' own figures'. The scheme envisaged an advanced construction technology and presented major safety and environmental problems. CE's costs were clearly too low, and once account was taken of its inflated revenue forecasts it also appeared to be unfinanceable. There were additional concerns about this scheme. First, Sherwood's commitment to the rapid completion of the link was at least questionable, given his ferry interests. Second, the project remained politically unacceptable in France.[136] Officials also made reference to the work of the Government's financial advisers, Schroder Wagg. The merchant bankers were suitably cautious, contending that the significant uncertainties about costs and revenues meant that none of the proposals possessed the 'credibility required for us to be confident that private sector financing will materialise'.[137] Schroders, who earlier had argued that more time was needed to evaluate the schemes, recommended that before making a final decision the uncertainties surrounding the CTG-FM and CE projects should be narrowed down. This would provide scope for the resolution of differences between the assessors and the promoters and increase the chances of choosing the option most likely to succeed. It would also allow time to explore the possible advantages of a merger between the two promoters, thereby combining the scheme which was 'potentially more innovative and appealing' [CE] with one that 'brings considerable contracting experience and greater credibility to financial markets' [CTG-FM]. Such an alliance could well 'maximise the chances of a CFL being successfully financed'.[138]

Whatever the merits of Schroders' recommendation, the political timetable simply did not allow for any delay. Even assuming that there was a clear consensus on the choice of scheme, things were tight. Ridley was due to meet Auroux, the Minister of Housing and Transport, on 7 January 1986, and on the following day the Cabinet's E(A) Committee were to consider the issue, with a full Cabinet debate earmarked for the 16th.[139] But on 23 December officials were told that Ridley had made up his mind. He wanted a drive-through link and, given EuroRoute's unsuitability, had come down firmly in favour of Channel Expressway.[140] In the circumstances the Secretary of State wished to consult colleagues about his negotiating stance before seeing Auroux, and an additional meeting of E(A) Committee was hastily arranged for 3 January. Committee officials thus had the task of getting as many senior ministers as possible to attend at short notice: 'the second eleven will not do'.[141]

Ridley's memorandum for E(A) Committee, while considered by one of his officials to be 'brave and oversimplified', did have the virtue of cutting through the mass of detail in order to present firm conclusions.[142] The Secretary of State repeated his view that the joint report did not represent an ideal basis for a decision. Nevertheless, 'delay would be fatal', he argued, and ministers had to 'work with what we have got'. Quickly eliminating both Eurobridge and EuroRoute, Ridley confined the choice to the two bored tunnel schemes. Looking at a range of what he called 'minor matters', including the environment, railway operation, local employment, driver appeal, security and safety, had proved inconclusive. But when finance was examined, on the promoters' own figures CE was the 'best bet'. CTG had come out ahead on the assessors' data, but the significance of this was summarily dismissed: 'there is no magic in the assessors' figures; they are just as likely to be wrong as the promoter'. Unable to choose these figures with confidence, Ridley changed tack. He was adamant that road vehicles should be able to drive through and argued that this feature would be good for competition in the cross-channel market. Raising an old hare, viz. the power of the trade unions to interrupt rail and shuttle services, the Minister noted that CE was 'effectively immune to industrial action'. The scheme was also more flexible and able to cater for any level of demand. Ridley conceded that CTG was 'undoubtedly the least risky scheme, as well as the cheapest', but felt that this was insufficient to counter the putative advantages of its rival: 'For all these reasons I would recommend Channel Expressway as the scheme most likely to appeal, and therefore to be financeable'. As for the 'French dimension', the Minister was hawkish. He was aware that the French preferred EuroRoute, but French opposition to CE did not provide a sound reason for 'choosing second best'. Furthermore, the anxiety in Paris for an early decision gave the British a strong bargaining position. Ridley therefore proposed to make a 'strong stand' in favour of CE when he met Auroux. His fall-back position was the Schroders' recommendation to keep both schemes in play, while exploring the collaborative possibilities. He did not propose to tell the French this, because 'we want to heighten their fears of having no deal to begin with, in order to maximize our negotiating hand'.[143]

Ridley's memorandum was circulated on a strictly limited basis, and with only two working days before the meeting there was little opportunity for departments to prepare briefs for their ministers.[144] If there was a common theme in the hastily concocted documentation, then it was that the Transport Secretary's stance was cavalier and heavy-handed. Treasury, Foreign Office and Cabinet Office staff all questioned his easy rejection of the assessors' figures. There was also unease about the way in which the EuroRoute scheme had been dropped, while CE's serious costing and ventilation problems had been ignored. The threat to CTG from the railway unions was exaggerated, since the shuttles were to be operated by the tunnel company's own employees, probably under a no-strike agreement.[145] Then there were the political considerations. Once again, the FCO found itself seeking to protect wider Anglo-French relations from the potential fall-out of actions on the Channel Fixed Link. There was dismay that Ridley was proposing 'a confrontational approach to what has always been a joint co-operative venture', while French objections to CE were considered to be more solidly grounded than he had suggested. In any case, the negotiating position was not as strong as the Transport Secretary was claiming. The French believed the Link to be 'more in our interest than theirs', and Mitterand could gain as much electorally from being seen to reject an 'Anglo-American Trojan horse' as from an announcement that the project was going ahead.[146]

If Ridley's strategy had been largely rejected, what did the ministerial briefings suggest as an alternative? In general, CTG was favoured. At the Treasury, the overriding objective was to avoid any financial guarantees and ensure that the Government clearly disassociated itself from the promoters' commercial assumptions. The most acceptable outcome would be no scheme at all, but beyond this officials sought to block EuroRoute and to facilitate acceptance of CTG as the least risky and economically most beneficial option.[147] The FCO wished to prevent Ridley from proposing CE to the French and to avoid postponing a decision. This left CTG as the only real option. Geoffrey Howe's response was a characteristic one. As his Private Secretary put it, 'the whole file simply adds to... [his] sense of foreboding and disbelief about the whole project'. If driven to a choice he would opt for CTG, but only because it was 'the least badly prepared. In the Secretary of State's words, some choice!'[148] However, there was no support for this view in the Policy Unit. Wybrew considered the CTG scheme to be backward-looking, a 'safe, uninspiring plodder' measuring up 'neither to the inspirational aims of statesmen nor the desire of the consumers . . . for a drive-through option'. He noted the irony in the situation. Both sides probably had a strong preference for a road scheme and he observed, with some prescience, that 'it would be a pity if Nicholas Ridley's dogmatic advocacy of Expressway forces both sides to compromise on CTG as the lowest common denominator'. Like the FCO Wybrew saw little point in confrontation, and suggested that the meeting with Auroux be used to test French reactions to a collaboration between the two promoters aimed at producing a drive-through plan.[149] The Cabinet Office's briefing for Thatcher was also important. It noted that the 'weight of evidence at present available favours the CTG option'. However, if ministers were not yet ready to make a choice, they could gain more time. The proposed announcement on 20 January might merely state that two schemes had met the guidelines, and it was the Governments' intention to proceed with bored tunnels, but that a final decision would be made after further analysis. Of course, there was 'no certainty that a few extra weeks or months will make the decision any easier or wiser'. What was important was that the E(A) Committee had to provide Ridley with firm instructions for his meeting with Auroux.[150]

Not for the first time, the recommendations of a Transport Secretary concerning the Fixed Link were given an awkward ride at a Cabinet committee. The debate followed the well-worn path. Ministers agreed that a drive-through scheme would be more attractive to the public, but there were serious environmental disadvantages with EuroRoute, while CE posed ventilation problems and there were considerable risks in boring such large tunnels through the limited chalk stratum. They therefore accepted that CTG was 'by far the best developed and the most likely to be financeable'. Further study of the schemes was constrained by the need for a decision before the imminent French elections. Summing up the discussion, Thatcher said that the CE's drive-through idea should not be eliminated at this stage. But Ridley should tell Auroux that the British Government favoured the CTG's proposal. He was also asked to sound the French out on the ploy that the 20 January announcement should merely confirm the intention to go ahead with a tunnel.[151]

Ridley considered that his consultation with colleagues had been 'rather inconclusive', and he therefore expected his meeting with Auroux in Paris on 7 January to be exploratory.[152] And so it proved. Ridley stuck to his guns, and the polarisation of views continued. Ridley produced arguments in favour of CE, but Auroux challenged these and expressed a preference for EuroRoute. When Ridley insisted that CE be retained, Auroux argued with equal force that EuroRoute be treated in the same way. There was agreement that CTG had no intrinsic weaknesses. Ridley reported that if the British Government had to make a choice now, they would go for CTG, but would do so 'with some regret'. Ridley's reference to the tactic of seeking further time and letting the financial markets decide was met by French insistence that a clear choice should be made by 20 January. With neither Minister giving ground, the three options remained on the table, and a further meeting would be necessary.[153] When Ridley spoke to E(A) Committee on the following day, he reported that French ministers had not yet discussed the report, and their position, as well as that of Mitterand, remained open. He suggested that he should now explore the possibility of a collaboration between CTG and CE on a road and rail tunnel, beginning with construction of the rail element. But the Committee saw problems in reconciling 'the economically irresponsible with the politically attractive'.[154] Ahead of the meeting Thatcher was advised that there was a 'strong case for biting the bullet now and going for the CTG proposal'; and Howe was also briefed to encourage a clear decision in favour of CTG.[155] Nevertheless, Ridley was able to keep his hopes of a drive-through scheme alive. With ministers apparently attracted by the idea of a four-tunnel road and rail link, he was asked to look immediately at the possibility of the promoters joining forces. With negotiations at a very delicate stage, and news that the Committee's earlier deliberations had been accurately reported in the press, the Prime Minister concluded with a stern warning that there should be no further leaks.[156]

There was more than a degree of ambivalence about the prospects of merger. Although both Schroders and the No. 10 Policy Unit had expressed support for the idea, the British assessors had concluded that it would bring little advantage to either CE or CTG. And Lyall, in briefing Mitchell, had questioned whether it should be the Government's role to 'arrange shotgun marriages between possibly unwilling partners'.[157] But even if a coalition could be facilitated, it might delay the legislative timetable, in addition to weakening the Governments' hand in negotiating the concession agreement.[158] Ridley himself commented that he did not see how a CE-CTG merger could be made to work, although he was happy to leave it as a fall-back position.[159] Nevertheless, these qualms, which had been conveyed to the E(A) Committee on 3 January, did not prevent the Transport Secretary from engaging in a hectic series of meetings – two with Henderson and one each with Broackes and Sherwood – on 8–10 January. The outcome was disappointing in that there appeared to be little or no prospect of any realignment in the groups. Indeed, the exercise merely served to stir up existing antagonisms, driven in part by the many rumours then in circulation. It was claimed, for example, that the French arm of EuroRoute was about to defect to Channel Expressway, along with two backers of France-Manche, Crédit Agricole and Bouygues.[160] The promoters also made further moves to make their schemes more palatable. Sherwood attempted to forestall technical concerns by offering various options for the boring of a pilot tunnel on the French side.[161] And, more significantly, CTG-FM promised to consider the inclusion of a drive-through facility at a later date, though this undertaking was heavily qualified: market conditions, technical factors and financing would have to allow it.[162]

On 12 January Ridley had a brief discussion with Thatcher. He told her that none of the groups was prepared to amalgamate. The French were blocking Channel Expressway and the British were refusing to accept EuroRoute, with the result that agreement could only be reached on CTG. Personally, he felt that 'this would be a rather disappointing result'. While it would be possible to go on insisting on the CE project to 'see if the French would crack before 20 January', this would produce a serious diplomatic row. It was likely, he concluded, that there would now be a 'clear cut perception on both sides that the CTG proposals would succeed'.[163] In fact, when Ridley met Auroux in London the next day the British Minister continued to carry the torch for Channel Expressway. The meeting lasted for some four hours. Auroux, now speaking with the formal approval of Mitterand, emphasised that CE remained unacceptable to the French and pointed out that the President, who was evidently 'attached to grand projects', favoured EuroRoute. Again the discussions proved inconclusive, although there was a more positive response to Ridley's suggestion that the CTG-FM scheme might be more acceptable if the promoters gave undertakings about adding a road tunnel.[164]

Ridley set out the latest developments in a note for the full Cabinet meeting on 16 January. Once more he was inclined to pursue a radical course. After reviewing the outcome of his talks with the promoters and the French, he offered his colleagues two options:

> 'a) To accept CTG, after obtaining from them the best possible undertakings we can about the later provision of drive-through capacity'; or
> 'b) To insist on CE, or on putting the choice between CE and CTG to the financial markets to decide'.

He admitted that option (a) was widely recognised to be 'the lowest common denominator'. The Government would be criticised for not choosing the drive-through link which public opinion appeared to favour, and would also face accusations that it had caved in to the French to help the Socialist Party's electoral ambitions. Option (b) would inevitably mean the postponement of an announcement on 20 January but would win plaudits for not rushing 'into what the public generally regard as the wrong decision'. Of course, with (b) there was the danger that no agreement would be reached, and thus the possibility that no Link would be built 'within our timescale'. Pinning his hopes on what he admitted was a 'risky course', he recommended that the Government should insist on Channel Expressway: 'I judge that the French would ultimately find a way either of accepting CE, or at least agreeing a market test'.[165]

Once again Whitehall failed to support Ridley's position. FCO officials briefed Howe to press for a decision firmly in favour of CTG.[166] A similar line was taken at the Treasury, which produced a note rehearsing the financial, technical and economic case against CE.[167] The advice given to the Prime Minister all pointed in the direction of CTG. David Norgrove, one of her private secretaries, expressed worries that Ridley was carrying his insistence on CE to damaging lengths. Wybrew now concluded that given the implacable French opposition to CE, CTG was the 'only tenable basis for a firm decision', and that this could be presented as the initial phase of a more ambitious scheme with a drive-through element.[168] Robert Armstrong, the Cabinet Secretary, also recommended CTG, adding the telling remark that 'it would be very difficult for the Government to defend and sustain a decision in favour of CE on the basis of the Assessment'.[169] Furthermore, on 15 January he had held a secret meeting with a personal emissary from the Elysée. The meeting with Louis Schweitzer, Fabius's Directeur de Cabinet, confirmed Mitterand's preference for EuroRoute and, above all, the strong French antipathy for CE. Armstrong asked Schweitzer whether, if CE was ruled out on the French side and EuroRoute on the British, the President would be prepared to consider CTG. Schweitzer replied that CTG was Fabius's personal preference, and he thought that Mitterand might be persuaded to choose CTG if it were presented positively, and the possibility of a drive-through link at some time in the future was kept alive.[170]

A decision was finally made at the Cabinet meeting on 16 January. Ridley set aside the recommendation in his memorandum and shifted ground. He told his colleagues that on transport grounds he still preferred CE, but now accepted that it was unrealistic to insist on the scheme in the light of French opposition. But he did not recommend CTG. Instead he returned to his fall-back position, suggesting that the announcement on 20 January should state that the two Governments intended to proceed with a bored tunnel, and that the financial markets would be allowed to decide between the two schemes. This would relieve the pressure on the Government for a decision, keep open the drive-through option, and go some way to meet public concern that the French were rushing the British into a decision. In the ensuing debate, it was argued that there would be difficulties in asking the financial markets to determine the scheme, not least that it would signal indecisiveness. There were still 'fundamental uncertainties' about CE's proposal: its costs, ventilation and tunnelling problems, and 'the strain of a 30-mile drive through the tunnel'.[171] Of the two schemes, CE's 'was the most likely to involve future Governments in public guarantees of expenditure', while CTG's, 'by operating trains which did not stop in the tunnel, was potentially the safest'. Thatcher, summing up, said that the Cabinet should decide whether to accept the proposal from CTG now or postpone a decision. Taking account of the timetable commitments, the satisfactory nature of the CTG bid and the likelihood of its acceptance by the French, the Cabinet agreed 'that the Channel Tunnel Group-France Manche should be chosen to construct the Channel Fixed Link'. Ridley was asked to continue his negotiations with the French, to secure the best possible terms for British Rail's involvement, and with CTG, to secure the minimum possible period of exclusivity for the Concession Agreement, and the firmest possible commitment to the future development of a drive-through facility. The decision was to be presented 'in as positive a light as possible', emphasising its 'historic nature'. The way was now clear for an announcement by Mitterand and Thatcher.[172]

When the two leaders met in Lille on 20 January the atmosphere was 'relaxed and warm throughout'.[173] Mitterand stated that he was 'perfectly content' about the choice of CTG-FM, persuaded by Thatcher's comment that the promoters had offered to submit proposals for an additional drive-through link by the year 2000. The Prime Minister pointed out that this project 'was the most fully worked out on every score'. Mitterand accepted that 'the commonsense view had prevailed even though he had pangs of nostalgia for Euro-route on aesthetic grounds'. Thatcher conceded that she had 'seen attractions in Euro-route at an earlier stage, but it was clear that the technical, security and environmental problems of it were substantial'. The President was 'very confident' about the Link's profitability, and wondered whether it might not be best to set a deadline for work on a drive-through element. Thatcher was more cautious. She agreed that the Link would lead to a rapid increase in traffic, but as to a drive-through option preferred not to be 'categoric at this stage', reminding Mitterand that Britain had also to consider the position of the ferries, which remained strategically important for troop reinforcement.[174] Their announcement to proceed, made at the Hotel de Ville, was in fact a hastily scribbled note on the back of the British briefing index (Figure 9.1). Mitterand then announced that France-Manche/CTG had been chosen. The agreed joint communiqué emphasised the winning project's technical feasibility, safety and attractiveness to users, and environmental acceptability. Construction was expected to begin in 1987 and to be completed in 1993. Reference was also made to the promoters' undertaking to submit a drive-through proposal by 2000.[175] Later on the same day Ridley addressed the Commons. 'The Channel tunnel', he said, was 'a massive and difficult project. It will be a challenge to our engineers, our technicians and our financial institutions. Equally, I believe that it will be of great benefit to travellers and exporters alike in giving them cheaper, quicker and more reliable access to the continent of Europe'.[176]

5. Treaty and concession

The successful promoter, CTG-FM, was naturally delighted to win the concession. Henderson accepted that 'an immense amount of hard work' was still required to meet the parliamentary timetable, complete the detailed design work and raise the finance. Nevertheless, he was confident that all the deadlines would be met and a tunnel would be operating by the spring of 1993.[177] British press reactions were fairly tepid after several days of intense speculation. The *Times* noted that 'the historic day' had 'proved an anticlimax for the British', and would 'be seen as another defeat for Mrs Thatcher at the hands of the unbending French'. The *Financial Times* noted that the two governments had 'played it safe'. It expected the choice to cause some disappointment in those who had wanted a road link. It was reported that the losing groups were aiming to fight back, and Sherwood had said 'we thought it was an open, fair bid, but found it was a closed shop'.[178] In fact, Sherwood went on the offensive in an attempt to subvert the decision. In a press release he lamented this 'sad day for the motorist' and went on to argue that the concession agreement as drafted contained so many uncommercial clauses as to deter equity investors and bank lenders. He attacked the French for not dealing fairly with Channel Expressway's submission, and claimed to have assurances that after the French elections a centre-right government would resort to blocking tactics to prevent the necessary legislation from being passed. Further complaints

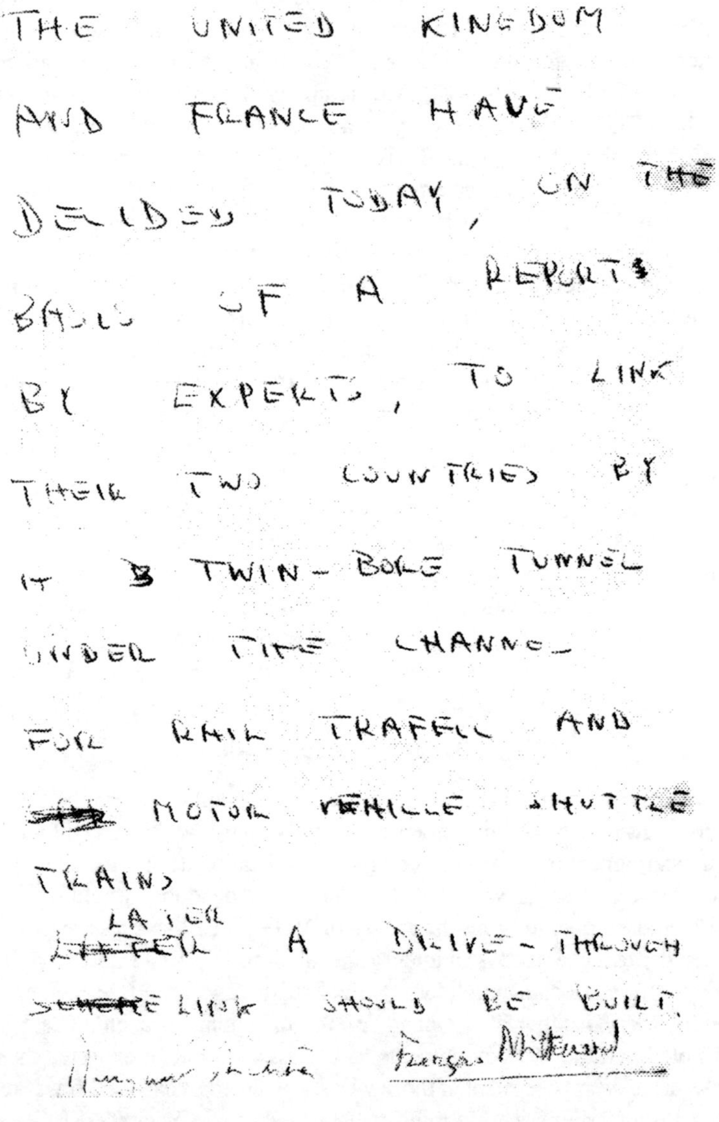

THE UNITED KINGDOM
AND FRANCE HAVE
DECIDED TODAY, ON THE
BASIS OF A REPORT
BY EXPERTS, TO LINK
THEIR TWO COUNTRIES BY
A TWIN-BORE TUNNEL
UNDER THE CHANNEL
FOR RAIL TRAFFIC AND
MOTOR VEHICLE SHUTTLE
TRAINS
LATER A DRIVE-THROUGH
LINK SHOULD BE BUILT.

Figure 9.1 Thatcher and Mitterand's signed announcement to proceed with a Channel Tunnel, 20 January 1986.

were made in a letter to Ridley, notably the suggestion that it was 'grossly unfair' that CTG appeared to have been given 'the option to build the Channel Expressway tunnels at some future date'.[179] Of course, as Lyall observed, it was doubtful whether Sherwood could claim any 'patented' right to a large diameter drive-through tunnel, especially as the Pilon scheme predated his project. But by the time that Ridley and Sherwood met, at the end of January, it was clear that the

American entrepreneur was now devoting his energies to saving his ferry business. He promised to mobilise public opinion against the CTG scheme and do all he could to obstruct the passage of the enabling bill.[180] Others were more forbearing. For all the earlier complaints about the assessment process, the British side of EuroRoute chose to go quietly, and Broackes gave Ridley an assurance that his group would not be seeking to 'create embarrassment'.[181] However, EuroRoute France made some threatening noises about suing the Governments. Its Chairman, Jacques Mayoux, argued that the reasons for rejecting the scheme could have been foreseen at the time that the guidelines were issued and, consequently, it had been misled into incurring expenditure which was always going to be abortive. But no lawsuit materialised and instead the French promoters put their efforts into preparing a new scheme combining elements of the EuroRoute and CE designs.[182] Last but not least, Ian MacGregor refused to let the demise of EuroRoute pass unrecorded. Fresh from his triumphs in defeating Arthur Scargill and the National Union of Mineworkers in the 1984–5 strike, he wrote to the *Times*, sending Ridley a copy. Claiming that he presided 'over more tunnelling work than any man alive', he warned: 'Experience makes me allergic to bored tunnels and their one certainty – that is their total unpredictability in safety, time and cost'.[183]

Ridley had told the Commons on 20 January that a White Paper would be issued as soon as possible, and little more than a week later, he arranged with John Biffen, Leader of the House, that the document should be debated before the Treaty was signed. With the latter scheduled for 12 February, there was little room for manoeuvre. The two ministers reserved 10 February for a debate and agreed that the White Paper should be published on the 4th. Fortunately, officials had already produced several versions of a draft text, and the timetable was kept.[184] The White Paper, entitled *The Channel Fixed Link*, was deliberately designed as a forward-looking document. It focussed upon the successful CTG-FM scheme, and its initial plans to raise capital. There were also sections dealing with the associated plans for through rail services and road infrastructure improvement in Britain; and the 'next steps' to be taken before construction could begin, viz. the Treaty, Concession Agreement, hybrid Bill and consultation with local authorities and other bodies. The material dealing with the assessment process was confined to two short annexes. One thing was made perfectly clear. The Government, in choosing one of the four projects, was anxious to state that the process did not imply endorsement of the prospectus of the successful promoter. And where finance and traffic were discussed, the promoters' data, and not the Government's own estimates, were used.[185] The Commons debate went relatively smoothly. Ridley indulged in some 'Opposition-bashing', and a Labour Party amendment calling, *inter alia*, for a public inquiry was comfortably defeated. The White Paper was then approved by 268 votes to 107.[186]

The next step was to sign the Treaty. As we have seen, work on this document had started in the previous summer and it proved to be a relatively straightforward task to finalise the text.[187] The choice of a venue for the signing ceremony gave officials more headaches, however. Lancaster House was first proposed, but the

Prime Minister preferred a venue outside London, and clearly somewhere in Kent had to be found, since she wished to provide assurances that the Government was alive to local anxieties about the project. Dover and Folkestone were ruled out because there were fears of large and hostile demonstrations. There were also practical considerations. A large and impressive hall was required as a backdrop, as were luncheon, meeting and press rooms. Two possibilities emerged: Leeds Castle; and the Chapter House of Canterbury Cathedral. Thatcher agreed that Canterbury was an imaginative choice.[188] On 12 February she welcomed Mitterand at RAF Manston, before a 30-minute drive to Canterbury. As in 1973, for reasons of protocol the Treaty was signed by the two Foreign Ministers, respectively Geoffrey Howe and Roland Dumas. However, to give the media the picture they most wanted, the two leaders were asked to sign the cathedral's visitors' book. Their luncheon menu of chilled melon and fillet of Scotch beef was graced by a Chaucer quotation:

> Destiny, paramount minister
> That in this world executes everywhere
> God's predetermined providence, is so strong
> Things thought impossible by everyone,
> Things which you'd swear could never ever be,
> Shall yet be brought to pass, though on a day
> That happens once a thousand years or so.

And unsurprisingly the speeches made much of the 'historic occasion' and the 'important milestone'. Thatcher referred to Napoleon and Churchill, Mitterand to the Entente Cordiale.[189] However, the event was marred by expressions of dissent, not least from the Mayor of Canterbury,[190] and eggs were thrown at the official cars, though local press reports were more supportive. The national press reaction in both countries was rather low-key. In Britain the preoccupation was with the Sikorsky rescue package for Westland Helicopters, an affair which raised doubts about the effectiveness of both public sector-private sector relations and European co-operation.[191]

The Treaty was modelled on that signed in 1973. In its 20 articles, it set out the basis for the Governments' commitment to the project. Article 1 declared that the link would be 'financed without recourse to government funds or to government guarantees of a financial or commercial nature'. Article 3 fixed the frontier between Britain and France in accordance with the continental shelf agreement of June 1982, and in Articles 4 and 5 reference was made to arrangements dealing with police, immigration, animal and plant health controls, and with defence and security matters. Articles 9–11 erected the machinery to safeguard the Governments' interest in financial, environmental and safety issues, and specifically the fiscal and customs regime, and the establishment of an Intergovernmental Commission and Safety Authority. Further articles ensured the freedom of the British and French concessionaires to determine commercial policy (Article 12);

defined the concessionaires' obligations, notably to deal with the Governments through a single executive (Article 13); made provision for compensation in the event of a political interruption or termination (Articles 15 and 16); set out the Governments' rights on termination of the concession (Article 17); and provided for the establishment of an arbitration tribunal to settle disputes (Article 19). As in 1973, government liabilities were to be shared on a 50–50 basis, and ratification of the Treaty waited upon the necessary legislation.[192]

With the Treaty determined, the Concession Agreement had now to be finalised. In fact, British and French officials had already devoted considerable time to the preparation of a text which was used in discussions with the four bidders in early January.[193] However, after exploratory talks with the winning group, CTG-FM, it was clear that the concession document was still very much a draft and moreover, one that was likely to change as a result of tough negotiations.[194] While the general provisions concerning the construction, financing and operation of the Tunnel had been accepted, and indeed were set out in the British Government's White Paper,[195] it was the precise detail that caused difficulty. After a first round of substantive talks, completed shortly after signature of the Treaty, Noulton drew the attention of Ridley and Mitchell to a number of areas in dispute. Three were considered important enough to warrant consultation with members of E(A) Committee: the length of the concession; the proposed financial structure; and the restoration of sites in the event of abandonment. CTG-FM had asked for a 60-year concession, starting from the ratification of the Treaty. Officials began by offering 50 years, though Noulton suggested that the additional years might be conceded in return for a relaxation of the promoters' demands elsewhere. The draft concession also specified minimum ratios of equity to debt and of contractors' equity to total equity. The first requirement was intended to prevent an over-reliance on bank debt, the second to bind the contractors to the success of the project. But CTG-FM regarded these demands as an 'unwarranted interference in their business', and Noulton suggested that they might be dropped. Finally, there was a requirement that on termination of the concession the concessionaire should remove structures, restore the land and make the tunnels safe. This was to apply even if the work had been completed, and CTG-FM argued that such wide powers were unreasonable. Officials offered to consider a more limited obligation.[196] Ridley accepted this negotiating position and put it to his colleagues. He also raised the issue of taxation. CTG and FM wished to be taxed only in their own countries, like shipping and the airlines, but the British Treasury had been disinclined to concede the so-called 'shipping article'. Ridley hoped that the Treasury would agree to concede this as part of the 'emerging negotiating package'.[197] The reaction of Ministers was generally encouraging.[198] John MacGregor, the Treasury Chief Secretary, was prepared to concede the 'shipping article', despite the estimated loss of £100 million to the British Exchequer. However, he asked that in return 'we should get satisfaction on the other outstanding issues'. In particular, he did not see that CTG-FM should have the right to compensation in respect of supplementary works required for safety, security or environmental reasons, nor was he prepared to provide a guarantee against discriminatory tax laws, or to change the basis of calculating compensation in the event of a political abandonment.[199]

Auroux was anxious to sign the concession agreement by 7 March, well ahead of the French elections on the 16th, and there was an element of brinkmanship in the final round of talks.[200] The now familiar quadripartite negotiations continued to throw up a range of issues, and differences were evident in the position of the two governments. At the final meetings held at the offices of the British lawyers Allen & Overy on 4–5 March, agreement was reached on most of the essential questions.[201] But British and French officials were unable to resolve three sticking points: exclusivity and the second link; the length of the concession itself; and the procedure for awarding construction contracts. The terms of all three had been agreed in principle before the announcement in Lille, but the French now sought modifications. On the first the French wanted to alter the arrangement whereby CTG-FM would enjoy a monopoly of the link until 2020, together with the right of 'first refusal' on a second link between 2000 and 2005. They preferred a shorter period of exclusivity, i.e. until 2010, and questioned the necessity for 'first refusal', a view which gained a measure of support from Paul Channon, the Trade and Industry Secretary.[202] As to the duration of the concession, the French favoured a period shorter than 60 years, while they also wanted to add a clause requiring the major construction contracts to be confirmed only after the Treaty had been ratified and the concession had taken effect. A further complication was the inability of CTG-FM and British Rail/SNCF to conclude satisfactory Heads of Agreement outlining the negotiating principles of a 'usage contract' for the railways' use of the Tunnel. Here, there was greater unanimity between London and Paris that the Concession Agreement could not be signed before the railway deal was settled.[203]

As with the exercise to choose a promoter, Ridley was in favour of adopting a firm stance with the French on the outstanding elements. If they remained intransigent he proposed to ask the Prime Minister to intervene directly.[204] In fact, this became necessary. On Sunday 9 March, Henderson told Ridley that CTG had been unable to reach an agreement with the railways because the French railways were continuing to press for lower tolls. The following day, Ridley asked Auroux to lean on SNCF.[205] There was also little progress with the other sticking points and on 13 March the Cabinet was informed that there was a real possibility that the timetable would not be met. Thatcher undertook to send a message to Mitterrand asking France to adhere to the arrangements agreed earlier and to proceed to signature of the Concession.[206] The move unlocked the door and the points at issue were settled the following day, although the exclusivity clause was negotiated up to the very last moment.[207] On the same day the Heads of Agreement between CTG-FM and the two railways were concluded. The Treasury also eased the overall bargaining process by agreeing to concede the 'shipping article' under a package of taxation issues to be incorporated into a subsequent Treaty protocol. At 6.30 p.m. on 14 March, the Concession Agreement was eventually signed by Auroux – in the final hours of the French socialist administration. Ridley signed the document in London.[208]

The Concession was a dense and complex legal document. In its 41 clauses and 4 annexes, it embraced 6 areas: purpose; construction; operation; common provisions; termination and disputes and laws. The Link would comprise a twin bored rail tunnel between the Pas-de-Calais and Cheriton. It would be undertaken at the concessionaires' risk, 'without recourse to government funds or to government guarantees of a financial or commercial nature' (Clause 2). The Concession was to remain in force for 55 years after the Treaty ratification, which was expected in the summer of 1987 (Clause 3). Before commencing construction the concessionaires were required to satisfy the Intergovernmental Commission that they had raised the necessary funds (Clause 5). Clause 6 provided for the appointment of 'one or more independent project managers'. Preliminary studies and preparatory works would be carried out within three years of the agreement coming into force, breakthrough of the service tunnel within seven years, and the construction completed within ten years (Clause 10). The Intergovernmental Commission was to monitor any proposed modifications to the design of the Link, the construction work itself, and in particular to establish whether the construction cost was compatible with the funds available. It was also given the duty of inspecting the completed facility (Clauses 7, 9, 11). Clause 12 gave the Concessionaires the freedom to determine tariffs and commercial policy. Clauses 31 and 32 dealt with lenders' security, which was extended to give lenders the right to substitute themselves for the Concessionaires under defined circumstances, including the establishment of a new concession. Rights were also asserted in the event of the two countries electing to take over and continue the project. Clause 34 gave the Concessionaires exclusive rights to a fixed link until 2020, with first refusal on a second, drive-through link until 2010.[209]

6. Conclusion

The eighteen months from October 1984 to March 1986 were significant ones for the Channel Tunnel project. A private sector promoter had been selected, a second treaty signed, and a concession agreement thrashed out. For all the assessment analysis, the choice of a promoter amounted in the end to a political decision taken by Ministers. The subsequent White Paper gave six reasons for choosing CTG. It offered the best prospect of attracting finance; carried the fewest technical risks; was the safest project from the travellers' viewpoint; presented no problems for maritime traffic; was least vulnerable to sabotage and terrorism; and had a containable environmental impact.[210] However, here some ex post facto rationalisation was at work. In the heady days of January 1986 the decision itself was a matter of horse-trading between the countries, taken amidst considerable inter-promoter intrigue. Many nursed the feeling that a compromise had been struck, and in both countries there was some disappointment that a drive-through link had not been endorsed, something which many British polls revealed the public wanted.[211] But it was also conceded that CTG-FM was proposing to undertake Europe's largest and most complex infrastructure project. In reality it was no less exciting or challenging than the other plans, and was certainly, as most observers recognised, the least risky and most financeable option.[212] Nor should the entrepreneurialism of the banks in the mid-1980s be forgotten. The Midland, for example, conceded that there were risks associated with this massive and complex project, but while some executives retained reservations about it, others were excited about the prospects of a return of 25–36 per cent on their lending.[213]

Progress had been made in a relatively rapid manner, in contrast with the longueurs of earlier periods. The factors responsible for this heightened sense of urgency included the exigencies of the electoral timetable, and the fact that since this was firmly a private sector project it was not burdened by the evaluation processes of the British Treasury, which accompanied public sector schemes. Last but not least, the determination of individuals made things happen. The successful revival of the project owed much to the intervention of enthusiastic, or at least purposeful, politicians, most of whom left the stage shortly after the Concession Agreement had been signed. Thatcher and Mitterand were very different political animals, but appeared to enjoy a peculiar chemistry. Their motives in supporting the Fixed Link were very different, however. For Mitterand it was a way of cementing his place in French history by connecting Britain to continental Europe. Thatcher, on the other hand, wished to endorse a facility which would symbolise a European Community espousing free trade and open markets, while acting as a practical demonstration of the efficacy of the private sector approach.[214] Here she would have been able to point to numerous optimistic signs: a marked revival of confidence in the City, with the stock market at a high; the successful privatisation of corporations such as British Telecom; and the placing of a contract for a road and rail tunnel in Hong Kong. There were even plans for a privately-funded road from London to Oslo. Once this would have been laughed out of court; now it was soberly reported in the *Financial Times*.[215] Of course, the two leaders owed a great deal to their respective Transport Ministers, Ridley and Auroux. Both were hands-on politicians. Ridley began as a pronounced sceptic but was won over to the idea, and once enthused, became like Peyton a committed figure, and was frequently involved in the detailed drafting of the critical documentation.[216] Elsewhere, there were equally committed people: within Whitehall Andrew Lyall, in the CTG Nicholas Henderson. All four left the project in 1986. In March Auroux lost office, Lyall retired, and Henderson was succeeded by Lord Pennock, a director of Morgan Grenfell and former director of ICI, BICC and Plessey. In May Ridley moved to Environment. These changes of personnel were not insignificant in that it was left to others to ensure that the optimism and co-operative spirit of 1986 did not become the disappointment of 1987, as had happened in 1974–5. Much was still to be done before a Tunnel was actually operational, not least the raising of capital by the promoters, and in Britain all the consultative processes connected with the passage of a hybrid Bill.

10

EUROTUNNEL

Finance and construction, 1986–90

1. The Channel Tunnel Bill, 1986–7

The French parliamentary elections of March 1986 produced the expected victory for the moderate right, and the neo-Gaullist Jacques Chirac became Prime Minister for a second time. However, his victory was not an overwhelming one, and with Mitterand having two years of his presidential term still to run, a period of somewhat uneasy 'cohabitation' or power-sharing ensued between right and left. Chirac, a fiercely ambitious politician who had stood unsuccessfully against Mitterand in the presidential elections of 1981, had had an uncomfortable experience of the Channel Tunnel. He had been Prime Minister when it was abandoned in 1975.[1] But his re-emergence did nothing to challenge the project. Indeed, when Foreign Ministers met on 14 April Jean-Bernard Raimond made it clear that the new French Government had the same intentions as the previous administration. Chirac repeated this sentiment when he met Thatcher at Chequers on the 26th, assuring her that the project enjoyed his 'unqualified support'.[2] The French proceeded to secure the legislation necessary for ratification of the Treaty, which was approved by the Senate in June 1987, together with a Déclaration d'Utilité Publique, obtained in May.[3]

For the British the legislative challenge was more urgent, since it was expected that the Conservatives would go to the country in 1987, probably in May or June. It was therefore highly desirable to pass the enabling legislation before the end of the parliament, to prevent the danger of it being lost in the wake of a general election, a possibility which might jeopardise the financing process.[4] The Channel Tunnel Bill was duly introduced in the Commons on 17 April.[5] This hybrid Bill, which provided the necessary powers for the compulsory purchase of land, and for construction and regulation of the link, including a London rail terminal at Waterloo and upgrading of the A20 road, was intended to receive royal assent within a year. However, the path was not entirely smooth for this rarely-used type of legislation. The Bill was deposited after the time limit for such measures, and therefore required special dispensation from the Standing Orders Committee in order to proceed.[6] In addition, the Department of Transport had circulated a draft timetable for the Bill to local authorities in Kent before it had been disclosed to the Commons. This breach of etiquette, which bordered on contempt, was fully exploited by the inveterate tunnel opponent, Jonathan Aitken.[7] The Tunnel concessionaires, now called Eurotunnel, were naturally concerned by the prospect of a substantial delay. When the Committee met on 20 May it heard arguments for delaying the Bill until the following session from Aitken, the Dover Harbour Board and Sealink (UK). On voting, the Committee was divided equally 5–5, and the chairman, deputy speaker Harold Walker, had already made it known that he would decline to use his casting vote. In fact, his decision helped to resolve the matter. Referred to the Commons itself on 3 June, the Bill was allowed to proceed, the resolution being passed by a comfortable majority (283 votes to 87).[8]

Aside from these procedural hiccups, and a substantial amount of debate, much of it familiar in content and presented by familiar names, the Bill proceeded relatively unscathed through its subsequent stages. First, there was a second reading on 5 June, introduced by the new Transport Secretary, John Moore. The Bill was then referred to a Select Committee, with David Mitchell, the Junior Minister, conceding an extra fortnight for individuals to lodge petitions.[9] The examination by a nine-member Select Committee, led by Alex Fletcher (MP for Edinburgh Central), began on 19 June and concluded with a report on 18 November, a fortnight after a motion was secured allowing the Bill to be reintroduced in its existing state in the new parliamentary session.[10] Of course, a fair amount of local opposition was mobilised, encouraged by Dover Harbour Board and the shipping interests, led by British Ferries' redoubtable lobbyist, Maureen Tomison. Nor were the local authorities in a mood to be co-operative. For example, at one stage an exasperated John Noulton was moved to complain of Kent County Council's 'inexplicable, obstructive and petty attitude'.[11] But it was the sheer scale of the enquiry that prevented the Committee from completing its work before the end of the session, as Ridley had intended.[12] There were 4,845 petitions against the Bill, and the Committee sat publicly for 34 days, taking some 220 hours of evidence. In an unprecedented move, six days were spent in hearings outside the Palace of Westminster, in Kent itself.[13] Unsurprisingly, there was a tension between those who were impatient to see off time wasters and filibusterers, and those who argued that the petitioners were not receiving due attention from the Committee. In the circumstances, Fletcher performed remarkably well in holding the ring.[14] After all this consultative ventilation, the Committee was generally favourable, since its powers did not extend to questioning the fundamental purposes of the Bill. However, there were some ripples of dissent, notably over fire safety, access to the Cheriton terminal, choice of Waterloo as the London terminal, inclusion of the A20 road improvement, and the absence of a public inquiry, all raised by the rookie MP for Fulham, Nick Raynsford, who held a press conference to air his 'minority report'.[15] Most of the Committee's 70 suggested amendments dealt with relatively minor matters and were either proposed or agreed by the Government itself. The most notable modification was support for a 'no subsidy' clause, which was taken up after pressure from the ferry interests, Dover Harbour Board and the British Ports Association. This made it a statutory requirement that the Tunnel be financed without recourse to Government funds or guarantees.[16] There was also provision for a firmer planning control regime, and a limitation on the disposal of spoil at Shakespeare Cliff.[17]

The Bill proceeded to Standing Committee on 2 December, and to 3rd Reading on 3 February 1987.[18] Amid the clamour generated by Aitken, Raynsford *et al.*, there was only one substantive change at this stage. Following an intervention from Peter Snape, the Government gave an undertaking to introduce a new clause requiring the British Railways Board to publish a plan indicating how it would increase the railways' market-share via 'the dispersal of traffic within Great Britain'.[19] A further clause required Eurotunnel to carry bicycles and mopeds on shuttle trains.[20] On completing its Commons stages Mitchell noted that 'After the longest pregnancy in the world ... we are about to witness the birth of the greatest civil engineering project ever undertaken in Europe'.[21] The Lords stages, 2nd Reading, and Select Committee, generated little excitement.[22] Among the items raised by 1,457 petitions, safety issues continued to be pressed, but the attacks made by shipping interests faded somewhat after the *Herald of Free Enterprise* disaster on 6 March.[23] When the Lords Committee reported on 6 May the only significant adjustments to the Bill were: a strengthening of the 'no subsidy' provisions, including a new clause preventing British Rail's international services from receiving grants; a refinement of the 'Snape clause', requiring British Rail to submit an action plan for its international services by the end of 1989; and an agreed alternative scheme for access to the Cheriton Terminal, introduced after an intervention from the Local Government Minister, Michael Howard, MP for Folkestone.[24] Unfortunately, the Government was unable to complete the parliamentary process before a general election was called on 11 May. There was, of course, a possibility that a change of government would interrupt the passage of the Bill, and indeed opposition spokesmen had promised that they would establish a public inquiry.[25] However, despite all the inevitable criticisms that an eight-year term by one party inevitably attracted, the election had a very limited impact upon the project. Thatcher duly secured a third successive victory on 11 June, the first Prime Minister to do so since Lord Liverpool in the 1820s. And the Bill, reintroduced by the newly-appointed Transport Secretary, Paul Channon, on 26 June, obtained its royal assent on 23 July 1987.[26] Once again there was a procedural hiccup, this time concerning the revised access to Cheriton terminal. The refusal of Standing Orders Committee to give a dispensation to the Lords amendment enlivened the final Commons stages on 8 and 21 July, though in the end the Government comfortably held off its opponents.[27] Indeed, the efforts made by DTp to ensure a continuing dialogue between the Government, Eurotunnel, and the local authorities, and above all, the determined and diplomatic response of the junior minister, David Mitchell, ensured that the process, if a little lengthier than anticipated, was relatively smooth. The Treaty was then ratified, at a special ceremony in Paris, on 29 July and the Concession became operational from that date. At the same time, the Intergovernmental Commission, which had been established in shadow form, was officially inaugurated by Channon and the French Transport Minister, Jacques Douffiagues.[28]

2. Eurotunnel: finance and contracts, 1986–7

In large measure the parliamentary process and the endeavours to secure finance for the project went hand in hand. But while royal assent was necessary, it certainly was not a sufficient condition for the Tunnel to proceed, and if the passage of the Bill had its moments, these were nothing compared with the trials and tribulations of the promoters. Here, of course, neither the British nor the French Government had a direct involvement, and on the British side the public record indicates that, at the higher levels of the Thatcher administration, monitoring was confined to a series of ad hoc briefings. It was for the private sector to determine organisational and financing matters, though the promoters were expected to work within the parameters agreed with the two governments. The first step was insisted upon by the banks. This was to split CTG-FM into two components: Eurotunnel, an Anglo-French consortium acting as promoters, owner and concessionaire; and Transmanche-Link (TML), representing the contractors who were to design and build the Tunnel. The Eurotunnel trademark appeared in April 1986, and the concern began to operate as a presiding and unincorporated partnership, though it could have no formal existence until the first tranche of equity was raised. Below the partnership, later referred to as 'Group', were the two public companies which had acquired CTG and FM and had the task of raising the capital: Eurotunnel PLC and Eurotunnel SA (Figure 10.1). The two holding companies had common boards of directors, which in turn made up the joint board of the partnership. At this initial stage the British Co-chairman was Henderson's successor, Raymond (Lord) Pennock, although there was no French counterpart until September, when André Bénard, a former MD of Royal Dutch Shell and senior adviser of Lazard Frères, was appointed.[29] TML was an Anglo-French joint venture of the ten CTG-FM contracting companies, established in October 1985.

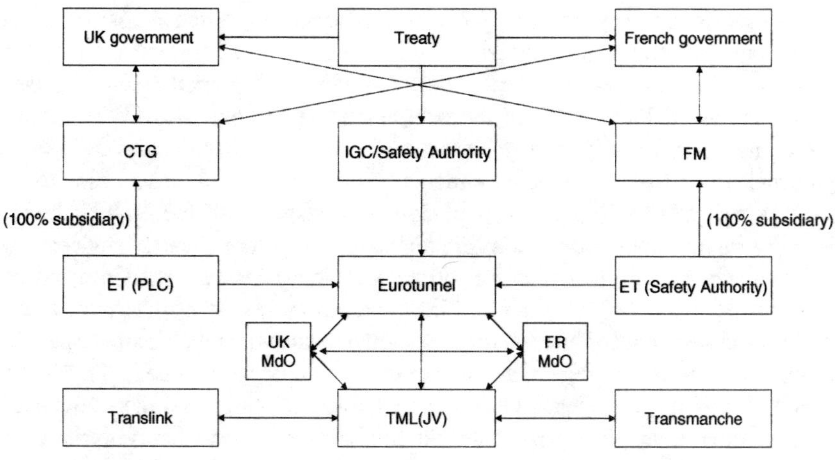

Figure 10.1 Channel Tunnel organisational chart.

Also divided into two parts, Translink Contractors and Transmanche Construction, it was led by John Reeve of Costain and Philippe Montagner of Bouygues, though the latter was quickly succeeded by François Jolivet of Spie Batignolles. Unfortunately, the reorganisation of the contractor-dominated CTG-FM left the new Eurotunnel organisations short of key staff, and for a time there was considerable instability within the respective organisations, just at the time when they faced their biggest challenge. In Britain a Bill had to be steered through Parliament, doubters in Kent and elsewhere had to be reassured and opponents disarmed. At the same time a challenging contract had to be negotiated, an agreement reached with the railways on usage, and unprecedented levels of finance raised.[30]

The negotiation of the construction contract took some months. Awarded to TML in May 1986, it was not signed until 13 August, after much horse-trading.[31] The 'technical banks', those institutions in the syndicate of underwriting banks which had undertaken to examine the contract, had been anxious that the contracting parties be tightly controlled. The advice they received from an American engineer, Howard Heydon, working for the consultants, Louis Berger, was scathing in its criticism of the draft contract. This apparently left much of the risk with Eurotunnel rather than TML. Some of the banks, notably Deutsche Bank and UBS, were unhappy that a fixed-price contract had been rejected in favour of a 'target-price' contract, commonly used in tunnelling projects, in which responsibility for overruns would be shared between the promoters and the contractor.[32] Under the contract TML was to design, build and commission the entire project in seven years, ready for the opening in May 1993. There were three elements: target cost works; lump sum works; and procurement items. The target cost works were the tunnels and underground structures, accounting for about half of the £2.6 billion contract cost. Here the contractor was to be reimbursed for actual costs incurred, plus a fixed fee of 12.36 per cent. If the costs exceeded the target, the contractor would meet 30 per cent of the excess, the total liability being limited to six per cent of the target cost. Lump sum works involved the terminal buildings and related infrastructure and other fixed plant. Any overruns would be met by the contractors. The main procurement items were the locomotives and shuttle trains. Eurotunnel would meet the costs of these and pay the contractor a fee of 11.5 per cent.[33] Eurotunnel then appointed independent project managers as the 'Maître d'Oeuvre' (MdO), in accordance with the requirements of the Concession: W.S. Atkins on the British side and SETEC on the French. Here, too, there was anxiety. The MdO had the task of monitoring the design, development and construction of the works, but the two firms appointed appeared to have only a limited degree of independence from the contractors. The strong suspicion that the contractors had established an over-dominant relationship with the concessionaires became firmly entrenched in banking circles in the course of 1986, and was an enduring element in the Channel Tunnel story.[34] Nevertheless, with these elements in place TML was now able to let contracts to suppliers, order the first Tunnel Boring Machines (TBMs), and begin preparatory work on site (see below).

The financing required was put at £5.5 billion, of which £1 billion would be raised as equity. There were to be three tranches. 'Equity 1' was to be provided by the founding shareholders, that is the ten construction firms and five banks, essentially a stock conversion of cash already provided. Under 'Equity 2' £200 million of share capital would be placed privately with financial institutions in Britain, France and elsewhere, timed to provide TML with the money to pay its initial bills. Finally there would be a public share offer of £750 million in 'Equity 3'. The capital was to take the form of Eurotunnel 'units', each giving one share in Eurotunnel PLC and in Eurotunnel SA, the intention being to ensure the indivisibility of the concern. In the meantime, Eurotunnel would sign informal loan arrangements with a syndicate of banks – 40 institutions had signed letters of intent by 28 May 1986 – though of course the loan capital could not be drawn down until the equity had been raised. When Noulton briefed Mitchell in May 1986, it was envisaged that Equity 1 would be raised in June 1986, with Equity 2 coming in the following month, together with agreement of the loan arrangements. Equity 3 would follow in mid-1987 following the ratification of the Treaty.[35] Parliamentary procedures (see above) played a part in the slippage of this timetable, but the problems were essentially financial. First of all Eurotunnel's preferred impact (underwriting) day for Equity 2, 17 July, met with opposition from the Bank of England, which wanted to make room for the intended sale of the Royal Ordnance Factories.[36] In the event this privatisation was postponed, but it soon became clear that financial institutions were not as enthusiastic about the Tunnel as had been expected. The project differed from the successful multi-billion privatisations of British Telecom and British Gas in its long gestation period and lack of tangible transferable assets, and with a flood of new issues imminent potential investors had made it clear that they required more information about it before agreeing to commit funds.[37] On top of this, Eurotunnel was in no position to make a placing given the delays caused by wrangling over the construction contract and disagreements over the loan arrangements.[38] On the day after the contract with TML was signed, it was announced that Equity 1 would be in place by 1 September, with £41 million taken up by the founder shareholders, together with a £9 million bank loan. This shareholder support, which was later raised to £47 million, cleared the way for Equity 2.[39]

The date for raising about £200 million under Equity 2 was now pushed into the autumn, and in the event the placing was not completed until 29 October 1986. While support was forthcoming from France and Japan, it had proved difficult to interest institutional investors in the City of London and in New York in such a risky issue. In particular, British pension fund managers were unsettled by the continuing opposition campaign mounted by Flexilink, and they were drawn to the more attractive possibilities of British Gas, which was privatised in December.[40] There was much speculation in the press, and it was evident that the placing had been badly handled by the company and its financial advisers: Morgan Grenfell, already under a cloud over the Guinness affair; and Robert Fleming, whose experience of major flotations was limited.[41] An attempt was made to draw the British Government into the affair. On 21 October Pennock informed Armstrong, the Cabinet Secretary, about his anxieties. He wanted the Prime Minister to be told about the situation, but Armstrong steered him towards the Bank of England instead. Two days later Pennock called on Armstrong. He reported that only £54 million of the British share of £75 million had been committed. The financial institutions did not feel that the estimated return – 17.7 per cent after tax and deferred until opening on a price of £12 plus 120FF per two-share unit – was generous enough. Pennock wanted to see Thatcher to elicit her support. He suggested that either the Prime Minister, or the Transport Secretary or the Governor of the Bank of England should 'get a few of the heads of institutions concerned together and "bang their heads together"'. Armstrong conferred with Sir Alan Bailey at the DTp and with David Walker at the Bank of England. Walker, who had been developing a more interventionist policy for the Bank in relation to corporate support operations,[42] used his influence to try to increase the British commitment but did not think it would be a good idea for either Thatcher or Moore to intervene, and Downing Street officials concurred.[43] Walker identified Trafalgar House and Hanson as possible supporters, and told Armstrong that it would be helpful if Lord Hanson were to get a signal of encouragement from Number Ten. Once again, Thatcher demurred, noting that to give such a signal would be 'quite improper'.[44] While the Government maintained its non-interventionist stance, the Bank of England's non-statutory activity produced results. With the help of the Governor, Robin Leigh-Pemberton, an arrangement was made to strengthen the Eurotunnel board by recruiting Sir Nigel Broackes of Trafalgar House, the former head of EuroRoute, and successful promoter of the third Dartford crossing. No finance was committed, but with the help of this last-minute confidence booster, the £206 million was raised. And despite their equivocation, British shareholders now owned 46 per cent of the shares, compared with 37 per cent held in France.[45] However, the mood was scarcely buoyant. As the *Economist* put it, 'If travellers prove half as reluctant to use it as institutional investors have been to invest in it, the Channel Tunnel is in deep trouble'.[46]

The overall perception in the City was that Eurotunnel was not performing well as a company, and matters were not helped by the relatively high turnover among senior managers. However, since the challenge was to convert a 'disparate group of banks and contractors into a smooth-running efficient transport company',[47] a relatively high turnover rate was inevitable, both at board level and lower down. At the top it was essential to dilute the contractor element on the Eurotunnel PLC, Eurotunnel SA and joint boards. Following the signature of the construction contract in August 1986, a raft of new people was introduced. In addition to the recruitment of Bénard as French Co-chairman, there were further moves to strengthen the joint board. On the British side there was an old hand from the 1970s Tunnel, Sir Alistair Frame, now Chairman of RTZ; the former CTG chairman, Sir Nicholas Henderson; Frank (subsequently Sir Frank) Gibb, Chairman and Chief Executive of Taylor Woodrow; and Denis Child, Deputy Chief Executive of NatWest. The French representatives comprised Jean-Paul Parayre of Dumez and Peugeot; Bernard Thiolon, Chief Executive of Crédit Lyonnais;

Patrick Ponsolle, Deputy Chief Executive of Suez; Jean Fontourcy, Deputy Chief Executive of Crédit Agricole; and Alexandre Dumont of Belgamanche. When Broackes was added after the placing of Equity 2, it could not be said that he was joining a lightweight team.[48] In addition, a new chief executive and deputy chief executive were appointed, with subsequent membership of the joint board. They replaced Colin Stannard and Jean Renault, who had been seconded from NatWest and Spie Batignolles to serve as joint chief executives of the shadow Eurotunnel.[49] The Chief Executive, Jean-Loup Dherse, formerly a World Bank vice-president, had worked with Lafarge and Pechiney and had had a brief experience of the 1970s Tunnel when with RTZ.[50] To balance the Anglo-French composition, Pennock brought in a former colleague from BICC, Michael Julien, as Dherse's deputy. Julien had acquired a reputation for troubleshooting as Executive Director for finance and planning at the Midland Bank, where he had helped the company out of the crisis left by its ill-judged purchase of Crocker Bank of California.[51] Lower down, the managerial hierarchy was thin, and there were barely a hundred staff before 1987. Nevertheless, in spite of the uncertainties associated with the project, some experienced people were recruited in 1986–7. They included: Colin Kirkland, a tunnel engineer seconded from Halcrow, who became Technical Director; Alain Bertrand from SNCF, who headed up an Operations Department; and Peter Behr, the head of a Project Administration and Control Department, who was seconded from the American giant, Bechtel.[52]

However, despite these changes City opinion remained firm in its belief that the Eurotunnel organisation lacked experience of transport and had insufficient capability to manage the contractors. This appeared to be confirmed in February 1987 with three high-level resignations in the space of a week. First, Pennock announced that he wished to stand down as Co-chairman. Then Broackes, who had at one time been seen as Pennock's successor, resigned from the board. Finally, Julien gave up the post of deputy chief executive. The reasons for these departures were quite different. Pennock inevitably took the flak for the Equity 2 difficulties and for public relations failings, including a botched TV campaign. Lacking charisma and the outward trappings of entrepreneurial flair, he was certainly no Broackes or Branson. More of a professional non-executive rather than an executive director, it was some time since he had tasted hands-on management. Furthermore, he had expected the job to be easier with a lower public profile than had transpired, and there were other calls on his time, not least from the beleaguered Morgan Grenfell, which had just appointed him to its restructured executive committee.[53] Broackes's insertion into Eurotunnel, while welcomed by Francis Bouygues, had never been fully accepted by the other contractors. There had been talk of giving Trafalgar House an eight per cent stake in TML, but when the British contractors refused to give up any of their interest Broackes had no option but to leave.[54] Julien's resignation as deputy chief executive was less expected. His departure was announced just before the name of Pennock's successor, Alastair Morton, was revealed, on 20 February. Reportedly unsettled by the boardroom rumour-mongering and unable to hit it off with Morton, he went off to an equally difficult assignment, rescuing Guinness from the mess left by its crisis-torn acquisition of Distillers.[55] Whatever the reasons for these moves, their conjunction did nothing to restore confidence in the fledgling company in the eyes of City analysts and financial pundits. Nor were Eurotunnel's French partners pleased by what they dubbed an 'Anglo-British problem'.[56] The new British Co-chairman, Morton, therefore took on a tricky brief, much as he had done when becoming Chief Executive of Guinness Peat in 1982. He was by no means a first-choice candidate. Several others had been canvassed, among them Sir Jeffrey Sterling of P&O, John Harvey-Jones of ICI, Sir Colin Corness of Redland, and Lord King of British Airways.[57] However, it was difficult to see any of these as other than kite-flying candidates. Morton, on the other hand, was highly regarded by Moore, Leigh-Pemberton, Walker, Pennock and Frame as a 'City dynamo' with the appropriate blend of leadership and management skills. Born 49 years earlier in Johannesburg and educated at Oxford and MIT, he had shown an aptitude for tough negotiating and for welding together a new organisation when Managing Director of the British National Oil Corporation, 1976–80. It was said that if you had breakfast with him, you negotiated whether the toast was brown or white. More significantly, while at Peats he had shown that he could turn round an ailing concern.[58] The appointment was not welcomed unequivocally. Morton himself was no stranger to boardroom squabbles, and there were question marks about his ability to heal the wounds of a divided board. But as the financial journalist Ivan Fallon noted, 'a hungry, ambitious and ruthless man with a dominating personality, and a huge desire to make his mark, might pull it off'. And the instigators of his appointment, by simultaneously recruiting Sir Kit McMahon, former deputy governor of the Bank of England and Chairman designate of Midland Bank, clearly hoped that Morton's volatility would be tempered by McMahon's urbanity and undoubted standing in the financial world.[59] There was also some strengthening on the French side, with the introduction of three bankers: Bernard Auberger, Chief Executive of Crédit Agricole, Renaud de la Genière of Suez, and Robert Lion of the Caisse de Dépôts.[60]

Morton, in contrast to Pennock, was prepared to work full time for Eurotunnel, which was just as well, since his initial tasks were considerable. He had to raise the company's profile, excite the City, and above all prepare a convincing prospectus for the third tranche of equity. Deciding the timing of the share issue was the main challenge. It had been assumed that Equity 3 would be handled in late June–early July 1987, after the Channel Tunnel Bill had received the royal assent. However, there were complications. The issue had to be made before Bastille Day, when the French money markets effectively closed for the summer. And there was a need to avoid another major British privatisation, that of the British Airports Authority (BAA). In January the Bank of England dismayed Eurotunnel by refusing it a mid-June/mid-July slot, but on becoming Chairman Morton was able to convince the Transport Secretary, Moore, that if Equity 3 were to be a success then it should be mounted before the summer break. Consequently, Moore wrote to the Treasury Financial Secretary, Norman Lamont, suggesting that in order to accommodate the company, the preferred impact day for BAA should be brought forward from 1 July to 17 June. Lamont agreed, though his officials, who had moved the BAA issue to the end of June to accommodate an earlier Eurotunnel request for July, found the request 'irritating and inconvenient'.[61] Eyebrows were therefore raised in Whitehall when Eurotunnel suddenly announced, on 6 April, that Equity 3 was being postponed until November, all the more so since the DTp had received no warning of such a possibility. Yet there were sound reasons for the delay: the slippage in the parliamentary timetable, the upheavals on the board, the protracted negotiation of the loan agreements, and, above all, the likelihood of a general election. Morton presented the decision in a positive light, and at the same time announced that Eurotunnel's team of financial advisers was being strengthened with the addition of Warburgs.[62] Some money was needed immediately, so that TML could continue with its preparatory work. The initial intention was that this would be raised via a private mini-equity issue of £75–100 million, but in June an interim financing package was agreed with a group of ten British, French and Belgian banks, led by Banque Indosuez and the Midland. The group agreed to provide a loan of £72.5 million, repayable from the proceeds of the share issue.[63]

In explaining the postponement of Equity 3 in April, Morton pointed out that two things needed to be settled if the issue were to succeed, one of which was the responsibility of the British and French Governments. First, he warned the two state railways that it was essential to settle the terms under which they would use the Tunnel, since this would provide a guaranteed income stream and therefore narrow the risks for potential investors. He also made it clear that he expected the rail provision to include a high-speed passenger service between London and Paris. Second, it was imperative to finalise the Credit Agreement with the banks, which had only been established on an informal basis.[64] The involvement of the railways is examined in Section 3 below. Suffice it to say here that after a prolonged period of negotiation over the specific terms, a Railway Usage Contract was eventually agreed between Eurotunnel and British Rail and SNCF in May 1987, with the signature of the contract following on 29 July. The Credit Agreement to secure the loan capital for the project needed to be in place if Equity 3, provisionally set for 18 November 1987, were to succeed.[65] After more tough negotiating, the £5 billion loan was formally underwritten by 50 banks at the end of August. Thirty per cent was provided by Japanese institutions, with 17 per cent from French banks, and 13 per cent each from Britain and Germany. American involvement was limited to 5 per cent.[66] These banks then looked to spread their risks through international syndication. Eurotunnel supported this task with Morton and Bénard travelling round the world's financial centres to drum up support. The process was greatly assisted by the European Investment Bank, which in May had agreed to lend £1 billion within the £5 billion framework.[67] The Bank's own appraisal reached the conclusion that the project was technically, economically and financially viable, even under the most adverse scenarios. It was expected that the debt could be paid off within 12 years.[68] At the beginning of November the Credit

Agreement was formally signed in London and Paris. Under this 1,400-page document, 198 syndicated banks contracted to provide project finance of £5 billion loan, £1 billion of which was to be in the form of a standby (contingency) credit. After syndication, support was provided as follows: Japan 23 per cent; France 18 per cent; Germany 13 per cent; and the United Kingdom 9.4 per cent.[69] According to Bénard and Morton, the Agreement 'was an uneasy compromise' between Eurotunnel's equity-raising needs and the banks' syndication needs.[70] Thus, a number of conditions were specified before the credit facilities could be employed. An expenditure of at least £700 million had to be made, progress was to be made under the construction contract, and the banks had to be satisfied with the future construction programme, including costs and duration of the works. Drawings could take place from July 1988, and the facilities would be available for 'a maximum period of approximately seven years' (i.e. to 1995). Repayments were set to commence after the end of the availability period and a schedule was designed to ensure full repayment by 15 November 2005.[71]

The final element was the placing of Equity 3, where private investors would be required to make a judgement on the project. Eurotunnel, together with its financial advisers, sought to build up interest via a series of reports from the company's financial advisers demonstrating the attractiveness of the investment.[72] Encouragement was also given by new forecasts showing that traffic would be some 10–20 per cent higher than had been predicted in 1986.[73] City opinion-formers, who continued to worry about the relationship between the client and contractor, were heartened when, in September, Dherse left the company to join the administration of the Vatican and was replaced by his deputy, Pierre Durand-Rival. An experienced French project manager, Durand-Rival, who took up the post with the new title of Managing Director, had a reputation for toughness to match that of Morton. He had recently launched a stinging attack on TML in a letter leaked to the press. Here he complained about delays in construction and the lack of adequate financial and cost information.[74] This plain speaking served to reassure investors that the relationship would not be a cosy one. There were also further moves to reinforce the organisation in the weeks before Equity 3. A joint study commissioned from the MdO and Bechtel produced a new management structure that promised more integrated project management and a substantial input from Bechtel.[75] In addition, substantial figures from British industry were recruited to the Eurotunnel joint board: Dr Tony Ridley, Chairman and MD of London Underground and former MD of Hong Kong's mass transit railway; Sir Robert Scholey, MacGregor's successor as Chairman of British Steel. They joined Robert Malpas, a British Petroleum MD and former ICI director, who had been appointed in April. All three had strong engineering backgrounds.[76]

It was difficult to gauge public opinion on the project at this stage. The press had tended to blow both hot and cold in the search for stories. At an early stage Lex of the *Financial Times* had noted that investors had to 'discount quite awesome financial, geological and traffic risks',[77] and the anti-Tunnel campaigners Flexilink were only too happy to spell these out at some length. Clearly this organisation had a vested interest in the Tunnel not being built, and its bleak assessment of Eurotunnel's prospects was only to be expected. On the other hand, the shipping lobby could justifiably claim to understand the cross-channel market, and its critical observations about traffic, tariff and revenue assumptions, which raised legitimate doubts about the ability of the Tunnel operator to cover interest and debt repayments and pay dividends, merited contemplation by potential investors. As the date for Equity 3 approached, it was arguing that no funds for dividends were likely to emerge earlier than 25 years after opening, while a major cost overrun could result in no dividend payments being made over the life of the concession. Insults and comparisons were traded, the promoters referring to the on- or under-budget successes of the Hong Kong Cross-Harbour Bridge and several gas and nuclear power plants, their opponents to overrun disasters such as the Seikan Tunnel in Japan, the Humber Bridge and the Thames Barrier.[78] This was not all. On 19 October the confidence of world markets was shattered when stock exchanges crashed. This naturally heightened anxieties in the build-up to Equity 3, though Eurotunnel was reported to be sanguine about the impact of 'Black Monday', observing that the long-term nature of the returns would insulate the issue from any adverse short-term market sentiment. The company was more concerned that once again there would be a clash with a British privatisation issue, this time of British Petroleum (BP). Morton pressed ministers to have the BP issue pulled. If this were done, Equity 3 would 'be a walk', he said.[79] The £7.2 billion BP offer went ahead as planned on 28 October, with Bank of England 'buy-back' support. However, in the aftermath of the stock market crash it proved to be a disappointing failure, and most of the stock was left with the underwriters. If nothing else, this was a severe psychological blow to Eurotunnel's financial prospects.[80]

Underwriting was of course critical to the success of Equity 3. Whatever the public interest in the stock, if financial institutions could be persuaded to underwrite the issue in full, then the project would continue.[81] A 'pathfinder' prospectus was issued on 5 November, and five days later Morton met Nigel Wicks, Thatcher's PPS, for one of a series of briefings given to senior figures in government. The Eurotunnel Co-chairman reported that the company was 'working against the odds' to achieve the underwriting. There were several reasons for pessimism. In Britain the coalition of support in the City was 'fragile', while the French issue 'was in terrible trouble'. Elsewhere, the Swiss had withdrawn from the equity market, and Deutsche Bank was also threatening to do so. The Treasury Permanent Secretary, Sir Peter Middleton, was told that the chances of success were only about 60 per cent. Morton made it clear that he was not asking for political help, but suggested that anything that Thatcher could say in support of the project would be welcomed.[82] The Bank of England, Treasury and DTp all advised that Thatcher should avoid a direct involvement, but a brief was prepared in case the matter was raised at Commons Question Time on 12 November. This was a possibility since only two days earlier Teddy Taylor and Jonathan Aitken, amongst others, had asked for an assurance that the Bank of England would refrain from buying shares in Eurotunnel.[83] In fact, no further questions were asked, and on 13 November Wicks informed Thatcher that the issue had been successfully underwritten. Morton 'sounded very happy'.[84]

Eurotunnel announced the successful underwriting operation on 16 November, the same day on which the actual prospectus was published. The £770 million offer was for 220 million units at £3.50, with each unit again giving an equal interest in both the British (40p) and French (10FF) Eurotunnel companies. The net yield on the issue price was expected to be 12 per cent in 1994, 42 per cent in 2003, and 654 per cent in 2041. As a further inducement to small shareholders, non-transferable travel perks were offered in the form of nominally-priced journeys on the shuttle, the precise number being linked to the size of the holding.[85] Investors were given until 27 November to make their applications.[86] In Britain, while more than 500,000 individual investors and institutions registered an interest, only 112,000 actually applied for shares, taking up 80 per cent of the issue. The underwriters were therefore left with the remaining 20 per cent. In France, individual investors took 57 per cent of the public offer, the remainder going to new institutional investors (15 per cent) and the underwriting financial institutions (28 per cent). Thus, Equity 3 was scarcely a resounding success. There was also the criticism that it had cost far too much. According to the *Financial Times*, at £68 million it was one of the most expensive stock exchange flotations mounted by a private company, and there was at least an argument that the issue, like its predecessor, should have been offered only to institutions.[87] Nevertheless, there was every reason for Morton, Bénard and the two Governments to breathe a collective sigh of relief. Given the risks, which appeared greater with the King's Cross Underground fire on 18 November, and the gloomy market environment of late 1987, the outcome was a reasonable one. The securing of Equity 3 had been central to the entire project. Without it, the loans would not have been forthcoming. Although the reaction of investors was rather lukewarm, financing was now assured and the real work of constructing the tunnel could begin.

3. The Railway Usage Contract, 1986–7

One of the critical steps in Eurotunnel's financing process had been the need to conclude the Railway Usage Contract (also known as the Usage Agreement). This set out the terms, both financial and operational, under which British Rail and SNCF would use the Tunnel for through rail services, and committed the railways to provide capacity sufficient to handle forecast traffic levels. The Agreement, which gave Eurotunnel an assured revenue stream and therefore provided evidence for the banks of the project's credibility, involved some tough bargaining between the concessionaires and the two state railways. As we have seen (pp. 222–3), in 1982 British Rail had been effectively excluded from promoting a fixed link, and its Channel Tunnel department had been wound down. Now, with the necessity to settle the Usage Contract and to plan for the new infrastructure,

British Rail once again had to take the Tunnel seriously. The Board responded by forming a new Channel Tunnel team, and giving one of its full-time executive members responsibility for the project. The team was headed by Malcolm Southgate, who took up the post of Director, Channel Tunnel in February 1986. He was an experienced operator and formerly General Manager of London Midland Region. In addition, Southgate reported directly to David Kirby, the responsible Board member. Kirby's appointment as Joint MD (Railways) in December 1985 was significant. He had handled Tunnel matters while combining the posts of Director of London & South East and General Manager of Southern Region in 1982–5, but British Rail accepted that it was important for the Tunnel negotiations to be seen to be handled at Board level. Kirby, a former MD of Sealink, was thus an ideal choice. The assignment of such senior managers to the Tunnel brief certainly contrasted with past experience.[88]

Initial Heads of Agreement, which set out the parameters of the Usage Contract, had been concluded in some haste, in order to allow the Concession Agreement to be signed on 14 March 1986.[89] However, the subsequent and necessary 'tidying-up' proved difficult to complete, mainly due to 'obduracy' on the part of SNCF. The French were particularly worried that their ambitious investment plans for a new high-speed line, justified on the basis of attracting significant levels of traffic, would be jeopardised by the tolls which Eurotunnel wanted to charge when traffic levels were high. They also argued for a general reduction in tolls, first to reflect the introduction of a lower rate of corporation tax in France, then, when this suggestion was resisted, to match a fall in the inflation rate. Eurotunnel's Chairman, Pennock, asked Moore to raise the issue with Douffiagues, but Noulton advised the Secretary of State against 'intervening in the commercial interests of a private sector group against a nationalised industry'.[90] Despite these obstacles, new Heads were finalised in early June with the expectation of imminent signature. The intention was to do so in time for Eurotunnel to include a reference to the terms of railway usage in its Equity 2 prospectus, which was planned for July (above, p. 290).[91] Unfortunately, a further problem arose at the eleventh hour. The tolling arrangements had been predicated upon the running of high-speed train services only, but under pressure from the French finance ministry, SNCF was insistent that tolls for trains run at conventional speeds should also be included. In fact, British officials agreed that the inclusion of both options would be a sensible move before the prospectus was issued. Nevertheless, Eurotunnel complained that to do this would prevent it from meeting its equity-raising timetable, and Stannard, one of the company's joint chief executives, telephoned the Department of Transport to warn that if the French persisted in their demands, Equity 2 would have to be postponed until September.[92] This stark assessment was no doubt a bargaining ploy, but in any case the scepticism of financial institutions, and the problems in finalising the Construction Contract were far greater factors in the decision to delay the raising of the equity.

In late September 1986 revised Heads of Agreement were signed. In exchange for ten train paths each way per hour (i.e. 50 per cent of tunnel capacity on opening), the two railways would pay the operating costs attributable to the passage of their trains, together with a variable toll per passenger or per tonne carried. The tolls were to taper with traffic levels and over time. High-speed and conventional-speed operating scenarios were now included, with the tolls for the latter some 20 per cent higher. A new element was the payment of a fixed annual toll of 7 million Units of Account (= £14 million in 1985 prices), which was included following doubts by British Rail freight managers about the sustainability of the freight traffic forecasts under the proposed tariffs. In contrast, if the Tunnel proved to be very successful commercially, British Rail and SNCF would benefit via a toll reduction, under a French-inspired provision known as 'retour de bonne fortune'. Both railways undertook to use their 'best endeavours' to invest in the necessary infrastructure and rolling stock, although the details were not, at this stage, enumerated. The Transport Secretary was informed that officials considered the deal to be satisfactory from British Rail's standpoint. Although the terms were not legally binding, it was envisaged that a formal usage contract would be completed by the end of the year.[93]

This expectation proved to be optimistic, however. Only limited progress was made by February 1987. Furthermore, the Eurotunnel team, led by Stannard, were now asking for significant modifications to the September Heads. First, they sought an 'absolute guarantee' from the railways that their Governments would sanction the necessary railway investment in both countries, something which obviously drew in the respective British and French ministries (see below). Second, they required revised terms for usage: an 8 per cent increase in the overall level of tolls; modifications to the formula governing the 'retour de bonne fortune' arrangement; and a guaranteed annual payment, referred to as a 'reservation fee'.[94] It was this final element that was to prove the greatest obstacle to a settlement. The term 'reservation fee' had been included in the September Heads, where it was defined as a pre-payment for each train path used. The railways expected it to be 'insignificant'. But by February Eurotunnel was arguing that if British Rail and SNCF were to be guaranteed half of the Tunnel's capacity, then they should pay for it. Thus, an annual, non-returnable, fee of £85 million was demanded over the length of the Concession, equivalent to 50 per cent of the tolls payable for the rail traffic forecast by Eurotunnel/SETEC to arise on opening in 1993. Over time, with rising traffic, the fee would obviously diminish as a percentage of total payments. Eurotunnel claimed that there would in fact be no cost to the railways because 'in normal circumstances there is no significant risk of it [the fee] not being completely offset by actual tolls'. Nevertheless the two railways found the proposal to put up 50 per cent of the initial toll payments 'totally unacceptable'.[95] Instead they suggested some form of assured minimum payment, detached from the right to use train paths. Eurotunnel, on the other hand, was adamant that it was not interested in variations unrelated to the notion of capacity reservation. British Rail and SNCF, responding positively to the impasse at the end of the month, offered to pay £50 million, that is 30 per cent of the tolls expected in the first year, an offer they considered to be a major concession.

This was equivalent to 2.5 millions Units of Account per train path in each direction, that is 25 million Units if all ten paths were used.[96]

Meanwhile, Whitehall officials, who were being fully briefed by both sides on the progress of the negotiations, expressed some concerns over the inclusion of the reservation fee. First, there was the possibility that the toll guarantee would be defined in such a way that it was effectively a lease and thus its discounted value would count as public expenditure in the first year. In fact, the Department argued successfully that the arrangement did not constitute a lease, and was able to secure the Treasury's agreement to this interpretation.[97] Second, and more crucially, there was the question as to whether the reservation fee involved a transfer of risk from Eurotunnel to the railways. Initially, Department officials understood that train paths could be given up at any time, with the fee reduced *pro rata*. On this basis, their view was that the proposal did not 'amount to any guarantee or transfer of risk whatever'. However, this judgement looked less secure when it became apparent that the period of notice to be given for a path cancellation was a year and that Eurotunnel was pressing to raise it to five years. It now appeared that there was indeed a risk transfer, although whether the balance of risk was acceptable was another matter.[98]

Eurotunnel's desire to improve the terms of the September Heads was of course driven by pressure from the financial institutions. The banks considered that the agreement as drafted was unfavourable to Eurotunnel: 'At high traffic levels it extracted too much of the cream. At low traffic it gave too little assurance of revenue'.[99] They argued that the terms needed to be improved to attract investors, and especially if they were to be tempted with the prospect of a 20 per cent return on equity. With Equity 3, at this stage, set for the summer of 1987, time for negotiation was short, and Eurotunnel was reported to be 'very uptight'.[100] For its part, the British Railways Board was uneasy about acceding to these demands. After all, one of the purposes of the Heads of Agreement was to insulate the railways from any attempt to renegotiate the deal if Eurotunnel experienced difficulties in raising finance. But neither did the railways wish to be seen to cause the project to founder. And officials realised that it would be plainly awkward for Ministers if British Rail prejudiced the viability of the Tunnel by refusing to accept higher tolls when it could actually afford to pay them.[101]

Morton's arrival as Eurotunnel Chairman in February 1987 brought a new urgency to the negotiations. He began with a measured appeal to British Rail Chairman, Bob Reid, and his SNCF counterpart, Philippe Essig, to break the deadlock by accepting the principles of a proposed package, including the railways' offer of £50 million (30 per cent of expected tolls) as a reservation fee.[102] This was followed up, on 18 March, with discussions between Morton and Bénard and the railways. At the meeting with Reid and Southgate, Morton emphasised that the usage contract had to 'impress the lending banks'. In order to achieve this it was vital that there be some 'front end loading of the tolls', to improve dividend prospects in the first two years of operation, and 'a hardening up' of the reservation fee element.[103] On the next day Morton met the Transport

Secretary, Moore, leaving him in no doubt that the railway agreement was 'the greatest threat to Eurotunnel'. He complained about SNCF intransigence, and emphasised that, of the outstanding issues, the reservation fee was the most important. Here he strongly disputed the notion that this represented a form of financial guarantee.[104] The railways' formal reply to Eurotunnel contained detailed responses to each of the points at issue. Reid and Essig indicated that while the package was not acceptable 'in its entirety', they were confident that the few remaining items could be resolved. An assurance was given that the contract would be signed before the end of the month.[105]

These good intentions were not realised, however, and in early April the negotiations were taken to the precipice. We have seen that when the postponement of Equity 3 was announced on 6 April, Eurotunnel had publicly increased the pressure on the railways to settle the contract. On the same day Morton and Bénard wrote to Reid and Essig in forceful terms, stating that Eurotunnel could not continue its activities unless a number of points were met. Among these was the demand that the reservation fee had now to be the equivalent of 80 per cent of forecast tolls. If accepted this would more than double the suggested reservation payment. It was coupled with a warning that the Eurotunnel Co-chairmen had 'now reached the limits of our negotiating powers and we cannot put off the deadline for settlement of the agreement any longer'.[106] British officials found Eurotunnel's tactics hard to fathom. It appeared that, with the railways on one side and the banks on the other, the company were 'dangerously close to painting themselves into a corner'.[107] Bailey, the Department's Permanent Secretary, felt that the predicament was probably genuine: 'it may be that Eurotunnel will not get agreement with the banks on the loan agreement they need unless there is some movement in the railways' position'. But he argued that the railways should be free to exercise their own commercial judgement at this stage. There were evident dangers in either the Department or the Treasury seeking to 'second-guess' them.[108] Nevertheless, a 'government steer' was given to Kirby and his team at British Rail. They were told that there was no objection from Whitehall to their increasing the reservation fee formula to 50 per cent of first year tolls, with a three-year notice of cancellation.[109] However, the negotiations were complicated by the fact that British Rail was unhappy with the traffic forecasts prepared for Eurotunnel by SETEC. Its own data, provided by Martin Vorhees Associates (MVA), were more cautious, and consequently, an 80 per cent formula would in fact equate to 94 per cent of the BRB/MVA forecast in the first year of operation. On the other hand, a British Rail risk assessment of the probability of not achieving 40, 50 and 60 per cent of the Eurotunnel/SETEC estimate was low (0.5, 1.5 and 5.0 per cent respectively), thus indicating that there was some latitude for bargaining.[110] Nevertheless, the railways' first response was to offer Eurotunnel a fee of £60 million or 30 million Units of Account, equivalent to 40 per cent of the latter's traffic forecast.[111]

Unimpressed with this offer, Morton raised the stakes by complaining that both the DTp and the Treasury were interfering in the negotiations. He insisted that the railways should be free to make a deal. 'Absent that', he told Moore on 22 April, and 'the Channel Tunnel may be dead within a fortnight'.[112] After further high-level talks on 5–6 May had failed, Morton wrote to Reid in similarly alarmist terms. He claimed that if an agreement were not reached at a final meeting on 11 May the project would be finished and Eurotunnel would issue a statement blaming the railways for the failure.[113] Even allowing for Morton's brinkmanship, this was undoubtedly a crisis point. When Morton met Moore again on 7 May, their discussion was almost entirely given over to the question of the reservation fee. Morton argued that agreement was necessary to send a positive signal to the market. A commitment by the railways to a low percentage of the SETEC forecast 'would be tantamount to a vote of no-confidence' in the traffic projections. If a satisfactory fee level could not be agreed, 'the railway companies clearly did not have sufficient confidence in the tunnel and it should not be built'. Moore accepted that matters were reaching a 'crunch-point', but while he offered to encourage British Rail to continue 'commercial discussions', he refused to be intimidated by Morton's Cassandra, and observed that if a deal could not be reached, and 'if Mr Morton's view was the tunnel could not therefore be built as a commercial proposition, so be it'.[114] Nevertheless, he regarded the position as serious enough to minute Thatcher and her senior colleagues. He told them that it could well be 'make or break', and that Morton had threatened to abandon the project if he did not get what he wanted.[115]

While agreement was sought on the three familiar issues – toll levels, retour de bonne fortune, and the reservation fee – the last element remained the most difficult. Eurotunnel lowered its demand from 80 to 66 per cent of tolls, with 60 per cent indicated as the minimum it would accept. However, it wanted the charge to be based not on the opening year, but on the expected traffic level over the first 15 years. And instead of a three- or five-year rolling cancellation period throughout the concession, Eurotunnel now proposed that the payments should remain fixed for 15 years, reflecting the maturity period of the concessionaires' loans. In addition, the explicit link between the fee and the entitlement to train paths was broken. Instead the railways were to be given 50 per cent of all available paths, including any additional capacity that might be added. With these changes, the fee was now referred to as the 'minimum usage charge' (MUC). There was a flurry of correspondence and discussion in Britain as British Rail, the DTp and the Treasury cleared their negotiating parameters. Both SNCF and the French Government were reportedly prepared to accept the 60 per cent-15 years formula, but British Rail had strong reservations about an arrangement that might be criticised as a public sector guarantee. And Moore and his officials were particularly wary of the proposal for a 15-year commitment. All were agreed that it would be helpful if some form of break-clause or carry-forward provision were inserted. Kirby felt that British Rail might have to accept the formula, and the line in Whitehall continued to be that this was a matter for the Board's commercial judgement.[116] Moore maintained his view that the DTp should adopt an advisory stance. Kirby was informed that if British Rail had to accept the new formula 'they are free to do so'.[117] Treasury officials advised their Chief Secretary, John MacGregor, that the deal was 'just about defensible', and recommended that no objection be raised. British Rail had calculated that there was a 6 per cent chance of a 60 per cent minimum exceeding actual tolls in 1993. This was regarded as being 'based on heroic assumptions', and did not allow for 'major uncertainties, such as greater airline competition'. Nevertheless, the transfer of risk was not considered to be large. With SNCF happy to accept the proposals, and the DTp prepared to endorse British Rail's judgement, it would be 'politically difficult' to seek to block 'an arguably commercial arrangement potentially leading to a collapse of the tunnel project'. MacGregor did not demur.[118]

The parties finally reached an agreement at a meeting held at Heathrow on 11 May. The railways obtained some concessions from Eurotunnel. The railways asked for the MUC to be expressed in monetary terms as a flat payment of 50 million Units of Account (£100 million in 1985 prices) per annum.[119] They also negotiated a reduction in the time-period from 15 to 12 years, and the insertion of a carry-over mechanism. The latter was to operate as follows. The 50 million Units would be paid in monthly instalments (of 4.167 million). When the MUC exceeded actual tolls, the excess would be carried forward to a special account, to be capped at 25 million Units. The fund would be drawn on to support payments higher than the MUC over a 36-month reference period (not the 60-months asked for by the railways). The schedule of standard toll payments remained as in the September 1986 Heads (see above). But the tapering mechanism with traffic increases was reduced from 1.57 to 1.1 per cent a year, giving Eurotunnel an additional 3 per cent in NPV, somewhat less than the eight per cent originally demanded. The threshold for 'bonne fortune' profit-sharing was also altered, applying when the company's internal return reached 18.25 per cent, instead of 17.3 per cent, again of benefit to Eurotunnel. All of this applied to both the high-speed and conventional-speed train scenarios, with the exception of the MUC, which at conventional speeds would be cut by 20 per cent.[120] The anticipated toll payments, comprising a fixed and variable element and subject to the MUC, are set out in Table 10.1. All sides welcomed the agreement, which was revealed publicly on 12 May. On the following day, Mitchell met Douffiagues in Calais, and revealed that the European Investment Bank [EIB] had agreed to provide Eurotunnel with a £1 billion loan. These events did much to stabilise Eurotunnel's prospects.[121]

After all the wrangling, the deal was felt to be a good one for both the railways and the concessionaires. As Reid told Mitchell, 'it gives EuroTunnel [*sic*] a somewhat firmer base on which to raise their Bank loans without prejudicing the BR case for investment'.[122] British officials were also satisfied with the outcome of negotiations in which they had taken a close interest.[123] But while the Transport Secretary and his civil servants had been at British Rail's elbow during the talks, there was little overt interference from the Government, contrary to Morton's suspicions. Once they had determined that the arrangement did not fall foul of Treasury definitions of public expenditure, officials were happy to trust British

Table 10.1 Toll payments agreed under the Railway Usage Contract, July 1987

	Volume range (m. per annum)	*Units of account*
Variable Toll		
Passenger toll		
For each passenger from	0 to and including 12	3.5
	12 to and including 16	3.0
	16 to and including 18	2.5
	18 to and including 19	2.0
	19 to and including 20	1.5
For each passenger above	20	1.0
Non-Bulk Freight Toll		
For each tonne	0 to and including 4	3.0
	4 to and including 5	2.5
	5 to and including 6	2.0
For each tonne above	6	1.5
Bulk Freight Toll		
For each tonne	0 to and including 3	1.0
	3 to and including 4	0.75
For each tonne above	4	0.25
Fixed Toll		
Fixed Annual Usage Charge	7 million units of account	

Source: Railway Usage Contract, Schedule VI.

Notes

The units of account are subject to an annual taper that has the effect of progressively reducing the variable toll for each volume range. For 14 years after the target commencement date the limits of the volume ranges are increased on an annual basis to 102% (passengers), 103% (non-bulk freight) and 102.5% (bulk freight) of what they were in the preceding year.

Rail's commercial judgement. Indeed, they were more concerned about being seen to intervene than about the danger that British Rail would settle on unfavourable terms. Did the Usage Contract represent a form of guarantee? On the conclusion of the 11 May talks, Thatcher was told that the contract 'does not constitute a Government guarantee and is within the limits of commercial prudence'.[124] However, as one Treasury official admitted, any contract between Eurotunnel and British Rail was 'in some sense a guarantee', because the Government would not let British Rail default on its legal obligations. It was more realistic to defend it as an 'arms length commercial relationship' between Eurotunnel as owners of the Tunnel and British Rail/SNCF as users. And, in any case, the strictures in the Channel Tunnel Act prevented the use of public funds to support the project.[125] On the other hand, the introduction of the MUC involved a significant transfer of risk from Eurotunnel to the public sector in Britain and France. Nick Wakefield of Warburgs, British Rail's advisers, calculated that, using the MVA forecasts, rail traffic would have to reach 70 per cent of that predicted in the first year (8.44 million passengers and 3.84 million tonnes of freight) to cover the MUC. In 2003, 63 per cent of the forecast would be needed

(17.4 million passengers and 7 million tonnes of freight).[126] However, in the late 1980s it was universally accepted that the actual toll payments would be *higher* than the MUC in other than exceptional circumstances. No one had reason to doubt that the expected traffic levels would materialise, and as Southgate put it (in 1992), the argument about the MUC was 'a damn great storm in a teacup'.[127] Furthermore, a substantial portion of the commercial risk was left with Eurotunnel. Wakefield had calculated that in total the MUC would be sufficient to amortise a loan of £1.6 billion. This figure represented about a third of the project's £4.7 billion cost. And although the Usage Contract may have provided some comfort to investors over the future use of the Tunnel, it was of no help in the construction phase, where Eurotunnel still bore the considerable risk.[128] It only remained for the Contract to be finalised. However, the process was subject to further delay, owing to arguments about the provision of railway infrastructure, and the nature of the revenue-sharing arrangement between British Rail and SNCF, items which had been running in parallel with the charging issue (see below). As a result, the Contract was not signed until 29 July 1987, the day on which the Treaty was ratified.

4. Infrastructure planning, 1986–7

While the British and French Governments were fairly detached from the negotiations over the Usage Contract, they had a more direct involvement in taking the first steps to provide the road and rail infrastructure connecting the Tunnel with national networks. Their commitments were referred to in the Concession Agreement, which stated that the Principals 'will use reasonable endeavours to carry out the infrastructure necessary for a satisfactory flow of traffic, to statutory procedures'.[129] Of course, much was to rest on the definition of 'reasonable endeavours'. Turning first to roads, the debate here was relatively subdued. Nevertheless, pressure was exerted from predictable quarters. Eurotunnel sought to maximise the provision of linkages to the terminals, and expressed doubts that some of the promised road-building would be completed in time for the Tunnel opening.[130] And Kent County Council, armed with the Kent Impact Study of August 1987, produced by David Mitchell's Joint Consultative Committee, pressed the Government to release special funds for the improvement of a whole series of roads, not all of which were essential to meet Tunnel traffic flows.[131] In France work began to extend the A26 motorway to Calais, together with an inter-regional motorway connecting Belgium with Calais, Boulogne and Le Havre. In Britain plans were also well advanced, since an improved road network was required to link the ports in Kent with London's orbital motorway, the M25, completed in October 1986. The main projects, devised or accelerated to coincide with the Tunnel's opening, were: completion of the M20 motorway, with the construction of the 14-mile Maidstone-Ashford section, plus widening of the Maidstone by-pass; upgrading of the A20 road between Folkestone and Dover, most of which was specified in the Channel Tunnel Act of 1987; improvements to the A259/A27, and Hythe-M20 (A261).[132] The work, which was the responsibility of the DTp's South East Construction Division, was started in January 1989, when Costain began work on the M20. In June 1990 the cost of the M20/A20 enhancements was estimated to be £220 million in November 1987 prices; the cost of the broader package of improved infrastructure was put at £588 million, of which schemes costing £268 million were expected to be completed by the end of 1993. In addition £75 million was to be spent on Tunnel-related local roads funded under the Transport Supplementary Grant system.[133] The process was a fairly smooth one, but was not entirely free of controversy. First there were critics opposing road-building on environmental grounds, who contrasted the generation of fierce opposition to a proposed high-speed rail line (see below) with the more muted reception given to road plans (except near Dover). However, environmentalists were more than matched by those who argued with Morton that the M20 and M25 were already inadequate for the transport demands required of them.[134]

The necessary railway infrastructure comprised not only the connections to the Tunnel system, but also an extensive investment in route improvements, rolling stock, terminals and depots. If the Governments found road planning a relatively straightforward matter, then they experienced considerable difficulties with the rail elements, and those who remembered the experience of the 1970s had a distinct feeling of déjà vu. Moreover, the issue was important because although the Tunnel itself was being privately financed, the railway components required significant levels of additional public expenditure on both sides of the Channel. And while many of the road improvements in Kent would undoubtedly have occurred without the Tunnel, the same could not be said of much of the Tunnel-specific railway investment. The railways' obligations were specified in the Railway Usage Contract. In time for the first full year of operation, British Rail and SNCF undertook to ensure that they had sufficient capacity to handle 17.4 million passengers, 5.2 million tonnes of non-bulk freight, and 2.9 million tonnes of bulk freight. The infrastructure needed to meet this requirement was set out in separate schedules. In Britain there was to be a terminal station at Waterloo, an international station in Ashford, associated new sections of line, a maintenance depot at North Pole in West London, and freight inspection facilities at Dolland's Moor, near Cheriton. British requirements were the same under both speed scenarios, since at this stage no separate high-speed rail link was planned on the British side.[135] Legislative powers for this work were given by the Channel Tunnel Act. In addition, as we have seen, the Act gave an encouragement to the provision of services beyond London, by requiring British Rail (in Section 40) to produce a report on how it would develop international traffic. In France SNCF accepted similar obligations.[136] However, the high-speed option included construction of a 320-kilometre dedicated line between the Tunnel and the outskirts of Paris. Here, there was a wider agenda, since SNCF, together with the Belgian, German and Dutch railways, were keen to use the potential through-rail traffic generated by the Tunnel as a means of boosting plans for a TGV-Nord and a high-speed rail network linking Paris, Brussels, Köln and Amsterdam [PBKA].[137]

The provision of rail infrastructure raised difficult questions on both sides of the Channel, since British Rail and SNCF had to defend their investment plans. In the course of an inter-ministerial meeting in February 1987, the French criticised the lack of train capacity in Britain during the evening peak, demanding seven trains an hour to the three offered by British Rail. Although the latter's managers maintained that the impact on traffic levels would be marginal, they had undoubtedly boxed themselves in with undertakings that domestic commuter services would be unaffected by Tunnel traffic. Their promise to opponents of the Channel Tunnel Bill that no international trains would run into Waterloo between 08.00 and 09.00 hours was a further source of annoyance to SNCF.[138] There was also French disquiet about the apparent imbalance in the magnitude of the respective railway investments.[139] However, these criticisms failed to mask the evident lack of unanimity in Paris. Douffiagues, for example, was a strong supporter of TGV-Nord, but the French Finance Ministry was doubtful about the project's viability.[140] In addition, there was disagreement about the exact route, and Raoul Rudeau, who had led the French Fixed Link Assessment Team in 1985/6, was appointed to chair a Commission of Enquiry to determine whether the line should serve Amiens or Lille.[141] Another hotly contested subject was the procurement of new trains. The British had assumed that contracts would be placed on a 50/50 basis, but the French wanted orders to reflect the level of infrastructure investment in the two countries, which would give the French railway manufacturing industry the predominant role. British officials were strongly opposed to this approach. Mitchell went so far as to tell Reid that he should ensure that the fleet was not 'based on a TGV look-alike built primarily by Alsthom'.[142] Last, but not least, there was the issue of revenue apportionment. This would normally have been calculated on a distance basis, but the matter became enmeshed with the debates about comparative capacities, journey times and investments. British Rail required sufficient revenue to justify its investment case, but the French wanted a greater share of the receipts in order to compensate them for perceived higher risks. This prolonged debate delayed the signature of the Usage Contract, much to Eurotunnel's annoyance. Although the final formula, devised by SNCF and taking journey times and capacities into account, was 'very complicated', Reid noted that it gave incentives to British Rail to reduce journey times and increase peak capacity. The two railways also agreed that the costs of the rolling stock would be apportioned according to the time spent on the respective networks, which officials felt would make it easier to argue for an equitable division of rolling stock procurement.[143]

Eurotunnel lost no opportunity to emphasise that the high-speed option was essential to the future of the entire project, and in February 1987 it asked the railways to guarantee that the Governments would approve the required investment. Of course, the railways were in no position to provide such assurances, and, pending the receipt of detailed schemes, neither were Ministers. Eurotunnel's stance was rather contradictory because while it wanted the high-speed case to be adopted, it was at the same time seeking to extract increased tolls from the investing railways. SNCF in particular needed to generate significant passenger numbers to justify the ambitious TGV-Nord scheme, and higher tolls would only militate against this.[144] However, with Eurotunnel continuing to exert pressure, Mitchell and Douffiagues agreed the wording of a joint communiqué when they met in April. The statement, supporting the high-speed option in principle, was to be released once the negotiations over tolls were completed, and it was expected that publication would be made when Mitchell visited the French tunnel works on 13 May. In fact, Douffiagues refused to issue the statement because the railways had not yet reached agreement on revenue-sharing.[145] Unsurprisingly, Morton kept up the pressure, telling the incoming Transport Secretary, Channon, that unless there was 'an unequivocal announcement of intentions for TGV [before the August Board meeting], Eurotunnel must be expected to call a halt to the project'. He repeated this threat when he met Channon for the first time, on 1 July.[146] In the circumstances Channon could do little to mollify him, though he expected to receive British Rail's investment case by the end of the week. Attempts to extract a decision in Paris were no more successful, and in the usual Whitehall refrain, French officials were reported to be in 'disarray'.[147]

British Rail's initial Channel Tunnel investment submission, made in November 1985, had estimated that an expenditure of £389 million (in January 1985 prices) was required for the fixed works and rolling stock under the preferred high-speed option. Ridley, endorsing the investment in January 1986 on the basis of a fully commercial operation, warned Reid that the figures submitted should be regarded as maxima.[148] Nevertheless, by the summer of 1987 the familiar mix of inflation, under-estimation and enhanced project scope, together with statutory and other obligations, had produced a sizeable increase in costs. In an attempt to present this embarrassing revelation more acceptably, British Rail resorted to something approaching sleight of hand. The project was now split into three parts: Phase I (£450 million in September 1986 prices), to meet the terms of the Usage Contract; Phase II (£250 million) for 'through services north of London, which were not envisaged in the original proposals'; and Phase III (£200 million) for increased line capacity. Thus, Reid was able to tell Channon that Phase I was 'broadly consistent' with the original submission (revised as £400 million in September 1986 prices). However, he was anxious to point out that the total investment was 'unlikely to be less than £700 m'.[149] Unsurprisingly, these revised proposals were not well received in the Treasury. The Chief Secretary, John Major, expressed dismay at the 'enormous increase' in costs, and was unhappy that the decision, required prior to signature of the Usage Contract, had to be taken within such a short timescale. But his officials advised him that there was little room for manoeuvre, and Major had to concede that, under the circumstances, British Rail should proceed. There were conditions, however. Neither the international station at Ashford, which had an extremely weak financial case, nor the through trains north of London, were approved at this stage. The exclusion of these items reduced the total cost to £550 million, a figure that Major regarded as a project ceiling. Stringent cost control, he told Channon, was essential.[150] Almost immediately expenditure of a further £70 million was added to British Rail's commitments following the conclusion of the revenue-sharing agreement. But Channon and Major were insistent that the £550 million ceiling should not be adjusted.[151]

The Usage Contract was signed in July, but Eurotunnel was now preoccupied with the raising of Equity 3, and consequently it continued to press the Governments via British Rail and SNCF for undertakings on the high-speed option. At the insistence of the banks, two deadlines had been inserted into the Contract. The first required government assurances, by 21 August, that there would be investment in high speed. In their absence, the Contract would be based on the conventional-speed scenario. Second, railways had by 21 September to certify that they had received the necessary government approvals for the railway investment. If these were not in place, then the Contract would lapse entirely.[152] Since the Government had already agreed to British Rail's high-speed proposals neither of these dates presented a difficulty in Britain, but in France an announcement on the TGV-Nord project was still awaited. However, if Eurotunnel thought that the specification of deadlines would force a decision, it was mistaken. The French let the first one pass, safe in the knowledge that the railways could meet their usage obligations without high speed. This move, while effectively turning the tables on Eurotunnel, caused some alarm within British Rail and the DTp, because no approval had been given for the conventional-speed option. Indeed, the investment case under this scenario was, at best, marginal.[153] As the second deadline approached, British officials watched the situation nervously and Eurotunnel continued to bluster about the project's imminent demise, but the French Government appeared unconcerned. Certainly it refused to be rushed into a timetable that it felt had been imposed on it. But in any case the TGV-Nord decision required the delicate balancing of complex political and economic considerations during the period of 'cohabitation', and also negotiations with neighbouring countries. And the Government did not think that the raising of Equity 3 would be compromised by a delay.[154] Given French procrastination, there was some surprise when the matter was raised by Chirac when he met Thatcher in Berlin on 25 September, just after the deadline's expiry (Eurotunnel, meanwhile, had agreed to a month's extension). The French Prime Minister complained about the meagre amount of British railway investment compared with the, as yet unannounced, investment in France. British officials were on the point of suggesting to Thatcher that she should respond to these accusations in 'robust terms' when Chirac announced, on 9 October, that the construction of the £1.2 billion TGV-Nord line, via Lille, had been approved.[155]

5. Monitoring construction and financing, 1987–90

The details surrounding the actual construction of the Channel Tunnel, Europe's largest infrastructure project, have naturally attracted the attention of several writers, and do not require elaboration here.[156] Not only were the scale and complexity of the operations immense, but the logistics of working in a confined space over such a large geographical area were challenging. At the peak of tunnelling activity in 1991, TML was employing a workforce, including sub-contractors, of nearly 14,000.[157] To summarise briefly, work began in earnest on the British side in the autumn of 1987, with the sinking of the first shaft at Shakespeare Cliff, and in December the first TBM began driving the 4.8-metre service tunnel. In France the first TBM was delivered to Sangatte in January 1988. In all, 11 TBMs were eventually deployed for 12 tunnel drives, in an operation that was to prove tougher than expected. In the first half of 1988 progress was slow on both sides of the Channel. First there were the expected difficulties with wet ground near the French coast, but the timetable was also affected by the failure of a TBM company, Somme Delattre, and the marine drive did not start until March 1988. In Britain, tunnelling was held up by the surprise discovery of wet ground near the coast, which caused a two months' delay. These difficulties came on top of the prolongation of the legislative and equity-raising processes (see above, pp. 285–7, 290–5), which, in the opinion of the MdO, had added three months to the timetable. With only 1.5 [from Britain] and 0.2 kilometres [from France] of seaward service tunnelling completed by July 1988, TML had failed to achieve a series of construction milestones, and was unable to meet the requirement of tunnelling 5.0 and 2.0 kilometres respectively by 1 November.[158] Nevertheless, the work gathered pace from the end of 1988, when there was a marked acceleration in the service tunnelling, and the driving of the main tunnels' marine sections began. An impressive 8 kilometres of tunnel were bored in the first three months of 1989, and although there were concerns about industrial relations and safety, a good rate of construction was maintained.[159] On 30 October 1990, the date, according to *Tunnels and Tunnelling*, 'when the seed of a brilliant idea became the flower of achievement', the two countries were physically joined when a British probe reached the French service tunnel works.[160] The full breakthrough was enacted with due ceremonial on 1 December, when about three-quarters of the total tunnelling had been completed. The main 7.6-metre twin bores were finished in June 1991, some six weeks ahead of programme (Table 10.2).[161]

The two governments were not required to take a direct interest in the conduct of the works. The mechanisms put in place by the Treaty (Articles 10 and 11) and the Concession entrusted supervision of the project to an Intergovernmental Commission (IGC), and safety in construction and operation to an advisory Safety Authority. Both bodies were assisted by the MdO (W.S. Atkins and SETEC), working in an independent capacity. The IGC, staffed by delegations of civil servants from the two countries and led initially by John Noulton and Michel Legrand, held its first meeting in May 1986, but was not officially inaugurated until ratification of the Treaty in July 1987. The Safety Authority, led initially by Major Charles Rose and Bernard Pilon, first met in July 1986. The British delegation included representatives of the Health and Safety Executive, the Railway Inspectorate and Kent Fire Brigade.[162] In 1986–7, of course, the supervision was fairly relaxed, being largely confined to the receipt of progress reports on the

Table 10.2 Progress with tunnelling, 1987–91

(i) Commencement and completion

	Boring commenced	*Boring completed*
United Kingdom		
Running Tunnel North		
Landward	August 1989	September 1990
Seaward	Mar 1989	May 1991
Running Tunnel South		
Landward	November 1989	November 1990
Seaward	June 1989	June 1991
Service Tunnel		
Landward	October 1988	November 1989
Seaward	December 1987	November 1990
France		
Running Tunnel North		
Landward	March 1990	November 1990
Seaward	December 1988	May 1991
Running Tunnel South		
Landward	January 1989	December 1989
Seaward	April 1989	June 1991
Service Tunnel		
Landward	June 1988	April 1989
Seaward	March 1988	December 1990

(ii) Boring completed (metres)

	United Kingdom			*France*			*Total*
	Running Tunnel North	*Running Tunnel South*	*Service Tunnel*	*Running Tunnel North*	*Running Tunnel South*	*Service Tunnel*	
Date							
12/87	—	—	140	—	—	43	183
6/88	—	—	2,784	—	—	1,218	4,002
12/88	—	—	8,432	—	—	3,992	12,424
6/89	1,116	310	14,648	1,148	1,102	6,694	25,018
12/89	3,191	1,703	21,820	3,845	5,253	9,889	45,701
6/90	12,087	9,999	26,482	10,131	10,482	14,861	84,042
12/90	19,296	18,643	30,414	17,786	14,917	18,869	119,925
6/91	26,072	28,079	30,414	23,272	22,122	18,869	148,828

Source: TML/Eurotunnel.

legislation, Treaty protocols, jurisdictional issues and so on. However, once the tunnelling started, the work of the IGC and Safety Authority began in earnest. Under the Concession Agreement, Eurotunnel had to obtain the approval of the IGC to outline designs, construction, operating rules and emergency procedures for Channel Tunnel operations. The process followed French practice in requiring Eurotunnel to submit 'avant projets', some 35 in all, providing detailed proposals for the design and construction of each major element of the system, for clearance by the IGC. Eurotunnel in turn depended on TML to provide the necessary documentation.[163] The procedure was a potential minefield, and the supervisory bodies were quickly drawn into detailed issues surrounding design features and the setting of safety standards over a wide area. Ranging from the design of shuttle fire-doors to seismic protection, many of them had cost implications. It is difficult to calculate the financial consequences of these requirements with any accuracy, but it is clear that legitimate concerns about safety in general, and fire safety in particular, had the effect of producing an additional cost burden for TML and Eurotunnel (see below, pp. 348–51). The process was exacerbated by the fact that, as with the Tunnel specification in general, safety standards had not been established in advance of the Concession Agreement. As one practitioner put it, 'the result was a moving target that became ever more demanding and costly to achieve as design and construction progressed'.[164]

The Governments' principal responsibility was to ensure that they committed public funds to the promised infrastructure provision. However, they also wished to reassure themselves that the Tunnel proper had good governance systems, that Eurotunnel and TML were maintaining a good working relationship, and that the project would be completed with limited time and cost overruns. Unfortunately, as is well known, the picture became gloomier and gloomier over time. The pressures on the contractors should not be underestimated. They were working to an imprecise contract in design terms, and had begun work in the midst of a world construction boom with a shortage of engineers and the pressures provided by inflation (6.9 per cent p.a., 1987–90). On top of this there were serious personality clashes among the major actors, a fact not lost on permanent secretaries in Whitehall.[165] In particular, Morton's penchant for brinkmanship and bullying, which was matched by his MD, Durand-Rival, plainly antagonised Andrew McDowall, TML's Chairman, and his colleagues, as did Eurotunnel's tendency to brief the press while holding TML to its contractual obligation to silence. In August 1988, with the first call on the banks due in three months' time, Morton accused the contractors of not taking the project seriously enough and at the same time he served a formal notice on them to expedite progress. TML retaliated by leaking the letter.[166] The lack of trust between the two companies was evident when Eurotunnel built up a Project Implementation Division [PID] from January 1988, thereby duplicating TML's project management function. The difficulties which the MdO had had in operating as a consulting engineer were accepted by both sides. But the move to an alternative approach, by separating the MdO's role of independent auditor from the supervision and control of the TML contract, while logical, was not without its drawbacks. Eurotunnel increased its project management staff to around 350, under the leadership of Joseph Anderson, who was seconded from Bechtel. In all 35 managers were seconded from the American firm, a move which plainly antagonised TML's engineers.[167] As the call on the banks approached, more optimistic noises emanated from Eurotunnel, its interim statement highlighting the marked improvement in the rate of tunnelling. At this stage the cost escalation appeared containable within the original funding arrangements, though by October 1988 the early tunnelling difficulties had contributed to an overspending of 7 per cent or £353 million, thereby raising the project's estimated cost from £4.87 to £5.23 billion (in July 1987 prices). However, Eurotunnel claimed that the extra costs would be offset by additional revenue, with new traffic forecasts promising an increase of 6 per cent in 1993–4, and 10 per cent in 2003.[168]

These initial concerns about cost escalation naturally worried the lending banks. While there were 210 financial institutions in the syndicate, they had delegated decision-making powers to 22 'instructing banks', which in turn worked through four 'agent banks' in their dealings with Eurotunnel. The latter comprised four of the founder shareholders (Midland, NatWest, Banque Nationale de Paris and Crédit Lyonnais). It was the instructing banks, some of whom had been prominent in assessing the construction contract of 1986, who now flexed their muscles in asking for further reassurances from Eurotunnel and TML. But the immediate prospects were bleak, since the continuing dispute between client and contractor had caused the former to withhold 12 per cent of claimed payments.[169] The news reached the Prime Minister's desk in December 1988 via an 'alarmist hand-wringing letter' from Channon's Private Secretary. While the DTp's view was that there was 'nothing for the Government to do except to watch developments', Thatcher regarded the position as more serious and suggested that the British and French Transport Ministers review the situation.[170] This proposed intervention was forestalled by more promising news. In January 1989 both Eurotunnel and TML accepted the argument for management changes, and their highly publicised squabbles, which had even provoked the French partners in TML to hold a special press conference in Paris in December 1988,[171] gave way to talk of 'accord'.[172] Eurotunnel and TML agreed to delay the opening by a month (now June 1993), to produce revised milestones, and settle all outstanding and disputed payments, with provision for a bonus to TML of £106 million if the new milestones were achieved. There was further optimism when the French Mitsubishi TBM broke though on the inland portion of the service tunnel on 27 April. The 'accord', effective from March 1989, was more the result of pressure from the instructing banks than concern expressed by the respective governments. Aware of 'difficulties of competence, personality and organisation at the top in TML and Eurotunnel', they insisted that these be sorted out.[173] And fundamental to the process was the demand that Eurotunnel and TML would effect management changes, with the removal of clashes of personality as important as the need for reinforcement. The first steps in this process were the appointment in January 1989 of Philippe Essig as Chairman of TML in place of McDowall, and, at Eurotunnel, the replacement of Durand-Rival by joint MDs, Tony Ridley and Alain Bertrand. In May an experienced American tunneller, Jack Lemley, became Chief Executive of TML, and later in the year John Noulton was recruited from the DTp. The changes, which were followed by the departure of McDowall, Reeve and Jolivet, were generally welcomed.[174] But although the banking syndicate agreed to allow further drawings on the loan, optimism was dented by Morton's April statement that the cost of the project could now be as high as £5.45 billion if TML earned its new bonuses. Furthermore, the banks' own assessment of the situation was gloomier still. Under the Credit Agreement, they monitored the project via a series of regular 'banking cases', prepared with the help of their technical advisers, Parsons–De Leuw Cather and Lahmeyer International. The December 1988 'case' forecast that the Tunnel would not open until February 1994, which indicated a project cost of £6.3 billion. The project was therefore found to be technically in default under the Agreement. While the banks elected not to enforce the default, worse was soon to come for Eurotunnel.[175]

Although tunnelling costs had been creeping up, Eurotunnel was confident that it could remain within the £6 billion financing limit. But there had been rumours that the contract for the shuttle vehicles, a procurement item with the risks borne by Eurotunnel, would be awarded at a cost greatly in excess of the £252 million envisaged in the 1987 prospectus. When the contract was announced in July 1989 the figure had risen to £600 million. This pushed estimated project costs close to the limit, and Eurotunnel was forced to admit that the total finance available would be insufficient to complete the project, and that the bankers would have to be asked for more money.[176] Eurotunnel's difficulties, which were reported to Thatcher by the new Transport Secretary, Cecil Parkinson, in September,[177] were confirmed when Morton presented a statement to the Stock Exchange on 2 October 1989. Eurotunnel now estimated the final cost of the project at 'just over £7 billion' in September 1985 prices, and Morton announced that the company would need to raise an additional £1.3–1.6 billion in 1990, a quarter of which would be in the form of a rights issue. He also revealed continuing and serious disagreements over projected costs with TML, who were working to a figure of £7.5 billion. The variation was mainly created by differences of opinion about the cost of the lump sum element in the contract, that is the terminals and fixed equipment, including signalling, where design changes and safety requirements were having a significant impact. On top of this, the banks' advisers, who remained sceptical about the chances of completion by June 1993, favoured a higher estimate for construction, which with financing costs implied a cost of £8.3 billion, a figure which was reported to the Treasury Chief Secretary.[178]

Eurotunnel's share price began to tumble as optimism faded. Floated at £3.50 in November 1987, the Units fell by £1 on the first day of London trading, but then rose steadily as favourable tunnelling reports were received. Having reached a high of £11.72 in early June 1989, the difficulties highlighted in July and October precipitated a slide, and the stock was trading at around £5.30 in mid

October.[179] At this stage TML attempted to put pressure on the IGC and the Safety Authority to relax safety requirements in the design specifications, particularly for the shuttle trains, in order to reduce costs. However, with some publicity being given to concerns about safety standards in general, and the autonomy of the Safety Authority in particular, the IGC was in no position to accommodate the contractors.[180] Essig then attempted to politicise the issue by writing to both Transport Ministers, seeking their help in encouraging the supervisory bodies to find 'cost-effective' solutions which would narrow the contractors' financial risks. After Anglo-French consultations this request to reduce safety standards in the interests of cost was firmly declined by Parkinson and Michel Delebarre.[181] TML was in some disarray at this time. The consortium had always been a more fragile alliance than presented publicly, and the British companies had found the early construction more challenging than their French colleagues. There were rumours that two of the companies, Taylor Woodrow and Wimpey, were prepared to withdraw unless a satisfactory deal were reached with Eurotunnel.[182] Certainly, these companies were known to be 'deeply unhappy' with the situation, and their chairmen, Sir Frank Gibb and Sir Clifford Chetwood, went so far as to ask the Governor of the Bank of England, Leigh-Pemberton, to act as a conciliator. Drawn into the matter, Parkinson once again fended off any suggestion that the Government might intervene, unless the negotiations were close to breakdown, and even then, as he made clear to Thatcher, he would tell the companies that the project would have to succeed as a private sector project.[183]

The instructing banks were alarmed by the news of higher cost estimates. This raised the prospect of their final return being deferred by 3–5 years, to 2008, and gave them little confidence that the figures would not rise still further. In September 1989 the lenders considered a number of options: they could stump up more money as and when required; close down Eurotunnel and find another operator; or replace TML with another contractor. The banks were determined to avoid the first option, but the other two were not, in practice, acceptable. Proposals were sought which would limit their exposure while getting the initial financiers, that is the agent banks and TML, to make a greater commitment themselves.[184] Having agreed a loan of £1 billion, albeit on a low-risk, senior creditor basis, the EIB was also monitoring progress, increasingly through the efforts of its managerial adviser, Tom Barrett. It had already expressed concerns about the quality of the project management, and discussed the deteriorating financial situation at its board meeting in October.[185] Morton's October statement went some way towards mollifying the banks and reflected their need for a quid pro quo. In particular, they had extracted the requirement that the cost to Eurotunnel of the target works (tunnelling) be capped, and that the lump sum exposure be clarified. In order to persuade the banks to commit additional finance, the warring parties had agreed that the MdO would conduct a cost assessment of the lump sum works and report in December. However, the Bank of England, which was being drawn further into the financing issue, continued to harbour anxieties. Leigh-Pemberton told the Chancellor, John Major, that there was a risk that the equity, which the Bank had encouraged behind the scenes, would be lost if an agreement between Eurotunnel and TML could not be reached. With Eurotunnel still technically in default, the Governor was also worried that the banks might elect to foreclose at this stage, before significant amounts of money were committed.[186] In fact, pending receipt of the report from the MdO, a decision was deferred. The banks continued to support Eurotunnel into the New Year, though to the accompaniment of 'threatening noises'.[187]

The MdO's report supported Eurotunnel's estimate of the lump sum elements, but did nothing to resolve the disputes between client and contractor.[188] In the first week of 1990 it was evident that the project was at a crossroads. Eurotunnel and TML were locked in argument, and in one element at least their aspirations were in apparent opposition. TML was interested in reducing the capital cost of equipment for which they bore the financial risks; Eurotunnel's interest lay in procuring equipment that would have low operating costs and perform to high standards of reliability.[189] TML was keen to have Morton removed from the firing line, and the banks were prepared to withdraw their support unless an agreement were reached. With guns pointing at several heads, a deal was struck, sufficient to enable the banks to allow a further credit of some £390 million to be drawn down. New Heads of Agreement were signed on 8 January, which transferred more responsibility for cost overruns to TML, but gave the contractors fairly generous treatment elsewhere.[190] Eurotunnel now agreed to share the additional tunnelling costs with TML by raising the target cost from £1.29 to £1.58 billion (in 1985 prices). TML was to pay 30 per cent of costs over that, but there was to be no cap. On procurement, the TML fee of 11.5 per cent was capped at £60 million. As to the lump sum elements – terminals and fixed equipment – the two sides agreed to a co-operative effort to reduce costs. Morton expressed satisfaction that the IGC had accepted the case for the non-segregation of shuttle passengers from their vehicles (see below, pp. 349–50), and that the two sides had agreed to reduce shuttle train speeds to 130 kph, a decision which would reduce ventilation costs. But the net effect of the revised contractual arrangements was to raise Eurotunnel's September cost estimate from £7.0 to £7.2 billion, though an updated estimate was promised in April 1990.[191]

The revision of the contract failed to end the antagonisms, however. Morton had blocked the idea of a joint communiqué, and his press statement provoked a highly publicised row with Peter Costain. A particular bone of contention was the observation that TML's UK tunnelling had been demonstrably less effective and more costly than that of the French.[192] Furthermore, TML was still claiming the right to pursue its lump sum claims via arbitration. In mid-February the banks were refusing to release funds unless the revised contractual arrangements were formally signed, but TML would not do so because it argued that Eurotunnel had not fulfilled its undertaking to make significant management changes, including the appointment of a new chief executive and a reduction in the size of the PID. Eurotunnel's decision to appoint Morton as Deputy Chairman and Chief Executive was regarded as unacceptable. TML had also decided to pursue its claim for the

February payment in the French courts.[193] At this point, with Eurotunnel close to bankruptcy after the Court had ruled that TML should be paid £62 million, and Bénard suggesting that the Tunnel might never be finished, the agent banks invited the Bank of England to mediate.[194] Leigh-Pemberton and Kent attempted to knock some sense into the adversaries, and achieved a measure of success. An agreement reached on 20 February produced the necessary management changes. A buffer between Morton and the contractors was established with the appointment of John Neerhout, another American and former Bechtel VP, as Eurotunnel's 'Project Chief Executive', with Ridley making way for him.[195] TML was paid, and with the banks releasing a further tranche of the loan capital, the crisis was averted. But with the posturing and brinkmanship drawing attention to personalities instead of the very real difficulties with the original contract, it had been a near thing. This new 'accord' was scarcely optimal. Neither Morton nor Neerhout could be described as project managers in the strict sense of the term, but the deal enabled the two sides to talk sensibly at least, though it certainly did not resolve issues of cost. The banks had agreed to release funds only until May, when it expected an agreed statement on final cost. And there were still serious disagreements between the parties, notably about the procurement of railway signalling.[196]

When Morton met Parkinson and his Transport Minister, Michael Portillo, in late February he brushed aside the crisis, and offered reassurances that henceforth the problem would be seen to be 'about money rather than personalities'. The raising of further funds was now a priority.[197] In March he was more specific, informing the Cabinet Secretary, Sir Robin Butler, that Eurotunnel would be seeking an additional £2.5 billion, with £0.5 billion in the form of equity. The news became public when Bénard and Morton presented Eurotunnel's 1989 results in April.[198] Raising further funds of this magnitude was no easy task, of course. Morton had revealed that construction costs had increased by a further £500 million, and the project costs had risen to £7.5 billion. The dispute with TML was still very much alive, and the unresolved claims now amounted to £700 million. The difficulties were compounded by the onset of an economic downturn.[199] Unsurprisingly, then, the refinancing process was a slow and painstaking one. The first step was to seek further support from the EIB, which would act as a psychological boost to sceptical financial markets. On 22 May the Bank agreed to extend its £1 billion loan by a further £300 million. However, the discussion at Board level had been 'long and difficult', and there was also some disappointment with the British Government's reluctance to make up its mind on the proposal to build a high-speed rail line to London, which was being promoted by a joint venture with British Rail (see below, p. 337).[200] On 31 May Eurotunnel was able to announce that it had secured a standby underwriting facility from British and French institutions for an equity issue of about £530 million, and that proposals had been agreed with the agent banks to provide a further £2 billion in loan capital. However, by this time, project costs had risen yet again, to £7.66 billion.[201] And although some progress was made with the loan from the banking syndicate, Eurotunnel was certainly not out of the wood. At an early stage it emerged that banking opinion was fragile. With the Japanese banks 'likely to be difficult to get on board', the agent banks were expected to have to make a disproportionately larger contribution to the £2 billion loan package. Morton also asked the Government to delay a decision on whether to support the joint venture proposing to build a high-speed rail line to London.[202] In the event, Parkinson's announcement that the Government had decided not to support the joint venture was made ten days after a mini prospectus was published on 4 June (see below, pp. 340–1).[203]

By mid-July it was clear that there were problems with the syndication of the banking loan. The banks had extended the default waiver with the condition that Eurotunnel should secure £1.8 of the £2.0 billion by the end of June, but Morton told Parkinson that the response from the banks had been mixed. Only £850 million had been offered, and Leigh-Pemberton complained to Major that the negotiations were 'tiresome and difficult'. The Governor also thought it would be a 'disgrace' if the City were unable to raise the capital for an infrastructure project of this kind.[204] In fact, London did take up its quota, but the task of persuading Tokyo to follow suit proved a greater challenge. Initially, only seven of the 38 Japanese banks in the syndicate agreed to make additional contributions in proportion to their existing loans.[205] While unfavourable reports of the project did not help, the poor response was also determined by conditions for participation set by the Japanese Ministry of Finance. These included: a full take-up by the British and French banks; a further commitment from the EIB; and 'positive support' from the British and French Governments.[206] As to the last requirement, both Eurotunnel and the agent banks had asked Parkinson whether pressure might be exerted on the Japanese institutions through their government. On 9 August Parkinson asked Thatcher whether she would be willing to write to the Japanese Prime Minister, Toshiki Kaifu, making plain the Government's support for the Channel Tunnel as a private sector venture. The Treasury, understaffed during the holiday period, was apparently unhappy with the idea of sending a letter, and attempted to remove any suggestion of a financial commitment.[207] In the hastily prepared, but nevertheless carefully worded letter, Thatcher emphasised the 'great importance' of the project and drew Kaifu's attention to the shortfall in the Japanese contribution to the credit.[208] However, the intervention appeared to have helped to sway some of the Japanese banks, despite the onset of internal financing problems and the uncertainties caused by Saddam Hussain's invasion of Kuwait (2 August).[209] On 14 September Parkinson was able to tell Thatcher that the Japanese commitment had increased from £160 to £290 million.[210] However, attempts to gain a further contribution from the EIB proved unsuccessful.[211]

At the beginning of September the syndication was still far from complete, and it was clear that the deadline set for the rights issue of 14 October would not be met. When Pen Kent, an associate director at the Bank of England, surveyed the state of play, he observed that there was 'serious risk of an accident because those playing brinkmanship miscalculate how near they are to the edge'. And yet he believed that 'somehow the financing will scramble home'. It was now anticipated that £1.35 billion of the £2 billion would be raised, the exact shortfall dependent on whether the £300 million contributed by the EIB was counted as part of the total. A 'final assault' on the laggards was expected to raise another £100–250 million, but it was evident that the instructing banks would have to decide whether collectively to make up the difference. However, Kent noted that the agent banks wished to resist 'heroic gestures' and avoid creating an 'unquenchable expectation that they would always stump up'.[212] By early October the loan deal was finally concluded. A total of £1.8 billion, the minimum specified in the equity underwriting agreement, comprised £1.549 billion from the syndicate, with the agent banks covering the shortfall of £251 million. The addition of the EIB loan allowed Eurotunnel to announce that funding of £2.1 billion had been secured, and a revised Credit Agreement, with higher fees and interest, was signed on 25 October.[213] An additional loan of £200 million from the European Coal and Steel Community was also promised.[214] With the loan capital secured, Eurotunnel went on in November to raise £566 million through a three-for-five rights issue of 199.4 million units, priced at a discounted £2.85 a unit. Travel perks again formed part of the offer, this time in the form of a 50 per cent reduction in fares, transferable to nominated individuals. Estimated yields were lower than in 1987: 10 per cent (gross) in 1998, 35 per cent in 2003.[215] Despite initial qualms, and the proximity of the more attractive privatisation of the regional electricity companies, the issue proved to be a success. Although the bearer unitholders (mainly French) were more enthusiastic in taking up the shares, only 16 per cent of the registered unitholding (mainly British) was unsubscribed for and this was sold in the market at a premium. Once again a crisis had been turned into something of a triumph.[216]

However, the 1990 financing package, coinciding with the much-publicised breakthrough of the service tunnel, offered only temporary relief from the problems facing the project. The prospectus for the rights issue revealed some worrying features. Costs were now shown as £4.21 billion for construction, and £7.61 billion for the project as a whole (in 1985 prices). These figures were, respectively, 56 and 61 per cent higher than those given in the Equity 2 prospectus of September 1986 (Table 10.3). While Eurotunnel sought to blame tunnelling for the cost increases, it was the other elements that were to be prove critical in escalating cost, a fact which had been understood for some time in the DTI.[217] TML's claims against Eurotunnel amounted to £953 million, but only £125 million related to the tunnelling. The bulk of the claims – £811 million or 85 per cent – related to the lump sum items (mechanical and electrical equipment, signalling, etc). The prospectus also revealed that TML were seeking a number of time extensions, notably a 55-week extension for the signalling, the subject of a dispute which had been taken to arbitration. The actual tunnelling had been a difficult, but containable contracting process; turning the tunnels into a piece of complex sophisticated and safe transport infrastructure was to prove an altogether different challenge.[218]

Table 10.3 Increases in Channel Tunnel construction and project costs, 1985–90 (£m., September 1985 prices)

	Original Proposal (September 1985)	*Equity 2 (September 1986)*	*Equity 3 (November 1987)*	*Rights Issue (November 1990)*
Contract	2,331	2,595	2,710	3,969
Contingency		109	132	239
Construction cost	2,331	2,704	2,842	4,208
Corporate costs	368	368[a]	n.a.	787
Inflation	896	607	n.a.	1,031
Financing	799	1,057	n.a.	1,582[b]
Project cost	4,394	4,736	n.a.	7,608

Source: CGT, Submission, September 1985; Eurotunnel, Preliminary Prospectus [Equity 2], September 1986, Pathfinder Prospectus [Equity 3], November 1987, Rights Issue, November 1990.

Notes

The figures in the Equity 3 prospectus were given in November 1987 prices, with project costs given as £4,874 m. For comparative purposes, the 1990 Rights Issue document restated the construction costs in September 1985 prices.

a Includes £5m. for purchase of work and studies carried out by Founder Shareholders.

b Includes £196 m. for net cash outflow during initial operating period.

Cartoon 7 Alastair Morton accuses TML of trying to force it into a corner, while Eurotunnel's share price begins to fall: Richard Wilson, *Times*, 4 October 1989.

The project had been close to foundering on three occasions in 1987–90: in the winter of 1988–9; the autumn of 1989; and in the spring and summer of 1990. The biggest crisis came in 1990, when the lending banks faced the prospect of extending their commitment beyond the point of no return. The evidence indicates that the British Government maintained an appropriate distance from the difficulties experienced by this private sector project, despite its highly political character, although the Bank of England did a great deal to lean on the City, and the Government applied informal pressure on the EIB and the Japanese banks. Nevertheless, although there were further storms on the horizon, 1990 marked the point at which the project was becoming a physical reality, while the financial commitments had proceeded too far to be easily reversed. It was a suitable point, perhaps, for one of the most enthusiastic Prime Ministers to end her involvement with the project. On 22 November 1990 Margaret Thatcher informed her Cabinet colleagues that she intended to step down as Prime Minister, and she was succeeded by John Major six days later.[219] While determined to maintain an arms-length relationship with Eurotunnel, she received progress reports when crisis threatened, and was happy to write to the Japanese Government in the midst of the funding problems in August 1990. She may have found no room for the Tunnel in her extensive memoirs, but there is little doubt that her known and publicised support for the idea of a link between Britain and the Continent helped to prevent the project from foundering when the prospect of abandonment beckoned.[220]

11

FROM TUNNEL TO TRANSPORT FACILITY, 1988–94

1. Completing the railway infrastructure, 1988–94

While the building of the Tunnel was bedevilled by delays and additional expense, the same could also be said of the railway infrastructure, though the publicity it attracted was much more limited. The story of the British share of the investment has already been told, from the perspective of the British Railways Board.[1] Here it is important to highlight the role played by the Government in the process. As we have seen (pp. 308–9), Channon and Major had capped spending on the Phase I works (London-Paris/Brussels core) at £550 million in August 1987. Following further appraisal work in January 1989 British Rail raised its estimate to £706 million, an increase of 16 per cent on the ceiling (now £607 million in Q3/1988 prices). However, the message from Euston House was that the financial return would be higher than that indicated in 1987.[2] Further revisions were made as the costs of the terminals and trains were firmed up. By July the estimate had risen to £884 million in 1988/9 prices, and in October it stood at £905 million, 46 per cent higher than the ceiling (£621 million in 1988/9 prices). With contingencies, the final cost was put at £1.1 billion, nearly 80 per cent higher.[3]

The DTp and Treasury lost no time in expressing concern about the increase in investment costs. The first intimation of a problem came when the Department was asked to authorise the British contribution to initial spending on the high-speed trains. In May 1989, shortly before he departed in a Cabinet reshuffle, Channon wrote to British Rail Chairman, Bob Reid, expressing dismay that the Phase I investment was likely to cost 'considerably more' than the sum he had authorised.[4] When the full extent of the increase emerged in the summer, the new ministerial team of Parkinson and Portillo was discomforted by the news. Not only was an increase in the cost of the passenger trains likely to contribute to a substantial overshoot of the Government's External Financing Limit (EFL) for railways, but British Rail was now expressing doubts about its ability to earn a commercial return on its investment in Channel Tunnel freight, even using a test discount rate of 7 per cent.[5] Treasury opinion was scathing, an official noting that 'We are left with the very unsatisfactory situation of a shaky project containing apparently uncommercial elements and with costs still running out of control'. And Lamont pointed out to Portillo that the Board's failure to 'manage within their 1989/90 provision, and to estimate with any accuracy the costs of their new rolling stock, is a most disturbing signal for the IFR [Investment & Financing Review] and for their management of large projects'.[6] There were mitigating circumstances of course, not least the undeveloped nature of the investment in 1987–8 and the procurement of trains from a single supplier. However, in October Portillo had no option but to remind Reid 'to ensure those responsible for projects are motivated to achieve not only specification but cost targets'. Irritated by an unsatisfactory response from Reid, and armed with Lamont's suggestion that a damage limitation exercise be mounted, the Minister suggested that management consultants be jointly commissioned to undertake an independent assessment of the cost control and project management of Phase I.[7] Touche Ross, who had recently investigated the railways' investment management, were duly appointed in November.[8] Their preliminary report in the following month identified past weaknesses in initial estimating, project definition and reporting, and in January 1990 their principal recommendation – that a task force be established to strengthen project management – was implemented. The consultants continued to work with British Rail in working up an action plan.[9] At the same time a team of engineering consultants, John Brown, was asked to review the status of Phase I, and in April this group was appointed to provide overall project direction.[10] The improvements were such as to convince the DTp that further authorisations of the component parts of the investment could proceed, though projects whose costs had risen by more than 10 per cent were to be reauthorised, and both the Department and the Treasury insisted on regular monitoring. In July John Brown confirmed the picture of a serious escalation in Phase I costs. These were estimated to be between £1.255 and £1.382 billion in Q3: 1989/90 prices, respectively 88 and 107 per cent higher than the Secretary of State's 1987 ceiling.[11]

Of course, it should be recognised that British Rail investment for the Channel Tunnel, with its 48 infrastructure and 10 rolling stock projects in 1990, was the largest the Board had ever undertaken.[12] The major elements were, for Phase I: route upgrading and resignalling; electrification of the West London and Tonbridge-Redhill lines; the Waterloo International Terminal; North Pole Depot; Dolland's Moor freight facility; TransManche Supertrains; and Class 92 locomotives; and for Phase II, North of London trainsets; Ashford International Station; and electrification of the North London line.[13] The size and complexity of the investments taken together demanded appropriate changes in British Rail's organisation, but there is evidence to suggest that this was not fully appreciated at first. As we have seen, when the Treaty was signed in 1986 Kirby and Southgate were appointed as responsible Board Member and Director, Channel Tunnel. However, the initial support was limited for such a multi-dimensional task, encompassing project management, business direction and negotiations with third parties, and it was quickly realised that the management had to be further strengthened to match the scale and complexity of the operation. Thus in November 1987 Kirby was succeeded by John Welsby, a former DTp senior economic adviser, who had impressed when rationalising the Board's engineering business. Southgate was given responsibility for overall project management, together with the development of a high-speed link. In 1989–90 the debate with government over cost overruns and project management weaknesses, together with Welsby's appointment as Chief Executive, prompted further changes. In December 1989 John Palmer, former Deputy Secretary, Public Transport at the DTp, who had departmental experience of the Channel Tunnel, became Managing Director, Channel Tunnel at British Rail. His remit was to provide a general oversight of the entire project, including the proposed Channel Tunnel Rail Link. John Brown's involvement resulted in a strengthened project management team headed by David Chalkley from John Brown as Project Director, and Bob Urie from British Rail as his Deputy. Finally, when Bob Reid I was succeeded as British Rail chairman by former Shell UK boss, Bob Reid II, in April 1990, the latter decided to become personally involved in the Channel Tunnel, as part of what later became a 'mega projects' portfolio. In the process Reid took charge of a newly-formed Channel Tunnel Investment Committee, with oversight of both Phases I and II.[14]

Of course, infrastructure management was only part of the story. It was also necessary to create institutions to plan train services and provide the necessary commercial expertise to exploit the investment. Here we should note that the passenger and freight bodies set up by British Rail to do this were very different. For the passenger business a new subsidiary company, European Passenger Services (EPS) was established. For freight, the Channel Tunnel was seen as the key part of a business strategy designed to transform the less profitable sectors of the rail freight business, which had been grouped together with the name Railfreight Distribution (RfD). Thus, in May 1988 the planning and operation of passenger services was placed under Richard Edgley, former deputy director of Network SouthEast, as Director of the newly-formed EPS. In the following October the requirements of freight were met by establishing RfD, consisting of Freightliners (containers), Speedlink (wagon-load traffic) and International Freight, as a separate entity under Ian Brown. Over the period 1988–94 a substantial amount of management effort was devoted to the preparation for Channel Tunnel services, and although initial thinking was that these would be operated in the public sector, the shadow of railway privatisation complicated the issue and affected subsequent organisational changes. In November 1990 EPS became a wholly-owned British Railways Board subsidiary, with John Palmer as Chairman and Edgley as MD. While the move gave the international services a sharper and distinct focus, and indeed was part of the Board's organisational ambitions in developing the concept of business sectors, it also made it easier to transfer EPS to the private sector when privatisation was placed firmly on the political agenda after 1992. In the meantime EPS managers worked on service planning, in conjunction with their counterparts in France, Belgium, Germany and Holland, developing an ambitious agenda for UK and continental daytime and sleeper services.[15] The RfD business presented a contrast in that there was trading before the Tunnel was opened. In fact, substantial operating losses were made, although there was some success in reducing the deficit via a policy of rationalisation, and notably the abandonment of Speedlink in 1991. It was evident that Brown's business plans rested upon high and, with hindsight, over-optimistic hopes for the Tunnel traffic. The expectation that 35 trains each way per day would be required by the end of the decade prompted plans for a substantial investment in freight. A network of intermodal terminals was established, while a number of joint ventures were created to develop specific parts of the business, notably the carriage of motor cars (Autocare Europe, Transfesa), and intermodal traffic operators (Allied Continental, Combined Transport, ICF, Unilog). Investments of £122 million in locomotives and £42 million in wagons (450 intermodal, 300 automotive) were undertaken.[16]

While the more focussed organisation at British Rail, and the involvement of John Brown, certainly led to improved project management of the infrastructure investment (Phases I and II), by 1990 the estimated costs of the major components had risen sharply, which in turn created doubts about the financial return with an eight per cent discount rate. It was easy to see how the passenger elements, including the Waterloo Terminal, North Pole Depot and the Chislehurst-Folkestone resignalling, had contributed to the additional costs. While there were ready explanations, the basic cause was the fact that the projects had not been scoped in detail in 1987/8, and both Waterloo and North Pole had been the subject of failed bids from the private sector. The original estimate for the Terminal had been £42 million, but when authorisation was given in May 1990 this had more than doubled to £100 million (in Q3: 1989/90 prices). In fact, the facility was redesigned with more capacity at peak periods, and some of the increase was explained by security and customs requirements. Nevertheless, only two months later John Brown redefined the project at a cost of £132 million, and the project was eventually reauthorised at this level in September 1991. British Rail made much of the fact that the Terminal was completed on time (May 1993) and under budget, but the final cost of £145 million (at May 1994) was 45 per cent higher than the 1990 authorisation. The North Pole Depot followed a similar course. Reckoned to cost £49 million after a rather cursory examination, its revised cost on authorisation in May 1990 was £76 million (Q3: 1989/90 prices). Reauthorised in September 1991 at John Brown's figure of £84 million, it was eventually completed at a cost of £76 million, well within the authorised amount but over 50 per cent higher than the original estimate.[17] Finally, the resignalling of the old Boat Train Route 1 was at £82 million (1990), then £89 million (1992), much higher than first envisaged (£13 million), but here British Rail had decided to upgrade the entire line, and authorisation was complicated by the fact that the infrastructure was to be shared with British Rail's subsidised Network SouthEast sector. Even so, the Tunnel component – about £55 million of the final cost of £92 million (Q3:1989/90 prices) – was over four times higher than the initial estimate.[18]

Another component to suffer from increased costs was the rolling stock, the TransManche Super Trains ordered by the British, French and Belgian railways from an international consortium headed by GEC and Alsthom. The British Government wanted to secure a fair share of the order for British industry, and in 1987 a former diplomat, Sir Ronald Arculus, was appointed to ensure this.[19] His intervention was moderately successful, but the negotiation with a single consortium produced problems of its own, contributing to escalating estimates. After a complaint from the German Wagon Builders Association, the European Commission also expressed concern about whether the procurement process, which had been confined to British, French and Belgian manufacturers, complied with EC competition law.[20] As we have seen, the uncertain cost of the trains, which required tri-voltage electrical systems, had sparked off Departmental anxieties about British Rail's project management, and when authorised at £356 million in December 1989, the cost was 37 per cent higher than the original estimate (in 1989/90 prices).[21] On top of this, there were technical and delivery problems, which suggested that project management was no better in the private sector. The dispute between the railways and the manufacturers, which engaged the attention of Sir Bob Reid II, Lord Weinstock (GEC) and successive transport ministers, concerned the contract performance and, in particular, the reliability profile of the trains.[22] The Commons Transport Committee, in its report on the adequacy of Britain's preparations for the opening, published in March 1992, was highly critical of the situation: 'We cannot be the only ones to view with some incredulity the fact that a Channel Tunnel can be built in less time than it takes to order and build the 34 trains which are to run through it'.[23] Morton fastened onto the wrangle between GEC-Alsthom (now a merged operation) and the railway companies, and sniffing an opportunity to sue, told the Commons Transport Committee that he doubted whether the trains would be ready in time for the Tunnel's opening. However, as events turned out the Eurostar trains, though over a year late in their delivery and affected by poor reliability, were brought into operation on 14 November 1994, while the passenger shuttles, which were Eurotunnel's responsibility, did not begin a limited service until 22 December, with a full service delayed until March 1995.[24]

The difficulty with the Phase II passenger commitments was not so much rising costs as economic viability. There was also a greater political content, the result of Peter Snape's amendment to the 1987 Channel Tunnel Act. Under Section 40, the Board was required to produce a report detailing how the British regions would be served by the Tunnel. There were heightened expectations of through passenger services from regional centres, and of local needs in Kent being served by an international station at Ashford. British Rail's report, published in December 1989, promised day services from Manchester, Wolverhampton, Edinburgh and Leeds to Paris and Brussels, and sleeper trains from Scotland and the West of England/South Wales. But Bob Reid I had sounded a note of caution in his preface. Invoking the commercial mantra provided by Section 42 of the Channel Tunnel Act, which prevented British Rail's international railway services from being grant-aided, he stated that trains would not be run merely because they were desirable.[25] Political interests, particularly in Wales and Scotland, were less willing to be bound by strictly commercial criteria, however. Although with hindsight some of the demands now appear rather fanciful, there is no doubt that in the late 1980s expectations of high traffic volumes through the Tunnel were widespread. The Commons Select Committee on Welsh Affairs, for example, in its Report on the implications for Wales in 1989, asked, *inter alia*, for passenger rail services to connect with Tunnel services, together with electrification of the London-South Wales line. When demand built up it expected to have through day- and night-time services.[26] In Scotland, Malcolm Rifkind, the Scottish Secretary, expressed 'keen disappointment' that there was to be no through day-time passenger service from Glasgow.[27] The Commons Transport Committee also took an interest in the subject. In its 1992 Report it was particularly critical of the lack of urgency in progressing a station at Ashford, and it also reported criticisms from local authorities that the constraints of Section 42 would leave 'a large swathe of the country without access to through night services to the continent'.[28] All this was indicative of expectations that, notwithstanding the contemporary recession, the future would see a rapid expansion in cross-channel traffic, and that the Tunnel would command a good share of it.

A substantial amount of commercial risk was therefore encouraged in the Phase II investment, the main elements of which were the regional day-time services, sleeper services, and the Ashford station. All were deemed to be of doubtful value using the Treasury's yardstick of financial worth. Following political pressure from Kent, the Ashford project was revived in 1990, three years after Channon's rejection, but was complicated by its association with the proposals for a high-speed line. A scheme incorporating works for the latter was costed at £94 million (1989/90 prices), four times higher than the more modest proposal in 1987.[29] Neither the DTp nor British Rail regarded the facility as a priority, given its marginal nature, but pressed by Morton and Eurotunnel in 1990–1, British Rail warned the Department that unless the station were authorised quickly it would not be ready in time for the opening and would therefore constitute a breach of the railways' Usage Contract.[30] The Department, on the other hand, was adamant that the station could not be afforded at the suggested cost (in January 1991) of £139 million. With Morton continuing the pressure with a scheme of his own, including a temporary 'Portakabin' provision designed to embarrass the Government, the Department pressed British Rail to examine cheaper options.[31] In February 1992 the Board came up with three such proposals, including a favoured option costing half that of the earlier scheme, but requiring further expenditure if a high-speed line were built.[32] However, departmental consideration was hindered, first by the absence of a detailed appraisal, second, by a general election, third, by further consideration of the high-speed line, and finally by the re-elected Conservative Government's plans for railway privatisation. It was some time before the station was eventually authorised as a private sector venture, one of the first under the Private Finance Initiative. The railway works – amounting to a not inconsiderable £60 million[33] – were funded by British Rail, but the station itself was built by John Laing in return for rent and a usage toll to be paid by EPS. Requiring a Government guarantee once EPS had passed into Government ownership (prior to its acquisition by London & Continental Railways), it was eventually completed in 1996. The project was a wonderful demonstration of the clash between economic imperatives and political expediency.[34]

Provision for services beyond London was also affected by doubts within British Rail and Whitehall as to whether the investment would make an appropriate return. There were also difficulties with the procurement. In 1991, it emerged that GEC-Alsthom was unwilling to produce day-time trains capable of splitting, and British Rail had no alternative but to abandon its ambitious plans in favour of a less complex and cheaper, non-splitting, alternative. Even so, there were difficulties. Not only was the return below eight per cent, even with somewhat optimistic traffic forecasts, but the trains would also compete with, and threaten the profitability of, British Rail's InterCity sector.[35] Nevertheless, despite Treasury scepticism, an investment of about £230 million in day and sleeper trains was eventually authorised by Malcolm Rifkind, Parkinson's successor as Secretary of State, in July and November 1991.[36] Unfortunately, the costs of modifying the railway infrastructure to handle the trains rose sharply over the course of 1992 and 1993, further prejudicing fragile returns, and the traffic forecasts were revised downwards in 1994. By this time opinion in British Rail, distracted by the prospect of privatisation, was that the day services, which would be loss-making, should be confined to the West Coast Main Line. The sleeper trains, financed by a leasing agreement, were ordered in July 1992, and an international joint venture company led by EPS was formed to operate them. However, while the stock was delivered in 1995–6, neither type of service was provided, because the subsequent owners of EPS, London & Continental Railways, were not prepared to go ahead.[37]

Freight preparations involved investments under both Phases I and II. Here the problem was escalating costs coupled with British Rail's growing doubts about the commercial viability, not only of Channel Tunnel freight, but also of its newly-constituted non-bulk sector, RfD. As we have noted, the strategy documentation produced by British Rail in the summer of 1989 suggested that the investment in freight would produce a negative return with both 7 and 8 per cent discounting. This caused some consternation in Whitehall, since the picture contrasted sharply with earlier indications of substantial profitability in 1987.[38] Pressed by both the DTp and Treasury to reappraise freight prospects, a revised strategy emerged in February 1990. Here, it was decided that for the Tunnel RfD would concentrate on trainload activities, notably intermodal and automotive traffics. Envisaging the need for 35 trains each way per day the core elements in the investment were: electrification of the Tonbridge-Redhill line, provision of 30 new dual-voltage locomotives and 750 wagons.[39] The new package promised an improved return but required a much larger capital investment. Estimated costs, initially put at £145 million, had already been raised to £225 million, an increase of 55 per cent.[40] After the February 1990 review, they rose still further, to £310 million (expenditure to 1994/5), and £345 million (to 1998/9). By February 1992 the estimate had increased to £408 million.[41] Procurement in all areas was to prove disappointing.

The cost of the complex Class 92 locomotives rose sharply from an initial £38 million to £102 million for 37 units in June 1991, a figure which was increased by £10 million in the following month, and reached £122 million by 1994.[42] Utilisation was hampered by delayed delivery and technical difficulties, some of them caused by Eurotunnel's own problems with signalling (see below). Freight services began in June 1994 without them; between February 1995 and June 1996 the locomotives were restricted to Tunnel use only; thereafter clearance was given to run through to Wembley, but not via the Tonbridge-Redhill line. Here the £24 million investment was rendered virtually redundant by the need for expensive additional work in track circuitry. A sizeable investment was made in freight terminals, at Dollands Moor, Wembley, and in regional centres, £87 million in all, but the commercial prospects remained poor. Treasury officials had been right to challenge the more up-beat forecasts produced by Ian Brown and RfD. As early as November 1989, one official suggested that 'there does not seem much room in the market at all for RFD . . . we are not persuaded that it is sufficient to bank on BR being able to turn its non-bulk businesses round in time to get Channel Tunnel business off on the right foot . . . The verdict of history is very much against them'. While this was a harsh view, the railfreight story was not a happy one, but both the nationalised railways and their sponsoring Ministry were fettered by the commitments given to Eurotunnel.[43] The situation led the Treasury to challenge the commercial wisdom of these undertakings. As Steve Robson put it in April 1990, 'My overall reaction is that BR should never have entered into the Usage Agreement. It has penalty terms which push them into the freight business despite the very low returns offered'.[44]

What investment was finally made in order to meet the obligations contained in the Usage Contract of 1987? When the Tunnel was officially opened in May 1994, the outturn costs of Phases I and II amounted to £1.45 billion in Q3: 1989–90 prices.[45] By this time it was clear that the return was much less secure than had been claimed initially, especially using a test discount rate of 8 per cent instead of the 7 per cent in use in 1987. With hindsight we can see that a sizeable proportion of the total investment, perhaps as much as a third, was made in patently unprofitable and even redundant areas. But it has to be remembered that the procurement was undertaken in a climate of general optimism about Tunnel prospects, amidst political pressure from the regions, and with fears of financial penalty should the infrastructure and trains not be ready in time for Eurotunnel's opening. In the course of the numerous reviews and appraisals, a number of exercises were undertaken to calculate the costs of not proceeding with the investment, either in whole or in part. With penalty payments and the cost of litigation, both from Eurotunnel and the French and Belgian railways, the calculations produced large sums as the prospective liability of the nationalised British Rail. In July 1990 a British Rail appraisal referred to an 'abandonment' NPV of −£772 million; a more confidential estimate of the Board's exposure in early 1991 produced a range from £403 to £1,454 million.[46] At regular intervals the Treasury made complaining noises about British Rail's project management,[47] and successive ministers were moved to challenge either specific elements of the investment or the extent of the total commitment to the Tunnel. However, given the legislative imperatives there was little that they could do but authorise the investment, after the due appraisal process. In fact, successive Secretaries of State, first Parkinson, then Rifkind (from November 1990), and finally John MacGregor (from April 1992), were only too anxious to claim credit for the government support they were giving to this private sector venture.[48] In fact, other issues were more pressing. Interest in the prospect of a high-speed rail link tended to dominate discussions in Whitehall, especially after 1990 (see below), and the general railway environment began to change radically while the investment was being undertaken, since after the re-election of the Major Government in April 1992 the impetus was firmly on the privatisation of British Rail. The attention of civil servants was engaged fully in handling matters concerning the disposal and sale of assets, rather than considering the dog days of a nationalised business.[49] Bob Reid, Welsby and other senior managers in British Rail, already sceptical about the traffic prospects offered by the Tunnel, were also distracted by the privatisation process. By the time the Tunnel was opened in May 1994, the rail infrastructure was under the control of a new body, Railtrack, and together with EPS had been turned into a Government-owned company (GoCo). Both were destined for the private sector.[50]

2. The Channel Tunnel Rail Link, 1988–94

Contrasting with the obligations placed on SNCF, the Usage Contract did not require British Rail to provide a dedicated high-speed rail link to the Tunnel. Indeed, in the mid-1980s British railway managers took the view that additional capacity would not be required in the foreseeable future. The first suggestion that the existing infrastructure in the south of England might ultimately constrain the growth of international rail services was contained in the Kent Impact Study produced for Mitchell's Joint Consultative Committee in August 1987. Mitchell then asked British Rail to undertake further work. The results of these endeavours were published as *Channel Tunnel Train Services* in July 1988.[51] We have seen that during the negotiations over the Usage Contract, the traffic forecasts prepared by British Rail's consultants, MVA, were lower than those prepared by SETEC for Eurotunnel and SNCF (pp. 301–5). Although Welsby and the Board continued to harbour serious doubts about the validity of SETEC's figures, the analysis of July 1988 was based on both sets of data.[52] Under the more optimistic scenario, capacity constraints would arise from the mid-1990s, but with the MVA data the problem was postponed until the turn of the century. Having rehearsed the options for increasing capacity, British Rail regarded the construction of a new route as the only realistic way forward. After rejecting the line proposed in 1974 via Tonbridge, Edenbridge and Croydon (p. 145 and Figure 6.1), together with a northerly route via Dagenham, the report presented four broad route corridors (Table 11.1 and Figure 11.1). The first, via Hollingbourne, was the most direct

Table 11.1 British Rail's four options for new route capacity, July 1988

Route	*Alignment*
1	North of Ashford-Charing-Hollingbourne-Snodland-tunnel-Longfield-Sidcup
2	As Route 1-Longfield-Swanley-Bromley
3	South of Ashford-Pluckley-Marden-Borough Green-tunnel-Swanley-Bromley
4	South of Ashford-Pluckley-existing line-Marden-Tonbridge-tunnels-Orpington-Bromley

Source: BRB, *Channel Tunnel Train Services* (July 1988), p. 11.

and offered the greatest opportunity for high-speed running. The other routes were cheaper, but were only suited to terminal sites in central or west London. Route 4, the most southerly, was not really a new route, but proposed the addition of new tracks alongside the alignment of the existing Boat Train Route 1. For the London terminal, 42 locations were quickly reduced to four: White City, in west London; St. Pancras; King's Cross Low Level, below the existing station; and Stratford in east London, above the existing station. Of these, King's Cross appeared to be the most attractive, and St. Pancras the least, since existing domestic services would need to be diverted to other stations. Cost estimates for combinations of route and terminal, forming 'Phase III' of British Rail's investment in Tunnel-related infrastructure, were put in the range £725 million (Route 2 and White City) to £1,200 million (Route 1 and King's Cross). There was a corresponding range of journey-time reductions, with Route 4 offering a saving of only 12–17 minutes on a journey of 70 minutes, while Stratford and Route 1 promised a saving of 34 minutes, although this advantage was largely offset by the inconvenience of the location in relation to central London.[53] Financial evaluations of the options indicated that with the MVA forecasts there would be no case for providing additional capacity 'until well into the next century', while with the SETEC figures a case could be made for provision by the turn of the century. However, the evaluations did not take into account the possible 'spin off' for domestic passenger services, and further work was needed to assess the potential for faster commuter services sharing the line. Overall, the tone of British Rail's response to Mitchell was cautious and did not represent an urgent demand for a new link. It was conceded that much remained to be done, and it would be two years before detailed survey and design work would enable a preferred route to be determined, an obvious prerequisite before parliamentary powers could be sought.[54] Clearly, many uncertainties remained about the traffic forecasts, and the Board wished to wait until the Tunnel had opened, and it could assess actual traffic levels, before committing itself to a large and risky investment.[55]

There was little dissent in Whitehall over the contents of the report. Ministers maintained a low profile, deciding that it would be best to distance themselves from the publication. Channon took the view that it was British Rail's report and it was for British Rail to defend it.[56] However, there were two sensitive issues requiring a political stance: the environmental implications; and the prospect of

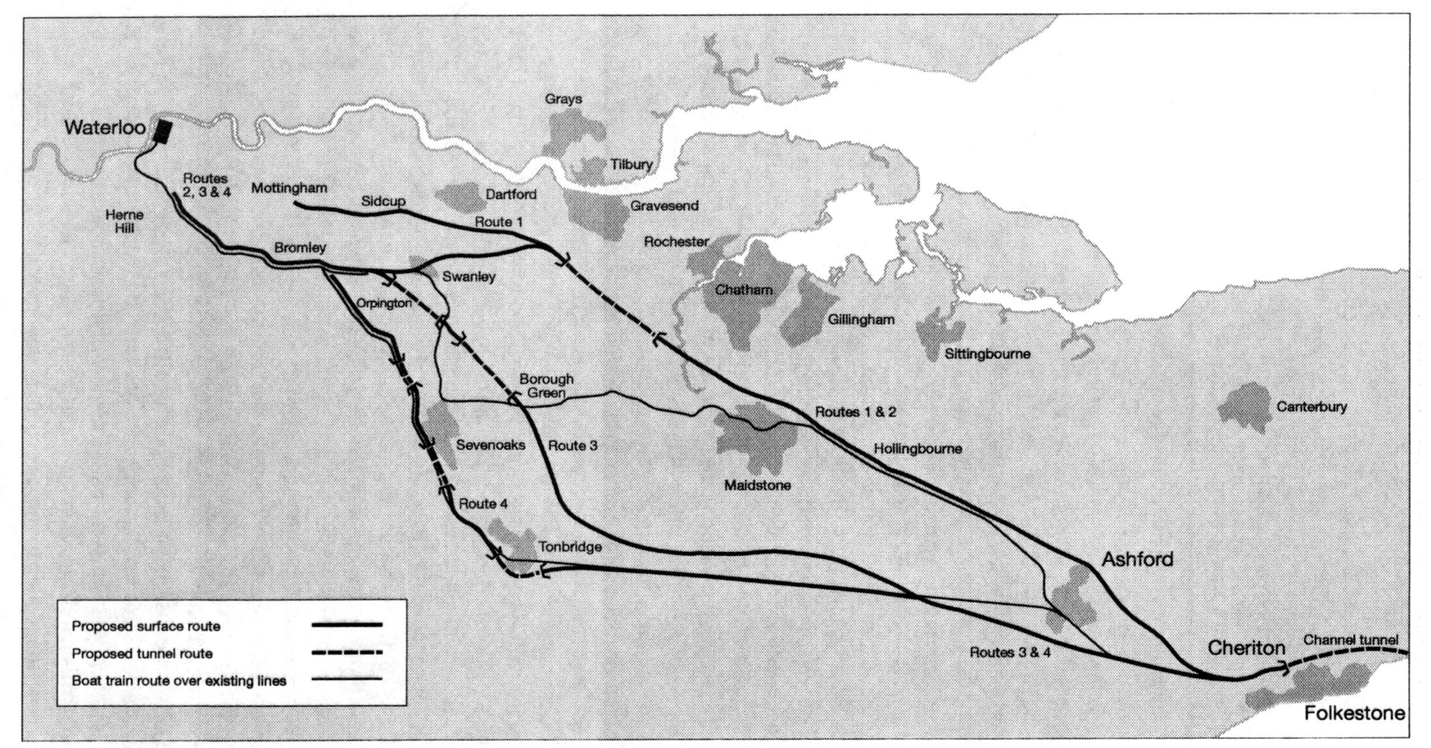

Figure 11.1a Channel Tunnel Rail Link: British Rail's four route options, 1988.

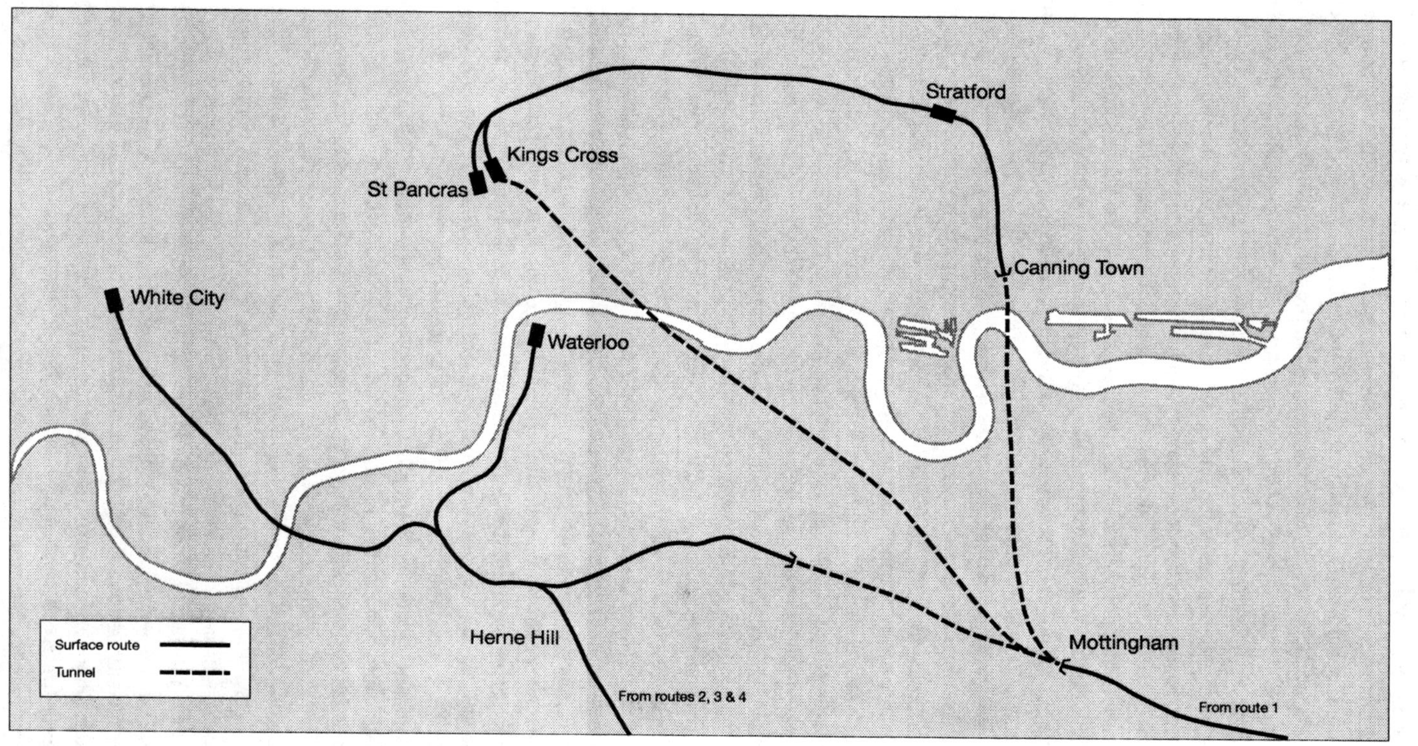

Figure 11.1b British Rail's four route options, 1988: London termini.

private financing. On the first, the Department had assured the Treasury that the publication of route corridors would not create blight, while both Channon and Ridley, now Environment Secretary, agreed that a public inquiry was to be avoided and felt that a private Bill should be deposited in the normal way.[57] The financing issue attracted some debate. During the course of British Rail's study, DTp officials had kept in mind the potential for private sector involvement through either financing, construction or operation of the new line, and in responding to the publication of the report, Channon welcomed the possibility.[58] There were complexities, of course. Should British Rail devise a scheme and then seek partners, or should the private sector be involved from the outset? What form would the financing take? Taking British Rail's more pessimistic traffic forecasts, would the private sector put up money without some form of implicit guarantee? Would such an arrangement transfer sufficient risk? Would it fall foul of the Treasury's 'Ryrie rules', which stipulated that the efficiency gains of private sector involvement should offset the higher financing? Such questions bore a striking similarity to those raised in the early 1980s about the funding of the Tunnel itself.[59]

At the same time, Morton was busy pressing his own idea for a Channel Tunnel rail link, comprising new and upgraded sections. The existing infrastructure would be sold to the private sector, enhanced and then leased back to British Rail. When Morton put the proposal to both Lamont and Channon, he was encouraged by Eurotunnel's latest and more optimistic traffic forecasts, which indicated that extra rail capacity would be required as soon as the Tunnel opened. British Rail, claimed Morton, was suffering from a 'lack of enterprise'. But there were distinct limits to Eurotunnel's entrepreneurial zeal: the company would not put up any money itself, but would instead adopt the role of 'promoters-cum-catalysts'.[60] As one Treasury official observed, 'although BR think he is wrong, we do not intend to obstruct anybody else who wants to put their money where his mouth is', adding that 'it would be very useful to be able to call the bluff of the lobby criticising BR for short-sightedness'.[61] And there had been some tentative interest from the private sector, notably from Trafalgar House and Costains, the latter unveiling 'Network Neptune', a project for a high-speed rail network linking the Tunnel with the North, Scotland, the Midlands, Wales and Central London.[62] In another development, British Rail prepared guidelines, with the help of Lazards, setting out the basis on which private sector firms would be invited to submit proposals. The Chairman, Bob Reid I, suggested that the Transport Secretary might make an announcement drawing attention to this initiative, and Channon readily agreed, incorporating it into his speech at the Conservative party conference in October.[63] A pre-qualification document, released in November, required Government clearance. Both ministers and officials were anxious to ensure that interested parties were not deterred, and that radical options were not ruled out.[64]

Unfortunately, British Rail's report created a storm in Kent, where the revelation of the route corridors produced planning blight across a wide area. At several meetings with Kent MPs and local authority representatives, Channon and Portillo were forced to concede that British Rail was not handling the issue well.

The clear message from all interested parties was that the options had to be narrowed down to a single preferred alignment as quickly as possible.[65] This gave momentum to the decision-making process. Compensation for property owners, a thorny matter, was one of the elements tackled. Here the difficulty was that the statutory provisions only applied to properties which were actually required for the line, and would not come into effect until the necessary parliamentary powers had been obtained, a process that could take at least three years. In November British Rail decided to relieve some of the problems of blight by going beyond its strict legal liability, in offering to make *ex gratia* payments in cases of genuine hardship.[66] However, the subject continued to provoke a good deal of agitation, which culminated in a Commons adjournment debate at the beginning of December, the first opportunity for MPs to discuss the proposal. Speaking for the Government, Portillo made it clear that the choice of route was British Rail's alone; the views of Kent County Council would be known in January 1989 and British Rail hoped to identify the preferred corridor shortly after that. The Minister emphasised that expenditure on associated environmental works would have to be included in the capital cost of the project. And in another gesture of appeasement on blight, he announced that British Rail was 'actively considering' making compensation payments when the route was announced.[67] The statement may have offered some reassurance in Kent, but it created alarm in Whitehall, where the Treasury regarded such proposals as 'excessive and unnecessary'.[68] The subsequent response of Kent County Council was less supportive, however. Accepting the argument for additional rail capacity but rejecting the existing route proposals, officers recommended consultation over more detailed alignments within a *single* corridor. The reaction of the DTp was that the report was as positive and as helpful as could be expected 'given BR's unhappy performance in Kent'.[69]

Meanwhile, away from Kent, there were difficulties with the selection of the second London terminal. King's Cross was the preferred choice of British Rail, being the location best able to accommodate both international and domestic traffic, the latter also including enhancements to the newly-opened Thameslink (Luton-Gatwick) services. But an equally important consideration was the fact that the area was the subject of proposals for development, led by Rosehaugh Stanhope. Much of it was on railway-owned land, and was thought to be worth at least £3 billion. This scheme was promoted in the King's Cross Railways Bill of November 1988. However, there was a complication, because in order to preserve the option of constructing a low-level international station there, it would be necessary to undertake substantial works at the same time as the rest of the development. Thus, the station was included in the Bill as a contingency.[70] The Treasury was most unhappy with the turn of events, fearing that British Rail's actions would effectively pre-empt the choice of terminal location. Matters came to a head in January 1989 when, following legal advice about the petitioning process for the Bill's second reading, British Rail suddenly announced that King's Cross was its preferred site for the international terminal. Officials were upset about this 'massive bounce', all the more so because a formal investment appraisal had not been submitted.[71] Supporters of the Stratford option, notably local MP Tony Banks, and the London Borough of Newham, were also unhappy.[72]

Assessing the situation at the end of January 1989, the Treasury was worried about the public expenditure implications: some £200–500 million in compensation; and £200 million for the preparatory work at King's Cross. Sunk costs of this magnitude would make the project 'inevitable'. And, Chief Secretary Major was warned, when Transport Ministers raised the issue they were 'likely to do so in something of a hurry'.[73] As predicted, the Rail Link came quickly to the fore, although the urgency emanated not, as expected, from the Department, which was involved in lengthy discussions with the Treasury, but from No.10. Stung by the way in which the new line had aroused hostility, the Prime Minister decided to take a personal interest in the project, and Channon, Ridley, Major and Portillo were called in to see her before a Cabinet meeting on 9 February.[74] It was agreed that a single proposal for the Rail Link should be pursued with 'maximum speed' in order to minimise blight, and while ideally the project should be financed in full by the private sector, a contribution from the public purse was not ruled out. This latter point was not of course to be disclosed to British Rail. The DTp was asked to produce a 'comprehensive paper' for discussion at a further meeting of Ministers in a fortnight's time. Reid I, Welsby and Kirby from British Rail were to be called in to make a presentation and, in order to allow Thatcher the option of taking part in revealing the chosen route, British Rail's announcement had to be made on 8 March.[75]

Channon's paper rehearsed the main areas of concern, giving particular attentions to environmental problems and the economics of the project.[76] Blight and compensation had been the subject of a continuing dialogue, and the package that British Rail intended to offer was set out by the Transport Secretary in separate correspondence. Once the route was announced, British Rail would purchase any property required for the construction of the line, together with any other property within a specified distance (100 metres in rural areas, 50 metres in built-up areas) if the owner claimed blight. Both Major and Ridley accepted that, in the circumstances, this was the minimum that could be done.[77] There were also issues of visual intrusion and noise, the latter mainly a consequence of high-speed running. Channon criticised British Rail for giving the impression that commercial requirements would preclude extensive environmental protection, but was quite clear that the cost of these desirable measures could not be subsidised by the Government. However, it was estimated that environmental protection would push the cost of the project up from £1 billion to £1.4–1.8 billion, and, as Welsby was eager to point out, at these levels the viability of the line would be compromised.[78] In spite of these legitimate concerns, there was a fairly widespread hope that the more optimistic traffic forecasts now in circulation would attract the interest of private capital. Certainly, at No.10 the Policy Unit thought that British Rail had moved too slowly to exploit potential new markets. A gung-ho paper referred to 48 million passenger trips and 60 million tonnes of freight by 2003, and to further growth produced by the 'M25 effect', and advised Thatcher that it was 'imperative' to involve the private sector.[79] In contrast, Treasury officials, naturally worried by a document which was 'unblemished by figures', and uneasy at the increasing degree of political commitment, advised their Chief Secretary that it should not be assumed 'that the private sector will build and finance it on acceptable terms'.[80]

Thatcher, Channon, Ridley, Major and Portillo met again on 23 February, augmented, at the Prime Minister's request, by senior officials. The mood was 'very much for cracking on with the building of the line as soon as possible'.[81] It was agreed that British Rail should make an announcement about their preferred route, provided that details relating to environmental protection, compensation and the timetable were 'fully worked through'. Then, in order to accelerate the process, it would be necessary to introduce a private Bill in the coming November.[82] Following a presentation to Ministers, British Rail announced its chosen route on 8 March. The line would run from Cheriton, through the centre of Ashford, and then follow the M20 to Detling, Upper Halling, Darenth and Swanley; it would then continue in tunnel to King's Cross, with a junction at Warwick Gardens (Peckham) providing a connection to Waterloo (Figure 11.2). Aside from the decision to serve Ashford directly, the route resembled option 2 in the 1988 report.[83] Enjoying the blessing of the Government, the Channel Tunnel Rail Link now required legislative action and serious negotiations with the private sector. In less than a year, it had been transformed from merely a cautious possibility into a project that appeared certain to go ahead. In the process, public expectations were raised, and, whatever the financial case, it had become politically difficult to backslide.[84]

It was over a year before Cabinet Ministers returned to the subject. During this period, British Rail undertook further work in defining the route, and there were lengthy negotiations with the private sector. The two issues were interrelated, since it was thought that the best prospects lay in a joint venture arrangement for *all* the international passenger services (including the Phase I investment), with British Rail taking an equity stake, and in limiting the scheme for financial reasons to the *above-ground* section between Cheriton and Swanley.[85] In November 1989 a joint venture was announced between British Rail and Eurorail Ltd., a consortium of Trafalgar House and BICC (Balfour Beatty).[86] At the same time, British Rail deferred the submission of a private Bill for the full route until November 1990, having abandoned the alternative of introducing a partial Bill for the above-ground section. The complexities of reaching agreement about the project and its financing had made it difficult to proceed immediately.[87] Over the ensuing months, the settlement of precise terms for the joint venture, and the working up of a financial case proved a severe challenge. Indeed, there was growing scepticism on all sides that the venture, known as European Rail Link, could be supported at all. An amended route was presented to Parkinson, now Transport Secretary, in February 1990, and a submission with financial projections followed at the end of March.[88] Thatcher was briefed on the matter in early May. The line

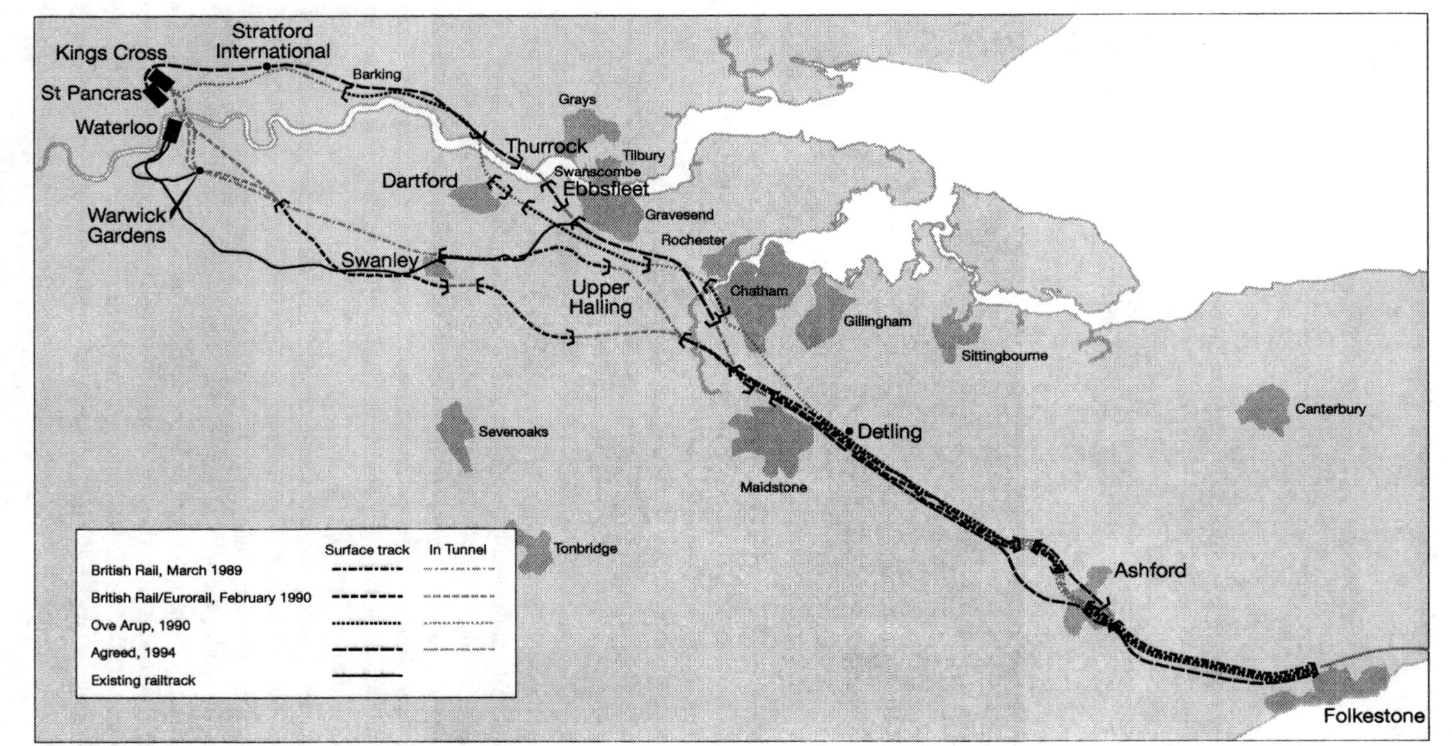

Figure 11.2 Channel Tunnel Rail Link: options, 1989–94.

now incorporated more running alongside the existing infrastructure in south London, with tunnelling confined to the section from Hither Green to King's Cross (Figure 11.2), changes which promised to reduce the estimated capital cost from £3.35 billion to £2.65 billion.[89] However, the latter figure still represented a considerable advance on earlier estimates, and even on very favourable assumptions, the project fell short of viability by at least £1 billion, on Eurorail's estimates. The demands of the private sector consortium stretched the Government's ability to support the project. Eurorail were looking for a capital grant of £500 million in recognition of benefits for commuter services using the line, together with an advantageous Government loan of £1 billion, covering the reassignment of British Rail's borrowing to fund its Phase I investment, and ranking below all other creditors in the event of default. Parkinson may have been ready to concede the grant, but not the loan, and the new British Rail chairman he had appointed, Bob Reid II, was also sceptical about the joint venture. The Transport Secretary therefore warned the Prime Minister that the terms would leave the Government open to attack for making an over-generous commitment while leaving most of the risk in the public sector. His recommendation was that British Rail should be instructed to abandon the joint venture, a decision which he conceded was unlikely to come as a surprise to Eurorail.[90] At the Treasury, Lamont agreed that the level of risk transfer was insufficient to justify the 'overt and covert subsidies' which the private sector partners required to earn a return ($12\frac{1}{2}$ per cent) on their small equity investment (a proposed 14 per cent).[91]

There was less unanimity about the next steps. Parkinson identified four options: find a more viable route; proceed with a public sector project; abandon the project; or keep the project alive with the minimum amount of work. Alternative routes were being developed by rival consortia (see below, p. 340) but none was thought to offer greater viability than the Eurorail proposals. In any case, there was a risk of opening up further areas of Kent and Essex to blight. Nor would the Link's financial viability be improved under public sector conditions, and Parkinson found it easy to reject this idea. Thus, on purely financial grounds, it made sense to abandon the project, but, of course, there were the familiar political arguments for not taking this position. There would be 'invidious comparisons' with France, which was pressing ahead with its high-speed line, and accusations that the Government was failing to exploit the full advantages of the Tunnel and the European Single Market in 1992. Another factor was the financial position of Eurotunnel. Here, Parkinson admitted that an abandonment could have a serious impact on the company's ability to raise additional money to complete the Tunnel.[92] Morton was lobbying furiously at this stage and although he disingenuously told Thatcher that the Rail Link was a project 'in which we are not involved and on which we are not depending', there was no doubting that a positive decision would assist Eurotunnel in its negotiations with the banks.[93] Against this background, the Transport Secretary thought that the best course of action was to keep the project alive by safeguarding the route. There was some opposition to this strategy from both the Treasury and the Policy Unit. Lamont contended that it would be 'very dangerous' to fix the route now 'for all time' since it might transpire in a few years' time that 'the safeguarded route was not the best one'.[94] The Policy Unit briefed the Prime Minister in uncompromising terms. It did not think the route should be protected merely because British Rail, with its property-development ambitions at King's Cross, happened to favour it. Short shrift was also given to the idea of making a 'precipitate statement' to assist Eurotunnel in its financing. The Government had 'no obligation to bail out its [Eurotunnel's] cost overruns either directly or indirectly by creating the expectations of a fixed link'.[95] When Thatcher met with Ministers on 24 May it was agreed that the joint venture should not proceed. However, the possibility of a Link was to be 'kept in play' via a compromise solution, in which the route between the Tunnel and the North Downs was safeguarded, with effect from September 1990, while the remainder of the line, including the terminal, was left open for 'further study', with the aim of maximising benefits to both international and commuter passengers.[96] These conclusions were confirmed at a meeting of E(A) Committee on 14 June, and later that day in a Commons statement.[97]

While the Eurorail proposals were being developed, other private sector promoters were working on rival schemes for the Rail Link. Two of these had been unsuccessful in the joint venture competition: Rail-Europe, a consortium of Laing, Mowlem, GTM, and subsequently Manufacturers Hanover and Bechtel; and Ove Arup, the consulting engineers. Rail-Europe began by promoting two easterly routes known as RACHEL (RAinham to CHannel TunnEL) and TALIS (Thames Alternative Link International System), but they eventually concentrated on the latter, a line through the Medway to Tilbury and Stratford. Ove Arup, acting with Colin Stannard and Kentrail, developed an ambitious scheme for a four-track line, with provision for international freight. This also followed an easterly route from Detling, crossing the Thames north of Dartford and proceeding to Stratford and King's Cross (Figure 11.2).[98] In 1990, an easterly route held some attraction for Ministers because of the possibility of a large development at Rainham marshes proposed by the Music Corporation of America.[99] The London Borough of Newham continued to press its case for a terminal at Stratford served by British Rail's southerly route. The Stratford plan, which was formulated in conjunction with Colin Buchanan & Partners, made 'gloomy reading' for at least one Treasury official, who noted that the route 'comes through my front room!'[100] At Parkinson's request, British Rail evaluated all the various options, engaging no fewer than 16 consulting firms in the process. The work encompassed new traffic and revenue studies, socio-economic and development benefits, and environmental impact. The resulting mountain of paper was considered by the British Railways Board in April and May 1991.[101]

At a special meeting on 2 May Board members backed the southerly route to King's Cross, which was shown to have the best financial return (4.2 per cent), and on the following day Bob Reid II passed on the decision to Rifkind, now Transport Secretary.[102] A week later Rifkind met Major, now Prime Minister. Railway privatisation was the main item of business, but the Rail Link was also discussed, with Rifkind emphasising that the Government was under strong pressure to reach an early decision. The Transport Secretary was asked to produce firm recommendations within two-three weeks, and a Rail Link Steering Group, comprising officials from the DTp, DOE, Treasury and the Policy Unit, was established to produce a report.[103] This intention quickly ran into difficulties when it became apparent that, notwithstanding British Rail's paper mountain, there was insufficient information to enable officials to properly assess the options. Nonetheless, Rifkind still hoped that a report would be ready by the end of June and that an announcement could be made before the July Recess.[104] Although the Department laid the blame for this delay squarely at the door of British Rail, there was at least a suspicion in No.10 that the DTp had not been firm enough with its railway corporation.[105] The receipt of additional information from British Rail towards the end of June did little to improve the situation, and there was pressure from the Steering Group to delay the report until the autumn.[106] On top of this the Treasury representative, Steve Robson, was expressing disquiet over the drafting of the report. Finding sections 'fundamentally flawed', he warned that unless officials provided advice, rather than merely handing on British Rail's work, he might be forced to write a dissenting note.[107] Nevertheless, the officials' report was completed in the first week of July, and Rifkind sent it to Major, Norman Lamont, now Chancellor, and Michael Heseltine, the Environment Secretary. It was a substantial document, with over 50 pages of analysis, eight annexes, and an 11-page memorandum from Rifkind. But in spite of all this work, the argument appeared to have moved little further forward, and the now familiar issues concerning the need for the new line, the financial case, and environmental factors were once again rehearsed.[108]

On this occasion, however, Ministers became actively involved in choosing the route, a decision which hitherto had been left to British Rail. It was over this issue and its handling that the debate became polarised. Rifkind advocated British Rail's southerly route, with its terminal at King's Cross, arguing that it was the best option in 'purely transport planning terms'. He wanted to 'confirm now' the need for a new line and announce that this route would form the basis for detailed consultations. Heseltine agreed that the international station should be located at King's Cross, but favoured the Arup route. Not only was it 'environmentally inoffensive', but it also suited his long-held ambitions to develop the East Thames gateway. His initial response was that there should be an announcement that the Link would be built, terminating at King's Cross, but that further work would be undertaken on *both* routes.[109] In contrast, Lamont's response was, in Major's words, 'wholly negative'. He was adamant that no commitment at all should be made, and argued that the decision whether to build a line should be left to the privatised railway companies.[110] Responding to his colleagues' criticisms, Rifkind appealed to wider factors, including the 'national interest' and the need for 'long-term vision'. Dealing with the Treasury's view that the return was so low that it would involve a loss to the economy of some £2 billion in NPV, he noted that it was at least 'positive' and contended that the 8 per cent requirement for nationalised industry investments was not 'absolute'. His conclusion was that a firm decision should be made to proceed with the Link along the preferred route, or else the project was dead.[111] The divergence of ministerial views was thus so great that consideration was postponed until September.[112] In the meantime Major charged the Policy Unit with producing a project review. Its analysis, undertaken by Jonathan Hill, confirmed that there was no economic justification for proceeding with the Link, but conceded that the political considerations were distinctly awkward. Indeed, it was pointed out that, faced with a similar decision in 1990, Thatcher and Parkinson had failed to 'bite the bullet and rule the CTRL out'. Searching for a compromise somewhere between 'signing up to huge public expenditure commitments' and 'leaving everything in grievous uncertainty', Hill suggested that the Government make an announcement that the easterly route would be safeguarded, but add that construction would be a matter for the private sector. This would offer Rifkind a selected route and the presumption of a go-ahead, Heseltine the opportunity to open up the East Thames corridor, and Lamont the postponement he desired, plus an assurance that there would be no public sector venture.[113]

When Rifkind met Heseltine in September, both were still batting for their favoured routes, but they were at least able to agree that a decision could not be delayed any further. And Heseltine was adamant that 'he would not allow Treasury to drive a wedge between us on this issue'.[114] The officials' steering group also produced a note setting out the efforts it had made to clarify some of the uncertainties identified in the July report. A revised financial assessment was included, showing that Ove Arup's easterly route would cost £377–514 million more to build and produce inferior benefits (£660–800 million NPV). However, the main emphasis lay in offering Ministers five options, ranging from 'Kill the Route' to 'Commitment to line and construction'.[115] Meanwhile, behind the scenes Hill sounded out the reaction of the three departments to his suggested compromise. He told the Prime Minister that the Treasury was prepared to agree to the safeguarding of a route, but remained worried that the more explicit the Government's statement was, the greater the possibility that public money might be made available. In these circumstances it naturally preferred Newham's southerly route to Stratford, because it was the cheapest, but ideally it wished 'to kill the scheme now'.[116] Heseltine was apparently pleased that the Arup route was to the fore, but he wanted the Government to be bolder in pressing ahead with the Link, advocating, as he had for the Tunnel itself in 1984–5 (above, pp. 255–6), the commitment of public money where necessary. There were signs of movement at the DTp. Rifkind had already hinted to Heseltine that he could live with either route as long as the terminus was at King's Cross, and Hill told Major that the Transport Secretary would not 'die in a ditch' over the choice. However, he had difficulty with the rest of the compromise solution since it left the future of the Rail Link too open-ended. He wanted British Rail to go beyond the safeguarding of the route and take forward the necessary planning and parliamentary procedures. And like Heseltine, he wanted to be able to announce something more positive. Precise words were now the obstacle to progress. If a statement were to be made in October, and there was some pressure to say something at the Conservative party conference in Blackpool, a commitment formula had to be devised that was capable of satisfying both the hawks and the doves.[117]

With time running short, Major convened a 'brass tacks' meeting with Rifkind, Lamont and Heseltine on 27 September. The Prime Minister threw his weight behind the Arup route. It was agreed that action should be taken to safeguard it and that an announcement would be made 'shortly'. However, the 'precise timing', and the 'precise nature of the Government's stance' were left for Ministers to settle.[118] The matter was urgent, since Rifkind was to speak at Blackpool on 9 October and the Commons would reconvene on the 14th. Nor were the immediate prospects good. In response to Rifkind's first draft of the statement, Heseltine wanted more emphasis on good news and the removal of uncertainty, and pressed Rifkind to bring forward this 'extremely popular announcement', rather than waiting for Parliament to reassemble. On the other hand, Lamont and the Treasury were unremitting in their efforts to censor any hint of commitment.[119] By 4 October Major was informed that the gap between Rifkind and Lamont was 'wide', the dispute centring on the work Rifkind wished British Rail to undertake on the easterly route after safeguarding. Thus, an announcement at the party conference appeared 'unlikely'.[120] Heseltine had warned of the danger of leaks if there was a delay, and so it proved. On 7 October, the *Independent* carried a report that the Government had rejected British Rail's route and instead had adopted the preference of the Environment Secretary.[121] The story enraged Bob Reid, who had not been briefed. He immediately wrote to Rifkind, then receiving no reply, went 'hot-foot' up to Blackpool to demand to know what was happening. There was a rather uncomfortable exchange between the two on 8 October, and ministerial discussions on the wording of the statement continued into the evening, when Rifkind wrote a personal letter to the Chancellor clarifying the basis on which he would make his statement. The next day, the text of a letter to Reid was made public, and Rifkind told the party conference that the Government had chosen an easterly route via Stratford to King's Cross. It was the Government's intention that the Rail Link should be taken forward by the private sector, but the precise financial arrangements would be dependent on the circumstances of the time. Existing capacity, he noted, would not be exhausted until 2005. The safeguarding of British Rail's preferred route was now revoked. Further confirmation of Government intentions came in a Commons statement on 14 October.[122] How was all this received? Predictably, British Rail was furious, following a wasted investment of some £250 million, and much was made of Reid's reference to a 'pantomime'.[123] Morton, too, was angered by the decision, telling the *Times* that he regarded it as 'a disaster'.[124] Nevertheless, the Government's decision was welcomed elsewhere, notably, with an election looming, in Tory marginal seats affected by British Rail's southerly route. This important political consideration, together with the developmental prospects in the east, however ill-developed, appealed not only to the Prime Minister but also to others in his Cabinet, notably the party chairman, Chris Patten.[125] The press portrayed the decision as a Cabinet defeat for Rifkind and a victory for Heseltine and Lamont.[126] In fact, Rifkind's actions were taken in a conscious effort to save the project in the face of Treasury perseveration. Further evidence of the latter's concern was provided by its close monitoring of the debate in the Commons, where Rifkind appeared to leave the door open to Government assistance, and its anxiety to restrain the extent of British Rail's work on the easterly route.[127]

In a written answer in December 1991 Rifkind confirmed that British Rail was proceeding with its work in refining the Arup route in preparation for its safeguarding. Reference was also made to the DOE's engagement of consultants to study the development potential of the East Thames corridor, and to the DTp's intention to appoint a merchant bank to advise the Government on involving the private sector.[128] British Rail took the work forward under the aegis of John Prideaux, who succeeded Palmer in leading on the Rail Link. In January 1992 he left InterCity to head New Ventures, then in August turned the new concern into a subsidiary company called Union Railways, becoming Chairman, with Gil Howarth, the Link's project director, as MD. The intention was to ring-fence the Link, together with the Heathrow Express project, in order to facilitate later privatisation. Union Railways engaged over 40 consultants, including Ove Arup, in a further substantial round of development work, undertaken in conjunction with the DTp, Treasury and DOE and completed in the autumn of 1992.[129] But the apparent smooth running of the project was suddenly upset. Union Railways' ensuing report achieved some notoriety within British Rail as a result of Prideaux's so-called 'ambush', in which he unexpectedly put forward St Pancras as a more suitable, and certainly much cheaper, location for the international terminal. This was clearly in opposition to the Board's long-cherished King's Cross scheme, and presented difficulties since the Bill was awaiting a third reading. After taking legal advice the report was considered by British Railways Board members in November 1992 on an informal basis only. Then, at a meeting in January 1993, the Board endorsed a document, stripped of the St Pancras option, for submission to the new Secretary of State, John MacGregor.[130]

In contrast with British Rail's previous efforts, MacGregor found the report, which had the endorsement of Samuel Montagu and W.S. Atkins, to be 'thoroughly professional', and he told Major so in February.[131] By adopting fewer tracks, steeper gradients and less tunnelling, and decoupling the Thameslink scheme, Union Railways were able to reduce the cost of the basic scheme to an estimated £2.3 billion. The 'reference case' for the Channel Tunnel Rail Link (CTRL) did not differ significantly from the Arup route of 1991. A 108-kilometre two-track main-line, capable of accommodating international freight trains, would run from the Tunnel to the north of Ashford, then via Detling and Swanscombe to Thurrock, Barking, then in tunnel via Stratford to King's Cross; reinstatement of the Gravesend (West) branch would provide a connexion to Waterloo.[132] Variations from the reference case were offered for five sensitive locations, but MacGregor proposed to accept only one of these, a short tunnel in the Medway valley. However, it was the possibility of saving money via the

St. Pancras alternative that caught ministerial eyes. Whitehall officials were already well aware of the idea, and in February Reid was required to submit an additional report detailing the option. Instead of tunnelling all the way to King's Cross, the Link would use the existing surface alignment of the North London line from Dalston to St. Pancras, where the station would be appropriated as an international terminus. The adoption of this plan would reduce the cost by more than £300 million and avoid the £1.4 billion expense of building King's Cross Low Level.[133] The Government's preference for St. Pancras was revealed, somewhat surprisingly, by the Chancellor, Lamont, in his budget speech on 16 March, when he confirmed that the CTRL would go ahead, and it was a further six days before MacGregor's fuller exposition set out the further work, including consultation exercises, that would be carried out by British Rail.[134]

This work was summarised in the report by Union Railways of October 1993. After further refinement of the route and other considerations – the terminal, intermediate stations, etc. – the revised estimate for the scheme was found to have risen to £2.6 billion. But the report enabled MacGregor to finalise most of the outstanding elements of the CTRL, which he regarded as the 'flagship of our private finance initiative',[135] and the plans were unveiled in a further Commons statement in January 1994. Here the Transport Secretary announced the safeguarding of a route which would finally remove all uncertainty and blight, and announced that the hybrid Bill mechanism would be employed, as it had been with the Channel Tunnel itself. The London terminus was confirmed as St. Pancras, and powers were to be sought to establish a separate Thameslink station at Midland Road. With the rejection of the King's Cross Low Level option came the withdrawal of British Rail's Bill and the removal of safeguarding in the area. Ironically, the proposed use of the North London line proved contentious for both engineering and environmental reasons, and the route now reverted to a tunnel from Stratford. Subject to satisfactory financing, MacGregor expected that there would be at least one intermediate station between Ashford and London: Stratford, Rainham and Ebbsfleet were the candidates. Planning directions to safeguard the route and the terminus were promised soon. MacGregor also emphasised that his decisions on the route were final. Any subsequent changes put forward by the eventual private sector partner 'must be within the area safeguarded'.[136] In Kent there were two outstanding sections to deal with: Ashford; and Pepper Hill, near Gravesend. The alignments here were subsequently determined in April 1994, a month before the Tunnel began operating.[137]

While the route of the CTRL was being refined during 1993/4, there was also a continuing debate about private sector involvement. MacGregor explained the position to Major in February 1993. Although the lower cost estimate produced by Union Railways had helped to improve the project's viability, with a 5 per cent return there was still 'no possibility' of the private sector taking full responsibility for construction without 'some form of public sector contribution'. Furthermore, this contribution would have to be large. As with the Eurorail joint venture proposal, around £1.5 billion was required in order to make a $12\frac{1}{2}$ per cent return for the private sector. But the maximum grant that could be justified within existing policies was £1.1 billion.[138] There were also competing claims on the public purse for other major transport infrastructure projects, such as the Jubilee Line Extension and London CrossRail. Indeed, Lamont pressed MacGregor to choose between the CTRL and CrossRail.[139] In his Budget speech in March the Chancellor conceded that the Government would make a financial contribution to the CTRL, in recognition of the benefits accruing to domestic rail passengers. A week later, MacGregor went further, and in the most explicit public admission to date promised that the project would receive 'substantial public sector support'.[140] But this was not the end. It became apparent that the money for the domestic passenger benefits, thought to be worth £700 million, would be insufficient to cover the estimated support required, put at some £1.7 billion by January 1994, and even allowing for regeneration benefits, there would still be a shortfall of £600 million. Ministers agreed that some means of supporting international benefits would have to be devised. As we have seen, Section 42 of the Channel Tunnel Act expressly prohibited the Government from making grants towards British Rail's international rail services. However, a way round this difficulty came with the realisation that the Act only forbade payments to British Rail: 'It does not prevent support being provided for a private sector project'.[141] MacGregor made this change of policy known during his announcement of the final route in January 1994. He hoped that it would be submerged in the general relief that the project was going ahead, but this substantial U-turn in Government policy was criticised by Labour spokesman Frank Dobson and his colleagues, and by Tory backbencher Teddy Taylor, and picked up by journalists such as Christian Wolmar and Simon Hoggart.[142] There was, of course, much more to be done. A period of negotiation had already begun to find a suitable private partner in a joint venture. Following advice received from Hill Samuel in September 1993, a competition was launched to find a bidder, who would take over both Union Railways and EPS. As a step towards privatisation, the Government turned EPS into a GoCo in May 1994 (Union Railways followed in April 1995). A hybrid Bill was published in November 1994.

Since 1988 the CTRL had passed through a number of manifestations. British Rail's *Channel Tunnel Rail Services* had quickly dismissed an easterly route through Kent and Essex, while St. Pancras was its least favoured option for the terminal. But by the time the Tunnel had opened, it was *these* options which had been endorsed and safeguarded by the Government. The process also had a lot to offer political scientists looking for a case study to demonstrate the way in which 'incrementalism' turned a project which all were agreed was unviable financially into something that had the air of inevitability about it. Nevertheless, in 1994 questions about when the Link would be built, its financial viability and, most critically, the details of its financing, were left to be settled. What was certain was that for some years to come, international passenger trains would speed through France on a new high-speed line but crawl through South-east England on the existing infrastructure.[143]

3. Completing construction, 1991–4

Boring the tunnels had proved to be a challenging affair; fitting them out, then transforming the facility into a piece of complex transport infrastructure, presented further logistical problems which tried the capabilities of all concerned. First, the tunnels required a large amount of fixed equipment: services such as electricity supply, lighting, ventilation, cooling, fire detection and suppression, and a transportation system for the service tunnel; and the rail track, signalling and train communication and control systems for the running tunnels. Then the several terminals and stations had to be constructed and fitted out. Finally, the rolling stock had to be ordered, built and commissioned. All this was of course subject to the monitoring and authorisation procedures of the IGC and Safety Authority before commercial operations could commence. The tasks involved were immense, and although manpower fell from its peak of 14,000 once the tunnelling itself was completed, the installation of so much equipment in 150 kilometres of tunnel was scarcely less problematic, with a TML workforce which remained above 10,000 until April 1993.[144] Indeed, the amount of material used was remarkable, the pipework alone extending to 550 kilometres, the electric cabling to 1,300 kms.[145] In the circumstances it is no surprise to find that design disagreements and delays continued to bedevil the project. When the running tunnels were completed in June 1991, the MdO noted the evident delays to the fixed works, which suggested that the opening date would slip to 15 September 1993. However, Eurotunnel held to its promise of 15 June for another eight months until it too conceded that September was a realistic date.[146] This target also proved unattainable. In its reports for June and September 1992 the MdO's view was that opening would be delayed until first, October, then December 1993, the latter date being conceded publicly by Eurotunnel in October 1992.[147] In fact, the Tunnel was handed over to Eurotunnel on 10 December 1993, when it was expected that after commissioning there would be a phased opening of services from March to May 1994.[148]

Delays in the installation of the fixed equipment were attributable partly to the difficulties experienced with design and procurement. In addition there was the continuing battle between Eurotunnel and TML over costs, a dispute which not only showed no sign of lessening but actually worsened in the period 1991–3. Examples of work that was adversely affected included the tunnel track and the signalling systems. The commissioning of a signalling system proved to be a protracted affair, the irony being that the delays stemmed from Eurotunnel's intervention in the tendering process in an attempt to progress the work. Costing an estimated £25 million, signalling was one of the key tunnel contracts. TML invited bids from manufacturers in 1987, and by November 1988 two consortia were in the running: the Tunnel Signalling Group [TSG], which included GEC and Westinghouse; and Eurosignal, including Balfour Beatty. At this point and before a technical and commercial evaluation of the bids had been completed, Eurotunnel insisted that TML select TSG, which was offering a system based on French TGV technology.[149] Eurosignal sought the help of the DTI in challenging the decision, while TML implied that Eurotunnel had been leant on by the French, and later claimed that the intervention prevented it from obtaining reasonable terms.[150] In fact, the selected contractor's price rose sharply, from about £30 to £70 million, over the course of 1988–9, partly as a result of satisfying British Rail concerns, and the negotiations were terminated. In March 1990 TML concluded a contract with Sofrerail, a subsidiary of SNCF, for the French TVM 430 system.[151] TML argued that Eurotunnel's action had led to an estimated 55-week delay, and it demanded an extension of time. Eurotunnel disagreed, and when the dispute went to the Project Disputes Panel, its adjudication, in February 1991, was in Eurotunnel's favour, although it criticised the company's intervention in the tendering process and agreed that this had contributed to the delay.[152] The choice of track system saw similar tensions between TML and Eurotunnel. When TML expressed a preference for the untried American Sonneville system, the approval process by the Safety Authority and IGC was necessarily protracted, though Lemley saw this as an attempt to exert pressure on TML to switch to French technology.[153]

There were also problems with the procedures for the formal approval of the design and of equipment and rolling stock, via the IGC and Safety Authority. As the project moved forward, the 'Avant Projet' system came under enormous pressure. In June 1989, Eurotunnel and TML were supposed to have presented 14 individual Avant Projets to the IGC, but only one had been submitted. There was then some acceleration. A year later the number of submissions had risen to 15, and when the tunnelling was completed in the summer of 1991, 28 of a total of 35 Projets had been presented. Of these, six were the subject of IGC objections.[154] Eurotunnel, TML and the MdO all expressed frustration with the slowness of this bureaucratic process, but British officials expressed only limited sympathy.[155] The peculiarities of the project were fully recognised. Since the plans for the Tunnel system had not been fully developed when work started, both design and construction proceeded apace, with insufficient time for leisurely monitoring. Financial and time constraints meant that Eurotunnel and TML could not wait for the IGC's approval of outline drawings before proceeding to detailed design; or, in some cases, for approval of the detailed design before proceeding to construction. The project was thus being approved 'in salami slices an element at a time'.[156] However, a number of measures were taken to speed up the process, with the IGC and Safety Authority reported to be 'bending over backwards' to accommodate the concessionaire and the contractor.[157] And as for the complaints of delay, officials pointed out that much of this was being caused by the paucity of detailed information from Eurotunnel and TML.[158]

We have already noted that in November 1989 Essig of TML complained to the British and French Transport Ministers about the IGC's excessive zeal on the safety issue. At that time, Morton chose to distance himself from Essig's allegations, telling Parkinson that Eurotunnel would not join in such attacks: 'Our position is that safety is not negotiable'.[159] He soon changed his tune. Although clause 27.7 of the Concession Agreement stated that the IGC and Safety Authority should give 'due consideration to the reasonable commercial objectives of the Concessionaires, including the avoidance of unnecessary costs and delays', there was a perception at Eurotunnel that stringent safety requirements were adding both directly and indirectly to costs.[160] During the first half of 1991 Morton embarked on an intensive round of high-level political lobbying, meeting Rifkind, Kenneth Baker, the Home Secretary, Michael Heseltine, the Environment Minister, and senior officials, the Cabinet Secretary and the Permanent Secretaries at Transport, Treasury and Home Office. His message was that absolute safety could not be guaranteed and that the additional cost burdens produced by alleged gold-plating were problematic for Eurotunnel. 'Sooner or later', he warned Rifkind, 'the point would be reached at which the project would no longer be viable'.[161] Uppermost in Morton's mind were the difficulties being encountered with the design of shuttle wagons (see below). Another example was the debate about seismic risks. Here the Concession Agreement contained a rather vague requirement that the works should 'withstand the effects of natural events predicted to occur once in 120 years'.[162] What exactly was required was a puzzle. There was broad agreement that the fabric of the Tunnel was compliant, but disagreement over the degree to which fixed equipment should be designed to withstand shocks. This resulted in prolonged discussions about the assumptions to be adopted in seismic studies. The episode demonstrated how a comparatively minor technical issue could produce significant differences in opinion and thus a great deal of time-consuming investigation.[163] The role of the Safety Authority was also questioned by the MdO. In May 1991 Peter Middleton, the British Executive MdO, wrote to Roger Freeman, the Transport Minister, recommending an urgent review of the workings of the Authority and the IGC. His letter was followed by a meeting with Freeman, attended by Morton. The Minister made soothing noises about appointments to strengthen the Authority, in particular to tackle the commissioning phase of its work, and promised that he would discuss the issue with Paul Quilès, in his second spell as French Transport Minister. The Authority was indeed strengthened with the addition of Allen Hall, the Deputy Chief Inspector of Mines, as 'Head of Safety Unit'. However, in subsequent correspondence, Freeman rejected the idea of a review, pointing out that any attempt to renegotiate parameters set out in the Treaty would merely lead to 'inordinate delay'.[164] In spite of the pressure exerted by Morton and others, Ministers refused to become embroiled in matters which were the clear responsibility of the two statutory organisations.

The prime instance of intervention was over the shuttle trains, where IGC/Safety Authority judgements were to have a critical impact on the rolling stock for both the passenger (tourist) and lorry (HGV) trains. Initial thinking on the design of the tourist shuttles was based on the segregation of car and coach passengers from their vehicles, but in subsequent discussions with the IGC, Eurotunnel and TML proposed a more convenient and economic design based on non-segregation. On 19 December 1989 the IGC informed Eurotunnel that it agreed to the development of such a design, but insisted on what the MdO considered to be 'a number of very onerous conditions', among them the requirement that the fire barrier pass doors be widened from the 'at least 600mm' specified in the Concession to 700 mm.[165] Eurotunnel, together with TML, who had proceeded to order the vehicles from a manufacturing consortium led by Bombardier of Canada on 14 December, accepted the variation. However, as the design work progressed, they found it would be difficult, and for engineering reasons around £6 million more expensive, to install 700 mm doors and in March 1990 expressed an intention to revert to the original design based on 600 mm.[166] The IGC stuck to its original decision, and in October, after much correspondence Morton asked the MdO to arbitrate.[167] The MdO found in favour of Eurotunnel and TML and a 600 mm width, but once again the IGC insisted that 700 mm doors be fitted on safety grounds, and the decision was eventually accepted by the concessionaires in April 1991.[168] The dispute caused some difficulties for Eurotunnel since construction had started in anticipation of a 'non-objection' from the IGC. The MdO was moved to criticise both sides, the IGC for adhering to the 700 mm principle, and Eurotunnel and TML for embarking on construction in advance of an IGC ruling.[169]

There were similar, but even more protracted, difficulties with the HGV shuttles, built by Breda and Fiat. Here, enclosed wagons were specified in Eurotunnel's original proposal to the two Governments in 1987, and the principle of segregation was agreed with the IGC in the following year.[170] But shortly before the contract with TML was signed in January 1990, there was a move from the closed to a semi-open design. This was partly the result of weight considerations in handling lorries of up to 44 tonnes, but it also formed part of the cost-saving package which Eurotunnel agreed with TML in early 1990 (see above, p. 316).[171] Pressing for a retrospective authorisation, the concessionaires became agitated when their efforts to effect the change met with firm resistance. However, the Safety Authority, concerned about the impact of a fire on lorry drivers and on following passenger trains, could not endorse such a radical change to the design without also receiving additional information. In particular, it sought a study of the feasibility of an in-tunnel fire detection system, and the details of Eurotunnel's freight policy and in particular, its stance on the carriage of dangerous goods. There were lengthy discussions on these aspects over the course of 1990, and it was not until January 1991 that Eurotunnel was able to submit detailed documentation.[172] Nonetheless, the Safety Authority was still unable to accept the design, and after its views, fully endorsed by the IGC, were conveyed to Eurotunnel in March, a considerable amount of further investigation ensued.[173] The MdO was happy with the semi-open concept, but the opposite view was taken by the consultants Electrowatt, in a risk assessment exercise undertaken for the Safety Authority.[174] Facing the prospect of an embarrassing rejection by the IGC and having lobbied Ministers hard, Eurotunnel eventually came up with the idea of retrospectively fitting cladding to the vehicles under construction, with a phased introduction of services. This revised approach was accepted by the Safety Authority, with conditions, in July.[175] Later on, minds changed again. In December 1991 Morton asked the IGC to reconsider its decision and allow Eurotunnel to proceed with the semi-open design.[176] Then in January 1992 the company submitted a new semi-open design, the main modification being the addition of on-board smoke detectors, together with an undertaking to provide headways of 4 km between the HGV shuttles and following trains. It justified the move with the assertion that the enclosed design would add some £130–200 million to costs.[177] In the negotiations that followed, some irritation was evident on both sides. For Eurotunnel there was annoyance that the IGC was creating difficulty with the HGV shuttles, while it had issued non-objections to proposals for freight trains and refrigerated containers in June and August 1991, services which were regarded as more hazardous. For the supervisory bodies, Eurotunnel's change of heart was frustrating, given the endorsement of the Commons Home Affairs Committee, in its Report on Channel Tunnel fire safety in December 1991, to the enclosed cladding design.[178] In the course of an in-depth examination of the issue at one of the Safety Authority's Guernsey meetings in March 1992, with the file documents now numbering 129, a difference of view emerged. French members were apparently more willing to endorse the semi-open design than some of their British colleagues.[179] Nevertheless, after further debate the Authority agreed to accommodate Eurotunnel on condition that further development and tests were undertaken to provide the necessary assurances about fire safety.[180] Nevertheless, with the Safety Authority uncertain about the prospects of Eurotunnel satisfying it on this score, the IGC referred the idea of conditional endorsement to Ministers before conveying its decision to Eurotunnel.[181] Discussions on fire safety and security then continued throughout 1992 and into the following year, and it was not until October 1993 that the IGC was able to issue a non-objection to the HGV shuttles.[182]

Morton was voluble in his criticisms of the statutory bodies for adding to the time taken to progress designs, and to the cost of the equipment, both of which had an impact on his relations with the banking syndicate. He also aimed a shot at individual members for failing to 'recognise that it was not possible to design for zero risk'.[183] However, it could scarcely be argued that Eurotunnel was unprepared for the supervisory system with which it had to work. Furthermore, in the absence of the Safety Authority and the IGC, Eurotunnel and TML would have had to deal individually with a number of health and safety authorities in the two countries, where the opportunity for delay and confusion would have been all the greater.[184] And on the safety question, it was extremely unlikely that the IGC, acting for the two governments, would be tempted to overrule the opinion of a body composed of experts. Indeed, the Safety Authority's independence was strengthened by a British Government undertaking that should a fundamental disagreement arise between the Authority and the IGC, the Transport Secretary would report the fact to Parliament.[185] The determination not to compromise on safety was also reinforced by the knowledge that a public campaign, orchestrated in Britain by the Consumers' Association and others, was continuing to complain of 'a stone wall of secrecy', implying that safety concerns were being treated in too cosy a fashion.[186] Given all the circumstances, it was difficult to disentangle the extent to which delays in completing the Tunnel were attributable to the problems with the procurement of rolling stock, or indeed, the extent to which the late deliveries of stock were a consequence of IGC decision-making. Such niceties proved to be no deterrent to Eurotunnel, which embarked on a campaign to extract some financial compensation from the Governments (see below, pp. 356–62). And this was by no means all that Eurotunnel had to worry about. Costs were rising, manufacturers' problems were increasing, the timetable was slipping, the bankers were growing uneasy, and there were continuing contractual difficulties with TML and the supplying firms. It is to these more serious issues facing the Tunnel project that we now turn.

4. Financial crises and disputes, 1991–4

The lull in the stormy relationship between Eurotunnel and TML, established by the agreement of February 1990, was soon broken, as was the breathing space provided by the rights issue in November and the successful tunnel breakthrough in December. In February 1991 the Delphic ruling of the Disputes Panel on the signalling claim (see above, p. 348) did more to open, rather than heal, the Eurotunnel-TML wounds. In April Morton, now Sir Alastair, reported that the shuttle trains would not be ready for opening in June 1993, and a full service would not be introduced until December. Eurotunnel's annual report, published in May, then revealed that TML's claim had increased from £953 million to £1.1 billion.[187] By October the project appeared to be in serious difficulties once again. Morton's letter to shareholders on 7 October produced another increase in the overall cost, to £8.05 billion, and another attack was launched on TML.[188] The latter was in no mood to roll over. With Keith Price from Morrison-Knudsen joining Lemley's senior management team, the consortium pressed its claim hard.[189] Indeed, the matter was urgent, since member companies were experiencing financial difficulties as the recession lengthened, and it was understood that TML was about to 'go cash negative' on its Tunnel operations. The contractors were now demanding that Eurotunnel allow them to convert the 'lump sum' element of the contract – for terminals and fixed equipment – into a cost-plus arrangement. Arguing that the cost had risen from £623 million to £1.274 billion (in 1985 prices), they required, with management fees, an additional £811 million.[190] Once again, Eurotunnel was faced with a delicate balancing act. As a Whitehall official put it, Eurotunnel and TML were 'like a husband and wife in some long-standing, dependent, but embittered marriage'.[191] It was clearly sensible to reach an agreement with TML, but any increase in projected costs would prejudice relations with the banks. Morton had already drawn the IGC's attention to the 'simple, stark truth' that Eurotunnel was 'barely within its (credit agreement) covenants', and the agent banks were nervous about being placed in the position of lenders of last resort.[192] On top of this TML raised the stakes by threatening to stop work on the Tunnel's ventilation system, which had been redesigned at a significantly higher cost, and by holding another special press conference in Paris to air their grievances. Eurotunnel responded by seeking an injunction to prevent a stoppage of the work.[193]

The situation was severe enough to engage the attention of Number Ten, which asked for a briefing from the DTp.[194] At the same time Morton wrote to Major. Reminding him that the Tunnel had been 'launched by the Conservatives as a private sector show-piece', he asked for an audience, which was refused. Major had no desire to meet him 'after his performance over CTRL'.[195] There were some conciliatory noises, not least from Peter Drew of Taylor Woodrow, and negotiations resumed between Neerhout, Eurotunnel's Chief Executive, and Lemley, his opposite number at TML. The lump sum claim was referred by Eurotunnel to the Disputes Panel, where a decision was promised in March 1992.[196] The Panel's ruling in March was favourable to TML in that it was argued that work affected by design changes should be valued at 'suitable rates'. The Panel therefore suggested that the two sides should negotiate to establish a revised figure for the lump sum element of the contract, and that in the meantime, Eurotunnel should pay TML an additional £50 million a month from the end of April 1992.[197] This requirement immediately jeopardised Eurotunnel's relationship with its bankers, since the 'funding margin' and 'cover ratio' were threatened, and there was also the deleterious impact of the late deliveries of rolling stock on the projected cash flow in the 'banking case' calculations.[198] But TML's position was equally precarious; the expectation was that without additional payments the consortium would make a loss of £280 million by the end of 1992.[199] Eurotunnel decided to refer the ruling to the arbitration of the International Chamber of Commerce in Paris, but the banks, also experiencing the pressures of recession, were unwilling to wait for the outcome, and they instructed the company to settle within the existing financial parameters. In order to secure a waiver from the banks regarding the technical breach of the credit agreement Eurotunnel reluctantly made the first £50 million payment to TML.[200] The situation remained tricky, exposing Morton's penchant for emotional outburst. When his attempts to keep the banks onside took a dent in May during the protracted negotiations with the IGC over the design of the HGV shuttles (see above, pp. 350–1), he sent a 'brusque letter' to Freeman, employed the word 'serious'

Cartoon 8 Escalating costs and financial crisis, October 1991, as seen by Peter Brookes, *Times*, 14 October 1991.

three times in the first three lines, and all but accused the Governments of trying to wreck his efforts with the banks by planning to double-cross him on the HGVs.[201] The Prime Minister and senior Ministers were briefed on the Eurotunnel-TML dispute again in the same month. MacGregor, the Transport Secretary, expressed alarm at the prospect, should brinkmanship turn into 'breakdown', that the costs of 'preserving the [Tunnel] fabric' would 'fall to HMG and the French Government', along with all the complications of terminating the concession and renegotiating a construction contract. This was a task which MacGregor was no doubt loath to take on in the midst of railway privatisation.[202] Major made no comment,[203] but Lamont, now Chancellor, was anxious to challenge the idea that the Government would automatically step in to maintain the Tunnel. If there were a failure, it was up to the banks to protect their investment while they sought another concessionaire.[204]

Eventually a deal was reached, though it was to take over a year to finalise. At the end of May 1992 a 'banking case' revealed Eurotunnel to be 'perilously close' to default. Nevertheless, the banks agreed to grant a waiver and allow a capital draw-down of £650 million, and Tunnel client and contractor entered into serious negotiations about all the disputed aspects of the project, including the opening date (by this time September 1993) and the commissioning process. Almost immediately the difference between the two sides narrowed. Agreement was reached on elements other than the lump sum works, and here the gap between demand and offer was reported to have been reduced to about £150 million in June, and £110 million in July (with TML demanding £1.3 billion, and Eurotunnel willing to offer around £1.19 billion).[205] But neither party was prepared to go the extra mile to resolve the dispute, and exasperated banks, perturbed governments and the Bank of England as 'honest broker' watched as the adversarial charade was played out over the course of 1992–3. The waters were muddied, first, by Eurotunnel's suggestion that TML might receive part payment in 'non-cash instruments', then by the concerns of the European Investment Bank. The proposal that TML should take on about £300 million in exercisable warrants and convertible, non-interest bearing preference shares, was unwelcome. Although the contractors had made substantial capital gains by selling on their original stake in Eurotunnel, they were not willing to accept new and less liquid paper at a discount. The EIB was pessimistic about the prospects for Eurotunnel, forecasting that the burden of increased construction costs and lower revenues would make it 'doubtful whether it would ever be able to repay the interest on its borrowings'. Insisting that the terms of the credit agreement be followed, it suggested three ways of averting a collapse: (1) Government funding in recognition of additional safety and environmental costs; (2) An equity investment by British Rail and SNCF and (3) An equity investment by TML.[206] Options (1) and (2) were scarcely acceptable to Whitehall, though the idea of the railways taking an investment was pressed by some of the banks, notably the EIB and the Midland.[207] However, something that did surface at departmental level, presumably as a result of banking contacts, was the notion that the Governments might be asked to extend the period of the Concession. Here the advantage was that it could be done 'without undermining the principle of no government funds'.[208]

The further negotiations, and the banks' attempts to impose discipline on the parties, need not be recounted in detail.[209] The agent banks were more willing to compromise than the EIB. Although it soon emerged from banking calculations that with later opening and lower growth projections, the Tunnel would cost £1 billion more than the existing provision of £8.7 billion, about 60 per cent of the funding had already been advanced, and it was felt that none of the major institutions would 'now wish to abandon such a heavy investment thus enabling someone else to profit'.[210] And although the British Government maintained its 'no subsidy' stance, the Prime Minister was given regular reports, and Transport Ministers kept a close watching brief on the situation, which extended to a series of meetings with the agent banks, and breakfast meetings with Morton.[211] MacGregor also agreed, in response to a request from Morton in August 1992, to say something supportive for the benefit of the Japanese banks, in a repetition, though more *sotto voce*, of Thatcher's intervention in 1990.[212] Close to agreeing heads of agreement in August 1992, the two sides continued to argue, and by this time TML appeared to be the unreasonable party, at least in banking eyes.[213]

The dispute dragged on for far longer than seemed advisable, facilitated by further banking waivers, and the complications created by arbitration rulings. An interim decision by the International Chamber of Commerce in September 1992 gave comfort to Eurotunnel by ruling against the additional £50 million monthly payment, and in November the banking syndicate gave the company a further waiver for 18 months to enable it to complete the project.[214] On the other hand, in January 1993 a Law Lords ruling gave comfort to TML, rejecting Eurotunnel's request for an injunction to prevent the contractors from walking off the site.[215] But the ICC's final decision in March was regarded by Eurotunnel as a 'stunning victory', finding against the idea of a 'global' claim and requiring TML to justify the individual components of its claim.[216] TML responded by challenging Eurotunnel's interpretation of the decision and resorted to intransigence, slowing down or disrupting the work on site. Equipment manufacturers followed suit, notably Bombardier, which halted production and slowed down delivery schedules for the passenger shuttle trains in an attempt to extract additional payments for the work caused by design changes.[217] These actions, which prejudiced the commissioning process, naturally raised doubts about the actual opening time of the facility. Eurotunnel had conceded in October 1992 that there would be no services at all until December 1993, and full operation would not begin until July 1994. The loss of valuable revenue during the summer peak was a real blow for Eurotunnel and its bankers, but so too was the increasing possibility that the 1994 summer season would also be missed. In April 1993 Eurotunnel admitted that it would require additional funding during the initial period of operation, and hinted that the dispute with TML might delay the opening until the middle of 1994.[218] With exasperation at a high level, the deadlock was finally broken in July 1993. Success was due to the replacement of Joe Dwyer of George Wimpey as TML negotiator by Neville Simms, Chief Executive of Tarmac, the intervention of Pen Kent of the Bank of England as mediator, and the patience of the French, who were content to let the Anglo-Saxon negotiators sort out their differences.[219] A press notice on 27 July announced that a deal had been reached which would ensure that the Tunnel would open for freight in March 1994, with a passenger service beginning in April or May. Essentially, the joint action needed to complete the project was separated from the claims about payment. TML agreed to co-operate fully in the commissioning process and hand over the Tunnel in December 1993; Eurotunnel agreed to make an additional payment to TML of £235 million. However, the arguments about the lump sum claim and other disputed elements, the subject of panel and arbitration references, were not settled but merely made the subject of a 'cease fire'. However, the truce allowed TML access to funds, while promising Eurotunnel a revenue stream from March 1994. The agent banks agreed to put up a further £120 million as a standby facility.[220]

By this time Morton was pursuing claims against the two Governments and their railways on a wider front, and in many ways the financial implications of the July 1993 deal made this matter more urgent. In a memorandum sent by Morton and Bénard to the British and French Transport Ministers in September 1992, the Concessionaires asserted that while a substantial part of Eurotunnel's financial strain was caused by the elements which had produced its dispute with TML, equally it was 'the direct or indirect consequence of Government action, or failure to act, and the consequence of action or failures by the state-owned railways of the two countries'. They therefore sought 'compensation and redress'. No fewer than seven specific 'grievances' were itemised: the capital and operating costs arising from the provision of equipment and services 'in excess of what the Concession envisaged or required'; the burden of excessive safety standards; the subsidy provided to the ferries and airlines by allowing them to retain duty-free sales for six years after the Tunnel opening; the injury caused by the existing terms of the Usage Contract with the railways, which had been signed in 1987 by an 'embryonic' and 'inexpert' Eurotunnel; the injury produced by the failure of British Rail and SNCF to procure rolling stock in time for commercial service in 1993; the failure of British Rail to put in place the promised infrastructure by 1993, and notably Ashford International station; and the threat to Eurotunnel presented by the plans to privatise Britain's railways. This formidable (though by no means incontestable) list was matched by a series of demands. Promising to submit a detailed case in due course, the Concessionaires proposed that in the meantime the two Governments should: (i) provide advance compensation in the form of an interest-free loan; (ii) instruct British Rail and SNCF to renegotiate the tariffs and related provisions of the Usage Contract, in order to give Eurotunnel the return it expected with the traffic and cost levels forecast 'at the outset of the project'; (iii) agree to pay Eurotunnel a six-year subvention equivalent to the benefit derived from its competitors as a result of duty-free sales (not allowed on trains); (iv) acknowledge that the IGC had required Eurotunnel to provide a safety standard equivalent to the maritime standard 'SOLAS 90', and advance the company an interest-free loan equivalent to the capital and operating costs not incurred by its ferry competitors, to be repaid when the latter attained the standard; and (v) confirm bi-national funding of the development of Euroscan security equipment, allowing Eurotunnel to operate without it until competing modes were equipped with it.[221]

As has already been suggested, Eurotunnel's actions, which were prompted by a further round of financial difficulties, could be viewed as opportunistic, since the company had fastened onto suggestions made by the agent banks, the EIB and the DTp about finding ways of assisting it in its financial plight without falling foul of the 'no subsidy' rule. These ideas, as well as Morton's threats of making a claim, were of long vintage. As early as August 1990, the Chairman of the Safety Authority, Bryan Martin, had been told by Morton that TML were basing their claim for more money in part upon the extra cost of safety measures required by the Safety Authority and the IGC.[222] Then in March 1991 the DTp had reassessed its position in the light of reports that Eurotunnel was waiting for an opportunity to build up claims for the delays and extra work resulting from IGC decisions. It was believed that Eurotunnel took as its starting point a fax which Andrew Lyall had sent to Sir Nicholas Henderson in January 1986, during the process of selecting a Tunnel promoter. This document, by which the company apparently 'set great store', stated that 'the Governments will consider claims arising from supplementary works or modifications, carried out at their request, which are in excess of generally applicable standards or technical regulations'.[223] As we have seen (pp. 281–2), in negotiating the actual Concession the idea of conceding a right to compensation in respect of supplementary works had been firmly opposed by John MacGregor when at the Treasury. And an investigation of the matter in 1989 had concluded that the Governments were not obliged to contribute to cost overruns, since the CTG had taken full responsibility for these during the negotiations of March 1986.[224] After taking legal advice the Department was able to confirm this position in May 1991, though it was noted that Eurotunnel was litigious, and a suit for damages 'would, at the least, be embarrassing'.[225] However, by this time the area of dispute had become much wider, going beyond Eurotunnel's relationship with the IGC to embrace its dealings with the railways, and the policy of a phased abandonment of duty-free sales on ferries and aircraft serving the EC after the establishment of the Single Market. The DTp therefore examined a wider list of possible claims, though the most substantial appeared to be that regarding the IGC's interventions on shuttle designs, where additional costs of £150–200 million were being aired. The emphasis was confirmed in November 1991 when Morton's exasperation with the IGC produced a formal complaint and an intention to claim which would run 'well into nine figures'. Morton also objected to the subsidies he alleged were enjoyed by the ferries: 'A further nine figure sum is at issue here'.[226] In December Morton and Bénard also wrote to Bob Reid II and Jacques Fournier of SNCF, setting out the extent of their dissatisfaction with the railways. The opportunity was provided by the EC's Directive 91/440, which required member states to give international train operators access to their rail networks. Eurotunnel asserted that the exclusivity of the Usage Contract appeared to be at odds with this requirement, thus strengthening its demand for renegotiation. There were also complaints about other aspects of the railways' actions: the likely late delivery of rolling stock; their intervention in the choice of signalling system; uncertainties over Ashford station and freight facilities; and British Rail's doubts about when new capacity would be needed.[227]

The correspondence produced a flurry of activity in Paris and London, and there were December meetings between Morton and Freeman, and between Morton, Bénard and the IGC. However, in the absence of specific claims all the Governments could do was to remind Eurotunnel of their compliance with the Treaty and Concession and await further documentation.[228] British Rail was more trenchant, refuting Eurotunnel's more exaggerated claims and defending its actions under the Contract.[229] Undaunted, Morton and Bénard maintained their lobbying activity. In May 1992 they reminded shareholders of their robust determination to secure what was due – 'from contractors, from governments, from the national railways, and so on'. When Morton visited Alan Rosling from the Number Ten Policy Unit in June he said that 'Government action/inaction' had had a deleterious effect on the project and that 'he would be seeking compensation for this'. However, his tone was altogether more cordial when he met Freeman five days later.[230] Thus, by the time of the September 1992 memorandum the two Governments had had considerable warning of the claims they might expect. Officials immediately turned to Eurotunnel's set of proposals. Some could easily be dismissed, for example the demand for advances and subventions, which clearly fell foul of the Treaty. But a formal reply was held up, first until Eurotunnel's bankers had decided to offer further support, in November, and then by French doubts about whether a reply was required. Morton's suggestion that a joint working party be set up to examine some of the claims also muddied the waters.[231] After necessary consultations with the French Transport Minister, Jean-Louis Bianco, it was not until February 1993 that official responses were sent. In MacGregor's letter to Morton, the Secretary of State affirmed that 'without further justification and detail . . . the Governments are not in a position to give full consideration to the grievances which you describe nor do they admit any liability for the potential losses described'. Eurotunnel was asked to submit a full case setting out the legal basis for claiming compensation. However, the dispute over the Usage Contract was deemed to be something for Eurotunnel to settle with the two railway corporations without government intervention.[232]

In the months following the Governments' non-committal replies, there was further correspondence between the DTp and Eurotunnel over aspects of the claims, and notably on the issue of ferry safety standards.[233] Morton and his colleagues were clearly preoccupied by the TML negotiations, though in May shareholders were told that compensation would be claimed from the Governments in the summer, and time was found to press the railways for a revision of the terms of the Usage Contract.[234] But it was not until after the July 1993 truce with TML that Eurotunnel was able to turn its attention to making a formal claim upon the Governments, and by this time officials in Whitehall were in fact looking at the possibility of offering something to the beleaguered company in order to keep the show on the road. Two ideas gained currency over the course of 1992–3: first, that notwithstanding their initial response, the Governments might indeed press the railways to renegotiate the Usage Contract to Eurotunnel's advantage; and second, that an extension of the length of the 55-year Concession might help the agent banks to persuade their fellow bankers to provide additional funding for the project. Both options were raised in a Departmental briefing for a meeting between MacGregor and Bianco in September 1992.[235] And by May 1993 the agent banks had made it clear that in return for offering more help they were expecting the Governments to provide some kind of assistance, and the EIB to relax the conditions attached to its loans. They were also keen to see a British undertaking that the existing arrangements with British Rail would continue after privatisation.[236] While the Eurotunnel-TML deal was being thrashed out, the Banks went so far as to state that as part of the package of further capital-raising required in 1994/5 they expected Eurotunnel to negotiate a 'minimum contribution' of £200 million from the Governments in one way or another.[237] But from Eurotunnel's perspective the process of working up a detailed claim was time-consuming, and time was short. Furthermore, the company's efforts to secure a voluntary renegotiation of the Usage Contract had come to nought, and in August the dispute was referred to the arbitration of the International Chamber of Commerce.[238] This left the focus firmly on the idea of extending the length of the Concession. Bénard and Morton raised the stakes somewhat by including the idea in a letter to Bianco's successor, Bernard Bosson, in June, and publicity was provided by references to it planted in the French press.[239] Morton drew MacGregor's attention to it in a letter on 14 July, and a fortnight later he was more specific. Having just finalised the deal with TML, he could now turn to his 'Financing Implementation Plan', which needed to be endorsed by the banking syndicate in November. With the banks seeking 'evidence of Government support', and the claims for compensation likely to run their course, the world's capital markets required a 'clear and obvious signal' that 'events beyond the individual control of Eurotunnel have contributed to a rise in total capital cost'. That signal was a lengthening of the Concession.[240] In more Machiavellian vein he had revealed that 'it didn't really matter where the money came from as long as there was some money, and there were ways of doing it that didn't involve the Treasury'.[241] The initial response of the two Governments was similar. At a Franco-British summit on 26 July Bosson identified a prolongation of the Concession as one of the ways of helping Eurotunnel, and MacGregor was happy to examine the matter further. At this stage both parties accepted Pen Kent's advice that such a dispensation was something of a last resort, to be used if the Japanese banks in particular failed to be supportive.[242] With Eurotunnel planning a further rights issue to coincide with the opening of the Tunnel in May 1994, and some of the banks, and in particular the EIB, unwilling to lend more without a substantive gesture from the Governments, the 'last resort' rapidly became a 'necessary response'.[243]

In August 1993 Morton combined 'carrot' with 'stick' when he intimated that Eurotunnel might drop its claims on safety as a 'trade-off' for a longer Concession.[244] And while Governments could not engage in a simple deal without a considerable amount of agonising, essentially the events of August–December followed the route set by Morton. First, the agreement of the Treasury and the French Finance Ministry had to be gained and this was by no means automatic.

In Britain, the Treasury's line appeared to have hardened after Morton revealed that a ten-year extension might be worth an additional £200 million in NPV, though a more substantial concern was the fear that the move would give a signal to the private sector in general that government contracts (including that for the CTRL) might easily be renegotiated if circumstances became difficult.[245] At the end of September the prospect of agreement appeared remote. Portillo, now Treasury Secretary, informed MacGregor that his department could not agree to an extension of the Concession. 'It would be a free good to Eurotunnel... [and] a substantial loss to the Exchequer.' The French Finance Ministry came to the same view.[246] Second, the two Transport Ministries had to work towards an agreed position. When Bénard and Morton pressed them in October to grant a 15-year extension, they both thought that 15 years was 'excessive', and were agreed that if an extension *were* given it was 'a card we could only play once'. Furthermore, they expected that in return Eurotunnel would abandon all current and future claims upon the Governments.[247] Finally, the intentions of the banking syndicate needed to be established. There were genuine difficulties here. On this occasion the four agent banks were not unanimous, and it was reported that the Banque Nationale de Paris was insisting that the two Governments each make a cash contribution of £200 million. In addition, both the EIB and the Japanese banks were more hawkish than before, while no one could predict the response of the banking syndicate, over half of whom were committed to the extent of only £20 million or less. The situation resembled an intense poker game, with each party waiting for the other to make the first move.[248]

Eurotunnel's more considered case for an extension was put to the Governments in November. It was noted that since the Concession had been signed the capital cost of the project had risen by 65 per cent, interest rates had been unfavourable, and the opening had been delayed by a year. In Document 1 of a three-part submission the company presented an assessment of the financial consequences of decisions taken by the Governments and the IGC in the areas of safety, security and the environment. An estimate of the 'cost consequences' in January 1993 prices revealed additional investment costs of £196 million for safety, £25 million for security and £215 million for environmental protection, £436 million in all; the impact on profit and loss over the life of the Concession was put at £618 million, the bulk of which was attributed to the segregation in shuttle trains of coaches, camper vans and caravans, a matter still under discussion with the Safety Authority (Table 11.2). In Document 2 the value of an extension of the Concession to Eurotunnel was expressed in NPV, using an 8 per cent discount rate. The value ranged from £11 million for a year's extension to £326 million for 45 years; for 15 years the figure was £226 million,[249] for ten years £171 million. Eurotunnel also asked for exclusivity to be extended from 2020 to 2030.[250] Meanwhile further efforts were made by the two transport ministries to get their finance ministries on board. In Britain there was a detailed correspondence between MacGregor and the Chancellor, now Kenneth Clarke. The Transport Secretary was convinced that an extension was a necessary element

Table 11.2 Eurotunnel's estimate of cost consequences of IGC and Governments' interventions, November 1993 (£ million, in January 1993 prices)

Element	*Additional investment cost*	*Additional operating costs/reduction in net revenue (over life of concession)*
Safety-related investments:		
Tourist shuttles	94.9	11.1
In-Tunnel fire detection	19.4	
Emergency communication	7.3	2.4
Seismic precautions	3.8	
Other	70.7	
Total	196.1	
Safety-Related Operating Constraints		544.0[a]
Security-related (Euroscan) investment	25.1	60.9
Environment-related investment	215.4	
Total	436.6	618.4

Source: 'Eurotunnel Request to the British and French Governments November 1993', 9 November 1993, p.9, and 'Request for Compensation to Governments: Costs', 16 December 1993, DTp file CHT9/0/18 Pt. 5.

Note
a If Eurotunnel's case were accepted, this would fall to £26 m.

in the refinancing package for the Tunnel. But Clarke felt that 'to give away such an extension would be a real worsenment [*sic*] in our position, potentially foregoing billions of pounds each year from 2042 to 2057'. The ferries 'would be loudly critical, and we would be hard put to explain, both to Parliament and in the EC, why we had bailed out a single quoted company, almost two-thirds of whose shareholders were French'. The extent of Treasury intransigence should not be exaggerated, however. Behind the posturing, the Treasury had already agreed to give the DTp discretion to negotiate government assistance with the development of the security scanning technology (up to £3 million), had offered to help in influencing the EIB, and had assisted Bénard's (unsuccessful) approach to the Japanese Ministry of Finance and JEXIM (The Export-Import Bank of Japan). It too had come to the view that a longer Concession might be offered if there were a sufficient trade-off. But there were limits: 'If we cannot strike a balanced deal', Clarke wrote, 'we must be ready to accept the demise of Eurotunnel'.[251]

Eventually, and after much nail-biting, a deal was brokered. With the Foreign Office keen for a settlement, the banks extending their deadline by a further month but continuing to press the Governments, and rumours reaching the press,[252] agreement was finally reached on 20 December. A ten-year extension was granted, conditional upon the raising of further finance and subject to the endorsement of the French Parliament and European Commission. Eurotunnel agreed to abandon all of its intended claims against the Governments in respect of acts or omissions prior to the date of the agreement. The company also agreed not to pursue a claim relating to the constraints on shuttle operating unless the IGC were to impose conditions which were more costly than those envisaged in its 'alternative proposal'. Eurotunnel's claims against British Rail and SNCF were left to run their course, but the company did undertake to 'examine constructively' the assignment of contracts when Britain's railways were privatised.[253] Both sides had conceded something. Eurotunnel had hoped for a 15-year extension and would have preferred to give up only the historic claims relating to safety investment (see Table 11.2).[254] The Governments, on the other hand, had wanted the abandonment of *all* claims, present and future.[255] There was an additional complication when both Treasury and DTp officials, feeling that Eurotunnel's case was a very weak one, insisted that it consent to the assignment of the railway contracts (including the Usage Contract) to private sector companies. In this context, the abandonment of Eurotunnel's claims against the railways was regarded as important in smoothing the tortuous path to privatisation. However, this element, which the EIB saw as a 'wrecking condition', was not surrendered.[256]

The extension of the Concession was clearly a political issue, with the calculations surrounding it highly speculative.[257] During the negotiations, the DTp and Treasury had involved themselves in an extended argument about its value to the two Governments. Several figures were put forward. The Treasury put a value on a 15-year concession of £493 million (based on selling the Concession in 2042 and using a 6 per cent discount rate), which contrasted with the £228 million placed on it by Eurotunnel (at 8 per cent). Of course, the calculation was highly sensitive to the choice of discount rate. As the DTp's advisers, Hill Samuel, observed, at 6 per cent Eurotunnel's figure would rise to £620 million.[258] But this was very much an abstract exercise. As a DTp official noted: 'is anyone going to take seriously cash flow forecasts which purport to peer 49–64 years into the future? This is the sort of timescale over which the transport scene can change beyond all recognition. In 1895 the motorcar did not exist; by 1959, it accounted for roughly half the UK passenger transport market'.[259] His opinion was confirmed by press reaction to the ten-year extension. The *Financial Times*, for example, reported one analyst as remarking that an assessment would involve 'the quantification of the unquantifiable'.[260]

December 1993 proved to be a critical month. On the 10th the Channel Tunnel was handed over by TML to Eurotunnel, and on the 15th Eurotunnel shareholders approved a £500 million rights issue to be undertaken in the spring. The resolution of the disputes with Bombardier and TML, the latter achieved in April,[261] the blessing of the banks, though the price paid was a narrowing of the debt-equity ratio,[262] and the extension of the Concession opened the way to life-saving funding. A week after the first commercial services (HGV shuttles) began on 19 May 1994, the issue was launched, offering shareholders three units for five at the discounted price of £1.325 + 11.25FF a Unit (£2.65). A total of £816 million was raised. Additional bank finance was then provided, beginning with the agent banks' standby facility of £120 million, then priority ranking credit amounting to £693 million, together with a further £50 million offered by Morgan Grenfell and Warburg. At the time of the official opening of the Tunnel on 6 May, the construction had cost £4.5 billion in 1985 prices (£5.5 billion in 1994 prices), and by June a total of £10.4 billion had been raised, £2.4 billion (23 per cent) in the form of equity.[263] Despite the escalation in cost, the numerous delays, the interminable squabbling and the incessant lobbying, Eurotunnel, led by Morton and Bénard, had completed the project and staved off another threat of insolvency and collapse at the 11th hour. Bénard, whose quieter, though no less effective, leadership achieved much in Paris, stepped down as Co-chairman in June 1994, and was replaced by Patrick Ponsolle; Morton stayed on until 1996, though in January 1994 he handed over the reins of Group Chief Executive to Georges-Christian Chazot.[264] Sir Alastair's achievement should not be undervalued. His sheer persistence, aggression and enthusiasm may have won him more critics than supporters – he could be abrasive and volatile, rarely seeing any point of view but his own. But there was no doubt about his commitment to the Tunnel, and most commentators were agreed that it would have been difficult to complete without someone of his 'unswerving drive'.[265] This was not the end of the story, of course, and there were to be many clouds on the horizon after the opening (see Chapter 12). While the private sector might take the credit for managing the project to completion, the British and French Governments had pitched in with as much as they could, given the constraints of the Treaty and Concession. A substantial element in our story has been the fact that, with the British Government's Private Finance Initiative in its infancy (Morton was recruited by the Chancellor to head a working group to advance it), the Conservative administration had been keen to support this bold venture as far as was possible. For all the talk of non-involvement and private sector responsibility, the Governments had been drawn into the project's affairs on a number of occasions and at a number of different levels. The British Government had been involved in providing its share of the agreed infrastructure and in initiating the joint venture for a high speed Rail Link. It had maintained a watching brief on Eurotunnel's fortunes during construction and fitting out and, thanks to Morton's lobbying, had been informally involved in its financial affairs, with intervention sometimes, as with Thatcher in 1990, fairly direct, at others, as with the Bank of England in 1993, less so. It may have been too late to turn back in the early 1990s, and several elements, once started, exhibited a political momentum of their own. However, political continuity over an extended period held the key to successful Anglo-French attitudes to the Channel Tunnel. In France Mitterand enjoyed two consecutive terms as President, from 1981 to 1995. In Britain Thatcher was Prime Minister from 1979 to 1990 and her party was in office until 1997. These regimes comfortably embraced both the start of the project and its completion in 1994, providing the continuity absent in the 1960s and 1970s. The stability thus produced in both countries undoubtedly aided the Tunnel project during its many shaky moments.

12

THE CHANNEL TUNNEL

Postscript, 1994–2005

1. The Tunnel opens: celebration and reality

The contractors' handover of the Tunnel on 10 December 1993, a celebratory luncheon held in the Tunnel on 26 February 1994, and the official opening on 6 May, were all lavish affairs, though the celebrations were constrained by the fact that full commissioning of the rolling stock had not been completed.[1] The lunch, organised by Eurotunnel, was held in a crossover chamber of the Tunnel. Echoing the promotional events organised in the nineteenth century by Brunel (Thames Tunnel) and Watkin (aborted 1880s Tunnel), the event was attended by former Prime Ministers Baroness Thatcher and Pierre Mauroy, and 800 or so British and French guests who tucked into scallops, seafood casserole, British and French cheeses, champagne, and an indeterminate, late 1980s claret.[2] 'After two centuries of dreaming and eight years of labour', the British and French heads of state, Queen Elizabeth II and President Mitterand, were able to meet for the official opening without travelling by sea or air. They were joined by the two Prime Ministers, John Major and Edouard Balladur, the Belgian Prime Minister Jean-Luc Dehaene, the EC President Jacques Delors, former Prime Minister Thatcher, Transport and other Ministers, and Bénard and Morton of Eurotunnel.[3] Although the European Parliament's idea of naming the facility the 'Winston Churchill – Jean Monnet Tunnel' had clearly fallen on stony ground,[4] there was much merry-making, the Louis Roederer champagne providing a distinguished alternative to the Pommery served at TML's handover party in December. With visits to both the Coquelles and Cheriton terminals and the sampling of both the 'Eurostar' train and Eurotunnel's 'Le Shuttle', there were brass bands and fireworks, and much pomp and ceremony. As the *Observer* noted, 'No blows were exchanged, no abuse uttered. And there were no nasty jokes about Waterloo, the Second World War, British cuisine, or the sexual predilections of British male politicians', though it was rather fanciful of *Le Figaro* to imagine that the link would 'abolish, psychologically, all the divorces and quarrels through the centuries'.[5]

The euphoria, if such it was, was short-lived. First of all, much more remained to be done before the Tunnel was a fully functioning transport system; second, it was not long before Eurotunnel's financial problems were once again exposed.

There were teething troubles in the early months of operating, rolling stock suppliers were late in their deliveries, and the process of authorising the use of passenger shuttles and trains took much longer than anticipated. It was not until 21 October 1994 that the IGC was able to authorise a full commercial Eurostar service, and that service did not begin until 14 November. The passenger shuttles were brought into service on a limited basis on 22 December, but a complete service, including the carriage of caravans and camper vans, was not available until 29 September 1995. Train operating was also restricted by the IGC for safety reasons. From 6 July 1994 there was a limitation of eight trains per hour in each direction; then twelve trains from 28 March 1995, a restriction which remained in force until March 1999.[6] Partly as a consequence of these delays and restrictions, the initial traffic and operating results for 1994 were well below expectations. Freight traffic was disappointing, and there was scarcely time for passenger traffic to build up. With the mountain of debt requiring servicing at the rate of nearly £2 million a day, the situation immediately brought the company's fragile

Cartoon 9 The Tunnel opens: *Private Eye*, 6 May 1994.

finances into question. Morton continued to exert pressure on the authorities on a number of fronts. He applied for a judicial review of the extension of duty-free facilities until 1999, and pressed the British Government for relief in relation to rates and withholding tax.[7] The first intimation that the company's difficulties were more severe than this tinkering could alleviate came in April 1995 with news of the 1994 results. Turnover at £30.6 million compared badly with the £137 million forecast in the Rights Issue document of May 1994, and although the net loss for the year of £386.9 million was closer to forecast (£382 million), the Co-chairmen, Morton and Ponsolle, could only report bluntly that 'Eurotunnel is at risk'. Then in June, when Morton visited John Major to talk about the Private Finance Initiative, he hinted that later in the year the Prime Minister might hear talk about 'public money and Eurotunnel'. The Treasury was informed that a 'series of gripes' would be submitted.[8] They duly appeared (see below, pp. 373–6).

2. 'Over time and over budget'

The Channel Tunnel (see Figure 12.1) had cost something under £5 billion to construct and double that to finance. Should this be characterised as a failure? The short answer is no. First of all, the challenges posed by Europe's largest piece of transport infrastructure were considerable. As we have seen, the logistics of tunnelling under the sea over such a length stretched the capabilities of the engineers. There were many uncertainties, and project managers could scarcely be criticised for the unexpected hazards encountered, particularly in relation to difficult ground. And while the technology of tunnelling may not have been novel, the technologies associated with the fitting out of the Tunnel were unquestionably at the cutting edge, and the differential increases in cost over estimate reflected this (Table 12.1). Second, the cost overruns and time delays, though clearly threatening Eurotunnel's commercial viability, were by no means large in relation to other 'mega projects'. The press fastened onto this observation at regular intervals. Eurotunnel's Rights Issue documentation in May 1994 revealed that the Tunnel had opened a year late, with construction costs some 57–64 per cent over the estimate in 1987, though total project costs, including financing, had risen more steeply (Table 12.1). But this was small beer compared with the Suez and Panama canals, both more than 50 times over budget, not to speak of Concorde (cost: seven times more than expected, with profoundly disappointing revenues), the Seikan Tunnel in Japan (14 years late), the Scottish Assembly building (costing ten times more than the initial estimate), or Gaudí's Sagrada Familia.[9] Academic research supports the contention that the Tunnel was progressed fairly well given the circumstances, which included its 'quadripartite' character (Britain, France, private and public sectors). A quantitative assessment of the capital cost of 52 large civil infrastructure projects, conducted by the Rand Corporation in 1988, found that the average cost overrun was 88 per cent, and the average delay 17 per cent (with a six-year project like the Tunnel equivalent to 12 months). Bent Flyvbjerg *et al.* placed the Channel Tunnel in the middle of a table of cost overruns for large transport projects, which

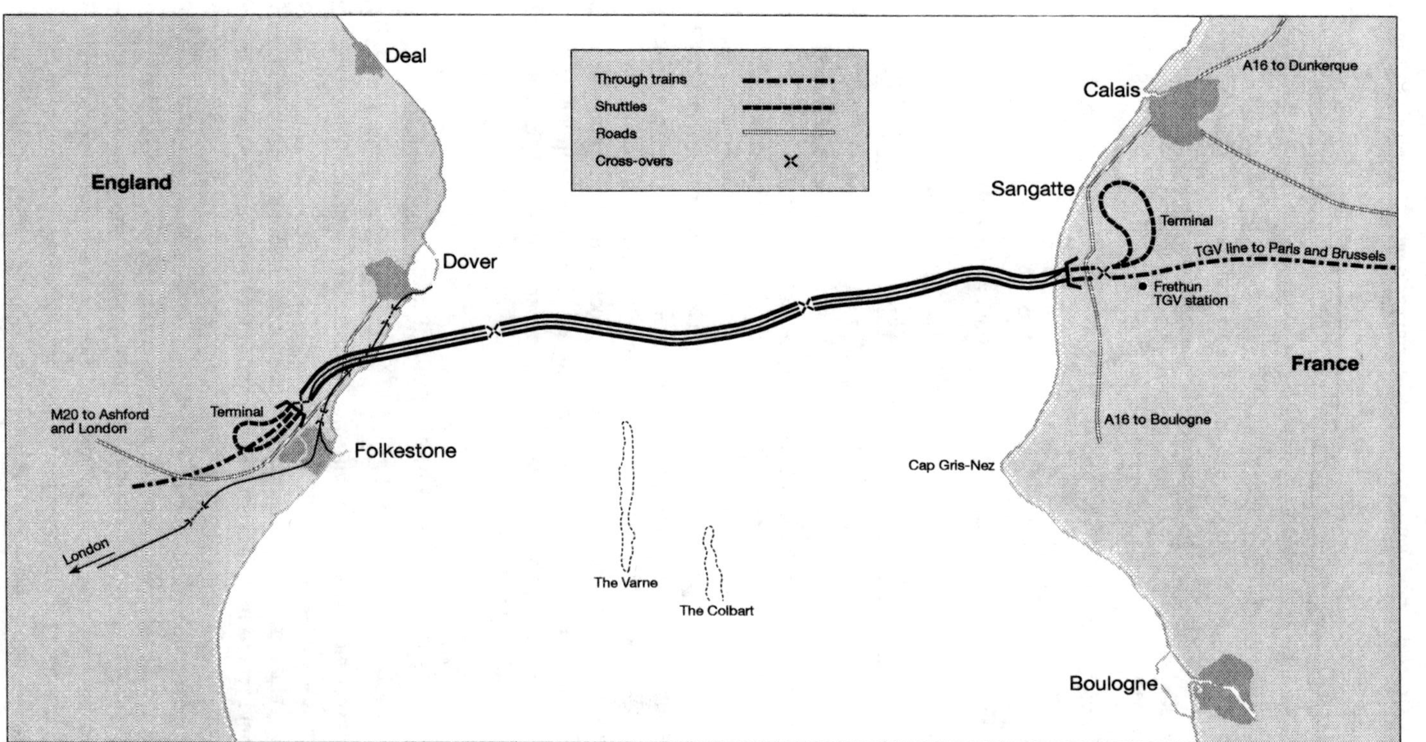

Figure 12.1 The 'Eurotunnel System', 1994.

Table 12.1 Channel Tunnel outturn, 6 May 1994, compared with November 1987 forecast [£ m., September 1985 prices]

	November 1987 Forecast	*Actual as at 6 May 1994*	*Increase [%]*
Construction costs			
Tunnelling	1,329	2,110	59
Terminals	448	553	23
Fixed equipment	688	1,200	74
Rolling stock	245	705	188
Bonuses	—	46	—
Direct works	—	36	—
Contingency	132	—	—
Total	2,842	4,650[a]	64
Project costs	November 1987 Forecast	Cash requirement to end 1998 est. in May 1994	Increase [%]
	4,550[b]	10,116	122

Source: Eurotunnel, Pathfinder prospectus, November 1987, Rights Issue document, May 1994.

Notes

a Includes £194 m. not spent. The overspend on £4,456 m. = 57%.

b Given as £4,874 m. in July 1987 prices: deflated by GDP mkt prices 2Q:87/3Q:85.

range from 196 to 26 per cent.[10] Judged in this context, the performance of TML and Eurotunnel, if leaving much to be desired on the public relations front, was satisfactory.[11] And unlike some earlier projects, it was clearly a misfortune for Eurotunnel to embark on a long construction process during a time of relatively high inflation, and then commence operating when the rate of inflation fell and prices became more stable. In such a situation, the weight of the debt burden remained stubbornly in place.

3. The Channel Tunnel's contribution to transport provision, 1994–2004

Although that most valuable of historical tools – hindsight – is in short supply, there has now been a decade of Tunnel operating, and it is possible to provide a tentative evaluation of its contribution to transport.[12] In Table 12.2 we summarise the Tunnel's record in terms of traffic carried from 1994. Despite a slow start and notwithstanding the setback of a serious fire on a freight shuttle on 18 November 1996, the railways' Eurostar business increased steadily on the London-Paris/Brussels routes, reaching 6 million passengers in 1997, 7 million in 2000 and 2004, and averaging 6.7 million a year, 1998–2004. The results were of course well down on the forecasts of 1987–94, and losses were experienced. The regional (north of London) and night sleeper trains fell by the wayside, though a winter ski service to Bourg-St-Maurice began in 1997, a direct summer service to Avignon was introduced in July 2002, and Britain's high-speed CTRL was partially opened in September 2003.[13] Eurotunnel's 'Le Shuttle' traffic built up well, though the ferries' retention of duty-free sales until 1999, and periodic outbursts of price cutting prevented the Tunnel from gaining a higher market share. Peaking at over 12 million passengers in 1998, patronage averaged 9.6 million a year, 1998–2004. Taken overall, passenger numbers in 2003 were only about 40 per cent of expectations in 1994. Freight was a mixed bag. The railways' trainload operations were clearly disappointing. Planned by British Rail on the British side, then progressed by the private sector after the sale of the RfD business to a consortium led by Wisconsin Central in 1997, the traffic remained well below Eurotunnel's expectations. The amount carried rose to 3.1 million tonnes in 1998, but then began to decline with the economic downturn in Europe, and the traffic in 2002 was only half that of the peak, by which time the business was being adversely affected by the moves made to combat the activities of unauthorised entrants ('asylum seekers').[14] On the other hand, Eurotunnel's HGV shuttles were more successful, in spite of the fire in 1996. The traffic grew steadily from just under 400,000 vehicles in 1995 to 1,300,000 in 2003 and 2004 (Table 12.2). Although the tonneage carried is impossible to calculate with accuracy, if we assume that the average pay-load per vehicle was nine tonnes, then 11.6 million tonnes were carried by 2003, 78 per cent of the level forecast by Eurotunnel in 1994 (14.85 m tonnes).[15] Eurotunnel's share of the roll-on roll-off traffic through the Channel ports in 1999 has been estimated at 26 per cent.[16]

Interested parties, and especially aggrieved shareholders, have suggested that the traffic forecasts were consciously fictitious, used to justify support for a private sector project with no subsidy. French sources have levelled the accusation at British officials.[17] This is unfair and, in fact, all forecasts, whether advanced by consultants, companies, civil servants, or academics, have proved to be wide of the mark.[18] One of the latter, Stefan Szymanski, has conceded that errors were made. There were deficiencies in estimating broad variables such as the rate of growth of the cross-channel market, and the assumptions made about the decline of the ferries after the Tunnel opened were premature. Eurotunnel itself was over-optimistic about its likely revenues, the product of assuming a market share and prices which did not materialise. On the other hand, there were few precedents if any for modelling the outcome of competition between a privately-owned fixed link and private sector ferries.[19] Clearly forecasting was and is a tricky business, and, indeed, it has been asserted that many transport mega projects have suffered from over-optimistic forecasts, especially where railway transport is involved.[20] Although a detailed analysis of the cross-channel market lies outside the scope of this book, we should observe that forecasting for the Tunnel was affected by the changing nature of the business over the quarter-century from 1980. In the passenger market, the leisure segment was greatly influenced by the fact that this was ceasing to be a simple geographical market, as 1970s forecasters had assumed, but was becoming more of a 'what you do with your spare time' market.[21] In this context, the competition offered by a deregulated airline industry might have been – and

Table 12.2 Channel Tunnel traffic, 1994–2004 ('000s)

Year	Passenger: Eurostar (pass. no.)	Shuttle (no. of vehicles) cars etc.	coaches	Total	Total Passengers (no.)	Freight: Railway (tonnes)	Shuttle (vehicles) (no.)	Total Freight (tonnes) estimate
1994[a]	n.a.	82	—	82	315	452	65	
1995	2,920	1,223	23	1,246	7,081[d]	1,350	391	
1996[b]	4,867	2,077	58	2,135	12,809[d]	2,361	519	
1997	6,004	2,318	65	2,383	14,653	2,923	256	
1998	6,038	3,351	96	3,448	18,405	3,141	705	
1999	6,593	3,260	82	3,342	17,550	2,865	839	
2000	7,130	2,784	79	2,864	17,018	2,947	1,133	
2001	6,947	2,530	75	2,605	16,313	2,447	1,198	
2002[c]	6,603	2,336	72	2,408	15,252	1,487	1,231	
2003	6,315	2,279	72	2,351	14,699	1,744	1,285	13,300[z]
2004	7,277	2,101	63	2,165	15,064[t]	1,889	1,281	13,400[z]
	(no.)	*(no.)*			*(no.)*	*(tonnes)*	*(tonnes)*	*(tonnes)*
1987 forecast: 2003	21,400	21,100			39,500	10,600	10,500	21,100
1994 forecast: 2003	17,120	18,650			35,770	10,450	14,850	25,300

Source: *TSGB 2003*, T5.26, *2004*, T6.18; Eurotunnel: *R&A 1994–2003* (restated figures used where given); Pathfinder Prospectus, November 1987, Rights Issue document, May 1994; News Release, 25 January 2005.

Notes

a partial opening.
b Tunnel fire 16 November 1996: passenger shuttles resumed 10 December 1996, full freight service 15 June 1997.
c disruption caused by clandestines (asylum seekers).
d 7,789 and 13,673 in MMC, 1997, para. 4.17.
t implied multipliers for shuttles = c.2.5 passengers per car, 37 passengers per coach.
z assumption 9 pay-load tonnes per vehicle + rail freight.

indeed was – anticipated, but few analysts foresaw the success of the low-cost airlines such as Ryanair and Easyjet from the mid-1990s. These companies not only challenged the established airlines but also had an impact on the cross-channel market as a whole. While their overall market share has been small, they affected all operators by transforming consumers' expectations about price. In addition they helped to narrow the market for international rail travel, though it should be pointed out that this narrowing was also encouraged by the more conservative business strategies of Eurostar after the privatisation of EPS.[22] The leisure market itself was subject to change. British holidaymakers continued to take their cars with them on visits to France, Belgium and Germany, but there were more short trips in the 1990s, encouraged by the ferries, which were able to increase the number of passenger vehicles carried by over 60 per cent in the five years before the Tunnel opened.[23] However, by 2002 the report on the international passenger survey (all journey types) revealed that France, the mainstay of UK residents' foreign visits in the past, had lost its place as the No.1 destination to Spain. And the Tunnel's popularity as a mode of transport for UK residents making foreign visits fell back after peaking in 1998. By 2002 it represented only 9 per cent of the total number of visits abroad. Travel to France was the core of Tunnel business, and longer-distance train travel has remained unattractive for both leisure and business passengers. Of course, this situation might easily change if the airlines are confronted with higher costs.[24] Nevertheless, the Tunnel has captured a sizeable share of 'near-European' passenger markets, and notably some 65 per cent of the London-Paris and 50 per cent of the London-Brussels markets.[25]

Eurotunnel's financial results were of course disappointing (see Table 12.3), and way below the documented expectations of 1987–94.[26] However, it is important to distinguish between (i) the operating results before financial operations; (ii) the underlying profit and loss; and (iii) the profit/loss after exceptional items, and notably the one-off gains produced by financial restructuring. Once the trials of late opening and the November 1996 fire had been overcome, Eurotunnel achieved a turnover of around £600 million a year over the period 1998–2004, and an operating margin of around 55 per cent. But after depreciation and financial charges, losses were severe and averaged £137 million a year, 1998–2004, before exceptional items. The company made much of the fact that 'cash breakeven' had been achieved in 2002, that is operating revenues were sufficient to cover both costs and interest charges. However, exceptional profits from financial operations were a key element in this statistic, and in any case, in the following year a considerable sum – £1.3 billion – was deducted as an impairment charge to reflect the fact that the discounted future value (at 7%) of cash flows was much lower than the net book value of the assets. A further £395 million was deducted in 2004. Unsurprisingly, the debt burden continued to dominate, and the disgruntled, mainly French, shareholders, disturbed by the unfulfilled promises of Eurotunnel's prospectuses, continued to challenge the company's directors in the courts. In April 2004 French shareholders, led by Nicolas Miguet, ousted the Board and installed a French-dominated management team, with Jacques Maillot

Table 12.3 Eurotunnel operating results and profit and loss, 1994–2004 (£m.)

Year	*Turnover: Shuttles*	*Railways*	*Total*	*Operating margin*	*Operating profit/(loss) after depreciation*	*Profit/(loss) after financial charges, tax ('underlying loss')*	*Exceptional profit*[c]	*Impairment charge*	*Profit/(loss) after exceptional items (exceptional profit, impairment charge, etc.)*
1994[a]	11	12	31	(320)	(465)	(1,103)	716[d]		(387)
1995	120	133	304	(64)	(200)	(925)			(925)
1996[b]	150	207	504	134	(29)	(716)			(716)
1997[b]	113	212	531	209	57	(611)			(611)
1998	210	213	666	334	184	(215)	279		64
1999	265	210	654	351	210	(94)	296		202
2000	315	208	600	345	208	(124)	0		(124)
2001	315	214	574	327	188	(147)	15		(132)
2002	349	227	609	348	207	(105)	407		302
2003	306	230	578	313	167	(148)	114	(1,300)	(1,334)
2004	285	234	555	294	171	(127)	(48)	(395)	(570)

Source: Eurotunnel, *R&A 1994–2004*. Restated figures used where given.

Notes

a Limited operating.
b Results affected by fire, 18 November 1996.
c From financial restructuring, etc.
d Capitalisation of own work.

as Chairman and Jean-Louis Raymond as Chief Executive. However, this radical step failed to produce immediate and effective solutions. Trading continued to be challenging in 2004, and with debt repayment and full interest payments set to resume at the end of 2005, and the Minimum Usage Charge expiring in 2006, the search for a stable debt management regime became even more urgent.[27] Maillot gave way to Jacques Gounon in February 2005, and when talks on a further debt restructuring began in April, it was Gounon who demanded that the creditors write off two-thirds of Eurotunnel's £6.4 billion debt. He declared himself entirely opposed to a debt-for-equity swap.[28] A challenge to his uncompromising approach was mounted by Miguet and Raymond, who resigned as Chief Executive, but the threat evaporated at shareholders' meetings in Calais in June. The meetings left nothing resolved, however, heralding a period of intense negotiation about Eurotunnel's future. The situation has clearly been complicated by the selling-on of much of the company's debt.[29]

4. The continuing relationship with government

Finance and the concession

Relations between the two governments and the private sector operator did not end on the opening of the Tunnel. First, the IGC and Safety Authority have continued to discharge their supervisory responsibilities in relation to safety issues, and aspects of the Tunnel franchise have attracted the attention of the European Commission. Second, the last ten years have seen further rounds of financial crisis, punctuated by appeals for government assistance. Third, the enduring responsibilities of the British, French and Belgian railways demanded the attention of their respective governments. In the British case, there were contractual complications arising from the completion of the railway privatisation process in 1994–7 (in particular, the reassignment of responsibilities under the Usage Contract), and the progressing of the CTRL. In this section we summarise the relationship between the two governments and Eurotunnel over financial matters, which led to the demand for a further extension of the Concession.

As we have seen, within months of the opening, Eurotunnel was facing yet another financial crisis, which provoked the company into sending the British and French Governments a further set of grievances and demands. In the late summer of 1995, after trading had been affected by a price war with the ferries, there was talk of a potential deficit of £5 billion, and on 14 September Eurotunnel announced the suspension of interest payments on its £8.7 billion junior debt, the expectation being that this would persist for 18 months.[30] With the revelation in early October that Eurotunnel had experienced a loss after depreciation and interest of £465 million in the first half of 1995, City analysts were expressing the opinion that the capital value of the concern was closer to a third of its book value.[31] With Eurotunnel's continued existence as a Concessionaire in some doubt, first Ponsolle, then Morton, presented their Governments with a lengthy series of demands. Ponsolle's eight-page letter, sent to Transport Minister Bernard Pons on 11 September, came with a 'heavy supporting tome' entitled 'Note technique de synthèse Eurotunnel', which itemised at length the company's complaints about duty-free sales, frontier and security controls, safety at sea and the granting of operating certificates.[32] Morton's letter, also eight pages long, was sent to the Transport Secretary Sir George Young, on 4 October. It demanded 'compensation for operational and commercial distortions to our financial disadvantage'. There was more than a slight resemblance to his grievance letter of September 1992 (above, p. 356). Then he had identified seven grievances; now there were more, with the addition of new concerns embracing the uncertainties created by the EC's Railway Directive 91/400, the need for a level playing field in the cross-channel market, and protests about security measures and frontier controls. And notwithstanding the assurances given when the Concession had been extended in December 1993,

Cartoon 10 The banks' continuing anxieties about Eurotunnel's fortunes, 1996. 'Damn! They have dug a Eurotunnel!': Plantu, *Le Monde*, 28–9 January 1996.

Cartoon 11 News of the Eurotunnel Concession extension, 1997: Kipper Williams, *Guardian*, 2 July 1997.

Eurotunnel repeated some of its earlier complaints in relation to safety requirements, Britain's failure to provide the promised railway infrastructure, and the fragmentation created by the privatisation of British Rail.[33] Although the submissions to the two governments were similar, Ponsolle provided a different emphasis when he called for the British Government to give an 'irrevocable' commitment to the CTRL, and asked for a review of the issue of government guarantees.[34]

Eurotunnel's efforts to 'share the pain around' by persuading the Governments to make some kind of contribution to its financial rescue initially met with resistance. Morton's suggestion that a joint working group be established to examine the idea of a credit support arrangement – a 'government-buttressed bridge' – smacked too much of a financial guarantee and was quickly rejected. The financial stakes were raised by the increasing restlessness of the 725,000 small shareholders (600,000 of them French), who were not impressed by allegations of earlier insider trading by some of the leading banks, and in February 1996 two *mandataires ad hoc* were appointed under French insolvency law by the Tribunal de Commerce of Paris.[35] However, the banks were not at this stage disposed to exercise their rights of substitution. They preferred a negotiated settlement of the financial difficulties, hoping that something might be offered by the Governments as goodwill.[36] For their part the Governments felt that the list of grievances was unconvincing. The outcome of the parallel dispute with the railways gave comfort to an obdurate stance. At the end of October the Arbitration Court of the International Chamber of Commerce found largely in the railways' favour. Eurotunnel's main claim was rejected. The arbitrators did not accept the argument that the railways should contribute to the Tunnel's construction cost overrun by either renegotiating the Usage Contract, or by making a cash payment of £2.3 billion.[37] The British Government, while having to steer a careful course between Scylla (Eurotunnel) and Charybdis (the railways), was encouraged by this news, and in December contested the allegations and resisted the demands for compensation.[38] The French Government followed suit.[39] Morton's hopes for a speedy resolution of the matter were disappointed. The British Government maintained its stance that the issue of financial restructuring was a matter for Eurotunnel and its bankers, arguing that the negotiations should be conducted without government intervention. It was therefore disposed to play the dispute 'long'. Morton made several efforts to provoke the Governments, for example in suggesting that they bore some responsibility for Eurotunnel's over-optimistic traffic forecasts, and in arguing that the transfer of British Rail's responsibilities under the Usage Contract to Railtrack, EPS (subsequently Eurostar [UK]) and RfD (via the 'Back-to-Back' Agreements of May 1994) was an assignment and therefore required Eurotunnel's consent. However, both were firmly resisted.[40]

Over the course of 1996 the work of civil servants was taken up in other aspects of the Tunnel – in awarding the Concession for the CTRL and progressing the hybrid Bill (see below, pp. 379–80). Of course, the efforts of Eurotunnel and the banks to produce a financial agreement continued to be closely monitored, and responses were required to more rounds of lobbying, notably from Eurotunnel's Director of Public Affairs, John Noulton, and from the British and French mandataires, Lord Wakeham and Robert Badinter. All mentioned the idea of a further extension of the Concession. These pressures became more urgent with the publication of the results for 1995, which revealed a loss of £925 million, reported to be the largest in British corporate history.[41] It was also necessary to respond to the developing views of the French Government, which, having been more bullish than the British in selling the idea of Eurotunnel to its citizens, was unhappy about the option of substituting another company, and was becoming more sympathetic to the idea of assisting the angry shareholders. After noises made within the French Trésor, President Jacques Chirac floated the idea of a 20–30 year extension when he met Major during his state visit in May.[42] The British, while seeing some merit in a relaxation of their negative stance, were unsympathetic to the notion of a further extension, feeling that it might provoke a legal challenge from the ferries and airlines and create difficulties with European Union rules on state aid. After further examination these obstacles were not regarded as insurmountable, but there remained the political danger of being seen to bail out lame ducks. On the other hand, it was understood that the French might oppose the substitution of Eurotunnel if a financial agreement were not reached. In July an ad hoc Cabinet meeting, chaired by the Deputy Prime Minister, Michael Heseltine, supported the strategy of waiting for the banks to do a deal with Eurotunnel; only then would the question of an extension be considered.[43] In the meantime, British officials looked for *quae pro quibus* to demand from Eurotunnel in return for a 34-year extension valued at a modest £100 million.[44]

Eventually, some progress was made. In July 1996, with agreement close, Morton announced that when the negotiations were concluded he would step down as Co-chairman in favour of Robert Malpas.[45] In early October the basic elements of a financial plan were in place and were made public. The burden of junior debt was addressed: £1 billion was to be swapped for equity, and £3.7 billion converted into new instruments (£1 billion of which was to be redeemed by 2003). Debt maturities would be lengthened, and below market-rate interest rates were to apply for seven years.[46] The deal was not dependent on an extension of the Concession, but on the 14th Morton and Ponsolle wrote to their respective Prime Ministers, Major and Alain Juppé, to request a further, and 'significant', increase. Now the emphasis was on using an extension to ensure that the banking syndicate, and more especially the shareholders, supported the restructuring. The latter were being presented with the prospect of a considerable dilution of control (to about 55 per cent, then to less than 40 per cent by 2003).[47] By this time it was clear that the French were more inclined to agree to the request than the British, who continued to insist on having something in return, either from Eurotunnel, or from France on a broader basis.[48] However, the stakes were raised on 30 October when Juppé put it to Major in somewhat strong terms that a 34-year extension, making 99 years in all, should be granted, and, although there were much more pressing issues, the subject was introduced by Chirac during the Franco-British summit meeting in Bordeaux in early November.[49] There was also pressure from the agent banks.[50] Still the British procrastinated, inviting another reference to that bête noire of Anglo-French diplomacy, 'feet-dragging'.[51] Negotiations were scarcely helped by the fire on 18 November, which temporarily halted commercial operating, by arguments over the financial value of an extension, or by action taken by SNCF in complaining to the European Commission about the support promised by the British Government when organising the privatisation of

RfD.[52] But outside the Treasury at least, some British officials were coming round to the view that it was not worth jeopardising good relations with France for something of uncertain value, the impact of which lay so far into the future.[53] Another important consideration was the impact on the financing of the CTRL project, which was scarcely helped by Eurotunnel's difficulties (see below).

In fact, the decision was taken by the incoming Labour administration led by Tony Blair, elected in May 1997, and by a new French Government, headed by Prime Minister Lionel Jospin, elected in June. Chirac asked Blair to look urgently at the issue when they met on 11 June, and there was some force in his position since Eurotunnel shareholders were due to vote on the financial restructuring package on 10 July.[54] After meetings between the three sides in Paris on 24 June, John Prescott, combining the posts of Transport Secretary and Deputy Prime Minister, reaffirmed British insistence on a *quid pro quo*, but was willing to agree to the French demand for a statement that the Governments were prepared, in principle, to grant an extension 'at least to 99 years'. The statement, issued on 1 July, indicated that the extension was subject to shareholder approval of the restructuring, an agreement between Eurotunnel and the Governments on ways and means to increase the rail freight business through the Tunnel, and satisfactory arrangements for the Governments to share in the post-2052 profits of the Concession.[55] At meetings of shareholders in Eurotunnel S.A. and Eurotunnel PLC nine days later the financial package was approved by a substantial majority.[56] The log-jam had been broken by positive reactions to Eurotunnel's proposal that there might be a profit-sharing arrangement as a *quid pro quo* – the French Government had suggested 50 per cent of pre-tax profits – and by French acquiescence, albeit reluctant, in Prescott's insistence that Tunnel rail freight be given some encouragement.[57] However, these elements were by no means easy to resolve, and horse-trading on the substantive detail ensured that it was not until December that the two Governments were able to agree an extension in principle.[58] Heads of Agreement were then signed in February 1998. They provided for a 34-year extension, that is from 2052 to 2086, dependent on the implementation of Eurotunnel's financial restructuring proposals. In return the company agreed to pay the Governments an annual sum, including corporation tax, equal to 59 per cent of pre-tax profits during the extension period. The extension was to benefit Eurotunnel only (if there was a substitution, the Concession would end in 2052; the company also retained the right to terminate the Concession in 2052). Eurotunnel also undertook not to challenge the Back-to-Back agreements, and it was agreed that the Usage Contract with the railways would not be extended (it would expire in 2052). By this time the sale of RfD to English Welsh & Scottish Railway (Wisconsin Central) had been cleared by the European Commission (in November 1997). The British Railways Board (backed by the DTp after privatisation) undertook to meet the Minimum Usage Charge payable by the British freight operator under the Usage Contract until 2005.[59] The two Governments gave undertakings to promote the development of international rail freight through the Tunnel, and Eurotunnel offered a special reduced toll arrangement for traffic from Germany, where the railways' share was small.[60] In turning the Heads into formal documentation there were some difficulties, particularly with the clarification of the profit-sharing mechanism, and it was not until the end of June 1999 that the French Parliament formally endorsed the extension (the British having produced a Command Paper in May).[61] There is no doubt that the second extension helped to prop up shareholder support, at least in the short run, but its impact on Eurotunnel's profit and loss account (a spreading out of depreciation payments with minimal impact on the valuation of the dividend stream) was limited when set against the overall problem of servicing the debt.[62]

5. The continuing relationship with government

The CTRL

Another enduring, and equally challenging, task for the British Government was to advance the project to build a high-speed rail line (CTRL) on the British side. As we have noted, by January 1994 the Government had agreed on a route and promised some public support for a flagship project of the Government's Private Finance Initiative, a joint venture with an estimated construction cost of £2.7 billion (Q4/92 prices). In February a competition was launched to find a bidder. After receiving enquiries from nine parties, four were selected in June for

Cartoon 12 The Channel Tunnel Rail Link's financing problems, 1998: London & Continental Railways ask the British Government for an additional £1.2 billion in support: as seen by Steve Bell, *Guardian*, 30 January 1998.

the post-qualification stage: Eurorail; Hochtief (Green Arrow); London & Continental Railways; and Union Link.[63] The consortia were asked to respond by March 1995 with proposals, specifying the amount of government support required (initially expected to be c.£1.7 billion), and the extent of their willingness to bear risk. In the meantime a hybrid Bill was laid before Parliament in November. In June 1995 two groups were shortlisted: London & Continental Railways (LCR) and Eurorail.[64] In February 1996, the winner was announced. LCR, a consortium made up of Bechtel, SBC (later UBS) Warburg, Virgin, National Express Group, SNCF/Systra and London Electricity, was awarded the contract to 'design, build, finance, operate and maintain' the CTRL.[65] The decision was also taken to include a station at Stratford in east London in addition to one at Ebbsfleet, and plans were announced to operate services beyond London, for example to Birmingham and Manchester.[66] In May a 'Development Agreement' was signed, granting LCR a 999-year Concession, and transferring Union Railways and Eurostar UK to the company. LCR, which was to operate as a fully integrated railway, unlike the privatised components of British Rail, would become eligible for government support totalling £1.4 billion (in 1995 prices) when 68 per cent of the project had been built. This was to be a combination of grant plus payment of a 'capacity charge' for use of the line by UK domestic services. Modest assistance from the European Union was also promised. In all, with the transfer of public rail assets and land to LCR, the amount of public support was reckoned to be as high as £5.7 billion by the Labour opposition.[67] The Channel Tunnel Rail Link Bill received a second reading in January 1995. It was then examined by a Commons Select Committee. Meeting for one year exactly (14 February 1995–14 February 1996), it was the longest running such committee in British parliamentary history, its 81 sessions comfortably beating the 57 for the Great Western Railway Bill in 1854. The Royal Assent was given on 18 December 1996.[68] The process was also accompanied by serious concerns about the impact of the project development process in terms of planning blight, which led to complaints by affected parties about the DTp's handling of the project from 1990 and to a reference to the Parliamentary Commissioner for Administration (Ombudsman). The Ombudsman, in a report published in February 1995, upheld the complaints of those deemed to have suffered from 'generalised blight'. The Department vigorously contested the findings, but after the matter had been referred to the PCA Select Committee, which endorsed the Ombudsman's findings, it offered to formulate a scheme of redress for cases of exceptional hardship. After consideration by an inter-departmental working group in 1996, this was eventually produced in March 1997. Both the passage of the hybrid Bill and the vexed issue of blight underlined the difficulties in progressing bold pieces of new infrastructure in a densely populated country with existing procedures.[69]

In 1997, as Eurotunnel concentrated on its financial restructuring and pushed the Governments for an extension to its Concession (see above), the CTRL came under pressure as Eurostar continued to disappoint, and cash flow problems emerged during the project development stage. Both the Major and Blair Governments were asked for assistance. Prescott, the incoming Minister, was reluctant to provide additional support, but, once again, government principle had to be balanced against the consequences of project failure and the consequent impact on future Public-Private Partnerships (PPPs). He was therefore willing to consider LCR's request that it be allowed early access to the proceeds of leasing the Eurostar trainsets.[70] Soon afterwards a more serious problem emerged. Capital market opinion turned against the company when revised traffic forecasts produced by LCR's consultants in September predicted much lower passenger numbers and revenue streams than at the time of the bid, thereby increasing the size of Eurostar's projected losses and prejudicing the prospects for a £5 billion debt – and equity-raising operation.[71] The company's plight, which amounted to a £750–1,000 million NPV gap in its finance forecasts, was fully evident by the end of the year. LCR attempted to extract additional government support, and also turned to Railtrack, the privatised rail infrastructure and property company, as a potential 'white knight'. There was also talk of rescheduling or scaling down the project.[72] In January 1998, with market sentiment remaining lukewarm, LCR asked the Government for £1.2 billion of support, in addition to the amount already pledged, now valued at £1.733 billion (in 1995 prices).[73] Prescott refused the request, but invited the company to resubmit.[74] After intensive negotiations with LCR and Railtrack under the name 'Project Airline', and numerous value-for-money calculations, the Government was able to accept revised proposals from LCR in June.[75] The rescue package for the project did not involve a significant increase in public funding, but the balance of risk certainly tipped in the direction of Government. There was a major restructuring of the company. Construction was divided into two parts: Phase I, 46 miles from the Tunnel to Fawkham Jnc. (nr. Ebbsfleet) (1998–2003); and Phase II, 24 miles from Southfleet to St. Pancras (2001–6). Railtrack Group undertook to manage the construction of Phase I, with a commitment to purchase for £1.5 billion; it would also hold an option to do the same with Phase II (£1.8 billion). Inter-Capital and Regional Rail Ltd, a consortium led by National Express, agreed to operate the Eurostar UK services under a management contract, thereby decoupling the CTRL from its direct dependence on the fortunes of Eurostar.[76] Finally, the Government agreed to add £100–330 million (later stated as £140–360 million) to its overall support in order to underpin Eurostar operations, and to guarantee £3.75 billion of the privately-raised debt in order to reduce financing costs.[77] In return it was to take a public stake in LCR yielding at least a 33 per cent share in pre-tax profits after 2020.[78] A 'golden share' established a dividend restriction until 2021, and gave the Government the right to veto a sale before 2011 but to insist on one at any time, with a 90 per cent share in the proceeds. At the same time the length of the Rail Link Concession was reduced to 90 years. The DTp could also draw comfort from the prospect of international and domestic social benefits and regeneration benefits in London and the Thames Gateway, though the National Audit Office later noted that the methodology employed was 'unconventional', some of the assumptions were 'questionable' and the findings were therefore highly speculative.[79]

In the circumstances, with a very real prospect that LCR would collapse, the new arrangement was a triumph of public-private policy-making, though the deal attracted criticisms from both the National Audit Office and the Public Accounts Committee, and the Government's commitment in terms of cash flow provision was put at a substantial £2.3–2.9 billion over the period 1998/9–2012/13.[80] With the deal in place, construction began on the £1.9 billion Phase I in October 1998, and the first tranches of government-backed bonds were issued in February 1999. Services on the Phase I section began on time in September 2003, after the UK rail speed record had been broken in July, with a speed of 334.7 kph. However, this was not the full story. A further restructuring was required in 2001–2. In April 2001 Railtrack Group, beleaguered after the train accidents at Ladbroke Grove and Hatfield, gave up its right to build and purchase Phase II.[81] Once Railtrack plc had entered into administration in October 2001, the Group's continued participation was jeopardised, and in June 2002 LCR agreed to acquire its interest in Phase I, with a provision to sell the operator agreement to Network Rail, Railtrack plc's successor.[82] Completion of the £3.3 billion Phase II section, on which work started in July 2001, is expected in 2007, but financial difficulties continue to bedevil Eurotunnel, LCR and Eurostar, and the British Government's exposure remains substantial. The CTRL, one of Britain's largest PPPs, has thus had a difficult history. Many lessons may be derived from it, including: the fragility of revenue forecasts for start-up businesses; the need to constrain the optimism of bidders; the importance of ensuring that the capital structure of a venture matches the risks involved; the problems created by pursuing enabling legislation before a bidder has been chosen; and the undoubted risks of transferring public assets to the private sector before secure financing is in place. If the British Government's Private Finance Initiative has raised the possibility of deploying extra funds and establishing efficiency gains via the application of 'private sector disciplines', then it has also shown how the private sector can get its forecasting wrong, and in these circumstances some of the risks have fallen on the public sector.[83]

6. Conclusion: the political economy of the 'mega project'

The Channel Tunnel was completed successfully without the direct involvement of public money. But construction costs and deadlines were exceeded, the Concession was revised twice, and the financial structure renegotiated. In ten years of operating, Eurotunnel has never paid a dividend and with its heavy debt burden, financial crisis has never been far away. At the time of writing [June 2005], there is considerable uncertainty following the shareholder revolt of April 2004, and the difficulty in reaching agreement on ways of tackling the company's debt burden. Looming on the horizon are the end of the Minimum Usage Charge and the start of the requirement to repay debts, both due in 2006. But it would be all too easy to dismiss the Tunnel as a failure. First of all it represents an enormous achievement in terms of construction, financial and political engineering. And in terms of transport provision, it has captured a large share of the cross-channel and London-Paris/ Brussels markets, even if the overall results have been much lower than initial expectations in the late 1980s, and the carriage of rail freight in particular has proved disappointing. However, the patent fact was that as an investment project the Tunnel cost too much, and revenues were much lower than forecast. Of course, had costs been closer to the original estimate of £2 billion for the tunnelling and £4 billion in total project costs, then Eurotunnel's profit and loss account would have been more satisfactory. But whatever the trading picture, the Tunnel remains a monument to the imagination, a potent symbol of what can be achieved in the face of scepticism and financial difficulty. No doubt some more surprises are in prospect, but few would currently challenge the view that the Tunnel is an essential piece of European transport infrastructure, with economic gains in France, even if the initial impact in Kent has been relatively modest.[84]

When Eurotunnel's preliminary prospectus was released in 1986 an American banker noted that the investment 'could hardly be less attractive'. He referred, somewhat cynically, to the five stages of a major project: 'Euphoria; Disenchantment; Search for the Guilty; Persecution of the Innocent; and Rewards for the Uninvolved'.[85] More seriously, the Channel Tunnel has several lessons to offer to those interested in the development and management of large projects.[86] It is important to work with a concessionaire that is distinct from the promoters (banks and construction companies) and which can act as project 'champion'; responsibility for risk-taking should be established and clearly defined among the several parties; it is difficult to finance large infrastructure schemes with evident social benefits but speculative private gains without public guarantees; and there is a real challenge in balancing project flexibility against the need to establish a strong framework of safety and service quality.[87] The way in which Eurotunnel was established, and, in particular, the nature of its contractual relations with TML and the railways, contributed to its difficulties. The tortuous relationship with TML owed much to the fact that the contractors were initially the promoters, and it took some time to appreciate that Eurotunnel's role was to establish a sophisticated piece of transport infrastructure and not just an engineered tunnel. At a critical stage Eurotunnel was a fledgling company, short of expertise, and there were clear information asymmetries between it and TML, and between the banks and TML. TML itself began as a loose confederation of five British and five French companies, and it took time before the individual members of the consortium were able to function effectively as a team. In this environment the construction contract invited difficulties, especially given the rudimentary nature of the design work before it was signed. Only the tunnelling was contracted for at a fixed price, with an incentive to restrain costs: the rolling stock was procured on a cost-plus basis, the equipment as a lump sum. It was no surprise to find that the latter elements gave rise to disagreements and disputes, or that construction costs rose. Graham Corbett, Eurotunnel's Finance Director from 1989 to 1996, offered a number of 'simple lessons' to follow in large infrastructure projects, such as: the need to keep credit arrangements flexible, including the introduction of public sector mezzanine finance at an early stage, the ability to protect against inflation and interest rate movements, and use of a performance-related element in rewarding debt; the need to avoid design and build contracts where the contractor is not going to be the operator; avoidance of unwieldy construction consortia; and above all, the need to embark on the design work *before* construction starts.[88] The over-optimism of successive traffic and revenue forecasts also came to haunt the company, and certainly produced a legacy in the Railway Usage Contract, with its Minimum Usage Charge that few felt would become operational. In all this, the responsibility lay firmly with the private sector players, although the two Governments presided over the arrangements and did not seek to challenge them.

The Tunnel also provides important and salutary lessons for government-industry relations, especially with international mega projects, in areas such as: the tension between economic and political evaluations of major investment schemes; and the tension between the Treasury and sponsoring departments in evaluating, distributing and managing risk in public-private ventures. Above all, it provided valuable experience for those embarking enthusiastically upon the British Government's Private Finance Initiatives. As we have seen, at several points in this long story the project foundered or was put on ice. One cannot emphasise enough how difficult it was for the 'tunnelistas' to wage their campaigns through the serried ranks of sceptics and opponents. Undoubtedly, much of the problem from the 1950s lay in uncertainty over ownership and governance issues. Should the Tunnel be built and operated by the public sector? Should it be constructed with private capital and operated publicly? Should it be constructed and operated by the private sector? These questions were not straightforward and were influenced by the fact that scepticism about the prospect of financial returns was an enduring feature from the early 1960s. There were to be two decades of fluctuating debate before a solution was found, and the one chosen has certainly not been free of criticism.

In this climate, the importance of critical actors should not be under-estimated. In the 1960s and 1970s there was the enthusiasm of Pisani and Castle (fleetingly); the unequivocal determination of Peyton; and the positive approach shown by civil servants such as Gingell, Barber, Kemp and Fogarty. In the mid-1980s the players were able to punch a more effective weight. There was the enthusiasm of Mauroy and Auroux, and the executive determination of Thatcher and Ridley; the effective civil service partnership of Lyall and Braibant; the entrepreneurial response of large contracting firms such as Costain and Dumez; and the risk-taking support (if later regretted) of the major British and French banks. But the initiation of the Tunnel project in 1986 was only the start of the challenge. As *Construction News* noted, when Thatcher and Mitterand announced their support in January 1986, 'many observers felt that they were watching little more than an elaborate public relations exercise'.[89] There had been many of these in the past, a plethora of reports, reconsiderations, holding operations, 'feet-dragging' and 'playing it long'. Even at this stage, the project would have foundered, as it had in the 1880s and the mid-1970s, without a continuity of political support from Thatcher and Mitterand, the extraordinary drive of Morton and the less strident but equally effective persistence of Bénard and Ponsolle, the critical intervention of the Bank of England at key points, and the nerve held by the sponsoring banks, harassed contractors, and key bureaucrats in the British and French finance and transport departments. The two Governments often pursued different agendas within the 'quadripartite quilt' of decision-making. For the French, the 1975 cancellation had been a major obstacle to a revival a decade later, but a determination to reverse economic decline and promote the regeneration of the Nord-Pas de Calais region was a major incentive. For the British, the insistence on full private sector financing proved the key to a change of heart, although, as we have seen, it often proved difficult to prevent the Governments from being dragged into the support of private enterprise, and, in any case, the public support offered in the form of road and rail infrastructure was substantial.[90] In all the British Government spent £3 billion on the project prior to opening, and has spent or committed at least £4 billion since then. Whether the Tunnel should have been built, or whether the Tunnel should have been built as a private sector venture, are legitimate questions to ask. However, the essential point to make is that it was built, and the history of the largest engineering project of the twentieth century, chaotic as it has sometimes been, represents the supreme triumph of political will and entrepreneurial optimism over economic scepticism.[91]

NOTES

1 BEGINNINGS, 1802–1945

1 Firm evidence of these early events is difficult to find. Much rests on Channel Tunnel Parliamentary Committee [CTPC], 'A Brief Historical Survey of the Channel Tunnel Project 1802–1929', February 1929, Churchill Archives Centre, Channel Tunnel Papers, CTUN5/1. There are many accounts of the tunnel project during the 19th century, deriving from common sources, e.g. Peter A. Keen, 'The Channel Tunnel Project', *Journal of Transport History*, III (1957–8), 133ff; Humphrey Slater and Correlli Barnett, *The Channel Tunnel* (1958); Thomas Whiteside, *The Tunnel under the Channel* (1962); A.S. Travis, *Channel Tunnel Story 1802–1967* (1967); Michael R. Bonavia, *The Channel Tunnel Story* (Newton Abbot, 1987); Donald Hunt, *The Tunnel: The Story of the Channel Tunnel 1802–1994* (Upton-upon-Severn, 1994); Keith Wilson, *Channel Tunnel Visions, 1850–1945: Dreams and Nightmares* (1994); and Richard Gibb, 'The Channel Tunnel Project: Origins and Development', in Richard Gibb (ed.), *The Channel Tunnel* (Chichester, 1996), p. 1ff.; Drew Fetherston, *The Chunnel: The Amazing Story of the Undersea Crossing of the English Channel* (New York, 1997). Verification of the Mathieu-Favier (often referred to as Albert) and Fox references is a challenge; they appear to originate in the writings of a mid-19th century tunneliste, Thomé de Gamond (see below), though plans by Mathieu dated 1803 have been found: see Bertrand Lemoine, *Le Tunnel sous la Manche* (Paris, 1994), pp. 12–14, and Frank Davidson, communication with author, 25 November 2001. References to the earlier work of Nicolas Desmarets [*not* Desmarest] in 1751 appear to be misplaced; he did not advocate the construction of a tunnel or bridge: Nicolas Desmarets, *L'Ancienne Jonction de l'Angleterre a la France ou le Détroit de Calais. Sa Formation par la Rupture de l'Isthme, sa topographie et sa constitution géologique. Ouvrage qui a remporté le prix au concours de l'Académie d'Amiens en l'année 1751* (Paris, 1875), and cf. Jean-Pierre Navailles, *Le Tunnel Sous La Manche: deux siècles pour sauter le pas 1802–1987* (Seyssel, 1987), pp. 22, 243, Lemoine, *Le* Tunnel, p. 12, and Frank Davidson, communication with author, 25 November 2001.

2 Aimé Thomé de Gamond, *Étude pour l'avant-projet d'un tunnel sous-marin entre l'Angleterre et la France* (Paris, 1857); Lemoine, *Le Tunnel*, pp. 22–6, Jean-Pierre Renau, *Louis Joseph Aimé Thomé de Gamond (1807–1876). Pionnier du tunnel sous la Manche* (Paris, 2001).

3 Low had an audience with Napoleon III in April 1867: *Channel Tunnel. Report of a Meeting of the Members of the Submarine Continental Railway Co. Ltd held at the Charing Cross Hotel on Friday the 20th January, 1882* (1882), pp. 14–15.

4 Scholars have drawn on the invaluable HC and HL, *Correspondence respecting the Proposed Channel Tunnel*, P.P.1875, lxxviii, C.1206, and *Correspondence with*

reference to the Proposed Construction of a Channel Tunnel, P.P.1882, liii, C.3358 (the latter contains a précis of the papers), E. Hertslet, Confidential 'Memo. respecting the Proposed Channel Tunnel between England and France', 13 March 1882, FO881/4601, and BoT papers, MT6/60/8, PRO. Cf. Travis, *Channel Tunnel*, pp. 12–15; Lemoine, *Le Tunnel*, pp. 30–1; Richard Rogers, 'England & the Channel Tunnel', University of Amsterdam PhD thesis, 1998, pp. 59–62. Grosvenor, 4th son of the 2nd Marquis of Westminster, was MP for Flintshire, 1861–86, and a director of the London & North Western Railway, 1870–1911 (Chairman, 1891–1911). He became Baron Stalbridge in 1886.

5 The Standedge Tunnel was 5,456 yards long. Charles Hadfield, *The Canals of the East Midlands* (Newton Abbot, 1966), p. 35, *The Canals of South and South East England* (Newton Abbot, 1967), p. 317, *The Canals of North West England: Vol. 2* (Newton Abbot, 1970), p. 323.

6 David Lampe, *The Tunnel: The Story of the World's First Tunnel Under A Navigable River dug beneath the Thames 1824–42* (1963); LUL, 'East London Line. A brief history of The Thames Tunnel', n.d.; Graham West, *Innovation and the Rise of the Tunnelling Industry* (Cambridge, 1988), pp. 110–15.

7 John Stretton, *An Illustrated History of Leicester's Railways* (Clophill, 1998), pp. 2–5; Alan Blower, *British Railway Tunnels* (Shepperton, 1964), pp. 13–16, 21–2, 73–4, 103–4; R.H.G. Thomas, *London's First Railway – the London & Greenwich* (1972), p. 27ff.; Jack Simmons and Gordon Biddle (eds), *The Oxford Companion to British Railway History* (Oxford, 1997), pp. 283, 544.

8 West, *Innovation and the Tunnelling Industry*, Chs.2, 11.

9 Jack Simmons, *The Railway in England and Wales 1830–1914: Vol. 1. The System and its Working* (Leicester, 1978), p. 162; George Dow, *Great Central: Vol. 1. The Progenitors, 1813–1863* (1959), p. 60ff. The Severn Tunnel was driven under the river Severn, while the Mont Cenis and St. Gotthard tunnels traversed the Alps.

10 With the Archway-East Finchley extension in 1939, the tunnel length was increased to 17 miles 528 yards. T.C. Barker and Michael Robbins, *A History of London Transport: Vol. 2. The Twentieth Century to 1970* (1974), pp. 112, 244–8; Simmons and Biddle, *Oxford Companion*, p. 298.

11 L.T.C. Rolt, *Victorian Engineering* (1970), pp. 190–2, 253–64; Blower, *Tunnels*, pp. 35–6; *Report of the Court of Inquiry… upon the Circumstances attending the Fall of a Portion of the Tay Bridge on the 28th December 1879*, P.P.1880, xxxix, C.2616.

12 The South Eastern's London to Folkestone and Dover line via Redhill and Tonbridge opened in 1843–4, the London Chatham & Dover's line to Dover via Chatham opened in 1861, and the South Eastern's shorter route via Sevenoaks in 1868.

13 Cf. Anthony Howe, *Free Trade and Liberal England 1846–1946* (Oxford, 1997), pp. 96–7, 186.

14 Cf. General Henry F. Ponsonby (Queen's PS)-Lord Derby (Foreign Secretary), 7 February 1875, Ponsonby-Benjamin Disraeli (Prime Minister), 9 February 1875, Ponsonby-Sir Stafford Northcote (Chancellor of Exchequer), 13 July 1875, Royal Archives, Windsor, RA VIC/B27/8, D6/17 and L13/199. This contrasts with the Queen's reported enthusiasm for a tunnel at an earlier stage: Keen, 'Channel Tunnel Project', 133.

15 The commission consisted of Capt. H.W. Tyler (BoT), C.M. Kennedy (FO), Horace Wilson (Solicitor to Office of Woods, Forests etc.), Ch. Gavard, C. Kleitz and A. de Lapparent. The tunnel concession was to be for 99 years; exploratory works were to start within a year from 1 July 1876; the British and French companies were to reach an agreement and declare intentions within 5 years of 2 August 1875 (with provision for an extension for a further 3 years); the tunnel was to be completed and opened within 20 years of the declarations. *Projet*, 31 May 1876. On the numerous twists and turns of the diplomatic negotiations see 'Channel Tunnel. Memorandum on the history of the scheme, 1867–88', MT10/500, PRO; 'Precis of Papers…', in

Correspondence, P.P.1882, liii, pp. ix–xiii; Hertslet, Memo. 1882, cit.; and, *inter alia*, Travis, *Channel Tunnel*, pp. 19–22; Wilson, *Channel Tunnel Visions*, pp. 10–22; Rogers, 'England & the Channel Tunnel', pp. 59–62.

16 A. Lavalley, *Submarine Railway (Between France and England). Report, 22 May 1877* (1877). The Chemin de fer du Nord co. held 50% of the capital of 2 m. francs [£80,000], and de Rothschild frères 25%. Rothschilds also had a controlling interest in the Nord.

17 Initially 354 shares were taken up with £2.50 of £20 called up: Channel Tunnel Co. List of Shareholders, 15 July 1874, BT31/1677, PRO.

18 N.M.Rothschild & Sons, Home Ledgers, 1876, 1877, V1/10/66–7, The Rothschild Archive, London.

19 South Eastern Railway Board Minutes, 19 November 1874, 11 February, 11 March, 6 May and 2 December 1875, 10 February and 6 April 1876, RAIL635/43–4, PRO; *Channel Tunnel* (1882), pp. 16–24. The Channel Tunnel Co. Shareholders' List for 22 August 1883 shows that 3,780 shares had been taken up, with a total of £38,600 called up. By 1885 *c.*£12,000 had been returned to shareholders: BT31/1677, PRO.

20 On Watkin and the Tunnel see T.R. Gourvish, 'Sir Edward Watkin', in David Jeremy (ed.), *Dictionary of Business Biography*, Vol. V (1986), pp. 682–5, and David Hodgkins, *The Second Railway King. The Life and Times of Sir Edward Watkin (1819–1901)* (Whitchurch, 2002). There are voluminous files in the PRO, e.g. MT6/62/10, MT10/392, and MT10/438.

21 Two members of the South Eastern Board, Joshua Fielden and John Bibby, opposed Watkin's plans for the Tunnel: South Eastern Railway Board Minutes, 10 and 24 September 1874, 11 March 1875, RAIL635/43, PRO.

22 Hawkshaw advocated a single-bore tunnel with ventilating shafts through the white chalk from St. Margaret's Bay; Low favoured a double-bore, self-ventilating tunnel through the deeper, grey chalk, and with Brady argued (rightly as events proved) that the St. Margaret's Bay site was flawed. Francis Brady-Sir Edward Watkin, 1 May 1874, in 'Channel Tunnel Minutes, Correspondence and Chairman's Observations', 8 March 1875, in South Eastern Railway Board Minutes, 11 March 1875, cit., correspondence in *Channel Tunnel* (1882), pp. 42–3, and cf. Travis, *Channel Tunnel*, p. 17ff., Rogers, 'England & the Channel Tunnel', pp. 64–76; Hodgkins, *Second Railway King*, pp. 447, 512ff.

23 Submarine Continental Railway Company, Report of Directors, August 1883, appended to South Eastern Railway Board Minutes, 16 August 1883, RAIL635/48, PRO; Hunt, *Tunnel*, pp. 42–3, 56–7; West, *Tunnelling Industry*, pp. 243–9. The first machine, designed by John D. Brunton in 1874, was used in French tunnelling, but with less success. Ibid., pp. 239–42. The Beaumont-English machine was subsequently employed in constructing the Mersey rail tunnel (1 mile 350 yards), opened in 1886: *Railway News*, 29 November 1885, p. 357; 23 January 1886, pp. 149–51.

24 Watkin, memorandum, 28 April 1875, South Eastern Railway Board Minutes, 6 May 1875, RAIL635/43, PRO; Sir Edward Watkin-Joseph Chamberlain, 23 August 1881, reply, 24 August 1881, Watkin-Chamberlain, 9 October 1881, reply, 15 October 1881, Watkin-Chamberlain, 17 October 1881, South Eastern Railway Board Minutes, 1 September, 13 and 27 October 1881, RAIL635/48, PRO (see also *Correspondence*, 1882, docs.188, 191, 192, 192a). See also Keen, 'Channel Tunnel Project', 138–9; Travis, *Channel Tunnel*, p. 26.

25 South Eastern Railway Board Minutes, 25 May, 17 August and 14 September 1882, RAIL635/48, PRO; Hodgkins, *Second Railway King*, pp. 526–30.

26 Cf. Sir Nathaniel de Rothschild-Watkin, 6 October 1881, Watkin-Rothschild, 14 October 1881 and reply, same date, Watkin-Rothschild, 17 October 1881, Watkin-Say, 27 January 1882, Say-Watkin, 5 February and reply, 8 February 1882, in South Eastern Railway Board Minutes, 13 and 27 October 1881, 2 and 16 February 1882,

RAIL635/48, PRO; Niall Ferguson, *The World's Banker* (1998), p. 815; Hodgkins, *Second Railway King*, p. 518.

27 CTPC, 'Historical Survey', cit.; Travis, *Channel Tunnel*, pp. 36–41. Cf. Albert Sartiaux, Note, *Revue Générale de Chemins de Fer et des Tramways* (April 1906), p. 311, and *Le Tunnel Sous-Marin entre la France et l'Angleterre. Conference faite à la Société industrielle au Nord de la France* (Lille, 1907); and Guy Monthier: 'Mais l'hostilité du gouvernement britannique à l'égard de la construction d'un tunnel... devait interrompre ces premières réalisations': speech, 17 January 1948, Churchill Archives Centre, Parliamentary Channel Study Group Papers, CTUN5/60.

28 Lt.-Gen. Sir John Adye, Memo. January 1882, Lt.-Gen. Sir Garnet Wolseley, 10 December 1881, in *Correspondence*, 1882, pp. 210–19.

29 Lord Tenterden and Sir Charles Dilke, notes, 5 March 1882, and 'Channel Tunnel. Note by Lord Tenterden on Sir E. Hertslet's Memorandum', 17 March 1882, FO881/4652, PRO, cit. in Wilson, *Channel Tunnel Visions*, pp. 29–32. Such views reached a wider public: cf. Admiral Lord Dunsany, 'The Proposed Channel Tunnel', *The Nineteenth Century*, XI (February 1882), 288–304; G. Valbert, 'L'Agitation Anglaise contre le tunnel de la Manche, *Revue des Deux Mondes* (June 1882); Rogers, 'England & the Channel Tunnel', p. 89ff.

30 The scientific committee, led by Major-General Sir Archibald Alison, reported in May 1882 by asking for numerous safeguards. It also found that neither of the two schemes then before parliament complied in full with these. Precis, in *Correspondence*, 1882, pp. xiv–xvi.

31 Clarke's views (when Commandant of the School of Military Engineering) were reported in 'Paper purporting to give the views of Colonel Sir Andrew Clarke...', in *Correspondence*, 1882, pp. 235–8.

32 *Report from the Joint Select Committee of the House of Lords and the House of Commons on the Channel Tunnel*, 10 July 1883, P.P.1883, xii, pp. xliv–xlv, and see Travis, *Channel Tunnel*, pp. 46–7; Wilson, *Channel Tunnel Visions*, pp. 33–47. Lansdowne was supported by Lord Aberdare, William Baxter and Arthur Peel, and opposed by the Earl of Devon, Earl of Camperdown, Lord Shute, Sir Henry Vivian, Sir Massey Lopes, and Edward Harcourt. Voting on draft reports by Lord Shute, Sir Henry Vivian and Sir Massey Lopes was 5–5 and they were therefore regarded as rejected. Lansdowne was less sanguine about the military risks later, in 1907: Wilson, *Channel Tunnel Visions*, pp. 66–7.

33 P.J.V. Rolo, *Entente Cordiale* (1969), and cf. Sir Eyre Crowe (Asst. U-Secretary of State, FO), Memo. 21 March 1920, Lord Hardinge (Permanent U-Sec, FO), Memo. 25 April 1920, cit. in Wilson, *Channel Tunnel Visions*, pp. 148–50; and Crowe, Memo. 17 June 1924, Committee of Imperial Defence [CID] Paper 123A, reaffirming CID 101A of 1 May 1920, CAB3/4, PRO. As late as 1949 the Foreign Office held the view that 'No-one can answer for the long-term friendship or political stability of France': Foreign Office Memo., 10 June 1949, Appendix B of Hugh Dalton (Chancellor of the Duchy of Lancaster), Memo. to Cabinet on 'Channel Tunnel', 15 July 1949, CAB129/36, PRO.

34 Cf. Paul M. Kennedy, *The Rise of the Anglo-German Antagonism 1860–1914* (1980).

35 Channel Tunnel Committee (a committee of the Economic Advisory Council), *Report*, 15 March 1930, P.P.1929–30, xii, Cmd.3513, para. 24; Hodgkins, *Second Railway King*, pp. 535–6, 626–8.

36 Note for example the reports of Col. Charles à Court Repington, 1895, cit. in Wilson, *Channel Tunnel Visions*, pp. 49–51.

37 *Railway News*, 22 December 1906, p. 1047; Albert Sartiaux, *Le Tunnel Sous-Marin entre la France et l'Angleterre. Conference faite à la Société industrielle au Nord de la France* (Lille, 1907).

38 There was also support for the tunnel from Gen. Sir William Butler, Maj.-Gen. Sir Alfred Turner, and Vice-Admiral Sir Charles Campbell. Travis, *Channel Tunnel*, pp. 53–5; Rogers, 'England & the Channel Tunnel', pp. 167–8.
39 CTPC, 'Historical Survey', cit.; Wilson, *Channel Tunnel Visions*, pp. 55–71.
40 Wilson, *Channel Tunnel Visions*, pp. 73–88; Hunt, *Tunnel*, pp. 70–1, 76ff. In 1907 the Admiralty had argued against the tunnel, maintaining that it was dangerous to rely on destroying it. In 1914 it was more supportive, but argued that it would only offer its support if the tunnel could be flooded or destroyed from the sea. However, this requirement served to undermine its military advantages, thus playing into the hands of the sceptics. It should be noted that the CID's decision was not announced until October 1916.
41 There is an abundant popular literature on the fears of invasion. Among the earliest examples are Cassandra, *The Channel Tunnel; or England's Ruin* (1876), and Grip, *How John Bull lost London, or the Capture of the Channel Tunnel* (1882). The most famous is the anti-German thriller, *The Riddle of the Sands* (1903), by Erskine Childers, a nephew of Hugh Childers (see above): John N. Young, *Erskine H. Childers President of Ireland: a Biography* (Gerrard's Cross, 1985), pp. 2–4. See also William le Queux, *The Invasion of 1910* (1906).
42 Baron Emile d'Erlanger followed Watkin (1887–1901) and Baron Frederick d'Erlanger (1901–11) as Chairman of the Channel Tunnel Co. Dent was General Manager of the South Eastern & Chatham Railway, 1911–20, Tempest was Chief Engineer and General Manager, 1920–3 and also Engineer for the Channel Tunnel Co. On the railway grouping in 1923 the latter became Joint General Manager of the Southern Railway, 1923–4.
43 Mick Hamer, 'La [*sic*] rêve de Napoleon…*et al*!', in Bronwen Jones (ed.), *The Tunnel: The Channel and Beyond* (Chichester, 1987), p. 274; Paul Varley, *From Charing Cross to Baghdad: A History of the Whitaker Tunnel Boring Machine and the Channel Tunnel 1880–1930* (Folkestone, 1992), pp. 80–1, 101–72.
44 Sir William Bull (Chairman, CTPC)-Ramsay MacDonald (PM), 31 May 1924, in CID121, CAB3/4, PRO; Bonavia, *Channel Tunnel Story*, p. 42; Wilson, *Channel Tunnel Visions*, p. 155.
45 Wilson, *Channel Tunnel Visions*, pp. 107–12.
46 See Note on 'Oeuvre du Comité Français du Tunnel sous la Manche', in Chemin de Fer du Nord archives, 202 AQ 722 File G80, Centre des Archives du Monde du Travail, Roubaix.
47 Wilson, *Channel Tunnel Visions*, p. 121ff.; Stephen Roskill, *Hankey, Man of Secrets. Vol. II 1919–1931* (1972), pp. 132–5; Richard S. Grayson, 'The British government and the Channel Tunnel, 1919–39', *Journal of Contemporary History*, 31 (1996), 127–9. Hankey was Cabinet Secretary, 1919–38.
48 Bull-MacDonald, 31 May 1924, cit.; 'Shorthand Notes of a Deputation to the Prime Minister…26 June 1924', CID 127A, CAB3/4, PRO. Bull, a solicitor, was Conservative MP for Hammersmith, 1900, Hammersmith (South), 1918–29.
49 CID Minutes, 1 July 1924, in CID 164A, CAB3/4, PRO; Report by the Chiefs of Staff Sub-Committee on the Channel Tunnel, 27 May 1930, CID 176A, CAB3/5, PRO; Chiefs of Staff Committee, Memo. on 'Channel Tunnel: Appreciation by the Chiefs of Staff' [Lords Tedder and Fraser and General W.J. Slim], 21 June 1949, Appendix A to Dalton, Memo. cit. CAB129/36, PRO; *Parl. Deb. (Commons)*, 5th ser.Vol. 175 (Session 1924), MacDonald, oral answer to Bull, 7 July 1924, *c*.1782–5; Hunt, *Tunnel*, pp. 81–2; Wilson, *Channel Tunnel Visions*, pp. 157–63. On Hankey's anti-tunnel lobbying cf. his Memo. on 'Summary of Previous Proceedings', 3 June 1924, CID 122A, CAB3/4, PRO, and Roskill, *Hankey*, p. 364.
50 Winston Churchill, 'Should Strategists Veto the Tunnel?', *Weekly Dispatch*, 27 July 1924, in Churchill Archives Centre, Churchill Papers, CHAR8/200B [also quoted elsewhere, e.g. in Rogers, 'England & the Channel Tunnel', p. 182].

51 Selfridge wrote articles on the Tunnel in the *Times* under the name 'Callisthenes', e.g. No. 3, 31 December 1928, p. 10, No. 49, 20 June 1929, p. 14; See also H. Gordon Selfridge-Sir William Bull, 19 January and 14 February 1929, Churchill Archives Centre, Channel Tunnel Papers, CTUN5/37; Reginald Pound, *Selfridge* (1960), pp. 114, 199–20.
52 Grayson, 'British Government and Channel Tunnel', 131.
53 William Collard, *Proposed London and Paris Railway: London and Paris in 2 hours 45 minutes* (1928), and see also his earlier *Proposed London & Paris Railway. London and Paris in $4\frac{1}{2}$ hours* (1895), where construction cost was put at £39 m. See also Philip Burtt, 'Proposed London and Paris High Speed Electric Railway Report', July 1929, in CAB58/125, PRO. Other schemes considered and rejected by the Committee included a bridge (Sir Murdoch MacDonald & Partners/A. Huguenin), a submerged tube, and a cross-channel jetty: Channel Tunnel Committee, *Report*, 1930, paras 39–42.
54 Channel Tunnel Committee, *Report*, 1930, paras 1–2, 47, 59, 177, and see summary in *Railway Gazette*, 21 March 1930, pp. 449–51. The Committee consisted of Peacock, Lord Ebbisham, Chairman, Blades East & Blades (stationers etc.), Sir Clement Hindley, Chief Commissioner of Indian Railways (1922–8), Sir Frederick Lewis of Furness Withy, and Sir Henry Strakosch, banker and chairman of the Union Corporation and *Economist* newspaper. It was assisted by three firms of consulting engineers: Livesey, Son and Henderson; Mott, Hay and Anderson; and Rendel, Palmer and Tritton. On post-war agitation for a tunnel, see *inter alia, Railway Gazette*, 31 January 1930, p. 157; Channel Tunnel Co., *Report and Accounts, 1919–39*, Churchill Archives Centre, Channel Tunnel Co. Papers, CTUN1/5.
55 Lord Ebbisham, Minute of Dissent, 28 February 1930, in Channel Tunnel Committee, Report, pp. 91–6. Ebbisham, until 1928 Sir George Rowland Blades, had been Mayor of London (1927–8) and President of the Federation of British Industries (1928–9). He was a director of the Southern Railway, 1928–45.
56 On Hankey's continuing anti-tunnel lobbying cf. the inclusion in the public record of a letter to the *Times* from Cecil Levita, 3 January 1929 (pointing out that French had become a critic of the Tunnel after the First World War), in Hankey, Memo. on 'The Channel Tunnel. Summary of Previous Proceedings', 18 January 1929, CID 164A, CAB3/4; his Memo. on 'The Channel Tunnel: Some Imperial Defence Aspects', 22 May 1930, CID 174A, CAB3/5, PRO; his evidence to the Channel Tunnel Committee, 11 November 1929, CAB58/125, PRO; and Roskill, *Hankey*, pp. 522–3. On Snowden see Grayson, 'British Government and Channel Tunnel', 136.
57 Duncan was Chairman of the Central Electricity Board (1927–35) and a director of the Bank of England (1929–40); Bevin was General Secretary of the TGWU (1921–40); Keynes, economist and Fellow of King's College, Cambridge, was subsequently a director of the Bank of England (1941–6). The other members were: Sir John Cadman, Chairman of Anglo-Persian [Iranian] Oil Co. (1927–41) and a director of the Suez Canal Co. (1935–9); Sir Alfred Lewis, a director of the National Provincial Bank; and G.C. Upcott, Deputy Controller of Supply Services, Treasury.
58 Treasury, Memo. 14 March 1930, and Report of Channel Tunnel Policy Committee of the Economic Advisory Council (Chairman: Sir Andrew Duncan), March 1930, CAB58/144, PRO, cit. in Wilson, *Channel Tunnel Visions*, pp. 171–2.
59 Inter-Departmental Conference, Memo. to Channel Tunnel Committee on 'Transportation Financial and Economic Aspects of the Channel Tunnel Scheme', March 1929, CAB58/122, PRO; Home Defence Sub-Committee, CID, Memo. on 'The Channel Tunnel', 19 May 1930, copy in T224/226, PRO; HMG, *The Channel Tunnel: Statement of Policy*, 4 June 1930, P.P.1929–30, xii, Cmd.3591, pp. 2–6; Wilson, *Channel Tunnel* Visions, pp. 173–5.
60 Grayson, 'British Government and Channel Tunnel', 133–4.

61 E. Godfrey (General Manager's office, Great Western Railway), paper, 16 January 1930, RAIL779/86, PRO, reproduced in full in *Railway Gazette*, 31 January 1930, pp. 156–60 and cf. editorials, ibid. pp. 152–3, and 21 March 1930, p. 438.

62 *Parl. Deb.(Commons)*, 5th ser. Vol. 240 (Session 1929–30), *c*.1687,1742; Dalton, Memo. cit. CAB129/36, PRO. Thurtle was Labour MP for Shoreditch from 1922, and Junior Lord of the Treasury, 1930–1. He was supported *inter alia* by William Wedgwood Benn, Secretary of State for India, Aneurin Bevan, Labour MP for Ebbw Vale, Winston Churchill, Conservative MP for Epping, James Chuter Ede, Labour MP for South Shields, Oswald Mosley, Chancellor of the Duchy of Lancaster, and Philip Noel-Baker, PPS to the Foreign Secretary.

63 Tedder *et al.*, 21 June 1949, citing Chiefs of Staff Sub-Committee Report, 27 May 1930, cit.

64 Rixon Bucknall, *Boat Trains and Channel Packets: The English Short Sea Routes* (1957), pp. 144–5; Charles F. Klapper, *Sir Herbert Walker's Southern Railway* (Shepperton, 1973), pp. 239–47.

65 Channel Tunnel Co., Notes of Meeting with Southern Railway Co., 29 April 1929, Churchill Archives Centre, Channel Tunnel Papers, CTUN5/40; Southern Railway Special Board Minutes, 9 May 1929, RAIL645/3, PRO. See also Michael R. Bonavia, *The History of the Southern Railway* (1987), pp. 52–61, 87–93, and Gerald Crompton, 'Transport', in Nigel Yates (ed.), *Kent in the Twentieth Century* (Woodbridge, 2001), pp. 124–32.

66 Walker, evidence to Channel Tunnel Committee, 12 July 1929, QQ.1107–16, and see also Precis of his evidence, Doc.62, 8 July 1929, CAB58/124, PRO.

67 Walker, evidence, 12 July 1929, QQ.1119, 1135, 1146–59, CAB58/124, PRO; 3 February 1930, QQ.2062–6, CAB58/126, PRO. Walker appears to have drawn on estimates prepared by his Assistant General Manager, Gilbert Szlumper: Rogers, 'England & the Channel Tunnel', p. 188. On Strakosch see P.L. Cottrell, 'Norman, Strakosch and the development of central banking: from conception to practice, 1919–1924', in Philip L. Cottrell (ed.), *Rebuilding the Financial System in Central and Eastern Europe, 1918–1994* (Aldershot, 1997), pp. 29–30; entry in *Oxford DNB* (2004).

68 Walker, evidence, 12 July 1929, Q.1134, CAB58/124, PRO; Walker-Capt. A.F. Hemming (Committee Secretary), 16 and 22 January 1930, CAB58/126, PRO, and see also *Railway Gazette*, 7 October 1949, p. 401. Walker was General Manager of the London & South Western Railway, 1912–23, Joint General Manager of the Southern 1923–4, sole General Manager, 1924–37 and Director, 1937–47. On the promoters' dismay see Charles Sheath (Secretary, Southern Railway)-Baron Emile d'Erlanger, 9 June 1930, and d'Erlanger's speech to the Channel Tunnel Co. AGM, 30 June 1930, Churchill Archives Centre, Channel Tunnel Co. Papers, CTUN1/18, 1/30.

69 Earl of Crawford, evidence to Channel Tunnel Committee, 14 October 1929, HO45/137–8, PRO, quoted *in extenso* by Wilson, *Channel Tunnel Visions*, pp. 183–6, who also quotes similar views expressed by Sir Maurice Hankey, pp. 191–2. The press provided numerous examples of such attitudes. Cf. Repington, in *Morning Post*, 13 March 1919, cit. in Wilson, *Channel Tunnel Visions*, p. 109: 'We shall have . . . a considerable infusion of Latin blood . . . The Latin races have great qualities, but they are different from ours, and things which alter the stock cause it to deteriorate'. For lingering (if lighthearted) elements in fiction cf. Kitty Tomlinson, *State Secret* (1997).

70 Campbell-Bannerman-Viscount Knollys (King's PS), 17 January 1907, RA PS/GV/R28/3, quoted in John Wilson, *C.B. A Life of Sir Henry Campbell-Bannerman* (1973), p. 593; Ian Holliday, Gérard Marcou, and Roger Vickerman, *The Channel Tunnel: Public Policy, Regional Development and European Integration* (1991), pp. 8–9; Grayson, 'British Government and Channel Tunnel', 139–40; Eve Darian-Smith, *Bridging Divides: the Channel Tunnel and English Legal Identity in the New Europe* (Berkeley and Los Angeles, 1999), pp. 84, 89–91.

71 *Railway News*, 13 January and 12 May 1939; Bonavia, *Channel Tunnel Story*, p. 58.
72 *Parl. Deb. (Commons)*, 5th ser. Vol. 340 (Session 1937–8), 1 November 1938, *c.*22–3; Vol. 357 (Session 1939–40), 8 February 1940, *c.*400–1.
73 John Farquharson, 'After Sealion: A German Channel Tunnel?', *Journal of Contemporary History*, 25 (1990), 409–30; Wilson, *Channel Tunnel Visions*, pp. 179–81.

2 NEW ASPIRATIONS: THE CHANNEL TUNNEL PROJECT, 1945–64

1 A useful survey of this period, focusing on the connexions with Britain's policy on Europe, is provided by Richard S. Grayson, 'The British Government, the Channel Tunnel and European Unity, 1948–64', *European History Quarterly*, 26 No. 3 (1996), 415–36.
2 Cripps, annotation on Dalton-Cripps, 16 May 1949, T224/226, PRO. Grayson notes that Christopher Mayhew, the Foreign U-Sec, was a lone enthusiast: 'Channel Tunnel and European Unity', 419.
3 Chiefs of Staff Committee, Memo. 21 June 1949, and Dalton, Memo. 15 July 1949, cit., CAB129/36, PRO.
4 Foreign Office Memo. 10 June 1949, cit., CAB129/36, PRO. For further evidence of Foreign Office scepticism see Grayson, 'Channel Tunnel and European Unity', 418.
5 Alan Lennox-Boyd, *Parl. Deb. (Commons)*, 5th ser. Vol. 530 (Session 1953–4), 21 July 1954, *c.*1333–4, reply to Edward Lance Mallalieu, Labour MP for Brigg (1948–74); Montgomery, speech to Navy League, October 1957, cit. in Thomas Whiteside, *The Tunnel under the Channel* (1962), p. 106, and *Times*, 25 September 1959.
6 Brian Colquhoun & Partners, Report to the Parliamentary Channel Tunnel Committee and Professor Cyril C. Means on 'Project for a Channel Tunnel. Resumé of Past History and Recommendations for Research and Investigations Necessary for Proposed Development', April 1957, pp. 13–14, copy in Prime Minister's papers, PREM11/3576, PRO; Prof. Cyril C. Means Jr (Technical Studies Inc.)-General Alfred N. Gruenther (Chairman, American National Red Cross), 19 March 1959, Technical Studies Inc. [TSI] archive, Vol. 37, Baker Library, Harvard Business School [HBS], Boston; Bonavia, *Channel Tunnel Story*, p. 58. One indication of the extent to which military objections had faded is provided by Brigadier J.M.W. Titley, who on retiring from the Army in 1958 applied for a job with the Channel Tunnel Co. He wrote, 'I believe my ancestor, Lord Wolseley, was one of the original advocates of the Tunnel': letter to Channel Tunnel Co., 11 September 1957, Churchill Archives Centre, Channel Tunnel Co. Papers, CTUN1/17.
7 Ministry of Defence Joint Administrative Officers' Committee, Report on 'The Channel Tunnel', 30 July 1953, Principal Administrative Officers' Committee Minutes, 5 August 1953, DEFE7/1625, PRO; Grayson, 'Channel Tunnel and European Unity', 422–3.
8 *Parl. Deb. (Commons)*, 5th ser. Vol. 537 (Session 1954–5), Harold Macmillan, Written Answer, 16 February 1955, *48*.
9 Earl Mountbatten of Burma (Chief of the Defence Staff)-Harold Watkinson (Minister of Defence), 17 November 1959, enclosing Chiefs of Staff Report on 'The Channel Tunnel Project', 16 November 1959, DEFE7/1625, PRO. This view was repeated subsequently. Cf. C.W. Wright (MoD)-W.W. Scott (MT), 30 June 1960, MT124/1420, and correspondence in 1961, MT124/1092, PRO.
10 Christopher Shawcross, Note, in Shawcross-Churchill, 31 January 1949, Churchill Archives Centre, Churchill's Papers, CHUR2/81, and cf. also Hugh Molson (Joint Parliamentary Secretary, Ministry of Transport & Civil Aviation), *Parl. Deb. (Commons)*, 5th ser. Vol. 536 (Session 1954–5), 2 February 1955, *c.*1239.
11 Cripps-Dalton, 31 May 1949, T224/226, PRO.

12 Board of Trade, Memo. June 1949, and Alfred Barnes (Minister of Transport), Memo. June 1949, in Dalton, Memo. 15 July 1949, cit., CAB129/36, PRO.

13 Alison Munro (Ministry of Transport & C.A.)-Robin Turton (Parl. U-Sec of State, FO), 10 February 1955, FO371/118138, PRO, also cit. in Alan S. Milward, *The United Kingdom and the European Community, Vol. I: The Rise and Fall of a National Strategy 1945–1963* (2002), p. 197. See also secret FO Memo. January 1957, FO371/130670, PRO.

14 Foreign Office Memo. 22 September 1956, cit. in FO Memo. January 1957, and see also C.M. Anderson (Assistant to Head of Western Dept. FO), brief for Cabinet Economic Policy Committee, 17 April 1957, FO371/130670, PRO; Cabinet Conclusions, 26 September 1956 (Anglo-French Relations), CAB128/30 Pt. 2, PRO.

15 Channel Tunnel Co., *R & A 1900, 1907, 1918, 1938*, Churchill Archives Centre, Channel Tunnel Papers, CTUN1/5. The d'Erlangers had once (in 1919) contemplated gifting their holding of Channel Tunnel shares to the Nation: see Emile d'Erlanger-Henry Cosmo Bonsor (Chairman, South Eastern & Chatham), 17 November 1919, Channel Tunnel Papers, CTUN1/19.

16 William Collard-Emile d'Erlanger, 28 May 1931, Collard-Robin d'Erlanger, 2 June 1931, Churchill Archives Centre, Channel Tunnel Co. Papers, CTUN1/24.

17 Channel Tunnel Co., *R & A 1940*, Churchill Archives Centre, Channel Tunnel Papers, CTUN1/5; John King, 'Leo Frederic Alfred D'Erlanger', and P.L. Cottrell, 'Sir Herbert Ashcombe Walker', in David Jeremy (ed.), *Dictionary of Business Biography*, Vol. II (1984), pp. 80–3, V (1986), pp. 628–34; *Directory of Directors*, 1939, 1946. Leo d'Erlanger (1898–1978) was instrumental in creating British Airways in 1935.

18 Christopher Shawcross, notes of dinner, 28 January 1947, and file note, 25 November 1948, Churchill Archives Centre, Parliamentary Channel Tunnel Study Group Papers, CTUN5/60. Bullock was Conservative MP for Waterloo, 1923–50, Crosby, 1950–3, and Vice-Chairman of the Franco-British Inter-Parliamentary Committee, 1945–9 (Chairman, 1950–3); Hicks was Labour MP for East Woolwich 1931–50, and Parl. Sec, Ministry of Works, 1940–5; Ernest Davies was Labour MP for Enfield, 1945–50, East Enfield, 1950–9, and PPS to Minister of State, Foreign Office, 1946–50 (Parl. U-Sec, 1950–1); Arthur Lewis was Labour MP for West Ham (Upton), 1945–50, West Ham (North), 1950–74, Newham (North-West), 1974–83; Noel-Baker was Labour MP for Brentford & Chiswick, 1945–50, Swindon, 1955–68. The secretary was Lt.-Cdr. Christopher Powell.

19 £45m. with ferro-concrete, £65m. with steel. Shawcross, notes, 28 January 1947, and file note, 25 November 1948, CTUN5/60. The same consulting engineers were used as in the 1930 exercise, viz. Livesey and Henderson; Mott, Hay and Anderson; and Rendel, Palmer and Tritton, with the addition of Brian Colquhoun & Partners. See Channel Tunnel Parliamentary Study Group Minutes, 16 March 1948, CTUN5/60.

20 Southern Railway Board Minutes, 28 July 1927, RAIL645/3, PRO; George Ellson-Walker, 7 February 1948, Churchill Archives Centre, Channel Tunnel Co. Papers, CTUN1/17; Minutes of Meeting, 16 March 1948; Walker, Statement to a joint committee of the Commons and Lords, 1 December 1948, Parliamentary Channel Tunnel Study Group Papers, CTUN5/60.

21 There was some irony in the fact that Lord Hankey, a staunch opponent of the Tunnel (above, pp. 10, 13, 15), was a British government director of the Suez Co.

22 Bonavia, *Channel Tunnel Story*, p. 60; Hubert Bonin, *Suez: du canal à la finance (1858–1987)* (Paris, 1987), pp. 205–9; Laurent Bonnaud, 'The Channel tunnel, 1955–75: when the Sleeping Beauty woke again', *The Journal of Transport History*, 3rd ser. 22 (March 2001), 7. In 1957–8 the Suez Co. converted itself into a French finance company and adopted the name Compagnie Financière de Suez: D.A. Farnie, *East and West of Suez: The Suez Canal in History 1854–1956* (Oxford, 1969), pp. 742–3.

23 Fetherston, *Chunnel*, pp. 55–6; Frank P. Davidson, communication with author, 15 November 2001. The original anecdote, which has the two French sisters, Izaline and Henriette Doll, granddaughters of banker Robert Schlumberger, making the crossing, is apparently inaccurate. Frank Davidson, *Macro: Big is Beautiful* (1986 edn), p. 39 and cf. Robert Allan (PUSS, FO), Minute, 22 December 1959, FO371/153942, PRO, Whiteside, *Tunnel under the Channel*, p. 104; Bonavia, *Channel Tunnel Story*, p. 60, and Bonnaud, 'Channel tunnel', 8.

24 Frank P. Davidson-Channel Tunnel Co., 14 December 1956, and Société concessionaire, 17 December 1956, TSI archive, Vol. 1, HBS.

25 See correspondence in TSI archive, Vols.1–3, HBS, and in particular Frank Davidson-General Maurice Hirsch, 21 February 1957, Vol. 2, Davidson-Kingman Douglass (Dillon Read & Co.), 3 April 1957, Davidson-Roger Geneau, 8 April 1957, Vol. 1; Means-Leo d'Erlanger, 1 May 1957, Vol. 1, Means-Alison Munro (MT), 1 May 1957, Vol. 2. The Prime Minister, Harold Macmillan, was also lobbied by Kingman Douglass, of Dillon Read & Co., bankers supporting the Americans. Douglass-Macmillan, 27 June 1957, Vol. 1; Lord Hood (Asst U-Sec, FO)-R.S. Isaacson (Commercial Counsellor, British Embassy, Paris), 7 March 1957, and replies, 26 March and 3 April 1957, Sir Herbert Brittain (2nd Sec, Treasury)-Hood, 11 April 1957, FO371/130670; Sir Leslie Rowan (2nd Sec, Overseas Finance, Treasury), Note, 2 April 1957, T224/226; Douglass-Macmillan, 27 June 1957, PREM11/3576, PRO.

26 Frank Davidson-George Brown (Brown & Root), 19 March 1957, TSI archive, Vol. 2, HBS. See also Davidson, *Macro*, p. 96.

27 Channel Tunnel Study Group [CTSG] Supervisory Board Minutes, 26 July 1957, 4 February 1958, TSI archive, Vol. 62, HBS. TSI also received support from the American R & D Corporation.

28 Valentine was a Member of the BTC, 1954–62, and a Member of the London Transport Executive, 1948–59 (he was Chairman of London Transport, 1959–65). The other members of the committee were: British co.: Leo d'Erlanger, and E.G. Whitaker (Unilever); French co.: Jacques Getten (Rothschild); Suez co.: Georges-Picot, Charles Corbin (Bank of France) and Lord Harcourt; and Technical Studies: John H. Ferguson (Cleary Gottlieb Friendly & Ball). In February 1958 Leroy-Beaulieu replaced Getten.

29 In 1959 participation in the Syndicate was set at 25% for each of the four main parties (the International Road Federation (Paris)'s stake being 4.17%). TSI representation on the supervisory board was then increased to three members. Membership was rather loosely handled, and subsequent meetings were attended by Ferguson, Frank and Alfred Davidson, George Ball (lawyer, Cleary *et al.*), and Thomas Lamont (J.P. Morgan). CTSG Supervisory Board Minutes, 26 January and 13 April 1959, et seq., TSI archive, Vols.63–4, HBS; CTSG, *Report 28th March 1960*, p. 3; Bonavia, *Channel Tunnel Story*, pp. 61–3; Hunt, *Tunnel*, pp. 91–2.

30 Brian Colquhoun & Partners, Report to the Parliamentary Channel Tunnel Committee and Professor Cyril C. Means on 'Project for a Channel Tunnel. Resumé of Past History and Recommendations for Research and Investigations Necessary for Proposed Development', April 1957, copy in Prime Minister's papers, PREM11/3576, PRO; Means-Colquhoun, 6 March 1957, TSI archive, Vol. 7, HBS. Technical Studies also commissioned four more preliminary reports.

31 US Presidential determination, 29 August 1958, TSI archive, Vol. 17, Means-d'Erlanger, 13 October 1958, Vol. 14, HBS.

32 Reports in TSI archive, Vols.78–80, 86ff., HBS. The other firms were: Craelius, Institut Technique du Bâtiment et des Travaux Publics, Telephonics Corporation, Marine Geophysical Services and Alpine Geophysical Associates, and Geophysical and Geological Consultants.

33 Report, TSI archive, Vol. 52, HBS. SOGEI also consulted Fourgerolle, Grands Travaux de Marseille and Solétanche.

34 Some were direct investors. For example, Baring Brothers invested £2,000 in the Channel Tunnel Co. in 1957: CTCo.-Baring Brothers & Co., 26 November 1957, Baring partners files, No. 206740, Baring Archives, ING Bank NV, London.

35 In addition, there were reports from Parsons, Brinckerhoff, Quade & Douglas, and from Richard Costain, Entreprises Campenon Bernard, Hyperion Constructors [joint venture led by De Long Corp], and Kaiser Engineers & Constructors on various crossings, including bridges, immersed tubes and hybrids, from the Bechtel Corporation, Brown & Root and Morrison-Knudsen on a bored tunnel, and from Dorman Long (Bridge & Engineering), Compagnie Française d'Entreprises and Merritt-Chapman & Scott, and from Steinman, Boynton, Gronquist & London, on bridges. See Reports in TSI Archive, Vols.47–51, 80–2, HBS; CTSG, *Report 28th March 1960*; Fetherston, *Chunnel*, pp. 55–74.

36 CTSG, *Report 28th March 1960*; ibid., *The Economic Benefits of a Channel Tunnel* (25 July 1960), copies in MT114/1090 and T298/249, PRO. Many of the supporting reports are also in the public domain. See e.g. MT144/87, PRO; TSI Archive, Vols.43–4, 86–9, HBS.

37 *Economist*, 5 October 1957, p. 57. The calculation excludes the 100,000 founders' (non-voting) shares.

38 Sir George Young (Minister, British Embassy, Paris)-P.F. Hancock (Head of Western Dept., FO), 2 January 1957, FO371/130670, PRO.

39 Anderson (FO), minute, 14 January 1957, FO371/130670, PRO.

40 Brittain-Hood, 11 April 1957, FO371/130670, PRO. Brittain's private view was more pessimistic: Brittain-Rowan, 8 April 1957, T224/226, PRO.

41 Brian Colquhoun's earlier operations in Iran had apparently ruffled the feathers of the International Bank for Reconstruction and Development. Anderson, minute, 17 April 1957, FO371/130670, PRO.

42 Brittain-E.W. Maude (PPS to Chancellor of Exchequer), 17 April 1957, T224/226, Cabinet EPC Minutes, 18 April 1957, CAB134/1674, Foreign Office, brief for Cabinet, 1 May 1957 (marked 'not used'), FO371/130670, PRO.

43 Harold Watkinson (Minister of Transport), Memo. C(57) 104, 30 April 1957, CAB129/87, Cabinet Conclusions, CC(57) 37th, May 1957, CAB128/31, PRO.

44 Anderson, minute, n.d. (May 1957), FO371/130670, PRO.

45 J.L. Harrington (Chief Shipping & International Services Officer, BTC), Report to Shipping & International Services' Sub-Commission, BTC on 'The Channel Tunnel Project', 8 March 1957, BRB.

46 British Transport Commission, Memo. on 'The Channel Tunnel', 10 May 1957, contained *inter alia* in T224/227, PRO.

47 A.T.K. Grant (U-Sec, Trade & Industry, Treasury)-R.R. Goodison (U-Sec, MTCA), 27 May 1957, T224/227, PRO.

48 M. Stevenson (U-Sec, Home, Overseas & Planning, Treasury)-Grant, 30 May 1957, T224/227, PRO.

49 As the memoirs of its Minister make clear: Harold Watkinson, *Turning Points: A Record of Our Times* (Wilton, 1986), pp. 67–87.

50 Watkinson, Memo. to Cabinet, 19 July 1957, CAB129/88, Cabinet Conclusions, 25 July 1957, CAB128/31, PRO; Grayson, 'Channel Tunnel and European Unity', 423. There was no time for Cabinet discussion: Cabinet Secretary's Notebook, 25 July 1957.

51 BTC, *R & A 1956*, and see T.R. Gourvish, *British Railways 1948-73: A Business History* (Cambridge, 1986), p. 175. Fuel rationing was applied from 17 December 1956 to 14 May 1957.

52 Sam Brittain, *Steering the Economy: the British Experiment* (1971), p. 207ff.; G.C. Peden, *The Treasury and British Public Policy, 1906–1959* (Oxford, 2000), pp. 488–93; Mark Jarvis, 'The 1958 Treasury Dispute', *Contemporary British History*, 12 (3) (Summer 1998), 22–50.

53 T.F. Brenchley (Assistant Head, African Dept., FO), Memo. 24 July 1957, FO371/130670.

54 Macmillan-Heathcoat Amory, 15 June 1959, and see also John Killick (Asst, Western Dept., FO)-Goodison, 15 July 1959, T224/227, and Juliet Collings (FO), Note, 13 July 1959, FO371/145656; Amory-Macmillan, 26 June 1959, PREM11/3576, PRO. Macmillan scribbled on a note of 17 July 1959 from his PPS Tim Bligh, 'I am rather against the Tunnel. But I suppose Cabinet should have some general talk about it': ibid.

55 S. Goldman (Asst Sec, Agriculture, Trade & Transport, Treasury)-B.D. Fraser (3rd Sec, Treasury), 14 July 1959, T224/227, PRO.

56 Watkinson, draft memo. to Cabinet on 'The Channel Tunnel', 13 July 1959, T224/227, and final memo. 16 July 1959 (circulated 17 July), CAB129/98; Cabinet Conclusions, 23 July 1959, CAB128/33, PRO. The departments were: Treasury, Foreign Office, Ministry of Defence, Board of Trade, and Ministry of Transport & CA.

57 See correspondence and notes for 1959 in T224/227, T236/6084 and FO371/145656-7, PRO.

58 Viz. the European Free Trade Area [EFTA], established by the Treaty of Stockholm of November 1959. Draft reports on 'The Psychological Impact on European Opinion' (n.d. 1959), FO371/145657, Draft 'Channel Tunnel. Report of an Official Study of certain Questions raised by the Tunnel Project', in Goodison-Goldman, 17 August 1959, T224/227, and Final 'Report by Officials', Annex to Ernest Marples (Minister of Transport), Memo. to Cabinet on 'Channel Tunnel', 1 February 1960, CAB129/100, and Goldman, Note, 21 December 1959, T224/228, PRO. See also Grayson, 'Channel Tunnel and European Unity', 424–7.

59 Jebb-Rumbold, 1 September 1959 and reply, 7 September 1959, FO371/145657, PRO.

60 Hailsham (LP of C)-Watkinson, 22 July 1959, T224/227, PRO.

61 Leslie O'Brien (Chief Cashier, Bank of England)-William Armstrong (3rd Sec, Treasury), 6 August 1959, T224/227, PRO. O'Brien's personal view was 'that, despite the development of air travel, this tunnel is probably going to be built in the end and that the best assurance that it would be worth the money is for private enterprise to take the job on': O'Brien-Sir Cyril Hawker and BOE Governors, 5 August 1959, Chief Cashier's Private File No. 224.15, Bank of England Archives, C40/1044. Both Hawker, an Executive Director, and Cyril Hamilton, a Deputy Chief Cashier, were more sceptical: Hawker, annotation, 5 August 1959, Hamilton-Brian Bennett (Assistant, Central Banking Info. Dept., BOE), 21 December 1959, ibid.

62 Wylie-S.Y. Dawbarn (Overseas Finance Divn., Treasury), 20, 24 and 28 August and 3 September 1959, T236/6084, and Goldman-Fraser, 3 September 1959, T224/227, PRO.

63 Sir Roger Makins (Joint Permanent Sec, Treasury), record of conversation with Alfred Davidson, 26 November 1959, Goldman (Treasury), Notes, 27 November and 21 December 1959, T224/228, Bill Harpham (British Embassy, Paris)-Edward Tomkins (Head of Western Dept., FO), 19 September 1959, FO371/145657, PRO.

64 Tomkins-Terence Bird (U-Sec, MTCA), 16 November 1959, T224/228; Sir Ivone Kirkpatrick-Sir Frederick Hoyer Millar (Permanent U-Sec, FO), 23 October 1959, Millar-Rumbold, 30 November 1959 and reply, 1 December 1959, FO371/145657, PRO.

65 Marples, Memo. 1 February 1960, cit.; and see Goldman, Note, 8 February 1960, T224/228; Selwyn Lloyd (Foreign Secretary), Memo. to Cabinet on 'Channel Tunnel', 5 February 1960, CAB129/100, PRO (also cit. in Grayson, 'Channel Tunnel and European Unity', 415 and 427).

66 Cabinet Conclusions, 18 February 1960, CAB128/34, PRO.

67 The consultants' traffic survey, for example, was a 3-vol. report extending to 595 pages.

68 Channel Tunnel Study Group, *Report 28th March 1960*, pp. 26–9. The BTC and SNCF had 'reached agreement, without commitment' with the CTSG's bankers about the required financial arrangements: BTC Memo. on 'Channel Tunnel: Proposed financial arrangements', 25 March 1960, MT124/1420, PRO. The arrangements went into some detail on tolls and tariffs (charges). The minimum toll payment was to be sufficient to cover bond interest and amortisation. Toll levels were to give the Tunnel Co. 70% of gross receipts (falling by 2/7ths after amortisation was complete). The toll would be adjusted for inflation (50% in relation to sterling, 50% in relation to the French franc). The Tunnel Co. would share with the railways any excess or 'super' profits i.e. 30–45% of the net revenue extant after paying 7% on equity. These arrangements bore some resemblance to the 'Usage Agreement' of 1987.

69 David Serpell, Note, 5 April 1960, Stevenson-Frank Figgures (U-Sec, Treasury), 14 April 1960, T319/409, PRO. The Bank of England confirmed the view that the guarantees precluded the project from being described as private: O'Brien-Armstrong, 4 May 1960, C40/1044, BOE.

70 Marples-Macmillan, 6 April 1960, PREM11/3576, copy with Heathcoat Amory's annotation, T319/409, PRO.

71 *Times*, 21 April 1960, p. 13; *Economist*, 23 April 1960, pp. 356–9, cit. in Whiteside, *Tunnel under the Channel*, p. 111, and 30 April 1960, p. 397. Silver City, which had begun services in July 1948, was controlled by P&O: *Financial Times*, 21 April 1960, p. 1.

72 'Note of meeting held in Mr. Serpell's room at the Ministry of Transport on Thursday 21st April, 1960', 25 April 1960, MT124/1420, PRO.

73 Stevenson, note on 'Suggested Financial Guarantees', 5 May 1960, Sir James Dunnett (Permanent Sec, MT)-Lee, 19 May 1960, and Stevenson, 'Note of Meeting' [with Lord Harcourt, CTSG, 19 May 1960], 20 May 1960, MT124/1420; Stevenson, brief for Sir Frank Lee (Joint Permanent Sec, Treasury), 18 May 1960, T319/409, PRO.

74 Cf. John Brunner (Economic Adviser, Treasury)-Stevenson, 23 May 1960; Rupert Raw (Adviser, Bank of England), Note on 'Channel Tunnel Company', 9 June 1960, with annotation from Baron Cobbold (Governor, Bank of England) to Sir Thomas Padmore and Sir Frank Lee; and Harpham-Tomkins, 16 June 1960, T319/409, PRO.

75 Goldman-Stevenson, 3 May 1960, T319/409, PRO.

76 General Sir Brian Robertson (Chairman, BTC, 1953–61), address to Europe House, 20 January 1960, extract in BRB 196-4-1 Pt. 2; Robertson-Marples, 19 May 1960, MT124/1420, PRO; Dr Richard Beeching (Chairman, BTC, 1961–3)-Dunnett, 12 March 1962, BRB 196-4-1 Pt. 3.

77 Stevenson-Goldman, 28 March 1960, T224/228, Lee, Note, 18 May 1960, T298/185, PRO; CTSG Steering Committee Minutes, 2 May 1960, TSI archive, Vol. 64, HBS; Gourvish, *British Railways*, pp. 300–1, 308ff. The other members of Stedeford's Special Advisory Group were Dr Richard Beeching of ICI, Frank Kearton of Courtaulds, and Henry Benson of Cooper Bros.

78 The work done at this time did not advance the argument very far: cf. Goldman-Stevenson, 24 June 1960, A.K. Ogilvy-Webb (Treasury)-Stevenson, 6 July 1960, 'Suggested Summary of Main Conclusions', 8 July 1960, T319/409, and Stevenson-R.W.B. 'Otto' Clarke (3rd Sec, Treasury), 20 July 1960, T319/410, PRO.

79 d'Erlanger-Macmillan, 15 July 1960, enclosing 'Memorandum containing certain modified proposals and explanations further to the Report of the Channel Tunnel Study Group, 14 July 1960', PREM11/3576; Harcourt-Lee, 28 July 1960, enclosing CTSG, *Economic Benefits*, cit., T319/410; 'Record of a Meeting held at the Treasury, 28th July 1960', n.d., MT124/1090, PRO.

80 The BTC was not happy with this suggestion. Cf. George Quick-Smith (Adviser (Special Projects), BTC)-Beeching, 27 July 1962, BRB 196-4-1 Pt. 3.

81 The calculation of economic benefits was criticised inside the Treasury, principally on the grounds that like was not being compared with like. The benefit return from

the tunnel was compared with the *revenue* return on ferries. See Ralph Turvey (Economic Adviser, Treasury)-Stevenson, 22 August 1960, and additional memo., August 1960, T230/739, PRO.

82 O'Brien was apparently known as 'Champagne Toby'. CTSG Supervisory Board Minutes, 13 May 1960, TSI archive, Vol. 63, HBS; Whiteside, *Tunnel under the Channel*, p. 111, and cf. CTSG, *Why Britain Needs a Channel Tunnel* (1962).

83 J. Mark (Treasury)-Lee, 28 July 1960, T319/410, PRO; 'Under the Sea', *Financial Times*, 29 July 1960); Stevenson-Clarke, 20 July 1960, cit.

84 At a meeting between Stevenson and Alfred E. Davidson on 9 September 1960 the latter hinted that the promoters might be prepared to give some ground on tax exemption: Stevenson-Serpell, 12 September 1960, enclosing 'Note for File', MT124/1090, PRO. A memorandum from the CTSG offering some concessions followed in October: 'Memorandum on the Taxation of the Proposed International Channel Tunnel Corporation', n.d., and see Serpell, minute, 28 October 1960, MT124/1091, PRO.

85 Marples, Memo. on 'The Channel Tunnel', EA(60) 83, 14 October 1960, enclosing 'Report by Officials', n.d., and Cabinet EPC Minutes, 2 November 1960, in MT124/1091 and T319/410; 'The Channel Tunnel: Report by Officials', n.d. [October 1960], ibid.; Cabinet Conclusions, 25 November 1960, CAB128/34, PRO.

86 *Times*, 4 April 1960, pp. 4, 11, 21 April 1960, pp. 12–13; MT, *Proposals for a Fixed Channel Link*, September 1963, P.P.1962–3, ix, Cmnd. 2137, Appdx.I. The 1960 scheme was similar to that estimated to cost £181 m. and offered to the CTSG by the same firms in 1958–9.

87 Serpell-Stevenson, 10 May 1961, Serpell-Tomkins, 1 August 1961, Collings, Note, 6 September 1961, FO371/158736, PRO; *Times*, 20 September 1961, p. 11, 4 October 1961, p. 9, 6 October 1961, p. 12; SEPM, *Le Pont sur La Manche*, 15 July 1961, and accompanying documents, in MT118/16 and FO371/158737, PRO. Subsequent supporters included the Société Générale and the Fédération Nationale Automobile.

88 Gourvish, *British Railways*, pp. 299–300. Moch had been Minister of the Interior, 1947–50 and Minister of Defence, 1950–1.

89 CTSG, 'The Economic Case for a Channel Tunnel', January 1961, in Kirkpatrick-Macmillan, 1 February 1961, and *Channel Tunnel The Facts Q A* (n.d.), in PREM11/3576; Harpham-Roderick Sarell (General Dept., FO), 26 September 1961, FO371/158737, PRO.

90 Cf. *Parl. Deb. (Commons)*, 5th ser. Vol. 638 (Session 1960–1), 11 April 1961, *c*.31–3, oral answers from Marples to John Rankin, Marcus Lipton and Gerald Nabarro.

91 MT, *Reorganisation of the Nationalised Transport Undertakings*, December 1960, P.P.1960–1, xxvii, Cmnd. 1248; *Times*, 9 December 1960, p. 6, 21 December 1960, p. 6; Treasury, *The Financial and Economic Obligations of the Nationalised Industries*, April 1961, P.P.1960–1, xxvii, Cmnd. 1337; Gourvish, *British Railways*, pp. 302–2, 307ff.

92 A formal treaty between the two countries was signed on 29 November 1962. See Keith Hayward, *Government and British Civil Aerospace: A Case Study in Post-War Technology Policy* (Manchester, 1983), pp. x, 54–6, 60–6, and Kenneth Owen, *Concorde and the Americans: International Politics of the Supersonic Transport* (Washington DC, 1997), pp. 16–20, 30–8.

93 Cf. Collings, Note, 6 September 1961, Sir Patrick Reilly (FO)-Millar, 13 September 1961, FO371/158736, PRO; Quick-Smith, 'Channel Bulletin No. 8', 7 July 1961, author's collection; *Parl. Deb. (Commons)*, 5th ser. Vol. 649 (Session 1961–2), 22 November 1961, R. Gresham-Cooke, question, *c*.1335; *(Lords)*, 5th ser. Vol. 245 (Session 1962–3), 20 December 1962, Lord Gladwyn, question, *c*.1237. Grayson emphasises the importance of the Tunnel in EEC considerations, but it was certainly not a major element. Later on, the dominant issue for tunnelistes was European *trade*. See Granville Ramage (FO), Note, 29 August 1962, FO371/165290, PRO; Grayson,

'Channel Tunnel and European Unity', 427–9; Milward, *United Kingdom and European Community*, I, and Kristian Steinnes, 'The European Challenge: Britain's EEC Application in 1961', *Contemporary European History*, 7 (1) (March 1998), 61–79.

94 Harpham-Peter Scott-Malden (U-Sec, MT), 3 August 1961, MT RA Divn, Aide-Memoire on 'The Channel Tunnel', August 1961, Sir Frank Lee-Dunnett, 15 September 1961, T124/1093, PRO; see also *Times*, 24 August 1961, p. 8.

95 'Note of a meeting between the French Minister of Public Works, Transport and Tourism, M. Robert Buron, and the British Minister of Transport, Mr. Ernest Marples,... 17th November 1961', n.d., MT114/363, PRO.

96 Quoted in *Times*, 18 November 1961, p. 8. He was more measured in the Commons: *Parl. Deb. (Commons)*, 5th ser. Vol. 649 (Session 1961–2), 22 November 1961, *c.*1336.

97 Sarell, Minute on 'Channel Tunnel/Bridge', 16 October 1961, FO371/158737, PRO.

98 MT, *Proposals for a Fixed Channel Link*, 1963. See also A.H. Watson, 'The Channel Tunnel: Investment Appraisals', *Public Administration*, 45 (Spring 1967), 1–21.

99 Maude was an Under-Secretary in the Treasury, Scott-Malden an Under-Secretary, Railways, MT, Bowen an Under-Secretary, BT, and Sarell, the former Consul-General in Algiers, was head of the General Dept., FO. Maude, Note on 'The Channel Crossing', 22 January 1962, T224/616, PRO. Vergnaud was Directeur du Cabinet, MPWT, Dargenton Conseiller Technique, MFEA, Mathieu Ingénieur Général des Ponts et Chaussees, MPWT, Lacarrière Chef du Service des Affairs Economiques et Itnternationales, MPWT, and Jordan Chef de Service des Affaires Générales et Transports Internationaux, MFA.

100 In all, there were 13 joint studies: engineering, operating, jurisdiction, and defence; traffic, tariffs, costs, revenue, users' surplus, and 'unquantifiables'; capital structure, guarantees, and taxation. Watson, 'Channel Tunnel', 4.

101 SETCM = Société d'Etude du Tunnel Complet routier et ferroviaire sous la Manche. Its report, 'Combined Channel Tunnel' of 1963, is in MT144/69, PRO.

102 Beeching-Dunnett, 12 March 1962, cit.; MT, 'Note of a meeting held in Mr Serpell's room... 20th September 1961', 26 September 1961, MT124/1093, Peter Lazarus (MT)-Serpell, 14 November 1961, MT124/1094, PRO.

103 Tunnel cost excluded financial charges but included cost of motor vehicle transporters, bridge cost included cost of rail connections on the British side. MT, *Proposals for a Fixed Channel Link*, 1963, pp. 4, 6, 26.

104 Ibid. pp. 6–10, 30–3. Later on, it was conceded that the forecasts for accompanied cars and freight had been 'over-cautious': Watson, 'Channel Tunnel', 20.

105 Ibid. pp. 4–5, 13; *Economist*, 28 October 1961, p. 375.

106 Alan Draper (Admiralty)-David Dell (MoD), 18 April 1962, DEFE7/1626; R.F. Stretton (FO)-Sarell, 27 June 1962, Dell-Ramage, 14 August 1962, FO371/165290, PRO.

107 Cabinet Conclusions, 18 July 1963, CAB128/37, PRO.

108 Marples, Note on 'Anglo-French Report on the Channel Crossing', 30 September 1963, with annex from Sir William Armstrong (Chairman, Economic Steering (General) Committee), 23 September 1963, C(63) 116, CAB129/114; Cabinet Conclusions, 8 October 1963, CC (63) 59th, CAB128/37, PRO.

109 MT, *Proposals for a Fixed Channel Link*, 1963, pp. 8, 11–12, 14, and see Maude, Note on 'Financing of a Channel Tunnel', 21 January 1963, T224/616, PRO.

110 MT, *Proposals for a Fixed Channel Link*, 1963, pp. 4, 13.

111 Watson, 'Channel Tunnel', p. 12. A.H. Watson was Director of Statistics, MT.

112 *Times*, 25 August 1961, p. 13.

113 Means-de Vitry *et al.*, 24 September 1957 and 21 April 1960, R. Gordon Wasson (V-P, Morgan Guaranty Trust)-Harcourt, 19 January 1960, TSI archive, Vols. 5, 97 and 104, carton #13, HBS.

114 Cabinet Economic Steering (General) Committee Minutes, 18 September 1963, CAB134/1887; Sub-Committee on the Fixed Channel Link, minutes and papers, 25 September–30 October 1963, CAB134/1899, PRO. The other members were: Peter Vinter (Treasury), M.S. Williams (FO), G. Bowen (BoT), J. Rogerson (H&LG), G.B. Blaker (Office, 1st SoS), and H. Wooldridge (DSIR).

115 Sub-Committee on The Fixed Channel Link Minutes, 18 and 24 October 1963; Report on the Fixed Channel Link (final version), 29 October 1963, paras I.1, II.5–9, II.19–21, III.1–15, CAB134/1899, PRO.

116 *Financial and Economic Obligations of the Nationalised Industries*, April 1961, P.P.1960–1, xxvii, Cmnd. 1337.

117 This contrasted with the government's view of Thorneycroft's resignation over the proposal to increase public expenditure by a 'marginal' 1%: Hailsham, cit. in Jarvis, '1958 Treasury Dispute', 45.

118 Cabinet Economic Steering (General) Committee Minutes, 1 and 8 November 1963, CAB134/1887; Treasury, Note on 'Channel Tunnel', ES(G) (63) 94, 5 November 1963, CAB134/1892; Reginald Maudling (Chancellor of the Exchequer), Note on 'The Fixed Channel Link', 20 November 1963, enclosing memo. from Armstrong, n.d., CAB134/1803, PRO. The comparisons with the Victoria Line and BOAC were made in Maudling, Memo. on 'Channel Tunnel – Investment', EP(63) 24, 3 December 1963, CAB134/1804, PRO. On PESC see Peter Hennessy, *Whitehall* (2001 edn), p. 175; Rodney Lowe, 'The Core Executive, Modernization and the Creation of PESC, 1960–64', *Public Administration*, 75 (Winter 1997), 601–15.

119 Cabinet Economic Policy Committee Minutes, 22 November and 10 December 1963, CAB134/1803; Marples, Memo. on 'The Channel Link', EP(63) 33, 9 December 1963, CAB134/1804, PRO; Maudling, Memo., 3 December 1963, cit. On the Treasury's further concerns about competing projects and its appeal to the need for 'prudence' see Maudling and Boyd-Carpenter (Chief Secretary to the Treasury), Memo. to Cabinet on 'Government Expenditure after 1968', CP(64) 19, 21 January 1964, CAB129/116, PRO.

120 Maudling, Memo. on 'The Channel Tunnel' (enclosing Treasury note on 'Constructing the Channel Tunnel without excessive strain on the economy', 7 January 1964), EP(64) 5, 8 January 1964, and further Memo. (enclosing Officials' note on 'The Channel Tunnel – the British Interest', 9 January 1964), EP(64) 6, 10 January 1964, CAB134/1806, PRO. On Sociétés d'Economie Mixte see Bank of England, Note, 24 July 1964, T230/739, PRO.

121 Scott-Malden, Note (criticising draft of EP(64) 6), 17 December 1963 ['this paper simply doesn't answer the question']; P.R. Sheath (RA Divn, MT)-Scott-Malden, 9 January 1964; Scott-Malden, Note (criticising EP(64) 5), 10 January 1964 ['the latest attempt to muddy the Channel waters'], and draft brief for the Minister, 14 January 1964, all in MT124/964, PRO.

122 Marples, Memo. on 'The Channel Tunnel', EP(64) 9, 13 January 1964, CAB134/1806, and see also Sir Charles Johnston (Dep-Sec, FO), brief for Lord Carrington (Minister without Portfolio), 14 January 1964, FO371/176343, PRO. On Treasury scepticism about EP(64) 9 see Vinter, Memo. 14 January 1964, T319/420, PRO.

123 Maudling, Memo. on 'The Channel Crossing', 21 January 1964, CP(64) 20, CAB129/116; Sir Burke Trend (Cabinet Secretary)-Alec Douglas Home (Prime Minister), 22 January 1964, PREM11/5161, PRO. Maudling's memo. was derived from Armstrong's memo., CAB134/1803, PRO.

124 Cabinet Conclusions, 23 January 1964, CM(64) 6th, CAB128/38, PRO; Cabinet Secretary's Notebook, 23 January 1964.

125 Maudling and Marples, Memos. to Cabinet on 'Channel Tunnel', CP(64) 29 and 30, 29 January 1964, CAB129/116, PRO.

126 Cabinet Conclusions, 30 January 1964, CM(64) 8th, CAB128/38, PRO; Cabinet Secretary's Notebook, 30 January 1964.
127 *Parl. Deb. (Commons)*, 5th ser. Vol. 688 (Session 1963–4), 6 February 1964, Marples, questions from G.R. Strauss, Arthur Holt, Sir William Teeling *et al.*, *c.*1351–4.
128 MT, 'Deputation to the Prime Minister from the Channel Tunnel Parliamentary Group. Note of meeting held in the Prime Minister's room at the House of Commons at 4 p.m. on 9th April 1964', 10 April 1964, PREM11/5161, PRO.
129 Marples-John Boyd-Carpenter, 27 April 1964, PREM11/5161, PRO; Maurice Couve de Murville (Minister for Foreign Affairs, France) and Sir Pierson Dixon (British Ambassador in Paris), 'Exchange of Notes. Establishment of Channel Tunnel Project Anglo-French Commission of Surveillance, Paris, 3 June 1964', FO93/33/481, PRO, printed as *Exchanges of Notes between the Government of the United Kingdom and Northern Ireland and the Government of the French Republic establishing a Joint Commission of Surveillance for the Geological Survey in connexion with the Channel Tunnel Project Paris, June 3, 1964*, July 1964, P.P.1964–5, xxxiii, Cmnd. 2416.
130 Norman Hillier-Fry (FO)-Johnston, 13 August 1964, enclosing MT Channel Tunnel Group, Memo. on 'State of play at 12th August, 1964', FO371/176345, PRO.
131 Cf. Roger Middleton, *The British Economy Since 1945: Engaging with the Debate* (Basingstoke, 2000), pp. 4–5, 86–9.
132 Cf. Terry Gourvish, *British Rail 1974–97: From Integration to Privatisation* (Oxford, 2002).
133 There were other distractions at Rambouillet, not least relations with the Soviet Union, Berlin, and nuclear weapons strategy. Philip de Zulueta (Macmillan's PS), Memo. on 'Points discussed with General de Gaulle at Rambouillet on March 12 and 13, 1960, 14 March 1960, FO/371/152096, also in PREM11/3576; Rumbold, Memo. on 'Channel Tunnel', 31 March 1960, FO371/153944; Juliet Collings (FO), brief for Selwyn Lloyd, 17 February 1960, FO371/153942, PRO. See also Alastair Horne, *Macmillan 1957–1986* (1989), p. 431.
134 Note the allegation that the British made an official, but informal, invitation to the French Government to discuss the Tunnel in December 1960, which was apparently misunderstood. See Means, Memo. 6 and 17 April 1961, TSI archive, Vol. 98, HBS.
135 Sir Pierson Dixon-Tomkins, 15 November 1960, reporting the views of Georges-Picot, FO371/153949; Harpham-Tomkins, 8 June 1961, MT124/1092; John Hay (PS, MT)-Serpell, 29 June 1961, Scott-Malden-R.C. Hope-Jones (FO), 11 September 1961, MT124/1093, Marples, Memo. to Cabinet EPC, EA(61) 95, 6 November 1961, CAB124/1692, PRO; Alfred Davidson-Frank Davidson, 13 December 1961, TSI archive, Vol. 104, HBS.
136 'Record of a Conversation at the Chateau de Champs at 3.15 p.m. on Sunday, June 3, 1962', and de Zulueta-Macmillan, 6 and 7 June 1962 [with Macmillan's annotation: 'I did not think that this part of the talk was in very serious vein. It was largely chat'], PREM11/4549, PRO.
137 Trend, Note to Macmillan on 'Channel Crossing', 17 July 1963, and see also Harpham-Tomkins, 19 November 1960, FO371/153949, Harpham-Sarell, 16 November 1962, FO371/165290, Marples-Macmillan, 6 July 1962, and 'Extract from Record of Conversation between the French Ambassador, M. de Courcel, and Sir Pierson Dixon in Paris on March 2, 1963', PREM11/4549, E. Whitmore (Treasury), Memo. on 'The Channel Tunnel', 18 March 1964, T319/424, PRO. Cf. also Bonnaud, 'Channel tunnel', 13.
138 John Fearnley (British Embassy, Paris)-Hillier-Fry, 25 February 1964, FO371/176343, PRO.
139 Vinter-Sir Richard 'Otto' Clarke (2nd Sec, Treasury), 23 April 1964, Vinter, Draft Note for Maudling, 7 May 1964, T319/426; Marples-Boyd-Carpenter, 27 April 1964, cit., with annotation by Alec Douglas-Home; Boyd-Carpenter-Marples, 1 May 1964,

Carrington-Boyd-Carpenter, 1 May 1964, PREM11/5161; Denys Brown (FO)-M.S. Williams (FO), 28 April 1964, FO371/176344; 'Provisional Report of a Meeting of British and French Officials in Paris on 8th May 1964', 12 May 1964, MT144/3, PRO. For a British Rail view see Llewellyn Wansbrough-Jones (Secretary, BRB)-Beeching *et al.*, 30 April 1964, BRB 196-4-1 Pt. 4.

3 ANOTHER FALSE START: THE WILSON GOVERNMENTS AND THE TUNNEL, 1964–70

1 Marples-Marc Jacquet (French Minister of Transport), 17 February 1964, copy in T224/616 and T319/423, O.F. Gingell (U-Sec, MT)-Lacarrière, 12 March 1964, MT144/3, J.J.B. Hunt (Treasury)-H.S. Lee (Treasury), 7 December 1965, T230/739, PRO. Somewhat confusingly, the CTSG's French members also set up a new committee under Louis Armand: press release, 5 May 1964, in BRB196-4-1 Pt. 4.

2 A joint group of railway officers led by M.A. Cameron (BTC) and Roger Hutter (SNCF) produced a report on railway operating, and a joint BTC/SNCF committee was established (consisting of G.W. Quick-Smith, H.E. Osborn, C.P. Hopkins, Roger Guibert and Jean Gorsat) to discuss financial operating and charging elements when the CTSG was preparing its 1960 report. See Report of the French and British Railway Officers on the Channel Tunnel, 1960, copy in MT114/363, PRO, and Quick-Smith, BRB 196-4-1 Pt. 2.

3 André Segelat (President, SNCF)-Beeching, 3 March 1964 (translation), and reply, 16 March 1964, BRB 196-4-1 Pt. 4. Beeching's initial response was cool: 'I find it difficult, however, to convince myself that such a joint working party can begin any serious work until the organisational structure for the overall control of the Tunnel project has been established.'

4 In addition to Shirley and Guibert, the initial members of the joint steering group were: John Ratter (BRB), Stanley Raymond (BRB), Fred Margetts (BRB), plus David McKenna (GM, SR, co-opted); and André Bernard (Dep Sec-General, SNCF), Roger Hutter (Directeur, Nord Region), and Philippe Graff (Chief Engineer, SNCF). Shirley, Memo., 18 September 1964, BRB Minutes, 24 September 1964, AN167/13, AN167/2, PRO.

5 For example, there is no reference to the Tunnel in Harold Wilson, *The Labour Government 1964–1970: A Personal Record* (1971), or R. Coopey, S. Fielding and N. Tiratsoo (eds), *The Wilson Governments 1964–1970* (1993), and only half a sentence in Ben Pimlott, *Harold Wilson* (1993), p. 625.

6 Tom Fraser, statement, 29 October 1964, MT144/75, PRO, reported e.g. in *Times*, 30 October 1964, p. 10, and cf. also 'Minutes of meeting held between the United Kingdom Minister of Aviation and the French Minister of Transport... 29th October 1964', MT144/75, Hiller-Fry-Fearnley, 30 October 1964, FO371/176345, and UK Channel Tunnel Coordinating Committee Minutes, 29 October 1964, MT144/5, PRO.

7 James Callaghan (Chancellor of Exchequer), press conference, 26 October 1964, *Times*, 27 October 1964, p. 10; Lee-Vinter, 20 November 1964, T319/427; Gingell-Scott-Malden, 27 November 1964, Gingell-Michael Custance (Dep Sec, MT), 1 December 1964, Sir Richard ('Otto') Clarke (2nd Sec, Treasury)-Sir Thomas Padmore (Permanent Sec, MT [1962–8]), 3 December 1964, MT124/1062, PRO.

8 Fraser-Callaghan, 2 December 1964, Patrick Gordon-Walker-Callaghan, 7 December 1964, T319/427, and see also MT144/93, PRO.

9 L. Petch (3rd Sec, Treasury)-Clarke, 3 December 1964, Clarke-Ian Bancroft (PPS to Chancellor), 3 December 1964, Lee-Vinter, 3, 4 and 17 December 1964, T319/427; Treasury Task Group on Government Expenditure Minutes, 22 December 1964, copy in MT124/1062, PRO.

10 Lee-Hunt, 5 August 1965, T319/432, PRO.

11 'Record of a Meeting in the Prime Minister's Room at the House of Commons on Tuesday, August 3, 1965', 3 August 1965, PREM13/466, PRO.
12 Its interest was confined to investment appraisal, relationship with overall transport policy, regional policy implications, and pricing. Cf. G.F.B. Corti (Asst Sec, DEA)-John Barber (Asst Sec, MT), 12 June 1968, MT144/92, PRO.
13 Wilson, *Labour Government 1964–1970*, pp. 8–9; Richard Coopey, 'Industrial Policy in the White Heat of the Scientific Revolution', in Coopey *et al.*, *Wilson Governments*, pp. 102–22; Alec Cairncross, *The British Economy since 1945: Economic Policy and Performance, 1945–1990* (Oxford, 1992), pp. 154–5, 171–2.
14 Both the Concorde and Polaris projects were subject to critical reviews, but the Labour government decided that the escape costs were prohibitively high. The TSR2 was abandoned. Wilson, *Labour Government 1964–1970*, pp. 40, 61–2, 90.
15 DEA, *The National Plan*, P.P.1964–5, xxx, Cmnd. 2764, September 1965, p. 131, and see A.H. Watson (MT)-K.F.J. Ennals (DEA), 4 August 1965, Kenneth Macdonald-H.S. Lee (Treasury), 4 August 1965, T319/432, PRO.
16 Scott-Malden-Denys Brown (FO), 12 February 1964, MT144/21, PRO.
17 Leo d'Erlanger (CTSG)-Padmore (MT), 20 February 1964, enclosing H.J.B. Harding, 'Channel Tunnel Site Investigation', same date, and MT, 'Notes of Minister's Meeting with Lord Harcourt [CTSG], 22nd February, 1964', MT144/21, PRO.
18 Scott-Malden-Brown, 11 February 1964, Gingell-Custance, 11 March 1964, MT144/21, PRO.
19 Vinter-H.W. Cauthery (MT), 28 February and 10 March 1964, MT144/18; Gingell, 'Brief for the Minister's Meeting with Mr. Harding [CTSG, 10 March 1964]', n.d., MT144/21, PRO.
20 'Note of a joint meeting of British and French officials... 25th March 1964', Note of a joint meeting of British and French officials and representatives of the Channel Tunnel Study Group... 25th March 1964', MT144/18, PRO.
21 MT and CTSG [CT Co., Chemin de Fer Sous-Marin, Compagnie Financière de Suez, Technical Studies Inc., Fédération Routière Internationale (Paris Office)], Agreements, 7 July 1964, MT144/20, PRO. The Commission was co-chaired by Col. Denis McMullen (MT Railway Inspectorate) and J. Mathieu. The British parliament was informed in a statement from Marples on 1 July 1964: *Parl. Deb. (Commons)*, 5th ser. Vol. 697 (Session 1963–4), *c.*1352–3. See also Hunt, *Tunnel*, pp. 104–5.
22 Gingell-H.W. Cauthery (MT), 7 July 1964, McMullen-Gingell, 8 July 1964, enclosing Commission of Surveillance Report on geological survey, 8 July 1964, MT144/10, PRO.
23 Commission of Surveillance, Report, 8 July 1964, cit., and draft Third Report, 18 August 1964, MT144/10; Commission of Surveillance Minutes, 20 August 1964, MT144/6, PRO.
24 'Channel Tunnel a Certainty', *Times*, 15 September 1964, p. 6, and see also *Railway Gazette*, 18 September 1964, p. 753.
25 See John Baker (MT CTG)-Gingell, 17 December 1964, Gingell, 'Note on Progress', 18 December 1964, Commission of Surveillance, 'Report by the British side', 2 February 1965, MT144/10, PRO; Hunt, *Tunnel*, p. 105. Only three boreholes had been completed by the end of 1964.
26 Both Wimpey-Forasol and the CTSG consultants appear to have underestimated the impact of bad weather on their operations. At the same time the handling of the contracting consortium by the CTSG and their consulting engineers clearly left something to be desired. A firm contract between the parties was not finally approved until August 1965. See Gingell, Note, 18 December 1964, cit.; Gingell, Aide-memoire on 'Boring Programme', 3 February 1965, MT CTG, Memo. on 'Geological and Geophysical Survey- Progress', n.d., UK CT Co-ordinating Committee Minutes, 4 February 1965, Bill Sharp (Asst Sec, MT)-Cauthery, 4 February 1965, MT CTG,

Memo. on 'The Marine Boring Programme', 8 April 1965, MT144/10, Commission of Surveillance Minutes, 23–4 August 1965, MT144/8, PRO.

27 W.N. Hillier-Fry (FO), Minute, 17 February 1965, FO371/181341; MT CTG, 'Note of a meeting held at the Ministry of Public Works and Transport, Paris ... 5 February 1965', Sharp-H.S. Lee, 5 April 1965, Gingell-Lord Harcourt (CTSG), 20 April 1965, MT144/10, PRO.

28 CTSG, 'Channel Tunnel: Site Investigations in the Strait of Dover 1964–1965', 1966, Vol. I, pp. 3–5, MT179/1 [for other volumes see MT179/2–9]; 'Joint report by British and French officials on the construction and operation of the Channel Tunnel', August 1966 [AF66], p. 2, copy in PREM13/1244; 'Channel Tunnel Site Investigation 1964–1965. Final Report of the Commission of Surveillance', September 1969, MT144/202, PRO; Hunt, *Tunnel*, p. 105.

29 Cf. Baker-Barber, 16 July 1969, MT144/153; McMullen, confidential note on 'Channel Tunnel Geological Survey Commission of Surveillance', October 1969, MT144/202, PTO.

30 Vinter-Lee, 25 May 1964, T319/426; Gingell-Hillier-Fry, 25 February 1965, FO371/181341; MT, Report on 'The Channel Tunnel: Progress with the French', 5 November 1965, enclosed in Fraser-Callaghan, 9 November 1965, MT144/26, PRO.

31 Cf. Hillier-Fry-F.C. Everson (Paris), 8 March 1965, FO371/181341, PRO.

32 Lee-Cauthery, 30 November 1964, T319/427, PRO. Much of the problem of length was caused by trying to consolidate finance papers drawn up by the Treasury and MT: MacDonald-Lee, 18 November 1964, ibid.

33 Cf. Brown, Minutes, 11 and 12 October 1965, FO371/181342, PRO; MT, Report, 5 November 1965, Fraser-Callaghan, 9 November 1965, cit.

34 W.W. Scott (MT)-A.N. [Michael] Halls (PPS to PM), 23 May 1966, PREM13/1244, PRO.

35 'Draft note of a meeting [Anglo-French] held at St Christopher House on 29th March, 1965', n.d., FO371/181341, PRO; Joint Report, August 1966, cit. pp. 18. As Vinter put it at an early stage: 'the French are probably pretty deeply wedded to some private participation; whereas given the demand for bond guarantee, which no-one has suggested giving up, we believe this to be rubbish'. Vinter-Petch, 8 May 1964, T319/426, PRO.

36 Macdonald-Lee, 1 June 1964, T319/426, PRO.

37 Michael Thornton (Dep Chief Cashier, BOE)-Lee, enclosing Bank of England, Note on 'Sociétés d'Economie Mixte', 24 July 1964, T319/429, PRO. On the Morrisonian public corporation see Jim Tomlinson, *Government and the Enterprise Since 1900* (Oxford, 1994), pp. 131–2, 193–6.

38 Vinter, 'Note of discussions in Paris on 2nd and 3rd February 1964', 6 February 1964, T319/423; Vinter, annotation, 12 March 1964, on Alan Whittome (BOE)-Macdonald, 11 March 1964, T319/424; 'Extract of a note (by Sir D. Rickett) of a conversation between the Chancellor of the Exchequer and the French Minister of Finance on 14th May, 1964', T319/426, PRO.

39 Whittome-Vinter, 7 April 1964, Lee-Vinter, 7 April 1964, enclosing note by Macdonald on 'Channel Tunnel: Finance', Vinter-I. De L. Radice (Treasury), 8 April 1964, 'Note of meeting held in Mr. Vinter's room on 9th April 1963 [*sic*: 1964] to discuss the financial aspects of the Channel Tunnel, T319/425, PRO.

40 Denys Munby (Economic Consultant, DEA)-Douglas Henley (Asst U-Sec, DEA), 18 January 1965 [*sic*: 1966], Alfred E. Davidson (CTSG)-Gingell, 6 April 1965, MT144/21; Cauthery-Lee, 12 May 1965, T319/428; Gingell-Fearnley [telephone conversation], 9 June 1965, FO371/181341; Sir Frank Lee (ex-Treasury, now Master of Corpus Christi College, Cambridge)-Vinter, 28 January 1966 [introducing 'Al Davidson'], T319/433; Vinter, Note for Record [meeting with Alfred Davidson, 19 February 1966], T319/434, PRO.

41 Lee-D.E. Thomson (BOE), 21 June 1965, Cauthery-Lee, 23 June 1965, Gingell-Custance, 30 June 1965, Gingell-Lord Harcourt (CTSG), 8 July 1965, T319/429, PRO.
42 CTSG, 'Reply to the questionnaire of 8th July, 1965', 27 July 1965, Lee-Macdonald, 29 July 1965, T319/429; Lee-Hunt, 5 August 1965, T319/432, PRO.
43 MT, 'Draft note of a meeting held on 5th August 1965, at 15.00 hrs...', 10 August 1965, Macdonald-Hunt, 13 August 1965, T319/432, PRO.
44 On Gingell's frustration see Lee, 'Note for the Record', 24 September 1965, T319/432, PRO.
45 Baker, 'Note of a meeting between Monsieur Billet (French MT)... and Mr. Baker on Tuesday, 28th September 1965', 30 September 1965, Vinter-Hunt, 11 October 1965, T319/432; Gingell-Brown (FO), 27 October 1965, Lee, 'Note for the Record', 1 November 1965, T319/430; Hunt-Vinter, 29 November 1965, T319/431; Henley-D.A.V. Allen (Permanent U-Sec, DEA), 3 November 1965, EW25/8; 'Note of a meeting to discuss the organisation and finance of the Channel Tunnel at the D.E.A. on 5th January, 1966', 7 January 1966, EW25/204, PRO.
46 Jacques Rigaud, 'Rapport sur les Problèmes Juridiques relatifs à une Société Internationale pour la Construction et l'Exploitation du Tunnel sous la Manche', August 1965, DTp file L5926, and see translation of Ch.1 in IT40/7/1 Pt. 1.
47 Rodgers-Gingell, 12 November 1965, FO371/181342; Lee-Hunt, 26 November 1965, Hunt-Vinter, 29 November 1965, T319/431; G.F. Rodgers (British Embassy, Paris)-Gingell, 22 November 1965, FO371/1812342, and 1 December 1965, MT144/26; Fraser-Callaghan, 13 December 1965, T319/431, PRO.
48 Brown-Rodgers, 7 January 1966, Brown-Garvey (FO), 28 January 1966, Gingell-Lacarrière, 13 January 1966, FO371/187405; MT CTG, 'Channel Tunnel Progress Report', enclosed in Castle-Callaghan, 20 April 1966, MT144/81, PRO; Joint Report, August 1966, cit. pp. 18–24.
49 Lee-Henley, 5 January 1966, Lee-Gingell, 10 January 1966, T319/433, PRO.
50 Bryan Harris (DEA)-Henley, 29 December 1965, Gingell-Lacarrière, 13 January 1966, Baker, 'Note of the Private Discussion between Monsieur Lacarriere, Mr Gingell, Monsieur Billet and Mr Baker... 21 January, 1966', 24 January 1966, T319/433, PRO.
51 Lee-Hunt, 27 January 1966, T319/433, PRO.
52 Lee-Vinter, 3 March 1966, T319/434, PRO.
53 Callaghan-Fraser, 6 December 1965, MT144/26, and cf. also earlier concerns in Austen Albu (Minister of State, DEA)-Brown, 19 November 1965, EW25/8, and Brown-Fraser, 23 November 1965, MT144/26; Fraser-Callaghan, 13 December 1965, cit. Use was made of French material, notably a report on 'Rentabilité Financier du Tunnel sous la Manche' of April 1965, which was sent to the MT on 13 December. See MT144/42, PRO.
54 Cf. Clarke-Vinter, 10 November 1965, T319/430, PRO. On the reappraisal see Baker-Gingell, 10 December 1965, and Baker, 'Note of the First Meeting of the Economic Steering Group... 16th December, 1965', n.d., etc., MT144/41, PRO.
55 Lee-J.J.B. Hunt (Treasury), 12 November 1965, T319/431, PRO. Lee also suggested that the electric traction might be delivered not by overhead wires but by third rail (the antiquated system used on British Rail's Southern Region), in order that the height (and therefore cost) of the tunnel might be reduced. Ibid. and Lee-Gingell, 29 October 1965, T319/430, PRO.
56 Callaghan-Fraser, 6 December 1965, cit.; Joint Report, August 1966, cit. p. 30; Crompton, 'Transport', pp. 138–40. The French were not informed to avoid giving the impression that the UK might be preparing to back out. Baker-Gingell, 10 December 1965, MT144/41; Lee-Hunt, 31 May 1966, T319/436, PRO.
57 Labour Party, *Let's Go with Labour for the New Britain* (1964) and *Time for Decision* (1966), in F.W.S. Craig (ed.), *British Election Manifestos 1959–1987* (Aldershot, 1990), pp. 49–50, 89.

58 Halls-Scott, 10 May 1966, and reply, 23 May 1966, with Wilson's annotation, and Michael Palliser (PS to PM)-Scott, 1 June 1966, PREM13/1244, PRO. On Halls see Dennis Kavanagh and Anthony Seldon, *The Powers Behind the Prime Minister: The Hidden Influence of Number Ten* (1999), pp. 14, 67–8.

59 MT, Note, 18 May 1966, enclosed with Scott-Halls, 23 May 1966, cit.

60 Castle-Callaghan, 20 April 1966, MT144/81, PRO. Castle suggested that the procedure be accelerated by having only relevant ministers consider the project, but the Treasury insisted that the full committee procedure be used. Albu-Castle, 31 May 1966, copy in FO371/187406, PRO.

61 Cabinet ED(O) Committee Minutes, 7 June 1966, CAB134/2713 (quotation from Eric Roll (DEA, Chairman, ED(O) Committee), Note to EDC, ED(66) 53, 9 June 1966, CAB134/2709), PRO. The quotation originated in a draft prepared for Roll by Robert Armstrong: Armstrong-Henley, 8 June 1966, copy, in FO371/187406, PRO.

62 MT, Note, 18 May 1966, cit.

63 Barbara Castle (Minister of Transport), Memo. to Cabinet EDC on 'Channel Tunnel', ED(66) 49, 3 June 1966, Annex 2, CAB134/2709; George Brown (First SoS and SoS for Economic Affairs), Memo. on 'Channel Tunnel', C(66) 79, 14 June 1966, CAB129/125, PRO.

64 MT Economic Steering Group, 'Channel Tunnel – Economic Reappraisal', 12 April 1966, MT144/89, PRO; Castle, Memo., 3 June 1966, cit., Annex 1.

65 Cabinet EDC Minutes, 13 June 1966, CAB134/2707; Castle, Memo., 3 June 1966, cit., Annex 3; Brown, Memo., 14 June 1966, cit.

66 On the origins of the hovercraft/ferries debate see Lee-Gingell, 21 September 1964, MT144/22; Lee-Vinter, 20 November 1964, Cauthery-Lee, 3 December 1964, T319/427, PRO. Albu, Minister of State, DEA, was another critic, having 'the gravest doubts' about the Tunnel's economics: A.C. Russell (Albu's PS)-Henley, 11 November 1965, EW25/8, PRO. Douglas Jay, President of the Board of Trade, also had doubts about a project he regarded as 'prestigious': C.W. Roberts (BoT)-Bowen, 13 November 1964, R.E. Abbott (PS to President, BoT), Minute, 27 April 1966, BT213/253, 375, PRO.

67 Stewart, Memo., ED(66) 51, 6 June 1966, CAB134/2709; Cabinet EDC Minutes, 13 June 1966, cit.; Brown, Memo., 14 June 1966, cit.; Trend-Wilson, 15 June 1966, PREM13/1244, Cabinet Conclusions, CC(66) 30th, 21 June 1966, CAB128/41, PRO; Richard Crossman, *The Diaries of a Cabinet Minister*, I (1975), p. 544 [Crossman was Minister of Housing]; Barbara Castle, *The Castle Diaries, 1964–70* (1984), pp. 133, 136.

68 Cabinet Secretary's Notebook, 21 June 1966, CO.

69 Castle, Memo. on 'Channel Tunnel', ED(66) 63, 23 June 1966, ED (66) 15th, 27 June 1966, CAB134/2709; Cabinet EDC Minutes, 27 June 1966, CAB134/2707, PRO.

70 CTSG, 'Channel Tunnel. Bored Tunnel: revised preliminary estimate of cost and programme of construction 30th June 1966', MT149/23; Scott-Palliser, 6 July 1966, enclosing MT, 'Channel Tunnel: Revised Cost Estimates', 1 July 1966, Brown-Castle, 11 July 1966, PREM13/1244; J.L. Clarke (DEA)-Henley, 6 July 1966, EW25/323, PRO; and see also Joint Report, August 1966, Annex 2, 'revised cost estimate', 5 July 1966.

71 FMV (66) 3rd meeting, 8 July 1966, item 1, PREM13/1244, and see also extract in EW25/343; Cabinet Conclusions, CC (66) 36th, 14 July 1966, CAB128/41, PRO.

72 Baker, Note, 7 July 1966, draft extracts from Communiqué, n.d. and briefing document, 8 July 1966, MT144/77; Brown, Minute, 5 July 1966, FO371/187407, PRO. Cf. also *Times*, 9 July 1966, pp. 1, 9, and 'Single Yellow for the Channel Tunnel', *Railway Gazette*, 15 July 1966, p. 548. Unlike the longer version, the shorter version made no reference to the details of the solution reached, e.g. the private construction/public operating model and the rights of the government to participate in the equity and acquire the assets in due course.

73 Castle, *Diaries 1964–70*, pp. 82, 91, 492. Castle tried unsuccessfully to have Padmore moved. Ibid. pp. 91–4, 114–17, 404; Crossman, *Diaries*, I, pp. 420, 428.
74 Castle, *Diaries 1964–70*, pp. 83, 85, 89; Gourvish, *British Railways*, p. 350.
75 Cf. Paris telegram to FO, No. 343, 26 April 1966, FO371/187405; Baker-Thomas Beagley (MT), 28 April 1966, MT144/81, Sir Patrick Reilly (British Ambassador, Paris), telegram to FO, 1 September 1966, MT 144/78, PRO. Pisani said de Gaulle was a strong supporter, 'not so much for technical or economic reasons, but because of his cosmic view of its long-term historical importance'.
76 Baker-Gingell, 25 February 1966, Castle-Callaghan, 25 May 1966, MT144/81, PRO.
77 Cabinet Conclusions, CC(66), 26th, 27th, 33rd, 36th, 39th, 26 May, 9 and 30 June, 14 and 21 July 1966, CAB128/41, PRO; Wilson, *Labour Government*, pp. 219–21, 235, 243–4. George Brown, reacting to a suggestion by Michael Stewart that Concorde and the Channel Tunnel be handled together, thought the former, about which there were serious doubts, was a quite different project: Stewart-Wilson, 21 June 1966, Brown-Wilson, 24 June 1966, PREM13/1244, PRO. He also noted: 'Foreign Office policy seems to be to harass and hurt the French as much as possible politically and ensure that *we* pay for it economically and financially!' J.L. Clark (Brown's APS)-Henley, 23 June 1966, EW25/305, PRO.
78 Castle, quoted in EDC Minutes, 13 June 1966, and at FMW (66) 3rd meeting, 8 July 1966, cit. In her diary Castle was more sanguine, claiming 'I'm all in favour of it': *Diaries 1964–70*, p. 133.
79 *Evening Standard*, 5 November 1964, p. 1, cutting in MT144/75, PRO.
80 Fearnley-Brown (FO), 15 June 1965, T319/429, PRO; Lee, Note, 1 November 1965, cit.
81 Rupert Raw (Adviser to Governor, BOE)-Leo Pliatzky (U-Sec, Treasury), 23 April 1964, enclosing BOE, 'Channel Tunnel – Finance and Planning Aspects in France', 17 April 1964, T319/426; Brown (FO)-Gingell, 15 October 1965, T319/429; Harris-Henley, 29 December 1965, cit.; Lee-Gingell, 10 January 1966, enclosing BOE note on 'Channel Tunnel: French budgetary and other requirements in relation to public bodies', n.d., T319/433, PRO.
82 Philip M. Williams and Martin Harrison, *Politics and Society in De Gaulle's Republic* (1971), pp. 65–6.
83 Stewart-Castle, 25 April 1966, Brown (FO)-Rodgers, 28 April 1966, FO371/187405, PRO; *Times*, 11 February 1966, p. 6, 15 March 1966, p. 12, 22 April 1966, p. 15, 28 April 1966, p. 16.
84 Baker-Beagley, 28 April 1966, cit.; Barber-Castle, 24 April 1967, MT144/68, PRO.
85 Baker-Padmore, 26 August 1966, MT144/78, PRO; Joint Report, August 1966, pp. 12–17, Annex 1 ['Commission of Surveillance: Assessment of the Reports of the Channel Tunnel Study Group and their Consulting Engineers', 14 June 1966], and Annex 2 ['Assessment by Commission of Surveillance of the Reports on the estimate of cost and programme of construction by the Channel Tunnel Study Group and their Consulting Engineers', August 1966]. The Commission was dissolved in April 1972: *Exchange of Notes between the... United Kingdom... and the... French Republic concerning the dissolution of the Joint Commission of Surveillance... 25 April 1972*, P.P.1971–2, xl, Cmnd. 5043, August 1972.
86 Joint Report, August 1966, pp. 27–9, 42–3, 57–8.
87 Scott-Malden-Castle, 1 August 1966, Castle-Callaghan, 6 September 1966 (copies to Wilson, Brown, Stewart, Jay), and replies, 6 September (Callaghan), 7 September (Brown), 8 September (Stewart), Baker, Note, 2 September 1966, MT144/78, PRO.
88 Sir Con O'Neill (Dep. U-Sec, FO)-Reilly, 26 August 1966, FO371/187409, Reilly, telegram, 1 September 1966, Baker, Notes, 2 and 5 September 1966, MT144/78, PRO.
89 Baker, revised 'Note of the Minister's Meeting with M. Pisani...', 12 September 1966, MT Press Release, 9 September 1966, MT 144/78, PRO. Castle claimed much

of the credit for the progress made: 'I find my open and direct method usually pays': Castle, *Diaries 1964–70*, p. 166.

90 Ibid. p. 166; Baker, 'Revised Draft Brief for the Minister's meeting with M. Pisani…', 5 September 1966, MT144/78; Barber-Scott-Malden, 6 October 1966, Reilly-Brown *et al.*, 10 November 1966, MT144/79, PRO.

91 Castle, *Diaries 1964–70*, p. 180, and see also FO371/187410, PRO. On press reactions see *Evening Standard*, 28 October 1966, *Financial Times, Daily Telegraph, Times, Guardian, Sun, Le Monde, Figaro*, etc., 29 October 1966, cuttings in MT144/79, PRO.

92 Joint communiqué, 28 October 1966, text in MT144/79 and FO371/187410, PRO.

93 Ministère de l'Equipment, Note d'Information, 26 October 1966, *Le Monde*, 28 October 1966, Barber-C. Hall (Principal Information Officer, MT), 1 November 1966, Castle-Pisani, 7 November 1966, MT144/79; B.O. White (FO)-Rodgers, 2 November 1966, FO371/187410; Philip Daniel (DEA)-Henley, 2 November 1966, EW25/343; and cf. *Le Figaro*, 28 October 1966, cutting in MT144/79, PRO.

94 Baker, Revised Note, 12 September 1966, *Le Figaro*, 28 October 1966, cit. Barber's Project Team was the successor to Gingell's Co-ordinating Committee.

95 Baker, Note for the Record, 12 December 1966, Barber, Note on 'Progress of Joint Work', 22 December 1966, Barber-Macé, 22 December 1966, Scott-Malden-Barber, 10 January 1967, Scott-Malden-Padmore, 2 February 1967, MT144/91, PRO.

96 Barber-Scott-Malden, 8 and 20 February 1967, 'Channel Tunnel Finance and Construction: Memorandum for the Information of Private Interests', 22 February 1967, MT144/80, PRO. The memorandum included construction cost and traffic data from AF66, but on the insistence of the French omitted estimates of revenue and charges.

97 *Parl. Deb. (Commons)*, 5th ser. Vol. 741 (Session 1966–7), 22 February 1967, Castle, *c.*1740; MT Press Release, 22 February 1967, MT144/80, PRO.

98 Hunt, *Tunnel*, p. 109; Barber-C.D. Foster (DG of Economic Planning, MT), 13 February 1967, MT144/69, PRO.

99 The two unsuccessful parties were: the New York financiers Kuhn Loeb; and Italian civil engineering contractors, Societá Italiana per Condotte d'Acqua. Letters, 19 and 22 May 1967, and 'Note by the joint Anglo-French project team' n.d., MT144/68; James Gibson (Treasury), 'Channel Tunnel: Observations on Applications from Financial Groups', n.d. [April 1967], MT144/69, PRO.

100 J.R. Coates (MT CT Division), Note, 10 April 1967, enclosing MT, 'Basis for Initial Discussions with Private Interests on the Financing and Construction of the Project: Submission to Minister', April 1967, MT144/90; 'Note of [Joint Anglo-French] meeting held at St. Christopher's House on 20th April 1967', 26 April 1967, MT144/91, PRO.

101 Barber-Scott-Malden, 7 April 1967, Castle, Minute, 19 April 1967, MT144/58; Castle-Callaghan, and Castle-Lord Campbell and Dr Balogh, 21 April 1967, MT144/59, PRO. 'Tommy' Balogh was a Fellow of Balliol College Oxford, 1945–73, and a Reader in Economics, 1960–73. He recommended Christopher Foster to Castle to head the MT's planning team in 1966. 'Jock' Campbell was Chairman of Booker McConnell, 1952–66 and the New Statesman Publishing Co. 1964–6. He recommended Peter Parker to Castle as a potential chairman of British Rail. Castle, *Diaries 1964–1970*, pp. 85, 89, 93, 285, 288, 294–5, 318, 331; Pimlott, *Harold Wilson*, pp. 116, 276–8.

102 Cf. Barber-Scott-Malden, 15 February 1967, MT144/80, and Balogh-Castle, 22 September 1966 [commenting on AF66], copies in PREM13/2429 and FO371/187409, PRO.

103 MT CT Divn, 'Note of Minister's meeting… 1st May 1967…', 8 May 1967, Castle-Stewart, Callaghan and Brown, 4 May 1967, MT144/59, PRO. It was Balogh who suggested the idea of an extended amortisation period (i.e. 40–60 years). However, it

is clear that he did so on the grounds that if tunnel revenues failed to grow as anticipated, the spreading of amortisation costs would enable transport costs to be lowered. See Sharp-Barber, 10 May 1967, Foster-Barber, 11 May 1967, P.D. Huggins (MT)-Coates, 12 May 1967, MT144/59, PRO.

104 Stewart-Castle, 10 May 1967, Fred Mulley (Minister of State, FO)-Castle, 12 May 1967, Callaghan-Castle, 12 May 1967, MT144/59, PRO.

105 Barber-Scott-Malden, 4 December 1967, enclosing MT CT Divn, 'Channel Tunnel: Finance Negotiations – State of Play', 4 December 1967, MT144/71, PRO. On the several meetings see MT144/62–7; on the proposals themselves see MT144/73, PRO.

106 Barber-Harcourt (British Chairman, CTSG), J. Colville (Hill, Samuel) and I.J. Fraser (S.G. Warburg), 22 December 1967, enclosing 'Framework within which Groups will be invited to put forward their modified and amplified proposals', n.d., MT144/73, PRO.

107 Barber-Scott-Malden, 5 March 1968, MT144/71, PRO.

108 Barber-Scott-Malden, 22 March 1968, MT CT Divn, 'Note of a meeting held in Mr. Scott-Malden's room…3rd April, 1968', 16 April 1968, Barker-Gibson, 19 April 1968, enclosing note for new Minister, Richard Marsh on 'State of Play', 16 April 1968, MT144/71; MT CTA Divn, draft paper on 'Channel Tunnel. Finance: Past History and Present Problems, December 1969', 3 December 1969, MT144/89, PRO.

109 'Draft Progress Report to U.K. Project Team on financial discussions with French Officials in Paris on 8th/9th April and subsequent events', n.d., MT144/71, PRO. On detailed aspects of the two countries' positions see Barber-Macé, 18 April 1968, MT144/95, PRO.

110 Stewart-Marsh, 9 May 1968 and reply, 23 May 1968, MT144/72, PRO. The way in which such clauses were inserted into the Bill, which was also subject to a guillotine, led Crossman, for example, to complain that it was 'an outrage of Cabinet Government because these subjects…have never been discussed either in Cabinet or in Cabinet Committee'. Crossman-Wilson, 7 May 1968, CAB164/914, PRO; Crossman, *Diaries*, III (1977), pp. 73–4. On parliamentary criticisms see *Parl. Deb. (Commons)*, 5th ser. Vol. 765 (Session 1967–8), 22 May 1968, Edward Heath, *c.*534–5, 23 May 1968, Heath, *c.*870–1, Peter Bessell, *c.*872, and Dame Irene Ward, *c.*893–5, and *Times*, 3 May 1968, p. 21, 20 May 1968, p. 1, 21 May 1968, p. 2, 24 May 1968, pp. 1, 8.

111 See, *inter alia*, David B. Goldey, 'A precarious regime: the Events of May 1968', in Philip M. Williams, *French Politicians and Elections 1957–1969* (Cambridge, 1970), pp. 226–60, Lucien Rioux and René Backman, *L'explosion de mai* (Paris, 1968), and Robert Gildea, *France Since 1945* (Oxford, 1996), pp. 51–5.

112 Some basic principles were established, e.g. that there should be a bonus return to the 'study period' equity capital. Barber-Scott-Malden, 28 June 1968, MT CT Divn, 'Note of a Meeting…2nd July 1968', 5 July 1968, 'Joint Recommendations of British and French Officials on the Choice of a Private Group for the Financing and Construction of the Channel Tunnel', annotations on a draft of 28 June 1968, MT144/73; Barber-Scott-Malden, 4 July 1968, MT144/96, PRO.

113 Marsh-Stewart, 15 July 1968, MT144/73, PRO.

114 The Airbus project provided another distraction. Barber-Scott-Malden, 2 August and 27 September 1968, CT Project Team Minutes, 7 October 1968, MT144/90; Barber-J.H.P. Draper (U-Sec, Nationalised Transport, MT), 16 October 1968, MT144/73, PRO.

115 *Parl. Deb. (Commons)*, 5th ser. Vol. 769 (Session 1967–8), 28 July 1968, Marsh, *c.*569–70, reply to Joseph Hiley, MP *et al.*

116 Barber-Scott-Malden, 25 September 1968, Marsh-Stewart, 1 October 1968, MT144/73; Marsh-Jean Chamant (French Minister of Transport), 27 September 1968, MT144/74, 18 October 1968, MT144/73, PRO.

117 *Parl. Deb. (Commons)*, 5th ser. Vol. 770 (Session 1967–8), 23 October 1968, Marsh, Written Answer, *305*.
118 Barber-Harcourt, Colville and Fraser, 23 October 1968, enclosing MT CT Divn, 'Notes for the Guidance of Private Groups…', October 1968, MT144/73, PRO.
119 Barber-Scott-Malden, 25 September 1968, cit.
120 MT CT Divn, 'Notes for Guidance', October 1968, cit.
121 *Financial Times*, 24 October 1968, p. 18.
122 *Times*, 24 October 1968, p. 21, 15 November 1968, p. 29, 4 December 1968, p. 2. The newspaper had suggested earlier that the project was in doubt and that Britain had withdrawn: 8 January 1968, p. 2; 15 January 1968, p. 1. See also *Railway Gazette*, 1 November 1968, pp. 781–2.
123 *Parl. Deb. (Commons)*, 5th ser. Vol. 787 (Session 1968–9), 25 July 1969, William Deedes (Ashford), Albert Costain (Folkestone & Hythe, Chairman, Richard Costain, 1966–9), David Crouch (Canterbury), *c.*2282–93.
124 MT CTA Divn, draft paper on 'Channel Tunnel. Finance: Past History and Present Problems, December 1969', MT149/89, PRO.
125 In October 1969 Marsh was replaced by Fred Mulley, but without Cabinet status; Chamant was succeeded by Raymond Mondon in June 1969, when Pompidou succeeded de Gaulle as President and Chabon-Delmas succeeded Couve de Murville as Prime Minister.
126 Cf. MT CTG, Note on 'Losses and Gains of the Proposed Solution for a Private Body to Design and Construct the Tunnel and a Public Body to operate it…', 18 February 1966, T319/434; Barber-D.L. Smithers (Treasury Solicitor, MT branch), 12 June 1967, MT144/84, PRO.
127 Harcourt (CTSG)-Minister of Transport, 14 July 1967, Barber-Harcourt, 24 August 1967, CTSG-Barber and Rapporteur Générale du Groupe du Travail Interministériel, 17 October 1967, MT144/84, PRO.
128 CTSG-Barber, 4 November 1968, Dallas Bernard (CTSG)-Barber, 12 November 1968, with enclosures, MT144/85, PRO.
129 MT CT Divn, paper on 'Channel Tunnel: Compensation to CTSG', 16 January 1969, 'Note of a meeting [Barber, Macé, Harcourt, Alfred Davidson, etc.]….5 January 1969', 22 January 1969, Peter Dixon (Treasury)-Barber, 16 January, and reply, 23 January 1969, MT144/85, PRO.
130 The CTSG were to receive £2.5 m. in stages during the construction period, and £0.5 m. in free shares. See Alfred Davidson, Memo. 2 April 1969, TSI archive, carton #13, f64, HBS; Alfred Davidson-Frank Davidson, 16 September 1969, ibid. f63; Barber-Draper, 16 May and 29 July 1969, Marsh-John Diamond (Treasury Chief Secretary), 31 July 1969, Scott-Malden-Harcourt, 11 August 1969 and reply, 15 September 1969, MT144/135; MT CT Project Team, Minutes, 5 November 1969, MT144/90, PRO. The final agreement was not signed until September 1971 (see Chapter 4).
131 Barber-Draper, 13 October 1969, MT144/96, PRO. On Chesapeake Bay see TSI archive, Vol. 85, HBS and www.cbbt.com.
132 Cf. Barker-Draper, 13 October 1969, MT144/96, PRO; Jean-Jacques Servan-Schreiber, *Le défi américain* (Paris, 1967).
133 Draft letter from Scott-Malden to Hunt, n.d. [June 1967], MT144/84, PRO.
134 Cf. criticisms of Morgan Grenfell in Anon., Note, 10 May 1968, Baring Brothers file, 206740, Baring Archive, ING; Coates, 'Note of a Meeting with Mr. Bernard of the CTSG [2 January 1969]', 3 January 1969, MT144/85, PRO.
135 MT CT Divn, draft paper on 'Channel Tunnel: Structure of the Operating Body', 30 May 1967, Barber-CT Project Team, 7 February 1969, enclosing draft 'Notes on the Structure of the Operating Authority', February 1969, MT144/90, PRO.
136 MT CTA Divn, 'Note of meeting…on 12th March 1969', 2 April 1969, MT144/132; MT CTA Divn, paper on 'Channel Tunnel Planning Council: Functions and

Structure', 10 April 1969, MT144/153; 'Note of the Secretary's [Serpell] Meeting with Sir Eugene Melville on Monday, 18 August 1969', Scott-Malden-Sir Eugene Melville, 6 January 1970, MT144/131, PRO.

137 E.J.D. Pearson (CTA/E Divn, MT), Loose Minute on 'Transport Services Vote – Outturn 1969/70', 11 December 1969, MT144/132, PRO.

138 Robert Long (Chief Commercial Manager, BRB)-Tom Beagley (Asst Sec, MT), 11 May 1966, enclosing BRB, Memo. on 'Channel Tunnel Organisation', May 1966, MT124/966, PRO; Joint Report, 1966, p. 25.

139 MT CT Divn, 'Note of meeting with representatives of the British Railways Board... 15th December 1967', 29 December 1967, MT144/119, PRO.

140 Baker-Scott-Malden, 9 September 1966, MT144/189, PRO.

141 Castle-Stanley Raymond (Chairman, BRB), 16 September 1966, BRB 196-4-1 Pt. 6; Raymond-Castle, 29 September 1966, and Barber, Note on 'Mr. Raymond's Letter', 3 October 1966, MT144/189, PRO.

142 MT's Office, 'Note of a Meeting held at the Grand Hotel, Brighton... 4th October 1966...', 6 October 1966, paras 23–5, John Morris (Joint Parl. Sec, MT)-Raymond, 24 October 1966, MT144/189, PRO.

143 Raymond-Castle, 11 November 1966, MT144/189; BRB Minutes, 8 December 1966, AN167/3, PRO. Robert Long, the Chief Commercial Manager, had handled Tunnel matters prior to this. On Bonavia's recollection of his appointment see his *Channel Tunnel Story*, p. 92. Raymond's difficult relationship with Castle culminated in his enforced resignation in October 1968: Gourvish, *British Railways*, pp. 358–60.

144 Ratter and Shirley (BRB), Memo. on 'Channel Tunnel Organization', 20 July 1967, BRB Minutes, 7 August 1967, AN167/17, AN167/3; Barber-Bonavia, 9 August 1967, MT144/189, PRO; List of Railway Officials, November 1968, BRB 196-4-1 Pt. 6. Legrand was Directeur, Nord Region, Parès was Directeur de la Comptabilité Générale et des Finances. The committee was 12-strong (including executive members) by 1970: List of Railway Officials, BRB 196-4-100.

145 Interview with Lord Peyton, 25 April 2002.

146 David McKenna (GM, Southern Region, BRB)-Wansbrough-Jones, 18 February 1965, BRB 196-4-1 Pt. 4.

147 Ratter-Raymond, 18 October 1966, BRB 196-4-1 Pt. 6.

148 Bonavia, *Channel Tunnel Story*, p. 92; MT CT Divn, paper on 'Channel Tunnel: Compensation to CTSG', 16 January 1969, cit., Appendix C; BRB Personnel files.

149 Baker, Note, 6 June 1966, MT144/189; P.R. Sheaf (Asst Sec, MT), 25 September 1969, MT149/89, PRO. Sheaf, annoyed by BRB's response to a request for a study of the costs involved in extending the continental (Berne) gauge to London, suggested that 'if the Railways get too difficult, we can always investigate the possibility of arranging our legislation to allow SNCF to operate the services on this side of the Channel!'

150 BRB, *Report & Accounts, 1965–72*. The first cross-channel service by hovercraft was in August 1968. Three BRB car ferries were introduced in 1965–9, and three more ordered in 1970 at a cost of £12 m. BRB Works & Equipment Committee Minutes, 20 February 1967, BRB; Investment Committee Minutes, 13 October 1970, AN109/297, PRO; Brian Haresnape, *Sealink* (Shepperton, 1982), pp. 88–9.

151 'Note of a meeting with representatives of the British Railways Board... 14th April 1969...', n.d., MT144/189, PRO. In the event, gloomy forecasts about the collapse of shipping services have proved to be wide of the mark.

152 Raymond-Castle, 29 September 1966, and Barber, Note, cit.

153 Baker, File note, 8 June 1966, reporting Long, MT144/189, PRO; BRB Works & Equipment Committee Minutes, 20 February 1967, cit.; BRB, *R & A 1968*, p. 21; Haresnape, *Sealink*, p. 89.

154 Under the 1968 Transport Act Freightliners Ltd passed to the National Freight Corporation, with BRB retaining a 49% stake.

155 BRB Press Release, 18 May 1966, copy in FO371/187406, PRO and cf. Jan Posner (Manager, International Container Services, BRB), reported in *Times*, 30 November 1966. About £9 m. was invested in Harwich containerisation (including two container ships) for services introduced in 1968. BRB Works & Equipment Committee Minutes, 17 May 1966, 7 February 1967, BRB; BRB, *R & A 1968*, pp. 22–3.
156 Gourvish, *British Railways*, pp. 397, 401–7, 493–6.
157 BRB, Report to Joint Steering Group on 'The Impact of the Channel Tunnel on British Railways', 16 November 1966, Labour Party Research Department, paper on 'The Channel Tunnel: Problems facing Anglo-continental Rail transport', n.d. [*c.*Jan. 1967], Baker, 'Note of a Meeting...4th January 1967...', 13 January 1967, MT144/189; K.F. Glover (Chief Statistician, MT)-Barber, 27 February 1969, Edward Kafka (MT)-Glover, March 1969, MT144/143, PRO.
158 Joint Report, August 1966, Tables 9.1–2, Raymond-Castle, 29 September 1966, BRB, Report, 16 November 1966, cit.; Long-Leonard Mills (U-Sec, MT), 5 September 1966, enclosing paper on 'Implications of the Channel Tunnel', September 1966, 'Note of the Minister [Richard Marsh]'s Meeting with Mr. Ratter on 7th November, 1968', n.d., MT144/189; Ratter, Memo. on 'The Channel Tunnel and British Railways', November 1968, BRB Minutes, 12 December 1968, AN167/19, AN167/4, PRO.
159 Beagley-Long, 20 April, and reply, 9 May 1966, MT144/189, PRO; BRB, Report on 'The Impact of the Channel Tunnel on British Railways', 16 November 1966, cit.
160 Beagley-W.A. Wood (MHLG), 7 June 1966, 'Note of a meeting held on 29th July 1966...[MT, BRB, Kent Co Co]', 15 August 1966, MT144/119; 'Note of a Meeting...on 2nd November, 1966' [MT, BRB], December 1966, MT, Note of a Meeting...on 16th February 1967...', 17 February 1967, MT144/189, PRO.
161 Bonavia-Barber, 22 December 1966, MT144/189, PRO.
162 Coates, Note for File, 3 May 1967, MT144/189, PRO. Delay was also encouraged by doubts (before the 1968 Transport Act) as to whether MT had powers to acquire land for tunnel purposes. Cf. Coates-Bonavia, 4 July 1967, MT144/119, PRO.
163 'Note of a meeting...[MT, BRB]...15th December 1967', MT144/119; MT CT Divn, 'Channel Tunnel British Terminals Working Party Interim Report', 11 April 1968, paras 1.5–6, MT144/120, PRO. Constant's appointment at the MT was matched by BRB in appointing James Manson as its tunnel engineer [Planning Officer (Channel Tunnel)] in November 1967.
164 Channel Tunnel British Terminals Working Party Interim Report, April 1968, cit. paras 7.1–10.
165 See BoT and MHLG, *The Third London Airport*, May 1967, P.P.1966–7, lix, Cmnd. 3259; Colin Buchanan, *No Way to the Airport: The Stansted Controversy* (Harlow, 1981), pp. 33–9; *Times*, 12–25 May 1967, *passim*.
166 Scott-Malden-Idwal Pugh (Dep Sec, MHLG), 24 July, and reply, 22 August 1968, MT CTE Divn, 'Note of a Meeting...on 26th August 1968', 27 August 1968, Scott-Malden, Minute, 12 September 1968, MT144/120, PRO.
167 Marsh, Memo. on 'Procedure for deciding on site of Channel Tunnel terminal facilities', EP (68) 39, 17 September 1968, CAB134/2766, Cabinet Ministerial Committee on Environmental Planning Minutes, EP(68) 10th, 19 September 1968, CAB134/2765, PRO.
168 Kent County Council, *The Channel Tunnel. A Discussion of Terminal Requirements on the British side and of possible locations for terminal facilities in Kent* (December 1968), copy in MT114/119, PRO.
169 Kent County Council Planning Committee, quarterly report, 19 February 1969, extract in MT144/143; MT CT Divns, Paper on 'Choice of Channel Tunnel Terminal Sites', May 1969, MT144/144, PRO.
170 British Railways' preference had been for Stanford. MT CT Divns, Paper, May 1969, cit. but see draft version, MT144/143; Draper-Constant, 13 May 1969, Brig. John

Constant (Asst Chief Engineer, MT)-P. Critchley (Asst Sec, MHLG), 22 May 1969, MT144/143; Marsh, Memo. to Ministerial Committee on Environmental Planning on 'Sites for the British Terminals of the Channel Tunnel', EP(69) 22, 9 July 1969, CAB134/2770, PRO; *Parl. Deb. (Commons)*, Vol. 787 (Session 1968–9), 22 July 1969, Marsh, written answer to Albert Costain, *353*, and MT Press Notice, 22 July 1969, MT144/145; BRB Channel Tunnel Division, Memo. on 'Channel Tunnel: Freight Yard Sites', 7 April 1970, MT144/146, PRO.

171 SoS for Industry, Trade and Regional Development, Minister of Housing and Local Government, and Minister for Welsh Affairs, White Paper on *South East England*, March 1964, P.P.1963–4, xxvi, Cmnd. 2308, para. 23; J.B. Cullingworth, *Environmental Planning 1939–1969. Vol. III: New Towns Policy* (1979), pp. 196–206, *Vol. IV: Land Values, Compensation and Betterment* (1980), pp. 239–51.

172 Official Committee on Environmental Planning Minutes, EPO (67) 13th, 26 July 1967, CAB134/2774; DEA and Official Committee on Environmental Planning, Working Group on the Channel Tunnel Report, 19 May 1967, paras 32–8, and Beagley (Asst U-Sec, DEA)-A.W. Peterson (Dep U-Sec, DEA) and J.C. Burgh (PS to SoS, DEA), 2 October 1967, enclosing draft note, n.d., EW25/370; Ministerial Committee on Environmental Planning Minutes, EP (67) 13th, 13 November 1967, CAB134/2762; Peter Shore (SoS for Economic Affairs)-Wilson, 24 November 1967, PREM13/2429, PRO.

173 MHLG, Press Notice, 26 March 1968, MT144/119, PRO, and see Cullingworth, *Environmental Planning. III*, pp. 246–52.

174 *Parl. Deb.* (*Commons*), 5th ser. Vol. 765 (Session 1967–8), 20 May 1968, Costain, Deedes and Crouch, *c.*193–8.

175 *Parl. Deb.* (*Commons*), 5th ser. Vol. 787 (Session 1968–9), 25 July 1969, Deedes, *c.*2282, Costain, *c.*2288. Later in 1969 Costain attempted to introduce a private member's motion on planning blight, and in February 1970 tried to get the 'area of interest map' published. See briefing papers, November 1969–February 1970, in MT144/147, PRO, and Costain's questions in *Parl. Deb. (Commons)*, 5th ser. Vol. 791 (Session 1969–70), 11 November 1969, c.163, and Vol. 796 (Session 1969–70), 24 February 1970, *269*.

176 Constant-Clerk, Kent Co. Co., 13 November 1969, Kent Co. Co., Press Notice, 19 December 1969, MT144/147, PRO.

177 Bonavia, *Channel Tunnel Story*, p. 86; Hunt, *Tunnel*, p. 118.

178 Padmore, Minute, 13 April 1967, MT144/58, and cf. his earlier opinion, reported in Brown-Garvey, 27 October 1966, FO371/187409, PRO.

179 Bonavia, *Channel Tunnel Story*, p. 86.

4 THE HEATH GOVERNMENT AND THE TUNNEL: REACHING AGREEMENT, 1970–2

1 1966: Con 253, Lab 363, Others 14; 1970: Con 330, Lab 287, Others 13. David and Gareth Butler, *Twentieth-Century British Political Facts 1900–2000* (Basingstoke, 2000), p. 237; Nick Tiratsoo, 'Labour and its critics: the case of the May Day Manifesto Group', in Coopey *et al.*, *Wilson Governments*, pp. 163, 168. On election tactics and experiences see David Butler and Michael Pinto-Duschinsky, *The British General Election of 1970* (1971), pp. 134–6, 166, 187; Wilson, *Labour Government 1964–70*, p. 774ff.; William Whitelaw, *The Whitelaw Memoirs* (1989), pp. 70–1; Heath, *The Course of My Life: My Autobiography* (1998), pp. 304–5.

2 F.W.S. Craig (ed.), *British General Election Manifestos 1959–1987* (Aldershot, 1990), pp. 112–59.

3 His autobiography contains two sentences on the Channel Tunnel (relating to the signing of the Treaty and the CT Bill): Heath, *Course of My Life*, p. 459. Wilson's had none.

4 Prime Minister and Minister for the Civil Service, *The Reorganisation of Central Government*, October 1970, P.P.1970–1, xx, Cmnd. 4506; Heath, *Course of my Life*, pp. 314–17; Hennessy, *Whitehall*, pp. 209–10, 220–3 and ff.; Kevin Theakston, *The Civil Service since 1945* (Oxford, 1995), pp. 111–12; Tessa Blackstone and William Plowden, *Inside the Think Tank: Advising the Cabinet 1971–1983* (1988), pp. 6–10.

5 The Channel Tunnel Divisions themselves remained intact. Constant-Manson, 17 November 1970, BRB CT file, CT120. On Walker's approach cf. Peter Walker, *Staying Power: An Autobiography* (1991), pp. 74–7.

6 Kevin Theakston, *Civil Service*, pp. 108–9; James Radcliffe, *The Reorganisation of British Central Government* (Aldershot, 1991), p. 80ff; Butler and Butler, *Political Facts 1900–2000*, pp. 34–5; John Peyton, *Without Benefit of Laundry* (1997), pp. 137–8, 143.

7 Cf. Robert Armstrong (Heath's PPS)- J.R. Coates (Peyton's PPS), 12 December 1970, in Prime Minister [Heath]'s papers on 'Transport: Channel Tunnel', Pt. 1, PREM15/1524, PRO; Heath, *Course of my Life*, pp. 354–63.

8 Dallas Bernard (Morgan Grenfell), Note, 17 September 1969, Baring Brothers file, 207258, Baring Archive, ING.

9 MT CTA Divn, 'Financing Proposals – Note for the Record', 10 November 1969, 'Note of Meeting held in the Treasury 25 November 1969', 28 November 1969, John Barber (MT), File note, 3 December 1969, T319/1135, PRO.

10 Barber-Draper, 8 December 1969, T319/1135; 'Points for discussion at the meeting of British and French Ministers of Transport at Paris on 17th December, 1969', n.d.; Barber-Sheaf *et al.*, 14 January 1970, enclosing draft note on 'Channel Tunnel: Remuneration of Private Interests', 12 January 1970; Barber-Draper *et al.*, 10 February 1970, enclosing draft submission to Minister on 'Channel Tunnel Finance Negotiations', 9 February 1970, MT144/157, PRO.

11 Pearson, 'Channel Tunnel Finance – Note for the Record', 11 March 1970, MT144/158, PRO.

12 It was envisaged that founders' shares (not remunerated during construction) would be exchanged for ordinary shares (paid 6% p.a. during construction) at a preferential or 'bonus' rate. The size of the 'multiplier' or conversion rate was the source of considerable debate. The group suggested 4.59, then 3.3, and numerous figures were discussed until agreement was reached at 2.8, a rate endorsed as more than reasonable by both the Bank of England and the MT's consultants, Hambros, and supported by the then Treasury Minister of State, William Rodgers. See Barber-Sheaf *et al.*, 15 December 1969, MT CTA Divn, 'Channel Tunnel – Finance Negotiations with the CTSG and the Hill Samuel Group – Note for the Record', 27 January 1970, MT144/157; Barber-Draper *et al.*, 10 February 1970, cit.; MT CTA Divn, 'Note of a Meeting with the Private Interests in Paris on 24th March 1970', April 1970, MT144/158; D.J.L. Moore (Treasury)-G.S. Downey (Treasury) *et al.*, 25 February 1970 and Downey, Minute, 26 February 1970, T319/1136, PRO.

13 Cf. Barber-Sheaf *et al.*, 19 January 1970, enclosing translation of letter from R. Macé to Barber, 15 January 1970, MT144/157; Barber-Draper *et al.*, 23 January 1970, enclosing translation of letter from R. Macé to Barber, 20 January 1970, T319/1135; MT, 'Note of a Meeting at the Ministry of Transport, London on 28th January 1970', 5 February 1970, MT144/157, PRO.

14 Barber, 'Note of discussion on Channel Tunnel finance', 5 February 1970, MT144/157, PRO.

15 Bernard Kelly (S.G. Warburg & Co.)-Barber, 13 April 1970, MT144/158, PRO.

16 Peter Kemp (CTA Divn, MT)-Sheaf *et al.*, 21 May 1970, Kemp, 'Note for the file', 27 May 1970, MT Project Team Finance Sub-group, 'Note of Meeting held on 28 May 1970 at Church House', n.d., MT144/158, PRO.

17 *Parl. Deb. (Commons)*, 5th ser. (Session 1969–70), Vol. 793, 9 December 1969, Frederick Mulley (Minister of Transport), oral answers to Michael Clark Hutchison (Edinburgh South), Albert Costain (Folkestone & Hythe) and Michael Heseltine (Tavistock), *c.*211–12; Vol. 594, 27 January 1970, Albert Murray (Parl. Sec, MT), oral answers to Robert Sheldon (Ashton-under Lyne) and Heseltine, *c.*1180–1; Vol. 796, 24 February 1970, Murray, oral answers to Heseltine, Arthur Dodds-Parker (Cheltenham), Geoffrey Wilson (Truro) and Lance Mallalieu (Brigg), *c.*957–8; Vol. 798, 24 March 1970, Mulley, written answer to Sheldon, *322–3*.

18 Cf. Barber-Draper, 8 June 1970, MT144/158; meetings held at St Christopher House, 11 and 17 June 1970, MT144/222 and T319/1136, PRO.

19 Kemp-Scott-Malden *et al.*, 3 July 1970, MT144/222 and T319/1137, PRO.

20 See John Peyton (Minister of Transport)-Maurice Macmillan (Treasury Chief Secretary), 10 July 1970, Prime Minister's Channel Tunnel papers, cit. Pt. 1. The only member of the original Hill Samuel group to drop out was the Midland Bank: John Colville (Exec. Dir., Hill Samuel)-Barber, 24 July 1970, MT144/222, PRO.

21 Lord Harcourt-J. Barber (MT), 15 July 1970, enclosing letter to Minister of Transport, n.d., MT144/159, PRO. A copy of the French version, Général Philippe Maurin-Roger Macé, 15 July 1970, is also on file.

22 'Note of meeting held on 7 July 1970 at St Christopher House', n.d., MT144/159, PRO.

23 *Parl. Deb. (Commons)*, 5th ser. Vol. 803 (Session 1970–1), 15 July 1970, Peyton, oral answers to Sheldon, and Costain (PPS, Duchy of Lancaster), *c.*1503–4; and see MT Press Notice, 15 July 1970, MT144/159, PRO. Press reaction was muted, since the Tunnel was overshadowed by the threat of a dock strike: *Financial Times*, 16 July 1970, p. 29.

24 Coates, Note, 3 January 1969, MT CT Divn, 'Channel Tunnel: Compensation to CTSG', 16 January 1969, MT144/85, PRO; Interview with Sir Peter Kemp, 15 October 2002.

25 Provision was also made to compensate the Group for expenses incurred [up to £50,000] if the governments chose to abandon the project before signing the Preliminary Agreement.

26 If the amount raised in equity failed to reach 15%, the governments were asked to meet the shortfall. A return of 6% during the construction period was suggested.

27 With the return increasing thereafter by 2–3% p.a. in real terms. The yield was to be equivalent to a discounted return of 8.9–9.5% over 50 years.

28 Proposals submitted with Harcourt-Barber, 15 July 1970, cit.

29 'Channel Tunnel Joint Co-ordinating Committee. Note of meeting held in Paris on 30 July 1970', Scott-Malden-Coates [a brief for Peyton], 4 August 1970, MT144/159, 'Note of Meeting in Paris September 14/15 1970', MT144/160, PRO and see also *Financial Times*, 16 July 1970, p. 29. Scott-Malden advised Peyton to read 'the excellent Anglo-French report published in 1963 (Cmnd. 2137)', but made no mention of the document of 1966.

30 Colville-Sir Alec Douglas-Home (SoS for Foreign and Commonwealth Affairs), 13 July 1970, Kemp-Scott-Malden and Draper, enclosing Gillian Brown (Marine & Transport Dept, FCO), note, 7 August 1970, MT144/159, PRO.

31 Colville and Harcourt suggested that 'he appeared to have doubts about the tunnel when he first took office; they thought his views had now changed': Brown, note, cit.

32 Coates-Scott-Malden, 14 September 1970, Scott-Malden-Draper, 15 September 1970, 'Note of Meeting held at St Christopher House on 17 September 1970', n.d., MT144/160, PRO. The French report had been produced by SETEC in 1969 (see below). Cf. *Economist*, October 1970, p. 80.

33 These involved a request for more precise abandonment terms, the inclusion of an exchange of assurances between the two governments, negotiation of the basis for rewarding ordinary shareholders, and an increase (if possible) in the size of the equity component.

34 Peyton (Minister for Transport Industries)-Anthony Barber (Chancellor of Exchequer), 26 October 1970, copy in PREM15/1524, PRO; 'Channel Tunnel: Draft Paper from the Minister to his colleagues', 15 October 1970, MT144/161, PRO.

35 Sir Val Duncan (RTZ)-Lord Gladwyn, 15 August 1969, and see also Bernard Kelly (Warburg)-Duncan, 14 August 1969, BOW756 (80/1.25.5 File 1), Rio Tinto plc archives, London (henceforth RT). 'Rollercoaster' appears in Allen Sykes (RTZ)-Duncan, 27 February 1970, ibid.

36 MT CTE Divn, 'Note of a Meeting…on 19th August, 1970 between Mr A Frame of Rio Tinto Zinc and CTE Division', 20 August 1970, MT144/160, PRO; Alistair Frame (RTZ)-Duncan Dewdney (Exec. Dir., RTZ), 9 October ['from a cautious start, I have become a great enthusiast for this project'] and 17 October 1969, BOW 756 (80/1.25.5 File 1), RT. On Frame see *Oxford DNB*.

37 Jehanne Wake, *Kleinwort Benson: the history of two families in banking* (Oxford 1997), pp. 367, 390; Terry Gourvish, ' "Beyond the merger mania": merger and de-merger activity', in Richard Coopey and Nicholas Woodward (eds.), *Britain in the 1970s: The Troubled Economy* (1996), pp. 236–40; Charles Harvey, *The Rio Tinto Company. An Economic History of a Leading International Mining Concern 1873–1954* (Penzance, 1981), pp. 305–10 and idem., 'RTZ Corporation PLC', *International Directory of Company Histories*, IV (Chicago, 1991), pp. 191–2; Bonavia, *Channel Tunnel Story*, pp. 100–1; Hunt, *Tunnel*, p. 122.

38 Duncan-Harcourt, 13 October 1969, BOW756 (80/1.25.5 File 1), RT; Fetherston, *Chunnel*, pp. 75–6. The concern to ensure good project management was reinforced by the knowledge that the Mont Blanc Tunnel, which lacked such expertise, had cost six times the estimate. Kemp, Note, 7 August 1970, cit.

39 Serpell-Scott-Malden, 22 December 1970, MT144/225, PRO; Margaret Elliott-Binns (Treasury)-John F. Slater (Asst. Sec, Treasury) and Peter Lazarus (U-Sec, Treasury), 28 September 1972, Treasury file 2PE 91/199/01 Pt. P; John Rosenfeld (Principal Finance Officer, Treasury)-Sir Idwal Pugh (2nd Permanent Sec, DOE), 12 December 1972, MT144/483, PRO; Interview with Sir Alastair Frame, 24 March 1982, RT; Constant, 'Feasibility Study', p. 17.

40 Constant (MT)-Sykes, 31 July 1970, Sykes-Duncan, 11 August 1970, BOW756 (80/1.25.5 File 1), RT; Scott-Malden-Coates, 2 September 1970, MT144/160, PRO; Constant, 'Feasibility Study', p. 15; www.ieee.ca/millennium/churchill.

41 RTZ, 'Rollercoaster. Record of a meeting held at RTZ on the 19th August 1970', BOW756 (80/1.25.5 File 1), RT; Kemp, Note, 7 August, cit.; John Barber (MT)-Scott-Malden, 21 August 1970, MT144/160, PRO.

42 RTZDE Board Minutes, 5 October 1970, 20 April 1971, RTZDE Report & Accounts, 1970–1, in SRR925, RT; *Daily Telegraph*, 6 October 1970, p. 18; *Times*, 18 February 1971, p. 19.

43 Barber-Scott-Malden, 18 September 1970, MT144/160, PRO.

44 'Note of a Meeting held on 6 October 1970 at St Christopher House', n.d., Kemp, Note for File, 12 October 1970, Note for File (meeting, 14 October 1970), n.d., Barber-Coates, 11 November, enclosing draft 'Note of meeting held at St. Christopher House on 16th October, 1970', MT144/161, PRO.

45 RTZ, 'Rollercoaster: the Presentation [*sic*] Situation', 14 July 1970, BOW756 (80/1.25.5 File 1), RT.

46 RTZ, 'Rollercoaster, Record of a meeting…', 19 August 1970, cit.

47 'Final draft memorandum to the Minister of Transport from Rio Tinto-Zinc Ltd., 16th October, 1970', n.d., MT144/161, PRO.
48 Cf. Peter W.G. Morris and George H. Hough, *The Anatomy of Major Projects. A Study of the Reality of Project Management* (Chichester, 1987), p. 25.
49 See Dewdney, Memo. 30 July 1970, RTZDE Board Minutes, CAR128, RT; Scott-Malden, Note for the Record, 9 October 1970, Barber, 'Discussion with M. Mace- Paris – 13th October, 1970', 27 October 1970, MT144/161, PRO.
50 Douglas-Home, annotation on J.A.N. Graham (Douglas-Home's PS)-Douglas-Home, 4 November 1970, Douglas-Home-Peyton, 9 November 1970, FCO76/191, PRO.
51 Maurice Macmillan (Chief Secretary, Treasury)-Peyton, 12 November 1970, FCO76/191, and see also Macmillan, Minute, 13 July 1970, T319/1137 and D.J.L. Moore (Treasury)-Lazarus, T319/1138, PRO.
52 M.W. Townley (William Whitelaw's PS)-J.B. Unwin (Maurice Macmillan's PS), 14 July 1970, T319/1137 and PREM15/1524; P.L.P. Davies (Whitelaw's PS)-D. Holmes (Peyton's PS), 29 October 1970, FCO76/191; Whitelaw-Peyton, 11 March 1971, MT144/166, PRO; Whitelaw, *Memoirs*, p. 74.
53 Peyton-Whitelaw, 9 November 1970, and reply, 11 November 1970, FCO76/191, PRO.
54 MT CTA Divn, 'Note of a meeting held at the Department of the Environment on 2nd December, 1970', December 1970, 'Secretary of State's Notes on Channel Tunnel', n.d., MT144/223; DOE CTA Divn, 'Note for the file', 8 December 1970, MT144/224; Harry Dudgeon (Head of Marine & Transport Dept., FCO)-J.K. Drinkall (Head of Western European Dept, FCO), 24 November 1970, Dudgeon-Ken Gallagher (Superintending U-Sec, FCO), 8 and 11 December 1970, Peyton-Douglas-Home, 10 December 1970, FCO76/191, PRO; Interview with Kemp, 2002.
55 Moore-Lazarus, 16 October 1970, cit.; Peyton-Douglas-Home, 10 December 1970, cit.; Christopher Soames (British Ambassador, Paris), Paris telegram No. 1248, 9 December 1970, FCO76/191; 'Tunnel sous la manche: signature probable de la convention en 1971' and 'L'Angleterre ne sera-t-elle plus une île?', *Le Figaro*, 10 December 1970, cutting in MT144/164, PRO.
56 Douglas-Home-Peyton, 14 December 1970, Douglas-Home-Soames, telegram No. 696, 14 December 1970, Soames-Douglas-Home, telegram no. 1265, 14 December 1970, FCO76/191; Coates, 'Note of the Minister's discussion with the British Ambassador in Paris on Wednesday 16th December 1970', 18 December 1970, FCO76/192, PRO.
57 Armstrong-Heath, 11 December 1970, and Armstrong's annotation, same day; Armstrong-Coates, 12 December 1970, PREM15/1524; Dudgeon-Gallagher, 17 December 1970, FCO76/192, PRO.
58 SETEC-Economie, 'Tunnel sous la Manche. Mise a Jour des études de trafic et de Rentabilité', 4 vols, Corbevoie, 1969, MT149/89 and MT179/58–61, PRO.
59 Peter Walker (SoS for the Environment), Memo. to Cabinet EPC on 'Cross-Channel Traffic and the place of a Channel Tunnel', EPC(70)67, 16 December 1970, CAB134/2789, PRO.
60 Cabinet EPC Minutes, EPC(70) 22nd, 21 December 1970, CAB134/2788, PRO.
61 Trend-Heath, 1 January 1971, PREM15/1524, PRO. The evidence suggests that Heath was irritated by Trend's 'measured' approach: cf. Hennessy, *Whitehall*, pp. 237–8.
62 Trend's words, Trend-Heath, 1 January 1971, cit.; Walker, Memo. on 'Channel Tunnel', CP(70)123, 31 December 1970, CAB129/154, Cabinet Conclusions, CM(71) 1st, 5 January 1971, CAB128/49; Moore-Lazarus, 31 December 1970, T319/1299, PRO.
63 John Barber (DOE), Memo. to Ministers's PSs, 1 January 1971, Peyton-Soames, 8 January 1971, Barber-Coates, 8 January 1971, MT144/164; Peyton-Rippon, 6 January 1971, FCO76/377, PRO.

64 Coates-Barber, 18 January 1971, Baron G. de Courcel (French Ambassador, London)-Peyton, 20 January 1971, enclosing translation of letter from Jean Chamant (French Minister of Transport), 19 January 1971, Peyton-Chamant, 22 January 1971, Coates-J.P.G. Rowcliffe (Peter Walker's PS), 25 January 1971, MT144/164; Coates, 'Note of the Minister for Transport Industries meeting with the French Minister of Transport on Friday, 22nd January, 1971', February 1971, Peyton-Harcourt, 27 January 1971, DOE Press Notice, 27 January 1971, MT144/165; Cabinet EPC Minutes, EPC(71) 3rd, 25 January 1971, CAB134/3377, PRO; *Parl. Deb. (Commons)*, 5th ser. (Session 1970-1), Vol. 810, 27 January 1971, Peyton, oral answer to Sheldon, *c.*525–6.
65 Barber-Scott-Malden, 25 January 1971, MT144/164, Elliott-Binns, 'Note for the Record', 27 January 1971, T319/1299, PRO.
66 Soames, Paris telegram No. 100 and 103, 27 January 1971, Barber-Dudgeon, 28 January 1971, Dudgeon-Gallagher, 2 February 1971, Dudgeon-J.R.A. Bottomley (Superintending U-Sec, FCO), 22 February 1971, and other papers in FCO76/377, PRO. There were similar problems in 1966 (See p. 62, above).
67 Harcourt-Peyton, 23 December 1970 and 29 January 1971, MT144/164–5; 'Note of a Meeting held in the Minister's room at the House of Commons on 27th January, 1971', February 1971, Coates, 'Note of the Minister's discussion with Lord Harcourt on Thursday 28th January 1971', 1 February 1971, Peyton-Harcourt, 1 February 1971, 'Note of a Meeting held on 4 February 1971 at St Christopher House', n.d., MT144/165, PRO.
68 Barber, 'Channel Tunnel – State of Play', 4 February 1971, MT144/165, PRO; Sykes (MD, RTZDE), Memo. on 'Rollercoaster: The Apparently Intransigent Attitude of the French Banks – pm. 3rd March 1971', 4 March 1971, BOW756 (80/1.25.5 File 2), RT.
69 Peyton-Walker, 15 February 1971, and see also Barber-Scott-Malden, 15 February 1971, with notes, and 'Note of the Minister's meeting with representatives of the British Banking Group on Tuesday, 16th February, 1971', 26 February 1971, MT144/165, PRO; Dewdney, ' "Rollercoaster". Conversation between D.A.C. Dewdney and General Maurin in London', 10 February 1971, BOW756 (80/1.25.5 File 2), RT. On RTZ's behind-the-scenes involvement note the private meeting of Peyton and Duncan, 15 January 1971, referred to in Duncan-Peyton, 20 January 1971, ibid.
70 Barber-Scott-Malden and de Courcel-Peyton, both 18 February 1971, Peyton-Soames and Peyton-Chamant, both 19 February 1971, MT144/165, PRO.
71 Peyton-Tony Barber, 22 February 1971, and Elliott-Binns-G.S. Downey (Treasury) *et al.*, 25 February 1971, T319/1299; Soames-Peyton, 29 December 1970, FCO76/192, PRO.
72 Macmillan-Peyton, 26 February 1971, T319/1299, Unwin, 'Note of a meeting held at the Treasury at 6.30 p.m. on Monday 8 March 1971', 9 March 1971, MT144/166, PRO.
73 Peyton-Tony Barber, 9 March 1971, PREM15/1524, PRO.
74 Coates, 'Note of the Minister for Transport Industries meeting with Representatives of the British Banking Group on Monday 8th March 1971', 10 March 1971, MT144/166; P.L. Gregson (Heath's PS)-Heath, 10 March 1971, with Heath's annotations, Gregson-Coates, 11 March 1971, Peyton-Heath, 11 March 1971, PREM15/1524, PRO.
75 Jellicoe-Peyton, Rippon-Tony Barber, Rippon-Heath, Gregson-Heath, all 12 March 1971, MT144/166 and PREM15/1524, PRO.
76 Peyton-Chamant, 15 March 1971, and cf. Brian Norbury (Trend's PS)-Gregson, and Gregson-Coates, both 15 March 1971, PREM15/1524, PRO.
77 DOE Press Notice, 23 March 1971, MT144/166, Peyton-Harcourt, 14 April 1971, with enclosures, MT144/167, PRO; *Parl. Deb. (Commons)*, 5th ser. (Session 1970–1), Vol. 814, 31 March 1971, Peyton, oral answer to Sheldon, *c.*1472–4; Hunt, *Tunnel*, p. 121.
78 The CTSU replaced the CTA (administration) and CTE (engineering) divisions.

79 Barber's role was taken on by Peter Kemp, who became an Asst Sec in the DOE, Press Notice, 25 March 1971, FCO76/385, Melville-Macé, 27 April 1971, FCO76/379, PRO; File on 'Operation Underground', Sir Eugene Melville Papers, Channel Tunnel Archive, University of Kent [Our thanks to Professor Roger Vickerman for permission to consult the archive]; Hunt, *Tunnel*, p. 121; Communication from Brig. Constant, 11 August 2002.
80 Cf. Peyton-Tony Barber, 30 March 1971, MT144/166, and Dudgeon-J.A. Turpin (Superintending U-Sec, FCO) and Crispin Tickell (Geoffrey Rippon's PS), 23 March 1971, FCO76/378, PRO.
81 Respectively, 5% and 1%. Dewdney-Duncan, 14 December 1970, Sykes and John Stanley (Planning Manager, RTZDE)-Turner, 3 June 1971, BOW756 (80/1.25.5 File 2), RT; Dewdney-Sir Eugene Melville (Special Adviser on Channel Tunnel Studies, DOE), 9 July 1971, enclosing 'Draft Paper for the RTZ Board', 1 July 1971, MT144/171, PRO.
82 MT144/167–74 and 298–9, and see also FCO76/379–81, PRO.
83 Cf. John Barber-Melville, 14 July 1971, Dudgeon-J.P. Cabouat (Ministère des Affaires Étrangères, Paris), 14 July 1971, Kemp, 'Note for the File', 12 August 1971, Kemp-Henry Woodhouse (Treasury Solicitor, DOE branch), 13 August 1971, Kemp-Macé, 27 August 1971, Kemp, 'Note for the Files', 6 September 1971, MT144/172; Kemp-Melville, 25 July 1971, MT144/298; Kemp-H.L. Smithers (Treasury Solicitor, DOE branch), 18 September 1971, MT144/173, PRO.
84 'Note on the Channel Tunnel', 26 May 1971, MT144/168; 'Draft Paper for the RTZ Board', 1 July 1971, cit.; Notes of meetings at Church House, 21–22 July 1971, Dewdney (MD, BCTC)-Melville, 23 July 1971, Melville-Scott-Malden, 23 July 1971, MT144/170; David Campbell (Marine & Transport Dept, FCO)-Dudgeon, 10 June 1971, FCO76/379, PRO. The cost of the additional work, referred to as 'overspill' [Melville], was initially put at £72,000; the BCTC offered to find £44,500, and the British Government agreed to contribute £27,500. It did not form part of the September 1971 agreement, and the sums were later scaled down to £68,000 (cost) and £23,500 (Government contribution). Melville-Dewdney, 8 September 1971, MT144/173, PRO; Kemp-Elliott-Binns, 22 June 1972, Treasury file 2PE 91/199/01 Pt. M, and reply, 29 June 1972, MT144/238, PRO.
85 Harcourt-Peyton, 22 September 1971, enclosing 'Heads of Terms for the Preliminary Agreement' and 'Terms of Transfer of Assets and Rights Owned by the Channel Tunnel Study Group', Chamant-Peyton, Peyton to Harcourt, Peyton-Chamant, all 22 September 1971, MT144/174, PRO; Soames, and Maurice Schumann (French Foreign Minister), *Exchange of Notes between the Government of the United Kingdom… and the Government of the French Republic concerning the Channel Tunnel Project. Paris, 22 September 1971*, November 1971, P.P.1971–2, xl, Cmnd. 4805.
86 Scott-Malden joined John Barber at Housing and Construction within the DOE. He was succeeded by Tom Beagley. *Civil Service List*, 1971–2.
87 Peyton, *Laundry*, pp. 149–50; Cabinet Secretary's Notebook, 5 January 1971, CO. The opposing ministers were Thatcher, Whitelaw, Reginald Maudling (Home Secretary) and Robert Carr (Employment).
88 Walker, *Staying Power*, p. 82; Interview with Sir Edward Heath, 2 October 2002.
89 Cf. Peyton-Whitelaw, 9 November 1970, cit.
90 On the 'artichoke' see Soames-Sir Denis Greenhill (Permanent U-Sec, FCO), 21 April 1971, PREM15/371, PRO.
91 A.H. Gray (Marine & Transport Dept., FCO)-E.J.D. Pearson (MT CTA Divn), 9 March 1970, FCO76/193, PRO. See also C.C. Wilcock (FCO)-E.G. White (FCO), 25 November 1970, FCO76/191, Campbell-Gallagher, 1 January 1971, FCO76/377, Sir William Nield (Permanent Sec, Cabinet)-Armstrong, 23 October

1970, PREM15/62, Francis Pym (Chief Whip)-Heath, 4 January 1971, PREM15/1524, PRO; *Times*, 11 February 1971, p. 13.

92 Rippon, annotation, 2 November 1970 on Dudgeon-Bottomley, 30 October 1970, FCO76/191, PRO. Cf. also Soames-Peyton, 29 December 1970, FCO76/192, PRO.

93 Lord Cromer (Barings)-Heath, 22 December 1970, PREM15/1524, PRO.

94 Peyton, *Laundry*, p. 150; Interview with Peyton, 25 April 2002.

95 Sykes-Dewdney, 5 September 1970, BOW756 (80/1.25.5 File 2), RTZ, and cf. Campbell-Dudgeon, 10 June 1971, cit.

96 The French underwriting contribution – £307,000 – took account of the work commissioned in 1968–9.

97 Harcourt-Peyton, 16 September 1971, enclosing 'Memorandum of Agreement' (first phase studies), Schedule 1; Melville-Coates, 20 September 1971, enclosing 'Summary of the Financing Proposals', n.d., MT144/174, PRO.

98 Melville-Elliott-Binns, 16 March 1972, Peyton-Barber, 21 March 1972, Elliott-Binns-Lazarus, 23 March 1972, Macmillan-Peyton, 24 March 1972, Peyton-Patrick Jenkin (Financial Secretary, Treasury), 18 April 1972, Treasury file 2PE 91/199/01 Pt. L.

99 See MT144/437–8, PRO, and DTp file FTS79/1/57, esp. Donald O'Connell (Asst Sec, DOE)-Geoffrey Wardale (U-Sec, DOE), 19 April 1972. Formal submissions from Harcourt and Maurin came in June: see Harcourt-Peyton, 9 June 1972, MT144/236, PRO.

100 Melville-Beagley, 5 May 1972, MT144/437, PRO; Pugh-Lord Rothschild (Director-General, CPRS), 24 August 1972, CPRS file Q9/2 Pt. 1.

101 Kemp-Len Creasy (Director of Civil Engineering Development, DOE) *et al.*, 20 April 1972; CTSU, 'Note of a meeting at Church House on 14 April 1972'; Kemp, 'Note of a meeting held at Church House 24 April 1972', 28 April 1972; Kemp-Creasy *et al.*, 1 May 1972, Treasury file 2PE 91/199/01 Pt. L.

102 Peyton-Barber, 8 May 1972, PREM15/1524; Campbell-T.W. Keeble (Head of United Nations (Economic & Social) Dept., FCO) and J.R.A. Bottomley (Superintending U-Sec, FCO), 31 May 1972, MT144/438, PRO. The figure of £366 m. was made public in Peyton's written answer to John Prescott on 19 July: *Parl. Deb. (Commons)*, 5th ser. (Session 1971–2), Vol. 841, 115.

103 Jenkin-Peyton, 22 May 1972, PREM15/1524, PRO.

104 Kemp-Creasy *et al.*, 30 June 1972, Treasury file 2PE 91/199/01 Pt. M; Walker, Memo. to Cabinet EPC on 'The Channel Tunnel', 19 July 1972, enclosing Peyton, Memo. and 'Channel Tunnel: Examination of the April 1972 Report', n.d., EPC(72)45, CAB134/3489, Cabinet EPC Minutes, EPC(72) 20th, 24 July 1972, CAB134/3487, PRO. The Tunnel memoranda were introduced by Walker in a covering memo., but it is clear that by this time Peyton enjoyed a semi-autonomous position vis-à-vis the project. Cf. Interview with Lord Armstrong, 25 July 2002.

105 'Examination of the April 1972 Report', cit., p. 3.

106 Lazarus-Elliott-Binns, 7 June 1972 and Elliott-Binns-Lazarus, 9 June 1972, Treasury file 2PE 91/199/01 Pt. M; Slater-Elliott-Binns, 5 July 1972; Douglas Henley (Dep Sec, Treasury), annotation [on Elliott-Binns-Slater and Lazarus, 21 July 1972], 21 July 1972, 2PE 91/199/01 Pt. N.

107 Slater-Elliott-Binns, 5 July 1972, Lazarus-Elliott-Binns, 7 June 1972, cit.; Elliott-Binns-Slater, 7 July 1972, Treasury file 2PE 91/199/01 Pt. N.

108 CTSU, 'Second Meeting of Working Group on 1972 Studies Report held at Church House on 1 May 1972', 23 May 1972, and cf. Slater-Lazarus, 5 May 1972, Treasury file 2PE 91/199/01 Pts. L and M. The divergence between RTZ and SITUMER had become evident at an early stage. Cf. Barber-Scott-Malden, 12 January 19761, MT144/164, PRO.

109 'Meeting of Working Group on the 1972 Studies Report held at Church House on 6 June 1972', n.d., MT144/438; Cabinet EPC Minutes, EPC(72) 18th and 21st, 17 and 27 July 1972, CAB134/3487, PRO; Monopolies Commission, *Cross-Channel Car Ferry Services: a Report on the supply of certain Cross-Channel Car Ferry Services*, 15 October 1973, published 10 April 1974, P.P.1974, viii.
110 H.N. Sporborg (Hambros Bank)-Melville, 8 May 1972, MT144/235, PRO; Slater-Lazarus *et al.*, 10 May 1972, Brendon Sewill (Special Asst., Treasury)-Anthony Barber, 11 May 1972, J. Kelley (Asst Sec, Treasury)-Slater, 16 May 1972, Treasury file 2PE 91/199/01 Pt. L; Elliott-Binns-Slater, 7 July 1972, cit.
111 Lazarus-Elliott-Binns, 7 June 1972, Elliott-Binns-Slater, 7 July 1972, cit.
112 Elliott-Binns-Lazarus, 9 June 1972, Slater-Elliott-Binns, 5 July 1972, Elliott-Binns-Slater, 7 July 1972, cit.; Lazarus-Slater, 7 July 1972, Treasury file 2PE 91/199/01 Pt. N.
113 'Examination of the April 1972 Report', cit., p. 8.
114 The adjustments followed a re-examination by RTZ/Coopers. Kemp-Creasy *et al.*, 30 June 1972, MT144/438, PRO.
115 Peyton, Memo., EPC(72) 45, Cabinet EPC Minutes, EPC(72) 20th, cit.
116 'Note of Meeting held on 8 December 1971', n.d., MT144/178, PRO.
117 'Note of a meeting between Mr Peyton (Minister (TI)) and M. Chamant (French Minister of Transport) held in M. Chamant's Office on 15 December 1971', MT144/178, PRO.
118 Kemp-Melville, 16 December 1971, MT144/178, PRO.
119 Melville-D.C. Renshaw (Peyton's PS), 13 December 1971, Scott-Malden-Peyton, 14 December 1971, MT144/178, PRO.
120 G.F. Naylor (Director, BCTC)-Melville, 'by hand', 11 January 1972, MT144/227; 'Note of meeting at Church House on 17 January 1972', MT144/228, PRO.
121 Chamant-Peyton, 21 January 1972 (with English translation), MT144/228, PRO.
122 Peyton-Chamant, 25 and 27 January 1972, Peyton-Harcourt, 26 January 1972 [and see Kemp, 'Note for the File', n.d.] and reply, 27 January 1972, Kemp, two 'Notes for the File', 31 January 1972, Harcourt-Peyton, 31 January 1972, MT144/228, PRO.
123 'Letter to the Minister [Peyton] from M. Chamant', n.d., received with French Embassy letter, 3 February 1972, MT144/228; Macé, referred to in 'Steering brief for the Minister's meeting with M. Chamant, 7.2.72', n.d., 'Note of meeting held in Paris on 7 February 1972', 9 February 1972, MT144/229, PRO.
124 Peyton-Harcourt, 15 February 1972, MT144/230, PRO.
125 Peyton-Heath, 16 February 1972, PREM15/1524, PRO. The discussion between Heath and Pompidou at Chequers was perfunctory: Campbell-Melville, 23 March 1972, MT144/232, PRO.
126 Chamant-Peyton, 8 March 1972 (English translation) and reply, 13 March 1972, draft agreement, 9 March 1972, enclosed in Harcourt-Peyton, 10 March 1972, MT144/231; DOE CTSU, 'Note of a Meeting held on 28 March 1972 at Lancaster House', 14 April 1972, MT144/233, PRO.
127 Peyton-Harcourt, 4 April 1972, MT144/233, PRO.
128 Melville-Renshaw, 24 January 1972, MT144/227; Kemp-Melville, 4 February 1972, MT144/229; J.S. Rooke (Minister (Economic), British Embassy, Paris)-Melville, 16 February 1972, MT144/230; Kemp, Note for the File on 'Meetings in Paris 15/16 March 1972', 20 March 1972, MT144/232, PRO.
129 See also Melville-Renshaw, 'Brief for the Ministers' [*sic*] meetings with Lord Harcourt on Monday 27th, and with M. Chamant on Tuesday 28th March', n.d., including 'Summary of British Group's draft Agreement No. 1, dated 9 March 1972' and 'Ministers Meeting 28 March 1972 Note by Officials', MT144/232; Kemp, 'Brief Note of a meeting held in Paris on 17 April 1972 to discuss Channel Tunnel financing', 19 April 1972, MT144/236, PRO.

130 See 'Note of Meeting held on 8 December 1971', MT144/178; Melville-Renshaw, 24 January 1972, cit.
131 Dewdney, File Note, 31 January 1972, MT144/228, PRO.
132 RTZ, 2nd draft annual conference paper, 4 January 1972, BOW 757 (80/1.25.5 File 1), RT.
133 Kemp-Melville, 16 February 1972, MT144/230; 'Ministers Meeting 28 March 1972 Note by Officials', cit.; Naylor and Stanley (BCTC)-BCTC Executive Committee, 14 April 1972, MT144/233, PRO.
134 Harcourt-Peyton, 10 March 1972, Peyton-Harcourt, 4 April 1972, cit.; Kemp-Melville, 14 March 1972, MT 144/231, PRO.
135 Kemp-Melville, 8 March 1972, MT144/231; Dr Denis Cross (Hambros Bank)-Melville, 11 April 1972, MT144/233, PRO.
136 Rooke-Melville, 14 April 1972, Melville-Rooke, 25 April 1972, MT144/233, Melville-Macé, 11 July 1972, MT144/239, PRO.
137 CTSU, Brief for 'Minister's meeting with Lord Harcourt and others of the British Channel Tunnel Company on Wednesday 8 December 1971', MT144/178; Melville-Renshaw, 24 February 1972, MT144/230, PRO.
138 'Note by British and French officials on the future operating body 15 March 1972', in Melville-Renshaw, 'Brief', cit.; Wardale-Melville, 24 March 1972, MT144/248, PRO.
139 'Aide-Memoire for Minister's talk with Lord Harcourt 22.12.71', n.d., MT144/178; CTSU, File note, 23 February 1972, MT144/230, PRO.
140 Kemp-Melville, 24 February 1972, with Melville's annotation, 16 March 1972, MT144/230; Harcourt-Peyton, 3 May 1972, MT144/236; CTSU, 'Channel Tunnel. Meeting of British and French Ministers of Transport 10 May 1972. Draft Joint Advice by Officials', n.d., MT144/235, PRO.
141 Melville-Renshaw, 11 May 1972, 'Notes prises au cours de la réunion du 10 mai à Paris entre les ministres des transports français et britannique', 12 May 1972; Peyton-Harcourt, 12 May 1972, MT144/235, PRO.
142 Melville-Peyton, 16 May 1972, MT144/235, PRO.
143 Dewdney-Peyton, 30 May 1972, MT144/235; Melville-Renshaw, 2 June 1972, MT144/236, PRO.
144 Melville-Beagley, 20 June 1972, MT144/236, PRO.
145 'Note of a Meeting held in Paris on 26 June 1972', n.d., Melville-Rooke, 28 June 1972, MT144/237; Kemp-Melville, 27 June 1972, and for a French view, conveyed by Maurin to Rooke, Rooke-Melville, 30 June 1972, MT144/238, PRO. The French were upset by a particularly sceptical article in the *Times* on 26 June.
146 Melville-Rooke, 11 July 1972, MT144/239, PRO. For the talks see Melville-Beagley, 4 July 1972, enclosing CTSU, Note for Peyton, MT144/238; CTSU, notes by British officials on meetings at Church House, 5–6 July 1972, July 1972, MT144/239, PRO.
147 See Macé, reported in CTSU, 'Note of a meeting held in the Secretary's [Idwal Pugh, Housing Construction & Transport Industries] room on 6 July 1972', 10 July 1972, MT144/238; Melville-Beagley, 12 July 1972, and O'Connell-Wardale, 12 July 1972, MT144/239; Kemp, Note for the File, 20 July 1972, MT144/241, PRO. Macé's intentions were difficult to read. As O'Donnell put it, 'Macé is such a dramatist that interpreting his underlying motivation must be a fine art': O'Donnell-Wardale, cit. and see also Kemp-Melville, 14 October 1971, MT144/176, PRO.
148 Peyton-Jenkin, 12 July 1972, Treasury file 2PE 91/199/01 Pt. N.
149 Soames-Peyton, 17 July 1972, MT144/240, PRO.
150 CTSU, 'Notes of Meeting, 20 July 1972', n.d., MT144/240, PRO. On further meetings and correspondence with the Group, 10–18 July 1972 see MT144/239–40, PRO.
151 Melville-Pugh, 26 July 1972, enclosing Kemp, 'Channel Tunnel: Note on Present Position', same date, Melville-Renshaw, 28 July 1972, MT144/241, PRO. Agreement No. 1 stated that the date of signing Agreement No. 2 could be deferred until no later

than 15 November 1973, but at the cost of the party requesting it. 'The Channel Tunnel Agreement No. 1', 20 October 1972 [British version], 2.3.5, Treasury file 2PE 91/199/01 Pt. Q.

152 Kemp, 'Note on Present Position', 26 July 1972, cit.

153 Elliott-Binns-Slater and Lazarus, 17 July 1972, Treasury file 2PE 91/199/01 Pt. N; Kemp, 'Note on Risk', 17 July 1972, MT144/240; 'Note of a Meeting held at 2 Marsham Street on 19 July 1972', n.d. MT144/241, PRO; Agreement No. 1, 5.1.2.

154 Harcourt-Peyton, 8 August 1972, MT144/242, PRO; Renshaw, 'Note of a meeting to discuss Channel Tunnel – 9 August 1972', 11 August 1972, Treasury file 2PE 91/199/01 Pt. N; Harcourt-Peyton, 10 August 1972 and reply, 11 August 1972, Peyton-Galley, 15 August 1972, Harcourt-Peyton, 18 August 1972, MT144/243, PRO.

155 Peyton-Barber, 15 August 1972, PREM15/1524, PRO.

156 DOE Press Notice, 16 August 1972, MT144/243, PRO. There had been some doubts as to whether such an interim statement was necessary, but Peyton's action, forced by the French, was endorsed by Heath. See Jenkin-Peyton, 16 August 1972, Treasury file 2PE 91/199/01 Pt. N; Heath, annotation on Peyton-Barber, 15 August 1972, cit.; Peyton-Robert Carr (Leader of the House), 17 August 1972, MT144/243, PRO.

157 J.A. Owen (Peyton's APS)-J.A. Page (Sir Idwal Pugh's PS), 18 August 1972, MT144/243; Melville-Macé, 18 September 1972, MT144/244, PRO.

158 Kemp, 'Note of meeting held in Paris on 21 September 1972', R.E. Adams (Treasury)-Kemp, 28 September 1972, Kemp-Melville, 29 September 1972, Peyton-Galley, 'personal and by hand', 3 October 1972; Melville, 'Note for the File', 4 October 1972, Wardale-Lazarus, 5 October 1972, MT144/245, PRO.

159 Frame, Note for File, 29 March 1972, BOW 1010 (80/1.25.10 File 1), RT.

160 Duncan-Harcourt, 17 August 1972 [two letters], BOW 757 (80/1.25.5 File 1), RT.

161 Draft Project Management Agreement, 17 July 1972; Creasy-Melville, 28 September 1972, MT144/482, PRO; Dewdney-Duncan, 21 September 1972, BOW 1010 (80/1.25.10 File 1), RT.

162 Melville-Renshaw, 19 September 1972 (two letters), MT144/244; Rooke-Melville, 22 September 1972, MT144/245, PRO.; Dewdney-Duncan, 19 and 21 September 1972, BOW 1010 (80/1.25.10 File 1), RT; Elliott-Binns-Slater and Lazarus, 28 September 1972, Treasury file 2PE 91/199/01 Pt. P.

163 Frame-Melville, 25 September 1972, Harcourt-Peyton, 26 September 1972, Treasury file 2PE 91/199/01 Pt. P, and see also MT144/482, PRO. Payments to RTZDE during Phase I were to be at the lower rate of £25,000 a month.

164 Creasy-Melville, 15 and 28 September 1972; Sir William Harris (DG Highways, DOE)-Melville, 26 September 1972, MT144/482, PRO. Precedents were traded. RTZDE referred to the 6% they claimed Bechtel charged, while the DOE referred to the Mangal Dam project in India, where Alexander Gibb & Partners apparently charged fees of under 0.1%.

165 Melville-Lazarus, 27 September 1972, Elliott-Binns-Slater and Lazarus, 28 September 1972, Slater-Melville, 29 September 1972, Treasury file 2PE 91/199/01 Pt. P; Dewdney-Duncan, 4 October 1972, RTZDE, Note on 'Channel Tunnel – Project Management Fee', 6 October 1972, Peyton-Galley, 6 October 1972, BOW 1010 (80/1.25.10 File 1), RT; Melville-Pugh, 5 October 1972, MT144/482, PRO.

166 Lazarus-Kelley, 3 October 1972, Treasury file 2PE 91/199/01 Pt. Q; Dewdney-Melville, 11 October 1972, MT144/482, PRO.

167 J.W.L. Lonie (Treasury)-Kelley, 3 October 1972, Treasury file 2PE 91/199/01 Pt. Q.

168 R.E. Adams (Treasury)-Kemp, 28 September 1972, Treasury file 2PE 91/199/01 Pt. P.

169 Wardale-Lazarus, 5 October 1972, MT144/245, PRO.

170 Slater-Lonie, 11 October 1972, Treasury file 2PE 91/199/01 Pt. Q; Lazarus-Wardale, 12 October 1972, MT144/246, PRO.

171 Melville, 'Progress Report – Friday 29 September 1972', Melville-Renshaw, 5 October 1972, MT144/245; Kemp-Renshaw, 18 October 1972, MT144/246, PRO; Slater-Kemp, 17 October 1972, Treasury file 2PE 91/199/01 Pt. Q.

172 *Exchange of Notes between the Government of the United Kingdom... and the Government of the French Republic concerning further Negotiations on the Channel Tunnel Project 20 October 1972*, November 1972, P.P.1972–3, xxxv, Cmnd. 5161; *Financial Times*, 21 October 1972, p. 17.

173 *Financial Times*, 23 October 1972, pp. 6–7, 16; Heath, *Course of my Life*, pp. 387–92.

174 Elliott-Binns-Slater and Lazarus, 25 September 1972, Treasury file 2PE 91/199/01 Pt. P; Peyton-Barber, 6 October 1972, Prime Minister [Heath]'s papers on 'Transport: Channel Tunnel', Pt. 2.

175 Agreement No. 1, esp. clauses 2.3.1–4, 3.2.1–2, 4.2.1–3, and 3rd schedule, p. 57; CTSG members, BCTC and Société Française du Tunnel sous la Manche [SFTM], Agreement, 20 October 1972, MT144/533, PRO. See also 'Channel Tunnel: Points in Agreement Number 1', in Elliott-Binns-Lazarus, 16 August 1972, Treasury file 2PE 91/199/01 Pt. N, and 'Note on Contents of Agreement Number 1', in Peyton-Barber, 6 October 1972, cit.

176 Agreement No. 1, clause 6.5.4.

177 See, *inter alia*, Elliott-Binns-Slater and Lazarus, 12 and 25 September 1972, Slater-Lazarus, 26 September 1972, Treasury file 2PE 91/199/01 Pt. P; Sporborg-Melville, 8 May 1972, MT144/235, PRO.

5 THE HEATH GOVERNMENT AND THE TUNNEL: TAKING THE PROJECT FORWARD, 1972–4

1 DOE Interdepartmental Committee on the Channel Tunnel [CTIC]: Composition and Terms of Reference, 15 September 1972, MT144/418; CTIC Minutes, 12 October 1972, complete set in Treasury file 2PE 91/145/09 [partial sets and papers in MT144/422, PRO and Cabinet Office file on 'Construction and Administration of a Channel Tunnel between Britain and France', 183/1].

2 DOE, Memo. on 'Channel Tunnel Legislative Programme', 6 October 1972, MT144/418, PRO.

3 Elliott-Binns-Slater, 17 January 1973, Treasury file 2PE 91/199/01 Pt. S; Elliott-Binns-Philip Cousins (Asst Sec, Treasury), n.d. [March 1974], Pt. AN; Brian Rigby (CTSU, DOE)-Gillian Ashmore (Rlys Divn, DOE), 31 May 1973, MT144/360, PRO.

4 Peyton, written answers, *Parl. Deb. (Commons)*, 5th ser. (Session 1971–2), Vol. 843, 20 October 1972, *150*, (Session 1972–3), Vol. 847, 28 November 1972, *100* [a copy of Agreement No. 1 was also deposited in the Lords library]; CTIC Minutes, 25 October and 10 November 1972, Treasury file 2PE 91/145/09; Hunt, *Tunnel*, pp. 129–30.

5 Cf. Elliott-Binns-Slater and Anthony Phelps (U-Sec, Treasury), 11 and 12 December 1972, Treasury file 2PE 91/145/05, and see also 2PE 91/199/01 Pts S-V.

6 Cf. Elliott-Binns-Slater and Phelps and Slater-Phelps, 23 February 1973, Treasury file 2PE 91/199/01 Pt. U.

7 Geoffrey Rippon (SoS for the Environment), Memo. to Cabinet EPC on 'Channel Tunnel: Public Presentation and Parliamentary Handling', EPC (73)7, 21 February 1973, enclosing Peyton, Memo., 21 February 1973, Cabinet EPC Minutes, EPC(73) 1st, 26 February 1973, CAB134/3598, PRO.

8 Maplin was recommended as the location for the third London airport by the Government in April 1971, overturning the choice of Cublington by the Roskill Commission in January 1971. The Maplin Development Bill received its second reading in the Commons on 8 February 1973, and its third reading on 13 June 1973. For Government concerns see PREM15/698, 1251–2, PRO.

9 Prior-Heath, 1 March 1973, Prime Minister [Heath]'s papers on 'Transport: Channel Tunnel', Pt. 2.
10 Heath, annotation, 12 March 1973, on draft Green Paper circulated by Peyton to Cabinet members, CP(73) 31, 8 March 1973, Prime Minister's Channel Tunnel papers, cit. Pt. 2.
11 The study, commissioned by the DOE, in association with Kent County Council and Dover and Folkestone BCs, was announced in October 1972. Cf. *Times*, 25 October 1972, p. 24.
12 DOE, *The Channel Tunnel Project*, March 1973, P.P.1972–3, xxxiv, Cmnd. 5256, esp. pp. v–vi, 4–5, 14, 21.
13 Reported in R.J. Alston (British Embassy, Paris)-Susan W. Fogarty (U-Sec, CTSU, DOE), 30 March 1973, MT144/374, PRO.
14 *Times*, 22 March 1973, p. 19 and see also pp. 6 and 25 [a more measured article by Richard Hope, editor, *Railway Gazette*].
15 A.J.P. Taylor, 'Who wants the Channel Tunnel?', *Sunday Express*, 25 March 1973, cutting in Treasury file 2PE 91/199/01 Pt. V.
16 *Economist*, 24 March 1973, p. 80.
17 *Channel Tunnel Project*, pp. 23–4; *Economist*, 24 March 1973, p. 80; Peter Bromhead, *The Great White Elephant of Maplin Sands: the neglect of comprehensive transport planning in Government decision-making* (1973), *passim*; Commons motion tabled by three Conservative MPs-Robert Adley (Bristol North-East), David Crouch (Canterbury) and John Wells (Maidstone), 22 March 1973, reported in *Times*, 23 March 1973, p. 6.
18 European Ferries Ltd., *The Channel Tunnel Project: An objective appraisal* (4 April 1973), copy in Treasury file 2PE 91/199/01 Pt. W, and see comment by Elliott-Binns in note to Miss E.L. Morhange (PS to Douglas Henley, 2nd Permanent Sec, Treasury), 10 May 1973, ibid. Pt. X. On Wickenden and European Ferries see Hunt, *Tunnel*, p. 132, and Crompton, 'Transport', pp. 139–44.
19 *Channel Tunnel Project*, pp. 6–8, 20–4.
20 The Studies in 1963 and 1966 had produced both Community and UK cost-benefit analyses. However, in 1972 neither RTZ, nor SETEC, nor the French Government was enthusiastic about a Community study. Furthermore, substantial differences in the methodological approach advocated by Coopers and SETEC created practical difficulties, and these were held to outweigh the advantages in producing a calculation to appeal to the EEC or the European Investment Bank should either express interest in the Tunnel. E.H.M. Price (Director, Economics (Transport Industries), DOE)-Humphrey Cole (DG Economics & Resources, DOE), 17 November 1972, MT144/473; Cole, Memo. on 'UK Cost Benefit Study of the Channel Tunnel – Situation Report', 23 November 1972, MT144/418, CTIC Minutes, 28 November 1972, Treasury file 2PE 91/145/09; Elliott-Binns-Slater and Lazarus, 28 November 1973, 2PE 91/145/05.
21 Studies were also made of operational safety and service interruption (including strikes, accidents and sabotage). See, for example, CTSU, Memo. on 'Interruption of Service', 16 May 1973, MT144/420, PRO.
22 J. Mathieu (Inspecteur Géneral des Ponts et Chaussées), reports on 'Construction du Tunnel Sous la Manche: Le tunnel immergé', 15 March 1968, and 'Tunnel sous la Manche: Avis sur les procédés de construction', 8 May 1968, MT114/115, PRO.
23 An ambitious scheme for a Euro-city and port complex on the Varne and Le Colbart Banks had been canvassed by an American promoter, Edgar Detwiler, in 1972. But the scheme was expensive and there were doubts about the safety of such hybrids. The much-heralded Chesapeake Bay bridge-tunnel-bridge had been damaged by ships on four occasions since 1964, and the engineer responsible for the project,

General L.J. Sverdrup, claimed that the bored tunnel was the 'only correct' option for the Channel Tunnel. See Detwiler (President, Liberian International American Corp.), 'Proposed European Common Market Channel Bridge, Industrial Area, City and Port Project', 20 April 1972, in FCO76/610, PRO; Sverdrup (Chairman, Sverdrup & Parcel)-Melville, 4 October 1972, and *Wall Street Journal*, 22 September 1972, p. 18 in MT144/418, PRO; Constant, 'Feasibility Study', pp. 8–9.

24 CTSU Memo. on 'Alternative Cross-Channel Fixed Links', 22 January 1973, MT144/418, CTIC Minutes, 29 January 1973, Treasury file 2PE 91/145/09; *Channel Tunnel Project*, pp. 27–8; DOE, *The Channel Tunnel*, September 1973, P.P.1972–3, xxxiv, Cmnd. 5430, pp. 44–6; Peyton, *Parl. Deb. (Commons)*, 5th ser. (Session 1972–3), Vol. 857, 15 June 1973, *c.*1869; www.pref.aomori.jp.

25 Peyton-Jenkin, 26 April 1973, Treasury file 2PE 91/199/01 Pt. X.

26 Economic Consultants Ltd., *The Channel Tunnel: Its economic and social impact on Kent* (May 1973); Peyton-Jenkin, 26 April 1973, Treasury file 2PE 91/199/01 Pt. X.

27 Elliott-Binns-Slater and Phelps, 9 May 1973, 2PE 91/145/08; CTSU, Note on 'Channel Tunnel – Economic and Social Implications for South East Kent', 30 April 1973, MT144/422, PRO; CTIC Minutes, 10 May 1973, Treasury file 2PE 91/145/09.

28 Harcourt-Peyton, 2 May 1973, MT144/422, PRO.

29 Cf. *Times*, 2 May 1973, referred to in D.J. Wright-K.G. MacInnes (both FCO), 3 May 1973, FCO file WRF 8/1/73 Pt. A.

30 Harcourt was authorised to reveal figures of £470 m. (1973 prices) and £820–30 m. (outturn): *Parl. Deb. (Lords)*, 5th ser. (Session 1972–3), Vol. 342, 2 May 1973, *c.*116–17.

31 Wright-McInnes, 3 May 1973, cit. and see also Wright, File note, 7 May 1973, FCO file WRF8/1/73 Pt. A. After Galley was succeeded as Minister of Transport by Yves Guéna, responsibility for the Tunnel passed to his junior minister, Secretary of State, Pierre Billecocq (April 1973–February 1974). See Melville-Sir Edward Tomkins (British Ambassador, Paris), 2 May 1973, ibid.

32 BCTC, Statement following completion of economic, technical and financial studies into the Channel Tunnel, 15 May 1973, copy in MT144/419, PRO; Elliott-Binns-Slater and Phelps, 14 May 1973, Treasury file 2PE 91/199/01 Pt. Y. The companies assumed growth rates of 2.8% for the UK and 4% for France, Germany and Italy, cf. 3.5% and 5% in the OECD forecast.

33 CTIC Minutes, 10, 23 and 30 May 1973, Treasury file 2PE 91/145/09; DOE brief on 'Channel Tunnel', PMVP(73)13, 11 May 1973, Prime Minister [Heath]'s papers on 'France March 1973'; extract from minutes of Pompidou-Heath meeting, 22 May 1973, Prime Minister's Channel Tunnel papers, cit. Pt. 3.

34 CTIC Minutes, 30 May, 4 and 5 June 1973, Treasury file 2PE 91/145/09; Phelps-Pugh, 30 May 1973, 2PE 91/145/08.

35 Phelps-Pugh, 30 May 1973, Treasury file 2PE 91/145/08; Phelps-Morhange, 26 March 1973, Elliott-Binns-Slater, 27 March 1973, Treasury file 2PE 91/199/01 Pt. V.

36 Elliott-Binns-Slater, 28 September 1972, Treasury file 2PE 91/145/05; Slater-Phelps, 6 February 1973, 2PE 91/199/01 Pt. S; Elliott-Binns-Slater and Phelps, 16 May 1973, Slater-Phelps, 21 May 1973, 2PE 91/145/08.

37 CTIC, Report on 'The Channel Tunnel Project: Outcome of Phase One Studies' [Pugh Report], in Rippon, Memo. to Cabinet EPC, EPC (73)30, 6 June 1973, CAB134/3599, PRO; Coopers & Lybrand, *The Channel Tunnel: A United Kingdom transport cost benefit study* (HMSO, June 1973), pp. 43–4; BCTC and SFTM, *The Channel Tunnel Economic and Financial Studies: A Report* (June 1973), pp. 62–3; DOE, *The Channel Tunnel*, September 1973, pp. 12–14, 16.

38 Kemp, Note for the File, 27 March and 5 April 1973, MT144/255, PRO. On Macé's behaviour, and especially his 'unannounced and uninvited visit' to the DOE on 9 May

1973, see Kemp-Peter Butter (Peyton's PS), 10 May 1973, and Kemp-Melville, and Note for the File, both 12 February 1973, MT144/255, PRO.

39 Melville-Macé, 14 March 1972, MT144/231, PRO.

40 CTSU, Memo. on 'Anglo/French Treaty', 4 May 1973, MT144/419, PRO; CTIC Minutes, 10 May 1973, cit.

41 CTIC Minutes, 10 May 1973, cit. On the development of this debate see 'Note for the File: Discussion with M. Macé – 23 January 1973', January 1973, and Kemp, Note for the File, 27 March 1973, MT144/255, PRO; Elliott-Binns-Slater and Phelps, 9 May 1973, cit.

42 Kemp-Slater, 28 November 1972, Treasury file 2PE 91/199/01 Pt. Q; Elliott-Binns-Slater, 26 January 1973, 2PE 91/145/08; CTIC Minutes, 29 January 1973, cit.; CTSU, Memo. on 'Abandonment of the Project', 25 January 1973, MT144/418, PRO; Peyton-Jenkin, 15 February 1973, 2PE 91/199/01 Pt. T; Jenkin-Peyton, 26 February 1973, 2PE 91/199/01 Pt. U; Lady Tweedsmuir (Minister of State, FCO)-Peyton, FCO file WRF8/1/73 Pt. A; Interview with Sir Peter Kemp, 15 October 2002. The option of 100% liability for the defaulting government was ruled out, not least because a game of 'chicken' might be played, with each government trying to manoeuvre the other into taking the decision to abandon.

43 Elliott-Binns-Slater and Phelps, 9 May 1973, cit.; CTIC Minutes, 10 May 1973, cit.

44 'Note of a meeting held in Paris on 17 May 1973', 22 May 1973, MT 144/255, PRO; CTIC Minutes, 21 and 23 May 1973, Treasury file 2PE 91/145/09; CTSU, Memo. on 'Anglo-French Treaty', 22 May 1973, MT144/420, PRO.

45 Cf. Fogarty, reported in DOE Channel Tunnel Agreement No. 2 Working Party [CTAWP] Minutes, 17 May 1973, MT144/268, PRO.

46 Rippon, Memo. to Cabinet EPC on 'The Channel Tunnel: Outcome of Phase One Studies', EPC (73)31, 7 June 1973, enclosing Peyton, Memo., 7 June 1973, Cabinet EPC Minutes, EPC(73) 8th, 11 June 1973, CAB134/3598–9, PRO.

47 Pugh Report, cit.

48 Tweedsmuir, Memo. to Cabinet EPC on 'Projects affecting Anglo-French relations', EPC (73)33, 8 June 1973, CAB134/3599, PRO. For a Treasury view ('a typically Foreign Office plea to be nice to the French on a series of unrelated issues') see C.J. Carey (Asst Sec, Treasury)-Leo Pliatzky (Dep Sec, Treasury), 8 June 1973, Treasury file 2PE 91/199/01 Pt. Z.

49 CPRS, Memo. to Cabinet EPC on 'The Channel Tunnel Project: Outcome of Phase I Studies', EPC (73)32, 7 June 1973, CAB134/3599, PRO. Fogarty, who had expected the report to be 'a tissue of misstatements', dismissed it as 'tendentious'. Fogarty-Pugh and Fogarty-Butter, both 8 June 1973, MT144/301, PRO.

50 'Financial Assessment. Note by Hambros Bank Ltd', Annex H of Pugh Report, cit.

51 Cabinet EPC Minutes, EPC(73) 8th, 11 June 1973, cit.; Barber-Heath, 12 June 1973, Prime Minister's Channel Tunnel papers, cit. Pt. 3.

52 *Parl. Deb. (Commons)*, 5th ser. (Session 1972–3), Vol. 857, 15 June 1973, Peyton, *c.*1867–73, Anthony Crosland (MP for Grimsby, shadow Environment Secretary), *c.*1874–84, and cf. also William Deedes (MP for Ashford), *c.*1885 and summary in Cabinet EPC Minutes, EPC(73) 10th, 28 June 1973, CAB134/3598, PRO. The attitudes of MPs may have been influenced by a much-publicised conference held at the Royal Society of Arts on 5 June: see *Times* and *Guardian*, 6 June 1973.

53 Hambros, Discussion paper on 'Channel Tunnel – Financial Viability', in Cross (Hambros)-Fogarty, 18 May 1973, MT144/268; Kemp-Melville, 16 May 1973, MT144/258; Melville-Pugh, 6 June 1973, MT144/484, PRO.

54 Frame-Peyton, 7 June 1973, MT144/272, PRO. The £106 m. = £85 m. (10% of cost) raised in cash, plus bonus shares.

55 Kemp-Melville, 11 June 1973, MT144/272, PRO.

56 CTSU, 'Draft Paper on Financing Arrangements', n.d., Rowe & Pitman, Note, 11 June 1973, Kemp-Melville, 13 June 1973, DOE CTAWP Minutes, 13 June 1973, MT144/268; Melville-Peyton, two letters, both 18 June 1973, MT144/272, PRO.
57 DOE CTAWP Minutes, 23 February 1973, MT144/266, PRO; Rowe & Pitman, Note, 11 June 1973, Kemp-Melville, 13 June 1973, cit.
58 Peyton-Billecocq, 20 June 1973 and reply, 22 June 1973, MT144/272, PRO.
59 CTSU, 'Draft Paper on Financing Arrangements', and Kemp-Melville, 13 June 1973, cit.
60 Elliott-Binns-Slater and Phelps, 25 June 1973, Treasury file 2PE 91/199/01 Pt. AB; Melville-Peyton, 26 June 1973, MT144/272, PRO.
61 John Page (Chief Cashier, BOE)-Melville, 27 June 1973, MT144/272, PRO.
62 Rippon, Memo. to Cabinet EPC on 'The Channel Tunnel Project', EPC (73)36, 26 June 1973, enclosing Peyton, Memo., Cabinet EPC Minutes, EPC(73) 10th, 28 June 1973, CAB134/3598-9, PRO, and see also Prior-Heath, 28 June 1973, Prime Minister's Channel Tunnel papers, cit. Pt. 3, and Gordon Campbell (SoS for Scotland)-Peyton, 24 July 1973, Treasury file 2PE 91/199/01 Pt. AD. As a CPRS aside had it: 'if our Tunnel terminal were at W. Hartlepool, the United Kingdom decision would be more straight forward'. J.M. Crawley (Asst Sec, CPRS)-J.C. Burgh (Dep Sec, CPRS), 5 June 1973, CPRS file Q9/2 Pt. 2.
63 Armstrong-Arthur Rucker (Prior's PS), Robin Butler (Heath's PS)-Gerard Wheeldon (Peyton's PS), Rucker-Wheeldon, both 14 June 1973, Prime Minister's Channel Tunnel papers, cit. Pt. 3.
64 Pliatzky-Morhange and David Howard (Jenkin's PS), 27 June 1973, Treasury file 2PE 91/199/01 Pt. AB.
65 Cabinet EPC Minutes, 28 June 1973, cit.
66 Kemp-Melville, 11 June 1973, cit.
67 Slater-Howard and Slater-Phelps, both 2 July 1973, Treasury file 2PE 91/199/01 Pt. AB; Melville-Peyton, 2 July 1973, MT144/272, PRO.
68 Peyton-Prior, 28 June 1973, Prime Minister's Channel Tunnel papers, cit. Pt. 3; 'Draft note of a meeting held in London on 3 July 1973', n.d., MT144/272, PRO; 'Draft letter to the companies', n.d. [handed to companies, 5 July 1973], Treasury file 2PE 91/199/01 Pt. AC.
69 Rippon, Memo. on 'The Channel Tunnel Project', CP(73)74, 2 July 1973, CAB129/170, PRO.
70 Cabinet Conclusions, CM(73) 35th, 5 July 1973, CAB128/52, PRO; Cabinet Secretary's Notebook, 5 July 1973, CO. See also Slater-Pliatzky and Bailey (Treasury), 4 July 1973, Treasury file 2PE 91/199/01 Pt. AB.
71 Peyton-Heath, 19 July 1973, Prime Minister's Channel Tunnel papers, cit. Pt. 3; Cabinet Conclusions, CM(73) 38th, 19 July 1973, CAB128/52, PRO.
72 Prior-Peyton, 20 July 1973, Prime Minister's Channel Tunnel papers, cit. Pt. 3. Prior made the point that the Opposition leader, Harold Wilson, had 'repeatedly pressed' him to confirm that no agreement would be signed on the Tunnel without the agreement of Parliament.
73 Butter-Christopher Roberts (Heath's PS), 23 July 1973, Prime Minister's Channel Tunnel papers, cit. Pt. 3; Peyton, *Parl Deb. (Commons)*, 5th ser. (Session 1972–3), Vol. 860, 24 July 1973, *c.*1414–15.
74 UK Chamber of Shipping, Memo., 20 July 1973, enclosed in Butter-Roberts, 23 July 1973, Prime Minister's Channel Tunnel papers, cit. Pt. 3.
75 Rippon, Memo. on 'Channel Tunnel', CP(73)85, 24 July 1973, CAB Conclusions, CM(73) 39th, 26 July 1973, CAB129/171, CAB128/52, PRO. See also Burke Trend, brief for Heath, 25 July 1973, Prime Minister's Channel Tunnel papers, cit. Pt. 3, and Cabinet Secretary's Notebook, 26 July 1973, CO.

76 'Note of meeting held on 10 July 1973 at 2 Marsham Street', n.d., MT144/273, PRO. The companies' position was subsequently confirmed in writing: Harcourt-Peyton, two letters, both 17 July 1973, Treasury file 2PE 91/199/01 Pt. AD.
77 Kemp, 'Note of a meeting held at Lancaster House on 31 July 1973', 1 August 1973, MT144/256, PRO; Peyton-Heath, 1 August 1973, Prime Minister's Channel Tunnel papers, cit. Pt. 4.
78 Butter, 'Note of a meeting held on 2 August', August 1973, MT144/273, PRO.
79 Cf. Slater-Phelps, 12 July 1973, Treasury file 2PE 91/199/01 Pt. AC.
80 Melville-Phelps, 11 July 1973, MT144/272, PRO; Harcourt-Peyton, 17 July 1973, cit.
81 Slater-Phelps, 12 July 1973, cit.; Kemp-Melville, 12 July 1973, MT144/255; Melville-Butter, 13 July 1973, MT144/273, PRO; Howard-Slater, 16 July 1973, Treasury file 2PE 91/199/01 Pt. AD.
82 Melville-Pugh, 19 July 1973, MT144/273, PRO.
83 Ibid. Calculations based on a multiplier of 1.9 and interest at 7%.
84 Melville, 'Note for the Record', 23 July 1973, MT144/273, PRO. The multiplier here was set at 1.62.
85 CTSU, Brief for Peyton, 30 July 1973, MT144/273, PRO; Kemp, 'Note of a meeting…31 July 1973', cit.; CTSU, 'Note of meeting held on 2 August 1973 at French Channel Tunnel Company's offices, Paris', 9 August 1973, MT144/255, PRO.
86 CTSU, 'Note of meeting', 9 August 1973, cit; Harcourt-Peyton, 3 August 1973, MT144/274, PRO.
87 Melville-Fogarty, 10 August 1973, PRO.
88 Melville, 'Note for the File', 28 August 1973, 'Dinner with M. Billecocq 29 August 1973 – Aide Memoire'[for Peyton], n.d., Kemp, 'Note for the File', 31 August 1973, Melville, 'Note for the File', 19 September 1973, MT144/256; CTSU, 'Note of a meeting held on 29 August 1973 at 2 Marsham Street', 30 August 1973, Jenkin-Peyton, 3 September and reply, 4 September 1973, MT144/274, PRO.
89 Rippon, Memo. on 'Channel Tunnel – Results of the Financial Negotiations', 4 September 1973, GEN 186(73)2, CAB130/702, PRO.
90 Melville-Peyton, 5 September 1973, MT144/274, PRO. Over the period 1981–2030 the Governments were expected to receive 79% of the net profits, after debt servicing (central estimate). In the White Paper, the higher figure of 85% was given by adding the debt payments to the Governments' share: DOE, *The Channel Tunnel*, p. 32.
91 Rippon, Memo. on 'White Paper on the Channel Tunnel', GEN 186(73)1, 31 August 1973, Cabinet Committee, Channel Tunnel Project, Minutes, GEN 186(73) 1st, 5 September 1973, CAB130/702, PRO; Prior-Heath, 3 August 1973, Prime Minister's Channel Tunnel papers, cit. Pt. 4. Cabinet members also agreed to provide government support for the funding gap between 31 July and signature of Agreement No.2.
92 *Parl. Deb. (Commons)*, 5th ser. (Session 1972-3), Vol. 857, 13 June 1973, *c.*1498–1654; Hunt, p. 137. An amending clause requiring further consultation was carried by 267–250, and the Bill secured a 3rd reading by the narrow margin of 255–246. On 23 October 1973 Lords' amendments were defeated by narrow margins (175–167, 170–164): Vol. 861, *c.*1004ff.
93 Cabinet Channel Tunnel Committee Minutes, 5 September 1973, cit.; Rippon-Heath, 3 and 7 September 1973, Prime Minister's Channel Tunnel papers, cit. Pt. 4. On Maplin and Shoeburyness see Lord Carrington (SoS for Defence)-Heath, 18 January 1973, Butler (Heath's PS)-W.F. Mumford (MOD), 8 May 1973, Prime Minister's papers on 'Transport: Third London Airport', Pt. 4; Robert Carr (Home Secretary), Memo. to Cabinet on 'Relocation of Defence Facilities from Shoeburyness', CP 73(47), 2 April 1973, Cabinet Conclusions, CM(73) 31st and 33rd, 14 and 21 June 1973, and Rippon, Memo. on 'The Maplin Project: Handling', CP(73) 94, 1 October 1973, CAB128/52, CAB129/169 and 171, PRO.

94 DOE Press Notices, 12 September 1973, Treasury file 2PE 91/199/01 Pt. AH.
95 *Times*, 13 September 1973, p. 17, cutting in FCO file WRF8/11 Pt. B. French press reaction is reported in Tomkins, telegram No. 1193, 14 September 1973, ibid.
96 Expenditure to 31 July 1973 = £5.1 m. cf. budget of £5.4 m. RTZDE Minutes, 3 December 1973, CA 128 (B1), RT.
97 DOE, *The Channel Tunnel*, cit.
98 *Times, Daily Telegraph, Daily Mail*, 13 September 1973, cuttings in FCO WRF8/11 Pt. B. At the Treasury Elliott-Binns remarked that the only new argument was the 'threat to the late spider orchid': Elliott-Binns-Slater, 13 September 1973, Treasury file 2PE 91/100/01 Pt. AH.
99 Channel Tunnel Opposition Association, *The Channel Tunnel – the reasons why it should not be built* (1973), and *The Channel Tunnel Project: An independent appraisal* (July 1973); Afco Associates, *The Channel Tunnel Project – an Answer* (June 1973) and *The Channel Tunnel Project: Key Issues* (October 1973), in CPRS file Q9/2 Pt. 2.
100 *New Scientist*, 11 October 1973, pp. 92–113, copy in Prime Minister's Channel Tunnel papers, cit. Pt. 5 and see R. Carpenter (Treasury)-Elliott-Binns and Slater, 19 October 1973, Treasury file 2PE 91/199/01 Pt. AH. On opposition see Rogers, 'England & the Channel Tunnel', pp. 248–57.
101 *Parl. Deb. (Commons)*, 5th ser. (Session 1972–3), Vol. 861, 25 October 1973, *c.*1494. Hunt called the amendment 'mean-spirited': *Tunnel*, p. 141.
102 Cabinet Conclusions, CM(73) 50th, 25 October 1973, CAB128/53, PRO. For Labour views see Tony Benn, *Against the Tide: Diaries 1973–76* (1989), entry for 22 October 1973, p. 73.
103 *Parl. Deb.* 25 October 1973, cit., Rippon, *c.*1494–1505, Crosland, *c.*1505–20, Ogden, *c.*1550–9, Peyton, *c.*1603–14. Conservative opponents included Angus Maude, *c.*1570–3. The White Paper was then endorsed by a margin of 243 to 187.
104 Channel Tunnel (Initial Finance) Act 1973, 1973 *c.*66.
105 *Parl. Deb. (Commons)*, 5th ser. (Session 1973–4), Vol. 863, 8 November 1973, *c.*1185–1248, Vol. 864, 12 November 1973 , *c.*163–210. Other critics included John Prescott, Richard Hornby (Tonbridge) and Sir John Rogers (Sevenoaks).
106 Cf. Peyton-Jenkin, 8 November 1973, Treasury file 2PE 91/199/01 Pt. AJ.
107 Harcourt-Peyton, 26 October 1972 (draft sent to DOE, 11 October), MT144/482, PRO.
108 Cf. John Rosenfeld (U-Sec, DOE)-Pugh, 1 December 1972, Melville-Pugh, 5 December 1972, MT144/483, PRO; Rosenfeld-Phelps, 21 December 1972, Treasury file 2PE 91/199/01 Pt. R.
109 Rosenfeld-Phelps, 2 and 8 January 1973, and Frame-Melville, 8 January 1973, MT144/484, PRO. SITUMER was to receive £1.44 m. fixed and up to £3.25 m. variable. The variable payments were to be cut on a sliding scale falling by 1/15 for each 1% overrun to 5%, and by 2/15 for each 1% up to 10%. On the background to the settlement see MT144/483–4, PRO.
110 Peyton-Jenkin, 19 January 1973, Treasury file 2PE 91/199/01 Pt. S and reply, 25 January 1973, MT144/483, PRO.
111 Cf. Frame-Melville, 10 August 1973, Kemp-Rosenfeld, 3 September 1973, MT144/484; Frame-Melville, 1 November 1973, MT144/485; Sir James McPetrie (Legal Adviser, CTU, DOE)-John Williams (CTU), 30 January 1974, MT144/486, PRO; Rosenfeld-Butter, and Rosenfeld-Elliott-Binns, both 14 November 1973, Treasury file 2PE 191/199/01 Pt. AK.
112 Melville-Harcourt, 17 November 1973, MT144/485; Melville-Macé, telex, 28 November 1973, MT144/486, PRO. Inflation was estimated at: 10% (1972), 11% (1973), 10% (1974), and 8% (1975–80).
113 Cf. 'Project Management Fee: Minister's meeting with Sir Mark Turner – 11 December 1972', n.d., MT144/483, and CTSU, 'Summary Note of Meeting on 4 January 1973',

5 January 1973, MT144/484, PRO. The proposal that the French banks should get the shares instead of SITUMER caused dismay on the British side: cf. Notes of Peyton's meeting with Harcourt and Merton (BCTC), 9 April 1973, MT144/484, PRO.

114 Billecocq-Peyton, correspondence, 21 December 1973–4 February 1974 (letter of 4 February telephoned to DOE on 1 February); Williams-Pugh, 28 January 1974, Rosenfeld-Williams, 30 January 1974, Fogarty-Harcourt, 4 February 1974, and Naylor (BCTC)-Williams, 25 February 1974, MT144/486-7, PRO; Agreement, 5 February 1974, CAR 646 (B1/R9/S10), RT.

115 Slater-Phelps, 16 July 1973, Treasury file, 2PE 91/199/01 Pt. AD; 'Channel Tunnel Agreement Number 2: Principal Points Outstanding on "Final Discussion Proof" dated 12 October 1973', n.d., MT144/275, PRO.

116 Cabinet Channel Tunnel Project Minutes, 5 September 1973, cit.; Melville-Peyton, 16 October 1973, enclosing Page-Melville, 11 October 1973, Treasury file 2PE 91/199/01 Pt. AH.

117 Butter-Melville, 18 October 1973, William Merton (Robert Fleming & BCTC)-Melville, 31 October 1973, Page-Pliatzky, 7 November 1973, MT144/275, PRO.

118 Melville-Merton, 16 November 1973, MT144/275, PRO.

119 Each Board was to have five government-appointed members, plus a minority of members nominated by the national company (1–3, dependent on the % of cost represented by risk capital).

120 FCO, *France No. 1 (1973). Treaty between the United Kingdom of Great Britain and Northern Ireland and the French Republic concerning the Construction and Operation of a Railway Tunnel System under the English Channel (with Exchanges of Notes and Letters and Agreements No. 2), 17 November 1973*, 20 November 1973, P.P.1973–4, xii, Cmnd. 5486, pp. iii–xxix (treaty), pp. xxx–xxxii (exchange of notes); DOE Press Notice, 17 November 1973, Prime Minister's Channel Tunnel papers, cit. Pt. 5.

121 The Channel Tunnel Agreement No. 2, 17 November 1973, copy in FCO, *Treaty*, pp. 1–100 (British agreement). The French agreement is reproduced on pp. 101–92.

122 £30.791 m. [347,931,000FF], 15 November 1973–1 July 1975, following the £5.685 m. [74,244,000FF] spent prior to 15 November 1973: Agreement No. 2, Schedule 2, Pt. 2, *Treaty*, p. 88.

123 See MT144/263–4, PRO.

124 I.e. for the British co. for each share 'f' = 12.65p, 'x' = 10×10^{-8}%, and 'y' = 3.45×10^{-8}%. The Treasury had set a ceiling of 6% interest under Section 65. In order to pay 7% the issue price was adjusted such that the rate was 5.635% net of tax (or 7% gross). See Companies Act 1948, 11 & 12 Geo.VI *c.*38, s.65 (1) (e), and correspondence in MT144/275, PRO. The clause originated in the 1907 Companies Act. However, it was never invoked, and was repealed in 1980. L.S. Davis (Asst Sec, DTI)-Lord Limerick (PUSS for Trade), 30 May 1973, MT144/258, PRO.

125 Agreement, No. 2, 6.1.3 (iv), *Treaty*, p. 54.

126 Bridges-Butter, 10 October and reply, 17 October 1973, Bridges-Heath, 17 October 1973, Rucker-Bridges, 30 October 1973, Tomkins, Paris telegram No. 1491, 5 November 1973, Prime Minister's Channel Tunnel papers, cit. Pt. 5.

127 Bridges-Butter, 12 November 1973, Prime Minister's Channel Tunnel papers, cit. Pt. 5; Peyton, *Laundry*, p. 150; Interview with Peyton, 25 April 2002. Heath, in his autobiography, is in error in asserting: 'I also signed, with President Pompidou, the Treaty for the Channel Tunnel': *Course of My Life*, p. 459.

128 On the oil crisis see Ian Skeet, *Opec: Twenty-five years of prices and politics* (Cambridge, 1988), p. 104, and James Bamberg, *British Petroleum and Global Oil, 1950–75: The Challenge of Nationalism* (Cambridge, 2000), p. 474ff.

129 *Parl. Deb. (Commons)*, 5th ser. (Session 1973–4), Vol. 865, 5 December 1973, *c.*1299–1410. On Cornish's intervention see *Financial Times*, 5 December 1973, cutting in Treasury file 2PE 91/199/01 Pt. AL.

130 J. Hobson (DOE)-Wardale, 1 November 1973, MT144/250, PRO; Elliott-Binns-Cousins, March 1974, cit.
131 Frame-Fogarty, 29 October 1973, MT144/492, PRO; Hunt, *Tunnel*, p. 143.
132 Meeting of Cabinet members on 5 January 1973 at 7.45 p.m., Cabinet Secretary's Notebook; Cabinet Conclusions, CM(74) 8th, 7 February 1974, CAB128/53, PRO; Heath, *Course of My Life*, p. 500ff. See also William Ashworth, *The History of the British Coal Industry, Vol. 5. 1946–1982: The Nationalized Industry* (Oxford, 1986), pp. 335–6, and Kenneth O. Morgan, *The People's Peace: British History 1945–1989* (Oxford, 1990), pp. 346–79.
133 Elliott-Binns-Cousins, March 1974, cit.; Interview with Lady Harrop (Margaret Elliott-Binns), 6 November 2002.
134 Cf. Prior-Heath, 3 August 1973, cit.; CTSU, 'Note of a meeting held on 29 August 1973 at 2 Marsham Street', 30 August 1973, MT144/274, PRO.
135 Kemp-Rosenfeld, 8 November 1973, MT144/275, PRO, Elliott-Binns-Cousins and Peter Harrop (U-Sec, Treasury), 23 May 1974, Treasury file 2PE 91/199/01 Pt. AO.
136 Cf. Pliatzky-Morhenge and Bailey (Treasury), 4 July 1973, Treasury file 2PE 91/199/01 Pt. AB.
137 Bonavia, *Channel Tunnel Story*, p. 86; Interview with Kemp, 2002.

6 ABANDONMENT, 1974–5

1 Harold Wilson, *Final Term: the Labour Government 1974–1976* (1979), pp. 10–11; David Butler and Dennis Kavanagh, *The British General Election of February 1974* (1974), *passim*; Edmund Dell, *A Hard Pounding: Politics and Economic Crisis 1974–1976* (Oxford, 1991), p. 8; David Butler, *British General Elections since 1945* (1995), pp. 27–30; Nick Tiratsoo, 'You've Never had it so Bad? Britain in the 1970s', in Tiratsoo, *From Blitz to Blair*, pp. 168–9.
2 *National Institute Economic Review*, 26 February 1974, referred to in Denis Healey's Budget statement, *Parl. Deb. (Commons)*, 5th ser. (Session 1974), Vol. 871, 26 March 1974, *c*.282, and cit. in Dell, *Hard Pounding*, p. 10. See also Butler and Kavanagh, *Election of February 1974*, pp. 10–24; Martin Holmes, *The Labour Government, 1974–79* (1985), pp. 1–4; Colin Thain and Maurice Wright, *The Treasury and Whitehall: The Planning and Control of Public Expenditure, 1976–1983* (Oxford, 1995), pp. 42–3; Denis Healey, *The Time of My Life* (1989), p. 392.
3 Hunt, *Tunnel*, p. 146.
4 F.W.S. Craig (ed.), *British General Election Manifestos 1959–1987* (Aldershot, 1990), pp. 161–211, quotation on p. 203.
5 Wilson, *Final Term*, p. 17, cit. in Kenneth O. Morgan, *The People's Peace: British History 1945–1989* (Oxford, 1990), p. 359; Holmes, *Labour Government*, pp. 1–2.
6 Morgan, *People's Peace*, p. 359.
7 *Parl. Deb. (Commons)*, 5th ser. (Session 1974), Vol. 870, 12 March 1974, *c*.47; Wilson, *Final Term*, p. 15.
8 Denis Healey (Chancellor of Exchequer), Memo. to Cabinet on ' Public Expenditure 1974–75', C(74) 4, 12 March 1974, CAB129/175, PRO.
9 Healey-Tony Crosland (SoS for Environment), 13 March 1974, Prime Minister [Wilson]'s Papers on 'Maplin and the Channel Tunnel', Pt. 1.
10 Cabinet Conclusions, CC(74) 3rd, 14 March 1974, CAB128/54, PRO.
11 Crosland-Healey, 15 March 1974, Prime Minister's Maplin/Channel Tunnel papers, cit. Pt. 1.
12 Ibid. with Wilson's annotation, and see also Robert Armstrong (Wilson's PPS)-Andrew Semple (Crosland's PS), and Crosland-Wilson, both 18 March 1974, Prime Minister's Maplin/Channel Tunnel papers, cit. Pt. 1.

13 *Parl. Deb. (Commons)*, 5th ser. (Session 1974), Vol. 871, Crosland, Written Answer to Sir Bernard Braine, 20 March 1974, *107* and Peter Shore (SoS for Trade), statement, 21 March 1974, *c*.1334.
14 Cabinet EPC Minutes, EC(74) 8th, 10 July 1974, CAB134/3738, PRO; *Parl. Deb. (Commons)*, 5th ser. (Session 1974), Vol. 877, Shore, statement, 18 July 1974, *c*.675–6.
15 Crosland, Memo. to Cabinet on 'Channel Tunnel', C(74) 8, 19 March 1974, CAB129/175, PRO.
16 CPRS, Memo. to Cabinet on 'The Channel Tunnel', C(74) 12, 19 March 1974, CAB129/175, PRO.
17 Lever was Chancellor of the Duchy of Lancaster, Mellish was Chief Whip, and Ross SoS for Scotland.
18 Jenkins was Home Secretary, Castle and Prentice SoS for Health and Education respectively.
19 Cabinet Conclusions, CC(74) 5th, 21 March 1974, CAB128/54, PRO; Cabinet Secretary's Notebook, 21 March 1974.
20 Crosland, Memo. to Cabinet on 'Channel Tunnel', C(74) 16, 26 March 1974, CAB129/175, PRO, and see also brief for Wilson by Sir John Hunt (Cabinet Secretary), 27 March 1974, Prime Minister's Maplin/Channel Tunnel papers, cit. Pt. 1. The DOE resisted the idea of engaging a second set of consultants. The idea originated in the CPRS, which had had some contact with McKinseys: Hugh Parker (McKinsey & Co.)-Lord [Victor] Rothschild (DG, CPRS), 25 January 1974, CPRS file Q9/2 Pt. 2; Elliott-Binns-Cousins and Harrop, 13 March 1974, referring to Hector Hawkins (CPRS), Treasury file 2PE 91/199/01 Pt. AN.
21 Peart was Minister of Agriculture, Varley and Williams SoS for Energy, and Prices and Consumer Protection respectively.
22 Cabinet Conclusions, CC(74) 7th, 28 March 1974, CAB128/54, PRO; Cabinet Secretary's Notebook, 28 March 1974. In fact, the latter stipulation was found to be incompatible with ratifying the Treaty, and was dropped in favour of an explicit undertaking to debate the Government's reassessment results before Phase III was signed. See Crosland-Edward Short (Lord President), 2 April 1974, and reply, 3 April 1974, Healey-Short, 4 April 1974, Prime Minister's Maplin/Channel Tunnel papers, cit. Pt. 1.
23 *Parl. Deb. (Commons)*, 5th ser. (Session 1974), Vol. 871, Crosland, statement, 3 April 1974, *c*.1267–8, and responses by Margaret Thatcher, *c*.1268, and John Peyton, *c*.1272. On Thatcher's earlier opposition see above p. 91.
24 Ibid. Vol. 872, 10 April, *c*.456, 30 April, *c*.960–1041, 3 May, *c*.1552; Vol. 875, 21 June 1974, *c*.948; Fred Mulley (Minister of Transport), Memo. to Cabinet Legislation Committee on 'Channel Tunnel Bill', LG(74) 15, 5 April 1974, CAB134/3783, PRO.
25 Ibid. Vol. 872, 30 April 1974, Mulley, *c*.961, Thatcher, *c*.967–8, vote, *c*.1038. Vocal critics included TGWU-MP Leslie Huckfield (Nuneaton), John Prescott (Hull, East), Roger Moate (Faversham), and Alan Clark (Plymouth, Sutton). The latter, in a maiden speech, repeated 19th century arguments against the Tunnel (*c*.982).
26 *Special Report from the Select Committee on the Channel Tunnel Bill*, 19 June 1974, P.P.1974, i. The only serious issue to emerge was the possibility, raised by Keith Wickenden and the shipping interests, that the existence of Treasury guarantees might encourage the Tunnel Authority to indulge in aggressive price-cutting.
27 Ibid. Vol. 873, 6, 9 and 15 May (SC membership changes), *c*.167, 742, 1393; David Butler and Dennis Kavanagh, *The British General Election of October 1974* (1975), p. 18.
28 BCTC, Prospectus, 18 February 1974, Treasury file 2PE 91/199/01 Pt. AM; *Financial Times*, 10 April 1974, p. 12, cutting in Pt. AN; 'Note of a meeting held in room

N18/07, 2 Marsham Street, at 2.45 p.m. on Tuesday 26 March 1974,' MT144/282, PRO. For details see MT144/279–83, PRO.

29 See Naylor-BCTC Board, 15 March 1974, Fogarty-Pugh, 9 April 1974, MT144/490; Fogarty-A.J.M. Morgan (Mulley's PS), 1 August 1974, etc., MT144/491, PRO.

30 George Jackson (RTZDE)-Harry Gould (DOE CTU), 19 February 1974, enclosing agreed Side Letter to Agreement No. 2, MT144/265, PRO; Channel Tunnel Progress Reports, 1974, BOW 1008A 80/1.25.6, RT; *Railway Gazette International*, September 1974, p. 353; Hunt, *Tunnel*, p. 138; Colin S. Harris *et al.* (eds), *Engineering Geology of the Channel Tunnel* (1996), p. 17.

31 See, *inter alia*, Catherine R. Schenk, 'Britain and the Common Market', in Coopey and Woodward, *Britain in the 1970s*, pp. 193–8.

32 Achille-Fould did have time to meet Mulley in Paris in May: Ronald Arculus (British Embassy, Paris), 'Note on Visit by the Rt Hon Fred Mulley (Minister for Transport) to Paris on 16 May: Channel Tunnel', 17 May 1974, FCO WRF8/13/74.

33 Cf. C.T.E. Ewart-Biggs, Memo. on 'Britain and France: the Requisites for an Understanding', 10 June 1974, Memo. on 'Visit by the Prime Minister to Paris', 11 June 1974, Michael Alexander (James Callaghan's APS)-Lord Bridges (Wilson's PS), 14 June 1974, and FCO, 'Talks between the Prime Minister and the President of France – 19 July 1974: Steering Brief', PMVP(74) 1, 12 July 1974, Prime Minister [Wilson]'s Papers on 'France June 1974'.

34 Armstrong, 'Record of a Conversation between the Prime Minister and the Foreign and Commonwealth Secretary and the French Prime Minister and Foreign Minister in the Office of the British Ambassador to N.A.T.O in the N.A.T.O. Headquarters in Brussels on Wednesday 26 June 1974 at 9.00 a.m.', 4 July 1974, Prime Minister [Wilson]'s Papers on 'Belgium June 1974'; Cabinet Conclusions, CC(74) 17th, 23 May 1974, 21st, 27 June 1974, CAB128/54, PRO; Cabinet Sec's Notebook, 27 June 1974; Hayward, *Government and British Civil Aerospace*, pp. 127–31, 142. The reference to '200 planes' appears in the Cabinet minutes and in Barbara Castle, *The Castle Diaries 1974–76* (1980), p. 124, but is not mentioned in the official 'Record of a Conversation'.

35 Bridges, 'Record of a meeting between the Prime Minister and the President of France held at the Elysée Palace in Paris on 19 July 1974 at 11.45 am', n.d., Wilson, 'Note of a meeting with President Giscard d'Estaing in Paris on Friday 19 July 1974', 21 July 1974, and Wilson, text of statement, 19 July, Prime Minister's Papers on 'France June 1974'; *Parl. Deb. (Commons)*, 5th ser. (Session 1974), Vol. 878, Tony Benn (SoS for Industry), statement, 31 July 1974, *c.*801–2.

36 Armstrong, 'Record', 4 July 1974, Cabinet Conclusions, 27 June 1974, and Cabinet Secretary's Notebook, 27 June 1974, cit.

37 Cavaillé-Mulley, 29 July 1974, and translation; Fogarty-Morgan, 30 July 1974, FCO file WRF8/2/74; *Parl. Deb. (Lords)*, 5th ser. (Session 1974), Vol. 353, 30 July 1974, Lord Shepherd (Lord Privy Seal), answer to Viscount De L'Isle, *c.*1241–2. On 10 July De L'Isle had introduced a debate expressing grave concerns about the rail link: *c.*676ff.

38 S.A. Price (Treasury)-John H. James (Treasury), 4 July 1974, James-Cousins, 31 July 1974, Treasury file 2PE 91/1270/01; Sir Edward Tomkins (British Ambassador, Paris), report to James Callaghan (Foreign Secretary) on 'The End of the Channel Tunnel Project', 14 March 1975, FCO file WRF8/4/75 Pt. C, subsequently printed as Diplomatic Report No. 187/75.

39 Wilson, Note, 21 July 1974, cit.; Arculus, 'Note of Conversation with M Dutet, Elysee, on 15 July', 15 July 1974, John Rhodes (PS, DOE)-Nick Stuart (Wilson's PS), 26 July 1974, Prime Minister's Papers on 'France June 1974'; Fogarty (DOE CTU)-Tom Shearer (Dep Sec, DOE), 22 July 1974 and telex to Roger Macé (Delegation au

Tunnel sous la Manche), same date, Macé-Fogarty, 23 June 1974, FCO file WRF8/2/74.

40 C.D. Foster-Fogarty, 10 April 1974, MT144/501, PRO.

41 Semple-Armstrong, 26 June 1974, Prime Minister's Maplin/Channel Tunnel papers, cit. Pt. 1; Fogarty-Semple and Morgan, 30 July 1974, Crosland-Sir Alec Cairncross, 2 August 1974, MT144/501, PRO; *Times*, 2 August 1974, p. 21.

42 Macé, Callou and their colleagues objected to the proposal that a series of sensitivity tests be applied to the main traffic demand model before a central case was defined. They argued that the results would enable the private companies to gain an advantage in subsequent negotiations on financing. They also objected to a more detailed examination of the 'fleet operating model', embracing the cross-channel ferry companies' competitive strategies. Here there was particular opposition to the assumption that peak pricing would be introduced before the Tunnel was opened, since the French objected to being led by the report of the British Monopolies Commission and argued that the study would help ferry operators to improve their competitive advantage. The issue was muddied by doubts as to the intentions of British Rail and SNCF in relation to their vessels. Cf. Fogarty-E.H.M. Price (U-Sec, DOE), 4 January 1974, Coopers & Lybrand and SETEC-Economie, Note on 'Economic Studies PHASE II', 10 January 1974, MT144/494; Fogarty-D.F. Hagger (Senior Economic Adviser, DOE), 11 April 1974, Hugh Sharp (DOE CTU), 'Channel Tunnel: Phase II Economic Studies. Note of meeting held at Church House on 2 May 1974', 3 May 1974, MT144/496, PRO.

43 See MT144/494–7, and, in particular BCTC and SFTM, Draft agreement with Coopers & Lybrand and SETEC-Economie, 13 February 1974, MT144/494, and final revision, July 1974, MT144/497; also David Burr (Asst Sec, DOE CTU)-Arculus, 11 July 1974, and Alastair Balls (Economic Adviser, DOE CTU)-Foster *et al.* (DOE), August 1974, MT144/497, PRO. See also DOE, 'Channel Tunnel Reassessment. Progress Report, July, 1974', Treasury file 2PE 91/111/08.

44 Frame-Fogarty, 30 April and 20 May 1974, Fogarty-Macé, 7 June 1974, Fogarty-Morgan, 10 June 1974, MT144/496, PRO.

45 DOE, 'Channel Tunnel Reassessment. Progress Report, July, 1974', cit.; Channel Tunnel Reassessment Steering Committee Minutes, 19 July 1974, Treasury file 2PE 91/111/08.

46 David McKenna (Member, BRB), Memo. 30 September 1970, BRB Minutes, 8 October 1970, AN167/6, 21, Philip James (Member, BRB)-McKenna, 1 October 1970, AN156/376, PRO.

47 McKenna, Memo. 8 October 1971, AN167/22, PRO; Rosenfeld-Elliott-Binns, 9 June 1972, Kemp-Elliott-Binns, 20 June 1972, Treasury file 2PE 91/199/01 Pt. M; Roy Hammond (Chief Secretary, BRB)-DOE, 13 October and 15 November 1972, MT144/162, PRO.

48 Bonavia-McKenna, 4 and 23 May 1972, McKenna-Melville, 24 May 1972, G.O. Jackson (RTZDE)-Bonavia, 20 July 1972, A.J. Powell (Planning Officer (Operating), Channel Tunnel, BRB)-Bonavia, 25 July 1972, AN191/166; Bonavia-McKenna, 26 September 1972, AN156/366; Bonavia-Jackson, 3 August 1972, Bonavia-Frame, 8 August and 16 November 1972, Bonavia-C.A. Tysall (Planning Officer (Technical), Channel Tunnel, BRB), 3 November 1972, AN191/167; Brian Rigby (CTSU, DOE)-Fogarty and Kemp, 13 October 1972, MT144/384, PRO. See also Michael R. Bonavia, *British Rail: the First 25 Years* (Newton Abbot, 1981), p. 207.

49 Wardale-Beagley, 5 May 1972, MT144/360, PRO.

50 In fact, a number of gauges were established under the auspices of the Union International des Chemins de Fer (UIC).

51 John Ratter (BRB)-Paul Draper (U-Sec, MT), [?] June 1969, with enclosure, 24 June 1969, MT144/118, PRO.

52 Eiichi Aoki *et al.*, *A History of Japanese Railways 1872–1999* (Tokyo, 2000), pp. 138–42; Jacob Meunier, *On the Fast Track: French Railway Modernization and the Origins of the TGV, 1944–1983* (Westport CT, 2002), pp. 5–6, 140ff.; Gourvish, *British Railways 1948–73*, p. 510; Terry Gourvish, *British Rail 1974–97: from Integration to Privatisation* (Oxford, 2002), p. 91.

53 MT CTA Divn, 'Note of meeting with British Railways Board... 29 October 1969', November 1969, MT144/140, PRO.

54 BRB, SNCB and SNCF, 'Prévisions de Trafic Voyageurs', No. 1, January 1971, AN191/216; McKenna, Memo. on 'Channel Tunnel', 2 February 1971, BRB Minutes, 10–11 February 1971, AN167/7, 22, PRO.

55 McKenna, Memo. on 'Channel Tunnel: Progress Report', 7 May 1970, BRB Minutes, 11 June 1970, AN167/6, 21; BRB and L&H, Agreement, 4 June 1970, AN191/184, PRO.

56 Livesey and Henderson, Report on 'Very High Speed Railway between London & Channel Tunnel', November 1970, pp. 11–12, 48, AN191/12, PRO; Bonavia-McKenna, 16 November 1970, AN191/185, PRO; McKenna, Memo. 2 February 1971, cit.; Bonavia, British Rail, p. 210, and *Channel Tunnel Story*, pp. 107–8.

57 Gourvish, *British Railways 1948–73*, pp. 507–9.

58 Bonavia-McKenna, 16 March 1971, BRB 196-4-1 Pt. 7.

59 Bonavia-C.L. Smith (MD, British Rail Property Board), 24 June 1970, 'Meeting in Dr. Bonavia's office, 29 June 1970, AN191/133; 'Note of DOE/BR Meeting on 30 June 1971 at Church House', n.d., MT144/118, and see also Bonavia-Melville, 30 September 1971, with enclosure, MT144/140, PRO; Bonavia, *Channel Tunnel Story*, pp. 93–5. The routes were via: Tonbridge and Sevenoaks (Boat Train Route 1); Maidstone (East) and Catford Loop; Tonbridge, Redhill and Croydon; and Tonbridge, Edenbridge and Oxted. Bonavia has recalled that the first was ruled out by the prohibitive cost of modifying the long tunnels, and that the second was the most viable, though speeds would be lower: *British Rail*, pp. 208–9.

60 Ken Peter (Asst Sec, LTP Divn, DOE)-Barber, 27 January 1971, Barber-Bonavia, 4 February 1971, Bonavia-Barber, 10 February 1971, MT144/118, PRO.

61 Sandy Morrison (CTA Divn, DOE)-Peter, 2 April 1971, MT144/118, and see also brief for DOE meeting with BRB, 30 June 1971, MT144/140, PRO. Brig. Constant annotated Bonavia's letter of 10 February thus: 'It seems hopelessly out of touch and uncooperative'.

62 GLC, Hammersmith BC and British Rail, 'Note of a meeting held at County Hall, S.E.1, on Thursday 6 May 1971', AN191/133, DOE's copy in MT144/118, PRO.

63 Bonavia-McKenna, 28 October 1971, enclosing 'Channel Tunnel – Choice of London Terminal', 26 October 1971, AN191/134; Bonavia-Constant, 22 November 1971, Constant, draft notes of a conversation with Bonavia, 22–3 November 1971, 23 November 1971, MT144/140, Melville-Renshaw (Peyton's PS), 26 November 1971, MT144/190, PRO.

64 Barber-Draper *et al.*, 18 March 1970, MT144/118, Morrison, Brief for Melville's dinner with Marsh and McKenna, 22 October 1971, n.d., Melville, Note for the File, 14 October 1971, MT144/140, PRO. See also Bonavia, *British Rail*, pp. 210–11, and *Channel Tunnel Story*, p. 104; Gourvish, *British Railways 1948–73*, p. 382; Marsh, *Off the Rails: An Autobiography* (1978), pp. 85–6, 158–60.

65 Cf. Gourvish, *British Railways 1948–73*, p. 507–9, 527–9, and *British Rail 1974–97*, pp. 84–5.

66 Lance Ibbotson (General Manager, Southern Region, BRB)-Bonavia, Ibbotson-William Reynolds (Executive Dir., S&O, BRB), both 17 February 1970, AN191/250, Arnold Kentridge (BRB)-David Bowick (Chief Executive (Railways), BRB), 29 December 1971, AN156/366, PRO. Livesey & Henderson had been engaged owing to constraints on Southern Region resources: Bonavia-Bowick, 22 December 1971, AN156/366, PRO.

67 Kemp-Andrew Lyall (Asst Sec, Rlys A Divn, DOE), 26 November 1971, Melville-McKenna, 7 December 1971, MT144/190, PRO.

68 O'Connell-Kemp, 21 December 1971, MT144/190, Marsh-McKenna, 8 December 1971, referring to the scepticism of Geoffrey Wardale and Peter Scott-Malden, AN191/269, PRO.

69 Lyall-Rosenfeld (DOE), 1 December 1971, Kemp-O'Connell, 23 December 1971, MT144/190, PRO.

70 A cheaper option, costing £65 m., would dispense with the new line from South Croydon to Edenbridge, but would not provide the UIC gauge. The use of APT technology also seemed unlikely, since it did not square with the French preference for new infrastructure.

71 Bonavia-Melville, 14 January 1972, enclosing Memo. on 'British Railways Proposed Route Strategy between the Channel Tunnel and London', 7 January 1972, MT144/381, PRO. On British Rail's development of the strategy see Bonavia-McKenna, 3 December 1971, AN191/269; McKenna, Memo. to BRB and Chairman's Conference, 3 January 1972, BRB Minutes, 13 January 1972, AN167/8, 23, PRO.

72 In March 1971 an inter-ministerial committee had given approval 'in principle' to SNCF's proposal for a high-speed line from Paris to Lyon, but decided to delay construction until the next planning period (*c.*1978). Formal government approval was secured thanks to Georges Pompidou in March 1974, in the wake of the oil crisis. It is clear that many politicians were hostile, including Couve de Murville and Giscard d'Estaing. See Meunier, *On the Fast Track*, pp. 157–8, 164–5; E.R. Powell, 'The TGV project: a case of techno-economic *dirigisime*?', *Modern & Contemporary France*, 5 (2) (1997), 200–2, 207.

73 Agreement No. 1, 7th Schedule. The French intended to electrify the Calais-Hazebrouck line, 'or such other rail investment', to permit a 130-minute journey time between Paris and the Calais terminal.

74 McKenna-Melville, 14 January 1972, BRB CT Dept., 'London Terminal – Passenger and Revenue Differences between Sites', 3 February 1972, AN191/135; Kemp, loose minute, 17 January 1972, O'Connell-Kemp, 17 January 1972, Lyall-Kemp, 18 January 1972, Melville-McKenna, 18 January 1972, BRB Press Release, 1 February 1972, Peter Hewitt (CTSU, DOE)-Kemp, 21 January 1972, MT144/381, PRO.

75 Brian Rigby (CTSU, DOE)-Kemp, 24 January 1972, MT144/381, PRO.

76 Lyall-Kemp, 18 January, Rigby-Kemp, 24 January 1972, cit.

77 Cf. for example Kemp-Constant *et al.*, 25 January 1972, MT144/381; Kemp-Bonavia, 28 February 1972, enclosing 'BRB Route Strategy to London: Note of some points to form the basis for initial discussion', AN191/145; Bonavia-Kemp, 1 March 1972, enclosing 'B.R.B. Replies…', MT144/381, PRO.

78 'Note of a meeting at British Railways Board Headquarters on Thursday 2nd March 1972', n.d., MT144/382; Kemp-Lyall, 21 March 1972, Kemp-Bonavia, 14 April 1972, MT144/381, PRO.

79 Bonavia-Kemp, 21 April 1972, MT144/381, PRO.

80 R.G. Clarke (Co. Planning Officer, Kent Co. Co.)-Melville, 10 April and reply, 14 April 1972, Melville-McKenna, 14 April and reply, 18 April 1972, Hewitt-Kemp and Melville, 19 April 1972, Bonavia, personal letter to Melville, 19 April and reply, 21 April 1972, MT144/381, PRO; *Modern Railways*, April 1972, G.M. Kichenside (editor), pp. 123 and 131–4. Cf. also Bonavia, *Channel Tunnel Story*, p. 110.

81 Rigby-Kemp, 18 April 1972, MT144/381, PRO.

82 Kemp-Bonavia, 3 May 1972, MT144/382, PRO.

83 Rigby, File note, 9 May 1972, Rigby-Morrison and Rigby-Kemp, 10 May 1972, MT144/382, PRO.

84 Bonavia-Kemp, 21 April 1972, BRB paper on 'Channel Tunnel: a possible B.R. low-investment route strategy', n.d., sent to Kemp [by Dewdney of RTZDE?], 25 April 1972, MT144/381, PRO. See also Peter Jackson (RTZDE)-Bonavia, 18 February 1972, Bonavia-McKenna, 21 April 1972, AN191/145, PRO.

85 Melville-McKenna, 30 May 1972, MT144/382, PRO.

86 McKenna-Melville, 22 June 1972, MT144/383, PRO.

87 Cf. Kemp-Melville, 23 June 1972, MT144/383, PRO. As Melville reminded McKenna: 'Your mind may wander over the Roskill episode; ours tends to wander over the Concorde!' Melville-McKenna, 26 June 1972, ibid. For evidence of exasperation with Bonavia's 'machinations' see Melville-Beagley, 3 July 1972, ibid.

88 Note of Minister (Transport Industries)'s meeting with the Chairman of BRB – 17 July 1972', n.d., and see also Rigby-Melville, 17 July 1972, MT144/383, PRO.

89 'Note of a meeting held in Room 531 on 26 July 1972 to discuss future work... on the... railway route strategy', n.d., MT144/383, PRO.

90 Maurice Constable (CTSU, DOE)-Kemp, 31 July 1972, John Seager (CTSU, DOE)-Bill Sharp (U-Sec, Railways, DOE), 31 July 1972, E.F. Glover (CTSU, DOE)-Creasy, 8 August 1972, MT144/383, PRO.

91 Melville, Note for the File, 9 November 1972, McKenna-Melville, 9 November 1972, MT144/384, PRO.

92 Bonavia-E.S. [*sic*] Fogarty, 8 November 1972, MT144/384, PRO.

93 Bill Sharp-Fogarty, 30 October 1972, DOE CTSU, 'Channel Tunnel Railway Route Strategy Working Party: Note of Second Meeting held on 1 November 1972', 7 November 1972, Fogarty-Bonavia, 13 November 1972, MT144/384, PRO.

94 Peyton-Marsh, 30 November 1972, MT144/384, PRO.

95 Sir Idwal Pugh (2nd Permanent Sec, DOE)-Bill Sharp, 15 December 1972, Fogarty-Melville, 19 December 1972, MT144/385, PRO.

96 Fogarty-Pugh, 26 January 1973, MT144/385, PRO.

97 BRB CT Dept., 'Route Strategy between London and the Channel Tunnel: Choice of London Passenger Terminal' (January 1973), AN156/366, endorsed by BRB Minutes, 8 February 1973, AN167/9; Bonavia-Fogarty, 25 January 1973, AN191/148, PRO. Costs were also estimated for three Victoria/White City hybrids, costing between £25.5 m. and £43.25 m. A more comprehensive estimate by the GLC put the costs at: White City £40.5 m.; Victoria/White City £55.75 m.; Victoria (High Level) £66.75 m.; Surrey Docks £75.5 m. Controller of Planning and Transportation, GLC, Report, 14 February 1973, MT144/394, PRO.

98 DOE CTSU, 'Note on a meeting held at Church House. 11 September 1972', n.d., Bonavia-R. Shaw (GLC), 25 September 1972, Fogarty-Melville, 13 October 1972, MT144/393, PRO.

99 GLC, *Channel Tunnel London Passenger Terminal: a document for consultation* (November 1972), esp. p 12, and GLC Strategic Planning Committee Report, 27 February 1973, agreed by GLC, 6 March 1973, in MT144/395, PRO. The 11 sites were: Battersea/South Lambeth Goods; Clapham Jnc.; Bishopsgate Goods; London Docks; Olympia/West Brompton; Bricklayers' Arms Goods; New Cross/New Cross Gate; White City; Victoria; Surrey Docks; and Isle of Dogs. Surrey Docks was chosen from a shortlist of three, the others being White City and Victoria. On the early expression of the preference see Kemp-Melville, 21 February 1972, Morrison, Loose Minute, 24 May 1972, MT144/393, PRO.

100 Cf. Tony Griffiths (Executive Director (Passenger), BRB), 'Draft Comparison of Victoria and White City as Terminals in London for the Channel Tunnel Railway', 8 January 1973, Griffiths-Bowick, 12 January 1973, Griffiths-Michael Bosworth (Deputy-Chairman, BRB), 31 January 1973, AN156/367, PRO.

101 Cf. GLC Report, 14 February 1973, cit.

102 Cf. Hewitt-Priestley (DOE), 15 November 1972, A.J. Harrison (Senior Economic Adviser, South-East Economics, DOE)-Fogarty, *et al.*, 15 December 1972, MT144/394, PRO.
103 DOE, *Channel Tunnel Project*, March 1973, para. 4.11.
104 DOE, *Channel Tunnel*, September 1973, para. 2.8.
105 Bowick-Pugh, 8 February 1973, MT144/395; BRB Minutes, 12 April 1973, AN167/ 9; Marsh-Bowick and McKenna, 18 May 1973, AN156/367, PRO.
106 CTIC, Report on 'The Channel Tunnel Project: Outcome of Phase One Studies' [Pugh Report], in Rippon, Memo. cit., 6 June 1973, CAB134/3599, PRO.
107 Fogarty-Morgan, 29 January 1974, GLC-DOE, 27 July 1973 and 2 January 1974, MT144/396; Report of GLC Planning and Transport Committees, 17–18 June 1974, extract in MT144/397, PRO.
108 Pugh-McKenna, 13 February 1973, AN191/148, PRO.
109 BRB CT Dept, 'Route Strategy between London and the Channel Tunnel' (February 1973), draft sent with Bonavia-Fogarty, 21 February 1973, final version with Bonavia-Fogarty, 5 March 1973, AN191/148, PRO.
110 'Route Strategy', pp 6–7.
111 Ibid. pp 8, 12–13, 15–16.
112 Fogarty-Bonavia, 13 March 1973, MT144/385, PRO.
113 Bonavia-Fogarty, 20 March 1973, MT144/385, PRO.
114 Price-Cole and, Peter-Fogarty, Cole-Pugh and Fogarty-Pugh, all 26 March 1973, DOE CTSU, 'Note of a meeting...on Tuesday 27 March...', 11 April 1973, MT144/385, PRO.
115 Fogarty-Pugh, 27 March 1973, MT144/385, PRO.
116 Fogarty-Melville, 31 January 1973, Fogarty-Callou, n.d. [February 1973], McKenna-Pugh, 19 February 1973, MT144/385; McKenna-Roger Hutter (SNCF), 19 February 1973, AN191/148, PRO.
117 Kemp-Fogarty, 5 March 1973, Fogarty-Pugh, 26 March 1973, with briefing documents, including a translation of Galley-Peyton, 28 February 1973, MT144/385, PRO.
118 Rigby-Fogarty, 6 March 1973, Fogarty-Pugh, 26 March 1973, MT144/385, PRO.
119 DOE CTSU, 'Minutes of a meeting held...on Thursday 29 March...', 10 April 1973, MT144/385, PRO.
120 Kemp-Lt.-Col. I.K.A. McNaughton (Chief Inspecting Officer of Railways, DOE) *et al.*, 2 April 1973, MT144/385, Kemp-Peter Barlow (BRB CT Dept.), 4 April 1973, Barlow-Bonavia, 10 April 1973, AN191/148; DOE CTSU, 'Note of a meeting...on 10 April 1973', 11 April 1973, Kemp-Fogarty, 10 April 1973, MT144/385, PRO.
121 Fogarty-Pugh, 10 April 1973, MT144/385, PRO.
122 Bonavia-McKenna, 29 March 1973, AN191/148, PRO.
123 Bonavia-Bill Reynolds (Executive Director, S&O, BRB), 3 April 1973, Bonavia-McKenna, 11 April 1973, AN191/148, Bonavia-Bosworth, 16 May 1973, AN191/149, PRO.
124 Bonavia-McKenna, 17 April 1973, enclosing 'Note for Chairman', same date, AN191/148, PRO.
125 DOE Railways 'A' Divn, 'Note of Minister's Meeting with Mr Richard Marsh on Thursday 26 April 1973', May 1973, MT144/386, PRO.
126 Bonavia-David Williams (BRB CT Dept.), 27 April 1973, AN191/149; McKenna-Peyton, 27 April 1973, MT144/386, PRO.
127 'Draft brief for Minister...', n.d., R.A. Channing (DOE Railways 'A' Divn)-Bill Sharp, 8 May 1973, Fogarty-Butter (Peyton's PS), 10 May 1973, MT144/386, and see papers in AN191/149, PRO.
128 Bonavia, Note on 'Meeting with the Minister, 10 May 1973', 11 May 1973, McKenna-Bowick, 16 May 1973, AN191/149, PRO; Bonavia-Bosworth, 16 May 1973, cit.

129 BRB, 'Channel Tunnel: BR Route Investment London-Tunnel' (amended draft), 18 May 1973, enclosed in Bosworth-Pugh, 17 May 1973, MT144/386, PRO.
130 Prior to this, Treasury briefings had been confined to information released through the DOE Channel Tunnel Agreement No. 2 Working Party [CTAWP]: see Treasury file 2PE 91/199/01 Pt. U.
131 DOE CTSU, Memo. on 'Railway Link to London', n.d. [May 1973], CTIC(73) 22, Annex A: 'Channel Tunnel Rail Link: Reasons for Rejecting Compromises between the "Recommended" Strategy and the "Low-Investment" Strategy', 9 May 1973, paras 5–17, 23–4, 27, MT144/420, PRO.
132 Ibid. Annex B: 'BR Route Strategy: London-Tunnel: Reasons for Rejecting a "Low-Investment" Solution', 18 May 1973, para. 18.
133 BR figures = 'lower estimate' given in Table 5.3 minus portal-to-portal passengers.
134 A rate of return matrix was included, with variations for 30% cost over-run, lower traffic forecasts, and three fares scenarios plus a toll rebate. The 17% figure was based on the central traffic forecast, a mid-range fare-split, no toll rebate, and no cost over-run. Ibid. Annex C: 'BR Route Investment, London-Tunnel', 18 May 1973, paras 1, 9, 14, 27–33.
135 DOE CTSU, Memo. on 'Railway Link to London', CTIC(73) 22, MT144/420; CTIC Minutes, 23 and 30 May 1973, Treasury file 2PE 91/145/09.
136 CTIC, Report on 'The Channel Tunnel Project: Outcome of Phase One Studies' [Pugh Report], cit. Annex E.
137 DOE CTSU Memo., CTIC(73) 22, para. 11. In fact, BRB was able to negotiate a more advantageous division of fares, recognising higher investment on the British side. Cf. McKenna-Melville, 24 September 1973, Evan Harding (Chief Secretary, BRB)-DOE [Fogarty], 15 November 1973, MT144/387, PRO.
138 Pugh Report, cit. summary and conclusions, para. 9, report, paras 44–5.
139 The increase of £2 m. was transmitted to the DOE on 15 June: Bosworth-Pugh, 15 June 1973, MT144/386; BRB Minutes, 14 June 1973, AN167/9, PRO.
140 Agreement No. 2, Schedule 3, paras 3–4. Reference was also made to the possibility of an additional terminal at Victoria. The French undertook to electrify the Calais-Hazebrouck and Lille-Bastieux lines.
141 *Treaty*, Article 4, p.v; Billecocq and Peyton, exchange of letters, 17 November 1973, pp. xxxiiii-v.
142 Fogarty-Sir Robert Marshall (2nd Permanent Sec, DOE), 4 September 1974, MT144/392, PRO.
143 Harding-Fogarty, 15 November 1973, enclosing Procedure Memorandum, n.d., and reply, 16 November 1973, MT144/387, PRO.
144 BRB, *Express Link with Europe: British Rail and the Channel Tunnel* (July 1973); DOE, *Channel Tunnel*, Plate 5.
145 Cf. CTSU contribution to Minister's brief, n.d. [October 1973], MT144/387; Edenbridge and District Society-Bonavia, 6 November 1973, MT144/361, Woldingham Association-Marsh, 18 November 1973, AN156/374, PRO. Rodgers was MP for Sevenoaks and Howe MP for Reigate.
146 'Draft Note of a meeting held on 30 October 1973', n.d., MT144/387, PRO.
147 Fogarty-Bonavia, 12 December 1973, 'Note of a meeting…on 29 January 1974', n.d., MT144/387, PRO; BRB, *Channel Tunnel: London-Tunnel New Rail Link: A Document for Consultation* ([?] January 1974), copy in MT144/388, PRO.
148 BRB, *London-Tunnel New Rail Link*, paras 1.15–17, 2.5, 2.9–10, 3.3, 4.3, 4.6, Plates 5–12. The disadvantages of an above-ground Chelsea-Croydon section included speed restrictions at Clapham Jnc., the need to rebuild Balham and Wandsworth Common stations, encroachment on Wandsworth Common, and an immense work-load for land referencing.
149 Ibid. para. 2.11 and see Fogarty-Morgan, 16 January 1974, Fogarty-Bonavia, 18 January 1974, MT144/388, PRO.

150 Bonavia-Fogarty, 11 March and 15 March 1974, the latter enclosing Ian Campbell (Executive Director (S&O), BRB)-Bowick, 14 March 1974, MT144/389/1; Mott, Hay & Anderson, report to A.W. McMurdo (Chief Civil Engineer, BRB) on 'Channel Tunnel Link South Croydon to Chelsea Basin: Route feasibility report' (March 1974), paras 3.5–7, 3.10, MT144/389/2, PRO.
151 Fogarty-John Williams (CTU DOE), 13 March 1974, DOE CTU, 'Note of a Meeting…on 20 March 1974', 26 March 1974, MT144/389/1, PRO.
152 'Note of a Meeting…on 22 March 1974', n.d., MT144/389/1; Harrop (Treasury)-Rosenfeld, 25 April 1974 [note: 'east' and 'west' routes were transposed!], MT144/390, PRO.
153 Morgan, 'Channel Tunnel Rail Link: Note of a Meeting on 9 April 1974', 9 April 1974, MT144/389/1; Marsh, Note for Papers, 9 April 1974, AN156/380; Marsh-Mulley, 15 May 1974, MT144/389/1, PRO.
154 Coopers & Lybrand, *United Kingdom transport cost benefit study*, Table 6.16; DOE, *Channel Tunnel*, Annex 10, Table 1.
155 Fogarty-Morgan, 2 April 1974, and see also Elizabeth Hitchins (CTU)-John Williams, 15 March 1974, 'Note of meeting…20 March 1974', cit., MT144/389/1, PRO; Rosenfeld-Harrop, 9 April 1974, Treasury file 2PE 91/199/01 Pt. AN.
156 Harrop-Rosenfeld, 25 April 1974, MT144/390. For earlier concern cf. Slater-Rosenfeld, 7 February 1974, MT144/388, PRO.
157 Peter Keen became Deputy Director (Channel Tunnel) in February 1974, when the project was put under Bowick's wing. He succeeded Bonavia, in May. Harding-Bill Sharp, 4 February 1974, MT144/360, PRO. Bonavia, who was then 65, was retained for a short time as 'Special Project Adviser' before retiring.
158 Bonavia-Bowick *et al.*, 19 April 1974, AN191/150 Pt. 2, PRO. See also Bonavia, *Channel Tunnel Story*, pp. 126–7.
159 Bonavia-Fogarty, 29 April 1974, MT144/390; Seager-Hitchins, 8 May 1974, MT144/389/1, PRO.
160 Fogarty-Sharp *et al.*, 21 May 1974, and see also Hitchens-Burr, 6 May 1974, 'Note for file' (informal meeting, 29 April 1974), MT144/389/1, PRO.
161 Fogarty-Peter Keen (Director (Channel Tunnel), BRB), 30 May 1974, MT144/390, PRO.
162 Fogarty-Pugh, 27 February 1974, Woodhouse (Principal Asst Solicitor, DOE)-Fogarty, 22 February 1974, MT144/385, PRO.
163 Fogarty-Morgan, 17 May 1974, with Mulley's annotation, and Morgan-Fogarty, 21 May 1974, MT144/390, PRO.
164 Notes of meetings to discuss the Channel Tunnel Rail Link on 17 and 25 June 1974, n.d., Fogarty-Shearer, 20 June 1974, MT144/390, PRO.
165 Mulley-Marsh, 26 June 1974 and reply, 28 June 1974, MT144/390, Mulley-Marsh, 3 July 1974, MT144/391, PRO.
166 *Parl. Deb. (Commons)*, 5th ser. (Session 1974), Vol. 876, Crosland, written answer, 1 July 1974, *69–70*. On opposition see RIBA, *Channel Tunnel Rail Link* (June 1974), a rather unfair attack on BR's consultation document, and press speculation about rising costs, e.g. *Daily Mirror*, 27 June, *Daily Telegraph*, 17 July 1974, cuttings in Treasury file 2PE 91/83/01. See also Bonavia, *Channel Tunnel Story*, pp. 120–2.
167 Bowick-Marsh, 10 and 21 June 1974, AN191/150 Pt. 2, PRO.
168 Marshall-Mulley, 14 June 1974, MT144/390, PRO. Sharp informed Fogarty on 25 June.
169 Keen-Fogarty, 26 June 1974, Fogarty-Shearer, enclosing brief for discussion with Marsh and McKenna, 28 June 1974, MT144/391, PRO.
170 Campbell and Keen, 'Channel Tunnel High Speed Rail Link: Report on Estimates June 1974', AN191/290, PRO.

171 Marsh-Mulley, 5 July 1974, and note Fogarty-Morgan, 15 July 1974, MT144/391, PRO.
172 £103.2 m., cf. £30.6 m. in BR's submission. See Burr-Shearer, 11 July 1974, MT144/391, PRO.
173 C.J. Currie (DOE)-Burr, 1 August 1974, Hitchins-Fogarty and Gould, 5 August 1974, MT144/392, PRO.
174 DOE CTU, Notes of meetings on 5 and 25 July 1974, MT144/391, PRO.
175 *Parl. Deb. (Commons)*, 5th ser. (Session 1974), Vol. 878, Mulley, written answer, 31 July 1974, *287*.
176 DOE Press Notice, 30 July 1974, MT144/391; 'Note of a meeting... in the House of Commons on 30 July 1974', n.d., MT144/392; Hitchins-Keen, 31 July 1974, MT144/360; Fogarty-McKenna, 6 August 1974, MT144/392, PRO.
177 *Parl. Deb. (Commons)*, 5th ser. (Session 1974), Mulley, written answer, 31 July 1974, *327*; BRB Press Release, 6 August 1974, AN191/150 Pt. 2, PRO. Mulley also promised that British Rail would purchase properties lying on any of the optional routes so identified.
178 Marsh-Mulley, 3 September 1974, enclosing BRB, 'Channel Tunnel Rail Link: Interim Report on Revised Cost Estimates and Expected Financial Return', 30 August 1974, MT144/392, PRO.
179 Fogarty-Marshall, 4 September 1974, with enclosure, MT144/392, PRO.
180 BRB, 'Interim Report', paras 19, 39; Fogarty-Shearer, 6 September 1974, MT144/392, PRO.
181 Cf. DOE Economics, Transport Divn, Draft paper on 'Channel Tunnel: Alternative Rail Investment Options', 23 August 1974, Burr-Morgan, 10 September 1974, DOE CTU, 'Note of a meeting... on 2 September', September 1974, MT144/392, PRO.
182 Mulley-Marsh, 17 September 1974, MT144/392, PRO; Mulley-Wilson (copies to Callaghan and Healey), 23 September 1974, Prime Minister's Maplin/Channel Tunnel papers, cit. Pt. 1.
183 Within Labour ranks Lords Chalfont and St. Davids defected to the Conservatives, and Lord Brayley resigned from the party. On the Conservative side Keith Joseph came out stridently for control of the money supply, and Margaret Thatcher promised a cut in the mortgage rate to 9½% by Christmas. *Times*, 23 and 26 September 1974, both p. 1; Butler and Kavanagh, *Election of October 1974*, pp. 2, 16, 25, 94–5, 102, 121–3; Margaret Thatcher, *The Path to Power* (1995), pp. 255–61.
184 CPRS, Memo. to Cabinet on 'Public Expenditure to 1978–79', Annex 2, CC(74) 102, 10 September 1974, CAB129/179, PRO, and see H.C.G. Hawkins (CPRS)-William Plowden (Asst Sec, CPRS), 8 August 1974, Crawley-Sir Kenneth Berrill (Head of CPRS), 29 October 1974, CPRS file Q9/2 Pt. 3.
185 Healey-Wilson, 24 October 1974, Prime Minister's Maplin/Channel Tunnel papers, cit. Pt. 1; Denis Healey, *The Time of My Life* (1989), pp. 393–4.
186 E.g. John Young, 'Final go-ahead on Tunnel certain to be postponed', *Times*, 21 September 1974, p. 4; 'Chunnel "May be Dropped" ', *Daily Telegraph*, 21 September 1974, p. 2.
187 *Parl. Deb. (Commons)*, 5th ser. (Session 1974–5), Vol. 881, 11 November 1974, *c*.35–139; Cabinet Conclusions, CC(74) 46th, 14 November 1974, CAB128/55, PRO. A similar motion was carried in the Lords: (Session 1974–5), Vol. 354, 12 November 1974, *c*.694–702.
188 Crosland, Memo. to Cabinet on 'Channel Tunnel', C(74) 135, 19 November 1974, CAB129/180, PRO. The Cabinet Secretary stated that Crosland had drafted his own 'ingenious' proposals: Hunt, Brief for Short, 20 November 1974, Prime Minister's Maplin/Channel Tunnel papers, cit. Pt. 1.
189 Cabinet Conclusions, CC(74) 48th, 21 November 1974, CAB128/55, PRO.

190 Hunt-Wilson, 27 November 1974, F.E.R. Butler (10 Downing St.)-C.J.S. Brearley (CO), 3 December 1974, Prime Minister's Maplin/Channel Tunnel papers, cit. Pt. 1; Hunt, Note on 'Cabinet Committee on the Channel Tunnel Project', CT(74) 1, 11 December 1974, CAB134/3731, PRO.
191 Richard Hope, 'British Rail axes £500 millions 150 mph Chunnel rail link', *Guardian*, 19 November 1974, p. 17.
192 By the time this was written British Rail were pessimistic about the possibilities: Marsh-Mulley, 18 November 1974, MT144/392, PRO.
193 Crosland-Harcourt, Cavaillé and Maurin, [26] November 1974, Department for Transport [DTp] file RA13/114/32 Pt. 4. For a bleak assessment of the prospects see Cross (Hambros Bank)-Burr, 25 September 1974, MT144/279, PRO.
194 Crosland, statement, *Parl Deb. (Commons)*, 5th ser. (Session 1974–5), Vol. 882, 26 November 1974, *c*.245–6, debate, 246–52.
195 Crosland-Bosworth, 26 November 1974, MT144/392, PRO.
196 Marsh-Mulley, 18 November 1974, cit.
197 Crosland, statement, cit. *c*.246; Bridges, 'Record of Conversation at Dinner at the Elysée on 3 December 1974', 6 December 1974, Prime Minister [Wilson]'s Papers on 'European Policy December 1974'; Sir Edward Tomkins (British Ambassador, Paris)-Sir Oliver Wright (Dep U-Sec, FCO), 3 January 1975, FCO file WRF8/4/75 Pt. A.
198 Mulley, Note on 'Meeting with French Secretary of State for Transport', n.d., MT144/302, PRO; David Ratford (Counsellor, Paris, FCO), Note, 4 December 1974, FCO file WRF8/2/74.
199 Shearer-Arculus, 4 December 1974, FCO file WRF8/9/74; Cavaillé-Crosland, 6 December 1974 (sent from French Embassy in London to DOE on 9 December), and translation, MT144/286 and 302, PRO.
200 Harcourt-Crosland, Maurin-Crosland, 10 December 1974, MT144/286, PRO.
201 Fogarty-Andrew Semple (Crosland's PS) *et al.*, 11 December 1974, MT144/286, PRO.
202 Fogarty-Morgan *et al.*, 10 December 1974, MT144/286, PRO.
203 Shearer-Morgan, 12 December 1974, MT144/287; Crosland-Harcourt, 17 December 1974, enclosing 'Revised Draft Channel Tunnel Supplementary Agreement 1974', 16 December 1974, MT144/286, PRO.
204 W. O'Hara (British Embassy, Paris)-Burr, 20 November and 18 December 1974, FCO file WRF8/5/74.
205 David McDonald (Crosland's Asst PS), 'Note of a Meeting held in Secretary of State's Office… 17 December 1974', 18 December 1974, Shearer-Morgan, 18 December 1974, MT144/286, PRO.
206 Harcourt-Cavaillé and Maurin-Cavaillé, 16 December 1974, MT144/286, PRO; CT Reassessment Steering Committee Minutes, 20 December 1974, cit.; *Parl. Deb. (Commons)*, 5th ser. (Session 1974–5), Vol. 883, 20 December 1974, *c*.2012–13.
207 Arculus-Shearer, 18 December 1974, MT144/286, PRO; John Peters (Asst Sec, CO)-Marshall and J.A. Hamilton (Dep Sec, CO), December 1974, Cabinet Office file on 'Channel Tunnel', 183/1 Pt. 5.
208 Shearer, telex to Macé, 19 December 1974, Harcourt-Crosland, 23 December 1974, MT144/286, PRO.
209 Peters-Marshall and Hamilton, 31 December 1974, Cabinet file 183/1 Pt. 5; Terry Heiser (Crosland's PS)-D.H.O. Owen (Elwyn-Jones's PS), 31 December 1974, Prime Minister's Maplin/Channel Tunnel papers, cit. Pt. 1.
210 Harcourt-Crosland and Maurin-Crosland, 2 January 1975, MT144/288/1, PRO.
211 MacDonald, 'Note of a meeting held in the Secretary of State's Office on… 6 January 1975', 7 January 1975, Mulley, Note, n.d. [7 January 1975?], MT144/288/1, PRO.

212 Tomkins-Wright, 3 January 1975, cit.; Kenneth James (Head of Western European Dept, FCO)-Fogarty, 8 January 1975, James-Morgan and M.I. Goulding (PS to Roy Hattersley, Minister of State, FCO), 10 January 1975, FCO file WRF8/4/75 Pt. A.
213 Fogarty-Shearer, 8 January 1975, MT144/288/1, PRO.
214 DOE CTU, 'Note of a Quadripartite Meeting held on 9 January 1975 at Church House', January 1975, Harcourt-Shearer, 9 January 1975 (enclosing draft notes), and see also Callaghan, telegram No. 8 to British Embassy, Paris, 10 January 1975, MT144/288/1, PRO, and James-Morgan and Goulding, cit.
215 Marsh-Mulley, 31 December 1974, MT144/392, PRO.
216 See Heiser, 'Note of meeting held in the Secretary of State's Office on 10 January 1975', 13 January 1975, MT144/288/1, PRO.
217 Keen-Bowick, 10 January 1975, AN191/270, PRO; Fogarty-Morgan, 13 January 1975, MT144/392, PRO; Marsh, *Off the Rails*, p. 196. The telephone calls were made on 10 January. The £100 m. saving was produced by dispensing with the UIC gauge: Keen, Major Projects Association [MPA] seminar transcript, in Philip Worthington (Executive Director, MPA)-Keen, 6 September 1982, author's collection.
218 Cabinet Conclusions, CC(75) 2nd, 14 January 1975, CAB128/56, PRO.
219 Crosland, Memo. to Cabinet Ministerial Committee on the Channel Tunnel Project on 'Channel Tunnel', CT(75) 1, 10 January 1975, CAB134/3873, PRO.
220 Cabinet Ministerial Committee on the Channel Tunnel Project Minutes, 14 January 1975, CAB134/3873, PRO, and see also Hunt-Wilson, 15 January 1975, Prime Minister's Maplin/Channel Tunnel papers, cit. Pt. 2. Committee members present were Elwyn-Jones, Crosland, Hattersley, and Joel Barnett (Chief Secretary, Treasury). Benn (Industry), Shore (Trade) and Lever (Duchy of Lancaster) were absent, though Lord Beswick (Trade Minister) and Clinton Davies (Parl. U-Sec for Trade) deputised, and Mulley and Peter Archer (Solicitor General) were also present.
221 Fogarty-McDonald, 15 January 1975, Callaghan, telegram No. 16 to British Embassy, Paris, 15 January 1975, MT144/288/2, PRO; Crosland-Cavaillé, 15 January 1975, Prime Minister's Maplin/Channel Tunnel papers, cit. Pt. 2.
222 Crosland-Wilson and Cabinet members, 15 January 1975, Prime Minister's Maplin/Channel Tunnel papers, cit. Pt. 2; Cabinet Conclusions, CC(75) 3rd, 16 January 1975, CAB128/56, PRO; Cabinet Secretary's Notebook, 16 January 1975.
223 Castle, *Castle Diaries 1974–76*, p. 281; Benn, *Diaries 1973–76*, p. 300.
224 Crosland statement, 20 January 1975, *Parl. Deb. (Commons)*, 5th ser. (Session 1974–5), Vol. 884, *c.*1021–3.
225 Callaghan, telegram No. 16, cit.; Cavaillé-Crosland, 18 January 1975, MT144/288/2, PRO.
226 Cabinet Conclusions CC(75) 4th, 21 January 1975, CAB128/56, PRO, and see also Tomkins-Sir Thomas Brimelow (Permanent U-Sec and Head of Diplomatic Service, FCO), 20 January 1975, Arculus-James, 29 January 1975, FCO file WRF8/4/75 Pt. B.
227 Tomkins, telegram No. 68 to FCO, 21 January 1975, Sir David Muirhead (British Ambassador, Brussels), telegram No. 14 to FCO, 22 January 1975, Bernard Wilcox (British Consulate, Lille)-Ratford, 27 January 1975, O'Hara, 'Record of a conversation with M Callou…', 30 January 1975, MT144/303, PRO; Arculus-James, 29 January 1975, cit.
228 *Times*, 18 January 1975, p. 1, 20 January 1975, pp. 2, 18; *Sunday Telegraph, Sunday Express, News of the World*, 19 January 1975, cuttings in DTp file IT4/5/66 Pt. 3; *Parl. Deb. (Commons)*, 5th ser. (Session 1974–5), Vol. 884, *c.*1023–34, 1094–1158. The Tunnel's defenders included Eric Ogden, Peter Snape, Robert Adley, John Peyton, David Crouch, and John Wells, its opponents included Leslie Huckfield, John Prescott, and Winnie Ewing. A motion to adjourn the House was defeated by 294 votes to 218.

229 Fogarty-Shearer *et al.*, 21 August 1975, enclosing 'Channel Tunnel: Experience of Project Abandoned January 1975. Notes for our Successors', August 1975, MT144/534, PRO; Tomkins, 'End of the Channel Tunnel Project', 14 March 1975, cit.; RTZDE Minutes, 4 August 1975, SRR0925 RT; There were also more public inquiries, e.g. by the *Sunday Times*: Keith Richardson *et al.*, 'Dark at the end of the Tunnel', *Sunday Times*, 19 January 1975, p. 49.

230 Hunt began a long professional association with the Tunnel project in Britain by becoming public relations consultant for CTSG in 1958.

231 Bonavia, *Channel Tunnel Story*, pp. 124–32.

232 Hunt, *Tunnel*, pp. 145–52. Crosland's biographers are silent on the Tunnel: Susan Crosland, *Tony Crosland* (1982); David Reisman, *Crosland's Future* (2 Vols., Basingstoke, 1996–7); Kevin Jeffreys, *Anthony Crosland: a new biography* (1999).

233 Morris and Hough, *Anatomy of Major Projects*, pp. 37–8, 195; Holliday *et al.*, *Channel Tunnel*, p. 11.

234 Gibb, 'Channel Tunnel Project', pp. 16–17, citing Peter Hall, *Great Planning Disasters* (1980), pp. 2, 7–8; Laurent Bonnaud, *Le Tunnel sous la Manche: deux siècles de passions* (Paris, 1994), pp. 175–226, and note p. 182.

235 Cabinet Conclusions, CC(74), e.g. 49th, 25 November 1974, CAB128/55, PRO. and cf. Healey, *Time of My Life*, pp. 380–1, 393 and Dilwyn Porter, 'Government and the economy', in Coopey and Woodward, *Britain in the 1970s*, p. 44.

236 Cf. M.L. Williams (Treasury)-James, 19 September 1974, J.B. Unwin (Treasury)-Rosalind Gilmore (Asst. Sec, Transport Industries Divn, Treasury), Gilmore-James, 27 November 1974, Treasury file 2PE 91/199/01 Pt. AP; James-Harrop, 16 October 1974, 2PE 91/1270/01; David Wright (Western European Dept., FCO)-James, 21 October 1974, FCO file WRF/8/9/74; Michael Scholar (Barnett's PS)-Gilmore, 13 January 1975, Treasury file 2PE 91/1297/02.

237 £159 m. in current prices: Gourvish, *British Rail 1974–97*, p. 88.

238 Cf. Tomkins, 'End of the Channel Tunnel Project', cit. para. 2.

239 Shearer, reported in BCTC, Notes of an informal BCTC meeting, 2 December 1974, CAR367, RT.

240 BCTC, informal meeting, 2 December 1974, cit.; RTZDE Minutes, 6 January 1975, SRR0925, RT.

241 Bowick-Marsh, 21 June 1974, AN191/150 Pt. 2; Bonavia, Note on 'Channel Tunnel Rail Link cost estimates: What went wrong?', 25 July 1974, AN191/19, PRO.

242 Gourvish, *British Rail 1974–97*, p. 11.

243 BR CT Policy Steering Group Minutes, 20 March 1974, AN191/270, PRO; Bowick-Marsh, 21 June 1974, cit.

244 Bonavia, *Channel Tunnel Story*, p. 132.

245 Cf. Rigby-Kemp (CTSU), 6 March 1972, MT144/381; Peter Kemp (Treasury)-James, 24 September 1974, Treasury file 2PE 91/83/01.

246 Mulley, reported in G.A. Wheeldon (Mulley's APS)-Fogarty, 20 June 1973, MT144/386; Fogarty-Morgan, 16 January 1974, MT144/388; Marshall-Shearer, 28 May 1974, MT144/360; Fogarty-Shearer, 20 June 1974, MT144/390, PRO; Mulley-Marsh, 17 December 1974, DTp file EPR21/1/5 Pt. 2; Interview with Peter Kemp, 15 October 2002.

247 M.R. Bonavia, *The Economics of Transport* (1936, 7th edn, 1954); Bowick-Marsh, 21 June 1974, cit.; Bonavia-Harding, 26 July 1974, AN191/19, PRO.

248 This term has been attributed to BRB member Cliff Rose: Peter Parker, *For Starters: The Business of Life* (1989), p. 206.

249 Trains arriving at or departing from London (Waterloo), 7.30–9.30 a.m.: Eurostar timetable, December 2002–June 2003, www.eurostar.com.

250 Fogarty, MPA seminar transcript, cit.

251 DOE, 'Channel Tunnel: Experience of Project Abandoned January 1975', cit., Note 2.
252 Woodhouse-Fogarty, 22 August 1975, MT144/535, PRO.
253 Bonavia-McKenna, 17 April 1973, AN191/148; Slater-Rosenfeld, 7 February 1974, MT144/388, PRO; Bonavia, Note, 25 July 1974, cit.
254 Kemp-James, 11 July 1974, Treasury file 2PE 91/199/01 Pt. AP; James-Harrop, 16 October 1974, 2PE 91/1270/01; Burr-Fogarty, 'Sero Venientibus Ossa', 30 May 1975, MT144/534, PRO.
255 *Parl. Deb. (Commons)*, 5th ser. (Session 1974-5), Vol. 884, Peter Snape (MP for West Bromwich East), 20 January 1975, *c.*1133.
256 'Draft Note of a meeting to discuss the Channel Tunnel project on 12 November 1974', n.d. MT144/503, PRO; see also Mulley-Crosland, 18 November 1974, DTp file FN5/3/25 Pt. 5.
257 Frame-Shearer, 22 May 1975, MT144/534, PRO; DOE, 'Channel Tunnel: Experience of Project Abandoned January 1975', cit.; RTZDE Minutes, 10 September 1975, SRR0925, RT.
258 DOE, 'Channel Tunnel: Experience of Project Abandoned January 1975', cit. Note 2.
259 Ibid. Note 2, 4.

7 KEEPING HOPES ALIVE, 1975–81

1 Agreement No. 2, cit. Section 6, and esp. paras. 6.1.3, 6.2.1, 6.2.9; Exchange of Notes, cit. p. xxxii.
2 Fogarty-Harcourt, 20 January 1975, Fogarty-BCTC and SFTM, 20 January 1975, quadripartite agreement, 20 January 1975, MT144/516, PRO.
3 Fogarty-Semple, 22 January 1975, MT144/522; Burr-Gilmore, 24 January 1975, Gilmore-Burr, same date, MT144/516, PRO and see also Treasury file 2PE 91/1297/03.
4 Fogarty-Morgan, and Burr-Gilmore, 28 January 1975, Burr-Naylor (BCTC), 12 February 1975, bipartite agreements, 27 January, 3 and 17 February 1975, MT144/516, PRO.
5 Cf. Brimelow-Tomkins, 27 January 1975, FCO file WRF8/4/75 Pt. B; O'Hara, 'Record of Conversation with M Callou', 30 January 1975, cit.; Kenneth James-Fogarty, 5 February and reply, 10 February 1975, MT144/522, PRO.
6 Touche Ross & Co., 'Report dated 3rd March 1975 to the Department of the Environment on the Expenditure incurred by the British Channel Tunnel Company Limited', Butt-D.J. Lyness (Asst Sec, DOE), 5 March 1975, MT144/519; Fogarty-Morgan, 3 March 1975, Fogarty-Harcourt, 4 and 13 March 1975, MT144/526, PRO.
7 I.e. £15,000 per month cf. £42,000, for six months, after which a fee equal to 35% of reimbursable costs. Fogarty-Naylor, 6 March 1975, Noulton-Shearer, 20 March 1975, BCTC Board Minutes, 21 March 1975, Fogarty-Semple *et al.*, 21 March 1975, Fogarty-Macé, 25 March 1975, MT144/526, and see also agreement, 21 March 1975, MT144/528, PRO.
8 D'Erlanger had been Hon. President of BCTC. See Fogarty-Semple et al., 21 March 1975, cit.; Peter Gallichan (Hill Samuel)-Noulton, 12 March 1975, Naylor-Fogarty, 7 March 1975, MT144/526, PRO.
9 Fogarty-Burr, 12 February 1975, McPetrie-Burr, 6 May 1975, MT144/533, PRO; Slaughter & May-Merton (CT Investments), 13 February 1975, TSI archive, carton #14 f11, HBS.
10 Alfred Davidson, Note, 15 October 1975, TSI archive, carton #13 f7, HBS.
11 Burr-Gould, 7 May and reply, 14 May 1975, Merton-Fogarty, 2 April 1975, Merton-Crosland, 17 October 1975, Noulton-Shearer, 11 November 1975, Rosenfeld-Merton, 13 November 1975, MT144/533, PRO.

12 Merton-Fogarty, 2 April, and reply, 18 April 1975, MT144/526, PRO.

13 Burr-McPetrie, 27 February 1975, MT144/516; Fogarty-Wright, 11 March 1975, Burr-Fogarty, 14 March 1975, with 'Note of Discussion with French Officials on 13 March 1975', Fogarty-Semple, 25 March 1975, with 'Channel Tunnel Abandonment: Cost Sharing between Governments', MT144/522, PRO.

14 Fogarty-Burr, 2 April 1975, Fogarty-Rosenfeld, 25 April and reply, 30 April 1975, MT144/519; Fogarty-Burr, 22 April 1975, MT144/523, PRO; Arculus-O'Hara, 22 April 1975, FCO file WRF8/4/75 Pt. C.

15 Burr-Morgan, 16 May 1975, MT144/524, PRO; O'Hara-Wright, 13 June 1975, FCO file WRF8/4/75 Pt. D.

16 Tomkins and J. Sauvagnargues (French Foreign Minister), *Exchange of Notes between the Government of the United Kingdom... and the Government of the French Republic relating to the Abandonment of the Channel Tunnel Project. Paris, 24 June 1975*, October 1975, P.P.1974–5, xxxviii, Cmnd. 6261.

17 Fogarty-Semple *et al.*, 27 June 1975, MT144/514, PRO.

18 Horace Parker (RTZDE)-Fogarty, 14 April 1975, enclosing 'Channel Tunnel State of Site Work on January 27, 1975', MT144/523, PRO.

19 Parker-Fogarty, 14 April 1975, cit.; Antony Terry, *Sunday Times*, 22 December 1974; Hunt, *Tunnel*, p. 150; Fetherston, *Chunnel*, p. 87.

20 Fogarty-Rosenfeld, 27 February 1975, MT144/522, PRO.

21 Edward Glover, Draft Note on 'Tunnelling Machines', December 1975, MT144/535, PRO and cf. Hunt, *Tunnel*, p. 150.

22 Fogarty-Gilmore, 24 January 1975, Treasury file 2PE 91/1321/01; Interview with John Noulton, 18 June 2003.

23 Mulley-Joel Barnett (Chief Secretary, Treasury), 28 January and 21 February, and replies, 30 January and 28 February 1975, Fogarty-Morgan, 13 February 1975, MT144/517, PRO.

24 In 1978: Memo. on 'Channel Tunnel – Dover Site', n.d. [1977], MT144/532, PRO; *Tunnels and Tunnelling*, 12 (9) (November 1979), p. 9.

25 *Parl. Deb. (Commons)*, 5th ser. (Session 1974–5), Vol. 895, Crosland, written answer to Roger Moate, 7 July 1975, *21*.

26 BCTC Project Management Committee Minutes, 19 December 1975, MT144/537, PRO.

27 DOE CTU, 'Channel Tunnel: Notes for our Successors', August 1975, cit. and see MT144/535, PRO.

28 Crosland, statement, 29 January 1975, cit.; *Parl. Deb. (Commons)*, 5th ser. (Session 1974–5), Vol. 887, Mulley, written answer to Moate, 28 February 1975, *268*.

29 See MT144/541, PRO.

30 BCTC Management Accounts, 21 May 1975, MT144/520; Noulton-Fogarty, 11 July 1975, Treasury file 2PE 91/1297/03; Noulton-Martin (DOE), 19 September 1975, and subsequent adjustments, MT144/541, PRO.

31 BCTC, 'Cost Report as at 31st December 1975', MT144/539, BCTC Reports & Accounts, 1975–7, MT144/538/2, PRO.

32 When William Rodgers (SoS for Transport) was asked by Gordon Wilson (MP for Dundee East) about the total cost in April 1979, he replied that 'Information... is not readily available': *Parl. Deb. (Commons)*, 5th ser. (Session 1978–9), Vol. 965, written answer, 2 April 1979, *552*. See also Bonnaud, *Le Tunnel*, p. 226.

33 CTAG Minutes, 7 October 1974, BS1/1, PRO.

34 Shearer-Cairncross, 24 July 1974, Cairncross Papers on Channel Tunnel Advisory Group, DC106/3/17, Glasgow University Archive Service (GUAS).

35 Arthur Knight (Courtaulds)-Crosland, 18 December 1974, MT144/501, PRO. None of the merchant bankers approached was able to give time to the committee.

36 Channel Tunnel Reassessment Steering Committee Minutes, 18 June and 6 September 1974, Treasury file 2PE 91/460/02; Crosland-Cairncross, 17 July 1974, Cairncross Papers, DC106/3/17, GUAS; Marshall-John Harvey-Jones (ICI), 18 September 1974 and similar letters, MT144/501, PRO; CTAG Minutes, 7 October 1974, cit.; DOE, *The Channel Tunnel and alternative cross Channel services. A Report presented to the Secretary of State for the Environment by the Channel Tunnel Advisory Group* (HMSO, 1975) [hereafter CTAG Report], Preface, p. v.
37 CTAG Minutes, 17 and 30 December 1974, 13 January 1975, BS1/1, PRO.
38 CTAG Minutes, 20 January and 3 February 1975, BS1/1, PRO; Cairncross-Crosland, 24 January 1975, MT144/501, PRO.
39 John James-Cousins and Harrop, 10 October 1974, Gilmore-Harrop, 25 November 1974, Treasury file 2PE 91/3/01; Gilmore-Burr, 11 December 1974, MT144/505; Burr-Naylor (BCTC), 17 October 1974, Frame (BCTC)-Burr, 21 November and reply, 27 November 1974, MT144/504, PRO; Channel Tunnel Reassessment Steering Committee Minutes, 20 December 1974, cit. In the end, the disparity between the consultants and the Treasury was not dramatic, e.g. for GNP growth in 1973–80 consultants: 1.75/2.5/3.25% cf. Treasury: 2.75/3.0/3.25%.
40 Alastair Balls (DOE CTU)-Coopers & Lybrand, 17 October 1974, Roger Chorley (Coopers & Lybrand)-Fogarty, 13 December 1974, MT144/506, PRO.
41 Cf. Balls-Fogarty, December 1974, MT144/506; Burr-Fogarty, 19 December 1974, MT144/505, PRO. See also CTAG Minutes, 21 October, 4 and 25 November 1974, BS1/1, PRO.
42 CTAG Report, para. 5.2.1.
43 Mulley-Marsh, 31 January 1975, AN191/151, PRO.
44 Marsh-Mulley, 12 February 1975, enclosing BRB, 'Channel Tunnel Rail Link Lower cost options for rail access to the tunnel: Preliminary assessment', 15 January 1975, MT144/392, PRO.
45 BRB, Preliminary assessment, January 1975, cit. pp. 1–2, 15, appendices A and B; Burr-Shearer, 19 February 1975, Hitchins, Note for File, 11 March 1975, MT144/392, PRO.
46 Gourvish, *British Rail 1974–97*, pp. 13–17, 521.
47 *Sunday Times*, 19 January 1975, p. 1; Morgan-Burr, 18 February 1975, Morgan-Semple, 21 February 1975, MT144/392, PRO; Keen, draft MPA seminar transcript, 1982, cit.
48 Fogarty-Burr, 13 February 1975, MT144/392, PRO; *Parl. Deb. (Commons)*, 5th ser. (Session 1974–5), Vol. 887, 26 February 1975, Crosland, written answer to Ronald Atkins (MP for Preston North), *142*.
49 See CTAG Report, para. 1.4.3, p. 52; information in BS1/6 and 1/9, PRO, and Cairncross Papers, DC106/3/5, GUAS.
50 CTAG Minutes, 17 February and 3 March 1975, BS1/1; Fogarty-Balls, 21 March 1975, MT144/514, PRO; CTAG Minutes, 24 March 1975, Jenny Williams (DOE)-Cairncross et al., 27 February 1975, Balls-Cairncross, 20 August 1975, Cairncross Papers, DC106/3/6, GUAS.
51 Morgan-D. Lipsey (Crosland's APS), 23 January 1975, and cf. Crosland, *Parl. Deb. (Commons)*, 5th ser. (Session 1974–5), Vol. 884, *c.*1029.
52 Burr-Wright (FCO), 11 April 1975, Crosland-Cairncross, 24 June 1975, MT144/514, PRO.
53 Fogarty-Morgan, 10 June 1975, MT144/514, PRO. Cairncross had not been impressed with British Rail managers (Peter Keen excepted): Jenny Williams-Sharp, 7 August 1975, DTp file RA 13/114/12 Pt. 7.
54 Crosland-Elwyn-Jones, 24 June 1975, Prime Minister [Wilson]'s Maplin/Channel Tunnel papers, cit. Pt. 2. Elwyn-Jones asked that a final meeting of his committee

should consider general issues arising from the Cairncross report: Elwyn-Jones-Crosland, 3 July 1975, ibid. and see also Peters-Hamilton, 30 June 1975, Cabinet Office file on 'Channel Tunnel', 183/1 Pt. 5.

55 Fogarty-Sharp, 10 June 1975, Crosland-Marsh, 24 June 1975, McKenna-Fogarty, 14 July and reply, 18 July 1975, Fogarty-Shearer, 9 and 18 July 1975, Fogarty-Neville Taylor (Director, Information, DOE), 18 July 1975, MT144/514, PRO.

56 *Parl. Deb. (Commons)*, 5th ser. (Session 1974–5), Vol. 896, Crosland, oral answer to Costain, *c*.551; DOE Press Notice, 23 July 1975, MT144/514, PRO.

57 CTAG Report, paras. 5.2.1, 5.2.6 and Annex A.

58 Ibid. para. 4.2.3, and see also 2.5.1–7, 4.2.1–2.

59 Ibid. paras. 2.6.21–4.

60 Ibid. paras. 2.7.2, 2.7.4, 2.7.7–9 and Section 4.4; Crosland, oral answer, 23 July 1975, cit. *c*.552.

61 CTAG Report, para. 4.4.6, and see Section 4 generally. The Group also examined the costs and benefits of postponing the Tunnel plus intermediate rail investment for five years (Section 4.5). Both the NPV and return rose, to £131 m. and 15%, but benefits would be foregone in the period of postponement, and there was the risk that the Tunnel's competitive position would be weakened by technological developments.

62 Ibid. paras. 5.1.1–5.

63 Ibid. paras. 5.3.2–5.

64 Ibid. paras. 5.4.3–4.

65 Ibid. paras. 5.1.7, 5.4.3–10.

66 *Times*, 24 July 1975, p. 3; *Guardian*, 24 July 1975, p. 5.

67 Cf. Callou, telex to Noulton, 22 July 1975, Callou-Fogarty, 24 July 1975, MT144/514, PRO and see also FCO file, WRF8/4/75 Pt. D. On press reaction cf. Ivor Rawlinson (British Embassy, Paris)-David Wright (FCO), 28 July 1975, and cuttings in MT144/514, PRO.

68 Shearer-Cairncross, 12 June 1975, MT144/514, PRO.

69 Hawkins (CPRS), note, 21 July 1975, Berrill-Pugh, 28 July and reply, 11 August 1975, CPRS file Q9/2 Pt. 3.

70 Fogarty-Sharp, 30 July 1975, MT144/514; McKenna-Fogarty, 24 July 1975, Fogarty-Gould, 29 August 1975, and further critical comments in MT144/515, PRO and DTp file EPR21/1/1.

71 Michael Bonavia, 'Cairncross and the Channel Tunnel rail link', *Railway Gazette International*, September 1975, pp. 351–3, and note DOE criticisms ['it would have been even more interesting had he taken the attitude expressed in the article when he was in office', Gould-Fogarty, 30 September 1975, MT144/515, PRO]; Alan Cornish (Afco Associates), letter to *Financial Times*, 4 August 1975, and Cornish-Crosland, same date, MT144/515, and see DOE criticisms in ibid.

72 Crosland, Memo. to Cabinet Ministerial Committee on the Channel Tunnel Project on 'Channel Tunnel: Report of the Advisory Group Chaired by Sir Alec Cairncross', CT(75) 2, 6 October 1975, CAB134/3873, PRO.

73 Cairncross, Minute, 31 May 1949, cit. in Grayson, 'Channel Tunnel and European Unity', 415, 420.

74 Cairncross Report, paras. 3.5.14–16 and cf. RTZDE, 'Observations on the Cairncross Report', 10 July 1975, RTZDE Board Minutes, 14 July 1975, SRR0925, RT.

75 Walter A. Barry Jr. (Vice-President, De Leuw, Cather & Co.)-Frank Davidson, 19 June 1975, TSI archive, carton #13 f6, HBS. See also David Williams (Planning & Investment Dept., BRB)-T.R. [Bob] Barron (Director of Planning & Investment, BRB), 28 September 1977, AN156/370, PRO; Frank Davidson, *Macro: Big is Beautiful* (1986 edn.), pp. 98, 212; Fetherston, *Chunnel*, p. 89.

76 RTZDE, 'Review of a Two-Tunnel System', August 1975, Frame-Frank Davidson, 20 August 1975, TSI archive carton #14 f.11–12; Al Davidson-Frank Davidson, 2, 9

and 15 October 1975, carton #13 f7, HBS. See also Barron, Memo. to BRB Railway Executive Committee [REC], 12 May 1977, AN156/370, PRO.

77 Jacques Bachelez (President, CGE-DE), 'Note sur un Projet de Tunnel Ferroviaire à voie unique sous la Manche', 18 September 1975, TSI archive, carton #13 f6, HBS; Frame, reported in RTZDE Board Minutes, 6 October 1975, SRR0925, RT.

78 Bachelez, Note, cit.

79 De Vitry-Hutter, 6 August 1975, Frank Davidson-Kenneth Galbraith, 21 October 1975, TSI archive, carton #13 f6; Al Davidson-Frank Davidson, 9 October 1975, reporting Sir Robert Marshall, f7; also Dallas Bernard-Al Davidson, 26 September 1975, carton #14 f11, HBS. See also RTZDE Board Minutes, 11 July 1977, SRR0925, RT.

80 Davidson, *Macro*, pp. 100–1.

81 RTZDE Board Minutes, 4 August, 10 September and 17 December 1975, SRR0925, RT.

82 Cf. Gould-Shearer, 22 December 1975, DTp file P65/1/60 Pt. 4; Bosworth-Peter Parker (Chairman, BRB), 14 October 1976, AN156/373, PRO.

83 RTZDE Board Minutes, 11 June 1976, SRR0925, RT; Frame-Marsh, 28 May, and reply, 18 June 1976, AN192/616, PRO.

84 Sir Douglas Wass (Permanent Sec, Treasury)-Sir Ian P. Bancroft (Permanent Sec, DOE), 19 March 1976, P.R.H. Wright (Wilson's PS)-Chris Brearley (PPS, Cabinet Office), 23 March 1976, Prime Minister's Maplin/Channel Tunnel papers, cit. Pt. 3. Wilson announced his resignation on the 16th: Cabinet Conclusions, CC(76) 10th, 16 March 1976, CAB128/58, PRO.

85 DOE, Note to Cabinet European Unit on 'New Proposal for Channel Tunnel', EUT(76) 7, 26 March 1976, Prime Minister's Maplin/Channel Tunnel papers, cit. Pt. 3.

86 Nigel Wicks (Callaghan's PS)-Jim Callaghan 26 April 1976, Sir Maurice Laing (Laing Construction Ltd)-Callaghan, 23 April 1976, Peter Shore (SoS for Environment)-Tony Crosland (SoS for Foreign & Commonwealth Affairs), 20 May, 17 June and 16 July 1976, Barnett-Crosland, 27 May 1976, Crosland-Shore, 19 July 1976, Prime Minister [now Callaghan]'s Maplin/Channel Tunnel papers, cit. Pt. 3. On Callaghan see David Butler and Dennis Kavanagh, *The British General Election of 1979* (1980), pp. 30–1; James Callaghan, *Time and Chance* (1987), pp. 390–4; Kenneth O. Morgan, *Callaghan: A Life* (Oxford, 1997), pp. 469–74.

87 CGE-DE and RTZDE, 'Channel Tunnel: Feasibility of a Single Track Scheme. Preliminary Note', February 1977, AN191/300, PRO.

88 Bowick-Parker (copied to Bosworth), 21 December 1976, Bosworth-Bowick, 23 December 1976, AN156/373, PRO. In October 1977 Bowick was appointed Chairman of the DGs of the Group of Nine Railways in Europe: BRB, *R & A 1978*, p. 30.

89 T.R. Barron became a part-timer in April 1978.

90 On earlier reservations see M.H. Harbinson (BRB)-Bowick *et al.*, 23 December 1975, Henry Sanderson (Executive Director (Passenger), BRB)-Harbinson, 29 December 1975, AN156/373, PRO.

91 Barron, Memo. to BRB REC, 12 May 1977, cit.; Barron, Memo. to BRB Chairman's Conference, 21 July 1977, Bowick to Bob Reid I (BRB Board Member, Marketing), 13 July 1977, AN156/370, PRO.

92 Barron, Memo. on 'Channel Tunnel', 28 July 1977, BRB REC Minutes, 1 August 1977, AN167/440, PRO.

93 Bowick-Reid, 13 July 1977, Bowick-Sanderson, 6 October 1977, AN156/370, PRO.

94 David Williams-Barron, 16 September 1977, Williams-Bowick, 23 September 1977, AN156/370, PRO.

95 Bowick-Parker, 4 October 1977, Campbell-Bowick, 10 October 1977, AN156/370; 'Cross Channel Rail Link: Note of discussion held in Paris 24 October 1977', 1 November 1977; Barron-Bowick, 25 October 1977, AN192/616; BRB REC Minutes, 30 October 1977, AN167/440, PRO.

96 Williams-Barron, 30 September 1977, Bosworth-Bowick, 7 October 1977, AN156/370, PRO; BRB REC Minutes, 30 October 1977, cit.; Pliatzky (Treasury)-Sir Peter Baldwin (Permanent Sec, DTp), 9 September 1977, Treasury file PE 106/443/01.

97 Williams-Barron, 28 September 1977, cit.; Bowick-Parker, 3 October 1977, Barron-Parker, 13 October 1977, enclosing 'Note of discussion, 13th October 1977', AN156/370, PRO.

98 Barron-Parker *et al.*, 30 December 1977, enclosing brief on 'Cross Channel Rail Link', AN192/616; David Williams-Barron, 16 February 1978, AN191/302, PRO; RTZDE Board Minutes, 11 June 1976, 11 July 1977, SRR0925, RT.

99 Cf. European Parliament resolution, 17 February 1975, in FCO file WRF8/6/75.

100 OJ C 207, presented to Council of Ministers, 5 July 1976. See Carlo degli Abbati, *Transport and European Integration* (EEC, Luxembourg, 1987), pp. 77, 137–9.

101 Parker-Jenkins, 2 December 1976, Peter Parker's Papers, PP11, and see also Bosworth-Parker, 14 October 1976, AN156/373, PRO.

102 Sir Nicholas Henderson (British Ambassador, Paris)-Parker, 30 June 1977, Parker-Henderson, 13 July 1977, AN156/370, PRO.

103 European Parliament Resolution, 4 July 1977; *Times*, 5 July 1977, pp. 5, 8; *Daily Express*, 7 July 1977, p. 11; *Parl. Deb. (Commons)*, 5th ser. (Session 1976–7), Vol. 927, Rodgers, oral answer to Philip Whitehead (MP for Derby North), 9 March 1977, *c.*1382; Vol. 935–2, Rodgers, answer to Costain, 20 July 1977, *c.*1595–6.

104 Bowick-Sanderson, 6 October 1977, and Barron-Parker et al., 30 December 1977, cit.; BRB REC Minutes, 7 November 1977, AN167/440, PRO.

105 European Council Decision, OJ L 54, 20 February 1978; BRB, *R & A 1978*, p. 30; John Whitelegg, *Transport Policy in the EEC* (1988), p. 21. The Tunnel was included in a list of projects drawn up by the Commission in November 1979: EC Commission, *A Transport Network for Europe: Outline of a Policy* (8/79).

106 *Times*, 3 April 1978, p. 3, 4 April 1978, p.3; *Sunday Telegraph*, 9 April 1978; European Commission, Durieux, written question No. 119/78, 14 April 1978, answer, 15 June 1978, extract in AN156/370, PRO.

107 Cairncross, letter to the *Times*, 8 June 1978, and see Barron-Cairncross, 8 June 1978, AN192/616, PRO.

108 *Parl. Deb. (Commons)*, 5th ser. (Session 1977–8), Vol. 949, Rodgers, oral answers to Peter Rost (MP for Derby South-East) and Gordon Bagier (Sunderland South), 3 May 1978 *c.*216–17, and see also answers on 1 March, 21 April and 7 June 1978.

109 DTp, 'Note of Discussions with Herr Gescheidle … 26 June 1978', July 1978, DTp file RA102/1/21 Pt. 1; Rodgers-Callaghan, 22 July 1978, Prime Minister's Maplin/Channel Tunnel papers, cit. Pt. 3; *Financial Times*, 27 June 1978, p. 6.

110 Barron (BRB) and Louis Lacoste (DG Adjoint, SNCF), 'Channel Tunnel. Joint Report on new proposal for a single track rail tunnel', August 1978, AN191/306, PRO.

111 BRB Minutes, 14 September 1978, AN167/44, PRO.

112 Barron-Lazarus (Dep Sec, DTp), 30 August 1978, DTp file FN 5/3/25 Pt. 5; Lazarus-Nicholas Monck (U-Sec, Treasury), 1 September 1978, Treasury file PE 106/443/02 Pt. A.

113 DTp, 'Note of a Meeting between the Secretary of State and the French Minister for Transport', 13 September 1978, DTp file RA102/1/21 Pt. 1; Sir Michael Palliser (Permanent U-Sec, FCO)-Sir John Hunt (Cabinet Secretary), 2 November 1978, Treasury file PE 106/443/02 Pt. A; Lazarus-Anthony Goldman (Rodgers's PS), 24 October 1978, DTp file FN 5/3/25 Pt. 5.

114 Lazarus-Goldman, 24 October 1978, cit.; Sarah Whitcombe (Rodgers's APS)-Lazarus, 26 October 1978, DTp file FN 5/3/25 Pt. 5.

115 Hugh Arbuthnott (British Embassy, Paris)-Tony Fairclough (Head of International Transport Divn, DTp), 18 December 1978, FCO file WRF178/1/78; Fairclough-Goldman, 29 December 1978, Fairclough-Goldman, 16 January 1979, enclosing 'Record of Meeting between Mr A J Fairclough... and M Collet... 12 January 1979', FCO file WRF178/1/79.

116 BRB Minutes, 14 December 1978, AN167/44; Parker-Rodgers, 1 February 1979, enclosing BRB, 'A Report on a Cross-Channel Rail Link', January 1979, AN192/616, PRO; BRB, *Cross Channel Rail Link* (February 1979), and *A Report on a Cross-Channel Rail link* (April 1979).

117 Whitcombe-Tim Lankester (Callaghan's PS), 5 February 1979, Prime Minister's Maplin/Channel Tunnel papers, cit. Pt. 3.

118 Cf. Cabinet Conclusions, CM(79) 6th, 1 February 1979; Morgan, *Callaghan*, pp. 501, 626–50, 655–74; Callaghan, *Time and Chance*, p. 513ff.

119 *Parl. Deb. (Commons)*, 5th ser. (Session 1978–9), Vol. 962, Rodgers, written answer to Bagier, 8 February 1979, *302*, and see also answers on 15 and 28 March 1979.

120 Cabinet Conclusions, CM(79) 14th, 29 March 1979; Butler and Kavanagh, *General Election 1979*, pp. 125–7; Morgan, *Callaghan*, pp. 684–5; Callaghan, *Time and Chance*, pp. 563–4; David Gowland and Arthur Turner, *Reluctant Europeans: Britain and European Integration 1945–1998* (2000), pp. 214–29; Nicholas Henderson, *Mandarin: The Diaries of an Ambassador 1969–1982* (1994), pp. 59, 94.

121 See Goldman-W. Sutherland (Baldwin's PS), 30 March 1977, Lazarus-Sutherland, 31 March 1977, Denis Fagan (International Transport Divn, DTp)-Lazarus, 6 July 1977, T.M. Kane (IT Divn, DTp)-Nevitt, 15 August 1977, John Low (Office of UK Permanent Representative to EC)-William Marsden (FCO), 30 June 1978, FCO file MWE178/1/78, and see also DTp file IT 401/014 Pt. 1.

122 Tiratsoo, *From Blitz to Blair*, p. 185; Butler and Kavanagh, *General Election 1979*, pp.166–8, 340; Morgan, *Callaghan*, pp. 686–98, Thatcher, *Path to Power*, p. 440ff.

123 'The Real Fight is for Britain', Liberal Party Manifesto 1979, cit. in Craig, *British General Election Manifestos*, p. 317.

124 Norman Fowler, *Ministers Decide: A Personal Memoir of the Thatcher Years* (1991), pp. 81–6, 125–6; Gourvish, *British Rail 1974–97*, p. 103.

125 Baldwin-Fowler, 11 May 1979, enclosing 'Channel Tunnel – Draft Submission to Secretary of State', in FCO file WRF178/1/79, and see also Rodgers-Parker, 7 March 1979, AN192/616, PRO.

126 Norman Fowler (Minister of Transport)-Margaret Thatcher (PM), 24 July 1979, and Thatcher's annotation, n.d., Prime Minister [Thatcher]'s papers on 'Transport: The Channel Tunnel', Pt. 1.

127 Fowler-Cairncross, 2 October 1979, DTp File IT40/2/6 Pt. 2, and for earlier approaches, Monck-Anthea Case (Treasury), 4 September 1978, John Rosenfeld (Principal Finance Officer, DTp)-Monck, 25 January 1979, Treasury file PE 106/443/02 Pt. A; Baldwin-Cairncross, 8 March and 2 April 1979, DTp files IT40/2/6 Pt. 2 and IT40/2/25 Pt. 11.

128 Angela Moss (DTp CTU)-Brian Payne (DTp CTU), 25 November 1979, DTp file IT40/2/22 Pt. 1; Fairclough-Barron, 10 July 1980, AN191/326, PRO.

129 Barron-Bowick, 6 March 1979, Barron-BRB members, 30 March 1979, AN192/616, PRO. Subsequently, a representative of SNCB attended the high-level directing group. Gerry Burt (Chief Secretary, BRB), Memo. on 'Cross Channel Rail Link', 22 March 1979, Barron, Memo. to BRB Railway Executive [RE] on 'Cross-Channel Rail Link: Patterns of Operation', 15 January 1980, AN192/617, PRO.

130 Barron, Memo. 15 January 1980, cit.; BRB RE Minutes, 21 January 1980, AN192/172; Williams, Memo. on 'Cross-Channel Rail Link: Operating Pattern: Meeting with SNCF, 19 September 1979', 20 September 1979, Barron-Parker,

13 December 1979, AN156/370; Barron-Lacoste, 26 March 1980, AN191/323, PRO; Hunt, *Tunnel*, p. 155.

131 BRB RE Minutes, 24 September 1979, AN192/172; Bob Reid I, reported in James Urquhart (Board Member, Operations & Productivity, BRB), 'Note for Papers', 4 October 1979, F.D. Pattisson (Chief Administration Officer, BRB)-Campbell, Reid and Urquhart (BRB), enclosing 'Note of Meeting 4 October 1979', 11 October 1979, AN156/370, PRO.

132 Parker-Roy Jenkins, 9 August 1979, AN192/616; David Williams, 'Note of Meeting held in Brussels, 1 October 1979', 10 October 1979, 'Notes of Meeting held in Brussels, Monday, 15 October 1979', Peter Parker's Papers, PP11; J.M. Crammer (Head of International Policy Office, BRB), 'Chairman's Reception for British MEP's in Strasbourg, 10 December 1979: An Appreciation', n.d., AN156/370, PRO.

133 See 'Channel Tunnel Island Project', August 1978, Nicolson-Parker, 18 September 1978, Nicolson (Co-Chairman, European Channel Tunnel Group)-Parker, 19 November and 1 December 1979, Peter Parker's Papers, PP11; Barron, File Note, 23 November 1979, AN191/319, PRO; *Financial Times*, 18 August 1979, p. 2.

134 Michael Posner (Part-time Member, BRB)-Barron, 19 April 1979, AN192/616, PRO; Barron, Notes of discussions with Cairncross, 12 November and 6 December 1979, Peter Parker's Papers, PP11.

135 Cairncross-Fowler, 23 January 1980, DTp file IT40/2/22 Pt. 1; 'Note of a meeting with the Minister of Transport 28 January 1980', IT40/2/25 Pt. 11.

136 Parker-Fowler, 5 October 1979, replying to Fowler-Parker, 4 October 1979, AN192/616, PRO.

137 Baldwin-Fowler, 18 February 1980, enclosing DTp CTU, 'Report by the Channel Tunnel Unit on the Initial Report of the BRB/SNCF Channel Tunnel Study', DTp file IT40/2/22 Pt. 2.

138 *Financial Times*, 26 February 1980, Barron-Parker *et al.*, 27 February 1980, AN156/370, PRO. Baldwin did drop hints that a bigger tunnel was required: cf. Barron, Memo. 30 January 1980, AN192/617, PRO.

139 BRB Management Brief, 5 March 1980, AN156/370, PRO; HC Transport Select Committee, *European Commission Green Paper on Transport Infrastructure. Minutes of Evidence, 5 March 1980: British Railways Board*, P.P.1979–80, xxviii, HC466-ii, QQ.82, 105–38.

140 Barron-Parker, 12 March 1980, AN192/617, PRO.

141 DTp, 'Note of Meeting on Channel Tunnel: Wednesday 5 March 1980', 6 March 1980, DTp file IT40/2/22 Pt. 2.

142 EC Commission, 'The Role of the Community in the Development of Transport Infrastructure', 14 November 1979, Doc 10808 (COM (79) 550 final), and see DTp, Background Paper, March 1980, in HC Transport Select Committee, *Transport Infrastructure. MOE, 25 March 1980: DTp*, P.P.1979–80, xxviii, HC466-iii, pp. 50–4, and HC Transport Select Committee, *Report on The European Commission's Green Paper on Transport Infrastructure*, May 1980, P.P.1979–80, xxviii, HC466-v, paras. 1–2.

143 *Parl. Deb. (Commons)*, 5th ser. (Session 1979–80), Vol. 981, Kenneth Clarke (PUSS, DTp), replying to Ogden, 17 March 1980, *c*.174–82.

144 *Parl. Deb. (Commons)*, 5th ser. (Session 1979–80), Vol. 981, Fowler, oral answer to Spriggs (MP for St Helens) and Whitehead, 19 March 1980, *c*.388–9, 392. On Downing Street reactions to the statement see Fowler-Thatcher, 10 March 1980, Nick Sanders (Thatcher's PS)-Thatcher, 18 March 1980, and Thatcher's annotation: 'I don't see that there is anything to make a statement about?': Prime Minister's Channel Tunnel papers, Pt. 1.

145 Lazarus-Rosenfeld, 10 March 1980, DTp file IT40/2/3 Pt. 1; Gourvish, *British Rail 1974–97*, pp. 234–5.

146 HC Transport Committee press release, 3 April 1980, DTp file IT40/5/6 Pt. 1. The decision was made on 25 March: P.P.1979–80, lii, 12 November 1980, p. 9.
147 Anne Davies, *Reformed Select Committees: The First Year* (Outer Circle Policy Unit, 1980), pp. 2–4; Priscilla Barnes, 'History and Rationale of the 1979 Reforms', in Gavin Drewry (ed.), *The New Select Committees: A Study of the 1979 reforms* (Oxford, 2nd edn., 1989), pp. 26–34, 254–67.
148 Fairclough-David Holmes (U-Sec, Finance Divn, DTp) and Genie Flanagan (Fowler's PS), 18 January 1980, DTp file IT40/5/6/ Pt. 1.
149 Baldwin-Fowler, 11 May 1979, cit.
150 Fairclough-D. Barclay (Baldwin's PS), 14 January 1980, enclosing paper to DTp Transport Policy and Management Board on 'Channel Tunnel – Questions concerning the handling of proposals', n.d., DTp file RA124/4/2 Pt. 4 and see Council for Science and Industry and Outer Circle Policy Unit, *The Big Public Inquiry* (June 1979), pp. 2–3, 18–26.
151 HC Transport Select Committee, *Transport Matters. Minutes of Evidence, 23 January 1980: Department of Transport*, P.P.1979/80, xxiii, HC381, Den Dover (MP for Chorley), Q.25 and Fowler's reply.
152 W. Deakin (DTp)-Fairclough, 7 February 1980, DTp file IT40/5/6 Pt. 1; Baldwin-Fowler, 19 February 1980, cit.
153 Fairclough-Jennifer Page (Asst Sec, DTp) *et al.*, 19 March 1980, DTp file IT40/5/6 Pt. 1; Anthony Goldman (Asst Sec, DTp)-Fairclough, 27 March 1980, IT40/5/66 Pt.5.
154 HC Transport Committee press release, 3 April 1980, cit. and cf. Burt, Memo. 9 April 1980, AN156/370, PRO.
155 HC Transport Select Committee, *Report on Channel Fixed Link*, February 1981 (3 Vols.), P.P.1980–1, xx, HC155; Gabriele Ganz, *Government and Industry: The provision of financial assistance to industry and its control* (Abingdon, 1977), p. 14, and Ganz, 'The Transport Committee', in Drewry (ed.), *The New Select Committees*, pp. 254–67.
156 Some were little more than 'assorted lunacies', including a submission from 'Pluto68' (Mr A.F. Jervis), who had asked Barclays Bank for £60 million: Cairncross Papers, DC106/3/8, GUAS. Peter Kemp, former DOE tunnelist, advanced one of the more imaginative ideas, viz. to fill the Channel in and build a road/rail causeway over it. Kemp-Kester George (Asst Sec, Transport Industries Divn, Treasury) and Case, 2 February 1979, and Kemp-Case, 12 March 1980, Treasury file PE 106/443/2 Pts A and C.
157 BRB, *Cross-Channel Rail Link* (April 1979) and *Cross Channel Rail Link* (March 1980).
158 HC Transport Committee, *Channel Fixed Link*, Vol. I, Report, paras 36–43, Annex B.
159 Coopers & Lybrand and SETEC-Economie, 'Study of the Community Benefit of a Fixed Channel Crossing', January 1980, AN191/322 Pts 1–2, PRO, and see also 'Draft Summary' (*c.*March 1980), DTp file IT4–0/2/22 Pt. 2; *Times*, 5 March 1980, p. 23, 7 March 1980, p. 7, *Economist*, 15 March 1980, pp. 46–8; *Modern Railways*, May 1980, p. 199.
160 Michael Pattison (Thatcher's PS)-Flanagan, 14 February 1980 and reply, 25 February 1980, Prime Minister's Channel Tunnel papers, Pt. 1; Pattison-Flanagan, 13 March 1980, DTp file IT40/2/22 Pt. 2. Heath continued to lobby for a bridge, after a meeting with Baron Philippe de Rothschild, who also met Thatcher: Heath-Cairncross, 6 March 1980, Cairncross Papers, DC106/3/8, GUAS; Thatcher-Lord Lever, 17 November 1980, FCO file WRF178/1/80.
161 Barron, 'Confidential. A Special Report to Board Members. The Channel Tunnel', 8 July 1980, and Memo. to BRB Executive on 'Channel Tunnel – Dual versus Mono Voltage Traction', 25 September 1980, AN192/617, PRO.

162 Cf. Barron-Lacoste, 16 December 1980, AN192/617, PRO.
163 Fowler-Parker, 2 April 1980, enclosing 'Report to Minister by Channel Tunnel Unit', n.d., with Cairncross, foreword, 18 March 1980, AN192/617, PRO. On DTp concerns about passing the report to BRB see Memos., February–March 1980, in DTp file IT40/2/22 Pt. 2. The report and foreword were subsequently published as part of the evidence submitted to the HC Transport Committee: *Channel Fixed Link*, Vol. II, MOE, 16 July 1980, Memorandum submitted by the Department of Transport, 20 June 1980, Annex A.
164 Parker-Fowler, 17 April 1980, AN192/617, PRO; Barron, Report, 8 July 1980, cit.
165 Barron, Report, 8 July 1980, cit.
166 Barron, Memo. on 'Channel Tunnel Diameter of Tunnel', 1 December 1980, AN156/371, PRO, and cf. Payne-M. Egerton (DTp) *et al.*, 18 December 1979, DTp file IT40/3/12 Pt. 1.
167 Edward Glover (CTU, DTp), Note on '1980 DTp Variant on BR/SNCF scheme', 22 May 1980, Fairclough-Payne, 29 May 1980, DTp file IT40/3/12 Pt. 1.
168 Parker-Fowler, 17 April 1980, cit.; 'Cross-Channel Rail Link; Note of Meeting between Department of Transport and BRB on 13 May 1980', n.d., DTp file IT40/2/3 Pt. 1.
169 Fowler-Parker, 15 May 1980, DTp file IT40/2/22 Pt. 3.
170 Parker-Fowler, 21 May 1980, DTp file IT40/2/3 Pt. 1; HC Transport Committee, *Channel Fixed Link*, Vol. II, MOE, 30 October 1980, 'Memorandum submitted by the British Railways Board commenting on the possible construction of a seven metre tunnel', October 1980. See also Payne-Fairclough, 18 August 1980, DTp file FN24/2/2 Pt. 1.
171 Barron, Memo. 1 December 1980, cit.; Barron, Memo. to BRB on 'Channel Tunnel: Single Track Rail Tunnel Scheme', 30 December 1980, AN167/72, PRO.
172 HC Transport Committee, *Channel Fixed Link*, Vol. II, MOE, 13 May 1980, Peter Fry (MP for Wellingborough), Q.314. On the use of 'mousehole' see J.M. Halligan (PS to Sir Kenneth Couzens (2nd Permanent Sec, Treasury), Note for Record, 4 February 1980, Treasury file PE 106/443/2 Pt. B; Baldwin-Couzens, 24 March 1980, Pt. C.; *Modern Railways*, May 1980, p. 199.
173 HC Transport Committee, *Channel Fixed Link*, Vol. II, MOE, 13 May 1980, Dover, Q. 315.
174 Barron-Parker *et al.*, 29 September 1980, Peter Parker's Papers, PP 12.
175 Barron, File Note, 28 May 1980, AN192/617; Barron-Parker *et al.*, 8 July 1980, Payne-Fairclough, 18 August 1980, cit.; Barron, File Note, 27 August 1980, AN156/371, PRO; Peter McIntosh (DTp CTU), File Note, 21 August 1980, DTp file FN24/2/2 Pt. 1.
176 John Dempster (Asst Sec, Finance Transport Industries Divn, DTp)- Anthea Case (Asst Sec, Transport Industries and General Policy Divn, Treasury), 9 May 1980, Richard Broadbent (Treasury)-Case, 29 May 1980, Case-Patrick Brown (Asst Sec, Finance Transport Industries Divn, DTp), 17 June 1980, Treasury file 106/443/2 Pt. C, and see also DTp file FN24/2/2 Pt. 1; John Wiggins (Asst Sec, Monetary Policy Divn, Treasury)-John Hobson (Finance Transport Industries Divn, DTp), 27 November 1979, RA124/4/2 Pt. 4; and Case-Wiggins and Peter Rees (Minister of State, Treasury), 27 November 1979, Treasury file PE 106/443/2 Pt. B.
177 Brown-Case, 30 July 1980 and reply, 19 August 1980, DTp file FN24/2/2 Pt. 1.
178 Clarke, reported in Jane Boys (DTp), 'Note of a meeting 3.15 pm 15th September 1980', 7 October 1980, DTp file IT40/2/25 Pt. 11.
179 *Parl. Deb. (Commons)*, 5th ser. (Session 1979–80), Vol. 981, Fowler, oral answer to Costain, 19 March 1980, *c*.390; Fairclough-Moss, 2 May 1980, DTp file IT40/5/6 Pt. 1.
180 HC Transport Committee, *Channel Fixed Link*, Vol. II, MOE, 11 November 1980, QQ.1682, 1690, 1694, Fowler's replies to Fry, Robin Cook (MP for Edinburgh Central), and Stephen Dorrell (Loughborough).

181 Ibid. QQ.1680,1683, 1688, 1699–1700, 1712, Fowler, replies to Sydney Bidwell (MP for Ealing, Southall), Fry, Sir David Price (Eastleigh), Dorrell, and Tom Bradley (Leicester East); Barron, Memos. 8 July and 29 September 1980, Boys, Note, 7 October 1980, cit.; John Bridgeman (U-Sec, Treasury)-Monck, 17 June 1980, Case-McIntosh, 14 and 15 July 1980, Treasury file PE 106/44/32 Pt. C.
182 Sir Anthony Rawlinson (2nd Permanent Sec, Treasury), Note for Record, 11 May 1979, Treasury file PE106/443/2 Pt. A; Frank Davidson (TSI), 'A Framework for Discussing a Channel Tunnel Concession', 2 August 1980, McIntosh-Al Davidson, 5 August 1980, DTp file FN24/2/2 Pt. 1; Barron-Parker *et al.*, 1 October 1980, enclosing Memo. on 'Channel Tunnel Study Group: Draft Proposals for Financing the Tunnel', 30 September 1980, Frank Davidson-Parker, 21 November 1980, AN191/314; Williams-Barron, 4 February 1981, AN191/333, PRO; Frank Davidson-Parker correspondence in TSI Archive, carton #13 f15, HBS.
183 McIntosh-Fairclough, 19 September 1980, McIntosh-Rosenfeld (now Dep Sec), 22 September 1980.
184 Transport Committee, *Channel Fixed Link*, Vol. II, MOE, 11 November 1980, Q.1688, Fowler's reply to Bidwell; Fairclough-Anthony Mayer (Fowler's PS), 14 November 1980, with briefing notes, including William Merton (Chairman, Robert Fleming & Co.)-Fowler, 5 November 1980, DTp file IT40/2/19 Pt. 3.
185 Barron, File Note on 'Private discussion with Alistair Frame... 12th August, 1980', 13 August 1980, AN192/617, PRO.
186 Palliser-Thatcher, 28 December 1979, enclosing copy of Giscard d'Estaing-Queen Elizabeth II, 17 December 1979, Sir Reginald Hibbert (British Ambassador, Paris), telegram No. 306 to FCO, 18 March 1980, Hibbert, 'France – Review of 1980', 6 January 1981, Prime Minister [Thatcher]'s File on 'Anglo-French Relations', Pt. 1; Margaret Thatcher, *The Downing Street Years* (1993), pp. 78–86; Geoffrey Howe, *Conflict of Loyalty* (1994), pp. 182–3.
187 Case-Wiggins and Nigel Lawson (Financial Secretary, Treasury), 7 December 1979, J.A. Thomson (Treasury)-Monck, 17 January 1980, Rachel Lomax (Senior Economic Adviser, Treasury)-Harry Walsh (CO), 24 January 1980, J.M. Halligan (Couzens's PS), Note, 3 March 1980, Treasury file PE 106/443/2 Pt. B; Lord Bridges (Dep U-Sec, FCO)-Michael Burton (Head of Maritime etc. Divn, FCO), 3 January 1980, FCO file WRF178/1/80; Cabinet Committee on Community Resource Transfers, EQR(80) 3rd, 28 January 1980; Sir Robert Armstrong (Cabinet Secretary)-Michael Alexander (Thatcher's PS), 18 March 1980, Cabinet Office file on 'Channel Tunnel', 183/1 Pt. 6.
188 DTp IT Divn, 'Note of a Meeting between the UK and French Ministers of Transport at 7.00 p.m. on 9 June 1980 in Mr Fowler's Office', July 1980, DTp file IT40/2/78 Pt. 1 and see also Case-Broadbent, 11 November 1981, Treasury file PE106/443/2 Pt. D. The two other problems raised by Le Theule were the French presidential elections in 1981 and the expiry of the SNCF statutes in 1982.
189 HC Transport Committee, *Channel Fixed Link*, Vol. II, MOE, 11 November 1980, Q.1712, Fowler's reply to Dorrell; Hunt, *Tunnel*, p. 160.
190 Mayer, 'Note of Meeting about Channel Tunnel 11 December 1980', 18 December 1980, DTp file IT40/2/78 Pt. 1; Hibbert, telegram No. 1015 to FCO, 12 December 1980, FCO file WRF78/1/80.
191 Fowler-Thatcher, 22 December 1980, Prime Minister's Channel Tunnel papers, Pt. 1.
192 BRB Minutes, 8 January 1981, AN167/47, PRO; Parker-Fowler, 27 January 1981, enclosing BRB, Report on 'Channel Tunnel Single Track Rail Tunnel Scheme', January 1981, Warburg-BRB, 27 January 1981, AN192/617; and for criticisms see McIntosh-Fairclough, 29 January 1981, Treasury file PE106/443/2 Pt. D.
193 Fowler-Parker, 13 February 1981, AN192/617, PRO.

194 Fairclough-Payne, 30 March 1981, Treasury file PE106/443/2; Cairncross-Mayer, 10 April 1981, DTp file IT40/2/25 Pt. 12.
195 HC Transport Committee, *Channel Fixed Link*, Vol. I, Report, paras 3, 131, 165–7. Dated 11 February 1981, the Report was published on 6 March: Transport Committee Press release, 6 March 1981, DTp file IT40/2/55 Pt. 1. For DTp reactions see Moss-J.H.H. Baxter (Asst Sec, DOE) *et al.*, 10 April 1981, ibid. and Moss-McIntosh, 8 February 1982, DTp file RA124/4/2 Pt. 9.
196 *Parl. Deb. (Commons)*, 5th ser. (Session 1980-1), Vol. 1, Fowler, oral answer to Whitehead and Ron Lewis (MP for Carlisle), 25 March 1981, *c.*907.
197 BRB Press releases, 6 March 1981, AN156/371, PRO; BRB, *Cross Channel Rail Link* (April 1981).
198 Parker-Fowler, 20 February 1981, DTp file IT40/2/77 Pt. 1; Barron, Confidential Memo. on 'Channel Tunnel: Diameter of Tunnel', 12 March 1981, AN192/617, PRO.
199 BRB, 'Notes of informal meeting held in Dijon, 15 May 1981', 21 May 1981, AN156/371, PRO. See also *Times*, 21 May 1981, p. 16.
200 Parker-Fowler, 18 May 1981, enclosing BRB and SNCF, 'Cross Channel Rail Link Joint Report', BRB, 'Corporate Effect Financial Assessment', May 1981, AN156/371; S.G. Warburg, 'A Study of the Financial Feasibility of the Channel Tunnel Project', 11 May 1981, AN191/66 Pt. 3, PRO.
201 Barron-Fairclough, 10 June 1981, enclosing BRB, 'Cross Channel Rail Link. Report on Examination of 7 Metre Tunnel with Road Vehicle Shuttle', June 1981, AN192/618, PRO.
202 See *inter alia*, GLC draft report, 19 February 1973, MT144/394, PRO; HC Transport Committee, *Channel Fixed Link*, Vol. II, MOE, 30 October 1980, QQ.1519–20, Barron and Malcolm Southgate (Chief Operations Manager, BRB), reply to Bradley, QQ.1519-20; Barron (Executive Director, CT, BRB), Memos. to BRB Railway Directing Group, 15 April and 3 June 1981, Burt-HC Transport Committee, 22 June 1980 [*sic*: should be 1981], AN192/618; Railway Directing Group Minutes, 15 April and 9 June 1981, AN167/451, PRO.
203 Rosenfeld-Baldwin and Mayer, 16 April 1981, Mayer, 'Note of Meeting about Channel Tunnel 24 April 1981', 28 April 1981, DTp CTU, 'Channel Tunnel: Note of Meeting on 7 May 1981', 11 May 1981, Fairclough-Rosenfeld, 12 May 1981, Payne-Fairclough, 28 May 1981, DTp file IT40/5/7 Pt. 1.
204 Stephen Newlove (DTp CTU), 'Note of Meeting held on 9 June 1981 . . .', 15 June 1981, Moss-Robin Bellis (DTp CTU) *et al.*, 15 June 1981, Fairclough-Rosenfeld, 16 June 1981, ibid.
205 David Sawers (U-Sec, TPRU, DTp)-Rosenfeld, 17 June 1981, Fairclough-Rosenfeld, 19 June 1981, Sawers-Rosenfeld, 22 June 1981, Brown-Rosenfeld, 30 June 1981, DTp file IT40/5/5 Pt. 1.
206 Payne-Rosenfeld, 1 July 1981, Rosenfeld-Mayer, 3 July 1981, ibid.
207 Moss-Payne and Fairclough, 10 April 1980, DTp file IT40/5/6 Pt. 1; Barron, Note on 'Channel Tunnel: Key Issues', 7 May 1981, David Williams-Burt, 30 June 1981, AN156/371, PRO.
208 CTD 1981, presentation to Fowler, May 1981, Tarmac, Press Release, 5 August 1981, DTp file IT40/2/31 Pt. 2.
209 For the record of meetings, August 1980-July 1981, see AN156/370–1, AN192/617–18, and especially Barron-Max Purbrick (Director of Civil Engineering, BRB), 13 May 1981, Nicolson-Barron, 23 June 1981, AN156/371.
210 Fowler-Parker, 8 July 1981, Parker-Fowler, 27 July 1981, David Williams-Burt, 27 August 1981, AN192/618; BRB Minutes, AN167/47, PRO.
211 J.D. Munro (John Laing Construction)-McIntosh, 3 July 1981, DTp file IT40/2/47 Pt. 2; Dover Harbour Board Channel Tunnel Study Working Party, Interim Report,

June 1981, IT40/2/36 Pt. 2. The Working Party comprised the DHB, European Ferries, P & O Ferries, and Sealink, assisted by Kent Co. Co., British Ports Association, the General Council of British Shipping, and the University of Oxford's Transport Studies Unit.

212 R.G. Ward (Chief Statistician, Treasury)-Patricia Brown (U-Sec (Economics), Treasury), 16 October 1979, Treasury file PE 106/443/2 Pt. B; McIntosh-Fairclough, 3 February 1981, F. Gale (DTp CTU)-Fairclough, 20 May 1981, DTp file IT40-4-4 Pt. 1; *Economist*, 1 March 1980, p. 55.

213 Holmes-Case, 22 July 1981, DTp file FN24/2/2 Pt. 1; Rosenfeld-Barron, etc., 5 August 1981, Brian Webber (DTp CTU)-McIntosh, 10 September 1981, IT40/2/52 Pt. 2, Broadbent-Case, William Ryrie (2nd Permanent Sec, Treasury) and Geoffrey Howe (Chancellor), 17 September 1981, Treasury file NIEA U/151/868/1 Pt. A.

214 Parker, *For Starters*, p. 225, and cf. *Modern Railways*, March 1986, p. 122.

215 Barron, Memo. 30 January 1980, cit.; Barron, Memo to BRB on 'Channel Tunnel', 30 July 1981, Kenneth Clarke-Parker, 7 August 1981, AN1192/618, PRO; Cairncross-Mayer, 4 June 1981, DTp file IT40/2/25 Pt. 12.

216 Cf. Baldwin-Fowler, 19 February 1980, cit.

217 Cf. Note of meeting, 5 March 1980, cit.; 'Note of a discussion on 29 September 1980 [David, Costet, Fairclough, Arbuthnot]', FCO file WRF178/1/80; Barron, File Note, 1 December 1980, AN192/617, PRO.

8 THE THATCHER GOVERNMENTS AND THE TUNNEL: FROM HOPE TO ETERNITY, 1981–4

1 Fairclough-Rosenfeld, 19 June 1981, DTp file IT40/5/5 Pt. 1; Burton-Fairclough, 1 July 1981, FCO file WRF178/1/81; Burton-Roy Osborne (WED, FCO), 4 August 1981, Burton-Rosenfeld, 7 August 1981, Gordon Downey (Dep Sec, Treasury)-Burton, 12 August 1981, Rosenfeld-Burton, 14 August 1981, MRY178/1/81 Pt. C; Broadbent-Case and Downey, 10 August 1981, Treasury file NIEA U/151/868/1 Pt. A.

2 Sir Antony Acland (Dep U-Sec, FCO)-Sir Robert Armstrong (Cabinet Secretary), 17 August 1981, Sir Anthony Duff (Dep Sec, Cabinet)-William Rickett (Thatcher's PS), 19 August 1981, Couzens-Acland, 19 August 1981, Baldwin-Acland, 21 August 1981, Prime Minister [Thatcher]'s papers on 'France: Visits of President Mitterand', Pt. 2; Burton-John Rosenfeld (Dep Sec and Principal Finance Officer, DTp), 7 August 1981, Alice Baker (Fowler's APS)-N.J. Kroll (Baldwin's PS), 21 August 1981, DTp file IT40/2/78 Pt. 1. On Fiterman see Crammer (BRB)-Parker, 24 June 1981, AN191/67, PRO, and David S. Bell and Byron Criddle, *The French Communist Party in the Fifth Republic* (Oxford, 1994), pp. 110, 234.

3 Christopher Cloke (Armstrong's APS)-Clive Whitmore (Thatcher's PPS), 21 August 1981, Pattison-Cloke, 28 August 1981, ibid. Pt. 2.

4 Ryrie-Acland, 25 August 1981, Francis Richards (Carrington's PS)-Michael Alexander (Thatcher's PS), 2 and 8 September 1981, ibid. Pt. 2; Broadbent-Thomas Burgner (U-Sec, Treasury) and Leon Brittan (Chief Secretary, Treasury), 7 September 1981, Treasury file NIEA U/151/868/1 Pt. A; Burgner-Rosenfeld, 3 September 1981, DTp file IT40/2/78 Pt. 1.

5 Baker, 'Meeting with M. Fiterman, French Minister of Transport – 10 September 1981', DTp file IT40/2/78 Pt. 1.

6 Heather Rowe (Deputy Head of Information, DTp), Note, 10 September 1981, Prime Minister's papers on 'Visits of Mitterand', Pt. 2.

7 'Record of a Conversation between the Prime Minister and the President of the French Republic . . . on 10 September 1981 at 1600 hours', Armstrong-Alexander,

10 September 1981, ibid. Pt. 2; 'Record of a Meeting between Sir Robert Armstrong and M Beregovoy . . . at 5.45 pm on . . . 10 September 1981', ibid. Pt. 3.

8 'Record of Plenary Discussion between the Prime Minister and the President . . . on Friday 11 September 1981', James Lee, Transcript of 'Press Conference given by the Prime Minister and President Mitterand . . . 11 September 1981', ibid. Pt. 3. See also Cabinet Conclusions, CC(81) 31st, 15 September 1981.

9 *Daily Mail, Guardian, Daily Express*, 11 September 1981, and Bernard Ingham (Thatcher's Chief Press Secretary), 11 September 1981, ibid. Pt. 2; *Times*, 12 September 1981, p. 1.

10 Barron, Memo. on 'Channel Tunnel', 30 July 1981, AN167/72; BRB Minutes, 6 August 1981, AN167/47, PRO.

11 Barron-Parker *et al.*, 3 September 1981, Williams-Burt, 24 September 1981, AN156/371; Burt-Board members, 17 September 1981, enclosing Barron, Memo. same date, AN192/618; BRB Minutes, 1 October 1981, AN167/47, PRO.

12 Howell was a right-winger with strong privatising sympathies. See David Howell, *A New Style of Government* (1970).

13 Parker-Howell, 1 October 1981, DTp file IT40/2/52 Pt. 2.

14 Barron, Memo. to BRB, 28 October 1981, AN167/73; BR/ECTG Joint Directing Group Minutes, 23 November 1981, AN191/28; Barron-Reid, 23 November 1981, AN156/371, PRO.

15 BRB Press Release, 11 December 1981, Reid-Parker *et al.*, 10 December 1981, BRB and ECTG, 'Presentation to the Secretary of State for Transport Friday 11 December 1981' [with Rothschild plan extended to 50, instead of 40, years], Barron-Parker *et al.*, 11 December 1981, Barron-BRB Members, 17 December 1981, AN156/371, PRO; DTp CTU, 'Note of Meeting with British Rail and European Channel Tunnel Group on 11 December 1981', DTp file RA124/4/2 Pt. 9.

16 Barron, Memo. 28 October 1981, cit.

17 Sir John Howard (Chairman and MD, John Howard & Co.)-Ian Gow (Thatcher's PPS), 20 August 1981, enclosing Ian MacGregor, 'EuroRoute: Free Enterprise Road and Rail Channel Crossing', 18 August 1981, and reply, 25 August 1981, Prime Minister's Channel Tunnel papers, Pt. 1. MacGregor lobbied the Foreign Secretary, Lord Carrington, on 7 September: FCO file MRY178/1/81 Pt. D.

18 Ian MacGregor, *The Enemies Within: The Story of the Miners' Strike, 1984–5* (1986), pp. 105–6. The Midland Bank's view was that the EuroRoute scheme would not help BSC much, but was a 'rather dramatic confidence-building project': Sir Donald Barron (Chairman)-Geoffrey Taylor (Group Chief Executive), 1 October 1982, Midland Bank Channel Tunnel files, ref. 10649, HSBC Archives, London [HSBC].

19 Mayer-Caroline Stephens (Thatcher's Personal Asst), 12 November 1981, enclosing brief, Prime Minister's Channel Tunnel papers, Pt. 1.

20 Michael Scholar (Thatcher's PS)-Mayer, 17 November 1981, ibid.

21 Gow-Alexander, 25 November 1981, with Thatcher's annotations, ibid. and cf. MacGregor, *Enemies Within*, pp. 107–8.

22 See the surviving DTp files, IT40/2/31 Pts 1–3, IT40/2/32 Pts 1–4, IT40/2/34 Pt. 2, IT40/2/35 Pts 1–2, IT40/2/38 Pt. 3, IT40/2/47 Pt. 2, IT40/2/77 Pt. 1.

23 Interview with Guy Braibant, 14 January 2005.

24 Fairclough-Rosenfeld, 29 September 1981, DTp file RA102/1/21 Pt. 1; Lyall-Burton, 7 October 1981, IT40/4/8 Pt. 1; Fairclough-K. Sriskandan (Chief Highway Engineer, DTp), 1 October 1981, IT40/4/13 Pt. 1; Anglo-French Directing Group Minutes, 10 December 1981, Treasury file NIEA U/15 1/868/1 Pt. C.

25 Cf. *Parl. Deb. (Commons)*, Fowler, oral answer, 25 March 1981, cit.

26 Interview with Braibant, 2005.

27 *Financial Times* and *Guardian*, 14 October 1981; Howell-Thatcher, 27 October 1981, Prime Minister's Channel Tunnel papers, Pt. 1.

28 Howell-Thatcher, 9 November 1981, ibid.

29 Brittan-Fowler, 26 May 1981 and reply, 4 June 1981, Treasury file NIEA U/151/868/1 Pt. A; Brittan-Thatcher, 16 November 1981, Prime Minister's Channel Tunnel papers, Pt. 1; Interview with Braibant, 2005.

30 Broadbent-Case, Ryrie and Howe, 17 September 1981, cit.; Kroll, 'Note of a meeting held on 21 September in Room N18/07 2 Marsham Street', and Ryrie-Baldwin, both 24 September, DTp file IT40/4/6 Pt. 1; Ryrie-Brittan, 24 September 1981, Treasury file NIEA U/151/868/1 Pt. A.

31 Broadbent-Case and Ryrie, 17 November 1981, Treasury file NIEA U/151/868/1 Pt. B.

32 Howell-Thatcher, 9 November 1981, cit.; 'Note of a bilateral meeting to discuss financial issues . . . 10 November 1981', Broadbent-Case and Brittan, 13 November 1981, Treasury file NIEA U/151/868/1 Pt. B.; McIntosh-Lyall and Payne, 11 November 1981, DTp file IT40/4/6 Pt. 1.

33 Rosenfeld-Mayer and Case-Ryrie, both 20 November 1981, Broadbent-Case, Ryrie and Brittan, 24 November 1981, ibid.

34 Case-Ryrie, 24 November 1981, ibid.; Broadbent-Case, Ryrie and Brittan, 24 November 1981, cit.; Broadbent-Case and Howe, 2 December 1981, Treasury file NIEA U/151/868/1 Pt. C.

35 F. Gale (DTp CTU)-Fairclough and Mayer, 3 June 1981, Boys-Rosenfeld and Mayer, 4 June 1981, DTp file IT40/2/25 Pt. 12.

36 Fairclough-Mayer, 11 September 1981, Howell-Cairncross, 16 September 1981, ibid.

37 Cairncross-Howell, 13 November 1981, ibid.

38 Ibid. and cf. Cairncross, Report on Fixed Channel Link, November 1981 draft, paras. 8.1, 8.5, 8.8, 8.11–24, Treasury file NIEA U/151/868/1 Pt. B.

39 Mayer, 'Note of Meeting about Sir Alec Cairncross's Report on Fixed Channel Link 25 November 1981', 3 December 1981, DTp file IT40/2/25 Pt. 12.

40 DTp CTU, 'Cairncross Draft Report of 13 November', 19 November 1981, enclosed in Rosenfeld-Mayer, 24 November 1981, ibid; Patrick Brown-Case, 20 November 1981, Treasury file NIEA U/151/868/1 Pt. B; John Stuttard (CPRS)-Gordon Wasserman (U-Sec, CPRS), 12 January 1982, CPRS file Q9/2 Pt. 4.

41 HC Transport Committee, *The Channel Link*, P.P.1981–2, xxiv, HC207, 3 March 1982, pp. 5–97 and see also McIntosh-Case *et al.*, 15 December 1981, Treasury file NIEA U/151/868/1 Pt. C; Lyall-Mayer, 12 January 1982, DTp file IT40/5/7 Pt. 2; Rosenfeld-Mayer, 15 January 1982, McIntosh-Mayer, 19 January 1982, RA124/4/2 Pt. 9.

42 Wasserman-Chris Turner (Adviser, CPRS), 24 November 1981, CPRS file Q9/2 Pt. 4.

43 Howell, Memo. to Cabinet Ministerial Committee on Economic Strategy [E Committee] on 'Fixed Cross-Channel Link', E(81) 121, 26 November 1981.

44 Brittan, Memo. to E Committee on 'Fixed Cross-Channel Link', E(81) 122, 27 November 1981.

45 CPRS, Note for E Committee on 'Fixed Cross-Channel Link', E(81) 124, 30 November 1981.

46 Cabinet E Committee Minutes, E(81) 37th, 3 December 1981, and cf. also Peter Gregson (Dep Sec, CO)-Thatcher, 2 December 1981, Prime Minister's Channel Tunnel papers, Pt. 1. See also Lyall-McIntosh *et al.*, 8 December 1981, DTp file IT40/5/7 Pt. 2.

47 Broadbent-Case, 31 December 1981, Treasury file NIEA U/151/868/1 Pt. C.

48 Nicholas Armour-Peter Vereker, and David Gladstone (Head of WED Dept, FCO), annotation, 14 December 1981, FCO file WRF178/1/81.

49 Anglo-French Directing Group Minutes, 10 December 1981, cit.; P.A. Hinckley (DTp)-R.S. Balme (Clarke's PS), 17 December 1981, enclosing Note on 'Technical Studies', DTp file IT40/6/1; Patrick Brown-Case, 16 December 1981, Treasury file NIEA U/151/868/1 Pt. C.

50 Lyall-Mayer, 17 December 1981, enclosing 'Note of Meeting between the Secretary of State and M. Fiterman in Brussels, 15 December 1981', Lyall-Rosenfeld and Mayer, 8 January 1982, DTp file RA124/4/2 Pt. 9.
51 Lyall-Rosenfeld, and Lyall, Note on 'Fixed Channel Link: Discussions in Paris, 14 January 1982', both 18 January 1982, ibid.
52 Lyall, Note, cit.
53 George Walden (First Secretary, British Embassy, Paris)-Richard Mark Evans (Minister (Economic), Paris), 16 January 1978, FCO file WRF178/1/78; Hibbert, Paris telegram No. 379 to FCO, 21 May 1981, MRY178/1/81 Pt. B.
54 Rosemary Spencer (Counsellor, British Embassy, Paris)-Lyall, 3 February 1982, DTp file RA124/4/2 Pt. 9; Lyall-Mayer, 8 February 1982, IT40/5/7 Pt. 2.
55 Lyall-Rosenfeld and Mayer, 8 January 1982, cit.; McIntosh-Rosenfeld and Mayer, 14 January 1982, DTp file IT40/5/7 Pt. 2; Howell-Thatcher, n.d. [19 January 1982], enclosing draft memo. for HC Transport Committee, and Scholar-Mayer, 25 January 1982, Prime Minister's Channel Tunnel papers, Pt. 1.
56 Lyall-Mayer, 21 January 1982, enclosing 'Joint Anglo-French Studies relating to a Fixed Link across the straits of Dover: Interim Report', English translation, 20 January 1982, DTp file RA124/4/2 Pt. 9.
57 B.S. Kalen (Economic Adviser (Public Enterprises), Treasury)-Herbert Christie (U-Sec (Economics), Treasury), 3 March 1982, enclosing 'Note of a meeting held on Friday 29 January 1982...', Treasury file NIEA U/151/868/1 Pt. D.
58 *Spirit of Free Enterprise*, catering for 1,326 passengers, 330 cars and 50 15-metre lorries, was launched in 1979. It was followed by *Pride of Free Enterprise* and *Herald of Free Enterprise* (both 1980), the latter suffering a serious accident off Zeebrugge in 1987. Sealink's *St. Anselm*, also launched in 1979, catered for 1,000 passengers, 310 cars and 62 12-metre lorries. It was followed by the *St. Christopher* (1980). SNCF's *Cote d'Azur* (1,400 passengers, 330 cars, 54 15-metre lorries), followed in 1981. *Motor Ship*, March 1980; John Hendy, *Ferry Port Dover: the development of cross-Channel vehicle ferries, their services and allied infrastructure* (Staplehurst, 1998), pp. 59–61, 95, 122.
59 Jonathan Sloggett (Deputy GM, Dover Harbour Board)-Lyall, 30 December 1981 and reply, 19 January 1982, DTp file GSP A2044 Pt. 1.
60 C.T.B. Smith (Senior Economic Adviser, Depts of Industry and Trade)-R.N. Simpson (Asst Sec, Shipping Policy Divn, Dept of Trade), 11 January 1981, DTp file GSP A2044 Pt. 1; Lyall-Rosenfeld and Mayer, 22 January 1982, IT40/5/7 Pt. 2; Lyall-Richard Goss (Professor of Maritime Economics, UWIST), 28 January 1982, IT40/2/36 Pt. 3.
61 E.g. funding should be undertaken in conditions of fair competition with the private sector, and higher interest rates should be offset by efficiency gains. Report of NEDC Working Party on Nationalised Industries' Investment, 28 September 1981, NEDC (81)53, and see NEDC Minutes, 5 October 1981, FG1/47, PRO. See also Geoffrey Howe (Chancellor), Memo. 26 May 1982, NEDC (82)31, and William Ryrie, *First World, Third World* (Basingstoke, 1999), p. 146ff.
62 Lyall-Rosenfeld and Mayer, 22 January 1982, cit.; Patrick Brown-Case, 21 January 1982, Broadbent-Case, 27 January 1982, Treasury file NIEA U/151/868/1 Pt. D.
63 Andrew Turnbull (Asst Sec, Treasury)-Case, 28 January 1982, ibid.
64 European Parliament [EP], 'Report for Committee on Transport on the construction of a Channel tunnel', 15 April 1981, EP Sitting and Resolution, 8 May 1981, Motion, 30 September 1981, and papers in DTp file IT4/5/66 Pt. 5.
65 E.g. the New Community Instrument (Ortoli facility), European Investment Bank, European Regional Development Fund, and the proposed Transport Infrastructure Fund. See DTp file IT40/4/8 Pts 1 and 2.

66 DTp Note to Cabinet Official Committee on European Questions on 'European Community Aspects of a Channel Fixed Link', EQO(82) 8, 27 January 1982; Official Committee on European Questions Minutes, EQO(82) 6th, 1 February 1982.
67 Howell, Memo. to E Committee on 'Fixed Cross-Channel Link', E(82) 7, 4 February 1982.
68 CPRS, Note for E Committee on 'Fixed Cross-Channel Link', E(82) 9, 5 February 1982.
69 Broadbent-Case, Ryrie and Howe, 8 February 1982, Treasury file NIEA U/151/868/1 Pt. D.
70 Interview with Lord Howell, 11 May 1999 [for Gourvish, *British Rail 1974–97*].
71 Brief for Howell on 'Note by the Central Policy Review Staff', n.d., DTp file RA124/4/2 Pt. 9.
72 DoT Shipping Policy Divn, Memo. to John Biffen (SoS for Trade) *et al.* on 'Fixed Cross-Channel Link', 8 February 1982, DTp file GSP A2044 Pt. 2.
73 Robin Simpson (Asst Sec, DoT Shipping Policy Divn)-Biffen, 8 February 1982, ibid.; Biffen-Howell, 8 February 1982, Prime Minister's Channel Tunnel papers, Pt. 1.
74 Walters-Thatcher, 5 February 1982, ibid.
75 Walters-Thatcher, 8 February 1982, ibid.
76 Walters-Thatcher, 5 February 1982, cit.; Gourvish, *British Rail 1974–97*, p. 155.
77 Mayer-Kroll, 9 February 1982, DTp file IT40/5/7 Pt. 2.
78 Cabinet E Committee Minutes, E(82) 4th, 9 February 1982.
79 Lyall-Rosenfeld and Mayer, 11 February 1982, DTp file IT40/5/7 Pt. 2. This view was shared by the DoT: Michael Franklin (Permanent Sec, DoT)-Knighton (Dep Sec, DoT), 18 February 1982, copied to Baldwin, Cabinet Office file on 'Channel Tunnel', 183/1 Pt. 6.
80 John Gray (Head of Maritime, Aviation & Environment Dept [MAED], FCO), Note for the File, 17 February 1982, Cabinet Office file on 'Channel Tunnel', 183/1 Pt. 6.
81 Fowler-Bradley (Chairman, HC Transport Committee) 27 November 1980, attached to Fowler's evidence, 11 November 1980, HC Transport Committee, *Channel Fixed Link*, Vol. II, MOE, p. 362; Howell-Carrington, 16 February and reply, 17 February 1982; Scholar-Thatcher, 17 February 1982 (with PM's annotation), Scholar-Mayer, 18 February 1982, Prime Minister's Channel Tunnel papers, Pt. 2; Mayer-Rosenfeld, 18 February 1982, DTp file IT40/5/7 Pt. 2.
82 HC Transport Committee, *The Channel Link*, P.P.1981–2, xxiv, MOE, Howell, Baldwin and Rosenfeld, 17 February 1981, including Howell, Memo. n.d. [18 January 1982], and QQ. 662–708; Lyall-Mayer, 12 February 1982, DTp file IT40/5/7 Pt. 2.
83 Lyall-Rosenfeld and Mayer, 16 February 1982, Mayer, 'Note of Meeting about Fixed-Channel Link 18 February 1982', 19 February 1982, DTp file IT40/2/78 Pt. 1.
84 Lyall-McIntosh *et al.*, 11 February 1982, DTp file IT40/6/1 Pt. 2.
85 Lyall-Rosenfeld and Mayer, 22 February 1982, DTp file IT40/5/7 Pt. 2.
86 Ibid. and Anglo-French Directing Group Minutes, 18 February 1982, DTp file IT40/6/1 Pt. 3.
87 Mayer-Lyall, 23 February 1982, DTp file IT40/5/7 Pt. 2.
88 Gourvish, *British Rail 1974–97*, pp. 101–7, 151–2, 154–64.
89 Lyall-Payne and McIntosh, 26 January 1982, DTp file RA124/4/2 Pt. 9.
90 Patrick Brown-Lyall, 18 January 1982, ibid.; Lyall-Rosenfeld and Mayer, 22 January 1982, cit.; John Palmer (U-Sec, Rlys, DTp)-Bob Reid (I) (Chief Executive, BRB), 28 January 1982, and David Miles (DTp Rlys A), 'Note of a meeting about the Channel Tunnel – 1 February 1982 held in Mr Reid's Office, BRB', 1 February 1982, AN156/372, PRO.
91 Payne-Lyall, 22 February 1982, DTp file IT40/3/12 Pt. 2.

92 Palmer-Lyall, 24 February 1982, ibid.; Barron-Reid, 23 February 1982, enclosing 'Note of Telephone Conversation with Andrew Lyall on Monday, 22nd February 1982', 22 February 1982, Barron-Reid, 25 February 1982, AN156/372, PRO.
93 BRB Minutes, 4 March 1982, AN167/48, PRO.
94 BRB Press Release, 1 February 1982; Gourvish, *British Rail 1974–97*, p. 116.
95 Parker-Howell, 10 March 1982, AN156/372, PRO. On Lyall's 'hints' see BR/ECTG Joint Directing Group Minutes, 25 February and 11 March 1982, AN191/28, PRO.
96 Howell-Parker, 26 March 1982, ibid.
97 Barron-Lyall, 11 January 1982, DTp file RA124/4/2 Pt. 9.
98 Ted Page (Taylor Woodrow Construction)-McIntosh, 9 October 1981, ACTG, presentation diagrams, 11 January 1982, DTp file IT40/2/38 Pt. 3.
99 Lyall-Rosenfeld, 12 January 1982, DTp file RA124–4-2 Pt. 9.
100 Patrick Brown-Rosenfeld, 13 January 1982, Rosenfeld-Lyall, 18 January 1982, ibid.; DTp CTU brief, 28 January 1982, and Lyall-Payne, 1 February 1982, DTp file IT40/5/18 Pt. 1. The Panel eventually ranked the promoters as follows: 1 CTD; 2 ACTG; 3 ECTG. Sriskandan-Lyall, 10 May 1982, ibid.
101 Spencer, Note on 'Fixed Channel Link: Call by Mr Lyall on M Braibant: 26 February', 1 March 1982, DTp file IT40/6/1 Pt. 3; Lyall-Rosenfeld and Mayer, 2 March 1982, IT40/5/7 Pt. 2.
102 Rosenfeld-Mayer, 2 March 1982, ibid.
103 Lyall-Mayer, 3 March 1982, and Mayer-Lyall, 5 March 1982, ibid.
104 Lyall-Rosenfeld and Mayer, 2 March 1982, cit.
105 Lyall-Mayer, 10 March 1982, enclosing brief for Howell's meeting with Carrington, DTp file IT40/2/78 Pt. 1.
106 Howell-Carrington meeting, 10 March 1982: DTp note in Lyall-Mayer, 11 March 1982, FCO record, 11 March 1982, DTp file IT40/2/78 Pt. 1.
107 Lyall-Rosenfeld and Mayer, 11 March 1982, DTp file 40/5/7 Pt. 2; Carrington-Thatcher, 17 March 1982, Prime Minister's Channel Tunnel papers, Pt. 2.
108 Howell-Thatcher, 16 March 1982, ibid.
109 Lyall-Kroll, 29 March 1982, DTp file IT40/7/1 Pt. 1.
110 Lyall-Mayer, 8 March 1982, DTp file IT40/2/78; Lyall-Mayer, 26 March 1982, Mayer-Lyall, 29 March and 6 April 1982, IT40/5/17 Pt. 2.
111 Lyall-Mayer, 5 April 1982, ibid.
112 Patrick Brown-Lyall, 10 March 1982, DTp file IT40/7/1 Pt. 1; Lyall-Mayer, 25 March 1982, IT40/5/17 Pt. 2. One suggestion was to insist that shareholders committed themselves to further calls of up to four times their initial stake.
113 Brown-Lyall, 10 March 1982, cit.; Lyall-Mayer, 5 April 1982, cit., enclosing 'Statement of Position Reached'. On legal opinion see Karl Newman (Lord Chancellor's Dept)-Robin Bellis (Asst Solicitor, DTp), 29 March 1982, John Siddle (Legal Adviser to FCO)-Bellis, 31 March 1982, Bellis-Lyall, 6 April 1982, Bellis-Payne, 15 April 1982, DTp file IT40/7/1 Pt. 1.
114 Lyall-Mayer, 25 March 1982, cit. and see also Lyall-Rosenfeld, 16 March 1982, DTp file IT40/4/6 Pt. 1; Brown-Lyall, 19 March 1982, IT40/7/1 Pt. 1.
115 Lyall-Brown, 18 March 1982, R.L. Wyatt (Asst GM (International), Midland Bank)-Rosenfeld, 8 April 1982, Lyall-Brown, 13 April 1982, John Noulton (DTp CTU)-Rosenfeld, 29 April 1982, ibid.
116 *Times*, 6 April 1982, p. 1.
117 Lyall-Mayer, 5 April, cit. There was further agonising about the bi-national co. at ministerial level, involving Douglas Hurd (FCO), Fiterman and Howell: see Mayer, 'Note of Meeting about Fixed Channel Link', 16 April 1982, Lyall-Mayer, 21 April 1982, DTp file IT40/5/17 Pt. 2; Sir John Fretwell (British Ambassador, Paris)-James Adams (Superintending U-Sec, FCO), 26 April 1982, FCO file MRY178/1/82 Pt. H.

118 Siddle-Bellis, 31 March 1982, Lyall-Bellis, 13 April and reply, 15 April 1982, DTp file IT40/7/1 Pt. 1.
119 Lyall-Meyer, 5 April 1982, 'Statement of Position Reached', cit.
120 Patrick Brown-Case, 14 April 1982, Treasury file NIEA U/151/868/1 Pt. D; 'Channel Fixed Link. Report of Anglo/French Study Group', n.d., summary of report and DTp CTU paper on 'Organisation for a Fixed Channel Link', both 16 April 1982, DTp file IT40/6/5 Pt. 3.
121 Report of Anglo/French Study Group, paras 6.1–4 and Annexes A and J.
122 DHB, *Final Report of the Channel Tunnel Study Working Party* (March 1982), and version with commercially sensitive data in DTp file IT40/2/77 Pt. 2; R.O. Goss and P.B. Marlow, Report on 'Cross-Channel Ferries and the Fixed Link', 4 March 1982, ibid. For unpublished criticisms see Lyall-McIntosh, 15 March 1982, Lyall-Howell, 17 March 1982, Webber-McIntosh, 23 March 1982, John Henes (Asst Sec, Shipping Policy Divn, DoT)-Webber, 1 April 1982, IT40/2/36 Pt. 5; Kalen, Note, 23 April 1982, Treasury file NIEA U/151/868/1 Pt. E.
123 Report of Anglo/French Study Group, paras 8.1–19, and see also Annex K; Summary Report, para. 8.
124 Report of Anglo/French Study Group, paras 10.1–16.
125 *Financial Times*, 10 April, *Sunday Times*, 11 April, *Daily Telegraph*, 14 April 1982. Cf. David Williams-Keen, 22 April 1982, AN191/238, PRO.
126 P.S. Jenkins (Howe's PS)-T.F. Mathews (Chief Secretary's PS), 19 April 1982, Treasury file NIEA U/151/868/1 Pt. D.
127 DTp CTU, 'Note of meeting about Fixed Channel Link, held 21 April 1982', April 1982, DTp file IT40/5/7 Pt. 3.
128 David Rowe (DTp CTU)-Mayer, 30 April 1982, ibid.
129 In addition, John Howard saw Baldwin (DTp) and Gow (Thatcher's PPS), Ken Groves (Chief Executive, EuroRoute) met Gray (FCO), and Ian Fraser (Chairman, Lazards) met Howe. See correspondence, etc. in DTp files IT40/2/42 Pt. 4 and IR40/2/77 Pt. 2, and Treasury file NIEA U/151/868/1 Pt. D; Williams-Keen, 22 April 1982, cit.; Parker, *For Starters*, p. 225.
130 Rowe-Lyall and Mayer and Mayer-Lyall, both 21 April 1982, DTp file IT40/2/42 Pt. 4.
131 Howell-Nicholas Edwards (SoS for Wales) *et al.*, 27 April 1982, Prime Minister's Channel Tunnel papers, Pt. 2.
132 James Prior (SoS for NI)-Thatcher, 4 May 1982, ibid.
133 Henes-Lord Cockfield (SoS for Trade), 30 April 1982, Jonathan Rees (Lord Cockfield's PS), 'Note of a Meeting with Mr MacGregor to discuss the Euroroute on Tuesday 4 May 1982', 6 May 1982, DTp file GSP2044 Pt. 4.
134 Howell, Memo. to E Committee on 'Fixed Cross-Channel Link', E(82) 40, 27 April 1982.
135 CPRS, Memo. to E Committee on 'Fixed Cross-Channel Link', E(82) 41, 30 April 1982, and see also Stuttard-John Sparrow (Head, CPRS), 22 April 1982, Cabinet Office file on 'Channel Tunnel', 183/1 Pt. 6.
136 Broadbent-Case and Ryrie, 23 April 1982, Treasury file NIEA U/151/868/1 Pt. E.
137 Ryrie-Howe, 26 April 1982, ibid.
138 Jonathan Rickford (Asst Solicitor, Depts of Industry and Trade)-R.M. Watson (DoT), 28 April 1982, Henes, Brief for Cockfield on 'Fixed Cross Channel Link', 30 April 1982, DTp CTU, 'Note of meeting held on 29 April 1982', 30 April 1982, DTp file GSP2044 Pt. 4.
139 Broadbent-Case and Howe, 30 April 1982, NIEA U/151/868/01 Pt. E.
140 Ridley-Howe, 29 April 1982, ibid.
141 Walters-Thatcher, 30 April 1982, Prime Minister's Channel Tunnel papers, Pt. 2. The term 'Son of Beeching' was coined by Ridley in reference to the imminent Serpell inquiry: Ridley-Howe, 29 April 1982, cit.

142 'Note for File. Channel Fixed Link: Meeting at Department of Transport 21 April', n.d., FCO file MRY178/1/82 Pt. G; Gray-Bridges, 23 April 1982, Bridges-Fretwell, 28 April 1982, Pt. H.
143 Gray-Bridges, 26 April 1982, Fretwell, Paris telegram No. 396, 27 April 1982, FCO file MRY178/1/82 Pt. H.
144 Gray-Bridges, 29 April 1982, enclosing 'speaking note', ibid.
145 Cabinet E Committee Minutes, E(82) 4th, 4 May 1982, 4.30pm. Attendees were Thatcher, Whitelaw (Home Secretary), Howe (Exchequer), Walker (Agriculture), Heseltine (Environment), Jenkin (Industry), Howell, Brittan (Treasury Sec), Lawson (Energy), Tebbit (Employment), Parkinson (Lancaster), Cockfield (Trade), Younger (Scotland) and Edwards (Wales). Pym was absent, addressing the Commons on the Falklands War prior to the news of the attack on *HMS Sheffield. Parl. Deb. (Commons)*, 6th ser. (Session 1981–2), Vol. 23, 4 May 1982, *c*.19ff.
146 Cf. Hunt, *Tunnel*, pp. 164–5; Holliday et al, *Channel Tunnel*, p. 13; Interview with Sir Peter Parker (for British Rail), 2 August 1999, and with David P. Williams, 13 November 2003; *New Scientist*, 27 May 1982, p. 551; *Times*, 17 June 1982, p. 3.
147 Cabinet Defence and Oversea Policy Committee: Sub-Committee on the South Atlantic and The Falkland Islands Minutes, OD(SA) (82) 25th, 4 May 1982, 6.30 p.m.
148 'Note for File. Meeting 21 April', cit.
149 Lyall-Mayer, 13 April 1982, DTp file IT40/5/17 Pt. 2; Gregson-Thatcher, 30 April 1982, Prime Minister's Channel Tunnel papers, Pt. 2.
150 Adams-Stephen Lamport (Hurd's PS), 5 May 1982, FCO telegram No. 219 to Fretwell, 5 May 1982, Gray-Adams, 6 May 1982, FCO file MRY178/1/82 Pt. H.
151 Fretwell, telegram No. 429 to FCO, 6 May 1982, FCO file MRY178/1/82 Pt. I.
152 Gray-Adams, Gray-Adams and Lamport, both 7 May 1982, FCO telegram No. 228 to Fretwell, 7 May 1982, ibid.; Noulton-Mayer, 7 May 1982, DTp file IT40/5/17 Pt. 2.
153 Fretwell, telegram No. 452 to FCO, 10 May 1982, Gray-Adams, 11 May 1982, Fretwell, telegram No. 458 to FCO and DTp, 11 May 1982, FCO file MRY178/1/82 Pt. I.; Interview with Noulton, cit. Rosenfeld also referred to the railway strike over flexible rostering as a 'complicating factor': Noulton, Note for the file, 11 May 1982, DTp file IT40/6/1 Pt. 5.
154 Gray-Adams, 11 May 1982, cit.
155 Howell-Thatcher, 12 May 1982, Prime Minister's Channel Tunnel papers, Pt. 2.
156 Pym-Thatcher, 14 May 1982, ibid.
157 *Parl. Deb. (Commons)*, 6th ser. (Session 1981–2), Vol. 23, 12 May 1982, *c*.738–40, Howell, responding to questions from Teddy Taylor (Southend East), Donald Stewart (Western Isles) and Roger Moate (Faversham).
158 John Coles (Thatcher's PS)-Thatcher, 30 April 1982, Prime Minister's papers on 'France. Visit of Monsieur Mauroy, PM of France, in May 1982'.
159 Thatcher, undated annotation to Coles-Thatcher, cit.; Coles-Richards, 4 May 1982, FCO file MRY178/1/82 Pt. I.
160 Lamport-Mayer, 30 April 1982, Richards-Coles, 13 May 1982, ibid.
161 Coles, 'Record of a Conversation between the Prime Minister and the Prime Minister of France at 1900 hrs on 15 May 1982 at Hopetoun House, Edinburgh', 17 May 1982, Prime Minister's papers on 'Visit of Mauroy'. There are other versions of the Thatcher-Mauroy conversation. Mauroy's ran something like this:

Thatcher: 'My dream is to take my car and drive directly to the Côte d'Azur'.
Mauroy: 'I also have a dream, which is to take the train from Lille to London'.
(Interview with Braibant, 2005)

162 See record of conversations in Prime Minister's papers on 'Visits of Mitterand', Pt. 3.

163 Cf. Fretwell, telegram No. 476 to FCO, 12 May 1982, FCO file MRY178/1/82 Pt. I; Lyall-Rosenfeld, 17 May 1982, DTp file IT40/6/1 Pt. 5.
164 Adams-Gray, 19 May 1982, Adams-Sir Peter Petrie (Minister, Paris Embassy), 20 May 1982, FCO file MRY178/1/82 Pt. I; Gray-Adams, 21 May 1982, Pt. J; Spencer-Lyall, 19 May 1982, DTp file IT40/6/1 Pt. 5.
165 It appears that Jean Deflassieux, Chairman of Crédit Lyonnais and a Socialist friend of Mauroy's, was a catalyst: Interview with Deflassieux, in Bernard Desjardins *et al.*, *Crédit lyonnais 1863–1986* (Geneva, 2003), p. 109; Interview with Braibant, 2005.
166 Noulton-Mayer, 26 May 1982, DTp file IT40/5/17 Pt. 2; Petrie-Adams, 26 May 1982, FCO file MRY178/1/82 Pt. J.
167 Gray-Adams, 27 May 1982, Gray-Adams and John M. MacGregor (PS to Malcolm Rifkind, PUSS, FCO), 27 May 1982, ibid.; Stuttard-Sparrow, 27 May 1982, CPRS file Q9/2 Pt. 4; DTp CTU, 'Note of meeting held on 26 May 1982 . . .', 26 May 1982, DTp file IT40/7/1 Pt. 1.
168 Howell-Thatcher, 7 June 1982, Scholar-Mayer, 11 June 1982, Prime Minister's Channel Tunnel papers, Pt. 2; DTp, *Fixed Channel Link. Report of UK/French Study Group*, June 1982, P.P.1981–2, liv, Cmnd. 8561.
169 *Parl. Deb. (Commons)*, 6th ser. (Session 1981–2), Vol. 25, 16 June 1982, Howell, answer to Phillip Whitehead (Derby North), *c.*940; DTp Press Release, 16 June 1982, DTp file IT40/4/13 Pt. 2.
170 Case-Brittan, 9 June 1982, Treasury file NIEA U/151/868/1 Pt. E; Sparrow-Howell, 9 June 1982, Brittan-Howell, 11 June 1982, Prime Minister's Channel Tunnel papers, Pt. 2.
171 Pym-Thatcher, 11 June 1982, ibid.
172 Howell, statement, cit.; Fiterman, statement in answer to M. Rieubon, 16 June 1982 [English translation, and French version of AF82 [*Manche: quelle liaisons?* (Paris, 1982)] in FCO file MRY178/1/82 Pt. J; Gray-Adams, 27 June 1982, ibid.
173 *Times*, 17 June 1982, p. 3; *Economist*, 19 June 1982, p. 20.
174 Franco/British Channel Link Financing Group-Lyall and Braibant, 9 August 1982 and Lyall's reply, 11 August 1982, DTp file IT40/6/1 Pt. 5. On the delay see Rosenfeld-Case, 15 July 1982, Treasury file NIEA U/151/868/1 Pt. E; Rosenfeld-Howell's PS (Mayer?), 15 July 1982, IT40/5/17 Pt. 2; Case-Rosenfeld, 19 July 1982, CPRS file Q9/2 Pt. 4.
175 Robert Henderson (Chairman, Kleinwort, Benson)-Baldwin, 18 May 1982, DTp file IT40/8/2 Pt. 1. See also Margaret Ackrill and Leslie Hannah, *Barclays: the Business of Banking 1690–1996* (Cambridge, 2000), pp. 211–14, 241–2; David Kynaston, *The City of London. Vol. IV: A Club No More, 1945–2000* (2001), pp. 340–4, 394, 429, 563–7, 601–3.
176 Kroll, 'Note of a meeting held on 8 June 1982 in Room N18/07', 11 June 1982, DTp file IT40/8/2 Pt. 1.
177 Franco/British Channel Link Financing Group-Lyall and Braibant, 9 August 1982, cit.
178 Lyall-David Peel (Asst Sec, DOE/DTp Manpower Services), 20 July 1982, DTp file IT40/4/13 Pt. 2.
179 E.g. Lyall-Eric Ballard (Director, John Laing), 16 June and 11 August 1982, DTp file IT40/6/1 Pt. 5.
180 Keen-Parker and Reid, 12, 19 and 21 May 1982, BRB 196-4-1 Pt. 13; Parker-Keen, 25 May 1982, Note of meeting on 3 June 1982, AN156/372, PRO; *Financial Times*, 10, 15 and 28 June 1982, cuttings in DTp file IT40/2/42 Pt. 4; Interviews with Parker and Williams, cit.
181 See *Financial Times*, 26 May 1982, p. 9, and Al Davidson, letter, *Financial Times*, 10 June 1982, and Noulton, Note for the File, 22 April 1983, DTp file IT40/2/43 Pt. 2.
182 Ballard-Lyall, 17 June 1982, DTp file IT40/2/47 Pt. 2.

183 Groves-Lyall, 16 June 1982, Toby Johns (Howell's APS), 'Note of a Meeting with Mr McGregor [*sic*] held on 30 June 1982', 1 July 1982, and papers in DTp file IT40/2/42 Pt. 4.
184 Jill Rutter (Howe's APS), 'Note of a meeting held in No. 11 Downing Street...on...28 September 1982', 28 September 1982, Treasury file NIEA U/151/868/1 Pt. E; Lyall-Noulton, 28 September 1982, DTp file IT40/2/42 Pt. 4.
185 Groves-Lyall, 7 July 1982, ibid.; Spencer-Roy Reeve (Asst, MAED, FCO), 15 November 1982, Spencer, Note for File, 29 November 1982, FCO file MRY178/1/82 Pt. L.
186 Adams, 'Note for the Record', 22 December 1982, ibid.; Lyall-Richard Bird (Howell's PS), 12 January 1983, DTp file IT40/5/17 Pt. 2; Keen, Note on 'Meeting with EuroRoute, 6 January 1983', 13 January 1983, AN156/372, PRO. Soames also lobbied Howell directly: Gray-Spencer, 18 January 1983, FCO file MRY178/1/83 Pt. A.
187 Rosenfeld-Case, 3 September 1982, Rosenfeld-Geoffrey Morgan (Asst Sec, Transport Industries, Treasury), 27 September 1982, Lyall-Morgan, 12 and 28 October 1982, CPRS file Q9/2 Pt. 4
188 Lyall-David Holmes (Principal Finance Officer, DTp), 18 and 29 November 1982, DTp file IT40/5/17 Pt. 2.
189 John-Lyall, 30 November 1982, Lyall-Bird, 3 December 1982, ibid.
190 Bird-Lyall, 15 December 1982, ibid.
191 Sean Bodkin (Howell's APS)-Noulton, 16 December 1982, ibid.
192 Lyall-Bird, 17 December 1982, ibid.
193 EEC Regulation 3600/82, 30 December 1982; Holmes-Bird, 31 January 1983, DTp file IT40/5/17 Pt. 2; *Parl. Deb. (Commons)*, 6th ser. (Session 1982–3), Vol. 38, 10 March 1983, Lynda Chalker (PUSS, DTp), written answer to John Wells (Maidstone), *472*; Abbati, *Transport and European Integration*, pp. 141–2.
194 Keen-Reid, 5 January 1983, AN156/372, PRO; Gourvish, *British Rail 1974–97*, pp. 174–81.
195 Lyall-Noulton, 3 May 1983, Noulton, 'Note of a meeting with the British banks on 5 May 1983', 9 May 1983, Noulton-Holmes, 9 May 1983, DTp file IT40/8/2 Pt. 4.
196 David Butler and Dennis Kavanagh, *The British General Election of 1983* (1984), p. 288ff; Craig, *British General Election Manifestos*.
197 *Financial Times*, 25 May 1983, p. 10, *Dover Express*, 27 May 1983, p. 1, and see Nicholas Comfort, 'Politics, Lobbying and Diplomacy', in Bronwen Jones (ed.), *The Tunnel: The Channel and Beyond* (Chichester, 1987), p. 45, and John Campbell, *Margaret Thatcher. Vol. Two: The Iron Lady* (2003), p. 312.
198 Lyall-Holmes *et al.*, 22 June 1983, with note on 'Channel Fixed Link', Holmes-R.S. Balme (Chalker's PS), 23 June 1983, DTp file IT40/5/17 Pt. 2.
199 MacGregor-Tom King (SoS for Transport), 13 June 1983, DTp, 'Note of Meeting with Ian MacGregor...7 July 1983', 12 July 1983, DTp file IT40/2/42 Pt. 6; Lyall-Holmes and Lyall-Balme, both 13 July 1983, FN24/3/8 Pt. 1; Lesley Stark (DTp)-Noulton and David Benson (DTp), 3 August 1983, enclosing Franco-British Channel Link Financing Group, 'Interim Report covering the first stage of analysis', July 1983, and cuttings from *Financial Weekly*, 15 July, p. 1, *New Civil Engineer*, 28 July, p. 6, and *Economist*, 5 August 1983, p. 56, Lyall-Brian Matthews (Senior Executive, Policy & Planning, Midland Bank (International)), 4 August 1983, IT40/8/5 Pt. 1; Lyall-King's PS, 4 August 1983, IT40/5/17 Pt. 2; *Parl. Deb. (Commons)*, 6th ser. (Session 1983–4), Vol. 45, 7 July 1983, Chalker, written answer to Gary Waller (Brighouse), *165–6*; David Mitchell (Transport Minister), answer to Price (Eastleigh), and Chalker, answer to Jonathan Aitken (Thanet South), 11 July 1983, *247*; Vol. 46, King, written answer to Howell, 21 July 1983, *227–8*, who surprisingly argued for a 6-metre tunnel.

200 Lyall-Holmes, 30 August 1983, Philip Wood (Asst Sec, DTp), Memo. on 'Private Operation of Channel Tunnel Rail Services', n.d., DTp file GSP2044 Pt. 7; Lyall-King's PS, 31 August 1983, IT40/8/5 Pt. 1; Spencer-Gray, 20 July 1983, FCO file MRY178/1/83 Pt. A.
201 DTp, 'Meeting to discuss the Fixed Channel Link... 1 September 1983', 5 October 1983, DTp file IT40/8/5 Pt. 1. Pontillon also met King's successor, Nicholas Ridley, in January 1984: see papers in IT40/2/17 Pt. 8.
202 Adams-Gray, 2 September 1983, FCO file MRY178/1/83 Pt. A; DTp, 'Meeting with Senator Pontillon to discuss Channel Fixed Link... 12 September 1983', 5 October 1983, DTp file IT40/2/17 Pt. 8.
203 Lyall-Holmes, 26 September 1983, DTp file IT40/8/5 Pt. 1; Holmes, 'Note of Informal Discussion between Secretary of State for Transport and French Minister of Transport – 6 October 1983', 10 October 1983, IT40/2/17 Pt. 8.
204 Thatcher, *Downing Street Years*, pp. 311–12; Gourvish, *British Rail 1974–97*, pp. 101, 547.
205 MacGregor-Nicholas Ridley (SoS for Transport), 21 October 1983, DTp file GSP2044 Pt. 7.
206 *Parl. Deb. (Commons)*, 6th ser. (Session 1983–4), Vol. 47, 24 October 1983, *c.*10, Ridley, oral answers to George Foulkes (Carrick), Den Dover (Chorley) and Donald Anderson (Swansea East).
207 Colin Stannard (Head of Development Projects, NatWest Bank)-Lyall, 17 October 1983, Lyall-Holmes, 18 October 1983, Lyall-Stannard, 19 October 1983, Holmes-Dinah Nichols (Ridley's PS), 19 October 1983, enclosing brief for Anglo-French summit on 20–1 October 1983 [subject not raised], DTp file IT40/8/6 Pt. 1.
208 *Parl. Deb. (Commons)*, 6th ser. (Session 1983–4), Vol. 50, 5 December 1983, Ridley, answer to Waller, *36*.
209 Lyall-Balme, 10 November 1983, Lyall-Michael Devereau (Head of Information, DTp), 21 November 1983, Stannard-Lyall, 20 January 1984, DTp file IT40/8/6 Pt. 1.
210 Lyall-Stannard, 23 January, Lyall-Ian Jordan (DTp), 24 January, and Stannard-Lyall, 27 January 1984, ibid.
211 Adams-Gray, 2 November 1983, FCO file MRY178/1/83 Pt. B.
212 Webber-Lyall, 16 September 1983 ['shoddy', 'abominably drafted', 'disjointed collection of random musings', 'dreadful', 'largely waffle', etc.], Lyall-Holmes, 26 September 1983 ['shoddy', 'incomprehensible'], Lyall-Stannard, 27 September 1983, DTp IT Divn, 'Interdepartmental Meeting on Channel Fixed Link 28 September 1983', 29 September 1983, DTp file IT40/8/5 Pt. 1.
213 Webber-Jordan, 28 November 1983, DTp file IT40/8/6 Pt. 1; Lyall-Adams, 29 November 1983, FCO file MRY178/1/83 Pt. B; DTp, 'Note of Interdepartmental Meeting to discuss Channel Fixed Link, 8 December 1983', DTp file GSP2044 Pt. 7; Lyall-Jordan, 23 January 1984, IT40/8/6 Pt. 1; Stannard-Lyall, correspondence, January 1984, cit.
214 Lyall-Holmes, 8 February 1984, DTp file IT40/8/6 Pt. 1.
215 The same was true of a further Ridley-Fiterman meeting on 21 March. Spencer-Lyall, 8 February 1984, Holmes-Nichols, 10 February 1984, DTp file IT 40/2/17 Pt. 8; Fretwell, Paris telegram No. 169 to FCO, 10 February 1984, Gray-Adams, 21 February 1984, FCO file MRY178/1/84 Pt. A; Adams-Gray, 21 February 1984, Robert Chase (Asst, MAED, FCO)-Adams, 27 March 1984, Pt. B.
216 Lyall-Devereau, 21 November 1983, cit.; Gray-Adams, 9 December 1983, FCO file MRY178/1/83 Pt. B; Adams-Gray, 30 January 1984, Ridley-Howe, 13 February 1984, Ronald Sindon (MAED, FCO)-Chase and Gray, 21 February 1984, MRY178/1/84 Pt. A.
217 Henry Derwent (Ridley's APS)-Holmes, 27 February 1984, enclosing 'Note of a meeting between the Secretary of State and representatives of the Midland and National Westminster banks 24 February 1984', DTp file IT40/8/2 Pt. 4.

218 Derwent-Holmes, 27 February 1984 (letter no. 2), DTp file IT40/8/6 Pt. 1; Gray-Sir Crispin Tickell (Dep U-Sec, FCO), 16 February 1984, FCO file MRY178/1/84 Pt. A.
219 D.J. King (Treasury)-Kingsley Jones (Asst Sec, Home & Transport Divn., Treasury), 1 March 1984, Treasury file NIEA U/151/868/1 Pt. E.
220 Robert Young (No. 10 Policy Unit)-Andrew Turnbull (Thatcher's PS), 7 March 1984, Prime Minister's Channel Tunnel papers, Pt. 2. On the demise of the CPRS see Hennessy, *Whitehall*, pp. 655–8.
221 Lyall-Nichols, 23 December 1983, Lyall-Jordan, 6 January 1984, MacGregor-Ridley, 15 December and 24 January 1984, Lyall-Nichols, 24 January 1984, DTp file IT40/2/42 Pt. 7; DTp, 'Note of meeting to discuss EuroRoute', 30 January 1984, IT40/8/8 Pt. 2.
222 Gow-Michael Alison (Thatcher's PPS), 23 February 1984, Turnbull-Nichols, 14 March 1984, Prime Minister's Channel Tunnel papers, Pt. 2.
223 Nichols, 'Note of Secretary of State's meeting with Rail Tunnel promoters… 21 September 1983', 21 September 1983, and Lyall's brief for meeting, 19 September 1983, DTp file IT40/2/71 Pt. 1.
224 *Financial Times*, 5 March 1984, p. 1, 6 March 1985, p. 6; Tony Gueterbock (CTG)-Malcolm Rifkind (Minister of State, FCO), 8 March 1984, FCO files MRY178/1/84 Pt. B. Cf. also Ty Bird, *The Making of the Channel Tunnel* (New Civil Engineer and Transmanche Link, 1994), p. 18.
225 Spencer-Lyall, 24 February 1984, Spencer-Gray, 21 March 1984, ibid. Pt. B; Valerie Ewan (British Embassy Paris)-Spencer, 4 May 1984, Malcolm Dougal (British Consul-General, Lille)-Spencer, 21 May 1984, ibid. Pt. C.
226 Bernard Pilon, 'Liaison Fixe Transmanche', September 1984, DTp file IT40/2/17 Pt. 12. It should be noted that Pilon lacked support within France, however.
227 Holmes-Nichols, 6 and 18 April 1984, Katharine Ramsay (Ridley's political adviser)-Ridley, 19 April 1984, Nichols-Holmes, 24 April 1984, DTp file IT40/8/8 Pt. 1; Holmes-Adams, 19 April 1984, FCO file MRY178/1/84 Pt. B.
228 Holmes-Nichols, 3 May 1984, DTp file IT40/8/8 Pt. 1.
229 Daniel Instone (DTp)-Holmes and Nichols, 1 May 1984, IT40/8/8 Pt. 1.
230 Ridley-Thatcher, [10] May 1984, Prime Minister's Channel Tunnel papers, Pt. 2.
231 Instone-Nichols, 17 May 1984, reporting responses of Thatcher, Peter Rees (Treasury Chief Secretary), Howe, Cockfield, *et al.*, DTp file IT40/8/8 Pt. 1. Howe continued to snipe: 'I have always been afraid that this grotesque project might acquire the remorseless inevitability of e.g. Greek entry to the EC': Howe, annotation on Gray-Adams, 11 May 1984, FCO file MRY178/1/84 Pt. C, and see also Howe-Ridley, 14 May 1984, IT40/8/8 Pt. 1.
232 Franco-British Channel Link Group-Lyall, 17 May 1984, ibid; *Finance for a Fixed Channel Link* (2 Vols., May 1984).
233 *Parl. Deb. (Commons)*, 6th ser. (Session 1983–4), Vol. 60, 22 May 1984, Ridley, written answer to John Wells (Maidstone), *380–1*.
234 Instone-Nichols, 21 and 22 May 1984, Jordan-Nichols, 22 May 1984, DTp file IT40/8/8 Pt. 1.
235 Holmes-Nichols, 6 April 1984, cit.
236 Gray-Adams, 11 May 1982, cit.

9 THE THATCHER GOVERNMENT AND THE TUNNEL: CHOOSING A PROMOTER, 1984–6

1 Instone-Ridley's PS, 22 June 1984, Instone-Kathleen Nash-Brown (DTp), 5 June 1984, DTp file IT40/8/8 Pt. 1; Hazel Duffy, 'Chunnel scheme rebuffed', *Financial Times*, 23 May 1984, p. 1; *Le Figaro*, 23 May 1984, cit. in Ewan-Nash-Brown, 23 May 1984, IT40/8/8 Pt. 1. Note also André Fontaine, in *Le Monde*, cit. in Spencer-Nash-Brown, 29 May 1984, ibid.; *Tunnels and Tunnelling*, July 1984, p. 10.

2 Franco-British Channel Link Financing Group, *Finance for a Fixed Channel Link*, May 1984, Vol. I, pp. 5–8.
3 Ibid. pp. 188–99 and cf. commentary in Robert Young-Turnbull, 7 March 1984, Prime Minister's Channel Tunnel papers, Pt. 2; Hunt, *Tunnel*, pp. 166–7, and Graham Anderson and Ben Roskrow, *The Channel Tunnel Story* (1994), pp. 4–5.
4 DTp, 'Note of a meeting held at Natwest Bank on 19 June 1984…', June 1984, Lyall-Holmes, 31 May 1984, Instone-Lyall, 22 June 1984, DTp file IT40/8/8 Pt. 1.
5 DTp, 'Note of a meeting… 18 July 1984', 20 July 1984, Lyall-Holmes, 20 July 1984, DTp file IT40/8/8 Pt. 2. Natwest's more assertive role had been evident from early 1983: cf. Elizabeth Cleary (DTp CTU)-Noulton and Lyall, 3 March 1983, IT40/8/2 Pt. 4.
6 Instone-Lyall, 23 July 1984, Holmes-Lyall, 6 August 1984, DTp, 'Note of zmeeting… 5 September 1984', 'Note of meeting with Nat West and Midland Banks, 11 October 1984', n.d., DTp file IT40/8/8 Pt. 2.
7 Groves-Lyall, 21 May, Groves-Rees, 24 May 1984, DTp file IT40/2/42 Pt. 7.
8 *Financial Times*, 14 September 1984, p. 8; Groves-Gordon Brunton (NEDO), 26 September 1984, DTp file IT40/2/42 Pt. 8.
9 Instone-Lyall, 22 June 1984, cit.; Frank Davidson-David Williams (BRB), 17 July 1984, AN191/189, PRO; Lyall-Jordan, 26 November 1984, DTp IT40/2/43 Pt. 2. The continuing interest of TSI in a possible compensation claim was a motivation: Lyall-Webber, 28 January 1985, DTp file FN24/3/1 Pt.1. The claim, resting largely on the assertion that the CTG-FM tunnel design derived from the work carried out for the CTSG by Charles Dunn for Bechtel, Morrison-Knudsen *et al.* in 1959, was rejected by both the DTp and Eurotunnel. See correspondence in TSI archive, carton #13, HBS and Fetherston, *Chunnel*, pp. 67–70.
10 Instone-Lyall, 22 June 1984, cit.; Derwent-Jordan, 11 October 1984, DTp file IT40/8/8 Pt. 2; Sir Nicholas Henderson (Tarmac and CTG)-Ridley, 23 October 1984, Prime Minister's Channel Tunnel papers, Pt. 2; R.J. O'Neill (Superintending U-Sec, FCO)-Len Appleyard (Howe's PS), 16 October 1984, FCO file MRY178/1/84 Pt. D; Henderson, *Channels and Tunnels*, pp. 9–10; Bird, *Making of the Channel Tunnel*, p. 22.
11 Leigh Lewis (David Young (Minister without Portfolio)'s PPS), 'Note of a meeting… 26th September, to discuss EuroRoute', 28 September 1984, Sir Nigel Broackes (Chairman, Trafalgar House)-Lewis, 3 October 1984, Lyall-Lazarus, 9 November 1984, Lazarus-Lyall, 13 November 1984, David Peretz (Asst Sec, Treasury), 'Note of a meeting at No. 11 Downing Street… 19 November 1984', n.d., Noulton-Lazarus, 21 November 1984, DTp file IT40/2/42 Pt. 8; *Financial Times*, 25 October 1984, p. 13.
12 Cf. Lyall-Holmes, 5 July 1984, DTp file IT40/2/17 Pt. 10.
13 Cf. Fretwell, Paris telegram No. 1316 to FCO, 26 November 1984, ibid. Pt. 11; FCO, Note to Cabinet Official Group on Bilateral Relations with Certain European Community Countries on 'Joint Report by Foreign Ministers of France and the United Kingdom to the Anglo-French Summit on 29/30 November 1984', 1 November 1984, MISC 76(84) 115. In French political circles there was a belief that British acceptance of the Tunnel was a quid pro quo for the Budget settlement: Interview with Braibant, 2005.
14 Instone-Lyall and Ridley's PS, 6 July 1984, Lyall-Ridley's PS, 9 July 1984, Lyall-Holmes, 20 July 1984, DTp file IT40/2/17 Pt. 10; Kate Timms (Counsellor (Agriculture & Economic), British Embassy, Paris)-Lyall, 20 July 1984, FCO file MRY178/1/84 Pt. C; Bell and Criddle, *The French Socialist Party*, pp. 122–3.
15 Timms-Lyall, 31 July 1984, Jean Auroux (French Minister of Transport)-Ridley, 16 October 1984, DTp file IT40/2/17 Pt. 10; Ewan-David Worskett (IT Divn, DTp), 10 August 1984, FCO file MRY178/1/84 Pt. C.
16 Lyall, Memo. on 'Responsibilities of French Transport Ministers', 16 August 1984, Andrew Lansley (Tebbit's PS), 'Note of a Meeting with M. Auroux, 5 September 1984', 10 September 1984, Lazarus-Ridley, 26 September 1984, Derwent-A.J.H.

Picton (Lazarus's PS), 27 September 1984, Ridley-Auroux, 4 October 1984, DTp file IT40/2/17 Pt. 10; Jeffrey Ling (Counsellor (Technology), British Embassy, Paris)-Ewan, 13 September 1984, FCO file MRY178/1/84 Pt. D. It was some time before Auroux's duties were clarified: cf. Ewan-Worskett, 7 November 1984, DTp file IT40/2/17 Pt. 10; Lyall-Ridley's PS, 27 November 1984, ibid. Pt. 11.

17 Ridley-Auroux, 4 October, and Lazarus-Ridley, 26 September 1984, cit.; Stannard-Lazarus, 22 October 1984 and reply, 24 October 1984, DTp file IT40/8/8 Pt. 2.

18 *Financial Times*, 1 October 1984, pp. 6, 48, 8 October 1984, p. 17, and cf. J.P. Anderson (MAED, FCO)-MacPherson *et al.* (FCO), 2 October 1984, FCO file MRY178/1/84 Pt. D.

19 Derwent-Lyall, 10 October 1984, DTp file IT40/2/17 Pt. 10.

20 Lyall-Holmes and Ridley's PS, 22 October 1984, 'Note of a Meeting on Channel Fixed Link with officials at French Ministry of Transport, 18 October 1984', n.d., DTp file IT40/9/1 Pt. 1.

21 French Embassy in London, Note on 'Speech of M. Francois Mitterand at a Dinner given by her Majesty the Queen (23 October 1984)', 24 October 1984, FCO file MRY178/1/84 Pt. D; Charles Powell (Thatcher's PS), 'Record of a Meeting between the Prime Minister and the President Mitterand on Wednesday 24 October…', 24 October 1984, Prime Minister [Thatcher]'s papers on 'France: Visits of President Mitterand', Pt. 4; Powell-Derwent, 24 October 1984, extract from press conference, 26 October 1984, in Timms-Lyall, 9 November 1984, DTp file IT40/2/17 Pt. 10, but see also French Embassy transcript, in MRY178/1/84 Pt. E.

22 See Petrie, Paris telegram No. 1273 to FCO, 15 November 1984, ibid. Pt. 11.

23 DTp, 'Note of a Meeting on the Channel Tunnel Fixed Link…Paris, 14 November 1984', November 1984, DTp file IT40/2/17 Pt. 11; DTp, 'Communiqué on Fixed Channel Link', 15 November 1984, ibid. Pt. 10; Cabinet Conclusions, CC(84) 37th, 15 November 1984.

24 Ridley-Thatcher, 24 October 1984, Prime Minister's Channel Tunnel papers, Pt. 2.

25 See Alex Galloway (John Gummer [Paymaster General]'s PS)-Derwent, 24 October, Lord (David) Young (Minister without Portfolio)-Thatcher, 30 October, John Neilson (Peter Walker [Energy Secretary]'s PS)-Derwent, Patrick Jenkin (Environment Secretary)-Ridley, John Wybrew (Policy Unit)-Turnbull and Tim Flesher (Thatcher's PS)-Thatcher, all 31 October, Michael Heseltine (Defence Secretary)-Thatcher and Flesher-Derwent, 1 November 1984, ibid.; Norman Lamont (Trade & Industry Secretary)-Ridley, 1 November 1984, FCO file MRY178/1/84 Pt. E. Peter Rees's was the most negative voice: Rees-Thatcher, 31 October 1984, Prime Minister's Channel Tunnel papers, Pt. 2. See also Lyall-Holmes and Ridley's PS, 9 November 1984, DTp file IT40/9/1 Pt. 1.

26 Young-Thatcher, 30 October, Gummer-Ridley, 8 November 1984, ibid.

27 Howe-Thatcher, 2 November 1984, ibid.

28 *Times*, 16 November 1984, p. 9; *Financial Times*, 12 November 1984, p. 28, 16 November 1984, p. 8. On the French press see Timms-Lyall, 16 November 1984, DTp file IT40/2/17 Pt. 10.

29 Note of Meeting, 14 November 1984, Petrie, telegram, 15 November 1984, cit; Lyall-Ridley's PS, 16 November 1984, DTp file IT40/2/17 Pt. 11.

30 French Embassy-FCO, 22 November 1984, Dr Christopher Woodman (Shipping Policy, DTp)-Ridley's PS, 22 November, and reply, 23 November 1984, Fretwell, Paris telegram No. 1294 to FCO, 22 November 1984, Colin Budd (Howe's APS)-Derwent, 26 November 1984, ibid.; Robin Christopher (WED, FCO)-Michael Jenkins (Superintending U-Sec, WED, FCO), 23 November 1984, FCO file WRF26/3/84 Pt. A.

31 Michael Llewllyn Smith (Head of WED, FCO)-Derek Thomas (Dep U-Sec, FCO), 28 and 29 November 1984, FCO files WRF178/1/84 and WRF26/3/84 Pt. C; David Broad (MAED, FCO)-Nichols, and Lyall, Note for the Record, both 28 November

1984, DTp file IT40/2/17 Pt. 11; Budd-Powell, 29 November 1984, Prime Minister [Thatcher]'s files on 'France: Visits to France', Pt. 4.

32 Powell, 'Record of a Conversation between the Prime Minister and President Mitterand... on Thursday 28 [*sic*: actually 29] November 1984', 29 November 1984, FCO file WRF26/3/84 Pt. C.

33 Lyall-Holmes, 3 December 1984, enclosing 'Note for the Record', and Sarah Straight (Ridley's APS)-Lyall, 4 December 1984, DTp file IT40/2/17 Pt. 11.

34 Lyall, 'Note for Record', cit. and cf. Derwent-Holmes, 16 November 1984, cit.

35 A final feasibility study would cost c.£20 m.: Dr J.C. MacDougall (Chief Executive, Midland Bank Int. Project Finance)-Geoffrey Taylor (Group Chief Executive, Midland Bank) *et al.*, 28 February 1984, Midland Bank Channel Tunnel files, ref. 10649, HSBC.

36 Lyall, 'Note for Record', cit.; and cf. Ridley, *'My Style of Government': The Thatcher Years* (1991), p. 158; David Dickinson, '12 Billion Pounds Under the Sea', *Independent on Sunday Magazine*, 18 January 1998, p. 10; Campbell, *The Iron Lady*, pp. 312–13.

37 Robin Butler (Thatcher's PPS), 'Note of a Meeting between the Prime Minister and the President of the French Republic... 30 November 1984', 30 November 1984, FCO file WRF26/3/84 Pt. C.

38 Ibid.; Timms-Lyall, 3 December 1984, DTp file IT40/2/17 Pt. 11.

39 Taken from Powell-Budd, 5 December 1984, enclosing 'Plenary Session, Anglo-French Summit, 30 November, 1984', 5 December 1984, ibid. and Lyall, Note for Record, cit.

40 Transcript of Press Conference, 30 November 1984, FCO file WRF26/3/84 Pt. C; Joint statement, 30 November 1984, DTp file IT40/2/17 Pt. 11.

41 Anderson and Roskrow, *Channel Tunnel Story*, p. 6; Fetherston, *Chunnel*, p. 96; Henderson, *Channel and Tunnels*, p. 7; Holliday *et al.*, *Channel Tunnel*, p. 13; Hunt, *Tunnel*, p. 168.

42 PM's Press Office, transcript of interview given by Thatcher to Philip Short (BBC Radio 4), and see also transcripts of interviews with John Simpson (BBC) and John Brunson (ITN), 30 November 1984, DTp file IT40/2/17 Pt. 11. See also *Financial Times*, 30 November 1984, p. 10, 10 December 1984, p. 5.

43 Timms-Fretwell and Lyall-Ridley's PS, both 18 December 1984, Timms-Lyall, 21 December 1984, DTp file 40/2/17 Pt. 11; Nichols, 'Note of points raised at the Secretary of State's round-up meeting on Thursday, 20 December', 20 December 1984, IT40/9/2 Pt. 1. On the differences in approach in Britain and France see Holliday *et al.*, *Channel Tunnel*, pp. 44–5; Andrew Lyall, 'The Channel Tunnel Saga', undated. I am grateful to Mr Lyall for providing this reference.

44 The British plenary team comprised officials from DTp, Treasury, FCO, Cabinet Office and No. 10 Policy Unit. The French also included an old tunnel hand, Philippe Lacarrière (see p. 46), though Embassy officials were not aware of it. See also Comfort, 'Politics, Lobbying and Diplomacy', p. 54; Henderson, *Channels and Tunnels*, p. 12.

45 Lyall-Holmes, 3 January 1985, DTp file IT40/2/17 Pt. 11; Lyall-Ridley's PS (wide circulation), 11 January 1985, IT40/9/1 Pt. 1.

46 Lyall-Ridley's PS, 11 January 1985, ibid.

47 Christopher-Bryan Cartledge (Dep Sec, CO), 29 January and 5 February 1985, Cabinet Office file on 'Channel Tunnel', 183/1 Pt. 7A.

48 Ibid.

49 Lyall-Ridley's PS, 20 December, and reply, 21 December 1984, DTp file IT40/2/17 Pt. 11; Lyall-Ridley's PS (marked 'for DTp eyes only'), 11 January 1985, IT40/9/1 Pt. 1; Brian Gilmore (U-Sec, Treasury)-Lawson, 4 December 1984, Gilmore-Rees, 10 January 1985, Treasury file CCPA151/1 Pt. A; Dius Lennon (Treasury), 'Note of a Meeting held at 5.15 p.m. 11 January', 14 January 1985, Broadbent (Rees's PS)-Peretz (Lawson's PPS), 16 January 1985, EPS QD514/674/15/1 Pt. E.

50 Treasury, 'The Channel Fixed Link: An Outline Assessment of Three Options', 4 January 1985 [subsequently revised as an agreed Treasury/DTp paper], Michael Spackman (Senior Economic Adviser, Treasury)-Woodman, 15 January 1985, IT40/10/3 Pt. 1; Derwent-Lyall, 14 January 1985, IT40/9/1 Pt. 1; Lyall-Lazarus and Lazarus-Lyall, both 21 January 1985, IT40/10/3 Pt. 1.
51 Nigel Lawson (Chancellor)-Ridley, 29 January 1985, DTp file IT40/9/1 Pt. 2.
52 Lyall-Lazarus, 4 February 1985, Ridley-Lawson, 5 February 1985, Lyall-Ridley's PS, 8 February 1985 (2 letters), Ridley-Lawson, 12 February 1985, ibid.
53 Ridley-Lawson, 12 February 1985, enclosing officials' note on 'Channel Fixed Link: Current Position in Anglo/French Negotiations', ibid.; Ridley, Memo. to Cabinet Ministerial Steering Committee on Economic Strategy: Sub-Committee on Economic Affairs [E(A) Committee] on 'A Channel Fixed Link: Guidelines for Promoters', with annexed note by officials and draft guidelines, E(A) (85) 11, 21 February 1985.
54 Cf. E. Strong (DTp)-Henes (Asst Sec, Shipping Policy, DTp), 9 May 1984, DTp file GSP A2044 Pt. 8; Roger Facer (Asst U-Sec, MOD)-Gray, 4 February 1985, FCO file MRY178/1/85 Pt. B.
55 Lawson-Ridley and Howe-Ridley, both 15 February 1985, DTp file IT40/9/1 Pt. 2.
56 Tebbit-Ridley, 18 February 1985, ibid.
57 Heseltine-Ridley, 19 February 1985, ibid. and 10 December 1985, DTp file IT40/10/19 Pt. 1.
58 DTP IT Divn, 'Note of an Anglo/French Meeting... on 4 February 1985', 5 February 1985, Cabinet Office file on 'Channel Tunnel', 183/1 Pt. 7A.
59 Christopher-Cartledge, 5 February 1985, cit.
60 Officials' note, in Ridley-Lawson, 12 February 1985, cit. See also Derwent-Lyall 19 December 1984, DTp file IT40/9/2 Pt. 1, and Lyall-Edward Osmotherley (Joint Head of Railway Directorate, DTp), 31 January 1985, Cabinet Office file on 'Channel Tunnel', 183/1 Pt. 7A.
61 Gowrie-Ridley, 18 February 1985, Jenkin-Ridley, 19 February 1985, DTp file IT40/9/1 Pt. 2.
62 Wybrew-Thatcher, 22 February 1985, Prime Minister's Channel Tunnel papers, Pt. 2.
63 Ibid. and see also Wybrew-Turnbull, 12 February 1985; Cf. Martin J. Wiener, *English Culture and the Decline of the Industrial Spirit* (Cambridge, 1985), and Correlli Barnett, *The Audit of War: the illusion and reality of Britain as a great nation* (1986). Both books enjoyed a wide currency in Conservative circles in the mid-late 1980s.
64 Preventing the spread of rabies had been a particular, long-standing, concern. Cf. correspondence in 1971, FCO76/385, in 1972, MAF287/185, in 1982, AN191/60 and 349, PRO, and in 1984–5, DTp file IT40/9/1 Pt. 2.
65 E(A) Committee Minutes, E(A) (85) 4th, 25 February 1985; and Dr Sir Robin Nicolson (Chief Scientific Adviser, CO)-Thatcher, Gregson-Thatcher, both 22 February 1985, Prime Minister's Channel Tunnel papers, Pt. 2.
66 Lyall-A.J.C. Poulter (PS to David Mitchell, PUSS for Transport), 28 February 1985, Derwent-Lyall, 1 March 1985, DTp file IT40/2/17 Pt. 11.
67 Ridley-Howe, 18 March and reply, 20 March 1985; Ridley's annotation on Lyall-Ridley's PS, 14 March, Derwent-Lyall, 19 March 1985, DTp file IT40/9/1 Pt. 2.
68 Lyall-Ridley's PS, 18 March 1985, enclosing ministerial brief; DTp, 'Note of the Secretary of State's Meeting with French Ministers Wednesday 20 March 1985', 22 March 1985, DTp file IT40/2/17 Pt. 12; Henderson, *Channels and Tunnels*, pp. 11–12.
69 Note of Meeting, 20 March 1985, cit. and see also Ridley-Howe, 28 March 1985, DTp file IT40/9/1 Pt. 2.
70 Lazarus-Armstrong, 21 March 1985, Prime Minister's Channel Tunnel papers, Pt. 2.
71 *Parl. Deb. (Commons)*, 6th ser. (Session 1984–5), Vol. 76, 2 April 1985, *c.*1078.

72 Gwyneth Dunwoody (Crewe & Nantwich), Howell (Guildford), Nicholas Winterton (Macclesfield), Bruce Millan (Glasgow Govan), Howard (Folkestone & Hythe), Aitken (Thanet South), ibid. c.1078–85.
73 Ridley, Memo. 21 February 1985, and Ridley-Howe, 28 March 1985, cit.
74 Howe-Ridley, 1 April 1985, Jenkin-Ridley, 3 April 1985, DTp file IT40/9/1 Pt. 12.
75 DTp, *Invitation to Promoters for the development, financing, construction and operation of a Channel Fixed Link between France and the United Kingdom* (April 1985), paras 05.1, 11.1, 11.4, 16.1–2, 31.1, and see also summaries in HC Transport Committee, Report on *Channel Link*, 2 December 1985, P.P.1985–6, xvi, HC50-I, paras 8–9; *Financial Times*, 3 April 1985, pp. 1, 9; Henderson, *Channels and Tunnels*, p. 22; Holliday *et al.*, *Channel Tunnel*, p. 14.
76 *Invitation to Promoters*, paras. 01.7, 03.3–6, 13.1, 14.3, 32.1, 34.3; Lyall-Ridley's PS, 29 March 1985, DTp file IT40/2/17 Pt. 12.
77 Henderson-Armstrong, 10 June 1985, Cabinet Office file on 'Channel Tunnel', 183/1 Pt. 8C, and cf. Henderson, *Channels and Tunnels*, p. 22.
78 Woodman-Ridley's PS, 22 May 1985, DTp file IT40/2/17 Pt. 12; Henderson, *Channels and Tunnels*, pp. 8, 12–32; Hunt, *Tunnel*, pp. 168–72; Bird, *Making of the Channel Tunnel*, p. 22.
79 Timms, Note for File, 30 April 1985, Cabinet Office file on 'Channel Tunnel', 183/1 Pt. 8A; Derwent-Powell, 10 May 1985, with Powell's annotation to Thatcher – 'Nico [*sic*] thinks you are tilted towards Euro-route', same date; Powell-Derwent, 13 May 1985, Prime Minister's Channel Tunnel papers, Pt. 3; Henderson, *Channels and Tunnels*, pp. 23–5.
80 Lyall-Woodman, 26 June 1985, DTp file IT40/2/17 Pt. 12.
81 Gray-Woodman, 22 May 1985, Cabinet Office file on 'Channel Tunnel', 183/1 Pt. 8B; Woodman-Christopher and Wybrew-Christopher, both 26 June 1985, Pt. 9A; Christopher-Woodman, 21 June 1985, Lyall-Lazarus, 26 June 1985, DTp file IT40/2/17 Pt. 12.
82 Comfort, 'Politics, Lobbying and Diplomacy', pp. 57–8; Anderson and Roskrow, *Channel Tunnel Story*, p. 13.
83 Cf. Lyall-Raoul Rudeau, 2 May 1985, Cabinet Office file on 'Channel Tunnel', 183/1 Pt. 8A.
84 Lyall, Memo. 17 October 1985, ibid. Pt. 11.
85 The British team was led by Paul Fifoot, the FCO's Deputy Legal Adviser, the French team by Gilbert Guillaume (Quai d'Orsay), Directeur des Affaires Juridiques at the Quai. See Cabinet Office file on 'Channel Tunnel', 183/1 Pts. 8A and 8B.
86 Christopher-Christopher Mallaby (Dep Sec, CO) and Armstrong, 29 October 1985, ibid. Pt. 11; Ridley-Howe, 25 November 1985, Prime Minister's Channel Tunnel papers, Pt. 3.
87 Cf. Ridley-Whitelaw (Lord President), 15 July 1985, Cabinet Office file on 'Channel Tunnel', 183/1 Pt. 9B, and follow-up correspondence, Pt. 10.
88 DTp, Note of Anglo/French Plenary Meeting, 20 May 1985, ibid. Pt. 8B, Woodman-Christopher, 15 July 1985, Pt. 9B.
89 Lyall-Christopher, 21 May 1985, ibid. Pt. 8B; DTp, 'Anglo-French Assessment Group. Note of Meeting held in London on 19 June 1985', 25 June 1985, Pt. 9A.
90 The advisers were: Schroder Wagg (finance), Binnie & Partners and Freeman Fox (engineering, project management), Hydraulics Research (hydrology), Land Use Consultants, Roger Tym, Roy Waller (environmental impact), and Beard Dove Project Management Partnership (co-ordination). DTp press notices, 13 and 30 August 1985, DTp file IT40/2/17 Pt. 13.
91 Cf. Lyall-Woodman, 31 July 1985, ibid. Pt. 12. Once again there was talk that the French were initially in disarray: cf. Woodman-Jordan, 22 and 25 April 1985, ibid. Pt. 12, Cabinet Office file on 'Channel Tunnel', 183/1 Pt. 8A; Lyall, 'Channel Tunnel Saga'.

92 Lyall, Memo. 17 October 1985, cit.; Noulton, communication with author, 23 February 2004; Interview with Sir David Mitchell, 9 June 2004.

93 CTG-FM's documentation is entitled 'Proposal for a Channel Tunnel', October 1985, DTp. On Expressway see James Sherwood (British Ferries/Sea Containers)-Woodman, 1 October 1985, FCO file MRY178/1/85 Pt. J. The five rejected proposals, 'ranging from the ingenious to the downright batty', were: Boothroyd Airship Co. (Milton Boothroyd, suspension bridge); Euro-Trans World Tunnels (Eric Munday/Julien Wieczorek); M.L. McCulloch (bridge/barrage); Eurolink (Andrew Prokopp, road bridge), twin rail tunnels (M. Steedley). The French also received a proposal from Theodorus J. Van der Putten (bridge/tunnel). *Financial Times*, 1 November 1985, p. 1; *Times*, 2 November 1985, p. 2; Comfort, 'Politics, Lobbying and Diplomacy', pp. 61–2; Navailles, *Tunnel Sous La Manche*, p. 206.

94 Ridley-Thatcher, 5 November 1985, Prime Minister's Channel Tunnel papers, Pt. 3; *Times*, 2 November 1985, p. 2.

95 Henderson, *Channels and Tunnels*, pp. 25–32; Bird, *Making of the Channel Tunnel*, p. 22; Hunt, *Tunnel*, p. 173; Fetherston, *Chunnel*, pp. 99–106; Anderson and Roskrow, *Channel Tunnel Story*, p. 26; Tom Rowland, 'Finance – Digging up the Money', in Jones (ed.), *The Tunnel*, pp. 8–9.

96 See material in DTp file IT40/2/42 Pts. 9 and 10.

97 Woodman-Jordan, 22 April 1985, FCO file MRY178/1/85 Pt. F; Lyall-Dougal, 20 August 1985, DTp file IT40/2/17 Pt. 12.

98 Sherwood-Ridley, 'Summary of the "Channel Expressway" Proposal', 31 October 1985, Treasury file CCP A/151/01; Interview with Mitchell, 2004. On Sherwood see Christopher-Woodman, 9 December 1985, Cabinet Office file on 'Channel Tunnel', 183/1 Pt. 13, and John Hunt (British Embassy, Washington)-Roger Beetham (MAED, FCO), 12 December 1985, DTp file IT40/2/76 Pt. 3; Fetherston, *Chunnel*, p. 105.

99 Lyall-Ridley's PS, 11 November 1985, Cabinet Office file on 'Channel Tunnel', 183/1 Pt. 12; Powell-Thatcher, 11 and 14 November 1985, DTp, Note on 'Channel Fixed Link', JMV(85) 4B, 18 November 1985, Prime Minister's papers on 'Visits of Mitterand', Pt. 5.

100 'Record of a meeting between the Prime Minister and President Mitterand…on Monday 18 November at 0900 hours', 'Record of the Plenary Session… 18 November 1985', 20 November 1985, ibid.; DTp Press Notice, 18 November 1985, DTp file IT40/2/17 Pt. 13.

101 DTp IT Divn, brief on 'Meeting with M Auroux – 3 June 1985', 31 May 1985, ibid. Pt. 12; Lyall-Woodman, 5 June 1985, Cabinet Office file on 'Channel Tunnel', 183/1 Pt. 8B; Ridley-Howe, 24 October 1985, Powell-Thatcher, 6 November 1985, Prime Minister's Channel Tunnel papers, Pt. 3; DTp, Note on 'Channel Fixed Link', 18 November 1985, cit.; J.S. Wall (Head of EC Dept., FCO), Memo. on 'Road Haulage Quotas', 4 November 1985, FCO file MRY178/1/85 Pt. K.

102 Letters giving the confidential undertakings on liberalisation were exchanged in March 1986, shortly after the Treaty was signed: Noulton-Ridley's PS, 29 January 1986, Straight-Noulton, 11 March 1986, DTp file IT40/12/19 Pts. 5 and 6.

103 'Record of the Plenary Session', cit.; Straight-Lyall, 19 November 1985, DTp file IT40/2/17 Pt. 13.

104 HC Transport Committee, *Channel Link*, December 1985, Vol. I, para. 11, p. xliv; *Times*, 5 December 1985, p. 1, 6 December 1985, p. 2; *Financial Times*, 6 December 1985, p. 11. Vol. II of the Report [HC50-II] comprised 105 pages of evidence and 30 memoranda from interested parties.

105 Bagier was MP for Sunderland South and a member of the National Union of Railwaymen. HC Transport Committee, *Channel Link*, December 1985, Vol. I, paras 15, 130, pp. xlii-iii.

106 *Guardian*, 24 October 1985, p. 24; *Sunday Observer*, 27 October 1985, p. 1; *Financial Times*, 1 November 1985, p. 1; HC Transport Committee, *Channel Link*,

December 1985, Vol. I, para. 28; *Parl. Deb. (Commons)*, 6th ser. (Session 1985–6), Vol. 88, 9 December 1985, Ridley, *c*.640, 642.

107 A public inquiry was demanded by Robert Hughes (Aberdeen North), John Silkin (Deptford), Stephen Ross (Isle of Wight), Bruce Millan (Glasgow Govan), Gwyneth Dunwoody (Crewe and Nantwich), Jonathan Aitken (Thanet South) and Roger Stott (Wigan). Ibid. *c*.652–4, 658–9, 667–8, 672, 686–7, 690–3, 705–6. As Mitchell put it, 'I think we underestimate the row we are inevitably in for on "no public enquiry" from an alliance of greens, little Englanders and all major ports': Carolyn Haskins (Mitchell's APS), Note, October 1985, DTp file IT40/10/18 Pt. 2.

108 Aitken, ibid. *c*.690; Sir David Price (Eastleigh), *c*.665. Unequivocal supporters of the Fixed Link included David Crouch (Canterbury), Sir John Wells (Maidstone), Ron Lewis (Carlisle), Sir John Osborn (Sheffield Hallam), Robert Adley (Christchurch), Dr John Marek (Wrexham) and David Gilroy Bevan (Birmingham Yardley).

109 Ibid. *c*.714; Christopher-Lyall, 14 February 1985, enclosing text on 'Commitments', para. 14, FCO file MRY178/1/85 Ct. C.

110 Lyall-Ridley's PS, 6 November 1985, DTp file IT40/9/1 Pt. 3; Powell-Richard Allan (Ridley's PS), 7 November 1985, Prime Minister's Channel Tunnel papers, Pt. 3.

111 Kingsley Jones, Memos. 4 and 8 November 1985, Treasury file CCP A151/1 Pt. A.

112 Powell-Allan, 7 November 1985, cit.

113 Woodman, Memo. 10 November 1985, Cabinet Office file on 'Channel Tunnel', 183/1 Pt. 11; Woodman-Ridley's PS, 11 November 1985, ibid. Pt. 12; Jones, Memo. 11 November 1985, Treasury file CCP A/151/1 Pt. A.

114 Lyall-Woodman, 11 November 1985, Lyall-Ridley's APS, 13 November 1985, DTp file IT40/2/17 Pt. 13; Note of Anglo/French Plenary Meetings, 12 and 19 November 1985, FCO file MRY178/1/85 Pt. L.

115 Jones, annotation on Memo. 4 November 1985, cit.; Lyall-Wybrew, 25 November 1985, Lyall-Woodman, 2 December 1985, DTp file IT40/2/76 Pt. 3; Woodman-Ridley's PS, 5 December 1985, Lyall-Woodman, 9 December 1984, IT40/2/17 Pt. 14.

116 Wybrew-Lyall, 20 November 1985, Cabinet Office file on 'Channel Tunnel', 183/1 Pt. 12.

117 Lyall-Jim Coates (U-Sec, Railways, DTp), 11 November 1985, ibid.; Lyall-Ridley's APS, 13 November 1985, cit.; David Bray (CE)-Woodman, 25 November 1985, DTp file IT40/12/19 Pt. 1. Bray was Chief Executive of British Ferries.

118 Note of Anglo/French Plenary Meetings, 26 November and 4 December 1985, ibid.; Sherwood-Lyall, 2 December 1985, Sherwood-Rudeau, 3 December 1985, DTp file IT40/2/76 Pt. 2.

119 Anglo/French Plenary Meetings, 12 and 19 November 1985, Lyall-Ridley's APS, 13 November 1985, cit.; Broackes-Ridley, 20 November 1985, DTp file IT40/12/19 Pt. 1.

120 Powell-Robert Culshaw (PS, FCO), 16 December 1985, Prime Minister's Channel Tunnel papers, Pt. 3.

121 Woodman-Lyall, 17 November 1985, DTp file IT40/10/26 Pt. 1; Christopher-Lyall, 20 November 1985, Cabinet Office file on 'Channel Tunnel', 183/1 Pt. 12.

122 Lyall-Coates, 11 November 1985, Woodman-Ridley's PS, 5 December 1985, cit.

123 Woodman-Ridley's PS, 5 December 1985, cit.

124 Sherwood-Lyall, 2 December 1985, Woodman-Ridley's PS, 5 December 1985, cit.; Lyall-Woodman, 9 December 1985, DTp file IT40/2/17 Pt. 14.; Lyall-Ridley's PS, 30 December 1985 (two letters), IT40/2/76 Pt. 2.; *Financial Times*, 25 November 1985, p. 9, 27 December 1985, p. 22, 28 December 1985, p. 9.

125 Lyall-Ridley's PS, 13 December 1985, Fretwell, Paris telegram No. 1121 to FCO, 13 December 1985, DTp file IT40/2/76 Pt. 2; Lyall-Woodman, 17 December 1985; Lyall-Bellis, 23 December 1985, ibid. Pt. 3.

126 *Invitation to Promoters*, para. 05.4; Jones-Gilmore, 18 September 1985, Cabinet Office file on 'Channel Tunnel', 183/1 Pt. 10.

127 Michael Gordon (MD, CTG)-Lyall, 28 November 1985, DTp file IT40/2/73 Pt. 5; Lyall-Woodman and Lyall-Lazarus, both 2 December 1985, IT40/2/76 Pt. 3; Lyall-Lazarus, 3 December 1985, ibid. Pt. 2.
128 Lyall-Woodman, 2 December 1985, cit.; *Times*, 26 November 1985, p. 21; Wybrew-Thatcher, 9 December 1985, Powell-Thatcher, 11 December 1985, with PM's annotation, and Powell-Wybrew, 11 December 1985, Prime Minister's Channel Tunnel papers, Pt. 3.
129 Robin Biggam (Chief Executive, EuroRoute)-Lyall, 4 and 5 December 1985, DTp file IT40/2/42 Pt. 11; Biggam-Lyall, 20 December 1985, Lyall-Ridley's PS, 23 December 1985, IT40/2/19 Pt. 1.
130 Woodman-Ridley's PS, 5 December 1985, cit.; Lyall-Ridley's APS, 9 December 1985, DTp file IT40/2/76 Pt. 3.
131 DTp, *The Channel Fixed Link*, February 1986, P.P.1985–6, l, Cmnd. 9735, para. 6 and see also DTp file IT40/12/17 Pt. 4. The full list was: civil engineering, project management etc.; financing & insurance; taxation; traffic & revenue; hydrology; frontier controls; marine safety; environment; marine environment (fisheries); adequacy of consultation; economic & employment implications; legal aspects; railway engineering; railway policy; road infrastructure; civil aviation safety and security and defence.
132 Ridley-Thatcher, 23 December 1985, enclosing Note by Officials on 'Channel Fixed Link: Assessment of Proposals', n.d., 'Assessment Report on Proposals for a Channel Fixed Link', Detailed and Summary Reports, both 20 December 1985, Prime Minister's Channel Tunnel papers, Pt. 3.
133 Lyall has expressed doubts that Ministers actually read the main report: Lyall, 'Channel Tunnel Saga', cit.
134 'Assessment Report on Proposals for a Channel Fixed Link', Detailed Report, December 1985, p. II/1.
135 Ibid. pp. V/23–6.
136 Note by officials on 'Channel Fixed Link: Assessment of Proposals', paras 50–2.
137 Ibid. para. 15; J. Henry Schroder Wagg, 'Financial assessment of proposals for a Channel Fixed Link', December 1985, para. 5.2, Prime Minister's Channel Tunnel papers, Pt. 3.
138 Schroders, 'Financial assessment', para. 6, and cf. Derek Netherton (Schroders)-Woodman, 29 November 1985, FCO file MRY178/1/85 Pt. L.
139 Straight-Noulton, 18 December 1985, DTp file IT40/12/19 Pt. 1. Auroux had succeeded Quilès in September 1985: Fretwell, Paris telegram No. 779 to FCO, 20 September 1985, FCO file MRY178/1/85 Pt. J.
140 Richard Bennett (Mitchell's PS)-Lyall, 23 December 1985, DTp file IT40/12/19 Pt. 1.
141 A.J. Wiggins (U-Sec, CO)-Christopher, 24 December 1985, Cabinet Office papers on 'Channel Tunnel', 183/1 Pt. 13.
142 David Norgrove (Thatcher's PS), annotation on Brian Unwin (Dep Sec, CO)-Thatcher, 2 January 1986, Prime Minister's Channel Tunnel papers, Pt. 4.
143 Ridley, Memo. to E(A) Committee on 'Channel Fixed Link', E(A) (86)1, 30 December 1985.
144 Unwin-Thatcher, 2 January 1986, cit.
145 Cf. Henderson-Ridley, 7 January 1986, DTp file IT40/2/73 Pt. 5; Henderson-Ridley, 9 January 1986 (2nd letter), Prime Minister's Channel Tunnel papers, Pt. 4.
146 Beetham-Appleyard, 31 December 1985, FCO file MRY178/6/86; Unwin-Thatcher, 2 January 1986, cit.
147 Gilmore-Robin Butler (2nd Permanent Sec, Treasury) and John MacGregor (Chief Secretary, Treasury), 2 January 1986, Treasury file EPS QD10/15A. On CTG-FM see Chase Investment Bank, 'Channel Fixed Link: A Report on the Availability of Debt Financing' (December 1985), DTp.
148 Appleyard-Beetham, 2 January 1986, FCO file MRY178/6/86.

149 Wybrew-Thatcher, 2 January 1986, Prime Minister's Channel Tunnel papers, Pt. 4, and cf. also Wybrew-Thatcher, 20 December 1985, ibid. Pt. 3.
150 Unwin-Thatcher, 2 January 1986, cit.
151 E(A) Committee Minutes, E(A) (86) 1st, 3 January 1986.
152 Straight-Holmes, 6 January 1986, FCO file MRY178/6/86.
153 Fretwell, Paris telegram No. 13 to FCO, 7 January 1986, Rodric Braithwaite (Dep U-Sec, FCO)-O'Neill, 7 January 1986, ibid.; Unwin-Thatcher, 7 January 1986, Prime Minister's Channel Tunnel papers, Pt. 4; Fetherston, *Chunnel*, p. 122.
154 E(A) Committee Minutes, E(A) (86) 2nd, 8 January 1986.
155 Unwin-Thatcher, 7 January 1986, cit.; FCO, 'Points to Make', n.d.; David Broad (MAED, FCO)-Braithwaite and Howe's PS, 7 January 1986.
156 Unwin-Thatcher, 7 January 1986, E(A) 2nd, cit.
157 Unwin-Thatcher, 2 January 1986, cit.; Lyall-Mitchell's PS, 24 December 1985, DTp file IT40/12/19 Pt. 1.
158 Holmes-Ridley, 2 January 1986, ibid.
159 J Cunliffe (Ridley's APS)-Lyall, 30 December 1985, ibid.
160 Lyall-Ridley's PS, 3, 8 and 10 January 1986, Straight-Lyall, Memos. on 'CFL: Meeting with Mr Sherwood – Wednesday 8 January', 'Meeting with EuroRoute – Thursday 9 January' and 'Meeting with Sir Nicholas Henderson – Friday 10 January', 8–13 January 1986, Sherwood-Ridley, 9 January 1986, ibid. Pts 1 & 2; Henderson-Powell, 9 January 1986, Henderson-Ridley, 9 January 1986 (3rd letter), Prime Minister's Channel Tunnel papers, Pt. 4; Henderson, *Channels and Tunnels*, pp. 52–3.
161 Cf. Lyall-Ridley's PS, 10 January 1986, DTp file IT40/12/19 Pt. 2.
162 Henderson-Ridley, 9 January 1986 (1st letter), Prime Minister's Channel Tunnel papers, Pt. 4; Straight-Lyall on 'CFL: Meeting with Sir Nicholas Henderson – Wednesday 8 January', 9 January 1986, DTp file IT40/12/19 Pt. 2.
163 Powell-Allan, 12 January 1986, Prime Minister's Channel Tunnel papers, Pt. 4.
164 Jones-Gilmore, 13 and 14 January 1986, Treasury file EPS QD10/15B; Beetham-O'Neill, 13 January 1986, FCO file MRY178/6/86; Unwin-Norgrove, 14 January 1986, Prime Minister's Channel Tunnel papers, Pt. 4.
165 Ridley, Memo. to Cabinet on 'Channel Fixed Link', C(86) 3, 14 January 1986.
166 Beetham-O'Neill *et al.*, 15 January 1986, FCO file MRY178/6/86.
167 Gilmore-MacGregor, 15 January 1986, enclosing Annex on 'The Case Against Channel Expressway', Treasury file EPS QD10/15B.
168 Norgrove-Thatcher, Wybrew-Thatcher, both 15 January 1986, Prime Minister's Channel Tunnel papers, Pt. 4.
169 Armstrong-Thatcher, 15 January 1986 [ref.A086/155], ibid.
170 Armstrong-Thatcher, 15 January 1986 [ref.A086/153], ibid. Auroux had warned Ridley that a presidential envoy might come to London, but the meeting with Armstrong took place without the initial knowledge of either Ridley or Howe. Armstrong-Powell, and Powell's annotation for Thatcher, 14 January 1986, ibid.; Straight-Lyall, 15 January 1986, DTp file IT40/16/1 Pt. 5; Beetham-O'Neill, 17 January 1986, FCO file MRY178/6/86.
171 Anxieties had been expressed in the Commons about the problems of driving in tunnels over long distances, notably by Tam Dalyell (Linlithgow) and Peter Snape (West Bromwich East). Cf. *Parl. Deb. (Commons)*, 6th ser. (Session 1985–6), Vol. 89, 18 December 1985, *c.*395–404.
172 Cabinet Conclusions, CC(86) 2nd, Minute 6, 16 January 1986.
173 Fretwell, Paris telegram No. 76 to FCO, 21 January 1986, FCO file MRY178/9/86.
174 Powell, 'Note of a Conversation between the Prime Minister and President Mitterand at the Prefecture in Lille on Monday 20 January 1986 at 10.45', Prime Minister's Channel Tunnel papers, Pt. 4.

175 'Channel Fixed Link: Joint British-French Communique', 20 January 1986, ibid.; French Embassy in London, Note of 'Speeches and Statements', 22 January 1986, FCO file MRY178/9/86.
176 *Parl. Deb. (Commons)*, 6th ser. (Session 1985–6), Vol. 90, 20 January 1986, *c.*19–20.
177 CTG News Release, 20 January 1986, DTp file IT40/2/73 Pt. 5; Henderson-Ridley, 22 January 1986, IT40/2/19 Pt. 3.
178 *Times*, 21 January 1986, p. 17; *Financial Times*, 21 January 1986, pp. 1, 24.
179 British Ferries News Release, 20 January 1986, DTp file IT40/12/19 Pt. 3; Sherwood-Ridley, 23 January 1986, IT40/2/76 Pt. 3.
180 Lyall-Ridley's PS, 27 and 28 January 1986, ibid.; Straight-Lyall, 30 January 1986, DTp file IT40/12/19 Pt. 5.
181 Allan-Lyall, 23 January 1986, DTp file IT40/2/42 Pt. 12; Broackes-Ridley, 24 January 1986, IT40/2/19 Pt. 6.
182 Lyall-Ridley's PS, 5 February 1986, Holmes-Lyall, 25 February, and reply, 3 March 1986, DTp file IT40/2/42 Pt. 13. The idea was to construct a EuroRoute-style bridge from the French coast to an artificial island in mid-channel, with a CE-style bored tunnel thereafter: Elizabeth Hopkins (DTp CFL Divn)-Mitchell's APS, 11 July 1986, ibid.
183 MacGregor, letter to *Times*, 7 January 1986 [published 9 January 1986, p. 15], enclosed in MacGregor-Ridley, 7 January 1986, DTp file IT40/2/42 Pt. 12.
184 See DTp file IT40/12/19 Pt. 5 and in particular Straight-Lyall, 29 January 1986; Ridley-Thatcher, 30 January 1986, Prime Minister's Channel Tunnel papers, Pt. 4.
185 DTp, *Channel Fixed Link*, 1986, para. 7, fn: 'The Government expressly asserts that it makes no representation, either express or implied, as to the viability of the project with any intention or desire that such representation be relied upon by any investor'.
186 *Parl. Deb. (Commons)*, 6th ser. (Session 1985–6), Vol. 91, 10 February 1986, *c.*686–734; Woodman-Lyall *et al.*, 6 February 1986, DTp file IT40/12/19 Pt. 6.
187 Fifoot-Noulton, 27 January 1986, FCO file MRY178/2/86 Pt. A.
188 Beetham-O'Neill, 24 January 1986, and note Thatcher-Christopher Gay (Chief Executive, Canterbury City Council), 12 March 1986, FCO file MRY178/10/86; Budd-Powell, 27 and 30 January 1986, with annotations by Powell and Thatcher, Prime Minister's Channel Tunnel papers, Pt. 4.
189 Mike Horne (No. 10 Press Office)-Ingham, Powell and Thatcher, 10 February 1986, ibid. Pt. 5; luncheon menu and speeches in FCO file MRY178/10/86.
190 The Conservative Mayor, Helen McCabe, reflected the opposition of the local council by refusing to attend the ceremony: Gay-Thatcher, 3 March 1986, ibid.; Darian-Smith, *Bridging Divides*, pp. 94–7, 115–18.
191 *Times, Financial Times* and *Guardian*, 13 February 1986; Timms-Beetham, 14 February 1986, and cutting from *Kentish Gazette*, 14 February 1986, FCO file MRY178/10/86.
192 FCO, *France No. 1 (1986). Treaty between the United Kingdom . . . and the French Republic concerning the Construction and Operation by Private Concessionaires of a Channel Fixed Link, with Exchanges of Notes, 12 February 1986*, P.P.1985–6, l, Cmnd. 9745, February 1986.
193 Noulton-Ridley's PS, 6 January 1986, Jones-John MacGregor, 6 January 1986, DTp file IT40/16/1 Pt. 4.
194 Noulton-Mitchell's PS, 29 January 1986, DTp CFL Divn, 'Note of a meeting between CTG/FM, UK government officials and French government officials on 27 January 1986', 12 February 1986, DTp file IT40/16/1 Pt. 6.
195 DTp, *Channel Fixed Link*, 1986, paras 53–60.
196 Noulton-Ridley and Mitchell's PSs, 18 February 1986, DTp file IT40/16/1 Pt. 8. There were also initial concerns about such issues as compensation, liability, lenders' security and nationality.

197 Straight-Noulton, 21 February 1986, ibid.; Ridley-Howe, 21 February 1986, Prime Minister's Channel Tunnel papers, Pt. 5.
198 Cf. Howe-Ridley, 25 February 1986, Wybrew-Thatcher, 24 February 1986, ibid.
199 John MacGregor-Ridley, 13 January and 25 February 1986, and reply, 28 February 1986, ibid. Pts. 4–5.
200 Auroux-Ridley, 24 February 1986, enclosed in Fretwell, Paris telegram No. 1 to DTp, Ridley-Auroux, 27 February 1986, DTp file IT40/2/17 Pt. 14.
201 Philip Daltrop (Allen & Overy)-Hopkins, 19 March 1986, enclosing note of meetings between the Governments and the promoters on 4 and 5 March 1986, DTp file IT40/16/1 Pt. 10.
202 Ridley-MacGregor, 28 February 1986, cit.; Lyall-Noulton, 28 January 1986, Paul Channon (SoS for Trade & Industry)-Ridley, 26 February 1986, DTp file IT40/16/1 Pts. 6 and 12.
203 Ridley-Auroux, 17 February 1986, FCO file MRY178/6/86; Jones-MacGregor, 6 March 1986, DTp file IT40/16/1 Pt. 10.
204 Straight-Noulton, 7 March 1986, ibid.
205 Henderson-Ridley ('by hand'), 9 March 1986, DTp file IT40/16/15 Pt. 1; Ridley-Auroux, 10 March 1986, IT40/16/1 Pt. 10.
206 Cabinet Conclusions, CC(86) 10th, 13 March 1986.
207 Powell-Resident Clerk, FCO, 13 March 1986, Howe, FCO telegram No. 168 to Paris, sent 14 March 1986, and Ridley-Howe, 24 March 1986, Prime Minister's Channel Tunnel papers, Pt. 5; Timms-Noulton, 17 March 1986, Cabinet Office file on 'Channel Tunnel', 183/1 Pt. 16.
208 Noulton-Ridley's PS, 6 March 1986, DTp file IT40/16/1 Pt. 10; Hopkins-Noulton, 18 March 1986, enclosing 'Heads of Agreement', 14 March 1986, DTp press notice, 17 March 1986, ibid. Pt. 12; Jones-MacGregor, 19 March 1986, Treasury file DT L/151/674/1605/1 Pt. D; Timms-Noulton, 17 March 1986, Cabinet Office file on 'Channel Tunnel', 183/1 Pt. 16.
209 DTp, *Channel Fixed Link Dated as of 14th March 1986... Concession Agreement*, P.P.1985–6, Cmnd. 9769, April 1986.
210 DTp, *Channel Fixed Link*, 1986, para. 15.
211 Unwin-Thatcher, 2 January 1986, cit.; Maureen Tomison (Communications Director, British Ferries)-Thatcher, 6 February 1986, DTp file IT40/2/76 Pt. 3.
212 Norgrove-Thatcher, 15 January 1986, cit.
213 Taylor, Memo. for Board meeting, 4 October 1985, Midland Bank Group Executive Committee Minutes, 2 October 1985, Midland Bank Channel Tunnel files, ref. 10649, HSBC.
214 Timms-David Dain (Head of WED, FCO), 12 May 1986, FCO file MRY178/6/86; Christopher-Timms, 20 May 1986, Cabinet Office file on 'Channel Tunnel', 183/1 Pt. 17; Ridley , *'My Style of Government'*, p. 158; Fetherston, *Chunnel*, p. 101.
215 *Financial Times*, 14 December 1984, p. 9, 2 November 1985, p. 1, 6 December 1985, p. 6, 13 February 1986, p. 1
216 See DTp file IT40/9/1 Pt. 5, and Interview with Mitchell, 2004.

10 EUROTUNNEL: FINANCE AND CONSTRUCTION, 1986–90

1 Sir Antony Acland (Permanent U-Sec, FCO)-Sir Peter Middleton (Permanent Sec, Treasury), 20 March 1986, DTp file IT40/2/17 Pt. 14; Andrew Knapp, *Gaullism since De Gaulle* (Aldershot, 1994), pp. 89–90; Andrew Knapp and Vincent Wright, *The Government and Politics of France* (4th edn., 2001), pp. 74–5, 112–14.
2 Record of Meeting of Foreign Ministers, Chevening, 14 April 1986, FCO file MRY178/6/86; Powell-Straight, 28 April 1986, enclosing extract of Thatcher-Chirac talks, 26 April 1986, Prime Minister's Channel Tunnel papers, Pt. 5.

3 Eurotunnel, Pathfinder Prospectus [Equity 3], 5 November 1987, p. 42.
4 Ridley-Thatcher *et al.*, 27 March 1986, enclosing DTp, Note on 'Channel Tunnel Bill', 26 March 1986, Prime Minister's Channel Tunnel papers, Pt. 5.
5 *Parl. Deb. (Commons)*, 6th ser. (Session 1985–6), Vol. 95, 17 April 1986, *c.*1035.
6 In the 1985–6 session private and hybrid bills had to be deposited on or before 27 November, at the start of the parliament, and public notice given on or before 11 December. John Biffen (Leader of the Commons), Ibid. Vol. 98, 3 June 1986, *c.*835–6.
7 Ibid. Vol. 96, 30 April 1986, Jonathan Aitken, *c.*947–8; Cabinet Conclusions, CC(86) 20th, 15 May 1986.
8 *Special Report from the Standing Orders Committee on Channel Tunnel Bill (Non-Compliance with Standing Orders)*, 20 May 1986, P.P.1985–6, xxxvii, HC418; *Parl. Deb. (Commons)*, 6th ser. (Session 1985–6), Vol. 98, 3 June 1986, *c.*868–71; Woodman-Ridley's PS, 20 May 1986, FCO file MRY178/13/86 Pt. B; Comfort, 'Politics, Lobbying and Diplomacy', pp. 70–1; Anderson and Roskrow, *Channel Tunnel Story*, p. 48. The Channel Tunnel Bill was the first to be referred to the Commons by the Standing Orders Committee since 1920, and the first hybrid bill to be considered for dispensation since 1957.
9 *Parl. Deb. (Commons)*, 6th ser. (Session 1985–6), Vol. 98, 5 June 1986, 2nd Reading (309–44) and Committal, *c.*1100–1332. Opponents included Aitken, Hughes, Roger Gale, Roger Moate, Teddy Taylor, Peter Rees and John Silkin. Committal of the Bill during an all-night sitting was unfortunately bound up with a filibustering manoeuvre designed to prevent Tam Dalyell's motion [to question Thatcher's conduct over the Falklands, Westland and Libya] being debated next day (cf. Ibid. Vol. 99, 9 June 1986, *c.*16–20).
10 *Parl. Deb. (Commons)*, 6th ser. (Session 1986–7), Vol. 103, 4 November 1986, Motion to reintroduce (174–3), *c.*877–923; HC, *Special Report from the Select Committee on the Channel Tunnel Bill*, P.P.1986–7, viii, HC34, 18 November 1986.
11 Noulton (U-Sec, IT Directorate, DTp)-Mitchell's APS, 1 August 1986, DTp file CHT2/1/4 Pt. 3.
12 Ridley-Thatcher, 27 March 1986, cit.
13 HC, *S.C. on the Channel Tunnel Bill MOE*, P.P.1985–6, xxxix, HC476 Pts I-IV; Interview with Mitchell, 2004. For further detail on the 2nd reading and committee stages see, *inter alia*, Comfort, 'Politics, Lobbying and Diplomacy', pp. 71–81; Fetherston, *Chunnel*, pp. 155–9.
14 Woodman (Asst. Sec, CFL Divn, DTp)-Mitchell's APS, Noulton-Mitchell's APS, both 18 July 1986, DTp file CHT2/1/4 Pt. 2; *Times*, 17 September 1986, p. 2.
15 Raynsford, press statement, 5 November 1986, in DTp file CHT2/1/4 Pt. 4. Raynsford had entered parliament after a by-election on 10 April 1986.
16 The clause ensured that any future government wishing to provide financial support would have to obtain legislative power to do so, and enabled third parties to challenge contraventions in the courts. Hopkins-Bellis, 27 August 1986, Noulton-Nick Finney (British Ports Association), 14 October 1986, Hopkins-David Revolta (Asst Sec, Treasury), 27 October 1986, DTp file CHT2/1/13 Pt. 1; HC, S.C. on Channel Tunnel Bill MOE, 18 November 1986, ibid. Pt. 2; HC, *Report from the Select Committee on the Channel Tunnel Bill*, 18 November 1986, paras 166–8.
17 HC, *S.C. on the Channel Tunnel Bill MOE*, P.P.1985–6, xxxix, HC476-IV, 5 November 1986; John Moore (SoS for Transport)-Biffen, 7 November 1986, Cabinet Office file on 'Channel Tunnel', 183/1 Pt. 17; HC, *Report from the Select Committee*, paras 59–83; *Times*, 29 November 1986, p. 4.
18 HC, *Minutes of Standing Committee A on Channel Tunnel (Recommitted) Bill*, P.P.1986–7, xv, HC147, 22 January 1987; DTp file CHT2/1/14 Pts 1 and 2, CHT2/1/21 Pt. 1; *Parl. Deb. (Commons)*, 6th ser. (Session 1986–7), Vol. 109, 3 February 1987, 3rd Reading (94–22), *c.*863–971.
19 Ibid. *c.*876–901.

20 Amendment introduced to replace that moved in Committee by Raynsford. Ibid. *c.*958–61.
21 Ibid. *c.*970–1.
22 *Parl. Deb. (Lords)*, 5th ser. (Session 1986–7), Vol. 484, 16 February 1987, *c.*897–985; HL, *Special Report from the Select Committee on the Channel Tunnel Bill*, P.P. (Lords) 1986–7, vi, HL138, 6 May 1987, with Minutes of Evidence (Vol. III in vii); Noulton-PS to Lord Brabazon (PUSS for Transport), 18 May 1987, DTp file CHT2/1/18 Pt. 6 and see also Pts. 1–5.
23 *Economist*, 14 March 1987, pp. 25–6; Anderson and Roskrow, *Channel Tunnel Story*, p. 64.
24 Peter Kirk (Mitchell's APS)-Noulton, 13 November 1986, DTp file CHT2/1/8 Pt. 1; Memo. on 'Channel Tunnel Bill: Filled Bill 27 April 1987 Main Amendments', DTp file CHT2/1/18 Pt. 6; *Parl. Deb. (Lords)*, 5th ser. (Session 1986–7), Vol. 487, 7 and 12 May 1987, *c.*246, 545; HL, Channel Tunnel Bill Amendments made by Select Committee, 6 May 1987, P.P. (Lords) 1986–7, ii, HL136.
25 *Parl. Deb. (Commons)*, 3 February 1987, 3rd Reading, Robert Hughes, *c.*965; see also *Times*, 10 January 1987, p. 4.
26 *Parl. Deb. (Commons)*, 6th ser. (Session 1986–7), Vol. 118, 26 June 1987, *c.*156; Vol. 120, 23 July 1987, *c.*534.
27 Ibid. Vol. 119, 8 July 1987, *c.*472–85; Vol. 120, 21 July 1987, *c.*218–94.
28 Sir Ewen Fergusson (British Ambassador, Paris), Paris telegram No. 753 to FCO, 30 July 1987, Prime Minister [Thatcher]'s papers on 'France: Prime Minister's visits to France', Pt. 5.
29 A French shell co. was incorporated on 18 December 1985, became Eurotunnel SA on 18 April 1986, and acquired FM on 30 May 1986. A British shell co. was established on 18 November 1985, becoming Eurotunnel Ltd on 25 February 1986, and acquiring CTG on 30 May; registration as a PLC followed on 1 July. Eurotunnel, Pathfinder Prospectus, November 1987, p. 83, and see also Preliminary Prospectus [Equity 2], 26 September 1986, pp. 87, 89.
30 Fetherston, *Chunnel*, p. 126ff; Noulton, cit. in ibid. p. 173.
31 For an insider's view see Colin J. Stannard, 'Managing a Mega-project – the Channel Tunnel', *Long Range Planning*, 23 No. 5 (1990), 51ff.
32 Noulton-Moore's PS, 28 May 1986, DTp file IT40/2/19 Pt. 19; Armstrong-Powell, 7 July 1986, Prime Minister's Channel Tunnel papers, Pt. 5; Fetherston, *Chunnel*, pp. 137–43, 155.
33 Construction contract, 13 August 1986, summaries in Eurotunnel, Preliminary Prospectus, September 1986, pp. 29–30, 77–81, Pathfinder Prospectus, November 1987, p. 44.
34 Maître d'Oeuvre contract, 13 August 1986, referred to in Eurotunnel, Preliminary Prospectus, September 1986, pp. 30–1, 81, Pathfinder Prospectus, 1987, p. 21; Fetherston, *Chunnel*, pp. 129, 131–2, 143; Bird, *Making of the Channel Tunnel*, p. 24; Interview with Patrick Ponsolle, 24 February 2003, Graham Corbett, 24 January 2005.
35 Noulton-Moore's PS, 28 May 1986, cit.; Rowland, 'Finance', p. 1ff.; A. Bénard and A. Morton, 'The private sector financing of the Channel Tunnel', in *The Channel Tunnel* (ICE Conference proceedings, September 1989), p. 31ff.
36 Ridley-Lawson, 15 May 1986, Prime Minister's Channel Tunnel papers, Pt. 5.
37 Revolta-Noulton, 24 June 1986, DTp file FN24/3/33 Pt. 1; *Guardian*, 10 July 1986, p. 19; *Financial Times*, 11 July 1986, p. 1; Rowland, 'Finance', pp. 3–5.
38 Noulton-PS to Sir Alan Bailey (Permanent Sec, DTp), 4 August 1986, ibid. See also *Times*, 11 July 1986, p. 21.
39 *Times*, 15 August 1986, p. 16; Eurotunnel, Preliminary Prospectus, 1986, p. 12; Pathfinder Prospectus, 1987, p. 14.
40 Cf. *Financial Times*, 29 July 1986, p. 21, 18 October 1986, p. 4, 28 October 1986, p. 8.

41 Ibid. 25 October 1986, p. 1; *Guardian*, 10 July 1986, p. 19; 24–7 October 1986, *passim*; *Times*, 25 October 1986, p. 2; Rowland, p. 18.
42 Interview with Pen Kent, 25 May 2005. A more neutral, intermediating role, known as the 'London Approach', was developed by Kent from 1988: Pen Kent, 'Corporate Workouts – A UK Perspective', *International Insolvency Review*, 6 (1997), 165–82.
43 Armstrong-Nigel Wicks (Thatcher's PPS), 21 and 27 October 1986, Wicks-Thatcher, 21 and 24 October 1986, Prime Minister's Channel Tunnel papers, Pt. 6.
44 Armstrong-Wicks, 27 October 1986 (minute 2), with annotations from Wicks and Thatcher, Wicks-Armstrong, 27 October 1986, ibid. The *Guardian* claimed that Thatcher had intervened personally: *Guardian*, 27 October 1986, p. 19.
45 Moore-Thatcher, 28 October 1986, Wybrew-Thatcher, 6 February 1987, ibid.; EIB Management Committee, Report to Board on 'Eurotunnel Project', 87/167, n.d. [April 1987], Treasury file EC ITPA/M12/1 Pt. A. See also *Times*, 28 October 1986, p. 21, 30 October 1986, p. 23; *Financial Times*, 28 October 1986, p. 44; Fetherston, *Chunnel*, pp. 171, 174–7; Philip Geddes, *Inside the Bank of England* (1987), pp. 121–2.
46 *Economist*, 1 November 1986, p. 66.
47 *Financial Times*, 18 October 1986, p. 4.
48 Eurotunnel, Preliminary Prospectus, 1986, p. 17; Hunt, *Tunnel*, p. 187.
49 Stannard stayed on for a time as head of the Commercial Division.
50 Interview with Jean-Loup Dherse, 11 January 2005.
51 *Banking World*, September 1986, p. 9. My thanks to Edwin Green for this reference.
52 Eurotunnel, Pathfinder Prospectus, 1987, p. 40; *Tunnels and Tunnelling*, February 1986, p. 5.
53 Bailey-Wicks, 4 February 1987, Wicks-Thatcher, 9 February 1987, Prime Minister's Channel Tunnel papers, Pt. 6; *Financial Times*, 3 February 1987, pp. 12, 40; *Sunday Times*, 8 February 1987, p. 61; *Times*, 11 February 1987, p. 1.
54 Wicks-Thatcher, 28 January 1987, Wicks-Bailey, 29 January 1987, Prime Minister's Channel Tunnel papers, Pt. 6; Interview with John Noulton, 28 June 2004; *Sunday Times*, 1 February 1987, p. 57, *Financial Times*, 2 February 1987, p. 5, 17 February 1987, p. 1; *Times*, 4 February 1987, p. 21.
55 *Financial Times*, 19 February 1987, p. 1; Rowland, 'Finance', pp. 38, 40–1; Eurotunnel, Pathfinder Prospectus, 1987, p. 39; Interview with Corbett, 2005.
56 *Financial Times*, 18 February 1987, p. 8.
57 Wicks-Thatcher, 28 January and 9 February 1987, cit. Other names raised included Sir Ian MacGregor, Sir Michael Edwardes (ex-British Leyland), Sir Owen Green (BTR), and Cecil Parkinson: *Sunday Times*, 8 February 1987, *Times*, 10 February 1987, p. 17, *Financial Times*, 11 February 1987, p. 6; *Construction News*, 12 February 1987, p. 1; Fetherston, *Chunnel*, pp. 188–90.
58 Robert Alastair Morton, CV, in D.J. Wiseman-P.S. Hall *et al.* (Treasury), 6 April 1987, Treasury file HE TP/R12/1 Pt. A.; Interview with Mitchell, 2004; *Tunnels and Tunnelling*, March 1987, p. 5.
59 Fallon, in *Sunday Times*, 22 February 1987, p. 62. McMahon and Pennock were Eurotunnel directors until February 1991.
60 *Times*, 21 February 1987, pp. 1, 17.
61 Noulton-Revolta, 29 January 1987 and reply, 23 February 1987, Revolta-J.P. McIntyre (Treasury), 4 February 1987, Moore-Lamont (Treasury Financial Secretary), 23 March 1987, J.G. Colman (Asst Sec, Treasury)-Lamont, 26 March 1987, David Moore (U-Sec, Treasury)-Lamont, 2 April 1987, Treasury file HE TP/R12/1 Pt. A; Jonathan Cunliffe (Moore's APS)-Noulton, 25 March 1987, DTp file CHT-A7/10 Pt. 1.
62 Revolta-McIntyre, and Eurotunnel Press Release, both 6 April 1987, ibid.; *Financial Times*, 7 April 1987, p. 1; Bénard and Morton, 'Private sector financing', p. 34.

63 Revolta-R.M. Bent (Treasury), and Noulton-Hopkins, both 12 June 1987, Treasury file, HE TP/R12/1 Pt. A; *Financial Times*, 18 June 1987, p. 1.
64 *Independent*, 7 April 1987, pp. 3, 19; *Times*, 7 April 1987, pp. 21, 23; *Economist*, 11 April 1987, p. 68.
65 Noulton-Hopkins, 18 May 1987, Treasury file HE TP/R12/1 Pt. A.
66 EIB, Information Note on 'Eurotunnel – Results of Credit Syndication', 87/253, November 1987, Treasury file EC ITPA/M12/1 Pt. A.
67 Bénard and Morton, 'Private sector financing', pp. 35–6; *New York Times*, 8 September 1987, p. D7; Fetherston, *Chunnel*, pp. 201–3.
68 Janet Barber (Treasury), Note for the Record, 30 March 1987, Roger Lavelle (Dep Sec, Overseas Finance, Treasury)-Lawson, 7 May 1987, Treasury file EC ITPA/M12/1 Pt. A; EIB Management Committee, Report on 'Eurotunnel Project', cit.
69 EIB, Information Note, November 1987, cit.
70 Bénard and Morton, 'Private sector financing', p. 35; Hunt, *Tunnel*, pp. 268–70.
71 Credit Agreement, 4 November 1987, summarised in Eurotunnel, Pathfinder Prospectus, 1987, pp. 47–51.
72 E.g. Warburg Securities, 'Eurotunnel: the Construction of the Fixed Link', and 'Eurotunnel: the Investment Opportunity', September 1987; Scrimgeour Vickers and County Nat West, 'Moving Ahead', July 1987, and Citicorp Scrimgeour Vickers and County Nat West, 'Eurotunnel: Get in at the ground level', September 1987. My thanks to Stefan Szymanski for these references.
73 E.g. for 2003: passengers, 39.5 m. [cf.36 m.], freight, 21.1 m. tonnes [17.6]. Eurotunnel, Preliminary and Pathfinder prospectuses, cit.; *Financial Times*, 30 July 1987, p. 6; *Sunday Times*, 16 August 1987, p. 47; *Economist*, 10 October 1986, p. 24.
74 *Sunday Times*, 20 September 1987, p. 69; *Financial Times*, 21 September 1987, p. 40; *Financial Times*, 24 September 1987, p. 28; Hunt, *Tunnel*, p. 203; Anderson and Roskrow, *Channel Tunnel Story*, pp. 77–9. Dherse retained his seat on the Eurotunnel joint board until early 1988. He has acknowledged that there was a need for a more experienced project manager to push the contractors: Interview with Dherse, 2005.
75 IGC UK Secretariat, 'Eurotunnel Management Structure: Note of Meeting on 11 November 1987', 20 November 1987, DTp file RPHP10/4/3 Pt. 8; IGC Minutes, 16 November 1987, CHT3/1/93 Pt. 1.
76 *Financial Times*, 14 October 1987, p. 48; *Who's Who*. Graham Corbett of Peat Marwick Mitchell also joined the company as financial adviser to the co-chairmen (effectively finance director, a title he was given in 1989). He joined the Board in 1991.
77 Lex, *Financial Times*, 23 June 1986, p. 40.
78 Flexilink, 'Questioning the Financial Viability of A Cross Channel Link', September 1986, and 'The Channel Tunnel: Some Weaknesses of the Financial Case', October 1987, esp. p. 7; *Lloyds List*, 27 October 1987, p. 10; *Financial Times*, 7 November 1987, p. 6; Sir Alfred Sherman and the Selsdon Group, 'A Conservative Case against a Fixed Link across the Straits of Dover', 1986. My thanks to Stefan Szymanski for some of these references.
79 Gilmore-Revolta, 20 October 1987, Morton-Lamont, 28 October 1987, Revolta-Moore, 28 October 1987, Treasury file HE TP/R12/1 Pt. A; Wicks-Thatcher, 28 October 1987, Prime Minister's Channel Tunnel papers, Pt. 6.
80 John Vickers and George Yarrow, *Privatization: an Economic Analysis* (Cambridge, MA, 1987), pp. 179–80; Hunt, *Tunnel*, p. 204; *Financial Times*, 23 October 1987, p. 48; *Sunday Times*, 25 October 1987, pp. 24, 34; *Guardian*, 29 October 1987, p. 21.
81 *Financial Times*, 3 November 1987, p. 8.
82 Wicks-Thatcher, 10 November 1987, Prime Minister's Channel Tunnel papers, Pt. 6; and copy with annotation by R.B. Saunders (Middleton's PS), Treasury file HE TP/R12/1 Pt. C.

83 Gilmore-Lawson, two memos., with copy of Noulton-APS to Paul Channon (SoS for Transport), all 11 November 1987, ibid.; Roy Griffins (Channon's PS)-Wicks, and Wicks-Thatcher, both 11 November 1987, etc., Prime Minister's Channel Tunnel papers, Pt. 6; *Parl. Deb. (Commons)*, 6th ser. (Session 1987–8), Vol. 122, 10 November 1987, *c.*529–30.
84 Gary Roberts (Treasury)-J.R. Lomax (U-Sec, Treasury), Treasury file HE TP/R12/1 Pt. C; Wicks-Thatcher, 13 November 1987, Prime Minister's Channel Tunnel papers, Pt. 6.
85 For registration fee of *c.*£10 and nominal charge of £1 each way: with 100 shares – 1 return journey in the first year of operation; 500 shares – 1 journey for first 10 years of operation; 1,500 shares – unlimited journeys for the Concession period.
86 Eurotunnel, Offer for Sale, 16 November 1987, printed in *Financial Times*, 18 November 1987.
87 Communication from Peter Ratzer (former Treasurer, Eurotunnel), 27 March 2005. See also *Financial Times*, 17 November 1987, p. 1, 28 November 1987, p. 1, 2 December 1987, p. 1; Fetherston, *Chunnel*, pp. 209–10; Anderson and Roskrow, *Channel Tunnel Story*, pp. 79–80. Note that the different methods of issuing in Britain and France mean that the percentages are not strictly comparable. It is not clear how much of the British share of Equity 3 was taken up by private investors. Estimates range from 38 to 52 per cent.
88 Interview with Malcolm Southgate, 30 September 1992, David Kirby, 13 January 1999, and Richard Edgley, 7 August 2000, for Gourvish, *British Rail 1974–97*, pp. 141, 320, 556.
89 BRB, SNCF, CTG and FM, Heads of Agreement, 14 March 1986, DTp file IT40/16/17 Pt. 1.
90 Ridley-Auroux, 10 March 1986, DTp file IT40/16/1 Pt. 10; David Pope (Railways Directorate, DTp)-Sandy Morrison (CFL Divn, DTp), 3 June 1986, Noulton-Moore's PS, 6 June 1986, DTp file CHT-A7/4 Pt. 1.
91 Eurotunnel, Briefing Note, 6 June 1986, ibid.; CTG, FM, BRB and SNCF, Draft Heads of Agreement, 3 June 1986, DTp file R39/1/1 Pt. 1; Interview with Andy Heslop, 1 July 2004.
92 David Miles (Head of Railways C Divn, DTp)-Moore's PS, 24 June 1986, Noulton-Maurice LeGrand (Head of French Delegation, Intergovernmental Commission [IGC], 25 June 1986, Hopkins-Noulton, 2 July 1986, DTp file CHT-A7/4 Pt. 1.
93 CTG, FM, BRB and SNCF, Draft Heads of Agreement, 24 September 1986, and see Ian Phillips (Director of Finance & Planning, BRB)-Coates, DTp, 10 September 1986, Miles-Moore's PS, 30 September 1986, DTp file R39/1/1 Pt. 1; Coates-Noulton, 7 January 1987, ibid. Pt. 3.
94 Coates-Noulton, 5 February 1987, DTp file CHT-A7/4 Pt. 1; Nick Wakefield (Warburg, advisers to BRB)-David Kirby (BRB), 5 February 1987, AN18/41, PRO.
95 As one of British Rail's negotiators has recalled, 'Ideally we didn't want half the capacity; what we wanted was toll rates that were more credible and more economic for the railways'. Interview with Heslop, 2004.
96 Malcolm Southgate (Director, Channel Tunnel, BRB), 'Usage Contract: Note of Proposed BR Position', n.d. [February 1987]; Andy Heslop (Project Manager, Channel Tunnel, BRB)-Kirby, 23 February 1987, enclosing Eurotunnel, Memo. on 'Railways' Usage Contract', in Colin Stannard (MD Commercial, Eurotunnel)-Southgate and Michel Walrave (SNCF), 17 February 1987, Southgate, 'Note of Discussion ET/SNCF/BR 23/2/87 in Paris', 24 February 1987, Wakefield-Southgate, 3 and 5 March 1987, AN18/41, PRO; Southgate and Walrave-Stannard, 19 February 1987, John Palmer (Dep Sec, Surface Transport Industries, DTp)-Coates, enclosing Stannard, Note on 'Railway Negotiations', 3 March 1987, DTp file R39/1/1 Pt. 3.
97 Coates-Noulton, 5 February 1987, cit.; Coates-Palmer, 6 March 1987, CHT-A7/4 Pt. 1; Jeremy Candfield (DTp)-Tony Boote (Treasury), 10 March 1987 and reply, 13 March 1987, Treasury file PE-TSS/H11/1 Pt. A.

98 Candfield-Boote, 10 March and 7 April 1987, Ian Cunningham (Treasury)-Boote, 8 April 1987, ibid.; Interview with Southgate, 1992, cit.
99 Miles, 'Note of Meeting with Mr John Bennett and Mr Roger Warby of National Westminster Bank', 21 November 1986, DTp file R39/1/1 Pt. 2.
100 Coates-Noulton, 5 February 1987, cit.; Sir Robert Reid (Chairman, BRB)-Moore, 28 January 1987, DTp file R39/1/1 Pt. 2; Mike Pitwood (DTp)-Tony Fortnam (DTp), 9 February 1987, DTp file CHT-A7/4 Pt. 1.
101 DTp FTI Divn, 'Note of a Meeting on 18 February between DTp and the Treasury', March 1987, DTp file CHT-A7/4 Pt. 1; Fortnam-Mitchell's PS, 20 February 1987, Coates-Bailey, 23 February 1987, DTp file R39/1/1 Pt. 3.
102 Morton and Bénard-Reid and Philippe Essig (President, SNCF), 5 March 1987, and Morton, personal note to Reid, 6 March 1987, AN18/41, PRO.
103 Southgate, 'Note of Discussion 18.3.87', 18 March 1987, ibid.
104 Cunliffe-Noulton, 25 March 1987, DTp file CHT-A7/10 Pt. 1.
105 Reid and Essig-Morton and Bénard, 19 March 1987, AN18/41, PRO.
106 Morton and Bénard-Reid and Essig, 6 April 1987, AN18/42, PRO.
107 Fortnam-Palmer, 9 April 1987, DTp file CHT-A7/4 Pt. 1.
108 Bailey-Palmer, 10 April 1987, ibid.
109 Fortnam-Bailey, 14 April 1987, ibid.
110 Southgate, Memo. on 'Channel Tunnel – Risk Assessment on Traffic Forecasts', 9 April 1987, and Candfield-Boote, 10 April 1987, Treasury file PE-TSS/H/11/1 Pt. A.
111 I.e. 1.5 m UACs per train path. Palmer-Bailey, 15 April 1987, DTp file CHT-A7/4 Pt. 1.
112 Morton-Moore, 22 April 1987, ibid.
113 Morton-Reid, 7 May 1987, ibid.
114 Cunliffe-Coates, 12 May 1987, ibid.
115 Moore-Thatcher, 8 May 1987, Prime Minister's Channel Tunnel papers, Pt. 6.
116 Coates-Moore's PS, 7 and 8 May 1987, C. Smith (Bailey's PS)-Coates, 15 May 1987, DTp file CHT-A7/4 Pt. 1; Boote-Colman and MacGregor, 7 May 1987, Treasury file PE-TSS/H/11/1 Pt. A; DTp, 'Note of a Meeting on Channel Tunnel issues held at 11.30 a.m. at BRB, 8 May 1987', May 1987, DTp file R39/1/1 Pt. 4; BRB Minutes, 7 May 1987, AN167/53, PRO.
117 Cunliffe-Coates, 11 May, Coates-Moore's PS, 11 May 1987, DTp file CHT-A7/4Pt. 1.
118 Boote-Nicholas Monck (Dep Sec, Industry, Treasury) and MacGregor, 8 May 1987, Jill Rutter (Major's PS)-Boote, 11 May 1987, Treasury file PE-TSS/H/11/1 Pt. A.
119 Broadly 60% of Eurotunnel's traffic forecast, but 63% in the first year.
120 BRB, 'Summary of Railways' Proposal of 11 May', and 'Summary of principal points agreed with Euro Tunnel [*sic*] and SNCF on 11 May 1987', 12 May 1987, Kirby-Morton, 12 May 1987, AN18/42, PRO; Coates-Moore's PS, 12 May 1987, DTp file R39/1/1 Pt. 4.
121 Cf. press releases from Eurotunnel and BRB, 12 May 1987, DTp file CHT-A7/4 Pt. 1 and R39/1/1 Pt. 4; DTp press notice, 13 May 1987, CHT-A7/4 Pt. 1; *Financial Times*, 13 May 1987, pp. 8, 48.
122 Reid-Mitchell, 13 May 1987, AN18/42, PRO.
123 Cf. Coates-Moore, 12 May 1987, cit.
124 Powell-Thatcher, 11 May 1987, Prime Minister's Channel Tunnel papers, Pt. 6.
125 Boote-Colman and MacGregor, 24 April 1987, Treasury file PE-TSS/H/11/1 Pt. A.
126 Wakefield-Kirby, 13 May 1987, AN18/42, PRO.
127 Interview with Southgate, 1992, and Heslop, 2004.
128 Boote-Monck and MacGregor, 8 May 1987, cit.
129 SoS for Transport, Ministre de l'Urbanisme etc., CTG and FM, Concession Agreement ('conformed copy'), 14 March 1986, Clause 2.1, Prime Minister's Channel Tunnel papers, Pt. 5.
130 Cf. Eurotunnel, Memo. 16 May 1990, HC Transport Committee, *Eurotunnel: Minutes of Evidence*, P.P.1989–90, xxxi, HC407, 16 May 1990, pp. 1–3.

131 Kent Impact Study Team, *Kent Impact Study: Channel Tunnel – A Strategy for Kent* (Channel Tunnel Joint Consultative Committee, August 1987). Kent Co. Co.'s actions were in no sense a sleight of hand. The authority was also anxious to improve access to the ports, and to stimulate areas adversely affected by the Tunnel.
132 More tangential schemes could be added to the list, including improvements to the A2 and M2, and the Third Dartford Crossing (bridge).
133 Background Note to PQ by William Hague, 28 June 1990, DTp file RPHP10/4/3 Pt. 12, and *Parl. Deb. (Commons)*, 6th ser. (Session 1989–90), Vol. 175, *w303*. The schemes costed were: M20/A20, A2/M2, and A27/A259 (but not the 3rd Dartford Crossing). See also John Henes, 'The Channel Tunnel – the effect in the UK', in *The Channel Tunnel* (1989), pp. 315–19.
134 HC Transport Committee, *Eurotunnel*, May 1990, Alastair Morton, Q. 88; and see also *Times*, 12 May 1986, p. 3.
135 BRB, SNCF, CTG and FM, Usage Contract, July 1987, proof copy, clause 3.2, Schedule II Pt. B1 and B2, DTp file R39/1/1 Pt. 5.
136 I.e. terminals at Fréthun, improvements at Paris (Nord), etc. Ibid. Schedule II Pt. C1 and C2.
137 Candfield-Boote, 2 April 1987, Treasury file PE-TSS/H/11/1 Pt. A.
138 Timms-Howe's PS, 26 February 1987, Beetham-Thomas, 6 March 1987, Fortnam-Mitchell's PS, 17 March 1987, FCO file MRY178/4/87 Pt. A; Candfield-Colman, 19 August 1987, Treasury file PE-TSS/H/11/1 Pt. C.
139 Timms-Howe's PS, 26 February 1987, cit.; Sir Ronald Arculus (Special Adviser, CT trains, DTp), 25 June 1987, Beetham-Howe's PS, 15 July 1987, FCO file MRY178/4/87 Pt. B.
140 Noulton-Lambert (Asst Sec, DTp), 25 March 1987, DTp file CHT-A7/4 Pt. 1; Timms-Beetham, 6 March 1987, FCO file MRY178/4/87 Pt. A.
141 Timms-Coates, 2 March 1987, ibid.
142 Mitchell-Reid, 30 April 1987, AN18/42, PRO. Moore appointed Sir Ronald Arculus as a special adviser to help negotiate an equitable division of the procurement. Bailey-Fretwell, 20 February 1987, Timms-Howe's PS, 26 February 1987, cit.; Pitwood-Fortnam, 23 March 1987, DTp, Note of Mitchell-Douffiagues meeting (31 March 1987), 3 April 1987, Beetham-Slater, 24 April 1987, FCO file MRY178/4/87 Pt. A; Arculus-Fergusson, 10 July 1987, Pt. B.
143 Pitwood-Coates, 5 June 1987, CHT-A7/4 Pt. 1; Fortnam-Channon's PS, 17 July 1987, Coates-Channon's PS, 22 and 23 July 1987 (enclosing Reid-Channon, 23 July 1987), Pt. 2; Channon-John Major (Treasury Chief Secretary), 24 July 1987, Treasury file PE-TSS/H/11/1 Pt. B.
144 Coates-Noulton, 5 February 1987, cit.; Fortnam-Palmer, 9 April 1987, DTp file R39/1/1 Pt. 3.
145 Candfield-Sheila James (Treasury), 13 April 1987, Candfield-Boote, 1 and 18 May 1987, with enclosure, Treasury file PE-TSS/H/11/1 Pt. A; Fortnam-Mitchell's PS, 28 April 1987, FCO file MRY178/4/87 Pt. A; DTp, Note of Mitchell-Douffiagues meeting (13 May 1987), 19 May 1987, Pt. B. Mitchell and the Belgian Minister, Hermann de Croo, signed a similiar communiqué on 19 May: DTp Press Notice, 19 May 1987, Treasury file PE-TSS/H/11/1 Pt. B.
146 Morton-Channon, 30 June 1987, Cunliffe-Coates, 1 July 1987, Prime Minister's Channel Tunnel papers, Pt. 6. Morton also pressed the matter with Thatcher's PPS, Nigel Wicks, and with Sir Alan Bailey.
147 Noulton-Coates, 24 June 1987, DTp file R39/1/1 Pt. 4; Fortnam-Beetham, 24 July 1987, FCO file MRY178/4/87 Pt. B.
148 Ridley-Reid, 23 January 1986, AN191/357, and see also Andy Heslop, Investment Appraisal, 8 November 1985, AN18/36, PRO.

149 BRB Minutes, 2 July 1987, AN167/53; Reid-Channon, 14 July 1987, cit. in Gourvish, *British Rail 1974–97*, p. 321.
150 Channon-Major, 10 and 17 July 1987, Boote-Monck and Major, 17 July 1987, Major-Channon, 20 July 1987, Treasury file PE-TSS/H/11/1 Pt. B.
151 Channon-Major, 24 July 1987, ibid. Pt. B; Major-Channon, 27 July 1987, Pt. C; Channon-Reid, 10 August 1987, cit. in Gourvish, *British Rail 1974–97*, p. 321.
152 Usage Contract, July 1987, clause 31 and 32.
153 Coates-Noulton, 31 July 1987, with enclosures, DTp file CHT-A7/4 Pt. 2; Pitwood-Fortnam, 27 August 1987, FCO file MRY178/4/87 Pt. B.
154 Fergusson, Paris telegram No. 852 to FCO, 4 September 1987, ibid.; Timms-Coates, 15 September 1987, Pt. C; Coates-Fortnam (2 Memos.), 11 September 1987, Fortnam-Bailey's PS, 16 September 1987, enclosing Morton-Reid, 28 August 1987, DTp file R39/1/1 Pt. 5.
155 Powell-Lyn Parker (FCO), 25 September 1987, Fergusson, Paris telegram No. 975 to FCO, 9 October 1987, FCO file MRY178/4/87 Pt. B; Cunliffe-Powell, 29 October 1987, Pt. C; *Construction News*, 15 October 1987, p. 3.
156 For detailed accounts see Anderson and Roskrow, *Channel Tunnel Story*, Fetherston, *Chunnel*, Hunt, *Tunnel*, Bird, *Making of the Channel Tunnel*, and Colin J. Kirkland (ed.), *Engineering the Channel Tunnel* (1995); *Tunnels and Tunnelling*, and *Construction News, passim*; Graham M. Winch, 'The Channel Fixed Link: Le Project du Siècle', UMIST Case Study, November 1998 (and his earlier working paper for Le Groupe Bagnolet, 1996).
157 At the peak (June 1991) 8,122 in Britain, 5,810 in France: MdO, Progress Report No. 22, 31 December 1991, DTp file CHT3/1/18 Pt. 13. Reports Nos.6–43 (31 December 1987–31 March 1997) are in CHT3/1/8 Pts. 1–19.
158 *Times*, 2 March 1988, p. 18; *Financial Times*, 25 July 1988, p. 34; Hunt, p. 213.
159 *Financial Times*, 17 January 1989, p. 9; *Independent*, 4 April 1989, p. 22; *Tunnels and Tunnelling*, November 1988, p. 10, May 1989, p. 19. There were 10 deaths during construction.
160 Ibid., December 1990, p. 5.
161 MdO, Progress Report No. 20, 30 June 1991.
162 From July 1987 Legrand served as Chairman of the IGC, with Rose Chairman of the Safety Authority, but the posts alternated on an annual basis between Legrand and Noulton, and between Rose and Pilon. In April 1989 John Henes succeeded Noulton, and Bryan Martin succeeded Rose. IGC Minutes, 1986–90, DTp file CHT3/1/93 Pt. 1; Safety Authority Minutes, 1986, 1989, in FCO file MRY178/17/86, MRY178/6/89 Pts. A-D.
163 List of Avant Projets, March 1989, in FCO file MRY178/6/89 Pt. A; Channel Tunnel Safety Authority, *Annual Report 1988/89*, pp. 2–3; List in March 1993 in ibid., *1992/93*, pp. 8–9; HC Home Affairs Committee, Report on *Fire Safety and Policing of the Channel Tunnel*, 17 December 1991, paras 5–6, P.P.1991–2, ix, HC23-I; Martin, Memo. tabled with evidence, 6 November 1991, ibid. *MOE and Appendices*, pp. 67–75, HC23-II.
164 Colin J. Kirkland, 'Introduction', and Richard Morris, 'Safety management', in Kirkland, *Engineering the Channel Tunnel*, pp. 11–12, 301; Graham Corbett, 'The Channel Tunnel – Managing the Financial Risk', paper delivered at International Tunnelling Conference, Basel, July 1996. For IGC see DTp files CHT3/1 series, minutes in CHT3/1/93 Pts. 1–3.
165 Cf. Sir Brian Hayes (Permanent Sec, DTI)-Bailey, 24 April 1989 and reply, 3 May 1989, Henes-Bailey's PS, 2 May 1989, DTp file CHT6/1/71 Pt. 2.
166 *Financial Times*, 23 August 1988, p. 1; *Tunnels and Tunnelling*, October 1988, p. 5.
167 IGC Minutes, 16 November 1987, DTp file CHT3/1/93 Pt. 1; *Observer*, 10 July 1988, p. 53; *Tunnels and Tunnelling*, March 1988, p. 14; Bird, *Making of the Channel Tunnel*, pp. 70, 90.

168 *Financial Times*, 4 October 1988, p. 27.
169 Noulton-PS to Michael Portillo (Transport Minister), 16 December 1988, Noulton-Channon's PS, 20 December 1988, DTp file CHT6/1/71 Pt. 1.
170 The letter was drafted by Noulton: Noulton-Channon's APS, 22 December 1988, ibid. See Roy Griffins (Channon's PS)-Lyn Parker (Howe's PS), 23 December 1988, FCO file MRY178/7/88 Pt. B; ibid. with Thatcher's annotation, and Powell-Griffins, 30 December 1988, Prime Minister's Channel Tunnel papers, Pt. 6; Beetham-Nicholas Bayne (Dep U-Sec of State, FCO), 6 January 1989, FCO file MRY178/2/89 Pt. A.
171 *Financial Times*, 14 December 1988, p. 2.
172 Noulton-Channon's PS, 4 January 1989, DTp file CHT6/1/71 Pt. 1; Neil Hoyle (Channon's PS)-Powell, 6 January 1989, Griffins-Powell, 16 January 1989, Prime Minister's Channel Tunnel papers, Pt. 6.
173 Henes-Bailey's PS, 2 May 1989, cit.; Interview with Corbett, 2005.
174 Noulton-Portillo's PS, 1 February 1989, FCO file MRY178/2/89 Pt. A; John Taberner (Eurotunnel)-Henes, 14 June 1989, DTp file CHT6/1/71 Pt. 2; *Financial Times*, 19 January 1989, p. 32, 8 May 1989, p. 31; *Independent*, 31 July1989, p. 21; *Tunnels and Tunnelling*, June 1989, p. 11. Lemley had been a VP of Morrison Knudsen.
175 Noulton-Portillo's PS, 1 February 1989, cit.; Beetham-Duncan Slater (Superintending U-Sec, MAED, FCO), 7 February 1989, FCO file MRY178/2/89 Pt. A; *Independent*, 4 April 1989, p. 22.
176 Eurotunnel, 1987 Prospectus, p. 23; *Financial Times*, 12 April 1989, p. 21, 22 July 1989, p. 22, 27 July 1989, p. 8.
177 Cecil Parkinson (SoS for Transport)-Thatcher, 14 September 1989, Prime Minister's Channel Tunnel papers, Pt. 7.
178 Case-PS to Norman Lamont (Treasury Chief Secretary), 18 September 1989, Treasury file HE TP/R/12/1 Pt. D; Eurotunnel, News Release, 2 October 1989, in Case-Lawson, 2 October 1989, Treasury file HE TP/R/12/1 Pt. D; *Financial Times*, 3 October 1989, pp. 1, 26; *Tunnels and Tunnelling*, November 1989, p. 15.
179 *Financial Times*, June and October 1989.
180 Beetham-Bayne and PS to Lord Brabazon (Minister of State, FCO), 20 October 1989, Beetham-Howe's PS, 3 November 1989, FCO file MRY178/2/89 Pt. B. Pressure to emphasise safety came from the Consumers' Association's *Which?*, April 1989, pp. 182–4, *New Scientist*, 23 September 1989, p. 20, *New Statesman*, 25 November 1989, pp. 42–7, and an intervention from John Prescott: see *Independent*, 19 October 1989, p. 28.
181 Philippe Essig (Chairman, TML)-Parkinson, 27 October 1989 and reply, 9 November 1989, Michel Delebarre (Ministre de l'Equipment etc.)-Essig, n.d., DTp file CHT6/1/71 Pt. 1.
182 Peter Burgess (Asst Sec, CT Divn, DTp)-Parkinson's PS, 1 December 1989, ibid.
183 Griffins-Henes, 3 November 1989, ibid.; Parkinson-Thatcher, 6 November 1989, Patricia Rennie (Parkinson's PS)-Dominic Morris (Thatcher's PS), 5 January 1990, Prime Minister's Channel Tunnel papers, Pt. 7.
184 Henes-Case, 14 September 1989, Treasury file HE TP/R/12/1 Pt. D.; Alan Houmann (Treasury)-James Mortimer (Asst Sec, Treasury) and Richard Allen (U-Sec, Treasury), 26 September 1989, EC ITPA/M/12/1 Pt. A.
185 Allen-Revolta, 15 December 1988, Treasury file HE TP/R/12/1 Pt. C; Allen-Wendy Preston (Treasury), 4 October 1989, EC ITPA/M/12/1 Pt. A; Interview with Corbett, 2005.
186 Case-John Major (Chancellor of the Exchequer), 7 November 1989, Minutes of Chancellor's bilateral meeting with Governor (BOE), 7 November 1989, Treasury file HE TP/R/12/1 Pt. D.
187 Case-Middleton, 16 and 20 November 1989, ibid.; Paul Gray (Thatcher's PS)-Thatcher, 17 November 1989, Prime Minister's Channel Tunnel papers, Pt. 7; IGC Minutes, 24 November 1989, DTp file CHT3/1/93 Pt. 1.

188 *Financial Times*, 1 December 1989, p. 10; *Times*, 19 December 1989, p. 23.
189 Eurotunnel, News Release, 11 January 1990, Treasury file HE TP/R/12/1 Pt. D.
190 Case-Sir John Anson (2nd Permanent Sec, Treasury), ibid.; Henes-Parkinson's PS, 26 January 1990, cit.; *Financial Times*, 10 January 1990, p. 22.
191 Eurotunnel, News Release, 11 January 1990, cit. and Eurotunnel, *Report and Accounts 1989*, p. 30.
192 Burgess-Anthony Fagin (Asst Sec, Construction Industry, DTp), 10 January 1990, Henes-Parkinson's PS, 26 January 1990, Rennie-Henes, 1 March 1990, DTp file CHT6/1/71 Pt. 1; *Financial Times*, 12 January 1990, p. 6.
193 Burgess-Parkinson's PS, 15 February 1990, ibid.; Case-Middleton, 15 February 1990, Treasury file HE TP/R/12/1 Pt. D.; *Financial Times*, 15–17 February 1990, *passim*.
194 Case-Middleton, 16 February 1990, ibid.; *Independent on Sunday*, 17 February 1990, p. 1; *Financial Times*, 19 February 1990, p. 1.
195 *Financial Times*, 21 February 1990, p. 24; *Independent*, 22 February 1990, p. 28; Interview with Kent, 2005.
196 Gray-Thatcher, 20 February 1990, Parkinson-Thatcher, 22 February 1990, Prime Minister's Channel Tunnel papers, Pt. 7; Henes-Davis (DTp), 28 February 1990, DTp file CHT6/1/71 Pt. 1; *Financial Times*, 22 February 1990, p. 10.
197 Rennie-Henes, 1 March 1990, cit.
198 Sonia Phippard (PS to Sir Robin Butler (Cabinet Secretary)), Note for Record, 22 March 1990, Cabinet Office file on 'Channel Tunnel', 183/1 Pt. 18; *Financial Times*, 24 April 1990, p. 29.
199 *Financial Times*, 25 April 1990, p. 22.
200 Allen-Wicks, 21 March 1990, Huw Evans (Dep Sec, Overseas Finance, Treasury), Note for the Record, 4 May 1990, EIB Management Committee, Report to Board on 'Eurotunnel II Project', 90/204, n.d. [May 1990], Pen Kent (Associate Director, BOE)-Case, 22 May 1990, Alison Cawley (EC1 Divn, Treasury)-Allen, 21 May 1990, Evans-Richard Wilson (Dep Sec, Industry, Treasury), 25 May 1990, Cawley-Middleton and Lamont, 24 August 1990, Treasury file EC ITPA/M12/1 Pts. A-C; *Financial Times*, 29 May 1990, p. 28.
201 Eurotunnel News Release, 31 May 1990, Treasury file HE TP/R/12/1 Pt. D; *Financial Times*, 1 June 1990, pp. 1, 20.
202 Case-Middleton, 21 May 1990, R.J. Evans (Middleton's PS)-Case, 22 May 1990, ibid.
203 Eurotunnel, Proposed Financing Programme, 4 June 1990.
204 Case-Middleton, 16 July 1990, Minutes of Chancellor's bilateral meeting with Governor (BOE), 16 July 1990, Wilson-Major's PPS, 27 July 1990, Treasury file HE TP/R/12/1 Pt. D; Allen-Case, 25 July 1990, EC ITPA/M/12/1 Pt. C.
205 Douglas Hurd (Foreign Secretary), FCO telegram No. 504 to Tokyo, 10 August 1990, FCO file MRY178/9/90.
206 Cawley-Middleton and Lamont, 24 August 1990, Treasury file EC ITPA/M/12/1Pt.C.
207 Ruth Flynn (Treasury), Note for File, 28 August 1990, Treasury file HE TP/R/12/1 Pt. D; Interview with Lord Parkinson, 19 September 2000.
208 Simon Whiteley (Parkinson's PS)-Powell, 13 August 1990, Thatcher-Toshiki Kaifu (Prime Minister of Japan), Prime Minister's Channel Tunnel papers, Pt. 7.
209 John Field (British Embassy, Tokyo), Tokyo telegram No. 708 to FCO, 23 August 1990, FCO file MRY178/9/90; Thatcher, *Downing Street Years*, p. 816; Richard Katz, *Japan: the System that Soured* (New York, 1998), pp. 7–10.
210 Parkinson-Thatcher, 14 September 1990, Prime Minister's Channel Tunnel papers, Pt. 8.
211 Cawley-Middleton and Lamont, 24 August 1990, cit.; Cawley-Evans, 28 and 30 August 1990, Treasury file EC ITPA/M/12/1 Pt. C; Roger Byatt (General Manager, Corporate and Institutional Banking, NatWest)-Pitt Treumann (Directeur, EIB), 29 August 1990, HE TP/R/12/1 Pt. D.

212 Kent-Evans, 5 September 1990, enclosing 'Eurotunnel – Early September Progress Report', 4 September 1990, Treasury file HE TP/R/12/1 Pt. E.
213 Evans-Case, 9 October 1990, Treasury file EC ITPA/M/12/1 Pt. C; *Independent*, 9 October 1990, p. 22; Eurotunnel, Rights Issue, November 1990, pp. 35, 69–73.
214 This loan, representing European steel used in the Tunnel's construction, did not materialise until November 1991. Cawley-Evans, 20 February 1991, Treasury file HE TP/R/12/1 Pt. E; Credit Agreement, 6 November 1991, DTp file CHT9/10/3 Pt. 6.
215 Eurotunnel, Rights Issue, November 1990, pp. 8, 65–8, and see also Eurotunnel, Rights Issue News Release, in DTp file CHT6/1/76 Pt. 1. The new travel privileges gave holders of 500 new units one transferable discounted return fare for the first 15 years of operation, holders of 1,500 units one return fare for the Concession period.
216 Case-Major, 5 September 1990, Treasury file HE TP/R/12/1 Pt. E; Communication from Ratzer, 2005. See also *Financial Times*, 25 October 1990, p. 25, 10 November 1990, p.IV; *Guardian*, 16 November 1990, p. 15, 6 December 1990, p. 18; *Sunday Independent*, 25 November 1990, p. 6; *Times*, 15 December 1990, p. 34; *Independent*, 15 December 1990, p. 17. The implied subscription rates were: France 98%, UK 84%, overall 92%.
217 Cf. Jim Broad (DTI)-C.B. Benjamin (U-Sec, Engineering Markets Divn, DTI), 9 January 1989, DTp file CHT6/1/71 Pt. 1; Broad-B. Steele (Asst Sec, European Market Branch, DTI), 28 April 1989, ibid. Pt. 2.
218 Eurotunnel, Rights Issue, November 1990, p. 31.
219 Cabinet Conclusions, CC(90) 37th, 22 November 1990.
220 Cf. Morton-Thatcher, 10 October and 26 November 1990, Prime Minister's Channel Tunnel papers, Pt. 8.

11 FROM TUNNEL TO TRANSPORT FACILITY, 1988–94

1 Gourvish, *British Rail 1974–97*, pp. 319–40.
2 Richard Edgley (Director, European Passenger Services [EPS], BRB), Memo. to BRB Investment Committee on 'Channel Tunnel Project: Updated Strategic Appraisal', 26 January 1989, enclosed in Jon Cunliffe (DTp)-Bill Guy (PE Group, Treasury), 19 April 1989, Treasury file PE TSS/H/11/2 Pt. E.
3 Andrew Jukes (Investment Adviser, BRB)-Coates, 7 July and 6 October 1989, DTp file FN5/3/145 Pts 5 and 6; Gourvish, *British Rail 1974–97*, pp. 321, 629.
4 Channon-Reid I, 4 May 1989, cit. in ibid. pp. 321–2. See also Channon-Major, 4 May 1989, Treasury file PE TSS/H/11/2 Pt. E.
5 The Treasury had recently increased the requirement to 8%. Portillo-Reid, 31 July and 30 August 1989, DTp file FN5/3/145 Pts. 5 and 6; Portillo-Lamont, 21 and 30 August 1989, Treasury file PE TSS/H/11/2 Pt. K; Gourvish, *British Rail 1974–97*, p. 630.
6 Phillip Morgan (Enterprise & Industry, Treasury)-Guy, 8 September 1989, Treasury file PE TSS/H/11/2 Pt. G; Lamont-Portillo, 29 August 1989, Pt. K; Guy-David Moore and Lamont, 18 September 1989, Pt. H.
7 Lamont-Portillo, 22 September 1989, ibid. Pt. K; Reid-Portillo, 13 October 1989, Charlotte Dixon (Asst Sec, Rlys CF Divn, DTp)-Coates and Portillo's PS, 23 October 1989, DTp file FN5/3/145 Pt. 7; Portillo-Reid, 25 October 1989, cit. in *Gourvish, British Rail 1974–97*, p. 322.
8 Reid-Portillo, 1 November 1989, Dixon-Portillo and Parkinson's PSs, 12 February 1990, DTp file FN5/3/145 Pt. 8; Portillo-Lamont, 17 November 1989, Treasury file Treasury file PE TSS/H/11/2 Pts. J and K; Cunliffe-Guy, 13 November 1989, Steven Reeves (Asst Sec, Rlys A Divn, DTp) and Glyn Williams (Director, Financial Planning, BRB)-John Everett (Touche Ross Management Consultants), 28 November 1989, R44/4/7 Pt. 1.

9 Touche Ross, 'Review of Channel Tunnel Link Phase I: Stage I Report', 15 December 1989, Cunliffe-Guy, 21 December 1989, ibid.; Touche Ross, 'Task Force Working Paper I', January 1990, draft 'master plan', referred to in ibid. Pt. 2.

10 Gourvish, *British Rail 1974–97*, pp. 322, 630. John Brown was a member of Trafalgar House, a partner in the Eurorail joint venture for the Channel Tunnel Rail Link (Phase III), which at this stage expected to acquire the Phase I assets.

11 £53 m. of the total was attributable to British Rail's Network SouthEast sector. John Brown Engineers & Constructors, Report on 'Project Definition Channel Tunnel Services', Vol. I, July 1990, AN192/614, PRO. John Brown figures presented in 'Q3/1989 prices', later held to be 'Q3:1989/90 prices': Jukes-Andrew Burchell (DTp), 1 May 1991, DTp file FN5/3/145 Pt. 13.

12 Reid-Portillo, 22 January 1990, DTp file FN5/3/145 Pt. 8; Derek Fowler (BRB), Memo. to BRB, 23 August 1990, AN167/77, PRO.

13 Gourvish, *British Rail 1974–97*, pp. 320, 324.

14 Ibid. pp. 320–2; John Palmer (MD, CT, BRB)-Dixon, 19 December 1990, DTp file FN5/3/145 Pt. 13; BRB Channel Tunnel Investment Committee Minutes, 5 October 1990, AN167/746, PRO.

15 BRB, *Report and Accounts, 1990–1*, p. 22, *1991–2*, p. 24, *1992–3*, p. 25; Gourvish, *British Rail 1974–97*, pp. 320, 325, 382.

16 BRB, *Report and Accounts, 1988–9*, p. 18, *1990–1*, p. 18, *1992–3*, p. 26, *1993–4*, pp. 24–5; Gourvish, *British Rail 1974–97*, pp. 283–5, 324–6.

17 Palmer-Jo James (DTp), 9 August 1993, DTp file R39/2/45 Pt. 3; R44/4/6 Pts. 1–3; Gourvish, *British Rail 1974–97*, pp. 323, 630. N.b. the files reveal considerable confusion over selection of the constant price base.

18 Ibid. pp. 323–5, 630; DTp file R44/4/5 Pt. 1.

19 Peter Kirk (Mitchell's APS)-Coates, 31 December 1986, DTp file CHT-A7/10 Pt. 1; Coates–Palmer, 5 May 1988, Pt. 3; Broad-Steele (DTI), 17 February 1988, DTI file R1/0/11 Pt. A; Wilf White (Treasury), draft note on 'Channel Tunnel Rolling Stock Procurement', 16 May 1989, Treasury file PE TSS/H/11/2 Pt. E.

20 The complaint from the Verband der Wagonindustrie in January 1988 was taken up by the Commission. The FCO recommended a low-profile response, and the complaint was subsequently withdrawn. See DTp, Memo. to Cabinet Official Committee on European Questions, EQO(89) 6, 12 January 1989; Tim Standbrook (MAED, FCO)-Hughes and Beetham (MAED), 19 January 1989, Denis Keefe (ECD[I], FCO)-Michael Arthur (Head of ECD[I]) and John Kerr (Superintending U-Sec, ECD(I)), 20 January 1989, FCO file MRY178/3/89; Clive Brewer (DTI)-John Altis (Cabinet Office), 23 December 1988, Henry Emden (OFT)-Martin Goulden (DTI), 29 September 1989, DTI file R1/0/11 Pts. B and C.

21 Parkinson-Reid I, 8 December 1989, DTp file R44/4/4 Pt. 1; DTp appraisal, June 1990, FN5/3/145 Pt. 11.

22 Cf. Judith Ritchie (Parkinson's APS)-Coates, 25 October 1990, S. Gooding (PS to Roger Freeman (Transport Minister))-J. Fells (Asst Sec, Rlys C Divn, DTp), 31 October 1990, Sir Bob Reid II-Malcolm Rifkind (SoS for Transport), 10 December 1990, Fells-Gooding, 7 January 1991, Ritchie-Coates, 1 July 1991, Freeman-Rifkind, 7 January 1992, DTp file R44/4/4 Pt. 1; Weinstock-Rifkind, 5 July 1991, CHT-A7/1 Pt. 1; Richard Edgley (MD, EPS), Briefing Note, 1 March 1992, R39/2/48 Pt. 2; Jim Betts (APS to John MacGregor (SoS for Transport))-M.R. Fawcett (Asst Sec, Int. Rlys Divn, DTp), 29 June and 11 November 1993, CHT-A7/10 Pts 5–6; Weinstock-MacGregor, 20 October 1993, Edgley-Nicholas Montagu (Dep Sec, DTp), 7 February 1994, Edgley-Ken Davenport (DTp), 10 February 1995, R39/2/48 Pt. 3.

23 HC Transport Select Committee, *Report on Preparations for the Opening of the Channel Tunnel*, Vol. I, March 1992, para. 27, P.P.1991–2, vii, HC12-I.

24 Morton, HC Transport Committee Report on *Preparations for the Opening of the Channel Tunnel: MOE*, 13 November 1991, QQ.151–7, P.P.1991–2, vii, HC12-II; Channel Tunnel Safety Authority, *Annual Report 1994/95*, pp. 2, 11; Gourvish, *British Rail 1974–97*, p. 325.
25 BRB, *International Rail Services for the United Kingdom* (December 1989), pp. 9–10; Gourvish, *British Rail 1974–97*, p. 327.
26 HC Select Committee on Welsh Affairs, Report on *The Channel Tunnel: Implications for Wales*, Vol. I, June 1989, paras 35–9, P.P.1988–9, xxi, HC191-I.
27 Malcolm Rifkind (SoS for Scotland)-Parkinson, 14 December 1989, Rifkind-Lamont, 16 January 1990, DTp file R44/4/9 Pt. 1.
28 HC Transport Select Committee, *Preparations for the Opening of the Channel Tunnel*, Vol. I, March 1992, para. 35. See also lobbying by Cornwall Co. Co. and northern England in DTp file R44/4/9 Pts. 1–2.
29 See DTp file FN5/3/146 Pts. 1–4.
30 Gourvish, *British Rail 1974–97*, p. 326; Gooding-Dixon, 28 August 1990, DTp file FN5/3/146 Pt. 4; Palmer-Dixon, 4 and 5 September 1990, R44/4/11 Pt. 1; Hugh Burns (PE2, Treasury), Note for the Record, 5 February 1991, Treasury file PE TSS/H/11/4 Pt. A.
31 Burchell-Coates and Freeman's PS, 11 February 1991, Rifkind-Reid, 20 May 1991, DTp file R44/4/11 Pt. 2; Rifkind-John Welsby (Chief Executive, BRB), 16 September 1991, Eurotunnel, 'Ashford International Passenger Station', September 1991, Freeman-Morton, 27 September 1991, Freeman-Reid II, 28 November 1991, Pt. 3.
32 Gourvish, *British Rail 1974–97*, pp. 326–7; Chris Humphrey (Freeman's APS)-David Rowlands (Rlys 1, DTp), 26 February 1992, Freeman-Reid II, 6 March 1992, Reid II-Rifkind, 11 March 1992, DTp file FN5/3/146 Pt. 7.
33 The railway works were initially authorised in March 1993 at £30.4 m. (excluding contingency) in Q2/92 prices. The revised authorisation in August 1995 was £60.0 m. cash, including contingency [= £50.8 m. *excluding* contingency in Q2/92 prices]. Martin Bucknall (DTp)-Eddie Gibbons, 21 March 1994, DTp file R39/2/45 Pt. 3; Alan Deighton (DTp)-Sir George Young (SoS for Transport), 28 July 1995, DTp file FN5/3/146 Pt. 10.
34 Edgley-Rowlands, 24 June 1993, ibid. Pt. 4; John MacGregor (SoS for Transport)-Lamont (Chancellor of Exchequer), 5 March 1993, Rutnam-Philip Wynn Owen (PS to Sir Terence Burns (Permanent Sec, Treasury)) and Stephen Dorrell (Financial Secretary, Treasury), 10 December 1993, Treasury file PXE EET/F/11/1 Pt. A; DTp file FN5/3/146 Pts. 8–10; BRB Channel Tunnel Investment Committee Minutes, 21 January 1994, AN167/746, PRO.
35 Gourvish, *British Rail 1974–97*, pp. 327, 632 and cf. Jukes-Coates, 20 July 1989, Ritchie, Note on 'Channel Tunnel Trains – Meeting with Lord Weinstock and Sir Bob Reid, Thursday 27 June', 1 July 1991, DTp file, R44/4/10 Pt. 1; Parkinson-Lamont, 6 December 1989, FCO file MRY178/3/89.
36 £230 m. in Q3:1989/90 prices. The authorisations were: day services, £108 m. (Q2/1989 prices); night services, up to £130 m. (Q2:1990/1 prices). See Rifkind-Reid II, 25 July 1991, Simon Judge (Treasury)-Burchell, 18 November 1991, Rifkind-Reid II, 25 November 1991, DTp file R44/4/10 Pt. 3.
37 Gourvish, *British Rail 1974–97*, pp. 327–8; *Modern Railways*, August 1997, p. 523; DTp file R44/4/10 Pts 3–4.
38 Cf. Jukes-Elizabeth Spiro (DTp), 27 June 1989, DTp file FN5/3/145 Pt. 5; Coates-Portillo's PS, 25 August 1989, ibid. Pt. 6; Reeves-Ian Brown (MD, RfD), 25 October 1989, R44/4/2 Pt. 1; Spiro-Reeves, n.d. [March 1990], ibid. Pt. 2.
39 Guy-Cunliffe, DTp file FN5/3/145 Pt. 7; RfD, Channel Tunnel Strategic Review, February 1990, R44/4/2 Pt. 2.

40 Over half the increase was explained by the earlier failure to count wagon leasing as investment. Cunliffe-Guy, 3 October 1989, DTp file FN5/3/145 Pt. 7.
41 In Q3:1989/90 prices. Ian Brown, Investment Submission, April 1990, DTp file R44/4/2 Pt. 3. See also Pitwood-Judge, 9 May 1990, ibid. Pt. 4; Dan Boyde (DTp)-James, 15 April 1992, R39/2/45 Pt. 1.
42 Rifkind-Reid II, 28 June and 24 July 1991, ibid. Pt. 6; Gourvish, *British Rail 1974–97*, p. 324.
43 Guy-Cunliffe. 9 November 1989, DTp file R44/4/2 Pt. 2; Gourvish, *British Rail 1974–97*, pp. 325–6.
44 Steve Robson (U-Sec, PE, Treasury)-Judge, 11 April 1990, Treasury file PXE EET/F/12/1 Pt. A. Of course, Treasury opinion at the time was that without its sanctioning the Usage Contract the project could be 'brought into question': Boote-Monck and Major, 17 July 1987, cit.
45 Gourvish, *British Rail 1974–97*, p. 324.
46 BR appraisal, July 1990, summarised in Spiro-Dixon, 2 November 1990, DTp file FN5/3/145 Pt. 13; Spiro-Peter Dodkins (DTp), 14 November 1989, ibid. Pt. 7; Gourvish, *British Rail 1974–97*, p. 320.
47 E.g. Judge-Pitwood, 15 March 1991, DTp file FN5/3/145 Pt. 13.
48 *Parl. Deb. (Commons)*, 6th ser. (Session 1988–9), Vol. 159, Parkinson, written answer, 3 November 1989, *346*; (Session 1989–90), Vol. 174, Parkinson, statement, 14 June 1990, *c.*482; (Session 1990–1), Vol. 196, Rifkind, statement, 14 October 1991, *c.*24; (Session 1993–4), Vol. 236, MacGregor, statement, 24 January 1994, *c.*34.
49 Cf. change of emphasis in DTp file FN5/3/145, e.g. Pts. 17–20; CHT-A7/10 Pt. 5. Monthly monitoring reports continued into 1994: R39/2/45 Pts. 1–3.
50 Gourvish, *British Rail 1974–97*, pp. 403, 421.
51 Kent Impact Study Team, *Channel Tunnel – A Strategy for Kent* (1987); DTp press notice, 14 August 1987, DTp file CHT-A7/14 Pt. 1; BRB, *Channel Tunnel Train Services: BR Study Report on Long-term Route and Terminal Capacity* (July 1988); HC Library Research Paper 95/2 on 'Channel Tunnel Rail Link Bill', 10 January 1995.
52 Cf. Welsby, Memo. to BRB on 'Review of Channel Tunnel Project', BRB Minutes, 31 March 1988, AN167/76, PRO; Gourvish, *British Rail 1974–97*, p. 329.
53 An early Treasury reaction was that Route 1 + Stratford was the most attractive: Guy-Moore, 17 June 1988, Treasury file PE TSS/H/11/1 Pt. D.
54 BRB, *Channel Tunnel Train Services*, pp. 7, 10–11, 16–20.
55 Welsby, reported in Fortnam-Coates, 2 September 1988, DTp file FN5/3/147 Pt. 3.
56 Fortnam-Channon's PS, 1 July 1988, ibid. Pt. 2; Griffins-Fortnam, 8 July 1988, DTp file CHT-A7/14 Pt. 1; Griffins-Gray, 13 July 1988, Prime Minister's Channel Tunnel papers, Pt. 6.
57 Fortnam-Mitchell's PS, 10 June 1988, Channon-Nicholas Ridley (SoS for Environment), 5 July 1988, DTp file CHT-A7/14 Pt. 1; Guy-Moore and Major, 12 July 1988 and 21 February 1989, Treasury file PE TSS/H/11/1 Pt. D and 11/2 Pt. C.
58 Coates-Bailey's PS, 18 November 1987, Palmer-Mitchell, 27 April 1988, DTp file CHT-A7/14 Pt. 1; DTp Press Notice, 14 July 1988, Prime Minister's Channel Tunnel papers, Pt. 6.
59 Colin Grimsey (Asst Sec, FTI Divn, DTp)-Moore, 14 June 1988, Guy-Mary Brown (Asst Sec, PE, Treasury) and Monck, 15 June 1988, Treasury file PE TSS/H/11/1 Pt. D; Cunliffe-Grimsey, 1 July 1988, Palmer-Fortnam, 22 August 1988, DTp file FN5/3/147 Pt. 2.
60 Morton-Lamont, 16 June 1988, Guy-Monck, 20 June 1988, Susan Feest (Treasury), 'Notes of a Meeting…on 20th June 1988', 22 June 1988, Treasury file PE TSS/H/11/1 Pt. D; Griffins-Fortnam, 12 August 1988, DTp file FN5/3/147 Pt. 2.
61 Guy-Brown and Monck, 15 June 1988, cit.

62 Palmer-Channon, 12 July 1988, DTp file FN5/3/147 Pt. 2; Grimsey-Moore, 14 June 1988, Guy-Monck, 20 June 1988, cit.
63 Coates-Moore and Fortnam-Channon's PS, both 4 October 1988, DTp file FN5/3/147 Pt. 3; *Times*, 15 October 1988, p. 24.
64 Griffins-Fortnam, 1 November 1988, Handley Stevens (U-Sec, Finance, DTp)-Fortnam, 3 November 1988, DTp file FN5/3/147 Pt. 3; Moore-Stevens, 11 November 1988, Treasury file PE TSS/H/11/1 Pt. E.
65 Griffins-Fortnam, 14 November 1988, Stephen Bramhall (Portillo's PS)-Fortnam, 16 November 1988, Pitwood-Fortnam, 28 October 1988, DTp file FN5/3/147 Pt. 3.
66 The move matched the DTp's response in relation to certain motorway schemes and Eurotunnel's actions in handling blight in Newington, Peene and Frogholt. Pitwood-Fortnam, 28 October 1988, Welsby-Coates and BRB Press Release, both 10 November 1988, ibid.
67 Portillo, *Parl. Deb. (Commons)*, 6th ser. (Session 1988–9), Vol. 142, 2 December 1988, *c.*1023–32, replying to motion introduced by Anne Widdecombe (Maidstone).
68 Moore-Stevens, 15 December 1988, Treasury file, PE TSS/H/11/1 Pt. E. Widdecombe's adjournment debate forced a DTp response somewhat earlier than had been anticipated, and without full consultation with the Treasury.
69 Chief Executive (Kent Co. Co.) *et al.*, report to Kent Co. Co. Development Planning & Transportation Committee on 'Channel Tunnel: British Rail High Speed Line Proposals', 17 January 1989, Fortnam-Portillo's PS, 17 January 1989, DTp file FN5/3/147 Pt. 5.
70 Stevens-Moore, 8 September 1988, Treasury file PE TSS/H/11/1 Pt. D; Gourvish, *British Rail 1974–97*, p. 329.
71 Fortnam-Portillo's PS, 11 January 1989, DTp file FN5/3/147 Pt. 4; Moore-Stevens, 19 January 1989, Pt. 5; Guy-Moore, 25 November 1988, Treasury file PE TSS/H/11/1 Pt. E; Grimsey-Moore, 11 January 1989, Stevens-Moore, 1 February 1989, PE TSS/H/11/2 Pt. A. The problem had been anticipated. On 9 September 1988 Bill Guy complained: 'We have seen this coming for ages…This is going to be the biggest bounce I have ever seen': annotation on Stevens-Moore, 8 September 1988, cit.
72 See Tony Banks (Newham North-West)-Portillo, 5 January and reply, January 1989, FN5/3/147 Pt. 4.
73 Moore-Stevens, 15 December 1988, cit.; Guy-Moore and Major, 31 January 1989, Treasury file PE TSS/H/11/2 Pt. A.
74 Gray-Thatcher, 8 February 1989, and briefing papers, Prime Minister's Channel Tunnel papers, Pt. 6.
75 Gray-Griffins, 9 February 1989, ibid.; Griffins-Fortnam and Fortnam-Channon's PS, both 9 February 1989, DTp file FN5/3/147 Pt. 6. In the event Thatcher met Welsby, Kirby and Edgley (in Reid's absence).
76 Griffins-Gray, 17 February 1989, enclosing 'New Channel Tunnel Rail Link – Paper by Secretary of State', n.d., Prime Minister's Channel Tunnel papers, Pt. 6.
77 Channon-Major, 13 February, and reply, 24 February 1989, ibid.; Ridley-Channon, 23 February 1989, DTp file FN5/3/147 Pt. 8. On British Rail's undertakings on noise see its pamphlet on *Noise and the New Channel Tunnel Rail Link* (December 1988), ibid. Pt. 6.
78 'New Channel Tunnel Rail Link – Paper by Secretary of State', cit. paras. 11–12; Welsby-Coates, 15 February 1989, DTp file FN5/3/147 Pt. 6.
79 Greg Bourne (No. 10 Policy Unit)-Thatcher, 22 February 1989, Prime Minister's Channel Tunnel papers, Pt. 6.
80 Moore-Major, 21 February 1989, Treasury file PE TSS/H/11/2 Pt. C.
81 Gray-Thatcher, 22 February 1989, Prime Minister's Channel Tunnel papers, Pt. 6; Moore-Major, 23 February 1989, Treasury file PE TSS/H/11/2 Pt. C.
82 Gray-Griffins, 23 February 1989, Prime Minister's Channel Tunnel papers, Pt. 6.

83 Reid I-Thatcher, 7 March 1989, with enclosures, Prime Minister's Channel Tunnel papers, Pt. 7; Maps in Gourvish, *British Rail 1974–97*, pp. 330–1.
84 *Parl. Deb. (Commons)*, 6th ser. (Session 1989–90), Vol. 168, 9 March 1990, Portillo, statement, *c.*1033.
85 A joint venture represented a dilution of earlier intentions. See Stevens-Moore, 5 June 1989, Treasury file PE TSS/H/11/2 Pt. F, and Major-Portillo, 15 June 1989, DTp file FN5/3/147 Pt. 10.
86 On the selection process see Gourvish, *British Rail 1974–97*, p. 332, DTp file FN5/3/147 Pts. 10–13, and Treasury file PE TSS H/11/2 Pts. F-J.
87 On the complexities surrounding the decision see Dixon-Edward Osmotherly (Dep Sec, PTR, DTp) *et al.*, 13 October 1989, Griffins-Dixon, 18 October 1989, DTp file FN5/3/147 Pt. 13, Parkinson-Thatcher, 27 October 1989, Gray-Griffins, 31 October 1989, ibid. Pt. 14; Parkinson, *Parl. Deb. (Commons)*, 3 November 1989, cit., *347*.
88 Coates-Rennie, 16 February and reply, 21 February 1990, DTp file FN5/3/147 Pt. 20; European Rail Link-Parkinson, 30 March 1990, ibid. Pt. 23.
89 European Rail Link-Parkinson, cit. In his presentation to Thatcher Parkinson rounded these figures down to £3bn and £2.5bn.
90 Interview with Parkinson, 2000; Potter-Thatcher, 4 and 10 May 1989, Parkinson-Thatcher, n.d. [May 1989], Prime Minister's Channel Tunnel papers, Pt. 7.
91 Lamont-Thatcher, 10 May 1990, ibid. and see Judge-Pitwood, 24 April 1990, DTp file FN5/3/147 Pt. 24.
92 Parkinson-Thatcher, n.d., Prime Minister's Channel Tunnel papers, Pt. 7.
93 Morton-Thatcher, 3 (2 letters), 17 and 22 May 1990, Potter-Thatcher, 23 May 1990, ibid. Morton argued that the real beneficiary of the CTRL would be 'Great Britain'.
94 Lamont-Thatcher, 10 May 1990, cit.
95 George Guise (No. 10 Policy Unit), 10 May 1990, Prime Minister's Channel Tunnel papers, Pt. 7.
96 See Parkinson-Thatcher, 17 May 1990, Guise-Potter, 23 May 1990, Potter-Whiteley, 25 May 1990, ibid.
97 Cabinet E(A) Committee Minutes, E(A) (90) 2, 14 June 1990; *Parl. Deb. (Commons)*, Parkinson, statement, 14 June 1990, cit. *c.*482–3.
98 Gourvish, *British Rail 1974–97*, pp. 333, 634. The route was also advocated by Maureen Tomison, formerly of British Ferries: Tomison (Decision Makers Ltd)-Hurd, 27 November 1989 and April 1990, FCO file MRY178/3/89 and MRY178/8/90 Pt. A.
99 Potter-Martin Stanley (Head of Solicitors Divn C, DTI), 11 May 1990, ibid.; Potter-Whiteley, 15 May 1990, Prime Minister's Channel Tunnel papers, Pt. 7. The proposal, for a theme park/film studio, did not materialise. It was described by a Treasury official as 'a bit of a googly': Judge, draft submission to Chief Secretary, 17 May 1990, Treasury file PE TSS/H/11/3 Pt. D.
100 Annotation on Report by Colin Buchanan & Partners, September 1989, Treasury file PE TSS/H/11/2 Pt. G.
101 Gourvish, *British Rail 1974–97*, p. 333; 'Rail Link Project: Comparison of Routes, Report to BRB', 25 April 1991, in DTp file FN5/3/147 Pt. 28 and see also Pts. 27 and 29.
102 Reid II-Rifkind, 3 May 1991, ibid. Pt. 27. The Report was published: BRB, *Rail Link Project: Comparison of Routes* (June 1991).
103 Potter-Whiteley, 10 May 1991, Prime Minister's Channel Tunnel papers, Pt. 8; DTp, 'Rail Link Steering Group – Note of the First Meeting, 14 May 1991', 16 May 1991, DTp file FN5/3/147 Pt. 29.
104 Coates-Rifkind's PS, 31 May 1991, ibid. Pt. 30; Jonathan Hill (No. 10 Policy Unit)-Potter, 31 May 1991, Rifkind-Major, 3 and 14 June 1991, Prime Minister's Channel Tunnel papers, Pt. 8.
105 Hill-Major, 6 June 1991, Potter-Major, 7 June 1991, ibid.
106 Coates-Rifkind's PS, 21 June 1991, DTp file FN5/3/147 Pt. 33.

107 Robson-Coates, 3 July 1991, passed to Rifkind, DTp file FN5/3/147 Pt. 34, and see also Treasury file PE TSS/H/11/4 Pt. H.
108 Rifkind-Major and 'Channel Tunnel Rail Link: Report by Officials', both 5 July 1991, Prime Minister's Channel Tunnel papers, Pt. 8.
109 Heseltine-Major, 12 July 1991, ibid.; Interview with Lord Heseltine, 6 February 2002.
110 Lamont-Major, 22 July 1991, with Major's annotation, 28 July, Prime Minister's Channel Tunnel papers, Pt. 8. Potter's view was that the memo. was 'a Steve Robson production if ever I saw one!' For the Treasury's position see file PE TSS/H/11/4 Pt. J.
111 Rifkind-Major, 25 July 1991, Prime Minister's Channel Tunnel papers, Pt. 8.
112 Whiteley-Coates, 19 July 1991, DTp file FN5/3/147 Pt. 35.
113 Potter-Major, 30 July 1991, enclosing, Hill, report on 'Channel Tunnel Rail Link', n.d., Prime Minister's Channel Tunnel papers, Pt. 9. See also Robson-Judge, 28 August 1991, Treasury file PE TSS/H/11/4 Pt. K.
114 Ritchie-Rowlands, 24 September 1991, DTp file FN5/3/147 Pt. 36.
115 Note by Officials, 24 September 1991, Prime Minister's Channel Tunnel papers, Pt. 9. The 5 options were: kill the route; choose the route but do no more; commit to the line/obtain statutory powers; commit to line/consult on routes; commit to line and construction.
116 Judge-Robson, 24 September 1991, Treasury file PE TSS/H/11/4 Pt. K.
117 Hill-Major, 24 September 1991, Potter-Major, 25 September 1991, Prime Minister's Channel Tunnel papers, Pt. 9, and see also Ritchie-Rowlands, 24 September 1991, cit.; Potter-Whiteley, 29 August 1991, DTp file FN5/3/147 Pt. 35; Robson-Judge, 18 September 1991, Treasury file PE TSS/H/11/4 Pt. K; and Sarah Hogg and Jonathan Hill, *Too Close to Call. Power and Politics – John Major in No. 10* (1995), p. 133.
118 Potter-Whiteley, 27 September 1991, Prime Minister's Channel Tunnel papers, Pt. 9; Ritchie-Rowlands, 27 September 1992, DTp file FN 5/3/147 Pt. 36.
119 Rifkind-Lamont, 2 October 1991, Heseltine-Rifkind, 3 October 1991, Lamont-Rifkind, 4 October 1991, Prime Minister's Channel Tunnel papers, Pt. 9.
120 Hill-Major and Potter-Major, both 4 October 1991, ibid.
121 *Independent*, 7 October 1991, pp. 1, 3; Interview with Bob Reid II, 1 February 2000; Potter-Whiteley, 8 October 1991, Prime Minister's Channel Tunnel papers, Pt. 9; Rifkind-Lamont, n.d. [8 October], enclosed in Whiteley-Rowlands, 15 October 1991, DTp file FN5/3/147 Pt. 36. Whatever the source of the leak, the *Independent* was incorrect in stating that the terminus would be at Stratford.
122 Rifkind-Reid II, 9 October 1991, ibid. Pt. 36; 'Transcript of Rifkind's Speech at 108th Conservative Conference', n.d., Pt. 37; DTp Press Notice, 9 October 1991, Whiteley-Potter, 11 October 1991, Prime Minister's Channel Tunnel papers, Pt. 9; *Parl. Deb. (Commons)*, Rifkind, statement, 14 October 1991, cit. *c*.24–6; press reactions, esp. *Sunday Times*, 13 October 1991, p. 33.
123 Gourvish, *British Rail 1974–97*, pp. 334–5, 635. Reid insisted on seeing Major, and was offered a private meeting. 'He would not expect even the existence, let alone the conclusions, of the discussion to be made public': Potter-Whiteley, 14 October 1991, Prime Minister's Channel Tunnel papers, Pt. 9.
124 Morton, reported in *Times*, 10 October 1991, p. 1, and see also *Sunday Times*, 13 October 1991, p. 33. See correspondence in Treasury file PE TSS/H/11/5 Pt. A.
125 Cf. Robson-Judge, 28 August 1991, Potter-Major, 4 October 1991, cit.; Rowlands-Rifkind's PS, 3 September 1991, DTp file FN5/3/147 Pt. 36.
126 E.g. *Independent*, 7 and 10 October 1991, Times, 10 October 1991, cit.; *Daily Mail*, 10 October 1991, p. 1. In fact, no Cabinet discussion took place.
127 Rowlands-Rifkind's PS, 27 September 1991, Jeremy Heywood (Lamont's PPS)-Whiteley, 10 October 1991, DTp file FN5/3/147 Pts. 36 and 37; Judge-Robson, 15 October 1991, Treasury file PE TSS/H/11/4 Pt. L.

128 *Parl. Deb. (Commons)*, 6th ser. (Session 1991–2), Vol. 200, Rifkind, 5 December 1991, *189–90*. On the background see Rifkind-Major, 22 November 1991, Prime Minister's Channel Tunnel papers, Pt. 9; *Sunday Independent*, 17 November 1991, p. 4.
129 See Treasury file PE TSS/H/11/5 Pts. A-K.
130 Prideaux later paid for this and other examples of an independent line, being dismissed by Reid as Chairman of the subsidiary in August 1993. Ministers were distinctly annoyed by the move, since they rated Prideaux highly, but there was little they could do. Gourvish, *British Rail 1974–97*, pp. 335–8; Alan Rosling (Policy Unit, No. 10)-Major, 20 August 1993, and subsequent correspondence, Prime Minister's Channel Tunnel papers, Pt. 10.
131 MacGregor-Major, 12 February 1993, Prime Minister's Channel Tunnel papers, Pt. 9.
132 *Rail*, 31 March-13 April 1993, pp. 4–5. MacGregor had announced the decision to provide two tracks, instead of four, but retaining freight capability, in May 1992: *Independent*, 21 May 1992, p. 6.
133 MacGregor-Major, 12 February 1993, cit. and 1 March 1993, Prime Minister's Channel Tunnel papers, Pt. 10. On the emergence of this option see Gourvish, *British Rail 1974–97*, pp. 336–7 and DTp file FN5/3/147 Pt. 42.
134 *Parl. Deb. (Commons)*, 6th ser. (Session 1992–3), Vol. 221, Lamont, 16 March 1993, *c.*194; MacGregor, 22 March 1993, *c.*609–14.
135 MacGregor-Major, 23 December 1993, Prime Minister's Channel Tunnel papers, Pt. 10.
136 *Parl. Deb. (Commons)*, MacGregor, statement, 24 January 1994, cit. *c.*19–21. On the background see Griffins-Grimsey (Head of Rlys 1 Divn, DTp) and MacGregor, 17 December 1993, DTp file FN5/3/147 Pt. 51.
137 MacGregor-John Gummer (SoS for Environment), 26 April 1994, Prime Minister's Channel Tunnel papers, Pt. 11.
138 MacGregor-Major, 12 February 1993, cit.
139 Heywood-Paul Coby (MacGregor's PS), 25 February 1993, Prime Minister's Channel Tunnel papers, Pt. 9. Lamont was inclined to abandon CrossRail, describing it as a 'bloated, gold-plated project', but following Major's intervention, both continued in play. See also MacGregor-Major, 3 March 1993, Rosling-Major, 8 October 1993, Pt. 10.
140 *Parl. Deb. (Commons)*, Lamont, 16 March 1993, cit. *c.*194; MacGregor, 22 March 1993, cit. *c.*610.
141 MacGregor-Kenneth Clarke (Chancellor), 11 January 1994 and reply, 14 January 1994, Treasury file PE TSS/H/11/7 Pt. A; Coby-Mary Francis (Major's PS), 21 January 1994, Prime Minister's Channel Tunnel papers, Pt. 11.
142 *Parl. Deb. (Commons)*, 6th ser. (Session 1993–4), Vol. 236, Frank Dobson, 24 March 1994, *c.*21; Wolmar, in *Independent*, 25 January 1994, p. 1, Hoggart, in *Guardian*, 25 January 1994, p. 6.
143 A notion raised by Mitterand when he opened the Paris-Lille TGV Link in May 1993: *Evening Standard*, 18 May 1993, p. 2, *Times*, 19 May 1993, p. 13.
144 MdO, Progress Report No. 28, 30 June 1993.
145 Kirkland, *Engineering the Channel Tunnel, passim*; Anderson and Roskrow, *Channel Tunnel Story*, p. 151.
146 MdO, Progress Report No. 20, June 1991, cit.; *Evening Standard*, 4 February 1992, p. 25, 10 February 1992, p. 1.
147 MdO, Progress Report No. 24, 30 June 1992, No. 25, 30 September 1993; *Financial Times*, 6 October 1992, p. 23.
148 MdO, Progress Report No. 30, 31 December 1993.
149 Broad-Goulden, 13 September 1988, Goulden-Brewer, 5 October 1988, DTI file R1/0/11 Pt. A; Hayes-Broad, 16 November 1988, Henes-Portillo's PS, 27 January 1989, Pt. B.
150 F. Rodgers (Chairman, Eurosignal)-Hayes, 22 June 1989, ibid. Pt. C.
151 Unlike the TSG proposal, Sofrerail's system excluded solid state interlocking. Andrew Davis (CT Divn, DTp)-Broad, 12 March 1990, DTp file R1/0/15 Pt. A;

Broad-Burgess, 17 May 1990, R1/0/11 Pt. D; MdO, Progress Reports No. 14, 31 December 1989, p. 139; No. 15, 31 March 1990, p. 136.

152 DTI, 'Note of a Meeting on 29 November 1990 with Robert Blood, TML', 27 December 1990, Broad, 'Channel Fixed Link – Signalling Contract', 18 January 1991, DTI file R1/0/11 Pt. D; Panel Decision, February 1991, in DTp file CHT6/1/71 Pt. 1; *Construction News*, 17 January 1991, p. 1.

153 See DTp file CHT3/1/32 Pts 1–2; MdO, Progress Report No. 15, March 1990, p. 135; Lemley, cit. in Fetherston, *Chunnel*, pp. 358–60.

154 MdO, Progress Reports No. 12, 30 June 1989, 16, 30 June 1990, No. 20, 31 July 1991.

155 Cf. IGC, Note of a meeting with Safety Authority and MdO, 16 March 1989, and meeting with Eurotunnel and MdO, 27 October 1989, DTp file CHT3/1/54 Pt. 1.

156 Briefing for Sir Robin Butler, in Scott Ghagan (Bailey's PS)-Phippard, 30 April 1991, DTp file CHT6/1/76 Pt. 1.

157 Burgess-Martin, 6 February 1991, DTp file CHT3/1/5 Pt. 3.

158 Ibid. and Burgess-Freeman's PS, 17 June 1991, DTp file CHT6/1/76 Pt. 1.

159 Morton-Parkinson, 6 November 1989, ibid.

160 Concession Agreement, 1986, Clause 27.7; Burgess-Freeeman's PS, 21 February 1991, DTp file CHT6/1/76 Pt. 1.

161 Whiteley-Burgess, 28 February 1991, Ghagan, Note on 'Meeting with Eurotunnel: 19 April 1991', 22 April 1991, Ghagan-Phippard, 30 April 1991, ibid.; Burgess-Graham Boiling (IND, Home Office), 4 July 1991, DTp file CHT6/1/25 Pt. 28. Note that Bénard also lobbied the French Government: Morton-Rifkind, 13 March 1991, CHT6/1/76 Pt. 1.

162 Concession Agreement, 1986, Annex AI.6.

163 MdO, Report No. 14, December 1989, p. 116, DTp file CHT3/1/54 Pt. 2; Burgess-Freeman's PS, 21 February 1991, cit. See also CHT3/1/68 Pts 1–2.

164 Middleton-Freeman, 22 May 1991, Burgess-Freeman's PS, 12 June 1991, Alison Bow (Freeman's APS)-Russell Sunderland (Dep Sec, Aviation etc., DTp), 24 June 1991, Freeman-Middleton and Freeman-Morton, both 16 July 1991, DTp file CHT3/1/54 Pt. 3.

165 IGC Minutes, 18 December 1989, DTpfile CHT3/1/93 Pt. 1; Legrand-Eurotunnel, with enclosure, 19 December 1989, CHT3/1/42 Pt. 1; MdO, Progress Report No. 14, 31 December 1989, p. 27.

166 Alain Bertrand (MD, Operations & Safety, Eurotunnel)-Legrand, 15 March 1990, DTp file CHT3/1/47 Pt. 1. The precise cost of the modification was uncertain. Cf. MdO, Progress Report No. 15, 31 March 1990, p. 141, Frances Evans (CT Divn, DTp)-Richard Woodward (CT Divn, DTp), 2 October 1991, CHT3/1/47 Pt. 4.

167 Beetham-Eurotunnel, 30 April and 14 May 1990, Henes-Morton, 12 July 1990, DTp file CHT3/1/47 Pt. 1; Henes-Eurotunnel, 1 August 1990 and reply, 2 August 1990, Morton-Henes, 5 October 1990, ibid. Pt. 2.

168 Peter Middleton (Executive MdO)-Henes, 5 November 1990, Burgess-Middleton, 20 November 1990, Taberner (Eurotunnel)-Henes, 21 March 1991, Martin-Legrand, 5 April 1991, Legrand-Eurotunnel, 8 April 1991, ibid. Pt. 3.

169 MdO, Progress Report No. 18, 31 December 1990.

170 IGC Minutes, 8 July and 7 October 1988, DTp file CHT3/1/93 Pt. 1; Henes-Roger Freeman (Minister for Public Transport)'s PS, 24 April 1992, CHT3/1/46 Pt. 5.

171 Alan Cooksey (Safety Authority and Railway Inspectorate, DTp)-Henes, 31 October 1989, Taberner-Robert Bailey (UK Secretary, Safety Authority), 17 January 1990, DTp file CHT3/1/46 Pt. 1; MdO, Progress Report No. 14, December 1989, pp. 142–3, No. 15, March 1990, pp. 140–1.

172 Taberner-Burgess, 11 July 1990, Bailey-Gérard Couvreur (Safety Authority, Paris), 18 July 1990, Henes-Eurotunnel, 23 July 1990, Eurotunnel documentation, 21–5 January 1991, DTp file CHT3/1/46 Pt. 1.

173 Pilon-Henes and Henes-Eurotunnel, both 28 March 1991, ibid. Pt. 2.

174 MdO, Report on 'Acceptability of the Semi-Open Wagon Concept for the HGV Shuttles', April 1991, Electrowatt, Report on 'Comparative Fire Risk Study of HGV Carrier Wagon Designs', May 1991, ibid.

175 Bow-Henes, 3 April 1991, ibid., Freeman-Morton, 21 May 1991, Martin-Bertrand, 21 May 1991, Taberner-Martin, 17, 21 and 28 June 1991, Martin-Legrand, 4 July 1991, ibid. Pts. 2–3.

176 Morton-Henes, 12 December 1991, ibid. Pt. 3. His letter arrived a month after he had told the HC Transport Committee: 'The revised [*enclosed*] design... has been agreed with the safety authority... There is the usual brinkmanship going on, with every side – Except us, of course! – striking irreconcilable postures'. Morton, HC Transport Committee Report on *Preparations for the Opening of the Channel Tunnel: MOE*, 13 November 1991, Q.142, P.P.1991–2, vii, HC12-II.

177 Eurotunnel documentation, in Bénard-Legrand and Bertrand-Martin, both 14 January 1992, ibid. Pt. 3; Burgess-Boiling, 16 March 1992, with enclosure, Pt. 4; Henes-Freeman's PS, 24 April 1992, Pt. 5.

178 HC Home Affairs Committee Report on *Fire Safety and Policing of the Channel Tunnel*, December 1991, para. 32, P.P.1991–2, ix, HC23-I.

179 Note on Guernsey meeting, 10–13 March 1992, DTp file CHT3/1/46 Pt. 3; Burgess-Henes, 2 April 1992, Pt. 4; Jeremy Beech (Safety Authority and Chief Fire Officer of Kent), Opinion, 21 April 1992, Pt. 5; Henes-Freeman's PS, 24 April 1992, cit.

180 Safety Authority, 'HGV Shuttles – List of Documentation', 5 March 1992, ibid. Pt. 3; Pilon-Eurotunnel, 3 April 1992, Pt. 4; Allan Hall (Safety Authority)-Martin, 13 April 1992, Roderick Allison (HSE)-Martin, 16 April 1993, Pt. 5.

181 Henes-Freeman's PS, 24 April 1992, cit.; Freeman-Earl Ferrers (Minister of State, Home Office), 27 April 1992 and reply, 28 April 1992, Henes-Eurotunnel, 30 April 1992, DTp file CHT3/1/46 Pt. 5.

182 Roger Lejuez (Chairman, Safety Authority)-Eurotunnel, 19 February 1993, Taberner-Legrand, 30 April, 1 June, 8 July and 27 August 1993, Legrand-Eurotunnel, 26 July 1993, ibid.; Edward Ryder (Chairman, Safety Authority)-Legrand, 28 September and 4 October 1993, Legrand-Eurotunnel, 5 October 1993, ibid. Pt. 6; Safety Authority, *Annual Report 1992/93*, pp. 15–17, *1993/94*, pp. 12–13.

183 Phippard, Note for Record, 1 May 1991, and see also Kenneth Sutton (PS to Sir Clive Whitmore, Permanent Sec, Home Office)-Boiling, 26 June 1991, DTp file CHT6/1/76 Pt. 1.

184 Freeman-Middleton, 16 July 1991, cit. This point was also made by the HC Home Affairs Committee Report on *Fire Safety and Policing of the Channel Tunnel*, December 1991, para. 7.

185 Rifkind-Morton, 19 March 1991, DTp file CHT6/1/76 Pt. 1; Burgess-Freeman's PS, 12 June 1991, cit.; Martin, Memorandum in evidence to HC Home Affairs Committee, 6 November 1991, cit. para. 5; *Parl. Deb. (Commons)*, 6th ser. (Session 1986–7), Vol. 115, Mitchell, written answer, 28 April 1987, *69*.

186 HC Home Affairs Committee Report on *Fire Safety and Policing of the Channel Tunnel*, December 1991, para. 14; *Which?*, May 1992, pp. 284–6.

187 Taberner (Eurotunnel)-Legrand, 8 April 1991, DTp file CHT3/1/54 Pt. 3; *Financial Times*, 9 April 1991, p. 1; *Guardian*, 2 May 1991, p. 12.

188 Eurotunnel, Letter to shareholders, 7 October 1991, cit. in *Times*, 8 October 1991, p. 22; *Independent*, 9 October 1991, p. 26.

189 Price replaced Jacques Thibonnier as MD.

190 Burgess-Henes and Martin, 5 September 1991, enclosing TML, 'Parameters for proposed negotiations between ET and TML', 27 August 1991, Whiteley-Barry Potter (Major's PS), 22 October 1991, enclosing DTp, Memo. on 'Channel Tunnel: Current Financial State', n.d., DTp file CHT6/1/71 Pt. 1.

191 Potter-Major, 25 October 1991, Prime Minister (Major)'s Channel Tunnel Papers, Pt. 9.

192 Morton-Henes (IGC), 24 June 1991, FCO file MDY178/15/19.
193 Henes-Rifkind's PS, 16 October 1991, DTp file CHT6/1/71 Pt. 1; Whiteley-Potter, 22 October 1991, cit. On TML's Paris press conference see Guy Milton (British Embassy, Paris), teleletter to FCO, 24 October 1991, Peter Costain (CE, Costain Group)-Rifkind, 1 November 1991, CHT6/1/71 Pt. 1; *Financial Times*, 24 October 1991, p. 23.
194 Potter-Major, 25 October 1991, cit.
195 Morton-Major, 21 October 1991, Prime Minister's Channel Tunnel Papers, Pt. 9; Major, annotation, 25 October 1991, on Potter-Major, cit. There was more to the refusal than mere pique, of course. A meeting might have encouraged Morton to expect some form of public sector support.
196 *Independent*, 25 October 1991, p. 22; Henes-Rifkind's PS, 11 November 1991, Costain-Freeman, 14 November 1991, DTp file CHT6/1/71 Pt. 1. See also Anderson and Roskrow, *Channel Tunnel Story*, p. 165ff.
197 Panel Decision, 26 March 1992, DTp file CHT6/1/71 Pt. 2.
198 Burgess-Simon Sargent (Asst Sec, PE Group, Treasury), 17 July 1992, DTp file CHT-A9/1 Pt. 2. Funding margin = difference between funds available and projected cash requirement; cover ratio = test of Eurotunnel's ability to repay debt within a given period of time.
199 Burgess-Michael Helston (DTp), 27 March 1992, Eurotunnel, News Release, 30 March 1992, DTp file CHT6/1/71 Pt. 1.
200 Morton and Bénard, Letter to Eurotunnel shareholders, 11 May 1992, in DTp file CHT3/1/46 Pt. 5.
201 Morton-Freeman, 18 May 1992, ibid.
202 MacGregor-Major, n.d. [received 29 May 1992], Prime Minister's Channel Tunnel papers, Pt. 9. The implications of a withdrawal by the banks were examined seriously within the DTp: cf. Burgess-Patrick Brown (Permanent Sec, DTp)'s PS, 18 June 1992, DTp file CHT-A9/1 Pt. 2.
203 Like Thatcher, Major made no mention of the Tunnel in his memoirs: John Major, *The Autobiography* (1999).
204 Sue Lewis (PE2, Treasury)-Sargent and Lamont, 5 June 1992, Lamont-Major, 8 June 1992, Treasury file PE TSS/H/11/5 Pt. E.
205 Julie Osborne (Patrick Brown's PS)-Montagu, 24 June 1992, Morton-Joe Dwyer (CEO, George Wimpey), 29 June 1992, Pen Kent (BOE), Note for Record, 31 July 1992, DTp file CHT–A9/1 Pt. 2.
206 Sargent-Robson and Sargent-Lamont, both 10 July 1992, Treasury file PE TSS/H/11/5 Pt. F. The EIB was also experiencing difficulties with its investment in Canary Wharf: Robson, Note for the Record, 23 April 1992, ibid. Pt. D.
207 Henes-Rowlands, 3 August, and reply, 18 August 1992, DTp file CHT-A9/1 Pt. 2. Rowlands found the idea 'quite crazy'.
208 Burgess-Sargent, 17 July 1992, ibid.
209 See, e.g. Morton and Bénard-Dwyer and Jean-Paul Parayre (Dumez), 1 September, reply, 3 September 1992, and ff., DTp file CHT6/1/71 Pt. 1.
210 Burgess-Sargent, 17 July 1992, cit.; Burgess-Freeman, 24 August 1992, DTp file CHT-A9/1 Pt. 2.
211 Humphrey-Patrick Brown, 25 August 1992, ibid.; Freeman-MacGregor, 26 April 1993, DTp file R39/7/5 Pt. 1; Coby-Francis, 16 September 1992, Prime Minister's Channel Tunnel papers, Pt. 9.
212 Patrick Brown-Coby, 14 August 1992, ibid.; Helston-Burgess, 26 August 1992, CHT6/1/25 Pt. 32; *Times*, 5 September 1992, p. 18. Freeman visited the Japanese Finance Ministry on 2 October: Mark Lennox-Boyd (PUSS for Foreign & Commonwealth Affairs), Tokyo telegram No. 691 to FCO, 2 October 1992, FCO file MDY178/11/92.

213 Rosling-Sarah Hogg (Head of Policy Unit, No. 10), 7 September 1992, Prime Minister's Channel Tunnel papers, Pt. 9; Sargent-Lamont, 4 September 1992, Treasury file PE TSS/H/11/5 Pt. G.
214 Eurotunnel News Release, 30 September 1992, DTp file CHT6/1/71 Pt. 1; Burgess-Freeman, 30 September 1992, Douglas Hurd (Foreign Secretary), FCO telegram No. 626 to Paris, 19 April 1993, ibid. Pt. 2.
215 *Financial Times*, 22 January 1993, p. 16; *Times*, 25 January 1993, p. 32.
216 ICC Decision, 25 March 1993, DTp file CHT6/1/71 Pt. 2; Morton-MacGregor, 19 April 1993, R39/7/5 Pt. 1.
217 *Financial Times*, 2 March 1993, p. 5, 22 April 1993, p. 33; *Times*, 31 March 1993, p. 21, 20 April 1993, p. 29. The dispute was not settled until December 1993: *Financial Times*, 25 November 1993, p. 24, 14 December 1993, pp. 18, 25.
218 Burgess-MacGregor, 19 April 1993, DTp file CHT6/1/71 Pt. 2; *Independent*, 6 October 1992, p. 23; *Times*, 31 March 1993, p. 21, 20 April 1993, p. 25.
219 See Coby-Henes and Henes-Burgess, both 15 July 1993, DTp file CHT6/1/71 Pt. 2; Interview with Kent, 2005. An EIB proposal for joint Anglo-French mediators was not pursued.
220 Coby-Russell Sunderland (Dep Sec, DTp), 27 July 1993, Morton-MacGregor, 29 July 1993, John Kingman (PE2, Treasury)-Lewis, 2 August 1993, DTp file CHT-A9/18 Pt. 1; Agent Banks-Eurotunnel Finance Ltd., 27 August 1993, CHT9/0/3 Pt. 6.
221 Bénard (France Manche) and Morton (CTG)-Ministers, 8 September 1992, DTp file CHT3/1/66 Pt. 2. SOLAS 90 = the International Maritime Organisation's 1990 standard for passenger ships; Euroscan = security scanning technology for vehicle inspections. Morton referred publicly to the claims in a statement on 5 October: *Independent*, 6 October 1992, p. 23.
222 Martin-Henes, 21 August 1990, DTp file CHT6/1/71 Pt. 1.
223 Burgess-Robin Bellis (Asst Treasury Solicitor), 4 March 1991, enclosing Lyall-Henderson, 16 January 1986, DTp file CHT3/1/66 Pt. 1.
224 Julian Jones (DTp)-Henes and Burgess, 25 October 1989, ibid.
225 Osmotherly-Rifkind's PS, 22 May 1991, ibid.
226 Morton-Rifkind, Morton-Patrick Brown, Morton-Henes, 27 November 1991, Bénard-Legrand, 28 November 1991, ibid.; IGC Minutes, 17 December 1991, DTp file CHT3/1/93 Pt. 2.
227 Bénard and Morton-Reid II and Fournier, 23 December 1991, DTp file R39/2/45 Pt. 2. The latter complaint originated in Rifkind's remarks to the party conference in Blackpool (above, p. 343), and a follow-up letter, published in the *Times* on 6 November 1991, p. 17. Rifkind revealed that his assertion that the existing infrastructure could cope with increasing traffic until *c.*2005 was derived from British Rail's report of April 1991. However, the report had not been so precise. See Morton-Freeman, 23 October 1991, CHT6/1/76 Pt. 2.
228 Legrand-Bénard, 17 January 1992, Henes-Morton, 22 January 1992, DTp file CHT3/1/66 Pt. 2; Henes-Burgess, 20 December 1991, CHT6/1/76 Pt. 2.
229 Reid II-Bénard and Morton, 6 February 1992, DTp file R39/2/45 Pt. 2.
230 Letter to Eurotunnel shareholders, 11 May 1992, cit.; Rosling-Hogg, 18 June 1992, Prime Minister's Channel Tunnel papers, Pt. 9; Helston-Henes, 22 June 1992, DTp file CHT6/1/76 Pt. 2.
231 Burgess-MacGregor, 11 September 1992, Bellis-Burgess, 15 September 1992, Morton-Freeman, 22 October 1992, Burgess-MacGregor, 17 December 1992, Burgess-Freeman and MacGregor, 21 January and 11 February 1993, DTp file CHT3/1/66 Pt. 2; Henes-Patrick Brown, 22 September 1992, R39/2/6 Pt. 15.
232 MacGregor-Morton, 16 February 1993, Bianco-Bénard (draft), DTp file CHT3/1/66 Pt. 2. The two Ministers conceded that the Governments would fund the testing of security equipment (Euroscan).

233 E.g. MacGregor-Morton, 5 March 1993, DTp file CHT6/1/76 Pt. 4.
234 Rowlands-Fawcett, 18 February 1993, Elizabeth Whatmore (DTp)-Fawcett and MacGregor, 20 April 1993, Freeman-MacGregor, 26 April 1993, DTp file R39/7/5 Pt. 1; Henes-Mike Thomas (Legal Adviser), 27 May 1993, CHT-A9/18 Pt. 1.
235 DTp, 'Briefing for Meeting with M. Bianco', 4 September 1992, DTp file CHT6/1/25 Pt. 32.
236 Burgess-MacGregor, 12 May 1993, Burgess-Sargent, 21 May 1993, DTp file CHT6/1/76 Pt. 4.
237 Colin Comery (Nat West, for Agent Banks)-Kent, 8 June 1993, DTp file CHT6/1/71 Pt. 2. The thinking here was that the banking syndicate would advance £200m., the EIB £200m., and the Governments £200m., leaving Eurotunnel to raise £500m. via a rights issue.
238 Morton-Reid II, and Eurotunnel News Release, both 20 August 1993, DTp file R39/7/5 Pt. 1.
239 Bénard and Morton, 'Memorandum aux Gouvernements', 16 June 1993, Burgess-Freeman and MacGregor, 30 June 1993, DTp file CHT6/1/76 Pt. 5; Helston-Bellis, 30 June 1993, CHT-A9/18 Pt. 1.
240 Morton-MacGregor, 14 and 29 July 1993, ibid.
241 Henes-Burgess, 15 July 1993, DTp file CHT6/1/71 Pt. 2.
242 Coby-Sunderland, 27 July 1993, cit.; Sunderland-Burgess, 29 July 1993, Coby-Sunderland, 30 July 1993, N.R.J. Abbott (British Embassy, Paris), Note on 'Franco-British Summit: Transport', 30 July 1993, Burgess-MacGregor, 6 August 1993, Burgess-Lewis, 9 August 1993, DTp file CHT-A9/18 Pt. 1.
243 Cf. Kingman-Lewis, 2 August 1993, cit.; Rosling, Note for the Record, 5 August 1993, Prime Minister's Channel Tunnel papers, Pt. 10.
244 Patrick Brown-Burgess, 25 August 1993, DTp file CHT-A9/18 Pt. 1.
245 Burgess-Brown, 13 September 1993, Mark Lambirth (Asst Sec, FTI, DTp)-Burgess, 25 August 1993, ibid.; Kingman-Lewis, 10 August 1993, PE TRA/J/2/1 Pt. A.
246 Portillo (Chief Secretary, Treasury)-MacGregor, 21 September 1993, Coby-Henes, 30 September 1993, ibid.; Peter Spiceley (Asst Head, AMD, FCO)-Burgess, 14 October 1993, FCO file MDY178/22/93.
247 Henes-Burgess, 13 September 1993, Coby-Henes, 30 September 1993, Morton-MacGregor, 4 October 1993, Burgess-MacGregor, 7 October 1993, DTp file CHT-A9/18 Pt. 1.
248 Burgess-MacGregor, 15 October 1993, Henes-MacGregor, 21 September 1993, Coby-Henes, 19 October 1993, Kent-Robson, 20 October 1993, Henes-Lambirth, 21 October 1993, ibid.; Morton-Patrick Brown, 21 April 1992, DTp file CHT6/1/76 Pt. 2; Coby-Francis, 26 November 1993, Prime Minister's Channel Tunnel papers, Pt. 10. The EIB was only prepared to offer funding in the form of Railway Advance Payment bonds, giving the lender priority over rail revenues: Agent Banks-Eurotunnel, 4 November 1993, CHT-A9/18 Pt. 2.
249 Later corrected to £228m.: Martin Anderson (Hill Samuel)-Henes, 30 November 1993, ibid. Pt. 3.
250 Bénard-Bosson, 5 November 1993, enclosing Bénard-Edouard Balladur (French Prime Minister), 5 November 1993 and 'Demande d'Eurotunnel aux Gouvernements Francais et Britannique Novembre 1993', 4 November 1993 [English version, 9 November 1993], ibid. Pt. 2. Document 3 gave details of the legal basis for the compensation claim.
251 MacGregor-Clarke, 22 October 1993, and reply, 3 November 1993, ibid. Research support of £6m. for security was agreed by the two countries in November: Coby-Henes, 30 November 1993, ibid. Pt. 3. On JEXIM see Morton-Sunderland and Huw Evans (Dep Sec, Overseas Finance, Treasury), 7 October 1993, Morton-HMG,

12 October 1993, ibid. Pt. 1; Morton-Lamont, 23 April 1993, Phil Wynn Owen (Private Secretary to Sir Terence Burns, Treasury Permanent Sec)-Clarke, 15 October 1993, Wynn Owen-John Kirby (Minister (Financial), British Embassy, Tokyo), n.d., Treasury file PE TRA/J/2/1 Pt. A; Communication from Ratzer, 2005.

252 Cf. Spiceley-Bone and Lennox-Boyd's PS, 22 October 1993, MRY178/22/93; Douglas Gurr (Brown's PS)-Henes and Burgess, 29 November 1993, Coby-Henes, 30 November 1993, DTp file CHT-A9/18 Pt. 3; *Evening Standard* and *Le Quotidien de Paris*, both 15 November 1993; *Le Monde*, 16 November 1993, p. 22.

253 Gurr-Henes, 21 December 1993, Eurotunnel and DTp News Releases, 29 December 1993, Copy of Agreement, signed on 29 December 1993, DTp file CHT9/0/18 Pt. 5; Ivan Wilson (U-Sec, PE, Treasury)-Clarke, 21 December 1993, Treasury file PE TRA/J/2/1 Pt. C; MacGregor-Clarke, 23 December 1993, Prime Minister's Channel Tunnel papers, Pt. 10. The Concession Agreement was formally amended on 29 June 1994 and published as Cm.2776 on 15 March 1995. It followed an earlier, minor amendment of 9 May 1988 (Cm.406).

254 Brown-MacGregor, 10 November 1993, DTp file CHT-A9/18 Pt. 2; Wilson-Wynn Owen, 16 December 1993, ibid. Pt. 4.

255 Henes-Michel Combes (French Transport Ministry), 2 December 1993, ibid. Pt. 2; Henes-Brown, 16 November 1993, ibid. Pt. 3; Gurr-Henes *et al.*, 2 December 1993, MacGregor-Clarke correspondence, 3–15 December 1993, Henes-Combes, 9 December 1993, ibid. Pt. 4.

256 Philip Wood (U-Sec, Rlys 2, DTp)-Henes, 14 December 1993, Fawcett-Henes, 15 December 1993, ibid. Pt. 4; Wynn Owen-Clarke, 2 November 1993, Rutnam-Wynn Owen, 12 November 1993, Treasury file PE TRA/J/2/1 Pts. B-C.

257 Cf. Clarke-MacGregor, 13 December 1993, DTp file CHT-A9/18 Pt. 4.

258 Rutnam-Henes, 16 November 1993, ibid. Pt. 3; Anderson-Henes, 30 November 1993, cit.

259 Lambirth-Burgess, 5 October 1993, DTp file CHT-A/9/18 Pt. 1; Burchell-Henes, 23 November 1993, ibid. Pt. 3.

260 *Financial Times*, 1 January 1994, p. xix.

261 Eurotunnel undertook to pay £70–85m. (£50–60m. in 1985 prices): Press Release, 5 April 1994.

262 The debt-equity ratio was *c.*5.0 for Equity 1–3, 3.7 for 'Equity 4' in November 1990 and *c.*1.0 for 'Equity 5' in May 1994. Cf. Corbett, 'Managing the Financial Risk', p. 2.

263 Eurotunnel, Rights Issue, May 1994, pp. 8, 10–11, 33–5, 79–83; Burgess-Brian Mawhinney (SoS for Transport), 3 August 1994, DTp file CHT6/1/25 Pt. 37.

264 Chazot had been with Alcatel and ADIA–France. Eurotunnel, Rights Issue, May 1994, pp. 7, 17.

265 *Times*, 10 December 1993, p. 29. See also Morton's obituaries, e.g. *Independent*, 4 September 2004, p. 48.

12 THE CHANNEL TUNNEL: POSTSCRIPT, 1994–2005

1 See Fetherston, *Chunnel*, pp. 371–9.

2 Nicholas Faith, *Sunday Independent*, 27 February 1994, p. 8; Simon Jenkins, *Times*, 28 February 1994, p. 14.

3 See FCO file MDT178/1/94 Pts. A-B, and Prime Minister's Channel Tunnel papers, Pt. 11.

4 IGC Minutes, 30 January 1989, DTp file CHT3/1/93 Pt. 1.

5 *Observer*, 8 May 1994, p. 10, *Le Figaro*, 6 May 1994, and see also *Evening Standard*, 6 May 1994, p. 7; *Times*, 7 May 1994, pp. 1, 3; *Independent*, 7 May 1994, p. 2.

6 MdO, Progress Report Nos.32–7, 30 June 1994–30 September 1995; *Financial Times*, 16 December 1994, p. 10; *Lloyd's List*, 30 September 1995, p. 10; information from Brian Restall and John Noulton of Eurotunnel.
7 Morton-Sir George Young (SoS for Transport), 14 September 1994 and 13 March 1995, Wynn Owen-Clarke, 18 April 1995, Treasury file PE TRA/J/2/1 Pt. D; Jason Myer (Patrick Brown's APS)-Mark Kelly (Sir Robin Butler's APS), 6 September 1994, DTp file CHT6/1/25 Pt. 37.
8 Eurotunnel Announcement, 10 April 1995, Robson-Saunders and Wynn Owen, 5 June 1995, Treasury file PE TRA/J/2/1 Pt. D; Wynn Owen-Clarke, 18 April 1995, cit.; Mary Francis (Major's PS)-Una O'Brien (Mawhinney's PS), 12 June 1995, Prime Minister's Channel Tunnel papers, Pt. 12.
9 *Financial Times*, 1 January 1994, p. xix, 16 September 2004, p. 25. Alternative calculations of cost overruns for Suez (× 20), Panama (× 3) and Concorde (× 12) are given by Bent Flyvbjerg, Nils Bruzelius and Werner Rothengatter, *Megaprojects and Risk: An Anatomy of Ambition* (Cambridge, 2003), p. 19.
10 The Channel Tunnel overrun was put at 80%. Flyvbjerg *et al.*, *Megaprojects and Risk*, p. 14.
11 Ed Morrow *et al.*, *Understanding the Outcomes of Megaprojects: A Quantitative Analysis of Very Large Civil Projects* (The Rand Corporation, Santa Monica, CA, March 1988), pp. v, 7, 18, 30–2, 45–6, referred to in Winch, Le Groupe Bagnolet paper, 1996, p. 24. The study compared outturn costs (*excluding* commissioning and start-up costs) with cost estimates at the 'detailed engineering stage'.
12 A detailed analysis of the Tunnel's impact on Kent is provided by Alan Hay, Kate Meredith and Roger Vickerman, 'The Impact of the Channel Tunnel on Kent and Relationships with Nord-Pas de Calais', report commissioned by Eurotunnel and Kent County Council, Centre for European, Regional and Transport Economics, University of Kent, June 2004.
13 Direct services to Paris Disneyland were also introduced, in June 1996. Trial connecting services from the regions proved a failure, May 1995–January 1997, and when the leasing arrangement for the sleeper trains was terminated in 1998, the DTp had to put up £109.5 m. in termination costs. The lack of regional services was lamented in the HC SC on Environment, Transport and Regional Affairs, *Report on Regional Eurostar Services*, January 1999, P.P.1998–9, xxvi, HC89.
14 Cf. *Guardian*, 3 September 2001, p. 1.
15 The economist Stefan Szymanski favours 12.5 tonnes: see '*Nostrae Culpae*: Forecasts and out-turns of cross channel competition between the ferries and the tunnel', in Bill Bradshaw and Helen Lawton Smith (eds.), *Privatization and Deregulation of Transport*, (Basingstoke, 2000), p. 413. On this basis, shuttle freight traffic in 2003 was 16.1 m tonnes, 8% higher than the 1994 forecast.
16 Hay, Meredith and Vickerman, 'Impact of the Channel Tunnel', 2004, p. 28.
17 E.g. Guillaume Pepy (Chairman, Eurostar), reported in *Sunday Times*, 28 September 2003, p. 30.
18 Cf. John Kay, Alan Manning and Stefan Szymanski, 'The Economic Consequences of the Channel Tunnel', *Economic Policy*, 8 (1989), 211–34.
19 Stefan Szymanski, '*Nostrae Culpae*', pp. 413–14, 420–3.
20 Flyvbjerg *et al.*, *Megaprojects and Risk*, pp. 22–5, 31–4.
21 My thanks to Roger Vickerman for this point.
22 Interview with Heslop, 2004; Hay, Meredith and Vickerman, 'Impact of the Channel Tunnel', pp. 23–4, 32–3.
23 MMC, *The Peninsular and Oriental Steam Navigation Company and Stena Line AB: A report on the proposed merger* (November 1997), para. 2.21.
24 *Travel Trends 2002* (2003), Tables 1.07–8; *Cross Channel Passenger Traffic*, 1997 edn.

25 Hay, Meredith and Vickerman, 'Impact of the Channel Tunnel', pp. 23–5; BBC News, 2 April 2004 [www.bbc.co.uk].
26 See Carmen Li and Bob Wearing, 'The Financing and Financial Results of Eurotunnel: Retrospect and Prospect', University of Essex Accounting Dept. WP No. 00/13, November 2000, Table 2.
27 *Times*, 10 May 2000, p. 25, *Financial Times*, 10 May 2000, p. 25; Eurotunnel News Release, 17 May 2000; *Daily Telegraph*, 18 March 2003, p. 25; *Observer: Business*, 11 April 2004, p. 3, 5 December 2004, p. 2.
28 *Financial Times*, 27 April 2005, p. 22; *Independent*, 27 April 2005, p. 58.
29 *Independent*, 11 June 2005, p. 44; *Guardian*, 18 June 2005, p. 28; *Financial Times*, 18–19 June 2005, pp. M1–2; *Observer Business*, 19 June 2005, p. 1.
30 Wynn Owen-Robson and J.P. McIntyre (EC Divn, Treasury), 5 September 1995, Clarke, 2 September 1995, Treasury file PE TRA/J/2/1 Pt. D; *Financial Times*, 15 September 1995, pp. 16, 18.
31 *Evening Standard*, 6 October 1995, p. 33.
32 Patrick Ponsolle (ET Co-Chairman)-Bernard Pons, 11 September 1995 and Eurotunnel: General Technical Review, September 1995 (French and English versions), Morton-Patrick Brown, 27 September 1995, DTp file CHT3/1/66 Pt. 3; Peter Moss (Head of CT Divn, DTp)- Graham Boiling (Home Office), 9 October 1995, ibid. Pt. 4; R39/7/5 Pts. 5–6.
33 Morton-Sir George Young (SoS for Transport), 4 October 1995, ibid. Pt. 4 and see also CHT9/0/18 Pt. 6 and R39/7/5 Pt. 6.
34 Ponsolle-Pons, 11 September 1995, cit.
35 Eurotunnel, Letter to shareholders, 12 February 1996, in DTp file CHT9/0/18 Pt. 7; *Le Monde*, 26 January 1996, p. 17, *Les Echos*, 1 April 1996, and *La Vie Française*, 13–19 April 1996, in CHT3/1/66 Pts. 6 and 7.
36 Moss-Grimsey, 15 February 1996, CHT3/1/66 Pt. 6.
37 ICC International Court of Arbitration, Award Sentence, 31 October 1995, DTp file R39/7/4 Pt. 5; *Times*, 1 November 1995, p. 25. Two issues were left outstanding: loss from insufficiency of rolling stock, and the adequacy of British infrastructure, 1994–5. Eurotunnel's grievances about the Usage Contract and privatisation were also rejected by the Tribunal de Commerce in May 1996: Ordonnance, 29 May 1996, DTp file CHT9/0/18 Pt. 8. Outstanding claims were abandoned in October 1996: Palmer-Malcolm Southgate (Dep MD, Eurostar (UK)), 23 October 1996, DTp file R39/7/4 Pt. 6.
38 Grimsey-Young, 10 October and 1 November 1995, Young-Morton, 13 October, 6 November and 4 December 1995, Morton-Young, 27 October 1995, DTp file CHT9/0/18 Pt. 6, and see also CHT3/1/66 Pts. 4–5; Morton-Major, 27 October 1995 and reply, 14 November 1995, Prime Minister's Channel Tunnel papers, Pt. 12.
39 Pons-Ponsolle, 22 December 1995, DTp file CHT3/1/66 Pt. 6.
40 Eurotunnel, Letter to shareholders, February 1996, cit.; Morton-Young, 22 December 1995, 15 and 17 January 1996, DTp file CHT9/0/18 Pts. 5–6. For rebuttals see Young-Morton, 12 January and 17 May 1996, John Palmer (BRB)-Grimsey, 16 January 1996, Patrick Brown-Morton, 11 March 1996, ibid. Pts. 6–8; Grimsey-Brown, n.d., papers in CHT3/1/66 Pts 7–8 and R39/7/5 Pt. 7.
41 *Observer: Business*, 20 June 1999, p. 2; Young-Lord Tugendhat (Chairman, Abbey National), 6 February 1996, DTp file CHT9/0/18 Pt. 7; John Noulton (Director of Public Affairs, Eurotunnel)-Grimsey, 25 January 1996, R39/7/5 Pt. 7; Robin Kealy (Head of AMD, FCO)-Peter Ricketts (British Embassy, Paris), 30 January 1996, CHT 3/1/66 Pt. 6; Lewis Atter (Young's PS)-Moira Wallace (Major's PS), 4 June 1996, Lord Wakeham-Major, 14 May and 29 September 1996, Prime Minister's Channel Tunnel papers, Pt. 12.

42 *Financial Times*, 16 May 1996, p. 24; Ricketts-Kealy, 18 April 1996, John Holmes (Major's PS)-William Ehrman (PS to Malcolm Rifkind (Foreign Secretary)), 15 May 1996, DTp file CHT9/0/18 Pts 7–8.

43 Deborah Phelan (CT Divn, DTp)-Roy Griffins (Head of Rail Link Divn, DTp), 22 April 1996, ibid. Pt. 7; Brown-Montagu, 11 July 1996, ibid. Pt. 9; Griffins, File Note on 'Eurotunnel', 27 June 1996, Mark Gibson (Heseltine's PPS)-Atter, 16 July 1996, Prime Minister's Channel Tunnel papers, Pt. 12.

44 These included a reduction in the tolls paid by RfD: Griffins-Moss, 30 April 1996, DTp file CHT9/0/18 Pt. 7; Philip Cox (Rlys Economics, DTp)-Moss, 20 May 1996, Robert Linnard (Asst Sec, DTp)-Montagu, 18 June 1996, Pt. 8; Cox-Linnard, 5 July 1996, Pt. 9.

45 Eurotunnel News Release, 24 July 1996, ibid. Pt. 10. Morton and Bénard retired from the Board in October, Ponsolle became Executive Chairman, and Chazot Group MD: News Release, 14 October 1996, Pt. 12.

46 Eurotunnel News Releases, 2 and 7 October 1996, ibid. Pts 11–12. The financial restructuring prospectus was published in May 1997: Eurotunnel, Prospectus, 29 May 1997.

47 Morton-Major, 14 October 1996, Prime Minister's Channel Tunnel papers, Pt. 13; Ponsolle-Juppé, 14 October 1996, DTp file CHT9/0/18 Pt.12. Shareholders were to be given the opportunity to build their stake up to 55% if an extension were granted. Eurotunnel News Release, 7 October 1996, cit. p. 7.

48 Michael Jay (British Ambassador, Paris), Paris telegram No. 1299 to FCO, 2 October 1996, Keith Shannon (2nd Sec, Technology, British Embassy, Paris), 'Eurotunnel: Record of Meeting between British and French officials, Paris, 16 October 1996', 18 October 1996, Atter-Wallace, 21 October 1996, Wallace-Major, 25 October 1996, Prime Minister's Channel Tunnel papers, Pt. 13. On press support for resistance see *Economist*, 12 October 1996, pp. 22–3, 99, 102.

49 Juppé-Major, 30 October 1996, Montagu-Young, 1 November 1996, Young-Major, 4 November 1996, Prime Minister's Channel Tunnel papers, Pt. 13; Holmes-Ehrman, 11 November 1996, Prime Minister's file on France: Relations, Pt. 20.

50 Lord Alexander (Chairman, NatWest)-Major, 30 October 1996, Prime Minister's Channel Tunnel papers, Pt. 13.

51 Atter-Wallace, 13 November 1996 and 18 February 1997, ibid.

52 Wakeham-Major, 3 December 1996, Atter-Wallace, 21 January and 18 February 1997, Young-Heseltine (Deputy PM), 1 January 1997, 'Meeting between the UK and French Governments and Eurotunnel: Wednesday 26 February 1997', ibid.

53 E.g. Rifkind-Major, 4 November 1996, Norman Blackwell and Jonathan Rees (No. 10 Policy Unit)-Wallace, 5 November 1996, ibid.; Schroders, advice, November 1996, DTp file CHT9/0/18 Pt. 13.

54 Note by Officials on 'Eurotunnel: Possible Extension to the Concession', 30 May 1997, John Prescott (SoS for Environment, Transport and Regions and Dep PM)-Tony Blair (PM), 9 June 1997, Cabinet Office file on 'Channel Tunnel Rail Link', R14/7 Pt. 4; Holmes (Blair's PPS)-Dominick Chilcott (PS to Robin Cook, Foreign Secretary), 12 June 1997, DTp file CHT9/0/18 Pt. 19.

55 Prescott-Blair, 30 June 1997, Cabinet Office file R14/7 Pt. 4; 'Eurotunnel: Statement by the Governments', 1 July 1997, DTp file CHT9/0/18 Pt. 20; John Prescott (Deputy PM), statement in DETR News Release, 1 July 1997, Pt. 21; *Financial Times*, 2 July 1997, p. 1.

56 Eurotunnel News Release, 10 July 1997, DTp file CHT9/0/18 Pt. 21.

57 Griffins-Montagu *et al.* and Cox-Griffins, 3 December 1996, Ponsolle-Montagu, 11 December 1996, Montagu-Young, 20 December 1996, ibid. Pt. 16; 'Meeting between the UK and French Governments and Eurotunnel on the Channel Tunnel Concession. Tuesday 24 June 1997', ibid. Pt. 20; *Financial Times*, 22 September 1997, p. 1. The suggestion that there be open access for freight operators in France,

and proposals to assist a private-sector freight company (EWS) were scarcely attractive to the new French Transport Minister, the Communist Jean-Claude Gayssot.

58 See DTp file CHT9/0/18 Pts 21–5, and especially DETR and Eurotunnel Press Notices, 19 December 1997, Pt. 25. There were further discussions at an Anglo-French summit on 6–7 November, and in discussions between Blair and Jospin on 18 December: Press Conference, 7 November 1997, Holmes-Chilcott, 10 November 1997, Pt. 23; Holmes-Richard Threlfall (Prescott's PS), 19 December 1997, Pt. 25.

59 NAO, *Report by the Comptroller and Auditor General on the Sale of Railfreight Distribution*, 26 March 1999, P.P.1998–9, xxxxvii, HC280; Committee of Public Accounts, Report on *The Sale of Railfreight Distribution*, 10 November 1999, lxxvi, HC601.

60 Eurotunnel Concession Agreement, 13 February 1998, DTp file CHT9/0/18 Pt. 25; *Parl. Deb. (Lords)*, 5th ser. (Session 1997–8), Vol. 587, 16 March 1998, Baroness Hyman, Written Answer to Lord Berkeley, 16 March 1998, w114–15.

61 DETR documentation for Anglo-French Summit, 3–4 December 1998, DTp file CHT6/1/9 Pt. 3, and see CHT9/0/18 Pt. 26; Dep PM and SoS for the Environment, Transport and the Regions, *The Channel Fixed Link: Amendment No. 3 to Concession Agreement, dated as of 29 March 1999*, May 1999, P.P.1998–9, cxxi, Cm.4350.

62 *Financial Times*, 20 December 1997, p. 18; Li and Wearing, working paper on 'Financing', cit.

63 Consortium members included: Eurorail-BICC, GEC, HSBC, NatWest and Trafalgar House; Green Arrow-Hochtief, Costain, Nishimatsu and Siemens; London & Continental-Bechtel, Warburg, Blue Circle (later replaced by Virgin) and London Electricity; Union Link-AEG, Holzmann, Mowlem and Taylor Woodrow. *Financial Times*, 12 May 1995, p. 10; Treasury file PE TSS/H/11/7, *passim*, and in particular Grimsey-MacGregor, 24 May 1994, Pt. J.

64 Project History, in www.dft.gov.uk; DTp, CTRL announcement, 31 August 1994, DTp file R39/2/45 Pt. 3; Brian Mawhinney (SoS for Transport), Written Answer, 3 July 1995, *Parl. Deb. (Commons)*, 6th ser. (Session 1994–5), Vol. 263 Pt. 2, w61–2.

65 Minority partners were Ove Arup and Halcrow, who with Systra and Bechtel formed Rail Link Engineering, the project managers. Virgin sold its stake in October 1998: www.dft.gov.uk.

66 Young (SoS for Transport), Statement, 29 February 1996, *Parl. Deb. (Commons)*, 6th ser. (Session 1995–6), Vol. 272, *c.*999–1001; Comptroller and Auditor General (NAO), Report on *Channel Tunnel Rail Link*, 28 March 2001, P.P.2000–1, xliii, HC302.

67 Clare Short (MP for Birmingham Ladywood), ibid. *c.*1002. EU support was put at £100 m. to 1999.

68 HC SC on the Channel Tunnel Rail Link, *Special Report and Minutes of Proceedings*, 14 February 1996, P.P.1995–6, xxxii, HC204, paras 23–4; *MOE*, 1995–6, P.P.1994–5, lxxi–ii, HC728i–lxi, 1995–6, xxxii, HC204i–x.

69 PCA (Ombudsman), *The Channel Tunnel Rail Link and Blight: Investigation of complaints against the Department of Transport*, 8 February 1995, P.P.1994–5, xxix, HC193; Sir Anthony Durrant, Chairman of SC on CTRL Bill, statement, 31 January 1996, *MOE*, HC204i-x, pp. 238–40; SC on the PCA, Report on *The Channel Tunnel Rail Link and Exceptional Hardship*, 19 July 1995, P.P.1994–5, xxxvi, HC270, and Report on *Government Proposals for Redress*, 20 March 1997, PP.1996–7, xli, HC453.

70 Prescott-Gordon Brown (Chancellor), 25 July 1997, Cabinet Office file R14/7 Pt. 5, and see also Treasury file PE TSS/H/87/3 Pt. A.

71 The initial set of traffic forecasts in 1995 envisaged 4.8–5.0 m. passengers in 1995/6, 9.0–9.5 m. in 1996/7, and 12.5 m. in 1997/8, rising to 30 m. + by 2018. They were scaled down sharply in September 1997, to 6.3 m. in 1997 and 10.5 m. in 2002; actual numbers, reduced by the effects of the Tunnel fire, were 5.1 m. in 1996/7 [4.9 m., 1996, 6.0 m., 1997]. See NAO, Report on *CTRL*, March 2001, cit., paras 1.11, 1.15;

LCR forecasts, 1995, in Treasury file PE TSS/H/11/8 Pt. G; 1997, in Philip Cox (DETR)-Mike Fuhr (DETR), 30 October 1997, PE TSS/H/87/3 Pt. B.

72 Prescott-Brown, 4 December 1997, ibid. Pt. 6.

73 In 1997 prices: £1.294bn + £2.014bn. NAO, Report on *CTRL*, March 2001, cit., para. 1.5 and Figure 3.

74 Prescott-Blair, 14 January 1998, Prime Minister (Blair)'s Rail Policy papers, Pt. 1; Prescott, statement, 28 January 1998, *Parl. Deb. (Commons)*, 6th ser. (Session 1997–8), Vol. 305, *c.*461–3.

75 DETR News Release, 3 June 1998, in Treasury file PEP/AE/3 Pt. 6.

76 The other members of IRR Ltd. were SNCF, SNCB and British Airways, the latter touting the prospect of a Heathrow–Paris service.

77 The additional support was not added to the PSBR on the grounds that the risk was small.

78 Later stated to be 35%.

79 NAO, Report on *CTRL*, March 2001, cit. and esp. Pt. 3. See also Prescott-Blair, 22 May 1998, Cabinet Office file R14/7 Pt. 5; Prescott, statement, 3 June 1998, *Parl. Deb. (Commons)*, 6th ser. (Session 1997–8), Vol. 313, *c.*367–70; *Guardian*, 4 June 1998, p. 27; HC Committee of Public Accounts, Report on *The Channel Tunnel Rail Link*, 21 March 2002, P.P.2001–2, lxxi, HC630, paras 4–5.

80 *Financial Times*, 6 June 1998, p. 11; NAO, Report on *CTRL*, March 2001, cit.; PAC, Report on *CTRL*, March 2002, cit.; 'CTRL and Eurostar: Government Cash Outflow' projections, 3 June 1998, Cabinet Office file R14/7 Pt. 5.

81 *Financial Times*, 11 February 1999, p. 30; *Modern Railways*, October 1999, p. 742; LCR Press Release, 3 April 2001; *M2 Communications Presswire*, 3 April 2001; *Times*, 4 April 2001, p. 25.

82 *Guardian*, 8 October 2001, p. 10; *Daily Telegraph*, 19 September 2002, p. 38; *Daily Star*, 4 October 2002, p. 47.

83 Cf. Rupert Bruce, 'A Tough Start for a U.K. Initiative', *Infrastructure Finance* (August–September 1995), 49–52; John Hall, 'Private Opportunity, Public Benefit?', *Fiscal Studies*, 19 no. 2 (1998), 121–40; NAO, Report on *CTRL*, March 2001, cit; HC PAC, Report on *CTRL*, March 2002, cit. Cf. also Treasury concern: Rutnam-Wynn Owen and Clarke, 6 January 1995, Treasury file TRA/J/17/1 Pt. A.

84 Hay, Meredith and Vickerman, 'Impact of the Channel Tunnel', 2004, pp. 46–65.

85 Malcolm Binks (Merrill Lynch Capital Markets, New York)-Al and Frank Davidson, 18 June 1986, TSI Archive, carton #13 f67, HBS.

86 Cf. Graham Winch, *Managing Construction Projects: An Information Processing Approach* (Oxford, 2002), pp. 13–15, 68, 402–3; Flyvbjerg *et al.*, *Megaprojects and Risk*, pp. 96–7.

87 European Conference of Ministers of Transport Paper, March 1999, ECMT/CS(99)21, in DTp file CHT6/1/25 Pt. 39.

88 Graham Corbett, in *Project Finance International*, 100 (3 July 1996), 69–71, and 'The Channel Tunnel – Managing the Financial Risk', paper to International Tunnelling Conference, Basel, 3–4 December 1996. See also Winch, *Managing Construction Projects*, p. 14.

89 *Construction News*, 10 March 1988, p. 30.

90 Cf. Sir Christopher Mallaby (British Ambassador, Paris) to Douglas Hurd (Foreign Secretary) on 'The Channel Tunnel', 24 May 1994, FCO file MDT178/3/94.

91 For speculations cf. *Independent*, 9 October 1996, p. 19; Christian Wolmar, in *Daily Mail*, 19 May 2004, p. 12.

INDEX

Achille-Fould, Aymar 139
Adye, Sir John 6
AF66 *see* Anglo-French Report of 1966
AF82 *see* Anglo/French Report of 1982
Agreement No.1 96–7, 101, 129; conclusion of 102–6
Agreement No.2 102, 129–31, 150, 152, 154, 171
Aitken, Jonathan 258, 265, 286–7, 296
Alsthom-Atlantique 244
Amory, Derick Heathcoat 24, 30
Anderson, C.M. 22
Anderson, Joseph 313
Anglo/French Report of 1982 227–8, 231, 236, 246–7
Anglo-French Entente Cordiale 9
Anglo-French report of 1966 60, 62, 146
Arculus, Sir Ronald 326
Argentinean invasion, of Falkland Islands 227
Armand, Louis 19–20, 51, 92
Armstrong, Sir Robert 87, 208, 275–6, 291
Armstrong, Sir William 41
Arnal, Claude 20
Ashford 68, 74, 76–7, 143, 145, 180, 305–6, 308, 323, 327, 336, 344–5, 356–7
ASLEF 132, 222
Asquith, Herbert 10–11
Atkins, Humphrey 221
Atkins, W.S. 289, 310, 344
Attlee, Clement 16
Auberger, Bernard 293–5
Auroux, Jean 250–1, 257, 271–3, 275, 281–2, 384
'Avant Projet' system 348

Badinter, Robert 376
Bagier, Gordon 265
Bailey, Sir Alan 291, 301
Baker, Kenneth 349
Baker, Prof. Arthur 178
Baldwin, Peter 11, 193, 195, 197, 211, 239, 289
Baldwin, Stanley 11
Balfour, Lord 11, 16
Balladur, Edouard 364
Balls, Alastair 178
Balogh, Thomas 64
Bank of England 7, 11, 25, 51, 60, 63, 92, 104, 119, 121, 129, 290–1, 293, 296, 315–18, 321, 354–5, 363, 385
Banking Group 1982–4 238–41; Report 1984 245–8
Banque de l'Union Parisienne 21
Banque Indosuez 239, 292, 294
Banque National de Paris 64, 239, 360
Barber, Anthony 84, 63–4, 66, 74, 88–9, 94, 143, 384
Barber, John 63–4, 66, 74, 89–90, 143, 384
Barron, Bob 187, 195–6, 223
Barron, Sir Donald 240
Basdevant, André 15, 17
BCTC *see* British Channel Tunnel Co.
Beagley, Tom 107
Beaumont, Col. Frederick 5
Bechtel 85, 292, 295, 313, 317, 340, 380–1
Beeching, Dr Richard 34, 71–2
Behr, Peter 292
Belgium 166, 305, 324, 371; railways 143, 154, 306, 325, 329, 373
Bénard, André 288, 291, 294–5, 297, 300, 317, 356–64, 385
Benn, Tony 47, 127, 135, 162, 165
Bennett, John 248
Bérégovoy, Pierre 208
Berger, Louis 289
Bernard, Dallas 80
Berrill, Sir Kenneth 185
Bertrand, Alain 292, 314
Bevin, Ernest 13
Bianco, Jean-Louis 358–9
Biffen, John 219, 231, 279
Billecocq, Pierre 112, 116, 119, 121–5, 129, 131, 194
Blair, Tony 378, 381
Bombardier 350

Bonavia, Michael 72, 74, 78, 133, 141–3, 146–8, 150–2, 156, 166, 168–9, 185
Bonnaud, Laurent 167
Bosson, Bernard 359
Bosworth, Michael 153
Boucher, Marcel 15
Bouygues 267, 274, 289
Bouygues, Francis 261, 292
Bowick, David 152–3, 188–9, 194
Box Hill Tunnel 3
Brabourne, Lord 127
Bradley, Tom 197
Brady, Francis 5
Braibant, Guy 211, 216, 221, 224–7, 235–6, 240, 243, 246, 249–50, 384
Brassey, Thomas 4
BRB *see* British Railways Board
Bridges, Lord 131, 234
Bright, John 4, 7
Brindley, James 2
Britain with Europe, linking of 1; channel tunnel project: abandonment of *see* Channel Tunnel project abandonment, versus bridge 33, channel tunnel company 18, channel tunnel study groups 19–20, 25–6, 42; *see also* Channel Tunnel Study Group, completion of *see* channel tunnel, opening of consortia for 65, economic obstacles 17–18, government attitude towards 21–6, Harrington report, on capital requirement 23, military advantages 17, official opinions French and English 16, 18, 42–3, 45, passenger traffic benefits 24, political obstacles 17–18, project status in 1964 39–45, Scott-Malden report 40–1, stance of United States 20, status of, for period 1964–70, *see* Wilson governments and the tunnel project; and Thatcher government: *see* Thatcher governments and the tunnel project; early proposals 2; free trade concept 4–10; inter war years 10–15, arguments against tunnel 14–15, ferry concept 14, response to, after 10; introduction of railways 3; island based projects 2; tunnel 1, routes of 1, services in 1; two gallery under-river tunnel 2
British Channel Tunnel Co. 91, 111–12, 119, 124, 128–30, 133, 138, 140–1, 167, 171–2, 175, 224
British Rail *see* British Railways Board
British Railways Board 29, 34, 40–1, 46, 53, 61, 79, 71–4, 77, 90, 120, 128, 136, 141–9, 151–8, 160–2, 165, 167–70, 177–78, 181, 184–90, 192–206, 209–10, 212, 216–17, 220, 222–3, 232, 234, 239–43, 246, 256, 258–9, 264, 267, 276, 282, 287, 294, 297–309, 317, 322–346, 348, 354, 356–9, 362, 369, 375–6, 378, 380
British Railways *see* British Railways Board
Brittain, Sir Herbert 22
Brittan, Leon 211–14, 231, 238
Broackes, Sir Nigel 249, 274, 279, 291–2
Broadbent, Richard 232–3
Bromhead, Peter 127, 178, 185
Brown, George 47, 50, 54, 56, 58, 64
Brown, Ian 324–5, 329
Brown, John 323–5
Brown, Patrick 236
Brown & Root 85
Bruckshaw, Professor J.M. 21
Brunel, Marc Isambard 2–3, 364
Brunlees, John 1, 4
Buchan, William 20
Bull, Sir William 11
Bullock, Capt. Malcolm 19
Burke, Richard 189, 194
Buron, Robert 34
Burr, David 173
Burtt, Philip 11
Butler, Rab 40, 43
Butler, Sir Robin 317

Cabinet (British) 16–18, 22–6, 31, 33, 38, 42–3, 46, 54, 56, 58, 60, 62, 64, 77, 80, 83–4, 87–93, 115–37, 139, 149, 153–4, 160–4, 193, 196, 202–4, 207–20, 225, 235, 242, 250–1, 255–7, 268, 271–6, 282, 291, 311, 321–2, 336–7, 343–9, 377
Cabinet Economic Policy Committee 84, 86–8, 93, 95, 101, 107–8, 115–17, 120–1, 149, 153
Cairncross, Sir Alec 140, 175–6, 178, 194, 197, 199–200, 204, 206, 212–13, 227, 231–2; *see also* Cairncross report
Cairncross report 175–85, 231–2; financial returns of the project 181; of passenger and freight traffic 180; rail costs and benefits of UK share 183; tunnel costs and benefits of UK share 182
Calais 1, 4, 33, 74, 166, 197, 216–17, 254, 303, 305, 373
Callaghan, James 47, 50, 53–4, 56, 64, 159, 165, 187, 190, 192
Callou, Roger 101, 106, 133, 163–4
Cambon, Paul 10
Campbell, Ian 155
Campbell, Lord 64
Campbell-Bannerman, Sir Henry 9, 15
Carrington, Lord 220–1, 225–6
Carvalho, Harold 19
Castle, Barbara 53–4, 56, 58, 59, 62–4, 71, 84, 92, 135, 137, 165, 280
Cavaillé, Marcel 139–40, 162, 165
CE *see* Channel Expressway
Chaban-Delmas, Jacques 19
Chadeau, André 216
Chalkley, David 324
Chamant, Jean 64, 68–9, 88–9, 93, 96–8, 100–1

Chamberlain, Joseph 6
Chamberlain, Neville 15
Channel Expressway 261, 264, 266–8, 271–9
Channel Tunnel Act of 1987 305, 326, 329
Channel Tunnel Bill 1986 285–8; petitions against 286; second reading 286; 'Snape clause' 287; third reading 287
Channel Tunnel bonds 27
Channel Tunnel Co. 4–6, 12–27, 33, 39, 65, 70, 81–2, 90–1, 141, 172–3, 224; *see also* Britain with Europe, linking of; scheme of 12
Channel Tunnel Committee 11
Channel Tunnel Group 244, 249, 252, 260–1, 265, 267, 270–9, 282–3, 357; *see also* CTG-FM
Channel Tunnel Parliamentary Committee 21
channel tunnel project *see* Britain with Europe, linking of
Channel Tunnel project abandonment 166–70; British Rail, involvement of 188, British Rail's 'mousehole' scheme 185–92, British Rail and SNCF report 190–2, boring concepts 185–7, mini tunnel project 187–8; October elections 159–66, compensation and infrastructure protection 171–5; Crosland observations 162–3, final 'quadripartite' meeting 164, Ministerial Committee decision 165–6; political crisis and new government 134–5; post abandonment status, Cairncross report 175–85; project status during 1980–1 201, financial problems 201–2, Transport committee report of 1980 203–4; railway dimension 141–8, British loading gauge, problem with 142, British Rail involvement 141, routes, decision on 143–4, stance of railway officials 144, traffic forecasts and benefits 143, 146–7; route strategy 148, British Rail objections 156, British Rail's terminals document 149–50, cost factor 157, interim report of Marsh 159, investment decisions 153–4, proposed route in 1973 151, rail link 160; Thatcher government interventions in revival 192–200, disagreement on the size of tunnel 199, railway intervention 198–9, Transport select committee report 196–8; Wilson government approach 135–41, Healey views of 137, introduction of channel tunnel bill 138, Shore, views of project 136
Channel Tunnel Rail Services 346
Channel Tunnel Study Group 20, 21, 27–8, 40, 44, 46, 48–52, 62–71, 80–2, 91, 106, 172, 186; 1960 report 26, 59, conclusion of 29, cost and time estimates 26, 28, economic benefits, of tunnel project 32, geological surveys 26, revised set of proposals 31, traffic estimates 26; 1963 report 35, conclusion of 38, economic and financial estimates 37, traffic forecast 36; agreement with British and French officials 44
Channel Tunnel, creating a transport facility: Channel Tunnel Rail Link 330–47, Channon's paper 336, compensation issues 335, expenditure implications 336, route options 333, 339–46, terminal selection 335; financial crisis and disputes 352–63, bank negotiations 354–5; concessionaires proposed 356, cost consequences of IGC and government interventions 361, credit agreements 354; project, completion of 347–52, IGC/Safety Authority judgements, impact of 349; railway infrastructure, completion of 322–30, investment costs in 322, railway investment management, report on 323, rolling costs 325–6, service limits 328
Channel Tunnel, opening of 364; celebrations 364–6; contribution to transport provision 368–73, channel tunnel traffic 370, operating profit and loss 371–2; cost overruns and time delays 366–8; CTRL 379–82; finance and concession 373–9; political economy of 382–5
Channon, Paul 281–2, 287, 308–9, 322, 331, 334, 336–7
Chazot, Georges-Christian 363
Chenu, Georges-Marie 251
Chetwood, Sir Clifford 315
Chevalier, Michel 2, 4–5, 20
Childers, Hugh 7
Chirac, Jacques 139, 162, 166–7, 285, 309, 377–8
Churchill, Winston 10–11, 17, 85, 280, 364
Clarke, Kenneth 195–6, 200, 204, 360–1
Clarke, Otto 47, 53
Clarke, Sir Andrew 7
Clarke, Sir George 9
Clyde tunnels 30
Cobden, Richard 4
Cockfield, Lord 232
Cole, Humphrey 107
Collard, William 11, 18
Colquhoun, Brian 20
Colquhoun report 21
Colville, Jock 81, 83
Committee of Imperial Defence 7, 10–11, 13
'Common Market' bloc 22
Compagnie Financière de Suez 82
Concorde project 34, 41, 46–7, 50, 58–9, 88, 91, 106, 108–9, 116, 134–7, 139, 156, 161, 167, 219–20, 226, 233–4, 366
Constant, Brig. John 74
Cook, Robin 138
Corbett, Graham 384
Corness, Sir Colin 293
Cornish, Alan 178

Costain, Albert 77, 131, 179
Costain, Richard 49
Cost-benefit analysis 31, 41, 92, 94, 111, 113, 176
Counter-Inflation Act 129
Counter-Inflation Policy 132
Cousins, Frank 47, 56
Couve de Murville, Maurice 58, 68
CPRS 79, 93, 107, 118, 136–7, 161, 163, 184–5, 213–14, 219, 231–2, 238, 244
Crawford, Lord 15
Creasy, Len 103
Crédit Lyonnais 33, 226, 239, 291, 313
Cripps, Sir Stafford 16
Crosland, Anthony 56, 118, 127, 135–7, 161–2, 164–5, 167, 175–8, 181, 185
Cross, Dennis 123
Crossman, Richard 56
'crowding-out' effect 18, 43
CTG *see* Channel Tunnel Group
CTG-FM 261, 268, 270–1, 274–6, 279, 281–4, 288
CTIC 149, 153–4

Dalton, Hugh 16
Dalyell, Tam 131
Davidson, Alfred 25, 70, 81, 186, 188, 201, 239, 249
Davidson, Frank 20, 81, 185–8, 188, 201, 249
Davies, Ernest 19
de Beaumarchais, Jacques 164–5
de Boer, Tony 210
de Gamond, Thomé 1–4
de Gaulle, Charles 24, 25, 38, 42, 45, 58–60, 80
de la Genière, Renaud 293
de Leuw Cather 21, 186, 314
de Monzie, Anatole 15
de Rothschild, Alfred 6
de Rothschild, Frères 21, 70
de Rothschild, Guy 88
de Vitry d'Avaucourt, Comte Arnaud 20
de Wouters d'Oplinter, Baron Charles 20
Deedes, William 68, 77
Dehaene, Jean-Luc 364
Delors, Jacques 211, 364
Dent, Sir Francis 10
d'Erlanger, Baron Emile 10, 18–19
d'Erlanger, Frederick 20
d'Erlanger, Gerard 19
d'Erlanger, Leo 19, 20, 24, 31, 33, 39, 69, 172
d'Erlanger banking family 11, 18–19, 21, 33
Dewdney, Duncan 85, 99
Dherse, Jean-Loup 292, 295
Dilhorne, Lord 43
Dilke, Sir Charles 6
Dillon, Read 20
Dobson, Frank 346
Dodds-Parker, Sir Douglas 131
Dorman Long 33, 210
Douffiagues, Jacques 287–8, 298, 303, 307–8
Douglas-Home, Sir Alec 38, 40, 42–3, 44, 81–4, 131
Drew, Peter 353
Dumas, Roland 280
Dumez 261, 291, 384
Dumont, Alexandre 292
Duncan, Sir Andrew 13
Duncan, Sir Val 84–5, 103–4
Dunwoody, Gwyneth 258, 265
Durand-Rival, Pierre 295, 312, 314
Dwyer, Joe 355

Ebbisham, Lord 13
Economist 30, 35, 109, 241
Edgley, Richard 324
Edwards, Nicholas 231
Elizabeth II, Queen 364
Elliott-Binns, Margaret 112
Ellson, George 19
Elwyn-Jones, Lord 161, 165
EPC *see* Cabinet Economic Policy Committee
EPS *see* European Passenger Services
Essig, Philippe 300–1, 314–15, 348
Eurobridge scheme 251, 260
Euro-Bridge Studies Group 198
European Channel Tunnel Group 194, 197, 200, 204, 209
European Ferries Ltd. 426
European Passenger Services 324
EuroRoute 210, 231, 235, 238–40, 251
Eurotunnel 285–386 *passim*; Channel Tunnel bill 1986 285–8, petitions against 286, second reading 286, 'Snape clause' 287, third reading 287; finance and contracts 288–97, cost of works 289, equity financing 290–5, organisational structure 288, underwriting 296; holding companies of 288; infrastructure planning 305–9, British Rail's initial investment plans 308; monitoring of 309–20, 1990 financing package 319, cost escalations and lending banks 313–15, 320, Intergovernmental Commission 310, tunneling, progress of 311; railway usage contract 297–305, initial agreements 298, modifications recommended by Eurotunnel team 299, Morton's interventions 300–1, toll payments agreed under 304

Fabius, Laurent 250–1, 276
Fairclough, Tony 193, 203, 211, 460
Fallon, Ivan 293
Farrer, Thomas 6
Fell, Arthur 10–11
Fetherston, Drew 174
Figgures, Sir Frank 84

Finance for a Fixed Channel Link 246
Financial Times 247, 277, 362
Fiterman, Charles 207–8, 211, 216, 235–6, 238, 242–3, 245–6, 250
Fleming, Robert 201, 290
Fletcher, Alexander 131, 286
Flyvbjerg, Bent 366
Foch, Marshal 10
Fogarty, Susan 107–8, 132–3, 139, 148, 150, 152, 154, 156–7, 159, 163–4, 172–4, 177–9, 185, 206, 384
Folkestone 280
Fontourcy, Jean 292
Foot, Michael 127, 135, 137, 162
Forasol 49
Forbes, James Staats 5–6
Foster, Professor Christopher 58, 140, 197–8
Fourcade, Jean-Pierre 173
Fournier, Jacques 357
Fowler, Norman 193–204, 207–9, 211, 224
Fox, Charles James 1
Fox, Sir Francis 7, 21
Frame, Alistair 84, 103, 132–3, 138, 140, 143, 147, 164, 172, 186, 189, 201, 291, 293
Franco-Prussian War of 1870–1 7
Fraser, Tom 46–7, 50, 53, 58
Freeman, Roger 349, 353, 358
Freeman Fox 85, 198
French, Sir John 10
Fretwell, Sir John 234
Friedman, Milton 220

Gabriel, Jean 138, 164
Galley, Robert 101–3, 151
Gentil, Paul 194
George, Lloyd 10–11
Georges-Picot, Jacques 20, 25, 88
Gibb, Richard 167
Gibb, Sir Frank 291, 315
Gingell, Overy 46–7, 53, 60, 384
Giscard d'Estaing, Valésy 51, 104, 139–40, 162, 186–7, 207
Gladstone, William 4, 19
Gladwyn, Lord 33, 84
Glenfield Tunnel 3
Glover, Ted 260
Godfrey, E. 13
Goguel, Professor Jean 21
Goodwin, Sir Reginald 149
Gordon-Walker, Patrick 47
Goss, Professor Richard 228
Gould, Harry 132, 174
Gounon, Jacques 373
Gowrie, Lord 256
Grands Travaux de Marseille 244
Grant, A.T.K. 23
Gray, John 236
Green Paper 1973 108–9, 111, 113, 117, 149
Grenfell, Henry 7
Griffiths, Jim 137
Griffiths, Tony 149
Grosvenor, Lord Richard 2, 4–6
Groves, Ken 239
Gscheidle, Kurt 190
Gueterbock, Tony 239
Guibert, Roger 46
Guichard, Olivier 139
Gummer, John 251

Hailsham, Lord 25
Halcrow, Sir William 21, 92, 132
Hall, Allen 349
Hall, Peter 167
Hambros Bank 64, 93, 99, 118–21, 123, 129
Hankey, Sir Maurice 10, 88
Harcourt, Lord 22, 70, 81, 83, 84, 85, 97–100, 103, 112, 123, 131–3, 164, 164, 172
Harding, Harold 21
Harecastle Tunnel 2
Harpham, Bill 45
Harrington, Leslie 23
Harris, Sir William 103, 107
Harvey-Jones, John 293
Hattersley, Roy 164
Hawkshaw, Sir John 1–5
Hay, John 45
Healey, Denis 135, 137, 159–60, 216
Heath, Edward 79–80, 85, 87, 89, 92, 104, 109, 112–13, 121–2, 125, 130–2, 134, 198
Heath government and channel tunnel project: agreement and treaty 128–32, money bill order, implementation of 128, other associated issues 128–9, 132, political instability of 1974 132, treaty, finalisation of 130; Agreement No.1 95–8, 101; Agreement No.2 102, 116–18, 130–1, problems with 116–18; Agreement No.3 130, 140, 162–3; conclusion of 102–6, parallel agreements of 104, problems with 103–4; fundamental points at issue 98–102, Melville's frank analysis of public-private partnership 100, split financing 99, taxation and tariff policies 99; interim studies and results 92–5, assumptions and methodology aspects of 94–5, initial results 93, 96, schedule of tasks 92; Lancaster House agreement 95–8, British and French official disagreements 97; negotiations with consortium 80–92, agreements with consortium group 82–3, Anglo-French group proposals 90, British and French official disagreements 80, 83–4, channel consortium 82, 90, Peter Walker's views 87–8, Peyton's views 87, stance of French banks 89; new ministries 79; project status in 1973 122–7, British and French official disagreements 123,

Heath government and channel tunnel project (*Continued*)
final round of negotiation 124–5, 127; remuneration issues 118–22, agreed package 126, Hambros strategy 121, proposed remuneration 120, reactions of British and French officials 119; review and consultation processes 107–16, British and French government views 112–14, cost benefit analysis for UK government 113, economic studies 111, estimated financial returns 113, Green paper 1973 108–9, 111, 113, 117, 149, Interdepartmental Committee, establishment of 107, traffic forecasts 114
Henderson, Sir Nicholas 189, 249, 260–1, 267, 274, 277, 282, 284, 291
Heseltine, Michael 231, 252, 255, 341–4, 349, 377
Heydon, Howard 289
HGV shuttles 349–51, 353, 362, 369
Hicks, George 19
Hill, Jonathan 342
Hill Samuel 64, 66, 69, 80–1, 83, 172, 201, 346
HMS Sheffield 235
Hoeffel, Daniel 202
Hoggart, Simon 346
Holmes, David 245
Horeau, Hector 1
Hough, George 167
Howard, Michael 258, 287
Howarth, Gil 344
Howe, Sir Geoffrey 155, 158, 231, 240, 243, 246, 251, 255, 274–5, 280
Howell, David 209–22, 225–6, 231–6, 238, 240–2, 244, 246, 258
Huckfield, Leslie 131–2
Hughes, Cledwyn 56
Hughes, Robert 265
Huguenin, A. 33
Hunt, Donald 78, 134, 166–7, 174
Hutter, Roger 72
hybrid Channel Tunnel bills 108, 130–1, 136, 157, 258, 260–1, 265, 279, 284–5, 345–6, 380

Ibbotson, Lance 144
Intergovernmental Commission (IGC) 280, 310, 312, 315–16, 347–53, 356–8, 360–2, 365, 373
Invitation to Promoters (1985 document) 258, 267

Jacquet, Marc 41, 43, 46, 49, 53
James, Philip 72
Japanese Ministry of Finance 318, 361
Japanese 'Shinkansen' services 142
Jebb, Sir Gladwyn 25
Jeffrey, Sir 293
Jellicoe, Lord 89
Jenkin, Patrick 93, 101, 123, 133, 210, 256
Jenkins, Roy 46, 56, 137, 165, 189, 194
JEXIM (The Export-Import Bank of Japan) 361
Jobert, Michel 131
John Laing Construction 186–7, 239, 264, 327, 340
Johnson, Sir Henry 144
Jolivet, François 289, 314
Jones, Elwyn 178
Jordan, Ian 260
Joseph, Keith 77
Jospin, Lionel 378
Julien, Michael 292
Juppé, Alain 377

Kaifu, Toshiki 318
Keen, Peter 156–7, 177, 223
Kemp, Peter 93, 100, 106–8, 116, 121, 132–3, 144–7, 152, 227, 384
Kent, Pen 196, 317–19, 355, 359
Kent County Council 74, 76, 286, 305, 335
Keynes, John Maynard 13
King, Lord 293
King, Tom 241–2
Kirby, David 232, 298, 301–2, 323–4, 336
Kirkland, Colin 292
Kirkpatrick, Sir Ivone 20, 26, 30, 39
Kleinwort Benson 84, 168, 201, 239
Knight, Arthur 175–6

Lacarrière, Philippe 34, 46–7, 53, 83
Lacoste, Louis 194
Laing, Sir Maurice 186–7
Lamont, Norman 293–4, 323, 333, 339, 341, 343–6, 354
Laniel, Joseph 19
Lansdowne, Lord 7
Latham, Arbuthnot 264
Lavalley, Alexandre 5
Lawson, Nigel 249, 255
Lazarus, Peter 104, 107, 190, 192, 196, 249–50
Le Figaro 247, 364
Le Monde 63
Le Theule, Joel 190, 202
Lea, David 175
Legrand, Michel 72, 310
Leicester & Swannington railway 3
Leigh-Pemberton, Robin 240, 291, 293, 315–18
Lemley, Jack 314, 348, 352–3
Leroy-Beaulieu, Paul 19–20
Lever, Harold 137
Lewis, Arthur 19
Lille 216, 237, 267, 276, 282, 307, 309
Lindsay, Sir Ronald 13
Lion, Robert 293
Liverpool, Lord 287

Livesay and Henderson 21, 143, 148, 158
Lloyd, Selwyn 26, 44
London and Greenwich Railway 3
London Chatham & Dover Railway 5–7
Louis-Dreyfus bank 64
Low, William 1–2, 5, 21, 26
Lyall, Andrew 146, 211, 216, 221–7, 235, 237, 240–3, 246, 249, 250, 253–5, 257, 260–1, 267, 274, 278, 284, 357, 384

'M25 effect' 337
MacDonald, Ramsay 11–13
MacDonald, Sir Murdoch 33
McDowall, Andrew 312, 314
Macé, Roger 63, 66, 81, 89, 97, 101, 106, 116, 124, 133, 140, 163–4
MacGregor, Sir Ian 210, 231–2, 234, 240–2, 244–5, 249, 279,
MacGregor, John 281, 295, 303, 330, 344–6, 354–5, 357–60
McIntosh, Peter 193
McKenna, David 72, 141–8, 151–3, 168–9, 179, 185
McMahon, Sir Kit 293
Macmillan, Harold 17, 24, 30–1, 38, 44–5,
Macmillan, Maurice 86
McPetrie, Sir James 116
Maillot, Jacques 371, 373
Major, John 308–9, 315, 321, 335–7, 340–5, 364, 366, 377, 381
Major Projects Association 169
Malcor, René 21
Mallalieu, Lance 17, 47
Malpas, Robert 295, 377
Manchester University 15
Manning, Cardinal 7
Maplin Development Bill 109, 125, 425
Marples, Ernest 26, 30, 33–4, 38–9, 41, 43, 49, 84
Marsh, Sir Richard 67–9, 76, 80, 144–9, 152–3, 156–9, 165, 177, 186
Marshall, Dr Edmund 138
Marshall, Sir Robert 157–8, 163–4, 186
Massigli, René 20
Mathieu, J. 34, 111
Mathieu-Favier, Jacques-Joseph 1, 194
Maudling, Reginald 41, 43–4, 51
Maurin, General Philippe 83, 97, 99, 131–2, 140, 162, 164
Mauroy, Pierre 216, 235, 237, 241, 245, 250, 253, 364, 384
Mayer, Pierre-Alain 216–17, 235, 237, 241, 245, 250, 253, 260, 364, 384
Mayer, Réné 19
Mayoux, Jacques 279
Means, Prof. Cyril 20, 39
Mekie, Eoin 30
Mellish, Robert 137
Melville, Sir Eugene 71, 96, 100–1, 106–8, 116, 118, 123–4, 129–30, 132, 144, 146–8, 150, 227
Mermaz, Louis 207
Merton, William 129, 164, 167, 173, 201
Messmer, Pierre 112, 139
Middleton, Peter (MdO) 349
Middleton, Sir Peter 296
Midland Bank 175, 226, 239–40, 243, 249–50, 284, 292–4, 313, 354
Migaux, Léon 21
Miguet, Nicolas 371, 373
Mills, Gordon 178
minimum usage charge 302, 373, 378, 383–4
Mitchell, David 244, 257, 274, 281, 286–7, 290, 303, 305, 307–8, 330–1
Mitterand, François 139, 203, 207–11, 237, 250, 252–3, 264, 267, 276–8, 284–5, 364, 384–5
Moate, Roger 128
Moch, Jules 33
Modernisation Plan 30
Mondon, Raymond 83, 88
'money' Bill 107, 122, 125
Mont Cenis tunnel 3
Montagner, Philippe 289
Montagu, Samuel 344
Montgomery, Lord 17
Moore, John 286, 291, 293, 298, 301–2
Morgan, J.P. 20
Morgan Grenfell 21–2, 80–1, 201, 284, 290, 292
Morgan Stanley 20, 90
Morris, Peter 167
Morrison-Knudsen 352
Morton, Sir Alastair 292–6, 300–2, 308, 312, 316–18, 326–7, 334, 339, 349, 351–3, 357–60, 363–4, 366, 376–7, 385
Mott Hay and Anderson 92, 103, 155, 155, 156
MUC, *see* minimum usage charge
Mulley, Fred 80–1, 128, 131–2, 135–6, 140, 155–60, 162–3, 170, 177–8
Munby, Denys 178

Napoleon 6
National Westminster [NatWest] Bank 226–7, 239, 243, 250
Naylor, G.F. 133, 167, 172
Neerhout, John 317, 353
Nicolson, Sir David 194
Night Ferry 14, 22
Noel-Baker, Francis 19
Nord railway 5, 7
Norgrove, David 275
Noulton, John 174, 236, 261, 281, 286, 290, 298, 310, 314, 376

O'Brien, E.D. 31
Ogden, Eric 127, 196

O'Hagan, Osborne 201
'ouvrage fixe' 34

Padmore, Sir Thomas 31, 47, 58, 78
Palmer, John 324, 344
Parayre, Jean-Paul 261, 291
Parès, R. 72
Paris riots 1968 68
Parker, Sir Peter 187–9, 193–6, 199, 202–3, 205, 209, 223, 239–40
Parkinson, Cecil 242, 314, 317–18, 322, 328, 330, 336, 339–42, 348
Patten, Chris 343
Paufique, Jean-Paul 250
Payne, Brian 193
Peacock, Edward 11
Peart, Fred 137
Pennock, Raymond (Lord) 284, 288, 290–3, 298
Peyton, John 80, 81, 83–5, 87–9, 91–3, 95–7, 100–3, 106–8, 111–12, 115–25, 128–31, 152, 154, 158, 168, 170, 194, 196, 284, 384
Phelps, Tony 115
Pilon, Bernard 245, 310
'Pilon tunnel' 245, 264, 278
Pisani, Edgard 53, 59–60, 62–3, 384
Pompidou, Georges 45, 58–9, 62, 80, 87, 91, 97, 104, 112, 130–2, 137, 139, 167
Pons, Bernard 374
Ponsolle, Patrick 292, 363, 366, 373–5, 385
Pontillon, Robert 241–2
Portillo, Michael 317, 322–6, 337, 360
Powell, Enoch 134
Powell, Roxanne 167
Prentice, Reg 137
Prescott, John 127, 378, 381
Price, Keith 352
Price, Sir David 265
Prideaux, John 344
Priestley, Robert L. 138
Prior, Jim 108
Public Expenditure Survey Committee mechanism 41
public sector borrowing requirement 17, 167
Pugh, Sir Idwal 76, 107, 111, 115–16, 120, 123, 148–9, 152–4, 157–8
Pugh Report 115, 117, 120, 154
Pym, Francis 234, 236, 238

Quilès, Paul 250–4, 257, 260, 349

RACHEL 340
railway companies, controlled by Watkin, Sir Edward: Manchester Sheffield & Lincolnshire 5; Metropolitan 5; South Eastern 5
railway usage contract 297–305, 329, 358–60; initial agreements 298; modifications recommended by Eurotunnel team 299; Morton's interventions 300–1; toll payments agreed under 304
Raimond, Jean-Bernard 285
Raoul-Duval, Fernand 5
Ratter, John 72, 74, 144
Raymond, Jean-Louis 373
Raymond, Stanley 71–4
Raynsford, Nick 286–7
Redpath Dorman Long 198, 204, 210
Rees, Peter 249
Reeve, John 289, 314
Reid, Sir Robert I 222, 242, 300–3, 307–8, 322–6, 333, 335
Reid, Sir Robert II 324, 326, 330, 339–40, 343, 345, 357
Renault, Jean 261, 292
Richard Costain 21, 49
Ridley, Adam 233–4, 266
Ridley, Nicholas 242–7, 249–61, 265–8, 271–9, 281–4, 286, 308, 333–6, 384
Ridley, Tony 295, 308, 314, 317, 334, 336–7, 384
Rifkind, Malcolm 327, 330, 340–3, 349
Rigaud Report 1965 52, 227
Rio Tinto-Zinc 84–85, 88, 90, 92, 94, 96, 99–101, 103, 123, 133, 141, 143, 165, 189, 201, 226, 291–2
Rippon, Geoffrey 83, 89, 92, 125
Robertson, Sir Brian 34, 72
Robson, Steve 329
Rodgers, Sir John 154
Rodgers, William 189–90, 192–3
Roederer, Louis 364
Rollercoaster (codename) 84–5
Rose, Major Charles 310
Rosenfeld, John, also known as Tony 107, 172, 204, 225, 231, 236, 239
Roskill, Stephen 175, 196
Rosling, Alan 358
Ross, Touche 172, 323
Ross, Willie 56, 137
Rothschilds 5–6, 21, 45, 70, 88, 209
Rowe and Pitman 119
RTZDE *see* RTZ Development Enterprises
RTZ Development Enterprises 85, 92, 98, 103, 128–9, 140, 146–7, 170, 172, 174, 177, 186–7, 190
RTZ *see* Rio Tinto-Zinc
Rudeau, Raoul 254, 257, 266, 307
Rumbold, Sir Anthony 25
Runcorn-Widnes bridge 30
Ryrie, William 211, 233

Safety Authority 280, 310, 312, 315, 347–51, 357, 360, 373
St. Gotthard tunnel 3
St. Margaret's Bay 5
Sapperton Tunnel 2
Sarell, Roderick 34

Sargent, J.R. (Dick) 175
Sartiaux, Albert 7
Sartiaux-Fox Channel Tunnel scheme 8
Say, Léon 5–6
Scargill, Arthur 279
Schmidt, Chancellor 186
Scholey, Sir Robert 295
Schroder, Wagg 268, 270–2, 274
Schweitzer, Louis 276
Scott-Malden, Peter, 34, 39, 63, 66, 72, 76, 83, 91, 96
Scott-Malden report 40–1
SCREG *see* Société Chimique Routière et d'Entreprise Générale
Second World War 15
Segelat, André 46
Selfridge, Gordon 11
Serpell, David 29–30, 33–4, 84–5
Serpell report on British Rail's finances 222, 241
Servan-Schreiber, Jean-Jacques 70
SETCM 35
SETEC 21, 86, 92, 94–5, 111, 140, 177, 184, 198, 289, 299, 302, 310, 330–1, 418
Severn Tunnel 3
SFTM *see* Société Française du Tunnel sous la Manche
Shackleton, Lord 85
SHAPE *see* Supreme Headquarters Allied Powers Europe
Sharp, Bill 107
Shawcross, Christopher 17, 19
Shearer, Tom 132, 163, 167, 172, 184
Sheffield, Ashton-Under-Lyne and Manchester Railway 3
Sheldon, Robert 128
Sherwood, James Blair 264, 266–7, 277–8
Shirley, Philip 46
Shore, Peter 127, 136–7, 187
Short, Edward 161
Short, Philip 254
Short, Renée 128
Silkin, John 265
Silver City Airways 30
Simms, Neville 355
Simpson, John 254
SITUMER 86, 92, 94, 103, 173, 128–9
Slater, John 94
Sloggett, Jonathan 260
Smith, Col. J.H. 6
Smith, Cyril 132
Smith, Dr William 21
Smith, Sir Herbert Llewellyn 9
Snape, Peter 138, 170, 287; *see also* 'Snape clause'
SNCF *see* Société Nationale des Chemins de Fer Français
Snowden, Philip 13
Soames, Christopher 88
Société Chimique Routière et d'Entreprise Générale 267
Société d'Etudes Techniques et Economiques *see* SETEC
Société du Chemin de Fer Sous-Marin Entre la France et l'Angleterre 4
Société Française du Tunnel sous la Manche 91, 171
Société Générale d'Exploitations Industrielles [SOGEI] 21
Société Nationale des Chemins de Fer Français 17, 20, 27, 29, 40, 45–6, 48, 51, 61, 66, 69–72, 82, 141–3, 145, 148, 184, 186, 188–203, 209, 216, 222, 241, 244, 259–60, 267, 282, 292, 294, 297–308, 330, 348, 354–7, 362, 378, 380
Southgate, Malcolm 298–300, 305, 323–4
Speed, Keith 131
Spencer, Herbert 7
Spie Batignolles 197, 261, 289, 292
Sriskandan, Kanagaretnam 224
Standedge Tunnel 2
Stannard, Colin 242, 248, 292, 298–9, 340
Stedeford, Sir Ivan 30
Stephenson, Robert 3
Sterling, Sir Jeffrey 293
Stevenson, Matthew 23, 29–31
Stewart, Michael 50, 54, 64, 67
Strakosch, Sir Henry 14
Submarine Continental Railway Co. 5–6
Suez Co. 20, 22, 24–5, 70
Sunday Express 109
Supreme Headquarters Allied Powers Europe 17
Sutcliffe, John 131
Sykes, Allen 99
Szymanski, Stefan 369

Talabot, Paulin 4
TALIS 240
Taylor, A.J.P. 109
Taylor, Teddy 296, 346
Tebbit, Norman 231, 250, 255
Teeling, Sir William 19, 43, 47
Tempest, Sir Percy 10, 19
Tennyson, Lord 6–7
TGV *see* Train à Grande Vitesse
Thames Tunnel 2–3, 364
Thatcher, Margaret 91, 138, 192, 196, 202, 210–11, 214, 219, 221, 225, 234–5, 237–8, 241, 244–5, 251–3, 257, 260–1, 264, 266–8, 273–4, 276–8, 280, 284–5, 291, 296, 304, 309, 314–15, 318, 321, 337, 340, 342, 363–4, 384–5
Thatcher governments and the tunnel project: Anglo-French joint study group report 224–31, final report of 227–31, Howell and Carrington, discussions of 225;

Thatcher governments and the tunnel project (*Continued*)
Anglo-French summit 247–54, alternative approach to project 248, Ridley-Auroux talks 251; Anglo-French talks 207–16, bored tunnel concept 210, British and French Transport ministry negotiations 211, Cairncross report 212–13, channel fixed link option 215, sponsorship arrangements 209; banking group studies 238–46, channel link options by 248, conclusion of 245, content of the report 242, French bankers attitude 240, Lyall's observations 241; Cabinet rejection of guarantees 216–24, Braibant's revelation 216, financing arrangements, issues relating to 217–18, railway officials interventions 222; competing bids, for concession grants 258–68, basic conditions for 259; project status in 1982 231–5, impact of attack on *HMS Sheffield* 235, negotiations with French 235–8, project status in 1984 254–8; promoter, selection of 268–77; comparison of promoter cost and revenue estimates 269, Ridley's memorandum 271–5, Schroders' recommendation 271; treaty and concessions 277–83, concession agreements 281, concession clauses and annexes 283, model of treaty 280
Thatcherite economic principles 220
Thatcherite private enterprise formula 257
Thatcher-Mauroy 'accord' 237
The Channel Fixed Link 279
The Channel Tunnel and alternative cross Channel services 179
The Channel Tunnel: London-Tunnel New Rail Link 155
The Channel Tunnel: the Facts 51
Thiolon, Bernard 291
Thompson, Sir Richard 128
Thomson, George 59
Thoresen, Townsend 217
Thoresen's Southampton-Cherbourg service 54
Thorneycroft, Peter 24
Thurtle, Ernest 13, 19
Times 30, 39, 49, 68, 73, 109, 127, 165, 189, 238, 251, 277, 279,
TML *see* Transmanche-Link
Tomison, Maureen 286
Tomkins, Sir Edward 163–6, 189
Tope, Graham 131
Townsend 30, 54, 217
Trafalgar House 249, 291–2, 333, 336
Train à Grande Vitesse 142
Transmanche-Link 288–90, 292–5, 310, 312–17, 319, 347–59, 362, 364, 366, 383
Transport Act of 1968 58, 67, 71
Transport and Road Research Laboratory 174
Treaty of Rome 22
Trend, Sir Burke 42, 88
TRRL *see* Transport and Road Research Laboratory
tube, immersed or submerged 1–2, 26, 35, 43, 48, 54, 61, 63, 111, 178, 186, 197–8, 204–5, 210, 213, 239, 266
Tunnel project 1974–5 134–71; and British Rail 141–8; March–September 1974 135–41; political crisis and a new government 134–5; second election and Labour doubts, October 1974–January 1975 160–5
Turnbull, Andrew 218
Turner, Sir Mark 84
Turvey, Ralph 178
Tweedsmuir, Lady 117
Twomey, Frank 128

UIC 'Berne' gauge 177
Urie, Bob 324
Usage Agreement, *see* railway usage contract

Valentine, Alec 20
Varley, Eric 137, 216
Vergnaud, Robert 34
Verret, Jean-Phillippe 251
Victoria, Queen 4
virgo intacta 15

Wakefield, Nick 304–5
Wakeham, Lord 376
Walker, David 291, 293
Walker, Harold 286
Walker, Peter 79, 86–9, 91, 106,
Walker, Sir Herbert 13–14, 19, 392
Walters, Alan 233–4
Warburg, S.G. 64, 67, 81, 200, 363, 380
Wardale, Geoffrey 104, 107
Wass, Sir Douglas 186
Watkin, Sir Edward 4–6, 364
Watkinson, Harold 22, 24–5
Webber, Brian 260
Weighell, Sid 190
Weinstock, Lord 326
Wells, John 131
Welsby, John 324, 330, 335–6
West London Relief Road 204
Whitaker, Douglas 10
White, Weld 81
Whitehall officials, final report by 31
Whitelaw, William 84, 86, 91
Wickenden, Keith 111, 178
Wicks, Nigel 296
Williams, David 193
Williams, Jenny 178
Williams, John 132
Williams, Shirley 137
Wilson, Alan 175

Wilson, Harold 46–47, 54–60, 64, 71, 78–81, 134–140, 144, 160–2, 167, 186–7
Wilson, Professor Gordon 186–187
Wilson, Sir Henry 10
Wilson governments and the tunnel project 1964–70: fundamental issues of 50–60, compensation issues 69, economic and financial returns of 55–6, financing alternatives 52–3, Fraser, Tom, progress report from 50, official views of British and French 51, political crisis 60, 68, traffic forecasts 57; geological survey of 1964–6 48–50, agreements signed for 48, tender of job contracts 48–9; infrastructure issues 74–8, channel tunnel terminal facility 76, option of channel tunnels 75, Terminals Working Party report 74; Labour party of Britain, views on channel tunnel 46–7; post 1966 54, Castle's revolution 58, meeting with Pompidou, Georges 58; private partnership in 60–70, Castle's view 62, 64, discussions with consortia 66, joint Commission of Surveillance report 60–2; railway dimension 70–4, BRB exclusion, impact of 71–2, debates within BRB 73; and white heat of the technological revolution 47
Wilson governments and the tunnel project 1974–6: Melville and McKenna meetings on 147; Cairncross Report 175–85; cross-channel passenger and freight traffic 180, tunnel costs and benefits, estimation 182–3; compensation and protecting the infrastructure, 1975 171–5; March–September 1974 135–41, Channel Tunnel Bill reintroduced 138; private sector companies role in 138–9; 'Mousehole' origin, 1975–9 185–92; project abandonment 165–70, factors contributing 166–7; rail link, route strategy 1973–4, 148–160, cost increase, analysis, 159; second election and Labour doubts, October 1974–January, 1975 160–5; final 'quadripartite' meeting 163–4; Wilson-Giscard talks, 140
Wimpey, George 21, 49, 204, 210, 244, 315, 355
Winterton, Nicholas 258
Wolmar, Christian 346
Wolseley, Sir Garnet 6
Woodhead Tunnel 3
Woodhouse, Henry 107, 169
Woodman, Dr Christopher 260
Wybrew, John 256, 267, 275
Wylie, Sir Francis 25
Wylson, James 1–2

Yom Kippur War 131
Young, Sir George 22, 374